Missouri
Ballards

Compiled by

Lynne D. Miller
Email: LMiller603@aol.com

Revised November 2020

Table of Contents

Introduction

This book is a Work in Progress and is subject to revision as new information becomes available. Corrections and additions are welcome and appreciated.   Please supply supporting documentation.

Please note that I have attempted to retain the original spelling used on all the legal documents. Early American history does not include uniform spelling. If a census taker spelled Ballard as Bullard, Bellard, Ballord, Ballar or any other way, I tried to keep that spelling, when transcribing that document, after first looking at the surrounding words to see how that person was using these letters in other words. Some census takers just didn't close the top of the "a".

Many Ballards could not read nor write in the 1800's. This is more evident by their signing with an "X" on various legal documents instead of their name.

Most early legal and military documents were full of spelling errors.

Dates of birth are more than likely incorrect on most census records but they do at least give us a time frame.

Census Records are great clues but often contain error. This is an interpretation of one census record transcription.
* 1900 - Living in Brookfield, Linn Co., MO - Ballard, Alexander L - Sept 1827 PA CT CT (PA represents him being born in Pennsylvania. CT is representing his father having been born in Connecticut. The second CT also represents the place of birth of his mother as Connecticut). I often find the date of birth to also be in error. I use that date until I find other documentation supporting their date of birth.

Lynne

Alexander Lane Ballard

Generation No. 1

1. *ALEXANDER LANE⁶ BALLARD (JOHN LEONARD⁵, JOSEPH⁴, WILLIAM³, NATHANIEL², WILLIAM¹) was born 17 Sep 1827 in Bradford Co., PA, and died 10 Dec 1905 in MO. He married ELIZA ELECTRA BRATT 1855. She was born 26 May 1837 in Allegany Co., NY, and died 10 Dec 1910 in Linn Co., MO.*

Notes for ALEXANDER LANE BALLARD:

Source: 1860 Potter County Pennsylvania Federal Census Records, 1870 Bradford County Pennsylvania Federal Census Records, 1880-1900 Linn County Pennsylvania Federal Census Records, Mike Ballard (cmballard@aol.com), Dr. John Ballard (john.ballard@ana.edu.au) McLaughlin Funeral Home Records Chariton Co MO

** 1860 - Living in Sharon, Potter Co., PA - Ballard, Alexander L 32 farmer PA, Eliza 24 NY, George E 3 PA, Ceola 1 PA, Cornelieus Pine 48, Edgar Henrington 21*
** 1870 - Living in West Burlington, Bradford Co., PA - Ballard, Alexander 42 farmer PA, Eliza 33 NY, Edmund 14 PA, Ceola 11 PA, Wm 9 PA, Wardie 5 PA, Clarrie B 3 PA, Minerva Van Liew 30 NY, Addie 9 PA, Edward Howard 30 VA, Van Alestine, Fanny 18 PA*
** 1880 - Living in Bucklin, Linn Co., MO - Ballard, Alexander 52 farmer PA Conn NY, Eliza E 43 NY, Edmond 23 PA, Ceola 21 school teacher PA, William 18 PA, Alonzo 15 PA, Eliza 8 PA*
** 1900 - Living in Brookfield, Linn Co., MO - Ballard, Alexander L - Sept 1827 PA CT CT, Eliza E - May 1837 - 6 children 5 living NY NY NY, George E - July 1856 PA*

More About ALEXANDER LANE BALLARD:
Burial: Rose Hill Cemetery, Brookfield, Linn Co., MO

More About ELIZA ELECTRA BRATT:
Burial: Rose Hill Cemetery, Brookfield, Linn Co., MO

Children of ALEXANDER BALLARD and ELIZA BRATT are:

> i.   GEORGE EDMOND⁷ BALLARD, b. 17 Jul 1856, PA; d. 22 Jul 1934, Norton Co., KS.
>
>   *More About GEORGE EDMOND BALLARD:*
>   *Burial: Rose Hill Cemetery, Brookfield, Linn Co., MO*
>
> ii. CEOLA BALLARD, b. 13 Apr 1859, PA; d. 29 Dec 1948, Adair Co., MO; m. WILLIAM M. CARPER; b. 1861; d. 1955.
>
>   *More About CEOLA BALLARD:*
>   *Burial: Forest-Llewellyn Cemetery, Kirksville, Adair Co., MO*
>
>   *More About WILLIAM M. CARPER:*
>   *Burial: Forest-Llewellyn Cemetery, Kirksville, Adair Co., MO*

2.   iii. JOHN WILLIAM BALLARD, b. 10 Jan 1860, Bradford Co., PA; d. 1933, Norcatur, Norton Co., KS.
3.   iv.   WARD ALONZO BALLARD, b. 13 Feb 1865, Bradford Co., PA; d. Mar 1948, Kirksville, Adair Co., MO.
4.   v.   LILA MAY BALLARD, b. 04 Jul 1871, PA; d. 02 Feb 1954.

Generation No. 2

2. *JOHN WILLIAM[7] BALLARD (ALEXANDER LANE[6], JOHN LEONARD[5], JOSEPH[4], WILLIAM[3], NATHANIEL[2], WILLIAM[1]) was born 10 Jan 1860 in Bradford Co., PA, and died 1933 in Norcatur, KS. He married JULIA CAROLINE BUTLER. She was born 04 Jul 1866 in IA, and died 06 Sep 1941.*

Notes for JOHN WILLIAM BALLARD:
Source: 1900-1910 Norton County Kansas Federal Census Records
** 1900 - Living in Rockwell, Norton Co., KS - Ballard, J W - Jan 1861 PA PA NY, Julias - July 1865 - 8 children 7 living IA PA AL, Alaxandria - Sept 1882 NE, Cara B - July 1884 KS, Dora M - Feb 1888 KS, Charlie B Mar 1881 KS, Jennie - June 1894 KS, John W - Oct 1896 KS, Frank E - Oct 1898 KS*
** 1910 - Living in Almena, Norton Co., KS - Ballard, John W 49 PA PA NY, Julia 43 - 9 children 8 living IA IN AL, Alexander L 27 NE, Charlie 18 KS, Jennie 15 KS, Willie 13 KS, Frank 11 KS, LeRoy 6/12 KS, Rachael Reagen 76 SC*

More About JOHN WILLIAM BALLARD:
Burial: Norcatur Cemetery, Norton Co., KS

More About JULIA CAROLINE BUTLER:
Burial: Norcatur Cemetery, Norton Co., KS

Children of JOHN BALLARD and JULIA BUTLER are:

  i. *ALEXANDER LANE[8] BALLARD, b. 17 Sep 1882, KS; d. 17 Apr 1954, Pipestone Co., MN; m. EMILY LONG, 17 May 1916, Troy, Pipestone Co., MN; b. 1890; d. 03 Jan 1965.*

   Notes for ALEXANDER LANE BALLARD:
   Source: 1920 Pipestone County Minnesota Federal Census Records, WWI & WWII Draft Registration
   ** 1920 - Living in Troy, Pipestone Co., MN - Ballard, Alexander 37 NE PA IA, Emily 29 MN Germany IA*

   More About ALEXANDER LANE BALLARD:
   Burial: Old Woodlawn Cemetery, Pipestone Co., MN

   More About EMILY LONG:
   Burial: Old Woodlawn Cemetery, Pipestone Co., MN

  ii. *CLARA BELL BALLARD, b. 20 Jul 1884, KS; d. 29 Jul 1955; m. WARREN B. REEVES; b. 21 Aug 1876; d. 02 Aug 1949.*

   More About CLARA BELL BALLARD:
   Burial: Mount Hope Cemetery, Almena, Norton Co., KS

   More About WARREN B. REEVES:
   Burial: Mount Hope Cemetery, Almena, Norton Co., KS

  iii. *JOEL A. BALLARD, b. 17 Feb 1886, KS; d. 11 Jul 1890.*

   More About JOEL A. BALLARD:
   Burial: Norcatur Cemetery, Norton Co., KS

  iv. *DORA MAY BALLARD, b. 1888, KS; d. 1968; m. WALTER L. SAUNDERS; b. 1878; d. 1970.*

   More About DORA MAY BALLARD:
   Burial: White Rock Cemetery, Republic Co., KS

More About WALTER L. SAUNDERS:
Burial: White Rock Cemetery, Republic Co., KS

5.   v.   *CHARLES BEDFORD BALLARD, b. 17 Mar 1891, Decatur Co., KS; d. 23 Jan 1962, King Co., WA.*
          vi.   *JOHN WILLIAM BALLARD, b. 27 Oct 1896, Norcatur, Norton Co., KS; d. May 1964; m. MILDRED*
                 ATKINSON; b. 25 Dec 1899, Norton Co., KS; d. 01 Aug 1991, Topeka, Shawnee Co., KS.

                 Notes for JOHN WILLIAM BALLARD:
                 Source: WWI & WWII Draft Registration Cards, Social Security Death Index

                 More About JOHN WILLIAM BALLARD:
                 Burial: Mount Hope Cemetery, Topeka, Shawnee Co., KS

                 More About MILDRED ATKINSON:
                 Burial: Mount Hope Cemetery, Topeka, Shawnee Co., KS

         vii.   *FRANK ELBRIDGE BALLARD, b. 26 Oct 1898, Norcatur, Norton Co., KS; d. 02 Nov 1978; m.*
                 FLORENCE HUBBART, 01 Jun 1929, Seattle, King Co., WA; b. 29 Sep 1902; d. 05 Aug 1946.

                 Notes for FRANK ELBRIDGE BALLARD:
                 Source: WWII Draft Registration Cards, Department of Veterans Affairs BIRLS Death File

                 More About FRANK ELBRIDGE BALLARD:
                 Burial: Mountain View Cemetery, Auburn, King Co., WA

                 More About FLORENCE HUBBART:
                 Burial: Mountain View Cemetery, Auburn, King Co., WA

        viii.   *LU ROY BALLARD, b. 10 Oct 1909, Almena, KS; d. 08 Jan 1982; m. MARY JANE BROWN; b. 12*
                 Jan 1910; d. 20 Dec 1989.

                 Notes for LU ROY BALLARD:
                 Source: WWII Draft Registration Card

                 More About LU ROY BALLARD:
                 Burial: Mount Hope Cemetery, Topeka, Shawnee Co., KS

                 More About MARY JANE BROWN:
                 Burial: Mount Hope Cemetery, Topeka, Shawnee Co., KS

3. *WARD ALONZO[7] BALLARD (ALEXANDER LANE[6], JOHN LEONARD[5], JOSEPH[4], WILLIAM[3], NATHANIEL[2], WILLIAM[1]) was born 13 Feb 1865 in Bradford Co., PA, and died Mar 1948 in Kirksville, Adair Co., MO. He married MARY SIGHTS Jan 1888, daughter of ISAAC SIGHTS and MARGARET WOODS. She was born 15 Dec 1866 in Bucklin, Linn Co., MO, and died 15 Mar 1929 in Bucklin, Linn Co., MO.*

Notes for WARD ALONZO BALLARD:
Source: 1900-1930 Linn County Missouri Federal Census Records
** 1900 - Living in Bucklin, Linn Co., MO - Ballard, Ward L - Feb 1865 PA PA NY, Mollie - Dec 1866 MO, Vena E - Oct 1888MO, H Ray - May 1890 MO, Mabel M - Oct 1891 MO, Myron W - July 1893 MO, Margaret E - Apr 1899 MO*
** 1910 - Living in Bucklin, Linn Co., MO - Ballard, Ward L 45 Pa PA NY, Mary 43 - 6 children 6 living MO, Vena C 21, Hubert R 19 MO, Mabel M 18 MO, Myron W 16 MO, Margarett E 11 MO, Edmond O 8 MO*
** 1920 - Living in Bucklin, Linn Co., MO - Ballard, Ward L 54 PA, Mary H 53 MO, Margaret 30, Edmond O 18*

** 1930 - Living in Bucklin, Linn Co., MO - Ballard, Ward L 65 wd PA PA PA, Ray H 39 MO, Rida B 32 dau in law, Edward R 14 NE grandson NE, Doris M 12 NE, Donald W 10 MO, Lloyd K 8 3/12 MO, Renneble E 5 9/12 MO, Mary M 4 3/12 MO, Margaret E 31 dau.*

More About WARD ALONZO BALLARD:
Burial: Wyandotte Cemetery, Bucklin, Linn Co., MO

Notes for MARY SIGHTS:
Source: Linn County Missouri Death Certificate

More About MARY SIGHTS:
Burial: 19 Mar 1929, Wyandotte Cemetery, Bucklin, Linn Co., MO

Children of WARD BALLARD and MARY SIGHTS are:

      i.   *VENA[8] BALLARD, b. 31 Oct 1888, Linn Co., MO; d. 27 Jan 1923, Flint, Genesee Co., MI; m. RALPH RAMSEY, 24 May 1919, Flint, Genesee Co., MI; b. 02 Aug 1888, Bucklin, Linn Co., MO; d. 21 Aug 1955, Bucklin, Linn Co., MO.*

        Notes for VENA BALLARD:
        Source: Genesee County Michigan Certificate of Death

        More About VENA BALLARD:
        Burial: Wyandotte Cemetery, Bucklin, Linn Co., MO

        More About RALPH RAMSEY:
        Burial: Wyandotte Cemetery, Bucklin, Linn Co., MO

6.   ii.   *HERBERT RAY BALLARD, b. 07 May 1890, Bucklin MO; d. 07 Feb 1968, Excelsior Springs, Clay Co., MO.*

     iii.   *MABEL M. BALLARD, b. 20 Oct 1890, Bucklin, Linn Co., MO; d. 20 Jul 1943, Genesee Co., MI; m. ERNEST W. SWAN; b. 18 Apr 1888, MO; d. Aug 1968, Corunna, Shiawassee Co., MI.*

        More About MABEL M. BALLARD:
        Burial: Greenwood Cemetery, Vernon, Shiawassee Co., MI

        More About ERNEST W. SWAN:
        Burial: Greenwood Cemetery, Vernon, Shiawassee Co., MI

     iv.   *MYRON WARD BALLARD, b. 28 Jul 1893, Linn Co., MO; d. 29 Sep 1955, Clearwater Co., ID; m. AUDRA MURIEL HUSTEAD; b. 09 Mar 1898, Linn Co., MO; d. 02 Aug 1974, Nez Perce Co., ID.*

        Notes for MYRON WARD BALLARD:
        Source: Clearwater County Idaho Certificate of Death

        More About MYRON WARD BALLARD:
        Burial: Riverside Cemetery, Clearwater Co., ID

        More About AUDRA MURIEL HUSTEAD:
        Burial: Lewis-Clark Memorial Gardens, Nez Perce Co., ID

     v.   *MARGARET E. BALLARD, b. 29 Apr 1899, Bucklin, Linn Co., MO; d. 16 Dec 1946, Linn Co., MO; m. EVERETT WHITE; b. 20 Apr 1904, Montgomery Co., KS; d. 04 Mar 1952, Bucklin, Linn Co., MO.*

Notes for MARGARET E. BALLARD:
Source: Linn County Missouri Certificate of Death

More About MARGARET E. BALLARD:
Burial: Wyandotte Cemetery, Bucklin, Linn Co., MO

Notes for EVERETT WHITE:
Source: 1940 Linn County Missouri Federal Census Records
** 1940 - Living in Bucklin, Linn Co., MO - White, Everett 35 KS, Margaret 40 MO, Geo W. Hubler nephew 12 KS, William Hubler nephew 13 KS, Ward L Ballard father in law 75 wd PA*

More About EVERETT WHITE:
Burial: Wyandotte Cemetery, Bucklin, Linn Co., MO

    vi.   EDMOND OSCAR BALLARD, b. 1902, Linn Co., MO; d. Aft. 1910.

4.   LILA MAY[7] BALLARD (ALEXANDER LANE[6], JOHN LEONARD[5], JOSEPH[4], WILLIAM[3], NATHANIEL[2], WILLIAM[1]) was born 04 Jul 1871 in PA, and died 02 Feb 1954. She married FRED SANFORD 26 Dec 1895. He was born 14 Jan 1862 in Iowa Co., WI, and died 02 Jan 1936 in Linn Co., MO.

More About LILA MAY BALLARD:
Burial: Bucklin Masonic Cemetery, Bucklin, Linn Co., MO

Notes for FRED SANFORD:
Source: 1900 Linn County Missouri Federal Census Records
** 1900 - Living in Bucklin, Linn Co., MO - Sanford, Fred T - Jan 1862 WI MA NY, Lila M - July 1871 PA PA NY, Ruby L - Oct 1895 MO, Grace J - Jan 1897 MO, Florence - Mar 1899 MO, Emma Pitcaron 18*

More About FRED SANFORD:
Burial: Bucklin Masonic Cemetery, Bucklin, Linn Co., MO

Children of LILA BALLARD and FRED SANFORD are:
    i.   RUBY L.[8] SANFORD, b. Oct 1895, Bucklin, Linn Co., MO; d. Aft. 1900.
    ii.   GRACE J. SANFORD, b. Jan 1897, Bucklin, Linn Co., MO; d. Aft. 1900.
    iii.   FLORENCE SANFORD, b. Mar 1899, Bucklin, Linn Co., MO; d. Aft. 1900.

Generation No. 3

5.   CHARLES BEDFORD[8] BALLARD (JOHN WILLIAM[7], ALEXANDER LANE[6], JOHN LEONARD[5], JOSEPH[4], WILLIAM[3], NATHANIEL[2], WILLIAM[1]) was born 17 Mar 1891 in Decatur Co., KS, and died 23 Jan 1962 in King Co., WA. He married EDNA CAROLINE RODINE. She was born 07 Sep 1887 in IL, and died 12 Jul 1984 in King Co., WA.

More About CHARLES BEDFORD BALLARD:
Burial: Evergreen-Washelli Memorial Park, Seattle, King Co., WA

More About EDNA CAROLINE RODINE:
Burial: Evergreen-Washelli Memorial Park, Seattle, King Co., WA

Child of CHARLES BALLARD and EDNA RODINE is:
    i.   CHARLES RICHARD[9] BALLARD, b. 04 Apr 1914, NE; d. 05 Jul 1993, Kirkland, WA; m. (1) RACHEL CRANDALL; m. (2) HELEN NICHOLS.

6. *HERBERT RAY[8] BALLARD (WARD ALONZO[7], ALEXANDER LANE[6], JOHN LEONARD[5], JOSEPH[4], WILLIAM[3], NATHANIEL[2], WILLIAM[1]) was born 07 May 1890 in Bucklin MO, and died 07 Feb 1968 in Excelsior Springs, Clay Co., MO. He married NIETA BELLE "RIDA" YONTZ, daughter of WILLIAM YONTZ and HARRIET SHOWALTER. She was born 05 Sep 1896 in Fairbury, NE, and died 10 Jan 1954 in St. Joseph, Buchanan Co., MO.*

Notes for HERBERT RAY BALLARD:

Source: 1920-1930 Linn County Missouri Federal Census Records, Clay County Missouri Standard Certificate of Death
** 1920 - Living in Linn Co., MO - Ballard, Herbert R 29 MO, Neita B 23 NE, Edwin R 3 10/12 MO, Doris M 2 1/12*
** 1930 - Living in Linn Co., MO with parents*

More About HERBERT RAY BALLARD:
Burial: Savannah Cemetery, Andrew Co., MO

Notes for NIETA BELLE "RIDA" YONTZ:

Source: Death Certificate # 204
** Birth listed as Jan 10, 1954 Fairbury, NE, death as Buchanan Co., St. Joseph, MO. Father listed as William Yontz. Mother listed as Harriet Showalter. Husband listed as Herbert Ray Ballard.*

More About NIETA BELLE "RIDA" YONTZ:
Burial: Savannah Cemetery, Savannah, Andrew Co., MO

Children of HERBERT BALLARD and NIETA YONTZ are:

    i.   *EDWIN R.[9] BALLARD, b. 1916, NE; d. Aft. 1930.*
    ii. *DORIS M. BALLARD, b. 09 Nov 1917, NE; d. 10 Jun 1984.*

        More About DORIS M. BALLARD:
        Burial: Savannah Cemetery, Andrew Co., MO

    iii. *DONALD W. BALLARD, b. 1920, Linn Co., MO; d. Aft. 1930.*
    iv. *LLOYD KEITH BALLARD, b. 19 Dec 1921, Linn Co., MO; d. 07 Jul 1934, Linn Co., MO.*

        Notes for LLOYD KEITH BALLARD:
        Source: Missouri State Board of Health Death Certificate # 25372
        ** 1934 - Linn County Missouri - died. Name listed as Lloyd Keith Ballard.*

    v.   *RENNEBLE E. BALLARD, b. 1924, Linn Co., MO; d. Aft. 1930.*
    vi. *MARY M. BALLARD, b. 1925, Linn Co., MO; d. Aft. 1930.*

Andrew Jackson Ballard

Generation No. 1

1. ANDREW JACKSON[1] BALLARD *was born Abt. 1832 in KY, and died Aft. 1880. He married (1)* SARAH J. WILCOX *04 Mar 1858 in Clark Co., KY.   He married (2)* HATTIE ELLEN JOHNSON *Bef. 1870. She was born 1852 in MO, and died Aft. 1880.*

Notes for ANDREW JACKSON BALLARD*:*

Source: 1860 Clark County Kentucky Federal Census Records, 1870-1880 Cooper County Missouri Federal Census Records

** 1860 - Living in Clark Co., KY - Ballard, Jackson 28 farmer KY, Sarah 19 KY*
** 1870 - Living in Clark Fork, Cooper Co., MO - Ballard, Jackson 38 farmer KY, Hettie E 18 MO, Emma 9 MO, Mollie 7 MO, James S. P. 5/12 MO*
** 1880 - Living in Prairie Home, Cooper Co., MO - Ballard, AJ 48 farmer KY VA KY H E 28 MO MO MO, SP 10 MO, S E A 8 MO, RL 6 MO, NA 3 MO, JA 1 MO*

Children of ANDREW BALLARD *and* SARAH WILCOX *are:*

    i.   MALE[2] BALLARD, *b. 31 Dec 1858, Clark Co., KY; d. 31 Dec 1858, Clark Co., KY.*

    ii.   EMMA BALLARD, *b. 10 Oct 1860, Clark Co., KY; d. 06 Feb 1930, Boone Co., MO; m.* WILLIAM RILEY ASHCRAFT, *06 Jul 1883, Cooper Co., MO; b. 09 Jan 1850, Cedar Co., MO; d. 11 Mar 1932, Boonville, Cooper Co., MO.*

        Notes for EMMA BALLARD*:*
        Source: Boone County Missouri Certificate of Death

        More About EMMA BALLARD*:*
        Burial: Walnut Grove Cemetery, Boonville, Cooper Co., MO

        Notes for WILLIAM RILEY ASHCRAFT*:*
        Source: 1900 Cooper County Missouri Federal Census Records
        ** 1900 - Living in North Moniteau, Cooper Co., MO - Ashcroft, William - Jan 1850 MO MO unk farmer, Emma - Feb 1860 1 child 1 living KY KY KY, Johnie - Feb 1887 MO MO KY*

        More About WILLIAM RILEY ASHCRAFT*:*
        Burial: Walnut Grove Cemetery, Boonville, Cooper Co., MO

Children of ANDREW BALLARD *and* HATTIE JOHNSON *are:*

2.   iii.   STERLING PRICE[2] BALLARD, *b. 07 Apr 1870, Cooper Co., MO; d. 26 Nov 1947, Kansas City, Jackson Co., MO.*

    iv.   SARAH E. A. BALLARD, *b. 03 Oct 1871, Cooper Co., MO; d. 13 Dec 1930, Kansas City, Jackson Co., MO; m.* ABRAHAM L. ALBERT LOWE, *14 Feb 1897, Jackson Co., MO; b. 10 Jan 1872, Sangamon Co., IL; d. 14 May 1960, Jackson Co., MO.*

        More About ABRAHAM L. ALBERT LOWE*:*
        Burial: Green Lawn Cemetery, Kansas City, Jackson Co., MO

    v.   ROBERT LEE BALLARD, *b. 28 Oct 1872, Cooper Co., MO; d. 11 Feb 1946, Boonville, Cooper Co., MO.*

More About ROBERT LEE BALLARD:
Burial: Walnut Grove Cemetery, Boonville, Cooper Co., MO

vi. NANCY A. BALLARD, *b. 09 Oct 1876, Cooper Co., MO; d. 31 Mar 1968, Kansas City, Jackson Co., MO; m. JAMES HURT BROWN; b. 01 Jul 1864, Moniteau Co., MO; d. 02 Nov 1941, Prairie Home, Cooper Co., MO.*

More About NANCY A. BALLARD:
Burial: Walnut Grove Cemetery, Boonville, Cooper Co., MO

More About JAMES HURT BROWN:
Burial: Walnut Grove Cemetery, Boonville, Cooper Co., MO

vii. JOHN ALEXANDER BALLARD, *b. 23 May 1879, Cooper Co., MO; d. 27 Sep 1955, Pettis Co., MO; m. VIRGINIA LEONA BURRELL, 06 May 1895, Boonville, Cooper Co., MO; b. 31 Oct 1877, Cooper Co., MO; d. 09 Nov 1972, Pettis Co., MO.*

Notes for JOHN ALEXANDER BALLARD:
Source: Social Security Records

More About VIRGINIA LEONA BURRELL:
Burial: Walnut Grove Cemetery, Boonville, Cooper Co., MO

Generation No. 2

2. STERLING PRICE[2] BALLARD (ANDREW JACKSON[1]) *was born 07 Apr 1870 in Cooper Co., MO, and died 26 Nov 1947 in Kansas City, Jackson Co., MO. He married KATIE GIBSON 01 Mar 1903 in Jackson, MO. She was born 1885 in VA, and died 1960.*

Notes for STERLING PRICE BALLARD:
Source: Jackson County Missouri Death Certificate, 1910 Johnson County Missouri Federal Census Records, 1920-1940 Jackson County Missouri Federal Census Records

** 1910 - Living in Round Grove, Johnson Co., MO - Ballard, Sterling 39 MO, Kate 25 VA, Bernell R 7, Lester M 4, Hettie 1 2/12 MO*
** 1920 - Living in Kansas City, Jackson Co., MO - Ballard, Sterling 40 MO, Katie 33 VA, Burnell R 16 MO, Lesta May 13 MO, Hattie C 16 MO, Edward Price 8 MO*
** 1930 - Living in Kansas City, Jackson Co., MO - Ballard, Stirling P 59 MO, Katie 43, Hettie C 28, Edward P 18*
** 1940 - Living in Kansas City, Jackson Co., MO - Ballard, Sterling P 70, Katie 55*

More About STERLING PRICE BALLARD:
Burial: Green Lawn Cemetery, Kansas City, Jackson Co., MO

More About KATIE GIBSON:
Burial: Green Lawn Cemetery, Kansas City, Jackson Co., MO

Children of STERLING BALLARD and KATIE GIBSON are:
i. BURNELL REED[3] BALLARD, *b. 07 Dec 1903, Johnson Co., MO; d. 31 Aug 1967, Leavenworth, KS; m. HAZEL G. BUCK, 08 Jan 1921, Jackson Co., MO.*

Notes for BURNELL REED BALLARD:
Source: Jackson County Missouri Marriage Records, Social Security Records

ii.   *LESTA MAY BALLARD, b. 14 Jun 1906, Johnson Co., MO; d. Jul 1979; m. (1) WILLIAM HOMER WARNER, 09 Nov 1924, Jackson Co., MO; b. 1905; d. 1953; m. (2) KELLY LEE KING, 26 Jul 1956, Excelsior Springs, Ray Co., MO; b. 1902; d. 1979.*

iii. *HETTIE CASAWAY BALLARD, b. 04 Feb 1909, Johnson Co., MO; d. 05 Feb 1992; m. JAMES ROBERT HARRISON; b. 1901; d. 1980.*

More About HETTIE CASAWAY BALLARD:
Burial: Green Lawn Cemetery, Kansas City, Jackson Co., MO

More About JAMES ROBERT HARRISON:
Burial: Green Lawn Cemetery, Kansas City, Jackson Co., MO

iv.   *EDWARD PRICE BALLARD, b. 13 Dec 1911, Jackson Co., MO; d. 02 Aug 1976, Kansas City, Jackson Co., MO; m. CHRISTINE SOPHIA STOCK; b. 17 Oct 1914, Moniteau Co., MO; d. 07 Sep 1977, Kansas City, Jackson Co., MO.*

Notes for EDWARD PRICE BALLARD:
Source: WWII Draft Cards

More About EDWARD PRICE BALLARD:
Burial: Green Lawn Cemetery, Kansas City, Jackson Co., MO

More About CHRISTINE SOPHIA STOCK:
Burial: Green Lawn Cemetery, Kansas City, Jackson Co., MO

Bennett D. Ballard

Generation No. 1

1. BENNETT D.[4] BALLARD (BLAND[3], THOMAS[2], WILLIAM[1]) was born 02 Oct 1802 in Albemarle Co., VA, and died 25 Oct 1858 in Hopkins Co., KY. He married (1) NANCY HOLLINGSWORTH in Duplin NC. She was born 1803. He married (2) BARBARA THORNHILL 25 Dec 1822 in Randolph Co., IL, daughter of HENRY THORNHILL. She was born 1805 in Albemarle Co., VA, and died 1840.

Notes for BENNETT D. BALLARD:
Source: 1830 Todd County Kentucky Federal Census Records, 1840 Christian County Kentucky Federal Census Records, Margie Garr, Madonna Mahurin (madlarry@vci.net)
** 1830 - Living in Todd Co., KY - Ballard, Bennett D*
Males - (under 5) 1, (40-49) - 1, Females: (under 5) - 3, (5-9) - 1, (20-29) - 1, Females slaves - 1
** 1840 - Living in Christian Co., KY - Ballard, Bennet D.*
Males: (under 5) - 1, (10-14) - 1, (30-39) 1, Females: (under 5) - 1, (5-9) 2, (10-14) - 2, (15-19) 1, (40-49) 1

Children of BENNETT BALLARD and BARBARA THORNHILL are:

2.   i.   FRANCES L.[5] BALLARD, b. Abt. 1826, Todd Co., KY; d. Oct 1874, Ozark Co., MO.
3.   ii.   HENRY THORNHILL BALLARD, b. 04 Nov 1826, Todd Co., KY; d. 02 Jul 1900, Webster Co., KY.
4.   iii.   ELIZABETH A. BALLARD, b. 01 Oct 1828, Christian Co., KY; d. 01 May 1907, Webster Co., KY.
5.   iv.   SARAH MARGARET BALLARD, b. 1830, Todd Co., KY; d. 1890, Williamson Co., IL.
6.   v.   MARY JANE BALLARD, b. 02 Jun 1832, Todd Co., KY; d. 13 Jun 1886.
      vi.   VIRGINIA C. BALLARD, b. 1834, Todd Co., KY; m. JOHN COBB, 19 Jul 1849, Hopkins Co., KY; b. Abt. 1832.

> *Notes for VIRGINIA C. BALLARD:*
> *Source: Marriage CD#2, Hopkins County Kentucky*

7.   vii.   BENNETT MARION BALLARD, b. 18 Aug 1836, Todd Co., KY; d. 16 Feb 1926, Huggins, Texas Co., MO.
8.   viii.   BARBARA ANN BALLARD, b. 1838, Hopkins Co., KY; d. 09 Jun 1880, Hopkins Co., KY.
      ix.   EMILY SUSAN BALLARD, b. 25 Aug 1838, Todd Co., KY; d. 15 Apr 1893, Todd Co., KY; m. JOHN COE JOYNER, 25 Aug 1856, Henderson Co., KY.

Generation No. 2

2. FRANCES L.[5] BALLARD (BENNETT D.[4], BLAND[3], THOMAS[2], WILLIAM[1]) was born Abt. 1826 in Todd Co., KY, and died Oct 1874 in Ozark Co., MO. She married RICHARD A. THOMPSON 05 Jul 1849 in Hopkins Co., KY, son of SANDERS THOMPSON and ISABELLA DOSSETT. He was born 03 Mar 1827 in KY, and died 08 Dec 1905 in Silverton, Douglas Co., MO.

Notes for FRANCES L. BALLARD:
Source: Marriage CD#2, Hopkins County Kentucky

Notes for RICHARD A. THOMPSON:
Source: 1860-1900 Ozark County Missouri Federal Census Records

** 1860 - Living in Ozark Co., MO - Thompson, Richard 33 KY, Francis L 36 KY, Benjamin S 9 AR, William H 8 MO, John W 6 MO, Alexander W 4 MO, Andrew 3 MO, Barbara E 1 MO*
** 1870 - Living in Ozark Co., MO - Thompson, Richard 42 farmer KY, Francis L 46 KY, Bennet S 19 AR, William H 19 MO, John M 16 MO, Alexander W 14 MO, Barbara E 10 MO, Anderson W 12 MO, Sarah F 8 MO,*

Mary J 7 MO, Richard A 5 MO, Sanders 82 NC
** 1880 - Living in Ozark Co., MO - Thompson, Richard 53 KY NC NC, Mary Jane 48 KY IN KY, Richard Andrew 15 MO, Hicks Franklin 10 MO*
***** There are two census listings for 1900*
** 1900 - June 12 - Living in Marion, Ozark Co., MO - Thompson, Richard N - Mar 1827 md 24 yrs 1876 - KY NC TN, Mary J - May 1832 9 children - 5 living md 24 yrs 1876 KY IN TN*
** 1900 - June 19 - Living in Barren Fork twp, Ozark Co., MO - Thompson, Richard N. - March 1827 53 yrs KY unknown unknown Farmer, Mary - March 1832, 8 children 5 living KY IN TN*

Children of FRANCES BALLARD and RICHARD THOMPSON are:

	i.	BENNETT SANDERS[6] THOMPSON, b. 09 May 1851, White Co., AR; d. 13 Oct 1928, Cherokee Co., OK; m. NAOMI "OMA" HILTON, 11 Jan 1872, Ozark Co., MO; b. 20 Nov 1855, Taney Co., MO; d. 28 Nov 1918, Cherokee Co., OK.
	ii.	WILLIAM H. THOMPSON, b. Abt. 1852, Ozark Co., MO; d. 03 Dec 1891.
9.	iii.	JOHN WESLEY THOMPSON, b. 24 Feb 1854, Ozark Co., MO; d. 02 Jun 1912, OK.
	iv.	ALEXANDER WINDFIELD THOMPSON, b. Abt. 1856, Ozark Co., MO; d. 23 Jun 1877, Ozark Co., MO.
	v.	ANDERSON WHITFIELD THOMPSON, b. 13 Mar 1857, Ozark Co., MO; d. 09 Mar 1925, Mountain Home Baxter CO AR; m. MANDA ANN MORRIS, Abt. 1877, POSS. ARK; b. Abt. 1860.
	vi.	BARBARA ELLEN THOMPSON, b. Abt. 1860, Ozark Co., MO; d. Aft. 1870.
	vii.	SARAH F. THOMPSON, b. Abt. 1862, Ozark Co., MO; d. Aft. 1870.
	viii.	MARY J. THOMPSON, b. Feb 1863, Ozark Co., MO; d. Aft. Jun 1900.
	ix.	RICHARD ANDREW THOMPSON, b. Abt. 1865, Ozark Co., MO; d. Aft. 1880.
	x.	HICKS FRANKLIN THOMPSON, b. 1870, Ozark Co., MO; d. Aft. 1880.

3.   HENRY THORNHILL[5] BALLARD (BENNETT D.[4], BLAND[3], THOMAS[2], WILLIAM[1]) was born 04 Nov 1826 in Todd Co., KY, and died 02 Jul 1900 in Webster Co., KY. He married (1) JUDITH L. TRUSTY 16 Mar 1853 in Hopkins Co., KY. She was born 04 Nov 1831 in White Co., IL, and died 09 Jan 1864 in Old Aaron Reynolds, Hopkins Co., KY. He married (2) SARAH DICKERSON 11 Jan 1865 in Hopkins Co., KY, daughter of ISHAM DICKERSON and ELIZABETH. She was born Abt. 1842 in NC, and died Bef. 1872. He married (3) ALSIE ALICE DICKERSON 06 Mar 1873 in Hopkins Co., KY. She was born 14 Feb 1844 in NC, and died 27 Jun 1915 in Webster Co., KY.

Notes for HENRY THORNHILL BALLARD:
Source: Margie Garr, Marriage CD#2 Hopkins County Kentucky, 1850 Hopkins County Kentucky Federal Census Records, 1860 Webster County Kentucky Federal Census Records, 1880 Kentucky Census Soundex

** He is listed as Henry Thornhill Ballard on his daughter Barbara's death certificate*
** 1850 - Living in Hopkins Co., KY - Ballard, Henry T 25 KY farmer (living in William Reynolds household)*
** 1860 - Living in Slaughtersville, Webster Co., KY - Ballard, Henry T 33 farmer KY, Judy L 28 IL, Sarah F 6 KY, Martha J 4 KY, Elizabeth L 2 KY, Susan 1/12 KY KY, Sarah L Reynols 21 domestic KY*
** 1870 - Living in Webster Co., KY - Bullard, H T 44 farmer KY, Martha 14 KY, Elizabeth 12 KY, Belle 10 KY, Marion 8 KY, Emley 4 KY, William 2 KY*
** 1880 - Living in Webster Co., KY - Ballard, Henry T 53, Allice 36, Martha J 24, Elizebeth 22, M. F. 18, Emily S 14, Wm .Henry 12, Mildred 6, Barbara M 5, Burnet W 4*
** 1900 - Living in Webster Co., KY - Ballard, Henry - May 1825 KY KY KY, Ailsey - Dec 1853 KY NC NC, Martha J - May 1862 KY, Ella M - May 1885, Millie Rice sister in law - Feb 1841 wd KY NC NC*

Children of HENRY BALLARD and JUDITH TRUSTY are:

	i.	SARAH FRANCES[6] BALLARD, b. 25 Dec 1853, Hopkins Co., KY; d. 07 Aug 1860.
	ii.	MARTHA JANE BALLARD, b. 23 Apr 1856, Webster Co., KY; d. 27 May 1937, Hopkinsville, Christian Co., KY.

Notes for MARTHA JANE BALLARD:
Source: Christian County Kentucky Certificate of Death

iii. ELIZABETH LANIER BALLARD, b. 06 Jan 1858, Webster Co., KY; d. 29 Jun 1906, Slaughters, Webster Co., KY; m. DAGNEY O. CATES, 20 Sep 1891, Webster Co., KY; b. 30 Aug 1846, Hopkins Co., KY; d. 14 Aug 1933, Webster Co., KY.

Notes for ELIZABETH LANIER BALLARD:
Source: CD#2 marriage records for Knott Co., KY

iv. SUSAN BELLE ELZADIA BALLARD, b. 13 May 1860, Webster Co., KY; d. Aft. 1870.
v. MARION FOREST BALLARD, b. 05 Apr 1862, Webster Co., KY; d. 29 May 1949, Sasafras Grove, Webster Co., KY; m. SARAH ALICE CROWLEY, 05 Jan 1888, Webster Co., KY; b. Abt. 1862.

Children of HENRY BALLARD and SARAH DICKERSON are:

10. vi. EMILY SUSAN[6] BALLARD, b. 28 Mar 1866, Webster Co., KY; d. 1957.
    vii. WILLIAM HENRY BALLARD, b. 22 Jan 1868, Webster Co., KY; d. 14 Nov 1896, Webster Co., KY; m. MARGARETTE LIZZIE RIDDLE, 28 Oct 1896, Webster Co., KY.

Children of HENRY BALLARD and ALSIE DICKERSON are:

viii. MILDRED DORA[6] BALLARD, b. 22 Nov 1873, Webster Co., KY; d. 13 Jun 1969; m. JOHN MORGAN NANCE, 20 Dec 1893, Webster Co., KY; b. 1870.
ix. BARBARA MELVING BALLARD, b. 22 Jan 1875, Webster Co., KY; d. 12 Mar 1958, Muhlenberg Co., KY; m. (1) WOODSON; m. (2) TOM G. WEBSTER, REV., 27 Sep 1899.
x. BENNET WARNER BALLARD, b. 12 Feb 1876, Webster Co., KY; d. 04 Apr 1958; m. CLARA CHANDLER; b. Abt. 1880.

Notes for BENNET WARNER BALLARD:
Source: 1900 Hopkins County Kentucky Federal Census Records
* 1900 - Living in Hanson, Hopkins Co., KY - Ballard, Bennett W - Feb 1876 KY living with sister's family Susan E Fowler

xi. ALICE CARNELIA BALLARD, b. 08 Jan 1879, Webster Co., KY; d. 1966; m. CHARLEY E. CROWLEY, 24 Feb 1897, Knott Co., KY; b. Abt. 1879.

Notes for ALICE CARNELIA BALLARD:
Source: KY Marriage CD #2 Knott Co., KY

xii. JAMES T. BALLARD, b. 23 Jul 1882, Webster Co., KY; d. Nov 1882, KY.
xiii. ELLA MAE BALLARD, b. 08 Jan 1885, Webster Co., KY; d. 23 Sep 1928, Evansville, Vanderburgh Co., IN; m. WILLIAM BLACKSTONE, 1903.

Notes for ELLA MAE BALLARD:

Source: Vanderburgh County Indiana Certificate of Death
* She had Tuberculosis

4. ELIZABETH A.[5] BALLARD (BENNETT D.[4], BLAND[3], THOMAS[2], WILLIAM[1]) was born 01 Oct 1828 in Christian Co., KY, and died 01 May 1907 in Webster Co., KY. She married (1) WILLIAM A. COBB 30 May 1848 in 3/30 Hopkins Co., KY. He was born 09 Feb 1825 in Todd Co., KY, and died 09 Jul 1884 in VA. She married (2) YANCEY OAKLEY 15 Aug 1857 in Hopkins Co., KY. He was born 07 Jun 1823 in Granville Co., NC, and died 07 Sep 1883 in Webster Co., KY.

Notes for WILLIAM A. COBB:

Source: 1850 Hopkins County Kentucky Federal Census Records
** 1850 - Living in Hopkins Co., KY - Cobbs, William A 25 VA, Elizabeth 22, Dolly C 4/12 (living with his parents)*

Notes for YANCEY OAKLEY:

Source: 1850 Hopkins County Kentucky Federal Census Records, 1860-1880 Webster County Kentucky Federal Census Records, Margie Garr

** 1850 - Living in Hopkins Co., KY - Oakley, Yancey 25, Sarah 21, Lockey E 4, Granville 2 KY*
** 1860 - Living in Webster Co., KY - Oakley, Yance 37 farming NC, Elizabeth 31 KY, Lockey E 14 KY, Greenville 12 KY, Judy 7 KY, Ellison 2 KY, Reacy 1 KY, Dolly A Cobb 10*
** 1870 - Living in Webster Co., KY - Oakley, Yance 45 NC Elizabeth 37 KY, Green 22 KY, Juda 15 KY, Ellison 12, Yance 9 KY, Resa 11 KY, Barbery 7 KY, Willis 3 KY, Edward 2 KY*
** 1880 - Living in Vanderburg, Webster Co., KY - Oakley, Yancey 54 farmer NC, Elizabeth L 48 KY, Green B 36 KY, Elison 22, Resie 21 KY, Yancey 15, Wilis 14 KY, Edie 16 KY, Barbrie 11 KY, Woodard 8 KY, Mennie Oakley 7 KY niece*

Child of ELIZABETH BALLARD and WILLIAM COBB is:

  i.   DOLLY C.[6] COBB, b. 14 Feb 1850, Hopkins Co., KY; d. 30 Apr 1926, Hopkins Co., KY; m. JOHN W. PATE; b. Abt. 1850.

   Notes for DOLLY C. COBB:
   Source: Hopkins County Kentucky Certificate of Death

Children of ELIZABETH BALLARD and YANCEY OAKLEY are:

  ii.   ELLISON W.[6] OAKLEY, b. 1858, KY; d. Aft. 1880; m. LUELLA SPRINGFIELD, 09 Jan 1884, Webster Co., KY.
  iii.   RHESA OAKLEY, b. 1859, KY; d. 27 Sep 1931, Webster Co., KY; m. AMANDA FAUCETT; b. 30 Aug 1863, Hopkins Co., KY; d. 22 Jan 1935, Webster Co., KY.
  iv.   YANCEY J. OAKLEY, b. 27 Jan 1861, Webster Co., KY; d. 03 Sep 1942, Slaughters, Webster Co., KY; m. (1) JOSEPHINE CHANDLER; m. (2) LAURA CHANDLER, 24 Dec 1885, Webster Co., KY; b. Abt. 1861.

   Notes for YANCEY J. OAKLEY:
   Source: Webster County Kentucky Certificate of Death

  v.   BARBARA OAKLEY, b. 22 Nov 1863, Webster Co., KY; d. 17 May 1914, Henderson Co., KY; m. PATRICK WILEY, 23 Dec 1896, Webster Co., KY; b. Abt. 1860.
  vi.   WILLIS E. OAKLEY, b. 18 Aug 1866, Webster Co., KY; d. 17 Mar 1939, Hopkins Co., KY; m. SUSAN MARION JOYNER; b. 29 Jun 1874, Webster Co., KY; d. 01 Sep 1939, Hopkins Co., KY.

   Notes for WILLIS E. OAKLEY:
   Source: Hopkins County Kentucky Certificate of Death

  vii.   EDWARD OAKLEY, b. 03 Jul 1868, Webster Co., KY; d. 02 Feb 1925, Webster Co., KY.
  viii.   WOODARD FRANKLIN OAKLEY, b. 22 Nov 1871, Webster Co., KY; d. 21 Dec 1954, Webster Co., KY; m. EULAR; b. 1884; d. 1968.

5. SARAH MARGARET[5] BALLARD (BENNETT D.[4], BLAND[3], THOMAS[2], WILLIAM[1]) *was born 1830 in Todd Co., KY, and died 1890 in Williamson Co., IL. She married* WILLIAM A. THOMPSON *16 Aug 1849 in Hopkins Co., KY, son of* SANDERS THOMPSON *and* ISABELLA DOSSETT. *He was born Jul 1831 in KY, and died 28 Jan 1907 in Los Angeles Co., CA.*

Notes for SARAH MARGARET BALLARD:
Source: Marriage CD#2 Hopkins County Kentucky

Notes for WILLIAM A. THOMPSON:
Source: 1880 Perry County Illinois Federal Census Records, 1900 Franklin County Illinois Federal Census Records, Margie Garr

** 1880 - Living in St. John, Perry Co., IL - Thompson, Wm 49 KY NC NC, Sarah M 50 KY VA VA, Wm S 21 MO KY KY*
** 1900 - Living in Frankfort, Franklin Co., IL - Living with son in law William Rogers*

Children of SARAH BALLARD and WILLIAM THOMPSON are:

11.	i.	BARBARA ISABELL[6] THOMPSON, b. May 1850, AR; d. 24 Apr 1910, Lake Creek, Williamson Co., IL.
12.	ii.	FRANCES ELIZABETH THOMPSON, b. 12 Dec 1851, AR; d. 19 Feb 1912, Pittsburg, Williamson Co., IL.
13.	iii.	JOHN WESLEY THOMPSON, b. 21 Oct 1856, St. Genevieve, MO; d. 07 Feb 1922, Los Angeles Co., CA.
14.	iv.	WILLIAM SAUNDERS THOMPSON, b. 25 Oct 1859, MO; d. 02 Dec 1945, Los Angeles Co., CA.

6. MARY JANE[5] BALLARD (BENNETT D.[4], BLAND[3], THOMAS[2], WILLIAM[1]) was born 02 Jun 1832 in Todd Co., KY, and died 13 Jun 1886. She married JOHN SHADRICK 09 Sep 1852 in Hopkins Co., KY. He was born 1816 in NC, and died 10 Jul 1886 in Hopkins Co., KY.

Notes for MARY JANE BALLARD:
Source: Marriage CD#2 Hopkins Co. Kentucky

Notes for JOHN SHADRICK:
Source: Daviess County Kentucky Certificate of Death, 1860-1880 Hopkins County Kentucky Federal Census Records

** 1860 - Living in Hopkins Co., KY - Shedrick, John 38 farmer NC, Mary J 27 KY, Barbra E 7 KY, Eliza J 4 KY, Malinda A 3 KY, Garland 10/12 KY*
** 1870 - Living in Hopkins Co., KY - Shadrick, John 53 farmer NC, Mary J 37 KY, Barbar E 17 KY, Eliza J 15 KY, Malinda 13 KY, William E 9 KY, John 7 KY, Robert F 4 KY, Anderson P 3 KY, Mary E 3 KY, Mascum 1/12*
** 1880 - Living in Hopkins Co., KY - Shadrick, John 64 farmer NC NC NC, Mary J 48 KY KY KY, Barbara E 26 KY, William E 19 KY, John 16 KY, Robt F 14 KY, Anderson P 11 KY, Mary E 11 KY, Henry J 10 KY*

Children of MARY BALLARD and JOHN SHADRICK are:

	i.	BARBARA E.[6] SHADRICK, b. 04 Nov 1853, Hopkins Co., KY; d. 16 Mar 1922, Daviess Co., KY.
	ii.	ELIZABETH J. SHADRICK, b. 1855, Hopkins Co., KY; d. Aft. 1880.
15.	iii.	MALINDA SHADRICK, b. 03 Mar 1857, Hopkins Co., KY; d. Aft. 1900.
	iv.	GARLAND SHADRICK, b. 1859, Hopkins Co., KY; d. Aft. 1860.
	v.	WILLIAM E. SHADRICK, b. 12 Jul 1862, Hopkins Co., KY; d. 24 Jun 1933, Hopkins Co., KY.

Notes for WILLIAM E. SHADRICK:
Source: Hopkins County Kentucky Certificate of Death

	vi.	JOHN STEPHEN SHADRICK, b. 15 Jun 1864, Hopkins Co., KY; d. 01 Mar 1941, Hopkins Co., KY; m. ANNIE AVERITT, 17 Nov 1886, Webster Co., KY; b. Abt. 1863.

Notes for JOHN STEPHEN SHADRICK:
Source: Hopkins County Kentucky Certificate of Death

	vii.	ROBERT F. SHADRICK, b. 1866, Hopkins Co., KY; d. 10 Feb 1932, Hopkins Co., KY.

viii. ANDERSON PASCAL SHADRICK, b. 11 Aug 1867, Hopkins Co., KY; d. 17 May 1945, Hopkins Co., KY; m. SARAH EMMA WILLIAMS, 20 Oct 1897, Webster Co., KY; b. 1880, Webster Co., KY; d. 1958, Evansville, Vanderburgh Co., IN.

Notes for ANDERSON PASCAL SHADRICK:
Source: Hopkins County Kentucky Certificate of Death

ix. MARY E. SHADRICK, b. 1868, Hopkins Co., KY; d. Aft. 1880; m. G. W. NANCE, 17 Dec 1893, Webster Co., KY; b. 1868, Hopkins Co., KY.

x. HENRY MASCUM SHADRICK, b. 05 Apr 1870, Hopkins Co., KY; d. 27 Sep 1925, Henderson Co., KY; m. CLEMENTINE MINTON.

Notes for HENRY MASCUM SHADRICK:
Source: Henderson County Kentucky Certificate of Death

7. BENNETT MARION⁵ BALLARD (BENNETT D.⁴, BLAND³, THOMAS², WILLIAM¹) was born 18 Aug 1836 in Todd Co., KY, and died 16 Feb 1926 in Huggins, Texas Co., MO. He married MARY GREEN 23 Feb 1860 in Jackson Co., AR. She was born 30 May 1845 in AL, and died 26 Oct 1919 in Huggins, Texas Co., MO.

Notes for BENNETT MARION BALLARD:
Source: 1880-1920 Texas County Missouri Federal Census Records, 1880 Missouri Federal Census Record Soundex, Margie Garr, JeffNC42@aol.com, Texas County Missouri Death Certificate

* 1880 - Living in Texas Co., MO - Ballard, B.M. 44 KY, Mary 35 AL, Barbra S 19 AR, Sarah F 17 AR, John C 12 IL, Grinstead 8 MO, Arthur B 4 MO, Charles W 5/12 MO
* 1900 - Living in Texas Co., MO - Ballard, Bennett - Aug 1836 KY TN TN, Mary - May 1845 AL GA AL, Barbra - Dec 1860 AR, Charles W - Dec 1879 MO
* 1910 - Living in Upton, Texas Co., MO - Ballard, Bennett 73 we KY NC VA, Mary 64 -11 ch 6 living AL GA NC, Charles W. 30 MO KY AL, Nora 27 MO KY AL
* 1920 - Living in Texas Co., MO with son Charles W Ballard

Children of BENNETT BALLARD and MARY GREEN are:
      i. BARBARA SUSANNA⁶ BALLARD, b. 10 Dec 1860, AR; d. 05 Jun 1908, Texas Co., MO.
      ii. SARAH FRANCES BALLARD, b. 10 Sep 1862, AR; d. 01 Jul 1895, Texas Co., MO.
      iii. WILLIAM HENRY BALLARD, b. Abt. 1864, AR; d. AR.
16.   iv. JOHN CALVIN BALLARD, b. 21 Oct 1867, Redbud, Randolph IL; d. 27 Mar 1959, Mountain Grove, Wright Co., MO.
      v. ALVA ANN BALLARD, b. 1870, Randolph Co., IL.
17.   vi. GUINSTAND DOUGLAS BALLARD, b. 16 Jul 1872, MO; d. 16 Dec 1941, Upton, Texas Co., MO.
18.   vii. ARTHUR BARRETT BALLARD, b. 08 Aug 1876, Texas Co., MO; d. 10 Aug 1936, Texas Co., MO.
19.   viii. CHARLES WALTER BALLARD, b. 20 Dec 1879, Texas Co., MO; d. 16 Mar 1968, Clay Co., MO.
      ix. NORA MINNIE BALLARD, b. 22 Mar 1883, MO; d. 17 Jun 1966, Mt. Grove, Wright Co., MO; m. GEORGE ALTIS.
20.   x. ROLLA MARION BALLARD, b. 10 Apr 1886, Huggins, Texas Co., O; d. 10 Dec 1956, Mt. Grove, Wright Co., MO.

8. BARBARA ANN⁵ BALLARD (BENNETT D.⁴, BLAND³, THOMAS², WILLIAM¹) was born 1838 in Hopkins Co., KY, and died 09 Jun 1880 in Hopkins Co., KY. She married WILLIAM MARION BROWN 23 Apr 1860 in Hopkins Co., KY. He was born Dec 1837 in Hopkins Co., KY, and died 1920 in Hopkins Co., KY.

Notes for WILLIAM MARION BROWN:
Source: 1860 & 1880 Hopkins County Kentucky Federal Census Records, 1870 Webster County Kentucky Federal Census Records, Marriage CD #2 Hopkins Co., KY, Margie Garr

** 1860 - Living in Slaughtersville, Hopkins Co., KY - Brown, William 25 farmer KY, Barbre M 21 KY*
** 1870 - Living in Webster Co., KY - Brown, William M 32 farmer KY, Barbra M 31 KY, Alexander 9 KY, Richard H 7 KY, Charles 5 KY, Ellenora 3, Mary L 2, Robert L 1/12 (hard to read) KY*
** 1880 - Living in Hanson, Hopkins Co., KY - Brown, William 42 cooper KY, Barbara 41 KY, Alexander T 19 KY, Charles M 15 KY, Elleanor 13 KY, Mary L 12 KY, Laura 10 KY, Emma 8 KY, William W 4 KY, Theodoria E 3 KY, Virdia 10/12 KY*

Children of BARBARA BALLARD and WILLIAM BROWN are:

      i.   ALEXANDER T.[6] BROWN, b. 1861, Hopkins Co., KY; d. Aft. 1891; m. NANCY WALLACE, 20 May 1891, Webster Co., KY; b. Abt. 1865.

      ii.   RICHARD HENRY BROWN, b. 10 Jan 1863, Hopkins Co., KY; d. 22 Mar 1940, Hopkins Co., KY; m. ROSA M. CRABTREE, 15 Mar 1883, Hopkins Co., KY; b. Abt. 1865.

21.   iii.   CHARLES MASON BROWN, b. 10 Jun 1865, Hopkins Co., KY; d. 21 Nov 1927, Webster Co., KY.

      iv.   ELLA NORA BROWN, b. 14 Jul 1867, Hopkins Co., KY; d. 15 May 1944, Pensacola, Mayes Co., OK; m. THOMAS S. PILANT, 23 Dec 1888, Slaughtersville, Webster Co., KY; b. Abt. 1865.

      v.   MARY L. BROWN, b. 12 Oct 1868, Hopkins Co., KY; d. 26 Nov 1915, Hopkins Co., KY; m. NOAH S. BAILEY, 22 Nov 1891, Hopkins Co., KY; b. Abt. 1865.

      vi.   ROBERT L. BROWN, b. Feb 1870, Hansen, Hopkins Co., KY; d. 04 Dec 1874, Hopkins Co., KY.

      vii.   LAURA BROWN, b. 1871, Hansen, Hopkins Co., KY; d. 1940; m. FRANCIS W. LIVINGSTON, 30 Jul 1893, Hopkins Co., KY; b. Abt. 1870.

     viii.   EMMA BROWN, b. 21 Feb 1872, Hopkins Co., KY; d. 16 Dec 1947, Hopkins Co., KY; m. JOHN CRABTREE, 20 Nov 1891, Hopkins Co., KY; b. 1866.

      ix.   WILLIAM W. BROWN, b. 21 Jan 1875, Hanson, Hopkins Co., KY; d. 18 Dec 1954, Webster Co., KY; m. NORA TAPP, 06 Jan 1897, Webster Co., KY; b. Abt. 1875.

      x.   THEODOSA E. BROWN, b. 1877, Hansen, Hopkins Co., KY; d. Aft. 1880; m. W. M. CRABTREE, 08 Dec 1897, Hopkins Co., KY; b. Abt. 1875.

      xi.   VIRDIA BROWN, b. 22 Jul 1879, Hansen, Hopkins Co., KY; d. 12 Jul 1919, Hopkins Co., KY; m. CHARLES FRANKLIN BLUE.

Generation No. 3

9. JOHN WESLEY[6] THOMPSON (FRANCES L.[5] BALLARD, BENNETT D.[4], BLAND[3], THOMAS[2], WILLIAM[1]) *was born 24 Feb 1854 in Ozark Co., MO, and died 02 Jun 1912 in OK. He married MARTHA JANE VANMETER 11 Mar 1874 in AR. She was born Nov 1857 in MO, and died 1942.*

Children of JOHN THOMPSON and MARTHA VANMETER are:

      i.   ELENORE[7] THOMPSON, b. 1877, MO; d. Aft. 1880.

      ii.   MARY THOMPSON, b. 1879, MO; d. Aft. 1880.

      iii.   EASTER ELSIE THOMPSON, b. 09 Jan 1886, AR; d. 01 Jun 1965, Muskogee Co., OK; m. JOSEPH ARTHUR HATHCOAT; b. 01 Jan 1878, Lawrence Co., AR; d. 18 Oct 1954, Wagoner Co., OK.

10. EMILY SUSAN[6] BALLARD (HENRY THORNHILL[5], BENNETT D.[4], BLAND[3], THOMAS[2], WILLIAM[1]) *was born 28 Mar 1866 in Webster Co., KY, and died 1957. She married MOODY TUCKER FOWLER 12 May 1886 in Webster Co., KY. He was born 16 Sep 1861 in KY, and died 21 Jul 1936 in Hopkins Co., KY.*

Notes for EMILY SUSAN BALLARD:
Source: Marriage CD#2 Knott Co., KY

Notes for MOODY TUCKER FOWLER:
Source: 1900-1910 Hopkins County Kentucky Federal Census Records, 1920 Vanderburgh County Indiana Federal Census Records, Hopkins County Kentucky Certificate of Death
** 1900 - Living in Hanson, Hopkins Co., KY - Fowler, Moody T - Sep 1862 KY NC NC, Susan E - Mar 1866 - 7*

children 6 living KY unknown NC, Virgel M. - Mar 1887 KY, Evey L - Dec 1888 KY, Arrola E - Apr 1893 KY, Cora M - Nov 1895 KY, infant son - Feb 1900 KY, Bennett W Ballard brother in law - Feb 1876 KY
** 1910 - Living in Hopkins Co., KY - Fowler, Moody T 48 KY NC NC, Susan E 40 - 8 children 7 living KY KY NC, Eva 21 KY, Arola 17 KY, Cora 14 KY, Oma 12 KY, Goebel 10 KY, Marvin -\11/12 KY*
** 1920 - Living in Evansville, Vanderburgh Co., IN - Fowler, Mooty F 58 KY NC NC, Susan E 53 KY KY NC, Eva L 30 KY, Cora M 24 KY, Oma 21 KY, Goble H 19 KY, Marvin T 10 KY*

Children of EMILY BALLARD and MOODY FOWLER are:

  i. VIRGIL M.[7] FOWLER, b. 06 Mar 1887, KY; d. 28 May 1915, KY.

    Notes for VIRGIL M. FOWLER:
    Source: Kentucky Certificate of Death (county of death is crossed out) Signatures are in Madisonville KY

  ii. EVA LILLIAN FOWLER, b. 03 Dec 1888, KY; d. 17 Nov 1979, Evansville, Vanderburgh Co., IN.

    Notes for EVA LILLIAN FOWLER:
    Source: Vanderburgh County Indiana Medical Certificate of Death

  iii. ARROLA ELIZABETH FOWLER, b. 27 Apr 1893, Madisonville, Hopkins Co., KY; d. 31 Jul 1964, Indianapolis, Marion Co., IN; m. HENRY CLAY SLATON; b. 28 Jul 1895, Hopkins Co., KY; d. 23 Jan 1939, Madisonville, Hopkins Co., KY.

    Notes for ARROLA ELIZABETH FOWLER:
    Source: Marion County Indiana Medical Certificate of Death

  iv. CORA MAE FOWLER, b. 07 Nov 1895, Hopkins Co., KY; d. 12 Apr 1979, Evansville, Vanderburgh Co., IN; m. WILLIAM DIXIE GRAHAM; b. 15 Nov 1895, KY; d. 27 Dec 1972, Tucson, Pima Co., AZ.

    Notes for CORA MAE FOWLER:
    Source: Vanderburg County Indiana Coroner's Certificate of Death

  v. OMA FOWLER, b. 26 Jan 1898, Hopkins Co., KY; d. 21 May 1973; m. WILLIAM L. WINTERNHEIMER; b. 28 Nov 1887, IN; d. 03 Apr 1971.

    Notes for WILLIAM L. WINTERNHEIMER:
    Source: 1930 Vanderburgh County Indiana Federal Census Records

    ** 1930 - Living in Evansville, Vanderburgh Co., IN - Winterwheimer, Wm L 43 IN IN IN, Oma 32 KY KY KY, Bettye J 7 IN, Iris W 3 10/12 IN, Moody T. Fowler father in law 68 KY NC NC, Emily S mother in law 64 KY MO KY, Eva L sister in law 41 KY, Marvin T brother in law 20 KY*

  vi. WILLIAM GOEBEL FOWLER, b. 05 Feb 1900, Slaughters, Webster Co., KY; d. 15 Aug 1924, Evansville, Vanderburgh Co., IN.

    Notes for WILLIAM GOEBEL FOWLER:
    Source: Vanderburgh County Indiana Certificate of Death

  vii. MARVIN T. FOWLER, b. 03 Jun 1909, Hopkins Co., KY; d. 29 Jan 1994, Evansville, Vanderburgh Co., IN; m. IMOGENE PRITCHETT, Bef. 1940; b. 02 Oct 1917, Madisonville, KY; d. 03 Jul 2009, Evansville, Vanderburgh Co., IN.

11. BARBARA ISABELL[6] THOMPSON (SARAH MARGARET[5] BALLARD, BENNETT D.[4], BLAND[3], THOMAS[2], WILLIAM[1]) *was born May 1850 in AR, and died 24 Apr 1910 in Lake Creek, Williamson Co., IL. She married WILLIAM*

CAMPBELL ROGERS 09 Feb 1872 in Williamson Co., IL. He was born Dec 1851 in TN, and died Aft. 1900.

Notes for WILLIAM CAMPBELL ROGERS:
Source: 1900 Franklin County Illinois Federal Census Records, 1910 Williamson County Illinois Federal Census Records
** 1900 - Living in Frankfort, Franklin Co., IL - Rogers, William C - Dec 1851 TN, Barbara - May 1850 AR, Mary - May 1875 IL, James M - Aug 1858 IL, Thompson, William father in law - July 1831 wd KY*
1910 - Living in Lake Creek, Williamson Co., IL - Rodgers, William 58 TN TN TN, Barbora J 59 AR KY KY, James M 21 IL

Children of BARBARA THOMPSON and WILLIAM ROGERS are:
  i. *SARAH E.[7] ROGERS, b. Abt. 1873.*
  ii. *MARSHALL ROGERS, b. 18 Feb 1874, Williamson Co., IL; d. 25 Nov 1961; m. CORA WILLIAMS.*
  iii. *MARY ROGERS, b. May 1875, IL; d. Aft. 1900.*
  iv. *MINNIE BELL ROGERS, b. 1877, IL; d. 21 Jan 1951, Williamson Co., IL.*
  v. *JAMES M. ROGERS, b. Aug 1888, IL; d. Aft. 1900.*

12. *FRANCES ELIZABETH[6] THOMPSON (SARAH MARGARET[5] BALLARD, BENNETT D.[4], BLAND[3], THOMAS[2], WILLIAM[1]) was born 12 Dec 1851 in AR, and died 19 Feb 1912 in Pittsburg, Williamson Co., IL. She married JOHN WESLEY WILLIAMS 30 Apr 1868 in Williamson Co., IL, son of ANTHONY WILLIAMS. He was born 24 Mar 1844 in KY, and died 08 Dec 1924 in Williamson Co., IL.*

Notes for JOHN WESLEY WILLIAMS:
Source: 1880 - 1910 Williamson County Illinois Federal Census Records, Williamson County Illinois Death Records

** 1880 - Living in Lake Creek, Williamson Co., IL - Williams, John Wesley 36 KY KY TN, Francis 28 AR KY KY, Laura A. 11 IL, William W 10 IL, John A 8 IL, George A 6 IL, Charlie B 3 IL, Margaret R 1 IL*
** 1900 - Living in Lake Creek, Williamson Co., IL - Williams, John W - Mar 1844 KY KY TN, Frances E - Dec 1851 - 8 children 7 living AR KY KY, George A - Mar 1875 IL, James L - Mar 1883 IL, Bertie A Odle grand au - Aug 1886 IL, Benjamin W Odle grandson - Nova 1889 IL*
** 1910 - Living in Lake Creek, Williamson Co., IL - Williams, John W 66 farmer KY KY TN, Frances E 58 - 8 children 5 living AR KY KY, George A 35 laborer IL*

Children of FRANCES THOMPSON and JOHN WILLIAMS are:

22. i. *LAURA ANN[7] WILLIAMS, b. Abt. 1869, Williamson Co., IL; d. 12 Aug 1907, IL.*
  ii. *WILLIAM WESLEY WILLIAMS, b. 04 Jun 1870, Williamson Co., IL; d. 23 Dec 1935, Williamson Co., IL; m. OLLIE; b. 04 Feb 1876; d. 24 Feb 1912.*
  iii. *JOHN A. WILLIAMS, b. 24 Feb 1872, Williamson Co., IL; d. 26 Jul 1944, Kane Co., IL.*
  iv. *GEORGE A. WILLIAMS, b. Dec 1875, Williamson Co., IL; d. Aft. 1910.*
  v. *CHARLES BURL WILLIAMS, b. 17 Feb 1877, Williamson Co., IL; d. 25 Aug 1957, Dixon, Webster Co., KY; m. SOFRONIE TAYLOR, 23 Nov 1907, Vanderburgh, IN.*

    Notes for CHARLES BURL WILLIAMS:
    Source: Social Security Records, Webster County Kentucky Certificate of Death

  vi. *MARGARET ROSA WILLIAMS, b. Abt. 1879, Williamson Co., IL; d. 1907.*
  vii. *ROY WILLIAMS, b. 29 Mar 1882, Williamson Co., IL; d. 06 Dec 1923, Williamson Co., IL; m. CORA; b. Abt. 1887, IL; d. Aft. 1910.*

    Notes for ROY WILLIAMS:
    Source: 1910 Williamson County Illinois Federal Census Records
    1910 - Living in Lake Creek, Williamson Co., IL - Williams, Roy 26 manager IL KY AR, Cora 23 - 1 child 0 living IL IL IL

viii.   JAMES LEROY WILLIAMS, b. 29 Mar 1882, Williamson Co., IL; d. 06 Dec 1923, Williamson Co., IL.

13. JOHN WESLEY[6] THOMPSON (SARAH MARGARET[5] BALLARD, BENNETT D.[4], BLAND[3], THOMAS[2], WILLIAM[1]) was born 21 Oct 1856 in St. Genevieve, MO, and died 07 Feb 1922 in Los Angeles Co., CA. He married NANCY ANNE WEAVER 21 Oct 1877 in Williamson Co., IL. She was born 20 Apr 1857 in Williamson Co., IL, and died 26 Aug 1922 in Los Angeles Co., CA.

Notes for JOHN WESLEY THOMPSON:
Source: 1880 Perry County Illinois Federal Census Records, 1900 Williamson County Illinois Federal Census Records, 1910 Los Angeles County California Federal Census Records

** 1880 - Living in St. John, Perry Co., IL - Thompson, John 24 KY KY KY, Nancy 21 IL MS TN, Lulu 5/12 IL*
** 1900 - Living in Lake Creek, Williamson Co., IL - Thompson, J. W - Oct 1857 MO KY KY, Nancy A - Apr 1857 - 10 children 7 living IL IL IL, Lula E - Jan 1882 IL, William E - Feb 1882 IL, Emery A. - Dec 1883 IL, Mary B - Oct 1884 IL, Gertie E - Nov 1887 IL, Henry H - Sept 1888 MO, Cecil - Nov 1897 IL*
** 1910 - Living in San Antonio, Los Angeles Co., CA - Thompson, John W 53 MO KY KY, Nancy A 54 - 11 children 8 living IL MS TN, William E 28 IL, Emery A 26 IL, Mary B 24 IL, Gertrude E 22 MO, Harry H 20 MO, Cecil V 12 IL, John A 9 IL*

Children of JOHN THOMPSON and NANCY WEAVER are:
> i.   LULU EMMA[7] THOMPSON, b. 25 Jan 1880, Perry Co., IL; d. 21 May 1965, Los Angeles Co., CA.
>
> *Notes for LULU EMMA THOMPSON:*
> *Source: Social Security Records*
>
> ii.   WILLIAM E. THOMPSON, b. 02 Feb 1882, IL; d. 21 Aug 1958, Los Angeles Co., CA.
> iii.   EMERY A. THOMPSON, b. Dec 1883, IL; d. Aft. 1910.
> iv.   MARY B. THOMPSON, b. Oct 1884, IL; d. Aft. 1900.
> v.   GERTIE E. THOMPSON, b. 02 Nov 1887, MO; d. 1956, Los Angeles Co., CA.
> vi.   HENRY H. THOMPSON, b. 17 Sep 1889, MO; d. 16 Nov 1921, Los Angeles Co., CA.
> vii.   CECIL THOMPSON, b. Nov 1897, IL; d. Aft. 1900.
> viii.   JOHN A. THOMPSON, b. Abt. 1901, IL; d. Aft. 1910.

14. WILLIAM SAUNDERS[6] THOMPSON (SARAH MARGARET[5] BALLARD, BENNETT D.[4], BLAND[3], THOMAS[2], WILLIAM[1]) was born 25 Oct 1859 in MO, and died 02 Dec 1945 in Los Angeles Co., CA. He married CLARA BETZ BEATS 03 Apr 1884 in Perry, IL. She was born 04 Jul 1862 in Perry Co., IL, and died 15 Oct 1947 in Los Angeles Co., CA.

Notes for WILLIAM SAUNDERS THOMPSON:
Source: 1900 Perry County Illinois Federal Census Records, 1910 Los Angeles County California Federal Census Records

** 1900 - Living in Du Quoin, Perry Co., IL - Thompson, William S - Oct 1859 MO KY KY, Clara - July 1862 - 5 children 4 living - IL Germany PA, Roy - Jan 1885 IL, Ray - Aug 1890 IL, Virgil - Oct 1891 IL, Margaret - Apr 1898 IL*
** 1910 - Living in San Antonio, Los Angeles Co., CA - Thompson, Clara 48 IL Germany, PA, Roy 24 IL, Ray 20 IL, Virgil 19 IL, Margaret 12 IL, Katherine 10 IL*

Notes for CLARA BETZ BEATS:
Source: Roman Catholic Diocese of Springfield Illinois Sacramental Records
** August the 17th - I Baptized Clara Beats born July the 4th 1862 Daughter of Nicholas and Margret Beats. Apr Nicholas and Mary Nugier. Thomas Cusac, CP*

Children of WILLIAM THOMPSON and CLARA BEATS are:

i. ROY[7] THOMPSON, b. Abt. Jan 1885, IL; d. Aft. 1910.
ii. RAY THOMPSON, b. Abt. Aug 1890, IL; d. Aft. 1910.
iii. VIRGIL THOMPSON, b. Abt. Oct 1891, IL; d. Aft. 1910.
iv. MARGARET THOMPSON, b. Abt. Apr 1898, IL; d. Aft. 1910.
v. KATHERINE THOMPSON, b. Abt. 1900, IL; d. Aft. 1910.

15. MALINDA[6] SHADRICK (MARY JANE[5] BALLARD, BENNETT D.[4], BLAND[3], THOMAS[2], WILLIAM[1]) was born 03 Mar 1857 in Hopkins Co., KY, and died Aft. 1900. She married THOMAS R. ROWE 17 Oct 1878 in Hopkins Co., KY. He was born Sep 1838 in KY, and died Aft. 1900.

Notes for THOMAS R. ROWE:
Source 1900 White County Arkansas Federal Census Records
** 1900 - Living in Searcy, White Co., AR - Rowe, Thos R - Sept 1838 KY KKY KY - Minister Gospel, Linnie A - Mar 1857 KY NC KY magnetic healer, Lula - June 1887 KY, Bonnie - May 1892 IL, Lacy F - May189 IL, Maud - Aug 1894 IL*

Children of MALINDA SHADRICK and THOMAS ROWE are:
i. LULA[7] ROWE, b. Abt. Jun 1887, KY; d. Aft. 1900.
ii. BONNIE ROWE, b. Abt. May 1892, KY; d. Aft. 1900.
iii. LACY F. ROWE, b. Abt. May 1889, IL; d. Aft. 1900.
iv. MAUD ROWE, b. Abt. Aug 1894, IL; d. Aft. 1900.

16. JOHN CALVIN[6] BALLARD (BENNETT MARION[5], BENNETT D.[4], BLAND[3], THOMAS[2], WILLIAM[1]) was born 21 Oct 1867 in Redbud, Randolph IL, and died 27 Mar 1959 in Mountain Grove, Wright Co., MO. He married MARY MILISSA WILSON 26 Dec 1889. She was born Jan 1873 in MO, and died Aft. 1930.

Notes for JOHN CALVIN BALLARD:
Source: LDS-IGI, 1900 Wright County Missouri Federal Census Records, 1910-1930 Texas County Missouri Federal Census Records
** 1900 - Living in Wright Co., MO - Ballard, John C Oct IL, Millissa Jan 1873 Married 11 yrs 5 children 4 living, Ollie M Feb 1891 MO, Alva A May 1895 MO, Walter S June 1898 MO, Douglas (brother) MO KY AL*
** 1910 - Living in Upton, Texas Co., MO - Ballard, John C 41 IL KY AL, Malissa 36 8 children 7 living MO, TN TN, Ollie M 18 MO IL MO, Bennett H 15 MO IL MO, Alva A 13 MO, Walter S 11 MO, Mamie 8 MO, Gladys E 5 MO, Arval A. 3 MO, Mary Z Wilson 62 Aunt in law TN TN TN*
** 1920 - Living in Upton, Texas Co., MO - Ballard, John C 53 IL, Mary M 45 MO, Mayme 17 MO, Gladys 14 MO, Arval 12 MO, Irena M 9 MO*
** 1930 - Living in Upton, Texas Co., MO - Ballard, John C 62, Melissa J 56, Arvil 22, Clarena 19*

Children of JOHN BALLARD and MARY WILSON are:
i. OLLIE MAY[7] BALLARD, b. 19 Feb 1892, MO; d. 04 Oct 1956; m. GEORGE A. TATE; b. 11 Jul 1889; d. 10 Aug 1978.
ii. BENNETT HARRISON BALLARD, b. 02 May 1894, Astoria, Wright Co., MO; d. 02 Sep 1971, Mount Pisgah Cemetery, Roby, Texas Co., MO; m. HATTIE KABLER; b. 10 Jul 1895; d. 17 Feb 1972.
iii. ALVA ANN BALLARD, b. 03 May 1896, Astoria, Wright Co., MO; d. 21 Jan 1958; m. GEORGE AUSTIN CLEAVER; b. 02 Sep 1895; d. 14 Oct 1960.
iv. WALTER SAMUEL BALLARD, b. 05 Jun 1899, Astoria ,Wright Co., MO; d. 05 Dec 1985; m. WILMA FANSIER.
v. MAYME INES BALLARD, b. 1902, Astoria ,Wright Co., MO; d. 1965; m. JOHN M. TRAPP.
vi. GLADYS ELFIE BALLARD, b. 07 Jul 1905, Astoria ,Wright Co., MO; d. 14 Feb 1992, Cabool, Texas Co., MO; m. JULIUS KOCH.
vii. ARVIL L. BALLARD, b. 21 Apr 1907, MO; d. Dec 1981; m. ROSELMA.
viii. CLARENA M. BALLARD, b. 03 May 1910, Texas Co., MO; d. 19 Nov 1986; m. PAUL FOSTER.

17. GUINSTAND DOUGLAS[6] BALLARD (BENNETT MARION[5], BENNETT D.[4], BLAND[3], THOMAS[2], WILLIAM[1]) *was born 16 Jul 1872 in MO, and died 16 Dec 1941 in Upton, Texas Co., MO. He married* REBECCA COFFMAN. *She was born 1879 in MO, and died 1955.*

Notes for GUINSTAND DOUGLAS BALLARD:
Source: 1910-1940 Texas County Missouri Federal Census Records, Texas County Missouri Standard Certificate of Death

** 1910 - Living in Upton, Texas Co., MO - Ballard, Guiney D 37 MO KY AL, Rebecca N 30 MO MO MO, Bevan 7 MO, Melvin 6 MO, Tony 4 MO, Zella 1 10/12 MO*
** 1920 - Living in Upton, Texas Co., MO - Ballard, Guinstard 46 MO, Rebecca 41 MO, Bevan 17 MO, Tony 13 MO, Zella 11 MO, Eula 9 MO, Willard 4 2/12, Raymone 1 9/12*
** 1930 - Living in Upton, Texas Co., MO - Ballard, Guinstand D 57 MO, Rebecca 51 MO, Willard B 14 MO, Raymond 12 MO*
** 1940 - Living in Upton, Texas Co., MO - Ballard G D 68, Rebecka 62, Melvin 36, Tony 34*

Children of GUINSTAND BALLARD *and* REBECCA COFFMAN *are:*

     i.   BEVAN M.[7] BALLARD, *b. 09 Jul 1902, MO; d. 10 Jul 1978; m.* VIANNA MARGARET HUTSELL.
    ii.   MELVIN BENNETT BALLARD, *b. 29 Oct 1903, Wright Co., MO; d. 08 Feb 1964, Butler Co., MO; m.* WILMA RANDALL; *b. 27 Dec 1922, Harlan Co., NE; d. 03 May 2010.*
    iii.   TONY BALLARD, *b. 18 Feb 1906, MO; d. 28 May 1971.*
    iv.   ZELLA BALLARD, *b. 21 Jun 1908, MO; d. 23 Apr 1993; m.* THEODORE CROSS.
    v.   EULA BALLARD, *b. 1911, MO; d. Aft. 1920.*
    vi.   WILLARD BALLARD, *b. 23 Oct 1915, MO; d. 13 Jul 1958.*
    vii.   RAYMOND BALLARD, *b. 28 Mar 1918, MO; d. 27 Nov 1968.*

18. ARTHUR BARRETT[6] BALLARD (BENNETT MARION[5], BENNETT D.[4], BLAND[3], THOMAS[2], WILLIAM[1]) *was born 08 Aug 1876 in Texas Co., MO, and died 10 Aug 1936 in Texas Co., MO. He married* MARY MAGDELINE "MAGGIE" CLEAVER *21 Aug 1898 in Texas Co., MO, daughter of* JOHN CLEAVER *and* JOSEPHINE BURCH. *She was born 12 Jul 1878 in Houston, MO, and died 19 Jul 1951.*

Notes for ARTHUR BARRETT BALLARD:
Source: Texas County Missouri Death Certificate, 1900 - 1920 Wright County Missouri Federal Census Records, 1930 Texas County Missouri Federal Census Records

** 1900 - Living in Montgomery, Wright Co., MO - Ballard, Arthur B - Aug 1876 MO, Mary M - July 1878, Mary J 7/1899*
** 1910 - Living in Montgomery, Wright Co., MO - Ballard, Arthur 33, Magga 32, Marry 10, Martha 2/12*
** 1920 - Living in Montgomery, Wright Co., MO - Ballard, Arthur B 43 MO, Maggie M 41, Arthur M 9, Claborne T 6*
** 1930 - Living in Morris, Texas Co., MO - Ballar, Arthur D 53 MO KY AR, Mary M 51 MO IN IN, Claybourne T 16 MO*

Notes for MARY MAGDELINE "MAGGIE" CLEAVER:
Source: Social Security Records

Children of ARTHUR BALLARD *and* MARY CLEAVER *are:*
    i.   MARY J.[7] BALLARD, *b. Jul 1899, Montgomery, Wright Co., MO; d. Aft. 1910.*
    ii.   ARTHA BALLARD, *b. 27 Jan 1910, Montgomery, Wright Co., MO; d. 04 Dec 2000; m.* WILLIAM RAY HUTSELL; *b. 21 Aug 1906, Texas Co., MO; d. 05 Feb 2002.*

        Notes for WILLIAM RAY HUTSELL:
        Source: 1940 Wright County Missouri Federal Census Records

* *1940 - Living in Van Buren, Wright Co., MO - Hutsell, Ray 34 MO, Artha 30 MO*

        iii.   ARTHUR M. BALLARD, b. 1911, Montgomery, Wright Co., MO; d. Aft. 1920.

23.   *iv.*   CLAIBORNE BALLARD, b. 18 Oct 1913, Montgomery, Wright Co., MO; d. 24 Mar 1971, Wright Co., MO.

19. CHARLES WALTER[6] BALLARD (BENNETT MARION[5], BENNETT D.[4], BLAND[3], THOMAS[2], WILLIAM[1]) was born 20 Dec 1879 in Texas Co., MO, and died 16 Mar 1968 in Clay Co., MO. He married EFFIE SHELLY 02 Oct 1912 in Texas Co. MO, daughter of JACK SHELLY and MAUDE DYE. She was born 05 Dec 1889 in MO, and died 04 May 1955 in Holden, Johnson Co., MO.

Notes for CHARLES WALTER BALLARD:
Source: 1920 Texas County Missouri Federal Census Records, 1930-1940 Johnson County Missouri Federal Census Records

* *1920 - Living in Upton, Texas Co., MO - Ballard, Charles W 40 MO, Effie 30 MO, Helen 6 MO, Hazel 5 MO, Etta 3 11/12 MO, Lauretta 1 9/12 MO, Bennett M 83*
* *1930 - Living in Holden, Johnson Co., MO - Ballard, Charles W 50 MO KY MO, Effie 40 MO US MO, Helen 16 MO, Hazel 16 MO, Etta 14 MO, Laurette 11 MO, Irene 7 MO, Faye 5 MO*
* *1940 - Living In Madison, Johnson Co., MO - Ballard, Charles 60 MO, Effie 50 MO, Hazel 25 MO, Loretta 21 MO, Irene 17 MO, Fay MO*

Notes for EFFIE SHELLY:
Source: Johnson County Missouri Death Certificate

Children of CHARLES BALLARD and EFFIE SHELLY are:
    i.   HELEN[7] BALLARD, b. 22 Aug 1913, MO; d. 05 Mar 2004; m. WILLIAM J. MCWHIRT; b. 01 Sep 1911; d. 26 Jun 1976.
    ii.   HAZEL BALLARD, b. 01 Sep 1914, MO; d. 25 Jun 2005; m. WHENHAM.
    iii.   ETTA BALLARD, b. 02 Jan 1916, Huggins, Texas Co., MO; d. 21 Jul 1989, San Diego Co., CA; m. ROWLAND.

        Notes for ETTA BALLARD:
        Source: Social Security Records, San Diego California Death Records

    iv.   LAURETTA BALLARD, b. 1918, MO; d. Aft. 1940.
    v.   IRENE BALLARD, b. 13 Jun 1922, MO; d. 17 Nov 1999.
    vi.   JANICE FAY BALLARD, b. 03 Jan 1925, MO; d. 24 Dec 2016.

20. ROLLA MARION[6] BALLARD (BENNETT MARION[5], BENNETT D.[4], BLAND[3], THOMAS[2], WILLIAM[1]) was born 10 Apr 1886 in Huggins, Texas Co., O, and died 10 Dec 1956 in Mt. Grove, Wright Co., MO. He married MARY ELIZABETH CANTRELL. She was born 1887 in Wright Co., MO, and died 14 Aug 1975.

Notes for ROLLA MARION BALLARD:
Source: 1910-1940 Texas County Missouri Federal Census Records

* *1910 - Living in Upton, Texas Co., MO - Ballard, Rolla M 24 MO, Elizabeth 23 MO, Lawrence 1 1/12 MO*
* *1920 - Living in Upton, Texas Co., MO - Ballard, Rolla 33 MO, Elizabeth 33 MO, Lawrence 11 MO, Andrew 9 MO, Wilbert 7 MO, Alma 4 4/12 MO, Ermal 2 2/12*
* *1930 - Living in Upton, Texas Co., MO - Ballard, Rolla M 44 MO, Mary E 43 MO, Lawrence 21 MO, Audrey 19 MO, Wilbert 17 MO, Alma 15 MO, Ermal 12 MO, Marie 10 MO, Ralph 7 MO, Gerald 5 MO*
* *1940 - Living in Upton, Texas Co., MO - Ballard, Rolla M 53, Elizabeth 53, Wilbert 28, Ermel 22, Mirie 20, Ralph 17, Gerald 15*

Children of ROLLA BALLARD and MARY CANTRELL are:
     i.   LAWRENCE[7] BALLARD, b. 31 Jul 1908, MO; d. 02 Nov 1976, Wright Co., MO; m. DOROTHY EDNA
        HOKE; b. 14 Sep 1913, Texas Co., MO; d. 20 Mar 2007, Wright Co., MO.
    ii.   AUDREY LILLIAN BALLARD, b. 14 Sep 1910, Huggins, Texas Co., MO; d. 25 Jun 1989, Texas Co.,
        MO; m. FRANK SMART; b. 07 Nov 1899; d. 04 Sep 1983.
   iii.   WILBERT EDWIN BALLARD, b. 24 Dec 1912, Huggins, Texas Co., MO; d. 09 Nov 1967; m. PANSY
        SKINNER; b. 29 May 1924; d. 07 Jul 2009.
    iv.   ALMA OPAL BALLARD, b. 17 Aug 1915, Huggins, Texas Co., MO; d. 08 Oct 1971, Texas Co., MO; m.
        ORAL TATE; b. 10 Mar 1910; d. 29 Nov 2000, Texas Co., MO.
     v.   ERMAL BALLARD, b. 03 Oct 1917, Huggins, Texas Co., MO; d. 22 Jan 2005; m. SMITH.

        Notes for ERMAL BALLARD:
        Source: Social Security Records

    vi.   MARIE R. BALLARD, b. 22 Mar 1920, MO; d. 05 Jul 2000, Cole Co., MO; m. WALTER E. MAXWELL; b.
        06 Jun 1909, Huggins, Texas Co., MO; d. 04 Apr 2002, Cole Co. MO.
   vii.   RALPH WARREN BALLARD, b. 30 Oct 1922, Huggins, Texas Co., MO; d. 06 Jul 1978; m. JUANITA
        HAMMONS; b. 20 Mar 1932.

        Notes for RALPH WARREN BALLARD:
        *Source: Social Security Records, Department of Veterans Affairs BIRLS Death File, WWII Draft
        Cards*

  viii.   GERALD CLEVELAND BALLARD, b. 24 Nov 1924, Texas Co., MO; d. 22 Nov 1998, Wright Co., MO; m.
        CLEDA J. MCKINNEY, 1951, Randolph Co., AR; b. 24 Mar 1929; d. 07 Dec 1997.

        Notes for GERALD CLEVELAND BALLARD:
        Source: Social Security Records, WWII Draft Cards

21. CHARLES MASON[6] BROWN (BARBARA ANN[5] BALLARD, BENNETT D.[4], BLAND[3], THOMAS[2], WILLIAM[1]) was born 10 Jun 1865 in Hopkins Co., KY, and died 21 Nov 1927 in Webster Co., KY. He married MARY FRANCES HOWELL. She was born 21 Apr 1870, and died 01 Jan 1959.

Notes for CHARLES MASON BROWN:
Source: Webster County Kentucky Certificate of Death

Child of CHARLES BROWN and MARY HOWELL is:
     i.   BULAH MAY[7] BROWN, b. 23 Oct 1891; d. 18 May 1914.

Generation No. 4

22. LAURA ANN[7] WILLIAMS (FRANCES ELIZABETH[6] THOMPSON, SARAH MARGARET[5] BALLARD, BENNETT D.[4], BLAND[3], THOMAS[2], WILLIAM[1]) was born Abt. 1869 in Williamson Co., IL, and died 12 Aug 1907 in IL. She married (1) ISAAC C. ODLE 15 Apr 1885 in Williamson Co., IL.   She married (2) THOMAS HENRY WEAVER 19 Oct 1892 in Perry, IL. He was born Bet. 04 Jan 1862 - 1864 in IL, and died 12 Aug 1929 in Franklin Co., IL.

Notes for THOMAS HENRY WEAVER:
Source: 1900-1910 Williamson County Illinois Federal Census Records

** 1900 - Living in Lake Creek, Williamson Co., IL - Weaver, T H - Jan 1865 IL TN TN, Laura A - Jan 1869 - 5
children 5 living IL KY MO, Berta - Aug 1886 IL, Benie - Nov 1889 IL, Bessie - Jan 1894 IL, Mabel - Oct 1896 IL,
Dola - June 1899 IL*
** 1910 - Living in Herrin, Williamson Co., IL - Weaver, Thomas H 45, Bessie 16, Mable 14, Dola 10, ORA 7*

Child of LAURA WILLIAMS and ISAAC ODLE is:

      i.   BENJAMIN WESLEY[8] ODLE, b. 29 Nov 1889, IL; d. 28 Dec 1941, Elko, NE.

      Notes for BENJAMIN WESLEY ODLE:

      Source: Nevada State Department of Health Standard Certificate of Death

Children of LAURA WILLIAMS and THOMAS WEAVER are:

      ii.   BESSIE[8] WEAVER, b. Abt. 1894, IL; d. Aft. 1910.
     iii.   MABEL WEAVER, b. Abt. 1897, IL; d. Aft. 1910.
     iv.   DOLA A. WEAVER, b. 1899, IL; d. 14 Feb 1921.
      v.   ORA WEAVER, b. Abt. 1903, IL; d. Aft. 1910.

23.   CLAIBORNE[7] BALLARD (ARTHUR BARRETT[6], BENNETT MARION[5], BENNETT D.[4], BLAND[3], THOMAS[2], WILLIAM[1]) was born 18 Oct 1913 in Montgomery, Wright Co., MO, and died 24 Mar 1971 in Wright Co., MO. He married OPAL MAE FLOYD. She was born 14 Feb 1914, and died 10 Mar 1948 in MO.

Notes for CLAIBORNE BALLARD:

Source :1940 Wright County Missouri Federal Census Records

** 1940 - Living in Montgomery Wright Co., MO - Ballard, Claiborn T 26 MO, Opal M 26 MO, Majorie R 4, Patsy J 1/12*

Children of CLAIBORNE BALLARD and OPAL FLOYD are:

      i.   MARJORIE R.[8] BALLARD, b. 02 Nov 1935, Wright Co., MO; d. 28 Jan 1978, Wright Co., MO.
     ii.   PATSY JOAN BALLARD, b. 16 Feb 1940, Wright Co., MO; d. 25 Oct 1991, Greene Co., MO; m. ROY KENNETH INMAN; b. 1938.

Bland Nixon Ballard

Generation No. 1

1. BLAND NIXON[1] BALLARD *was born Jul 1800 in Kershaw Co., SC, and died 21 Feb 1861 in Waynesville, Pulaski Co., MO. He married* MARGARET SMELSER *Abt. 1822 in Overton Co., TN, daughter of* JOHN SMELSER *and* CATHERINE HIGGINS. *She was born 16 Jan 1800 in Overton Co., TN, and died 05 Aug 1870 in Pulaski Co., MO.*

Notes for BLAND NIXON BALLARD:
Source: Mike Weber (popo@ctwok.com), Janet Acree (acreerc@poncacity.net), 1830 Putnam County Indiana Federal Census Records, 1850-1860 Pulaski County Missouri Federal Census Records, US General Land Office Records, Old Settlers Gazette 2002 pg 10

** 1830 - Living in Putnam Co., IN - Free White Persons - Males - 30 thru 39 -1 - Free White Persons - Females - Under 5 - 1 Free White Persons - Females - 5 thru 9 - 2 - Free White Persons - Females - 20 thru 29 -1- Free White Persons - Under 20 -3 - Free White Persons - 20 thru 49 - 2 -Total Free White Persons 5*
** 1833 - Living in Sangamon Co., IL*
** Pulaski Co., MO - Served as Sheriff from Jan 1, 1836 through Jan 3, 1868, Collector, Circuit and County Clerk, Member of the State Legislature, Probate County Judge 1858*
** 1849 - Land grant - Aug 1, 1849 - Pulaski Co., MO 41 acres*
** 1850 - Living in Pulaski Co., MO - (hard to read), Ballard, Bland N 51 NC, Margarit 50 TN, Bland N Jr 16 IL, Morning 14 MO, Minerva Anne 7 MO, Eliza York 7, John York 6*
** 1860 - Living in Pulaski Co., MO - Ballard, BN 60 farmer SC, Margaret 59 TN, BN Jr. 26 IL, Minerva 17 MO, Jane York 17 MO, John York 15 MO*

More About BLAND NIXON BALLARD:
Burial: Laughlin Cemetery, Pulaski Co., MO

Children of BLAND BALLARD *and* MARGARET SMELSER *are:*

2.	i.	ELIZA JANE[2] BALLARD, b. 24 Oct 1824, Roane Co., TN; d. 26 Mar 1898, Richmond, Pulaski Co., MO.
3.	ii.	CATHERINE BALLARD, b. 31 Mar 1830, Pulaski Co., MO; d. 12 Jan 1914, St. Louis Co., MO.
	iii.	JAMES W. BALLARD, b. 21 Mar 1833, IN.
4.	iv.	BLAND NIXON BALLARD, JR., b. 10 Feb 1834, Sangamon Co., IL; d. 19 May 1900, MO.
5.	v.	MATILDA MOURNING BALLARD, b. 08 Mar 1836, Pulaski Co., MO; d. 14 Oct 1903, MO.
6.	vi.	MINERVA ANN BALLARD, b. 02 Jun 1841, Pulaski Co., MO; d. 25 Mar 1910, Pulaski Co., MO.

Generation No. 2

2. ELIZA JANE[2] BALLARD (BLAND NIXON[1]) *was born 24 Oct 1824 in Roane Co., TN, and died 26 Mar 1898 in Richmond, Pulaski Co., MO. She married* SAMUEL LUTHER GIBSON *08 Sep 1839. He was born 11 Mar 1820 in St. Louis, MO, and died 22 Feb 1883.*

More About ELIZA JANE BALLARD:
Burial: Oaklawn Cemetery, Pulaski Co., MO

Notes for SAMUEL LUTHER GIBSON:

Source: 1850-1880 Camden County Missouri Federal Census Records

** 1850 - Living in Camden Co., MO - Gibson, Samuel 29 farmer MO, Eliza 25 TN, Mary 10 MO, Sarah 8 MO, George 6 MO, Charlotte 10/12 MO, Land Morris 18 farmer, Mariah Gibson 20, Laticia 10*
** 1860 - Living in Camden Co., MO - Gibson, Samuel 39 MO, Eliza J 36 TN, Sarah R 16 MO, George N B 13 MO,*

Charlotte 10 MO, Mariah 7 MO, Samuel 5 MO, Eliza ME 1 MO
** 1870 - Living in Camden Co., MO - Gibson, Samuel 50 MO, Lizzie J 47 IN, Mariah J 10 MO, Samuel L 15 MO, James B 9 MO, Alice 6 MO, Lilly B 4 MO, Albert 4/12 MO*
** 1880 - Living in Camden Co., MO - Gibson, Samuel 60, Eliza J 56, James B 18, Alice Isadore 16, Lillie B 13, Elbert Q 10*

More About SAMUEL LUTHER GIBSON:
Burial: Old Laughlin Cemetery, Camden Co., MO

Children of ELIZA BALLARD and SAMUEL GIBSON are:

7.   i.   *MARY MARGARET[3] GIBSON, b. 04 Oct 1841, Camden Co., MO; d. 02 Feb 1927, Pulaski Co., MO.*
8.   ii.   *SARAH GIBSON, b. Abt. 1844, Camden Co., MO; d. Aft. 1880.*
9.   iii.   *GEORGE GIBSON, b. 22 Sep 1845, Camden Co., MO; d. 27 Jul 1916, OK.*
10.   iv.   *CHARLOTTE GIBSON, b. 31 Dec 1851, Camden Co., MO; d. 09 Oct 1888.*
    v.   *MARIA JANET GIBSON, b. 12 Apr 1852, Camden Co., MO; d. 03 Jun 1936, Richland, Pulaski Co., MO; m. MILLER FRANCIS ELLIS, 30 May 1875, Camden Co., MO; b. 22 Nov 1848; d. 01 Feb 1897.*

More About MARIA JANET GIBSON:
Burial: Oaklawn Cemetery, Richland, Pulaski Co., MO

More About MILLER FRANCIS ELLIS:
Burial: Oaklawn Cemetery, Richland, Pulaski Co., MO

11.   vi.   *SAMUEL L. GIBSON, b. 27 Nov 1855, Camden Co., MO; d. 24 Jun 1911, MO.*
    vii.   *ELIZA GIBSON, b. 1859, Camden Co., MO; d. Aft. 1860.*
12.   viii.   *JAMES BLAND GIBSON, b. Aug 1861, Camden Co., MO; d. 1909.*
    ix.   *ALICE ISADORE GIBSON, b. 1863, MO; d. Aft. 1880.*
13.   x.   *LILLIE BELLE GIBSON, b. 30 Jul 1867, MO; d. 11 Jun 1939.*
    xi.   *ELBERT Q. GIBSON, b. 1870, MO; d. Aft. 1870.*

3.   *CATHERINE[2] BALLARD (BLAND NIXON[1]) was born 31 Mar 1830 in Pulaski Co., MO, and died 12 Jan 1914 in St. Louis Co., MO. She married JOHN JORDAN LAUGHLIN. He was born 14 Apr 1818 in Lincoln Co., MO, and died 21 Jan 1875 in Pulaski Co., MO.*

Notes for CATHERINE BALLARD:
Source: 1880 Pulaski County Missouri Federal Census Records

** 1880 - Living in Cullen, Pulaski Co., MO - Laughlin, Catherine 48 farmer IN TN TN, Margaret 30 MO Charles 28 MO, Samuel 26 MO, John 18 MO, James 16 MO, Sarah E 9 MO*

More About CATHERINE BALLARD:
Burial: Laughlin Cemetery., Ft. Leonard Wood, Pulaski Co., MO

Notes for JOHN JORDAN LAUGHLIN:
Source: 1850-1870 Pulaski County Missouri Federal Census Records, Pulaski County Missouri Wills Vol A-C

** 1850 - Living in Pulaski Co., MO - Laughlin, John J 30 farmer MO, Catharine 21 IL, Margaret L 2/12 MO*
** 1860 - Living in Pulaski Co., MO - Loughlin, John J 40 farmer MO, Catharine 28 IN, Margarett L 10 MO, Charles N 8 MO, Samuel H G 6 MO, Bland B 3 MO, Matilda R 1 MO, George Templeton 21 laborer MO, Rebecca Stewart 16 MO*
** 1870 - Living in Cullen, Pulaski Co., MO - Laughlin, John 51 farmer MO, Catherine 40 IN, Margaret S 20 MO, Charles 18 MO, Samuel 11 MO, Matilda 11 MO, John 8 MO, James 6 MO*
** 1875 - January 11 - Pulaski Co., MO - In view of the uncertainty of life and the certainty of death and being in poor health but of Sound mind, I John J Laughlin in the presence of Almighty God and these witnesses do make this*

my last will and Testament. My Executor hereinafter to be named is empowered and enjoined to give my body a Christian burial and all necessary expense incidental then to be paid from any funds that shall come into his or her hands as proceeds from my property. It is my Will and command that all Just debts against my Estate Shall be paid. To My beloved wife Catherine Laughlin I give and bequeath all lands and Real Estate that I am professed of to hold and for her use during her life time and at her death the title of Said lands and Real Estate Shall descend to and be held by my children named as follows Charles N Laughlin, Samuel H Laughlin, John S Laughlin, Joseph J Laughlin, Margaret L Laughlin, Sarah E Laughlin for their use and benefit during their lifetime after which said Lands and Real Estate Shall be the property of the heirs or legal Representatives of those of my Children herein before mentioned. Those of my Children herein before named are by the terms of this my will and testament Restrained from Selling or bargaining away in any manner their interest herein bequeathed to them as it is my will and wish that my land property be for their use and benefit after the death of my beloved wife during their life time and then to descend to their heirs and legal Representatives. To my daughter Matilda R Long formerly Matilda R. Laughlin I give and bequeathed of one Dollar to be paid within Six Months after this will Shall go into Effect with this further provisions that in the the equivalent of both in money, all moneys that shall remain in the hands of my executor arising from the Sale of my personal property or from any other Source Shall be placed on interest and So remain until youngest child becomes of age and then equally divided between Charles N Laughlin, Samuel H Laughlin, John S Laughlin, Matilda R Long and Sarah E Laughlin or in the event of any of them being dead to their heirs or legal Representatives. Should any of these Children herein before named die without issue their portion Shall be apportioned to those living Mary E. Casteel, formerly Mary E Laughlin excepted from the number. I hereby name and appoint my beloved wife Catherine Laughlin Executrix of this my last will and testament I hereby enforce upon my executrix herein named that She Council and advise with my neighbor and friend Elijah J Christeson in the transaction of the business and carrying out of the provisions of this will. I hereby make and cancel all former wills bequests and leave this as my last will and testament dated this 11th day of January AD 1875. J. J. Laughlin - Signed and Sealed in presence and witnessed by B. F Kinter, Thos. J Christeson .

Proof of Will - State of Missouri County of Pulaski } In the County Court in vacation. Be it Remembered that on this Twenty Third day of February in the year of our Lord one Thousand Eight Hundred and Seventy five before me .E E. Williams

Clerk of the County Court in Vacation held and in for the County of Pulaski and State of Missouri personally appeared B. F Kinter and Thomas J. Christeson who being Sworn upon their oaths deposed and Says that they were present and Saw John J. Laughlin sign the foregoing instrument purporting to be the last will and testament of him the said John J Laughlin and heard him publish and declare the same to be his last will and testament and that at the time of Signing the Same the said John J Laughlin was of Sound and Deposing mind and that these deponents attesting witnesses subscribed their name thereunto as witnesses to the Same in the presence of the testator and of each other and at the request of the Said John J. Laughlin. B. T Kinter, Thomas J. Christeson.

Subscribed and Sworn before me E. J Williams Clerk of the county Court in Vacation the day and year first aforesaid. E. E Williams Clerk County Court

The foregoing will and Proof was filed for Record Feby 24th 1875. E. E. Williams Clerk, By B. Slmay DC

More About JOHN JORDAN LAUGHLIN:
Burial: Laughlin Cemetery., Ft. Leonard Wood, Pulaski Co., MO

Children of CATHERINE BALLARD and JOHN LAUGHLIN are:

    i.   CATHERINE[3] LAUGHLIN, *b. Pulaski Co., MO; d. Bef. 1875.*

    ii.

    ii.   ISABELLE LAUGHLIN, *b. 1847, Pulaski Co., MO; d. Bef. 1875.*

    iii.   MARGARET LUTESIA LAUGHLIN, *b. 16 Apr 1850, Pulaski Co., MO; d. 09 Mar 1886, Pulaski Co., MO; m. PERRY.*

        More About MARGARET LUTESIA LAUGHLIN:
        Burial: Laughlin Cemetery, Ft. Leonard Wood, Pulaski Co., MO

    iv.   CHARLES NIXON LAUGHLIN, *b. 08 Jan 1853, Pulaski Co., MO; d. 22 Oct 1882.*

More About CHARLES NIXON LAUGHLIN:
Burial: Laughlin Cemetery, Ft. Leonard Wood, Pulaski Co., MO

     v.   SAMUEL HENRY LAUGHLIN, b. 1856, Pulaski Co., MO; d. Aft. 1880.
    vi.   BLAND BALLARD LAUGHLIN, b. 1857, Pulaski Co., MO; d. 1963.
    vii.   ROSA MATILDA LAUGHLIN, b. 1859, Pulaski Co., MO; d. 1877.
    viii.   JOHN RUBEN LAUGHLIN, b. 1861, Pulaski Co., MO; d. Aft. 1875.
    ix.   JOHN STERLINE LAUGHLIN, b. 19 Dec 1862, Pulaski Co., MO; d. 16 Jul 1902, Pulaski Co., MO.

More About JOHN STERLINE LAUGHLIN:
Burial: Laughlin Cemetery, Ft. Leonard Wood, Pulaski Co., MO

    x.   JOSEPH JAMES LAUGHLIN, b. 24 Jan 1864, Pulaski Co., MO; d. 28 Apr 1911, Pulaski Co., MO; m. DORA ESTELLA LOGAN; b. 27 Jul 1870, Pulaski Co., MO; d. 10 Sep 1957, Waynesville, Pulaski Co., MO.

More About JOSEPH JAMES LAUGHLIN:
Burial: Laughlin Cemetery, Ft. Leonard Wood, Pulaski Co., MO

More About DORA ESTELLA LOGAN:
Burial: Waynesville Memorial Park, Waynesville, Pulaski Co., MO

    xi.   SARAH ELIZABETH LAUGHLIN, b. 23 Nov 1870, Pulaski Co., MO; d. 14 Feb 1961, Lebanon, Laclede Co., MO; m. (1) WILKES BOOTH RIGSBY, 03 Dec 1896; m. (2) WILLIAM L. ANDERSON, 08 Sep 1901.

More About SARAH ELIZABETH LAUGHLIN:
Burial: Mitchell Cemetery, Waynesville, Pulaski Co., MO

4. BLAND NIXON[2] BALLARD, JR. (BLAND NIXON[1]) *was born 10 Feb 1834 in Sangamon Co., IL, and died 19 May 1900 in MO. He married (1) SARAH WHITE 1867. She was born 07 Feb 1844 in Springfield, Greene Co., MO, and died 22 Mar 1878 in Pulaski Co., MO. He married (2) ELIZABETH FRANCES BRADFORD Bef. 1880, daughter of NEELY BRADFORD. She was born 31 Jan 1842 in Phelps Co., MO, and died 30 Dec 1932 in Versailles, Morgan Co., MO.*

Notes for BLAND NIXON BALLARD, JR.:

Source: 1870 -1900 Pulaski County Missouri Federal Census Records, Stephen Ballard, Old Settlers Gazette 2002 pg 10

** 1861 - Enlisted in 1861 Company A, under Col. Stein Confederate Army.*
** 1870 - Living in Pulaski Co., MO - Ballard, Bland N 33 farmer IL, M. Sarah 26 MO, M. Margaret 1 MO*
** 1880 - Living in Cullen, Pulaski Co., MO - Ballard, Blan 43 IL SC TN, Elizabeth 37 MO KY KY, Maggie 12 MO, Olive 10 MO, Cora 8 MO, Charles 6 MO, Sallie 3 MO, Lucy 6/12 MO*

** 1893 - Dec 3 - Pulaski Co., Missouri Will Records: (Using original spelling)*
I Bland N Ballard of Cullen Township Pulaski County State of Missouri over twenty one years of age and of Sound mind and Memory and understanding but considering the uncertainty of this transitory life do make and publish this my last will and testament in the maner and form following To wit - I will that my body be intered in a deasent and Christian like maner and first that all my Just debts be paid and I will and devise to my beloved wife Elizabeth F Ballard the following described Real Estate living being and Situated in Pulaski County State of Missouri To wit - SW 1/4 NE 9/4 and N 1/2 lot 1 SW 1/4 Section 7 T 35 R 11 Containing eighty acres more or less and pt SW 1/4 and pt of E 1/2 of SE 1/4 Sec 36 T 36 R 12 Containing ninety nine acres more or less for and during her natural life or widowhood together with all my personal property choses in action and money and at her death the above described real estate to equally divided among my three sons Charles, Samuel and Neely Ballard Share and Share alike

(Should any of my sons died before reaching.... hard to read) and I will and bequeath to my daughters Maggie Hamilton, and Cord Hamilton, Ollie Sallie Lucy and Winnie Ballard each such and amount of my personal estate together with they have received hereto fore as will make them Shear & Equal with and Share either of my sons if there Should be a suficient amount. I further will that my Interest in Town... in Waynesville Pulaski County Missouri and my interest in pt lot one N E 1/4 Section (3) F 34 R 12 be sold at the discresion of my executor here in after named. I further will that my executor extend to J J York Sufficient time to pay Balance due on the following described real Estate to wit N E NE Section 22 and the NW 1/4 and SW 1/4 of SW 1/4 Section 14 all in T 35 R11 but when they become satisfied that he will not be able to pay said indebtedness in a reasonable time they may proceed to take possession of the Same I further will that my minor Children have a good comon School education and that the expenses there of be not deducted from their distribution shares of the Estate. I hereby Constitute and appoint Elizabeth F Ballard and W L Bradford my executors of this my last will and testament and they be not required by the Probate Court to enter into Bond as executors of my Said Estate Given under my hand this 3rd day of December AD 1893. B N Ballard
We attest the above and foregoing will by subscribing our names hereto in the presents BN Ballard the testator and we all so attest the sanity of the Testator. This 3rd day of December 1893. William C Kees, Samuel Laughlin, W. L Bradford, L Tice MD
** State of Missouri County of Pulaski} SS In the Probate court I W L Vaught judged of the Probate Court of Pulaski County State of Missouri having examined the foregoing Instrument purporting to be the last will of B. N. Ballard Deceased and Signed by B N Ballard and hearing the Testimony of W C Keer, W L Bradford Samuel Laughlin and L Tice and Subscribing witnesses thereto in relation to the execution of the same do declare and adjudge said instrument to be the last will and Testament of the said B. N Ballard deceased late of Pulaski County Missouri and the same is hereby admitted to Probate.*
In Testimony whereof I have hereunto set my hand and affixed the seal of said court at my office at Waynesville this the 6th day of August AD 1900 W. L Vaught, Judge of Probate

More About BLAND NIXON BALLARD, JR.:
Burial: Laughlin Cemetery, Ft. Leonard Wood, Pulaski Co., MO

More About SARAH WHITE:
Burial: Laughlin Cemetery, Ft. Leonard Wood, Pulaski Co., MO

Notes for ELIZABETH FRANCES BRADFORD:
Source: Civil War Pension Files, 1900 Pulaski County Missouri Federal Census Records
** 1900 - Sept 17 Widow pension, soldier Bland N Ballard, Widow Elizabeth F Ballard. Service A 48 Missouri Inf. filed in MO. Certificate No 685.306 application 726.717*
** 1900 - Living in Cullen, Pulaski Co., MO - Ballard, Elizabeth - Jan 1842 wd - 4 children 4 living MO MO KY, Samuel G. - June 1881 MO, Neely B - Feb 1884 MO, Winnie - Jan 1886 MO, Sallie E - June 1879 MO step daughter*

More About ELIZABETH FRANCES BRADFORD:
Burial: Laughlin Cemetery, Ft. Leonard Wood, Pulaski Co., MO

Children of BLAND BALLARD and SARAH WHITE are:

	i.	MARGARET "MAGGIE"³ BALLARD, b. 1869, Pulaski Co., MO; d. Aft. 1893; m. HAMILTON.
14.	ii.	OLIVE BALLARD, b. 04 Jan 1871, Waynesville, Pulaski Co., MO; d. 02 Oct 1956, St. Louis Co., MO.
15.	iii.	CORA CATHERINE BALLARD, b. 30 Jul 1872, Pulaski Co., MO; d. 05 Oct 1902, Phelps Co., MO.
16.	iv.	CHARLES BALLARD, b. 12 Jul 1875, Pulaski Co., MO; d. 12 Jun 1902, Waynesville, Pulaski Co., MO.
	v.	SALLIE BALLARD, b. Jun 1879, Pulaski Co., MO; d. Aft. 1893.

Children of BLAND BALLARD and ELIZABETH BRADFORD are:

	vi.	LUCY³ BALLARD, b. 1879, MO; d. Aft. 1893.
	vii.	SAMUEL GIBSON BALLARD, b. 09 Jun 1880, MO; d. 08 Jan 1961, Pima Co., AZ; m. EDITH; b. 1888; d. 1978.

More About SAMUEL GIBSON BALLARD:
Burial: South Lawn Memorial Cemetery, Tucson, Pima Co., AZ

More About EDITH:
Burial: South Lawn Memorial Cemetery, Tucson, Pima Co., AZ

17.   viii.   NEAL "NEELY" BRADFORD BALLARD, b. 16 Feb 1884, MO; d. 21 Oct 1987, Phelps Co., MO.
       ix.   WINNIE BALLARD, b. 17 Jan 1886, MO; d. 30 Dec 1985; m. LUNA WHEELER; b. 23 Feb 1885, Pulaski Co., MO; d. 09 Dec 1964, Springfield, Greene Co., MO.

More About WINNIE BALLARD:
Burial: Waynesville Memorial Park, Pulaski Co., MO

More About LUNA WHEELER:
Burial: Waynesville Memorial Park, Pulaski Co., MO

5. MATILDA MOURNING[2] BALLARD (BLAND NIXON[1]) was born 08 Mar 1836 in Pulaski Co., MO, and died 14 Oct 1903 in MO. She married JAMES P. BRITTAIN. He was born 04 Feb 1831 in McMinn Co., TN, and died 22 Aug 1878.

More About MATILDA MOURNING BALLARD:
Burial: Dixon Cemetery., Dixon, Pulaski Co., MO

More About JAMES P. BRITTAIN:
Burial: Dixon Cemetery., Dixon, Pulaski Co., MO

Child of MATILDA BALLARD and JAMES BRITTAIN is:
     i.   HORACE GREELEY[3] BRITTAIN, b. 1872.

6. MINERVA ANN[2] BALLARD (BLAND NIXON[1]) was born 02 Jun 1841 in Pulaski Co., MO, and died 25 Mar 1910 in Pulaski Co., MO. She married BRAMLETT WHITE VAUGHAN. He was born 15 Sep 1827 in Adair Co., KY, and died 14 Jun 1894 in Pulaski Co., MO.

More About MINERVA ANN BALLARD:
Burial: Laughlin Cemetery, Ft. Leonard Wood, Pulaski Co., MO

Notes for BRAMLETT WHITE VAUGHAN:
Source: 1870-1880 Pulaski County Missouri Federal Census Records

* 1870 - Living in Roubideaux, Pulaski Co., MO - Vaughn, Bram 38 farmer KY, Minerva 29 MO, F. James 17 MO, Mary 10 MO, Oliver 5 MO, F Benjamin 7/12 MO
* 1880 - Living in Roubideaux, Pulaski Co., MO - Vaughn, Bramley 53 farmer KY KY KY, Menerva 40 MO TN TN, Oliver 13 MO, Ben F 12 MO, Samuel B 7 MO, Ora L 3 MO, Harry E 9/12 MO

More About BRAMLETT WHITE VAUGHAN:
Burial: Laughlin Cemetery, Ft. Leonard Wood, Pulaski Co., MO

Children of MINERVA BALLARD and BRAMLETT VAUGHAN are:
     i.   WILLIAM BLAND[3] VAUGHAN, b. 21 Apr 1864, Pulaski Co., MO; d. 04 May 1864, Pulaski Co., MO.
     ii.   OLIVER BRAMLETT VAUGHAN, b. 02 Jun 1865, Phelps Co., MO; d. 03 Feb 1943, Jasper Co., MO; m. MARY EMMA YORK; b. 12 Jan 1869, Pulaski Co., MO; d. 17 Oct 1959, Jasper Co., MO.

More About OLIVER BRAMLETT VAUGHAN:
Burial: Centerville Cemetery, Jasper Co., MO

More About MARY EMMA YORK:
Burial: Carterville Cemetery, Jasper Co., MO

   iii.   ANDREW JOHNSON VAUGHAN, b. 24 Jul 1867, Pulaski Co., MO; d. 24 Jul 1867, Pulaski Co., MO.
   iv.   SAMUEL BALLARD VAUGHAN, b. 29 May 1872, Pulaski Co., MO; d. 17 Jun 1948, Pulaski Co., MO; m. IDA JANE MATTHEWS.

Notes for SAMUEL BALLARD VAUGHAN:

Source: Social Security Records, Pulaski County Certificate of Death

   v.   ORA LEA VAUGHAN, b. 16 Dec 1874, Pulaski Co., MO; d. 29 Mar 1938, Pulaski Co., MO; m. ANDY DENIS PIPER; b. 07 Apr 1876, Wayne Co., OH; d. 01 Aug 1961, Greene Co., MO.

More About ANDY DENIS PIPER:
Burial: Laughlin Cemetery, Ft. Leonard Wood, Pulaski Co., MO

   vi.   CHARLES LUTHER VAUGHAN, b. 04 May 1877, Pulaski Co., MO; d. 13 Sep 1968, Greene Co., MO; m. SUSIE J. CLARK; b. 15 Sep 1884, Pulaski Co., MO; d. 20 Feb 1973, Greene Co., MO.

More About CHARLES LUTHER VAUGHAN:
Burial: Maple Park Cemetery, Springfield, Greene Co., MO

More About SUSIE J. CLARK:
Burial: Maple Park Cemetery, Springfield, Greene Co., MO

   vii.   HARRY EDWIN VAUGHAN, b. 04 Sep 1879, Pulaski Co., MO; d. 29 Aug 1966, Ozark Christian Co., MO; m. (1) PEARL M. GAN; b. 18 Mar 1894, Pulaski Co., MO; d. 07 May 1975, Springfield, Greene Co., MO; m. (2) ROSA E. CROSSLAND; b. Abt. 1880; d. 26 Feb 1907.

More About HARRY EDWIN VAUGHAN:
Burial: Maple Park Cemetery, Springfield, Greene Co., MO

More About PEARL M. GAN:
Burial: Maple Park Cemetery, Springfield, Greene Co., MO

More About ROSA E. CROSSLAND:
Burial: Bloodland Cemetery, Pulaski Co., MO

Generation No. 3

7. MARY MARGARET[3] GIBSON (*ELIZA JANE[2] BALLARD, BLAND NIXON[1]*) *was born 04 Oct 1841 in Camden Co., MO, and died 02 Feb 1927 in Pulaski Co., MO. She married WILLIAM ROBERT HARRISON. He was born 20 Sep 1834 in KY, and died 22 May 1919 in Richland, Pulaski Co., MO.*

More About MARY MARGARET GIBSON:
Burial: Oaklawn Cemetery, Richland, Pulaski Co., MO

More About WILLIAM ROBERT HARRISON:
Burial: Oaklawn Cemetery, Richland, Pulaski Co., MO

Children of MARY GIBSON and WILLIAM HARRISON are:

      i.   JAMES SAMUEL[4] HARRISON, b. Feb 1860, Richland, Pulaski Co., MO; d. 13 Nov 1959, Laclede Co., MO.

         More About JAMES SAMUEL HARRISON:
         Burial: Oaklawn Cemetery, Richland, Pulaski Co., MO

     ii.   GEORGE ROBERT HARRISON, b. 18 May 1864, Camden Co., MO; d. 04 Jan 1964, Jasper Co., MO.
   iii.   DANIEL HARDEN HARRISON, b. 26 Oct 1866, Camden Co., MO; d. 14 May 1908, Camden Co., MO; m. FELICIA DOROTHY TABOR; b. 16 Nov 1876, Pulaski Co., MO; d. 10 Oct 1965, Laclede Co., MO.

         More About DANIEL HARDEN HARRISON:
         Burial: Mount View Church of Christ Cemetery, Camden Co., MO

    iv.   ELMER ROSCOE HARRISON, b. 28 Nov 1873, Camden Co., MO; d. 27 Dec 1942, Pulaski Co., MO; m. MOLLIE LEDBETTER; b. 10 Dec 1883, Pulaski Co., MO; d. 27 Apr 1946, Pulaski Co., MO.

         More About ELMER ROSCOE HARRISON:
         Burial: Oaklawn Cemetery, Richland, Pulaski Co., MO

         More About MOLLIE LEDBETTER:
         Burial: Oaklawn Cemetery, Richland, Pulaski Co., MO

     v.   ORA M. HARRISON, b. 21 Feb 1878, Camden Co., MO; d. 09 Jul 1932, St. Louis City, MO.

         More About ORA M. HARRISON:
         Burial: Oaklawn Cemetery, Richland, Pulaski Co., MO

    vi.   CHARLES BLAND HARRISON, b. 25 Jun 1887, Camden Co., MO; d. 27 Feb 1970, Pulaski Co., MO.

         More About CHARLES BLAND HARRISON:
         Burial: Oaklawn Cemetery, Richland, Pulaski Co., MO

8. SARAH[3] GIBSON (ELIZA JANE[2] BALLARD, BLAND NIXON[1]) *was born Abt. 1844 in Camden Co., MO, and died Aft. 1880. She married JOHN C. DAVIS. He was born Abt. 1843 in MO, and died Aft. 1870 in Camden Co., MO.*

Notes for SARAH GIBSON:
Source: 1880 Camden County Missouri Federal Census Records

** 1880 - Living in Auglaize, Camden Co., MO - Davis, Sarah 36 MO, George W 13, Fredrick 9, Eliza J 7*

Notes for JOHN C. DAVIS:
Source: 1870 Camden County Missouri Federal Census Records

** 1870 - Living in Auglaize, Camden Co., MO - Davis, J. C 27 MO, Sarah 26 MO, George W 3 MO, Samuel J 1 MO*

Children of SARAH GIBSON and JOHN DAVIS are:
      i.   GEORGE W.[4] DAVIS, b. 1867, MO; d. Aft. 1870.
     ii.   SAMUEL J. DAVIS, b. 1869, MO; d. Aft. 1870.
   iii.   FREDERICK R. DAVIS, b. 1871, MO; d. Aft. 1880.
    iv.   ELIZA J. DAVIS, b. 1873, MO; d. Aft. 1880.

9. GEORGE[3] GIBSON (ELIZA JANE[2] BALLARD, BLAND NIXON[1]) was born 22 Sep 1845 in Camden Co., MO, and died 27 Jul 1916 in OK. He married PARADINE LUCY DAVIS 17 Feb 1867 in MO. She was born 16 Jan 1851 in Laclede Co., MO, and died 15 Dec 1882 in Pulaski Co., MO.

Notes for GEORGE GIBSON:
Source: 1870-1880 Camden County Missouri Federal Census Records
** 1870 - Living in Auglaize, Camden Co., MO - Gibson, GB 24 MO, Paradine 19 MO, Samuel 2 MO, Parley A 8/12 MO*
** 1880 - Living in Auglaize, Camden Co., MO - Gibson, George 33 MO MO IL farmer, Paradine S 29 MO, Samuel W 11 MO, Harley A 9 MO, Warren D 7 MO, Laura E 4 MO, George 3 MO, Infant 6/12 MO*

More About GEORGE GIBSON:
Burial: Grand Army of the Republic Cemetery, Miami, Ottawa Co., OK

More About PARADINE LUCY DAVIS:
Burial: Dowty Cemetery, Laclede Co., MO

Children of GEORGE GIBSON and PARADINE DAVIS are:

      i.   SARAH W.[4] GIBSON.
      ii. SAMUEL GIBSON, b. 1868, MO; d. Aft. 1880.
18.   iii. PARLEY ORLANDO GIBSON, b. 01 Nov 1869, Camden Co., MO; d. 11 Jul 1947, Camden Co., MO.
      iv. WARREN DELMAR GIBSON, b. 21 Jan 1872, Pulaski Co., MO; d. 26 Oct 1961, Delaware Co., OK; m. MABEL M. FARIS; b. Nov 1882, MO; d. 1968.

             More About WARREN DELMAR GIBSON:
             Burial: Olympus Cemetery, Grove, Delaware Co., OK

             More About MABEL M. FARIS:
             Burial: Olympus Cemetery, Grove, Delaware Co., OK

      v. LAURA E. GIBSON, b. 1876, MO; d. Aft. 1880.
      vi. GEORGE OSCAR GIBSON, b. 12 Oct 1877, MO; d. 04 Oct 1924; m. ELIZA; b. 1875; d. 1935.

             More About GEORGE OSCAR GIBSON:
             Burial: Grand Army of the Republic Cemetery, Miami, Ottawa Co., OK

             More About ELIZA:
             Burial: Grand Army of the Republic Cemetery, Miami, Ottawa Co., OK

     vii. ARTHUR H. GIBSON, b. 1879, MO; d. Aft. 1880.
   viii. BERTHA I. GIBSON, b. 1881, MO.

10. CHARLOTTE[3] GIBSON (ELIZA JANE[2] BALLARD, BLAND NIXON[1]) was born 31 Dec 1851 in Camden Co., MO, and died 09 Oct 1888. She married HENRY E. WARREN 04 Mar 1869. He was born 29 Jun 1844 in Grainger Co., TN, and died 20 Dec 1933 in Pulaski Co., MO.

More About CHARLOTTE GIBSON:
Burial: Oaklawn Cemetery, Richland, Pulaski Co., MO

Notes for HENRY E. WARREN:
Source: 1870 Pulaski County Missouri Federal Census Records
** 1870 - Living in Liberty, Pulaski Co., MO - Warren, Henry E 26 Dry Goods Merchant, Charlotte 20, Eliza 5/12*

More About HENRY E. WARREN:
Burial: Oaklawn Cemetery, Richland, Pulaski Co., MO

Children of CHARLOTTE GIBSON and HENRY WARREN are:
     i.   *ELIZA⁴ WARREN, b. 1869.*

    ii. *HENRY ERNEST WARREN, b. 30 May 1877, Richland, Pulaski Co., MO; d. 19 Jan 1960, Richland, Pulaski Co., MO; m. OLIVE RAY LINGSWEILER, 04 Jun 1904; b. 02 Nov 1884, Richland, Pulaski Co., MO; d. 11 Mar 1966, Waynesville, Pulaski Co., MO.*

        More About HENRY ERNEST WARREN:
        Burial: Oaklawn Cemetery, Richland, Pulaski Co., MO

        More About OLIVE RAY LINGSWEILER:
        Burial: Oaklawn Cemetery, Richland, Pulaski Co., MO

   iii. *CHARLES WESLEY WARREN, b. 23 Dec 1872, Richland, Pulaski Co., MO; d. 14 Feb 1966, Greene Co., MO; m. FLORENCE BROCK; b. 11 Nov 1876, KY; d. 04 Jun 1938.*

        More About CHARLES WESLEY WARREN:
        Burial: Oaklawn Cemetery, Richland, Pulaski Co., MO

        More About FLORENCE BROCK:
        Burial: Oaklawn Cemetery, Richland, Pulaski Co., MO

11. *SAMUEL L.³ GIBSON (ELIZA JANE² BALLARD, BLAND NIXON¹) was born 27 Nov 1855 in Camden Co., MO, and died 24 Jun 1911 in MO. He married VIRGINIA WRINKLE 18 Jun 1902 in Linn Creek, Camden Co., MO. She was born Abt. 1882 in TN, and died Aft. 1910.*

Notes for SAMUEL L. GIBSON:
Source: Camden County Missouri Marriage Records, 1910 Pulaski County Missouri Federal Census Records

** 1910 - Living in Liberty Ward, Pulaski Co., MO - Gibson, Samuel L 54 MO MO TN, Virginia 28 - 2 children 1 living TN TN TN, Earl S 7 MO, Mattie Bowling servant 19, Walter W Wrinkle brother in law 17 MO TN TN*

More About SAMUEL L. GIBSON:
Burial: Oaklawn Cemetery, Richland, Pulaski Co., MO

Children of SAMUEL GIBSON and VIRGINIA WRINKLE are:
     i.   *EARL⁴ GIBSON, b. Abt. 1903; d. Aft. 1910.*
    ii. *VIVIAN VIRGINIA GIBSON, b. 14 Feb 1905; d. 09 Jul 1905.*

        More About VIVIAN VIRGINIA GIBSON:
        Burial: Oaklawn Cemetery, Richland, Pulaski Co., MO

12. *JAMES BLAND³ GIBSON (ELIZA JANE² BALLARD, BLAND NIXON¹) was born Aug 1861 in Camden Co., MO, and died 1909. He married JENNIE LUCINDA TRAW. She was born 25 Mar 1863 in Camden Co., MO, and died 08 Nov 1963 in Jackson Co., MO.*

Notes for JAMES BLAND GIBSON:
Source: 1900 Cole County Missouri Federal Census Records

** 1900 - Living in Jefferson, Cole Co., MO - Gibson, James B - Aug 1861 MO TN TN physician, Jannel L - Mar 1864 - 16 or 10 (hard to read) - 6 living - MO MO MO, Alice - May 1883 MO, Autis B - Apr 1884 MO, John E - Apr*

1886 MO, Samuel V - Jan 1888 MO, Ione J. - Dec 1891 MO, Schley - June 1899 MO

More About JAMES BLAND GIBSON:
Burial: Oaklawn Cemetery, Richland, Pulaski Co., MO

Notes for JENNIE LUCINDA TRAW:
Source: Jackson County Missouri Certificate of Death, 1920 Atchison County Kansas Federal Census Records, 1925 Atchison County Kansas State Census Records

** 1920 - Living in Atchison Co., KS - Gibson, Jennie 56, Maud 36, Aleta 18, Robert 16*
** 1925 - Living in Atchison Co., KS - Gibson, Jennie L 62, Maud 42, Oleta 23, Letha Jones 21, Chas Anton 40*

More About JENNIE LUCINDA TRAW:
Burial: Oaklawn Cemetery, Richland, Pulaski Co., MO

Children of JAMES GIBSON and JENNIE TRAW are:

i.   *MAUDE ALICE[4] GIBSON, b. 09 May 1883, MO; d. 25 Apr 1972.*

      More About MAUDE ALICE GIBSON:
      Burial: Oaklawn Cemetery, Richland, Pulaski Co., MO

ii.   *AUTIE BLAND GIBSON, b. 18 Sep 1884, MO; d. 07 Sep 1984; m. OVID HARVEY BELSHE; b. 19 Oct 1886, Miller Co., MO; d. 25 Aug 1958, Greene Co., MO.*

      More About AUTIE BLAND GIBSON:
      Burial: Oaklawn Cemetery, Richland, Pulaski Co., MO

      More About OVID HARVEY BELSHE:
      Burial: Oaklawn Cemetery, Richland, Pulaski Co., MO

iii.   *SAMUEL V. GIBSON, b. 15 Jan 1888, Cole Co., MO; d. 21 Jun 1949, Cole Co., MO; m. BERTHA SMITH; b. 1891; d. 1962.*

      More About SAMUEL V. GIBSON:
      Burial: Riverview Cemetery, Jefferson City, Cole Co., MO

      More About BERTHA SMITH:
      Burial: Riverview Cemetery, Jefferson City, Cole Co., MO

iv.   *SIMEON J. GIBSON, b. 15 Jan 1890, Pulaski Co., MO; d. 31 Dec 1891.*

      More About SIMEON J. GIBSON:
      Burial: Oaklawn Cemetery, Richland, Pulaski Co., MO

v.   *L. RUSSELL GIBSON, b. 27 Nov 1891, MO; d. 08 Jan 1892.*

      More About L. RUSSELL GIBSON:
      Burial: Oaklawn Cemetery, Richland, Pulaski Co., MO

vi.   *IONE J. GIBSON, b. 26 Dec 1892, Richland, Pulaski Co., MO; d. 18 Feb 1979, Peoria Co., IL; m. OSCAR SEEBER, 27 Jun 1917, Atchison, KS; b. 02 Jan 1893, Clay Co., KS; d. Jul 1982.*

      More About IONE J. GIBSON:
      Burial: Springdale Cemetery and Mausoleum, Peoria, Peoria Co., IL

More About OSCAR SEEBER:

Burial: Springdale Cemetery and Mausoleum, Peoria, Peoria Co., IL

   vii.   SCHLEY GIBSON, b. Abt. 1899, MO.
  viii.   OLETA T. GIBSON, b. 30 Jun 1901, Jefferson, MO; d. 28 Dec 1992, Holden, Johnson Co., MO; m. WILLIAM L. GORDON; b. 20 May 1893, Rushville, Buchanan Co., MO; d. 15 Apr 1989, Holden, Johnson Co., MO.

Notes for OLETA T. GIBSON:
Source: Social Security Records

More About OLETA T. GIBSON:
Burial: La Monte Cemetery, La Monte, Pettis Co., MO

More About WILLIAM L. GORDON:
Burial: Le Monte Cemetery, La Monte, Pettis Co., MO

   ix.   ROBERT EMERSON GIBSON, b. 10 Dec 1903, Jefferson, MO; d. Aug 1978; m. LULEEN F. ELLIS; b. 1909; d. 1998.

Notes for ROBERT EMERSON GIBSON:
Source: WWII Draft Cards, Social Security Records

More About ROBERT EMERSON GIBSON:
Burial: Sunset Memory Gardens, Atchison Co., KS

More About LULEEN F. ELLIS:
Burial: Sunset Memory Gardens, Atchison, Atchison Co., KS

13. LILLIE BELLE[3] GIBSON (ELIZA JANE[2] BALLARD, BLAND NIXON[1]) was born 30 Jul 1867 in MO, and died 11 Jun 1939. She married JAMES MONROE LIGHT. He was born 19 Feb 1863 in MO, and died 17 Feb 1916.

Notes for JAMES MONROE LIGHT:
Source: 1900 Camden County Missouri Federal Census Records, 1910 Lamb County Texas Federal Census Records

** 1900 - Living in Auglaize, Camden Co., MO - Light, J M - Jan 1863 MO IN MO, Lillie B - July 1866 - 3 children 3 living - MO MO TN, Hattie B - Sep 1884 MO, Frances E - Jan 1888 MO, Margerit - Nov 1897 MO*
** 1910 - Living in Lamb Co., TX - Light, James M 44 MO MO MO, Lillie B 41 - 5 children 5 living MO MO MO, Hattie B 24 MO, Francis E. 22 MO, Maggie M 13 MO, Levena 8 MO, Samuel M 6 MO*

Children of LILLIE GIBSON and JAMES LIGHT are:
19.   i.   HATTIE BELLE[4] LIGHT, b. 15 Sep 1884, Camden Co., MO; d. 04 Dec 1972, Hale Co., TX.
       ii.   FRANCES ELBERT LIGHT, b. Abt. Jan 1888, Camden Co., MO; d. Aft. 1910.
     iii.   MARGARET "MAGGIE" LIGHT, b. Abt. Nov 1897, Camden Co., MO; d. Aft. 1910.
     iv.   LAVENA LIGHT, b. 1901, Camden Co., MO; d. Aft. 1910.
      v.   SAMUEL MONROE LIGHT, b. 1903, Camden Co., MO; d. Aft. 1910.

14. OLIVE[3] BALLARD (BLAND NIXON[2], BLAND NIXON[1]) was born 04 Jan 1871 in Waynesville, Pulaski Co., MO, and died 02 Oct 1956 in St. Louis Co., MO. She married LEROY JASPER HOBBS. He was born 1860, and died 1948.

Child of OLIVE BALLARD and LEROY HOBBS is:

i.   JOE L.[4] HOBBS, b. 1895; d. 1918.

15. CORA CATHERINE[3] BALLARD (BLAND NIXON[2], BLAND NIXON[1]) was born 30 Jul 1872 in Pulaski Co., MO, and died 05 Oct 1902 in Phelps Co., MO. She married THOMAS PHELIX HAMILTON. He was born 13 Dec 1868 in Dent Co., MO, and died 08 Jan 1945 in Newburg, Phelps Co., MO.

Notes for THOMAS PHELIX HAMILTON:
Source: 1900 Phelps County Missouri Federal Census Records
* 1900 - Living in Spring Creek, Phelps Co., MO - Hamilton, Thomas P - Dec 1869 MO MO MO, Cora - July 1872 - 5 children 5 living MO KY KS, Minnie F - Dec 1891 MO, Birt L - Feb 1893 MO, Zelma L - Nov 1895 MO, Robert F - Dec 1897 MO, Grace D - Feb 1900 MO

More About THOMAS PHELIX HAMILTON:
Burial: Hamilton Cemetery, Phelps Co., MO

Children of CORA BALLARD and THOMAS HAMILTON are:
      i.   MINNIE F.[4] HAMILTON, b. Abt. 1892, MO; d. Aft. 1900.
     ii.   BERT LAVIGGA HAMILTON, b. 10 Feb 1894, MO; d. 13 Sep 1928, St. Louis City, MO.

        More About BERT LAVIGGA HAMILTON:
        Burial: Hamilton Cemetery, Phelps Co., MO

    iii.   ZELMA L. HAMILTON, b. Abt. 1896, MO; d. Aft. 1900.
    iv.   ROBERT F. HAMILTON, b. Abt. 1898, MO; d. Aft. 1900.
     v.   GRACE D. HAMILTON, b. Abt. 1900, MO; d. Aft. 1900.

16. CHARLES[3] BALLARD (BLAND NIXON[2], BLAND NIXON[1]) was born 12 Jul 1875 in Pulaski Co., MO, and died 12 Jun 1902 in Waynesville, Pulaski Co., MO. He married ELVA DUNCAN. She was born 26 Sep 1877, and died 19 May 1905 in Waynesville, Pulaski Co., MO.

Notes for CHARLES BALLARD:
Source: Obituary

* Pulaski County Democrat - 4 Jul 1902
Charles Ballard died at his home near Waynesville, June 12, 1902, of typhoid fever after a short illness, aged 24 years. Everything that skilled physicians and loving hands could do was all in vain; the Lord had need for him and called him away. His sisters and step-mother were with him and administered to every want until the end came. His companion had proceeded him just three weeks. But we weep not as those that have little faith. While we have lost him we hope our loss is his gain. He is free from all care and trouble and has paid the debt we all must pay. While his body moulders in the tomb the soul is safe in Heaven. where there will be no hour of parting and God shall wipe all tears away. He leaves two small children and four sisters to mourn his loss. The interment took place at the Laughlin cemetery at 12 o'clock Saturday.

More About CHARLES BALLARD:
Burial: Laughlin Cemetery., Ft. Leonard Wood, Pulaski Co., MO

More About ELVA DUNCAN:
Burial: Laughlin Cemetery., Ft. Leonard Wood, Pulaski Co., MO

Child of CHARLES BALLARD and ELVA DUNCAN is:
      i.   CLARENCE A.[4] BALLARD, b. 1897; d. 1969.

17. NEAL "NEELY" BRADFORD[3] BALLARD (BLAND NIXON[2], BLAND NIXON[1]) was born 16 Feb 1884 in MO, and died 21 Oct 1987 in Phelps Co., MO. He married IDA ETHEL LAMBETH 04 Jul 1905 in Phelps Co., MO. She was born 12 May 1888 in MO, and died 06 Apr 1986.

Notes for NEAL "NEELY" BRADFORD BALLARD:
Source: 1910-1920 Pulaski County Missouri Federal Census Records, 1930 St. Louis County Missouri Federal Census Records, Phelps County Missouri Marriage Records

* 1910 - Living in Cullen, Pulaski Co., MO - Ballard, Neal B 27 MO MO MO, Ida 25 - 2 children 2 living MO MO MO, Ray L 3, Ethel 8/12 MO, Benjamin F Fuller hired man 18 MO
* 1920 - Living in Cullen, Pulaski Co., MO - Ballard, Neal B 36 MO, Ida E 32 MO, Ray L 12 MO, Ethel V 10 MO, Samuel 8 MO, Lucy Buckner 20 servant MO
* 1930 - Living in University, St. Louis Co., MO - Ballard, Neal 46 MO MO MO, Ida 42 MO MO MO, Lee 6 MO

More About NEAL "NEELY" BRADFORD BALLARD:
Burial: Rolla Cemetery, Phelps Co., MO

More About IDA ETHEL LAMBETH:
Burial: Rolla Cemetery, Phelps Co., MO

Children of NEAL BALLARD and IDA LAMBETH are:
    i.   SON[4] BALLARD, b. 21 Mar 1906, Pulaski Co., MO; d. 21 Mar 1906.

       More About SON BALLARD:
       Burial: Laughlin Cemetery, Ft. Leonard Wood, Pulaski Co., MO

    ii.   RAY BALLARD, b. Abt. 1907, Pulaski Co., MO; d. Aft. 1920.
    iii.   ETHEL BALLARD, b. 06 Jul 1909, Waynesville, Pulaski Co., MO; d. 17 Jul 1928, Rolla, Phelps Co., MO.

       More About ETHEL BALLARD:
       Burial: Laughlin Cemetery, Ft. Leonard Wood, Pulaski Co., MO

    iv.   SON BALLARD, b. 18 Dec 1910, Pulaski Co., MO; d. 18 Dec 1910, Pulaski Co., MO.

       More About SON BALLARD:
       Burial: Laughlin Cemetery, Ft. Leonard Wood, Pulaski Co., MO

    v.   SAMUEL BALLARD, b. Abt. 1912, Pulaski Co., MO; d. Aft. 1920.
    vi.   LEE NIXON BALLARD, b. 01 Apr 1924, Phelps Co., MO; d. 16 Jun 2004.

       Notes for LEE NIXON BALLARD:
       Source: Social Security Records

Generation No. 4

18. PARLEY ORLANDO[4] GIBSON (GEORGE[3], ELIZA JANE[2] BALLARD, BLAND NIXON[1]) was born 01 Nov 1869 in Camden Co., MO, and died 11 Jul 1947 in Camden Co., MO. He married ELIZABETH "LIZZIE" DODSON ARMSTRONG. She was born 26 Aug 1878 in MO, and died 07 Mar 1972.

Notes for PARLEY ORLANDO GIBSON:
Source: 1900 Camden County Missouri Federal Census Records
* 1900 - Living in Auglaize, Camden Co., MO - Gibson, Harley, - Nov 1869, Lizzie - Aug 1878, Lucy - Oct 1895, John A - Dec 1897

More About PARLEY ORLANDO GIBSON:
Burial: Armstrong Cemetery, Camden Co., MO

More About ELIZABETH "LIZZIE" DODSON ARMSTRONG:
Burial: Armstrong Cemetery, Camden Co., MO

Children of PARLEY GIBSON and ELIZABETH ARMSTRONG are:

> i.   LUCY[5] GIBSON, b. Oct 1895, Camden Co., MO; d. Aft. 1900.
> ii. JOHN A. GIBSON, b. Dec 1897, Camden Co., MO; d. Aft. 1900.

19.   HATTIE BELLE[4] LIGHT (LILLIE BELLE[3] GIBSON, ELIZA JANE[2] BALLARD, BLAND NIXON[1]) *was born 15 Sep 1884 in Camden Co., MO, and died 04 Dec 1972 in Hale Co., TX. She married* JOSEPH EDWARD OURSBOURN *04 Sep 1912 in Camden Co., MO. He was born 30 Jan 1885 in Camden Co., MO, and died 20 Sep 1972 in Camden Co., MO.*

Notes for HATTIE BELLE LIGHT:
Source: Hale County Texas Certificate of Death

More About HATTIE BELLE LIGHT:
Burial: Oaklawn Cemetery, Richland, Pulaski Co., MO

Notes for JOSEPH EDWARD OURSBOURN:
Source: 1920-1930 Camden County Missouri Federal Census Records

** 1920 - Living in Auglaize, Camden Co., MO - Oursbourne, Joe E 34, Hattie V 35, Willie R 6, Jos Aubrey 4, Robert M 2, Ernest C*
** 1930 - Living in Auglaize, Camden Co., MO - Oursbourn, Joe E 45, Hattie B 45, Willie R 16, Aubrey J 15, Robert M 12, Earnest C 10, Laverne S 8, Cecil F 5, Mildred L 2*

More About JOSEPH EDWARD OURSBOURN:
Burial: Oaklawn Cemetery, Richland, Pulaski Co., MO

Children of HATTIE LIGHT and JOSEPH OURSBOURN are:

> i.   ATHOL C.[5] OURSBOURN, b. 05 Apr 1906.
> ii. WILLIAM R. OURSBOURN, b. 19 Aug 1913, Camden Co., MO; d. 05 Apr 1988; m. ELIZABETH KATHLEEN SCOTT; b. 07 Jan 1918, Pulaski Co., MO; d. 06 Jun 2010, Lebanon, Laclede Co., MO.
> iii. ROBERT MONROE OURSBOURN, b. 03 Jul 1917, Camden Co., MO; d. 21 Aug 2011, Richland, Pulaski Co., MO; m. BARBARA MARIE PARKER; b. 11 Jan 1920, Camden Co., MO; d. 03 Jun 2010, Springfield, Greene Co., MO.
> iv. ERNEST C. OURSBOURN, b. 07 Nov 1919, Camden Co., MO; d. 22 Jul 1994.
>
>   *More About ERNEST C. OURSBOURN:*
>   *Burial: Oaklawn Cemetery, Richland, Pulaski Co., MO*
>
> v.   LILLIAN L. OURSBOURN, b. 19 Mar 1922, Camden Co., MO; d. 29 Mar 1986; m. HENRY OLIVER WILLIAMS; b. 26 Feb 1915, MO; d. 16 Dec 1985.
>
>   *More About LILLIAN L. OURSBOURN:*
>   *Burial: Oaklawn Cemetery, Richland, Pulaski Co., MO*
>
>   *More About HENRY OLIVER WILLIAMS:*
>   *Burial: Oaklawn Cemetery, Richland, Pulaski Co., MO*

vi.   CECIL F. OURSBOURN, b. 23 Dec 1924, Camden Co., MO; d. 29 Nov 1998, Lebanon, Laclede Co., MO; m. NATHALEE HAMMOCK; b. 07 Aug 1926, Richland, Pulaski Co., MO; d. 04 Jan 2002.

More About CECIL F. OURSBOURN:
Burial: Beulah Baptist Church Cemetery, Montreal, Camden Co., MO

More About NATHALEE HAMMOCK:
Burial: Beulah Baptist Church Cemetery, Montreal, Camden Co., MO

vii.   MILDRED L. OURSBOURN, b. 27 Apr 1927, Camden Co., MO; d. 18 Feb 2001; m. MELVIN DORAL CARROLL; b. 12 Aug 1924; d. 31 Aug 2003.

More About MILDRED L. OURSBOURN:
Burial: Beulah Baptist Church Cemetery, Montreal, Camden Co., MO

More About MELVIN DORAL CARROLL:
Burial: Beulah Baptist Church Cemetery, Montreal, Camden Co., MO

viii.   AUBREY JOSEPH OURSBOURN, b. 22 Feb 1915, Camden Co., MO; d. 23 Aug 2005; m. MARY ELIZABETH OLIVER; b. 07 Jan 1915, Richland, Pulaski Co., MO; d. 23 Feb 2005, Olton, Lamb Co., TX.

More About AUBREY JOSEPH OURSBOURN:
Burial: Olten Cemetery, Olton, Lamb Co., TX

More About MARY ELIZABETH OLIVER:
Burial: Olton Cemetery, Lamb Co., TX

Caleb Ballard

Generation No. 1

1. CALEB[2] BALLARD (MR.[1]) *was born Jul 1835 in IL, and died Aft. 1910. He married* CYNTIIA ANN PYLES. *She was born Jul 1836 in IL, and died Bet. 1900 - 1910.*

Notes for CALEB BALLARD:
Source:1850 Wayne County Missouri Federal Census Records, 1860, 1870 Iron County Missouri Federal Census Records, 1880 Crawford County MO, 1900 Benton Wayne County MO
** 1850 - Living in Wayne Co., MO - Ballard, Caleb 13 IL, Levi Ballard 10 IL. They are apparently brothers living with John Hall 85 and Nancy 63*
** 1860 - Living in Arcadia, Iron Co., MO - Ballard, Caleb 24 IL, Cynthia A 23 IL, Rebecca A 4 MO, James L 1 MO, David Young 30 VA*
** 1860 - The United States of America Graduation Certificate No. 28800} To all to whom these presents shall come, Greeting: Whereas Caleb Ballard, of Iron County, Missouri has deposited in the General Land Office of the United States, a Certificate of the Register of the Land Office at Jackson whereby it appears that full payment has been made by the said Caleb Ballard according to the provisions of the Act of Congress of the 24th of April, 1820, entitled: As act making further provision for the sale of Public Lands," for The East half of Section twenty in Township twenty seven North, of Range one West, in the District of Lands subject to sale at Jackson, Missouri containing three hundred and twenty acres according to the official plat of the Survey of the Lands, returned to the General Land Office by the Surveyor General, which said tract has been purchased by the said Caleb Ballard.*
** 1870 - Living in Iron Co., MO - Ballard, Caleb 32 IL, Cynthia 29 IL, James S 11 MO, John 5 MO, Phillip S. 2 MO*
** 1876 - Living in St. Francois Co., MO - Ballard, Caleb, Cintha, James, John, Caleb S*
** 1880 - Living in Courtois, Crawford Co., MO - Ballard, Calob 44 laborer IL SC SC, Cintha A 43 IL SC KY, James 20 MO, John 14, Sherman 13 MO*
** 1890 - Veterans Schedule - Name: Caleb Ballard, Rank: Private, Role: Veteran Residence Date: Jun   1890, Residence Place: Union, Iron, Missouri, USA, Enumeration District: 60, Enlistment Date: 1863,   Discharge Date: 1865, Regiment or vessel: 29 Missouri Inf, Company: E, Length of service: 2 Yrs*
** 1900 - Living in Benton, Wayne Co., MO - Ballard, Caleb - July 1835 IL NC NC, Cynthia A - July 1836 IL KY KY, Lizzie 8 - July 1891 MO MO IL grand daughters*
** 1910 - Living in Wayne Co., MO - Ballard, Caleb 74 wd IL NC NC (near neighbor of Sherman)*

Notes for CYNTIIA ANN PYLES:
Source: James L Ballard Madison County Illinois Death Records (names his parents)

Children of CALEB BALLARD *and* CYNTIIA PYLES *are:*

       i.   REBECCA A.[3] BALLARD, *b. Abt. 1856, MO; d. Aft. 1860.*
2.   ii. JAMES L., BALLARD, *b. Jul 1859, MO; d. 05 May 1933, Granite City, Madison Co., IL.*
3.   iii. JOHN BALLARD, *b. Jul 1865, MO; d. 1923.*
      iv. CALEB PHILLIP SHERMAN BALLARD, *b. 26 Feb 1868, Des Arc, Iron Co., MO; d. 29 Sep 1946, Des Arc, Iron Co., MO; m.* SARAH LOUISE; *b. 26 Feb 1868; d. Aft. 1946.*

        Notes for CALEB PHILLIP SHERMAN BALLARD:
        Source: 1910 Wayne County Missouri Federal Census Records, Iron County Missouri Death Certificate
        ** 1910 - Living in Wayne Co., MO - Ballard, Sherman 42 MO IL IL, Lulu 34 MO GA SC*

        More About CALEB PHILLIP SHERMAN BALLARD:
        Burial: Masonic Cemetery., Piedmont, Wayne Co., MO

2. *JAMES[3] L., BALLARD (CALEB[2] BALLARD, MR.[1]) was born Jul 1859 in MO, and died 05 May 1933 in Granite City, Madison Co., IL. He married SARAH MCMANUS 27 Nov 1881 in Crawford, MO. She was born 16 Mar 1862 in MO, and died 09 May 1931 in Madison Co., IL.*

Notes for JAMES L., BALLARD:
Source: Pam Reichnaner, 1900 Wayne County Missouri Federal Census Records

** 1900 - Living in Benton, Wayne Co., MO - Ballard, James - July 1859 MO MO MO, Sarah - Mar 1862 MO Ireland MO, Charley - July 1881 MO, Anna - Dec 1885 MO, Alice - May 1888 MO, Mamy - Mar 1892 MO, Eddie - Nov 1897 MO*

More About JAMES L., BALLARD:
Burial: Sunset Hill Cemetery, Edwardsville, Madison Co., IL

More About SARAH MCMANUS:
Burial: Sunset Hill Cemetery, Edwardsville, Madison Co., IL

Children of JAMES L. and SARAH MCMANUS are:

      i.   *CHARLES[4] BALLARD, b. Jul 1881, MO.*

     ii.   *ANNA ADELINE BALLARD, b. 28 Dec 1885, Des Arc, Iron Co., MO; d. 21 Mar 1964, Granite City, Madison Co., IL; m. WILLIAM FRANKLIN MANN; b. 05 Jun 1876, Reynolds Co., MO; d. 18 Jan 1962, Granite City, Madison Co., IL.*

            More About WILLIAM FRANKLIN MANN:
            Burial: Sunset Hill Cemetery, Glen Carbon, Madison Co., IL

    iii. *ALICE MYRTLE BALLARD, b. 08 May 1888, Wayne Co., MO; d. 03 Jan 1935, St. Francois Co., MO; m. GEORGE BATES; b. 24 Sep 1877, Wayne Co., MO; d. 07 Aug 1924, St. Louis Co., MO.*

            More About ALICE MYRTLE BALLARD:
            Burial: Valhalla Cemetery, Bel-Nor, St. Louis Co., MO

            More About GEORGE BATES:
            Burial: Valhalla Cemetery, Bel-Nor, St. Louis Co., MO

     iv. *MAMIE ETHEL BALLARD, b. 15 Mar 1892, Granite City, Madison Co., IL; d. 17 May 1944, Granite City, Madison Co., IL; m. (1) OBERT DEVER ALLEN; b. 10 Aug 1881, Putnam Co., TN; d. 21 Nov 1968, Madison Co., IL; m. (2) CHARLES ROSS NORRIS; b. 02 Nov 1900, IL; d. 30 Oct 1933, Granite City, Madison Co., IL.*

            Notes for MAMIE ETHEL BALLARD:
            Source: Social Security Records

            More About MAMIE ETHEL BALLARD:
            Burial: Sunset Hill Cemetery, Glen Carbon, Madison Co., IL

            More About OBERT DEVER ALLEN:
            Burial: Sunset Hill Cemetery, Glen Carbon, Madison Co., IL

            More About CHARLES ROSS NORRIS:
            Burial: Sunset Hill Cemetery, Glen Carbon, Madison Co., IL

v. EDWARD SHERMAN BALLARD, b. 27 Nov 1897, Wayne Co., MO; d. 05 Dec 1965, St. Louis Co., MO; m. AMY LOUIS BEHRENDS; b. 20 Feb 1906, MO; d. 21 Sep 1936, Madison Co., IL.

More About EDWARD SHERMAN BALLARD:
Burial: Sunset Hill Cemetery, Glen Carbon, Madison Co., IL

More About AMY LOUIS BEHRENDS:
Burial: Sunset Hill Cemetery, Glen Carbon, Madison Co., IL

vi. NELLIE JEWELL BALLARD, b. 12 Dec 1901; d. 22 Jun 1958; m. RICHARD BRICE MCCONNELL; b. 08 Feb 1902; d. 28 Mar 1976.

More About NELLIE JEWELL BALLARD:
Burial: Mt. Hope Cemetery, San Diego, San Diego Co., CA

More About RICHARD BRICE MCCONNELL:
Burial: Mt. Hope Cemetery, San Diego, San Diego Co., CA

3. JOHN[3] BALLARD (CALEB[2], MR.[1]) was born Jul 1865 in MO, and died 1923. He married ELIZABETH GRAHAM. She was born Mar 1867 in OH, and died 1923.

Notes for JOHN BALLARD:
Source: 1900 Wayne County Missouri Federal Census Records, 1910 Crawford County Missouri Federal Census Records

** 1900 - Living in Benton, Wayne Co., MO - Ballard, John 35 - July 1865 MO IL IL, Elizabeth - Mar 1867 OH OH OH , Hattie - Oct 11 1888 MO MO OH, Bessie 3 - June 1896 MO MO OH, Ora 1 - May 1899 MO MO OH*
** 1910 - Living in Meramec, Crawford Co., MO - Ballard, John 44 MO, Elizabeth 43 OH, Bessie 13 MO, Ora M 10 MO, Maud N 8 MO*
** 1920 - Living in Saint Louis Co., MO - Ballard, John 5(1) (hard to tell second number), Elizabeth 51 OH, Bessie 22 MO, Maud 12 MO, Wilma Whitworth 5 grand child MO*

Children of JOHN BALLARD and ELIZABETH GRAHAM are:

    i. HATTIE[4] BALLARD, b. Oct 1888, MO.
   ii. BESSIE BALLARD, b. Jun 1896, MO; d. Aft. 1920.
  iii. ORA BALLARD, b. May 1899, MO; d. Aft. 1910.
  iii. MAUD N. BALLARD, b. 1902, MO; d. 1975.

David Crawford Ballard

Generation No. 1

1. DAVID CRAWFORD[5] BALLARD (JOHN[4], THOMAS HORACE[3], THOMAS[2], WILLIAM[1]) *was born 11 Jun 1779 in VA, and died Aft. 1853 in Ray Co., MO. He married ELIZABETH HUCKSTEP 03 Sep 1811 in Bond 8/26/1811 Orange Co., VA. She was born Abt. 1791 in VA, and died Aft. 1850.*

Notes for DAVID CRAWFORD BALLARD:
Source: Ray County Missouri Wills, 1850 Ray County Missouri Federal Census Records, Dr. John Ballard

** The following are marriages listed in The Harris Papers, Orange Co. taken from the Orange Co. Marriage Resister #1, 1757-1867:   Peter Harris and Isaac Goodall witness marriage of David C. Ballard & Elizabeth Huckstep, 1811*
** 1850 - Living in Ray Co., MO - Ballard, David C 52 VA, Elizabeth 44 VA, Richard L. 20 VA*
** 1853 - Ray Co., MO - Will - I David Crawford Ballard of the county of Ray and State of Missouri, do make and publish this my last will and testament, hereby writing and making absolutely null and void all wills and Codicils thereto by me at any time hereto from made.*
First, I direct that my body be decently interred and that my funeral be conducted in a manner corresponding with my estate and condition in life.
Second, I direct that my funeral expenses and all my debts be paid as soon after my decease as possible, out of the first moneys that shall come to the hand of my executors hereinafter named, out of any portion of my estate real or personal.
Third, I direct that all of my estate real and personal, be inventoried and appraised in all respects according to the laws of the State of Missouri, governing the administration of estates of deceased persons in Cases where no will is made.
Fourth, Should it become necessary to sell any portion of my estate in Order to the payment of my debts and funeral expenses, (??? can't read) that my beloved wife Elizabeth Ballard shall in all cases have the privilege of Selecting and determining what property, weather real or personal shall be first sold for that purpose. And if she fail or refuse to make such Selection within a reasonable time after being notified, thereto by my executors in each particular case, then my executor on to proceed and sell according to the requirements of law as if no such privilege were hereby given.
Fifth, I direct that my whole estate, real and personal subject whoever to the payment of my debts and funeral expenses as above mentioned) shall immediately upon my decease (?) and remain in my beloved wife Elizabeth Ballard during her natural life or widowhood and at her death or marriage to be disposed of as hereinafter provided in
Sixth, I direct that upon the death or marriage of my wife, if she survive me, and if she does not then upon my decease, my whole estate real and personal be sold by my executors in the manner and on the terms required by law in sale of the property of deceased persons for payment of debts, in the ordinary course of administration, hereby giving to my said executors as full and complete proven to convey said estate under such sale, as would be given them by law if said sale, were made as aforementioned in the ordinary order of a administration or as I myself would have if living.
Seventh, I devise that the net proceeds of my whole estate up on the sale mentioned in the last preceding clause be disposed as follows, viz; I Give to my sons Thomas G and Richard L out of said proceeds the sum of one hundred dollars each of them.
Eight, Whereas my son John B. Ballard is now indebted to me in the sum of three hundred and twenty one dollars and eighty cents ($320.87) for money by me paid for him as specified in a deed of Trust executed by him in my farm, dated the 6th day of March AD 1846, and recorded in the Recorders office of Ray County aforesaid in Book "E" page 337 now if my said Son John B. Ballard shall not have paid to me or my executors the said sum of money then the amount due thereupon by then, without interest at the time of the distribution wherein after mentioned, shall be counted in and considered as a portion of the then which shall be coming to him said distribution; I direct that the remainder of said proceeds, after deducting the sum of two hundred dollars above bequeathed in the seventh clause hereof and subject to the limitation specified in the Clause be equally divided among my children John B. Ballard, James E, Willis H, Thomas G and Richard L Ballard and Lucinda Maupin the share of the said Lucinda Maupin to

be only loaned to her for the term of her natural life but to belong to and at her death next in the heirs of her natural life, but to belong to and at her death next in the heirs of her body.

Ninth, I do hereby make and appoint my sons Thomas G Ballard and Willis H. Ballard Executors of this my last will and testament.

In testimony whereof I have hereunto set my hand and seal this 1st day of December A. D. 1847. D. C Ballard (seal) Attested by us in the Summer of the Testators. R. (hard to read), Edward Lewis witnesses.

Children of DAVID BALLARD and ELIZABETH HUCKSTEP are:

	i.	LUCINDA⁶ BALLARD, d. Aft. 1847; m. MAUPIN.
2.	ii.	JOHN B. BALLARD, b. 1814; d. Aft. 1853.
3.	iii.	JAMES E. BALLARD, b. 22 Nov 1817, VA; d. 03 Feb 1893.
4.	iv.	WILLIS H. BALLARD, b. Abt. 1822; d. Aft. 1880.
	v.	RICHARD L. BALLARD, b. 1830, VA; d. Aft. 1850.
5.	vi.	THOMAS GARLAND BALLARD, b. Apr 1830, VA; d. 01 Oct 1917, Ray Co., MO.

Generation No. 2

2. JOHN B.⁶ BALLARD (*DAVID CRAWFORD⁵, JOHN⁴, THOMAS HORACE³, THOMAS², WILLIAM¹*) *was born 1814, and died Aft. 1853. He married NANCY N.. She was born Abt. 1815 in VA, and died Aft. 1850.*

Notes for JOHN B. BALLARD:
Source: 1850 Ray County Missouri Federal Census Records
** 1850 - Living in Ray Co., MO - Ballard, John B 36 farmer VA, N. N 35 VA, Mary C 15 VA, Ellen E 11 TN, Mildred 10 VA, William L 8 MO, Lucy 6 MO, Thomas R 2 MO*

Children of JOHN BALLARD and NANCY N. are:

	i.	MARY C.⁷ BALLARD, b. Abt. 1835, VA; d. Aft. 1850.
	ii.	ELLEN E. BALLARD, b. Abt. 1839, TN; d. Aft. 1850.
	iii.	MILDED BALLARD, b. Abt. 1840, VA; d. Aft. 1850.
	iv.	WILLIAM L BALLARD, b. Abt. 1842, MO; d. Aft. 1850.
	v.	LUCY BALLARD, b. Abt. 1844, MO; d. Aft. 1850.
	vi.	THOMAS R. BALLARD, b. Abt. 1848, MO; d. Aft. 1850.

3. JAMES E.⁶ BALLARD (*DAVID CRAWFORD⁵, JOHN⁴, THOMAS HORACE³, THOMAS², WILLIAM¹*) *was born 22 Nov 1817 in VA, and died 03 Feb 1893. He married MATILDA. She was born Abt. 1828, and died Bet. 1870 - 1880.*

Notes for JAMES E. BALLARD:
Source: 1850 Ray County Missouri Federal Census Records

** 1850 - Living in Ray Co., MO - Ballard, James E 33 farmer VA, Matilda 22 KY, Adeline 1 MO*
** 1860 - Living in Ray Co., MO - Ballard, James 44 miller VA, Matilda 30 KY, Adaline 10 KY, Jas 2 MO, (living with another family, (Saml Ballard looks like Rolland)*
** 1870 - Living in Richmond, Ray Co., MO - Ballard, James 53 retired merchant VA, Matilda 43 KY, James J 12 MO, Lemuel Boon 79 KY*
** 1880 - Living in Sedan, Chautauqua Co., KS - living with daughter Addie Hancock - Ballard, James 64 father in law and James Jr. 22 brother*

More About JAMES E. BALLARD:
Burial: Greenwood Cemetery, Sedan, Chautauqua Co., KS

Children of JAMES BALLARD and MATILDA are:

6.	i.	ADELINE⁷ BALLARD, b. Abt. 1849; d. Aft. 1880.
	ii.	JAMES E. BALLARD. JR., b. 1859; d. 1923; m. LOUISE VAN OSTIN, 08 Sep 1876, Chautauqua Co., KS.

More About JAMES E. BALLARD. JR.:
Burial: Greenwood Cemetery, Sedan, Chautauqua Co., KS

4. WILLIS H.[6] BALLARD (DAVID CRAWFORD[5], JOHN[4], THOMAS HORACE[3], THOMAS[2], WILLIAM[1]) *was born Abt. 1822, and died Aft. 1880. He married ELIZA JANE ROGERS 21 Nov 1842 in Albemarle Co., VA. She was born Abt. 1825 in VA, and died Aft. 1900.*

Notes for WILLIS H. BALLARD:
Source: 1850 -1860 Ray County Missouri Federal census Records, 1870, 1880 Saline County Missouri Federal Census Records
** 1850 - Living in Ray Co., MO - Ballard, Willis H 27 VA, Eliza J 27 VA, Mary E 7 MO, Lucinda J 5 MO, Matilda 3 MO, George R 1 MO*
** 1860 - Living in Richmond, Ray Co., MO - Ballard, W H 37 Hotel proprietor VA, E J 36 VA, Tilla 12 MO, Walter 7 MO, Eugenia 5 MO, (hard to read (fe) 4 MO*
** 1870 - Living in Arrow Rock, Saline Co., MO - Ballard, W H 48 VA merchant, Eliza G 47 VA, Walter L 18 clerk in store MO - Millie B 13 MO, Richard 11 MO, Willie 6 MO*
** 1880 - Living in Arrow Rock, Saline Co., MO - Ballard, WH 58 farmer MO, E J 56, Dick 21, WD (17), Millie ? Lasear 23 daughter & ch: Lida 6, Blanch 4, not named 1 MO*

Children of WILLIS BALLARD and ELIZA ROGERS are:
     i.   *MARY E.[7] BALLARD, b. Abt. 1843.*
     ii.   *LUCINDA J. BALLARD, b. 1845, MO; d. Aft. 1850.*
     iii.   *MATILDA "TILLA" BALLARD, b. 1847, MO; d. Aft. 1860.*
     iv.   *GEORGE R. BALLARD, b. 1849, MO; d. Aft. 1850.*
     v.   *WALTER L. BALLARD, b. 01 Apr 1852, MO; d. 23 Mar 1913, Kansas City, Jackson Co., MO.*

          Notes for WALTER L. BALLARD:
          Source: Missouri State Board of Health Certificate of Death.
          ** Buried in DeWitt Missouri*
          ** Occupation: Traveling Salesman*

          More About WALTER L. BALLARD:
          Burial: 26 Mar 1913, DeWitt MO

     vi.   *EUGENIA BALLARD, b. 1855, MO; d. Aft. 1860.*
  7.   vii.   *RICHARD L. "DICK" BALLARD, b. 1858, MO; d. Aft. 1900.*

5. THOMAS GARLAND[6] BALLARD (DAVID CRAWFORD[5], JOHN[4], THOMAS HORACE[3], THOMAS[2], WILLIAM[1]) *was born Apr 1830 in VA, and died 01 Oct 1917 in Ray Co., MO. He married (1) SARAH PRICE Bef. 1850. She was born 1830 in VA, and died Bet. 1860 - 1870. He married (2) SARAH LUCINDA TAYLOR 27 Oct 1874 in Ray Co., MO. She was born 09 Oct 1847 in MO, and died 10 Mar 1932 in Jackson Co., MO.*

Notes for THOMAS GARLAND BALLARD:
Source: Ray County Missouri Death Certificate, Richard O. Ballard (richamy@knology.net), 1850, -1910 Ray County Missouri Federal Census Records
** 1850 - Living in Ray Co., MO - Ballard, Thomas G 22 VA, Sarah R 18 VA, Alice B 7/12 MO, Richard T. Gillespie 16 TN, Joseph S Shoop 35 NY (next door to David Ballard)*
** 1860 - Living in Ray Co., MO - Ballard, Tho G 31 VA, Sallie 27 VA, Allice 10 MO, L. P 7 MO, C. L 5 MO, LE 3 MO, Tho W. 1 MO*
** 1870 - Living in Richmond, Ray Co., MO - Ballard, Thomas 42 VA, Alice 20 MO, Livingston 18 MO, Laura 15 MO, Leclerc 13 MO, Thomas 11 MO, Sallie 4 MO*
** 1880 - Living in Ray Co., MO - Ballard, Thos 50 dry good merchant VA VA VA, Sallie 31 MO MO VA, Daisy 3 MO, Fenton 1 MO, Eliza 3/12 MO*

** 1900 - Living in Richmond, Ray Co., MO - Ballard, Thomas G - Apr 1830 VA VA VA, Sallie T - Oct 1847 - 5 children 5 living VA VA VA, Fente - Nov 1878 MO, Lida T - Mar 1880 MO, Bessie D - June 1882 MO, Linnie - May 1890, Taylor, Eliza J mother in law - Dec 1823 wd VA VA VA*
** 1910 - Living in Richmond, Ray Co., MO - Ballard, Thomas G 80 md 2x VA VA VA, Sallie T 63 - 5 children 4 living, VA, Sam T 19 MO VA VA, Eliza J Taylor mother in law 87 - 6 children 3 living VA VA VA*

More About THOMAS GARLAND BALLARD:
Burial: 03 Oct 1917, Richmond Cemetery, Richmond, Ray Co., MO

More About SARAH LUCINDA TAYLOR:
Burial: Richmond Cemetery, Richmond, Ray Co., MO

Children of THOMAS BALLARD and SARAH PRICE are:

	i.	ALICE[7] BALLARD, b. 1850, MO; d. Aft. 1870; m. WILLIAM D. KING, 1873, Ray Co., MO.
8.	ii.	LIVINGSTON PRICE BALLARD, b. 16 Jun 1853, Waverly, Lafayette Co., MO; d. 27 Apr 1914, Manitou Springs, El Paso Co., CO.
	iii.	LAURA BALLARD, b. 1855, MO; d. Aft. 1870.
9.	iv.	LECLERK EDWIN BALLARD, b. 25 Nov 1856, MO; d. 01 Apr 1921.
10.	v.	THOMAS WILLIS BALLARD, b. 24 Feb 1858, MO; d. 29 May 1910, Buckley, Pierce Co., WA.
	vi.	SALLIE BALLARD, b. Bet. 1860 - 1869, MO; d. Aft. 1870.

Children of THOMAS BALLARD and SARAH TAYLOR are:

	vii.	DAISY[7] BALLARD, b. 1873, MO; d. Aft. 1880.
	viii.	FENTON BALLARD, b. 1879, MO; d. Aft. 1900.
	ix.	ELIZA BALLARD, b. 1880, MO; d. Aft. 1880.
	x.	LIDA T. BALLARD, b. Mar 1880, MO; d. Aft. 1900.
	xi.	BESSIE D. BALLARD, b. Jun 1882, MO; d. Aft. 1900.
11.	xii.	SAMANTHA TAYLOR "SAM" BALLARD, b. 15 May 1890, Richmond, Ray Co., MO; d. 14 Jul 1942, Callaway Co., MO.

Generation No. 3

6. ADELINE[7] BALLARD (JAMES E.[6], DAVID CRAWFORD[5], JOHN[4], THOMAS HORACE[3], THOMAS[2], WILLIAM[1]) was born Abt. 1849, and died Aft. 1880. She married S. KEN C. HANCOCK. He was born Abt. 1843 in TN, and died Aft. 1880.

Notes for S. KEN C. HANCOCK:
source: 1880 Chautauqua County Kansas Federal Census Records
** 1880 - Living in Sedan, Chautauqua Co., KS - Hancock, S. Ken C 37 farmer TN TN TN, Addie 30, Ida 1, James Ballard 64 father in law, James Jr. 22 brother in law teamster*

Child of ADELINE BALLARD and S. HANCOCK is:

	i.	IDA[8] HANCOCK, b. Abt. 1879, KS; d. Aft. 1880.

7. RICHARD L. "DICK"[7] BALLARD (WILLIS H.[6], DAVID CRAWFORD[5], JOHN[4], THOMAS HORACE[3], THOMAS[2], WILLIAM[1]) was born 1858 in MO, and died Aft. 1900. He married CALLIE BECK 17 May 1899 in Knox Co., MO.

Notes for RICHARD L. "DICK" BALLARD:
Source: 1900 Jackson County Missouri Federal Census Records

** 1900 - Living in Kansas City, Jackson Co., MO - Ballard, R T - Sep 1858 MO VA VA, Kally - Apr 1878 MO IN IL, Eliza mother - May 1822 wd 10 children 6 living VA VA VA, R. T son- Mar 1900 MO MO MO*

Child of RICHARD BALLARD and CALLIE BECK is:
12.   i.   RICHARD T.[8] BALLARD, b. 1900, MO; d. 05 Feb 1942, Spokane, Spokane Co., WA.

8.   LIVINGSTON PRICE[7] BALLARD (THOMAS GARLAND[6], DAVID CRAWFORD[5], JOHN[4], THOMAS HORACE[3], THOMAS[2], WILLIAM[1]) *was born 16 Jun 1853 in Waverly, Lafayette Co., MO, and died 27 Apr 1914 in Manitou Springs, El Paso Co., CO. He married JANE ISABELLE SEVERANCE 07 Jun 1883 in Axtell, Marshall Co., KS, daughter of JOHN SEVERANCE and ELIZABETH WESTCOTT. She was born 28 Feb 1862 in Truxton, Cortland Co., NY, and died 29 Dec 1953 in Manitou Springs, El Paso Co., CO.*

Notes for LIVINGSTON PRICE BALLARD:
Source: Richard O. Ballard (richamy@knology.net), 1880 Buchanan County Missouri Federal Census Records, 1900-1910 Reno County Kansas Federal Census Records

** 1880 - Living in Buchanan Co., MO - Ballard, Livingston P. 28 MO traveling salesman*
** 1900 - Living in Reno Co., KS - Ballard, Price June 1854 MO VA VA, Isabel Feb 1862 NY NY NY, Lloyd May 1884 KS, Elizabeth Oct 1885 KS, Agness Feb 1888 KS, Florence Sept 1889 KS, John Jan 1900 KS*
** 1910 - Living in Reno Co., KS - Ballard, Livingston P 57 MO VA MO, Isabel 48 NY NY NY, Florence P 20 KS, John G 10 KS*

Children of LIVINGSTON BALLARD and JANE SEVERANCE are:
13.   i.   LLOYD SEVERANCE[8] BALLARD, b. 16 May 1884, KS; d. Aft. 1920.
        ii.   ELIZABETH WESTCOTT BALLARD, b. 25 Oct 1885; m. ADAMS.
        iii. AGNES BELLE BALLARD, b. 07 Feb 1888.
14.   iv.   FLORENCE PRICE BALLARD, b. 20 Sep 1889, Peoria, Franklin Co., KS.
15.   v.   JOHN GARLAND BALLARD, b. 10 Jan 1900, Hutchinson, Reno Co., KS; d. 18 Jul 1952, Amarillo, Potter Co., TX.

9.   LECLERK EDWIN[7] BALLARD (THOMAS GARLAND[6], DAVID CRAWFORD[5], JOHN[4], THOMAS HORACE[3], THOMAS[2], WILLIAM[1]) *was born 25 Nov 1856 in MO, and died 01 Apr 1921. He married (1) ELLA B. SHELDON. She was born Jul 1864 in PA, and died 04 Oct 1948. He married (2) NANCY ELVIRA BROWN Bef. 1888. She was born 18 Sep 1864 in Allegheny Co., PA, and died Aft. 1900.*

Notes for LECLERK EDWIN BALLARD:
Source: 1900 Valley County Nebraska Federal Census Records, 1910-1920 Douglas County Nebraska Federal Census Records

** 1900 - Living in Ord, Valley Co., NE - Ballard, LeClerc - Nov 1856 MO VA VA, Nancy E - July 1864 - 4 children 4 living PA PA PA, Wilson L - Aug 1887 NE, Mary E - Dec 1888 NE, William G - Apr 1894 NE, Acsa G - Aug 1898 NE, * 1910 - Living in Omaha, Douglas Co., NE - Ballard, Leclerc 52 MO VA VA, Ella 45 - 4 children 4 living PA PA PA, William 16 NE, Asca 11 NE, Charles M Hitchman son in law 24 PA PA PA, Edna Hitchman daughter 21 NE*
** 1920 - Living in Omaha, Douglas Co., NE - Ballard, Leclerk E 63 MO VA VA, Ella N 52 PA PA PA, Acsa 21 NE*

More About LECLERK EDWIN BALLARD:
Burial: Forest Lawn Memorial Park, Omaha, Douglas Co., NE

More About ELLA B. SHELDON:
Burial: Forest Lawn Memorial Park, Omaha, Douglas Co., NE

Child of LECLERK BALLARD and ELLA SHELDON is:
        i.   ASCA G.[8] BALLARD, b. 24 Aug 1898, NE; d. 30 Jun 1977; m. KENNETH JAMES BUNNELL; b. 10 Jun 1903, Omaha, Douglas Co., NE; d. 19 Jul 1981.

More About ASCA G. BALLARD:

Burial: Forest Lawn Memorial Park, Omaha, Douglas Co., NE

More About KENNETH JAMES BUNNELL:
Burial: Forest Lawn Memorial Park, Omaha, Douglas Co., NE

Children of LECLERK BALLARD and NANCY BROWN are:
> ii.   WILSON LECLERC[8] BALLARD, b. 22 Aug 1888, NE; d. Aft. 1900; m. (1) REBECCA GALLINGER, 17 Oct 1919, Salt Lake Co., UT; m. (2) DOROTHY JUNE BEAUREGARD, 15 Feb 1934, Sevier, UT.
> iii. MARY EDNA BALLARD, b. Dec 1888, NE; d. 23 Oct 1940, Lancaster, NE; m. CHARLES M. HITCHMAN; b. Abt. 1886, PA; d. Aft. 1910.
> iv.   WILLIAM G. BALLARD, b. 19 Apr 1894, NE; d. 10 Jun 1984, Multnomah Co., OR.

10.   THOMAS WILLIS[7] BALLARD (THOMAS GARLAND[6], DAVID CRAWFORD[5], JOHN[4], THOMAS HORACE[3], THOMAS[2], WILLIAM[1]) was born 24 Feb 1858 in MO, and died 29 May 1910 in Buckley, Pierce, WA. He married RHODA B. VAN NOSTIN 20 Jul 1878 in Chautauqua, KS. She was born 10 Oct 1860 in Bloomington, McLean Co., IL, and died 26 May 1948 in Parkland, Pierce Co., WA.

Notes for THOMAS WILLIS BALLARD:
Source: Pierce County Washington Death Certificate, 1900 Lincoln County Oklahoma Federal Census Records, 1910 Pierce County Washington Federal Census Records
** 1900 - Living in Lincoln Co., OK - Ballard, Thomas W - Feb 1858 MO MO MO, Rhoda - Oct 1860 - 8 children 6 living IL OH IL, John - July 1884 MO, Roy - Jan 1889 KS, Beulah - Sept 1891 TX, Thomas - Nov 1893 TX, Charles - Apr 1895 TX*
** 1910 - Living in Pierce Co., WA - Ballard, Thomas W 52 MO VA KY, Rhota 49 - 8 children 6 living IL OH IL, Roy 21 KS, John 25 KS, Thomas 16 TX, Sylvester 15 TX*

More About THOMAS WILLIS BALLARD:
Burial: Buckley Cemetery, Pierce Co., WA

More About RHODA B. VAN NOSTIN:
Burial: Buckley Cemetery, Pierce Co., WA

Children of THOMAS BALLARD and RHODA VAN NOSTIN are:

> 16. i.   WILLIAM PRICE[8] BALLARD, b. 10 Oct 1879, Chautauqua Co., KS; d. 12 Nov 1954, Pierce Co., WA.
>   ii.   CLARA L. BALLARD, b. 1880.
>   iii. JOHN GARLAND BALLARD, b. Jul 1884, MO; d. 07 Nov 1966, Pierce Co., WA.
>   iv.   MARY A. BALLARD, b. 13 Apr 1886, Chautauqua Co., KS; d. 07 Jul 1888.
>   v.   ROY CARR BALLARD, b. Abt. 1889, KS; d. 09 Jan 1958, Tacoma, Pierce Co., WA; m. ITLE ALICE DINSMORE, 01 Nov 1911, Edwards, King Co., WA.

> *Notes for ROY CARR BALLARD:*

> *Source: Pierce Washington Certificate of Death*

>   vi.   BEULAH LEOTA BALLARD, b. 03 Sep 1891, TX; d. 27 Aug 1949, Pierce Co., WA; m. RYAN.

> *Notes for BEULAH LEOTA BALLARD:*
> *Source: Pierce County Washington Certificate of Death*

>   vii. THOMAS VAN NOSTIN BALLARD, b. Nov 1893, TX; d. 07 Aug 1939, Seattle, King Co., WA; m. MABEL F.

> *Notes for THOMAS VAN NOSTIN BALLARD:*
> *Source: King County Washington Certificate of Death*

17.   viii.   CHARLES SYLVESTER BALLARD, b. 03 Apr 1895, TX; d. 08 Jun 1987, CA.

11. SAMANTHA TAYLOR "SAM"[7] BALLARD (THOMAS GARLAND[6], DAVID CRAWFORD[5], JOHN[4], THOMAS HORACE[3], THOMAS[2], WILLIAM[1]) was born 15 May 1890 in Richmond, Ray Co., MO, and died 14 Jul 1942 in Callaway Co., MO. She married DAVID W. LONG. He was born 04 Aug 1888 in Ray Co., MO, and died 14 Jan 1932 in Ray Co., MO.

More About SAMANTHA TAYLOR "SAM" BALLARD:
Burial: Richmond Cemetery, Richmond, Ray Co., MO

More About DAVID W. LONG:
Burial: Richmond Cemetery, Richmond, Ray Co., MO

Child of SAMANTHA BALLARD and DAVID LONG is:
     i.   SARAH L.[8] LONG, b. Abt. 1913, MO; d. Aft. 1930.

Generation No. 4

12. RICHARD T.[8] BALLARD (RICHARD L. "DICK"[7], WILLIS H.[6], DAVID CRAWFORD[5], JOHN[4], THOMAS HORACE[3], THOMAS[2], WILLIAM[1]) was born 1900 in MO, and died 05 Feb 1942 in Spokane, Spokane Co., WA. He married MABEL M. EMERICK 11 May 1921 in Billings, Yellowstone, MT. She was born Abt. 1900 in MO, and died Aft. 1940.

Notes for RICHARD T. BALLARD:
Source: 1930 King County Washington Federal Census Records, 1940 Spokane County Washington Federal Census Records, Spokane Washington Death Records

* 1930 - Living in Seattle, King Co., WA - Ballard, Richard T 31, Mabel M 30, Richard T 8
* 1940 - Living in Spokane, Spokane Co., WA - Ballard, RT 40, Mabel 40, Richard Jr. 18

Child of RICHARD BALLARD and MABEL EMERICK is:

     i.   RICHARD THOMAS[9] BALLARD, b. 19 Feb 1922, Billings, Yellowstone, MT; d. 11 Jun 1998, Clark, WA.

          Notes for RICHARD THOMAS BALLARD:

          Source: Montana Birth Records, WWII Draft Cards

13. LLOYD SEVERANCE[8] BALLARD (LIVINGSTON PRICE[7], THOMAS GARLAND[6], DAVID CRAWFORD[5], JOHN[4], THOMAS HORACE[3], THOMAS[2], WILLIAM[1]) was born 16 May 1884 in KS, and died Aft. 1920. He married LEOTA AULT 22 May 1908. She was born 1885 in MO, and died 1979 in KS.

Notes for LLOYD SEVERANCE BALLARD:
Source: 1910 Summit County Ohio Federal Census Records, 1920 Sedgwick County Kansas Federal Census Records

* 1910 - Living in Akron, Summit Co., OH - Ballard, Loyd 25 boarder KS MO MO
* 1920 - Living in Sedgwick, Wichita Co., KS - Ballard, Lloyd S 36 KS MO NY, Leota 35 KS, OH OH, Philip 7 KS

Children of LLOYD BALLARD and LEOTA AULT are:
     i.   PHILLIP[9] BALLARD, b. 1913.
     ii. RICHARD WESCOTT BALLARD.

14. FLORENCE PRICE[8] BALLARD (LIVINGSTON PRICE[7], THOMAS GARLAND[6], DAVID CRAWFORD[5], JOHN[4], THOMAS HORACE[3], THOMAS[2], WILLIAM[1]) was born 20 Sep 1889 in Peoria, KS. She married JAMES PHILLIP ANTHONY.

Child of FLORENCE BALLARD and JAMES ANTHONY is:
> i.   JAMES[9] ANTHONY.

15.   JOHN GARLAND[8] BALLARD (*LIVINGSTON PRICE[7], THOMAS GARLAND[6], DAVID CRAWFORD[5], JOHN[4], THOMAS HORACE[3], THOMAS[2], WILLIAM[1]*) was born 10 Jan 1900 in Hutchinson, Reno Co., KS, and died 18 Jul 1952 in Amarillo, Potter Co., TX. He married SADIE CLAUDIA CURTIS 08 Jun 1927 in St. Andrews Episcopal Church, Amarillo, Potter Co., TX, daughter of JAMES CURTIS and SADIE EPPLER. She was born 04 Sep 1903 in Amarillo, Potter Co., TX, and died 18 Nov 1979 in Amarillo, Potter Co., TX.

Notes for JOHN GARLAND BALLARD:
Source: Richard O. Ballard (richamy@knology.net), Listed with son James Henry Curtis Ballard in the Marquis Who's Who in the South and Southwest.

Children of JOHN BALLARD and SADIE CURTIS are:
> i.   JOHN GARLAND[9] BALLARD, b. 09 Mar 1928, Amarillo, Potter Co., TX; m. ANN THATCHER, 05 Apr 1952, TX; b. 05 Sep 1929, OK City OK.
> ii.   MARY ELIZABETH BALLARD, b. 10 Nov 1932, Amarillo, Potter Co., TX; d. 18 Nov 1987, Scott Co., KY; m. JOHN COLUMBUS WARD, JR., 27 Oct 1951, Amarillo, Potter Co., TX; b. 11 Mar 1928, KY.
> iii.   JAMES HENRY BALLARD, b. 27 Dec 1934, Amarillo, Potter Co., TX; d. 24 Oct 1996, Amarillo, Potter Co., TX; m. BARBARA HELEN LLOYD; b. 19 Jul 1936, Huntsville, Madison Co., AL.
>
> > *Notes for JAMES HENRY BALLARD:*
> > Source: Richard O. Ballard (richamy@knology.net)

16.   WILLIAM PRICE[8] BALLARD (*THOMAS WILLIS[7], THOMAS GARLAND[6], DAVID CRAWFORD[5], JOHN[4], THOMAS HORACE[3], THOMAS[2], WILLIAM[1]*) was born 10 Oct 1879 in Chautauqua Co., KS, and died 12 Nov 1954 in Pierce Co., WA. He married (1) JESSIE MAUD HAUN. She was born Sep 1879 in KS, and died Aft. 1900. He married (2) ALICE M.. He married (3) LAURA F..

Notes for WILLIAM PRICE BALLARD:
Source: 1900 Lincoln County Oklahoma Federal Census Records
* 1900 - Living in Lincoln Co., OK - Ballard, William - Oct 1879 KS MO IL, Jessie - Sept 1879 1 child 1 living KS TN IL, Clarence - Sept 1899 OK

More About WILLIAM PRICE BALLARD:
Burial: Woodbine Cemetery, Pierce Co., WA

Child of WILLIAM BALLARD and JESSIE HAUN is:
> i.   CLARENCE[9] BALLARD, b. Sep 1899, OK; d. Aft. 1900.

17.   CHARLES SYLVESTER[8] BALLARD (*THOMAS WILLIS[7], THOMAS GARLAND[6], DAVID CRAWFORD[5], JOHN[4], THOMAS HORACE[3], THOMAS[2], WILLIAM[1]*) was born 03 Apr 1895 in TX, and died 08 Jun 1987 in CA. He married MARION C. PHILLIPS 26 Nov 1927 in Whatcom Co.,, WA. She was born 29 Jul 1899 in MA, and died 29 Jul 1987 in CA.

Notes for CHARLES SYLVESTER BALLARD:
Source: 1930-1940 King County Washington Federal Census Records

* 1930 - Living in Seattle, King Co., WA - Ballard, Charles S 35 TX MO IL, Marion C 30 MA Wales Canada
* 1940 - Living in Seattle, King Co., WA - Ballard, Charles S 45 OK, Marion 40 MA, Phillis 9 WA

Child of CHARLES BALLARD and MARION PHILLIPS is:
> i.   PHILLAS[9] BALLARD, b. Abt. 1931, WA; d. Aft. 1940.

Elijah G. Ballard

Generation No. 1

1. ELIJAH G.³ BALLARD (JOSEPH², JOHN¹) was born 25 Jun 1848 in Orange Co., IN, and died 30 Sep 1931 in Carroll Co., MO. He married CATHERINE COOK 15 Dec 1875 in Edgar Co., IL, daughter of ISAAC COOK and SUSANNA SHANNON. She was born 01 May 1856 in Edgar Co., IL, and died 15 Oct 1923 in Wakenda, Carroll Co., MO.

Notes for ELIJAH G. BALLARD:
Source: Will of Elijah Ballard, Carroll County Missouri Death Certificate, 1880 Illinois Federal Census Record Soundex, 1880 Vermillion County Illinois Federal Census Records, 1920-1930 Carroll County Missouri Federal Census Records, Carol (Jonesy6iron@earthlink.net) , The National Archives Soldier's certificate No. 882413 Elijah G. Ballard, Rank - Pvt, Service: Co. C. 11" Ind. Vol, Inf. Can No. 18096, bundle 28, Illinois Marriage Record index

* 1864 - Volunteered May 4, 1864 to serve in the military. Served Company "C" 133rd Indiana Volunteers.
* 1864 - Discharged from Military Sept 5, 1864, had typhoid fever.
* 1865 - Re-enlisted in Company "C" 11th Indiana Volunteers March 3, 1865
* 1880 - Living in Vermillion Co., IL - Ballard, Elijah 31 IN KY KY, Catharine 24 IL OH OH, Effie 7/12 IL, Rollo 8 (nephew) IN

* 1890 - Pension records #324.190 - In claim No 324.190 of Elijah G. Ballard Company "C" 133rd regiment, Ind. Volunteers, State of Illinois, County of Edgar} ss; On this 28 day of March one thousand, eight hundred and Ninety personally appeared before me A Notary Public within and for the County and State aforesaid, Leroy O. Jenkins, MD., who being duly sworn, according to law, on oath states: That the affiant is aged years, a resident of Paris Ills, occupation Physician is well acquainted with Elijah G. Ballard, Co. "C" 133rd Regiment, Indiana Volunteers and has known him for about __ years. ....stated: Since 1880 at which time I made a statement for above named soldier, I have treated him at various times for heart troubles and a Rheumatic trouble of the lumbar and Cervical muscles also at times of any kidney trouble he is not able to perform more than half the manual labor of an able bodied man. I have known him for about fifteen years. That affiant has no interest, direct or indirect in the prosecution of this claim for pension. Affiant's Post Office Address Paris, Illinois Leroy O. Jenkins MD Sworn to and Subscribed before me a Notary this 28 day of March AD 1890 by Leroy O. Jenkins, MD. and I hereby certify that the contents of the above affidavit were fully made known and explained to affiant before swearing to the same, that he is respectable and entitled to credit, and that I have no interest, direct or indirect, in the prosecution of this claim, including the words..... inserted, and the words...... erased. Witness my hand and official seal, at Paris, IL Certificate on file. Signed by Jessie Trogdon, Notary Public

* 1900 - Living in Van Horne twp, Carroll Co., MO - Ballard, Elijah J June 1849 married 24 years, Catherine J Feb 1856 IL OH OH, Effie Nov 1879 IL IN IL, Claud June 1882 IL IN IL

* 1910 - Living in Carroll Co., MO - Ballard, E G 61 IN KY KY, wife (no name) 54 IN IL IL, Flora 27 OH Ger OH, Claudine 5 MO, Florine 3 MO

* 1915 - Pension records - Elijah G. Ballard - Carrollton MO date of birth June 25, 1848 Orange County, Indiana Co. C, 11th Regiment, Indiana Volunteers. It appears in Elijah G. Ballard's own handwriting on the Bureau of Pensions form #3-389, date stamped April 23 or 28, 1915. He indicates his wife's name as Cathrine Cook Ballard, married December 15, 1875. He indicates "I am living with my first wife," but in the question before that he says "no previous marriage by either of us.
* 1915 - Living in Carrollton MO: Civil War Pension Index (Supplied by JONESY6IRON@ aol.com) - Name of Holder: Ballard, Elijah G. - Service: C11 Ind. Inf. & C133 Ind. Inf. Date of Filing:1879 Dec 29, Class: Invalid, Application No. 324.190   Certificate No. 882413
* 1915 - Pension document - Department of the Interior #3-389 Bureau of Pensions. Washington, DC January 2, 1915. Sir: Please answer, at your earliest convenience, the questions enumerated below. The information is requested future use, and it may be of great value to your widow or children. Use the enclosed envelope, which requires no stamp. Very respectfully, GM Saezgabey??? Commissioner. Stamped April 28, 1915. Elijah G. Ballard, Carrollton MO 882413 Act May RR7.Date and place of birth? June 25, 1848 Orange Co. Indiana. The

name and organizations in which you served? Co C 11th regiment Indiana. What was your post office at enlistment? New Goshen Vigo Co Indiana. State your wife's full name and her maiden name. Catherin Cook Ballard. When, Where and by whom were you married? Dec 15, 1875 Co of Edgar State Ills Wesley Chapel by Robert Stevens minister. Is there any official or church records of your marriage? Non that we no of. Were you previously married? No previous marriage. If your present wife was married before her marriage to you, state the name of her former husband, the date of such marriage and the date and place of his death or divorce. No previous marriage by either of us. Are you living with your wife, or has there been a separation? I am living with my first wife. State the names and dates of birth of all your children, living or dead. Elmer Ballard dead borned July 15 1876. Effie Ballard born November 3, 1879. Claud F or J. Ballard born June 23 1882. Date: April 25 1915 signed Elijah g. Ballard

** 1920 - Living in Carroll Co., MO - Ballard, E. G 71 IN KY KY, Catherine 63 IL OH OH*
** 1930 - Living in Carroll Co., MO - Ballard, Elijah G 81 IN ? KY (living with son Claud)*
** 1931 - Oct 6 - Carrollton, Carroll Co., MO - Elijah G. Ballard - Last Will And Testament - I, Elijah G. Ballard of Carrollton, Carroll County, Missouri, being of lawful age and sound mind, and realizing the frailties and uncertainties (sp) of the present life, do hereby make, publish and declare this my last Will and Testament, as follows:*

1. I direct that all my just debts, legal obligations and funeral expenses be paid out of my personal estate by my Executrix hereinafter mentioned.

2. In the event that I, Elijah G. Ballard, do not, during my lifetime, erect a suitable tombstone beside the grave of my departed wife, Katherine Ballard, I hereby direct my Executrix to appropriate sufficient monies out of my personal estate to erect a suitable tombstone beside the graves of my departed wife, Katherine Ballard and myself, such monies to be considered as funeral expenses, and I expressly authorize my Executrix, if my personal estate be insufficient to pay my funeral expenses and all my just debts, to sell the whole or any part thereof of my real estate as maybe sufficient for that purpose.

3. I give and bequeath to my beloved nephew, Rollie Ballard, the sum of One Hundred Dollars ($100.00).

4. I give and bequeath to my beloved daughter, Effie Jenkins, all of my household effects, such as furniture, dishes, rugs, pictures and all other articles of such nature to be hers absolutely.

5. And lastly, all the rest, residue and remainder of my estate whatsoever, real, personal and mixed, and wherever situate, I give devise and bequeath to my dutiful son, Claude Ballard, my beloved daughter, Effie Jenkins and unto Effie Osborne Dickson, equally, share and share alike, forever.

I appoint my daughter, Effie Jenkins, Executrix of this my last Will and Testament serve without bond, revoking any former Will by me made.

In witness whereof, I have hereunto subscribed my name, this ___ day of ___ 1924.

The foregoing instrument was at this time therefore signed and declared by the said Elijah G. Ballard, to be his last Will and Testament, in the presence of us, who at his request and in his presence, and in the presence of each other, have subscribed our names as witnesses thereto. Ed Jenkins, Dudley D. Thomas Jr, M J Schmidt

Notes for CATHERINE COOK:
Source: Carroll County Missouri, Certificate of Death

Children of ELIJAH BALLARD and CATHERINE COOK are:

   i. ELMER[4] BALLARD, b. 15 Jul 1876; d. 15 Jul 1876.
2. ii. EFFIE BALLARD, b. 03 Nov 1879, IL; d. 12 Oct 1961.
3. iii. CLAUDE FRANKLIN BALLARD, b. 23 Jun 1882, Vermilion Co., IL; d. 19 Nov 1963, Carrollton, Carroll Co., MO.

Generation No. 2

2. EFFIE[4] BALLARD (*ELIJAH G.[3], JOSEPH[2], JOHN[1]*) *was born 03 Nov 1879 in IL, and died 12 Oct 1961. She married EDWARD MANSFIELD JENKINS 07 Aug 1901 in Carroll Co., MO. He was born 18 Apr 1879, and died 14 Oct 1962.*

More About EFFIE BALLARD:
Burial: Rose Hill Memorial Park, Tulsa, Tulsa Co., OK

Notes for EDWARD MANSFIELD JENKINS:
Source: 1910-1920 Carroll County Missouri Federal Census Records, 1930-1940 Tulsa County Oklahoma Federal Census Records

** 1910 - Living in Carrollton, Carroll Co., MO - Jenkins, Edward 31 laborer MO IN MO, Effie 30 - 2 children 1 living IL KY IL, Hazel 7 MO, Effie Osborne 15 servant AR*
** 1920 - Living in Carrollton, Carroll Co., MO - Jenkins, Edward 40 MO MO KY, Effie 39 IL IN IL, Hazel 17 IL*
** 1930 - Living in Tulsa, Tulsa Co., OK - Jenkins, Ed M 50 MO KY MO, Effie 50 IL IL IL, (boarders) Lester & Lucile English, Hurley and Ethel Hunt*
** 1940 - Living in Red Fork, Tulsa Co., OK - Jenkins, Ed M 61 MO, Effie 60 IL*

More About EDWARD MANSFIELD JENKINS:
Burial: Rose Hill Memorial Park, Tulsa, Tulsa Co., OK

Child of EFFIE BALLARD and EDWARD JENKINS is:
4.   i.   HAZEL M.⁵ JENKINS, b. 24 Nov 1902, Carroll Co., MO; d. 02 Feb 1980, Broken Arrow, Tulsa Co., OK.

3. CLAUDE FRANKLIN⁴ BALLARD (ELIJAH G.³, JOSEPH², JOHN¹) was born 23 Jun 1882 in Vermilion Co., IL, and died 19 Nov 1963 in Carrollton, Carroll Co., MO. He married FLORA LESSER. She was born 19 Sep 1882 in OH, and died 09 Feb 1962 in Carrollton, Carroll Co., MO.

Notes for CLAUDE FRANKLIN BALLARD:
Source: 1910-1930 Carroll County Missouri Federal Census Records

** 1910 - Living in Carroll Co., MO with parents - Ballard, Claud 27 IN IL IL, Flora 27 OH Ger OH, Claudine 5 MO, Florene 3 MO*
** 1920 - Living in Carrolton, Carroll Co., MO - Ballard, Claud 37 IN IL IL, Mrs. Claud 37 OH Ger OH, Claudine E 15 MO, Florene H 13 MO*
** 1930 - Living in Carroll Co., MO - Ballard, Claud F 47 IL IN IN, Flora F 47 OH Ger OH, Claudine 25 MO, Florene 23 MO, Elijah G 81 father KY*

More About CLAUDE FRANKLIN BALLARD:
Burial: Oak Hill Cemetery, Carrollton, Carroll Co., MO

More About FLORA LESSER:
Burial: Oak Hill Cemetery, Carrollton, Carroll Co., MO

Children of CLAUDE BALLARD and FLORA LESSER are:
    i.   CLAUDINE E.⁵ BALLARD, b. 22 Aug 1904, Carrollton, Carroll Co., MO; d. 11 Apr 1999, Carrollton, Carroll Co., MO; m. MARVIN O. WHITNEY; d. 11 Aug 1968.
    ii.   FLORENE H. BALLARD, b. 1907, MO; d. Aft. 1930.

Generation No. 3

4. HAZEL M.⁵ JENKINS (EFFIE⁴ BALLARD, ELIJAH G.³, JOSEPH², JOHN¹) was born 24 Nov 1902 in Carroll Co., MO, and died 02 Feb 1980 in Broken Arrow, Tulsa Co., OK. She married WILBUR B. WINFREY. He was born 24 Feb 1891 in Carroll Co., MO, and died 14 Jul 1976 in Tulsa, Tulsa Co., OK.

More About HAZEL M. JENKINS:
Burial: Rose Hill Memorial Park, Tulsa, Tulsa Co., OK

Notes for WILBUR B. WINFREY:

Source: 1940 Wagoner County Oklahoma Federal Census Records
** 1940 - Living in Coal Creek, Wagoner Co., OK - Winfrey, Wilber 49 MO farming, Hazel 37 MO, Gene 17 MO,*
Wanald 15 MO, Billie L 12 OK, Floria A 6 OK

More About WILBUR B. WINFREY:
Burial: Rose Hill Memorial Park, Tulsa, Tulsa Co., OK

Children of HAZEL JENKINS and WILBUR WINFREY are:

      i.   GENE E.[6] WINFREY, DR., b. 17 Nov 1922, Carroll Co., MO; d. 07 Feb 2013, Loganville, Walton Co.,
GA; m. WANA JEAN BENTON; b. 19 Apr 1925; d. 18 Jun 2017.

        More About GENE E. WINFREY, DR.:
        Burial: Georgia Memorial Park, Marietta, Cobb Co., GA

        More About WANA JEAN BENTON:
        Burial: Georgia Memorial Park, Marietta, Cobb Co., GA

     ii.   WANALD CLARK WINFREY, b. 21 Jun 1924, Carrollton, Carroll Co., MO; d. 14 Oct 2010, Tulsa Co.,
OK; m. GLYNNA L. DIXON, 02 Nov 1973, Broken Arrow, Tulsa & Wagoner Co., OK; b. 09 Nov 1941.

        More About WANALD CLARK WINFREY:
        Burial: Park Grove Cemetery, Broken Arrow, Tulsa Co., OK

5.   iii.   BILLIE LORENE WINFREY, b. 09 Mar 1928, Tulsa, Tulsa Co., OK; d. 25 Sep 2019, Tulsa, Tulsa Co.,
OK.

     iv.   GLORIA ANN WINFREY, b. 02 Mar 1934, Tulsa, Tulsa Co., OK; d. Dec 1981; m. ROYCE CLINTON
FULLER, 27 Jul 1956, Tulsa Co., OK; b. 03 Jan 1933; d. 24 May 2019, Denver Co., CO.

        Notes for GLORIA ANN WINFREY:
        Source: Social Security Records

        Notes for ROYCE CLINTON FULLER:
        Source: Tulsa County Oklahoma Marriage Records

        More About ROYCE CLINTON FULLER:
        Burial: Fort Logan National Cemetery, Denver, Denver Co., CO

Generation No. 4

5. BILLIE LORENE[6] WINFREY (HAZEL M.[5] JENKINS, EFFIE[4] BALLARD, ELIJAH G.[3], JOSEPH[2], JOHN[1]) *was born 09 Mar
1928 in Tulsa, Tulsa Co., OK, and died 25 Sep 2019 in Tulsa, Tulsa Co., OK. She married CLARENCE MOSLEY.*

Children of BILLIE WINFREY and CLARENCE MOSLEY are:

     i.   RICK[7] MOSLEY, m. TAMI.
     ii.   VICKY JEAN MOSLEY, b. 20 Nov 1952; d. 30 Aug 1992; m. DONALD EUGENE KINDLE; b. 15 Aug 1950;
d. 09 Apr 2002.

        More About VICKY JEAN MOSLEY:
        Burial: Rose Hill Memorial Park, Tulsa, Tulsa Co., OK

        More About DONALD EUGENE KINDLE:
        Burial: Rose Hill Memorial Park, Tulsa, Tulsa Co., OK

Francis Marion Ballard

Generation No. 1

1. FRANCIS MARION[1] BALLARD *was born Feb 1843 in KY or TN, and died 1904 in AR. He married* SUSANNAH WAGONER *27 Aug 1865 in Saline Co., IL. She was born 1844 in IL, and died 27 Apr 1922 in White Co., AR.*

Notes for FRANCIS MARION BALLARD:
Source: Saline County Illinois Marriage Records, 1870 Saline County Illinois Federal Census Records, 1880 Texas County Missouri Federal Census Records, 1880 Missouri Federal Census Record Soundex, 1900 Izard County Arkansas Federal Census Records, Bob Foley (Bobfoley@aol.com), Farris Ballard (fdballard@home.com), ynonamarie@webtv.net

** 1870 - Living in Saline Co., IL - Ballard, Francis M 26 KY, Susan 26 IL, Joseph W 8 IL, Mary J 4 IL, Wm C 1 IL*
** 1880 - Living in Texas Co., MO - Ballard, Francis 37 TN, Susannah 35 IL, Mary J. 13 IL, William 12 IL, Frances 9 IL, James M 7 MO, Richard 3 MO, Alvis D 7/12 MO, Luis 5-7/12 MO*
** 1900 - Living in Bryan Izard Co., AR - Ballard, Francis M Feb 1843 KY KY VA, Susie A Jun 1844 IL TN IL, married 35 years 12 children - 9 living, Riley M June 1883 MO, Elizabeth N Jan 1886 AR*

Notes for SUSANNAH WAGONER:

Source: 1920 LeFlore County Oklahoma Federal Census Records

** 1920 - Living in Milton, LeFlore Co., OK - Ballard, Susana 75 living with her daughter Betty Hill*

More About SUSANNAH WAGONER:

Burial: Union Hill Cemetery, White Co., AR

Children of FRANCIS BALLARD *and* SUSANNAH WAGONER *are:*

2.	i.	MARY JANE[2] BALLARD, b. 27 Aug 1866, Saline Co., IL; d. 08 Jan 1960, Crawford Co., AR.
3.	ii.	WILLIAM CALVIN BALLARD, b. 07 Jan 1869, Saline Co., IL; d. 08 Jan 1958, Grand Prairie, Dallas Co., TX.
4.	iii.	FRANCIS ALBERT MARION BALLARD, b. 14 Feb 1871, Saline Co., IL; d. 25 Mar 1967, Stanislaus Co., CA.
5.	iv.	JAMES MONROE BALLARD, b. 04 Apr 1873, Texas Co., MO; d. 30 Jul 1949, Harrisburg, Poinsett Co., AR.
6.	v.	RICHARD IRVING BALLARD, b. 05 Apr 1877, Texas Co., MO; d. 14 Feb 1962, Haskell Co., OK.
	vi.	ALVIS D. BALLARD, b. 23 Oct 1879, Texas Co., MO; d. Texas Co., MO.
7.	vii.	LEWIS SAMUEL BALLARD, b. 23 Oct 1879, Texas Co., MO; d. 12 Jan 1962, Hot Springs, Garland Co., AR.
	viii.	JOSEPH PATTERSON BALLARD, b. Abt. 1881, Saline Co., IL; m. REBECCA A. CURTIS.
	ix.	RILEY MARTIN BALLARD, b. 23 Jun 1884, Texas Co., MO; d. 16 Nov 1944, Wild Cherry Izard Co., AR; m. LAURA WILLIAMS, 03 Oct 1903, Baxter Co., AR; b. 1882, AR; d. 1963, AR.
8.	x.	ELIZABETH NAYWASIE BALLARD, b. 31 Jan 1886, Mountain Home, Baxter Co., AR; d. 13 Nov 1972, Jasper Co., TX.

Generation No. 2

2. MARY JANE[2] BALLARD (FRANCIS MARION[1]) *was born 27 Aug 1866 in Saline Co., IL, and died 08 Jan 1960 in Crawford Co., AR. She married* GEORGE MASON FOLEY *02 Oct 1885 in Batesville AR. He was born 16 Mar 1863 in TN, and died 29 Aug 1920 in Crawford Co., AR.*

Notes for MARY JANE BALLARD:
Source: Crawford County Arkansas Certificate of Death

More About MARY JANE BALLARD:
Burial: Gill Cemetery, Van Buren, Crawford Co., AR

Notes for GEORGE MASON FOLEY:
Source: 1910 Independence County Arkansas Federal Census Records, 1920 Crawford County Arkansas Federal Census Records

** 1910 - Living in Magness, Independence Co., AR - Foley, George 54 TN TN TN, Mary J 43 - 8 children 8 living MO, Melzona 21 AR, Myrtle F 17 AR, Carolla 15 AR, Richard 13 AR, Riley 8 AR, Effie 5 AR, Jessie 10/12 AR*
** 1920 - Living in Richland, Crawford Co., AR - Foley, George 57 TN TN TN, Mary J 52 IL TN IL, Melzonie 30 AR, Richard 21 AR, Riley 18 AR, Effie 14 AR, Opal 10 AR*

Children of MARY BALLARD and GEORGE FOLEY are:

     i.   SARAH ETHEL[3] FOLEY, b. 28 Nov 1887, AR.
    ii.   MELLZONA FOLEY, b. 28 Aug 1889, AR; d. Aft. 1920.
   iii.   MYRTLE FOLEY, b. 11 May 1892, Izard Co., AR; d. 06 Apr 1968, Crawford Co., AR; m. HAMILTON.

        Notes for MYRTLE FOLEY:
        Source: Crawford County Arkansas Certificate of Death

        More About MYRTLE FOLEY:

        Burial: Gill Cemetery, Van Buren Co., AR

    iv.   CAROLIA "CARLIE" FOLEY, b. 23 Feb 1895, Baxter Co., AR; d. 06 Apr 1981, Van Buren, Crawford Co., AR; m. WILLIAM F. HODGE, 18 Jul 1916, Crawford Co., AR; b. 1891; d. 1950.

        Notes for CAROLIA "CARLIE" FOLEY:
        Source: Baxter County Arkansas Certificate of Birth

        More About CAROLIA "CARLIE" FOLEY:
        Burial: Gracelawn Cemetery, Van Buren, Crawford Co., AR

        Notes for WILLIAM F. HODGE:
        Source: Crawford County Arkansas Marriage Records

        More About WILLIAM F. HODGE:
        Burial: Gracelawn Cemetery, Van Buren, Crawford Co., AR

     v.   RICHARD M. FOLEY, b. 16 May 1898, AR; d. 02 Sep 1950, Sebastian Co., AR; m. PEARL G. TANKERSLEY; b. 02 Nov 1911; d. 27 Dec 1989.

        More About PEARL G. TANKERSLEY:
        Burial: Gill Cemetery, Van Buren, Crawford Co., AR

    vi.   RILEY SAMUEL FOLEY, b. 16 Mar 1902, Batesville, Independence Co., AR; d. 11 Oct 1971, Van Buren, Crawford Co., AR; m. (1) ELETHA CONLEY, 26 Dec 1924; b. 12 Feb 1903, Crawford Co., AR; d. 24 Nov 1936, Ft. Smith, Sebastian Co., AR; m. (2) JEWELL THISSEN, 12 Dec 1942, Van Buren, Crawford Co., AR.

        More About ELETHA CONLEY:

Burial: Gracelawn Cemetery, Van Buren, Crawford Co., AR

9.   *vii.*   EFFIE ELLEN FOLEY, *b. 26 Aug 1905, Batesville, Independence Co., AR; d. 02 Nov 1983, Van Buren, Crawford Co., AR.*

      viii.   OPAL LEE FOLEY, *b. 29 May 1909, AR; d. Aft. 1920.*

3. WILLIAM CALVIN[2] BALLARD (FRANCIS MARION[1]) *was born 07 Jan 1869 in Saline Co., IL, and died 08 Jan 1958 in Grand Prairie, Dallas Co., TX. He married* ALPHA BAKER *04 Jan 1903 in Randolph Co., AR. She was born 17 Apr 1886 in AR, and died Sep 1983 in Benton AR.*

Notes for WILLIAM CALVIN BALLARD:
Source: 1910 Van Buren County Arkansas Federal Census Records, 1920 Lawrence County Arkansas Federal Census Records

** 1910 - Living in Union twp, Van Buren Co., AR - Ballard, William 41 IL KY MO, Alpha 24 MO KY MO, Lewis 5 AR, Berdie 3 AR, Olen 5/12*
** 1920 - Living in Cache, Lawrence Co., AR - Ballard, W. C 51, Alpha 33, J. L C 15, Bertie 12, Riley O 10*

More About WILLIAM CALVIN BALLARD:
Burial: Restland Memorial Park, Dallas, Dallas Co., TX

More About ALPHA BAKER:
Burial: Restland Memorial Park, Dallas, Dallas Co., TX

Children of WILLIAM BALLARD *and* ALPHA BAKER *are:*

      i.   JAMES LOUIS CALVIN[3] BALLARD, *b. 01 Jan 1905, Walnut Ridge, AR; d. 15 Nov 1960, Dallas Co., TX.*

           Notes for JAMES LOUIS CALVIN BALLARD:
           Source: Dallas County Texas Certificate of Death

      ii.   BERTIE ANN BALLARD, *b. 03 Apr 1907, AR; d. 15 Dec 2001, MO; m.* HATLEY TILLMAN, *19 Oct 1927, Lawrence Co., AR; b. 28 Aug 1907, Lawrence Co., AR; d. 29 Sep 1964, St. Louis Co., MO.*

           More About BERTIE ANN BALLARD:
           Burial: Lawrence Memorial Park, Lawrence Co., AR

           More About HATLEY TILLMAN:
           Burial: Lawrence Memorial Park, Lawrence Co., AR

      iii. RILEY OLEN BALLARD, *b. 18 Nov 1909, Heber Springs, Cleburne Co., AR; d. 14 Jun 1982; m.* RUTH J. RISENHOOVER, *18 Oct 1930, Lawrence Co., AR; b. 10 Feb 1915.*

           Notes for RILEY OLEN BALLARD:
           Source: Cleburne County Arkansas Birth Certificate

           More About RILEY OLEN BALLARD:
           Burial: Lawrence Memorial Park, Walnut Ridge, Lawrence Co., AR

4. FRANCIS ALBERT MARION[2] BALLARD (FRANCIS MARION[1]) *was born 14 Feb 1871 in Saline Co., IL, and died 25 Mar 1967 in Stanislaus Co., CA. He married* MARY LEE DOBBS *17 Mar 1901 in Independence Co., AR. She was born 13 Apr 1883 in Izard Co., IL, and died 17 Jul 1991 in Bakersfield, Kern Co., CA.*

Notes for FRANCIS ALBERT MARION BALLARD:
Source: 1910 Haskell County Oklahoma Federal Census Records, 1930 Crawford County Arkansas Federal Census Records, 1940 Jackson County Missouri Federal Census Records
** 1910 - Living in San Bois, Haskell Co., OK - Ballard, Francis M 39 md 2x IL TN IL, Mary L 26 - 4 children 3 living AR AR US, Wacey C 8 AR, James U 6 AR, Stephen L 2 AR, Charles R. Wagener 18 MO hired hand*
** 1930 - Living in Van Buren, Crawford Co., AR - Ballard, Albert 67 MO, Mary 48 AR, Lee 22 AR, Hazell 16 OK, Elva 12 OK, Willie 11 OK, Irene 9 OK*
** 1940 - Living in Kansas City, Jackson Co., MO - Ballard, Albert E 70 IL, Mary L 57 AR, Essie May 13 AR*

More About FRANCIS ALBERT MARION BALLARD:
Burial: Greenlawn Cemetery and Mortuary, Bakersfield, Kern Co., CA

More About MARY LEE DOBBS:
Burial: Greenlawn Cemetery and Mortuary, Bakersfield, Kern Co., CA

Children of FRANCIS BALLARD and MARY DOBBS are:

> i. WACIE C.³ BALLARD, b. 24 Mar 1902, Independence Co., AR; d. 21 Nov 1991, Bryon Co., OK.
> ii. ROY EURAL BALLARD, b. 17 Dec 1903, Sharp Co., AR; d. 01 Nov 1988, Ft. Gibson, Muskogee Co., OK; m. LILLIE MAE EASTWOOD; b. 10 Jul 1903; d. 13 Nov 1983.
>
> *More About ROY EURAL BALLARD:*
> *Burial: Citizens Cemetery, Ft. Gibson, Muskogee Co., OK*
>
> *More About LILLIE MAE EASTWOOD:*
> *Burial: Citizens Cemetery, Ft. Gibson, Muskogee Co., OK*
>
> iii. FRANCIS EDGAR ALLEN BALLARD, b. 07 Feb 1906, AR; d. 07 Mar 1907, AR.
> iv. STEVE LEE BALLARD, b. 01 Apr 1908, Izard Co., AR; d. 05 Aug 1992; m. MAMIE LOUISA STEELE, 24 Sep 1934, Crawford Co., AR; b. 21 Nov 1914, Crawford Co., AR; d. 05 Dec 2000, Clinton Co., MO.
>
> *Notes for STEVE LEE BALLARD:*
> *Source: WWII Draft Cards*
>
> *More About STEVE LEE BALLARD:*
> *Burial: Lathrop Cemetery, Lathrop, Clinton Co., MO*
>
> *More About MAMIE LOUISA STEELE:*
> *Burial: Lathrop Cemetery, Lathrop, Clinton Co., MO*
>
> v. RICHARD LOUIS BALLARD, b. 18 Jan 1911, Batesville, Independence Co., AR; d. 07 Oct 1988, Kern Co., CA.
> vi. HAZEL JEAN BALLARD, b. 13 Nov 1913, McCurtain Co., OK; d. 19 Jan 1983, Merced Co., CA; m. FLOYD RAY COKER; b. 13 Nov 1910, Wetumka, Hughes Co., OK; d. 12 Apr 1999, Weeks, Scott Co., AR.
>
> *More About HAZEL JEAN BALLARD:*
> *Burial: Hills Ferry Cemetery, Newman, Stanislaus Co., CA*
>
> *More About FLOYD RAY COKER:*
> *Burial: Hills Ferry Cemetery, Newman, Stanislaus Co., CA*

10. vii. ELVA LO EDITH BALLARD, b. 12 Jul 1916, OK; d. 12 Jan 2004.
> viii. WILLIE MARIE BALLARD, b. 14 Jul 1918, OK; d. Aft. 1930; m. HUBERT JAMES HOOPER, JR.,

04 Aug 1934, Crawford Co., AR; b. 14 Jan 1913, Sevier Co., AR; d. 28 Nov 2001, Cass Co., MO.

ix.   VIRGINIA IRENE BALLARD, *b. 09 Dec 1920, OK; d. 28 Dec 1998, Riverside, CA; m. JAMES HOWARD STEELE, 04 Jun 1938, Jackson Co., MO; b. 06 Jul 1917, Crawford Co., AR; d. 01 Nov 1983, Cedar Co., MO.*

x.   ELSA MAE BALLARD, *b. 11 Jan 1927; d. Aft. 1940; m. ROBERT M. MCCARROLL, 27 Nov 1964, Riverside, CA.*

5. JAMES MONROE[2] BALLARD (*FRANCIS MARION[1]*) *was born 04 Apr 1873 in Texas Co., MO, and died 30 Jul 1949 in Harrisburg, Poinsett Co., AR. He married (1) M. A. HALE 10 Nov 1889 in Whiteville, Baxter, AR. He married (2) MATTIE VIOLET ANDREWS 26 Jun 1894 in Union, Baxter Co., AR. She was born 17 Feb 1873 in AR, and died 12 Jul 1937. He married (3) JESSIE MORRIS 06 Mar 1940 in Harrisburg, AR.*

Notes for JAMES MONROE BALLARD:
Source: 1900 Izard County Arkansas Federal Census Records, 1920 White County Arkansas Federal Census Records, 1930 Jackson County Arkansas Federal Census Records, Baxter County Arkansas Marriage Records, JW9@aol.com

** 1900 - Living in Guthrie, Izard Co., AR - Ballard, James M - Apr 1873 MO TN IL, Mattie M - Feb 1873 - 4 children 3 living AR TN AR, Nora R - Dec 1894 AR, Jacob I - Sept 1896 AR, James C - July 1899 AR*
** 1920 - Living in Jackson, White Co., AR - Ballard, Jim 46 MO, Viola 46 AR, Calvin 20 AR, Jeff 14 OK, Leone 12 OK, Charley 9 AR, Clara 7 AR, Cora 4 AR*
** 1930 - Living in Barren, Jackson Co., AR - Ballard, J. M 57, Viola 57, Calvin 30, Bessie 18*

More About MATTIE VIOLET ANDREWS:
Burial: Shiloh Cemetery, Poinsett Co., AR

Child of JAMES BALLARD and M. HALE is:
> i.   GLADYS[3] BALLARD, *b. 1943, Harrisburg AR.*

Children of JAMES BALLARD and MATTIE ANDREWS are:

ii.   PERLEY[3] BALLARD.

iii.   NORA BALLARD, *b. 12 Jul 1895, OK Territory; d. Jun 1960, Alicia AR; m. ALONZO STAGGS.*

11.   iv.   JACOB "JAKE" IRVIN BALLARD, *b. 22 Sep 1896, Baxter Co., AR; d. 23 Dec 1974, Batesville, Independence Co., AR.*

v.   JAMES CALVIN BALLARD, *b. 12 Jul 1899, AR; d. 01 Jan 1976, Harrisburg, Poinsett Co., AR; m. PAULINE FLEETWOOD, 22 Feb 1942, Poinsett Co., AR; b. 11 Apr 1927, OH; d. 11 Jun 2012, Harrisburg, Poinsett Co., AR.*

> *More About JAMES CALVIN BALLARD:*
> *Burial: Shiloh Cemetery, Poinsett Co., AR*

vi.   WILLIAM JEFFERSON BALLARD, *b. 09 Nov 1904, Haskell Co., OK; d. 09 Aug 1955, Bradford Co., AR; m. BESSIE RILEY, 27 Jun 1929, Jackson Co., AR; b. 12 Mar 1912, White Co., AR; d. 24 Dec 1952, Pulaski Co., AR.*

vii.   LEONIA BALLARD, *b. 06 Sep 1907, OK; d. 1991, IL.*

viii.   CHARLEY BALLARD, *b. 26 Jan 1910, Poinsett Co. AR; d. 20 Jun 1985, Cleburne Co., AR.*

ix.   CLORIA EMMA BALLARD, *b. 02 Mar 1912, Craighead Co., AR; d. 1984, White Co., AR.*

> *Notes for CLORIA EMMA BALLARD:*
> *Source: Arkansas State Department of Health Delayed Certificate of Birth*

x.   CORA ETHEL BALLARD, *b. 27 Aug 1915, White Co., AR; d. 04 Jan 1921, Craighead Co., AR.*

Notes for CORA ETHEL BALLARD:
Source: White County Arkansas Certificate of Birth, Craighead County Arkansas Certificate of Death

6. RICHARD IRVING[2] BALLARD (FRANCIS MARION[1]) *was born 05 Apr 1877 in Texas Co., MO, and died 14 Feb 1962 in Haskell Co., OK. He married MARTHA. She was born 02 Mar 1884 in Fulton Co., AR, and died 21 Apr 1932 in Haskell Co., OK.*

Notes for RICHARD IRVING BALLARD:
Source: 1910 Izard County Arkansas Federal Census Records
** 1910 - Living in Izard Co., AR - Ballard, Richard 33 MO TN IL, Martha 26 AR TN AR, Susie 7 AR, Stella 4 AR, Loyd 4/12 ? AR*

More About MARTHA:
Burial: Hoyt Cemetery, Haskell Co., OK

Children of RICHARD BALLARD and MARTHA are:
> i. SUSIE[3] BALLARD, *b. 1903, AR; d. Aft. 1910.*
> ii. STELLA CORA BALLARD, *b. 12 Apr 1906, Izard Co., AR; d. 20 Mar 1988; m.* WILLIAM PERRY TUCKER; *b. 11 Oct 1899; d. 20 Sep 1962.*
>
> > *Notes for STELLA CORA BALLARD:*
> > *Source: ynonamarie@webtv.net*
> >
> > *More About STELLA CORA BALLARD:*
> > *Burial: San Bois Cemetery, Kinta, Haskell Co., OK*
>
> iii. LLOYD BALLARD, *b. 1910, AR.*

7. LEWIS SAMUEL[2] BALLARD (FRANCIS MARION[1]) *was born 23 Oct 1879 in Texas Co., MO, and died 12 Jan 1962 in Hot Springs, Garland Co., AR. He married (1) MABEL MCDANIEL Bef. 1894. He married (2) ROSY A. YOUNG 15 Dec 1895 in Baxter Co., AR. She was born Aug 1880, and died Abt. 1902 in AR. He married (3) ELIZABETH MARIAH SHERRIL 24 Sep 1903 in Izard Co., AR. She was born 25 Jun 1883, and died 13 Nov 1941.*

Notes for LEWIS SAMUEL BALLARD:
Source: 1900 Izard County Arkansas Federal Census Records

** 1900 - Living in Union twp, Izard Co., AR - Ballard, Louis S Oct 1879 MO, Rosy A July 1888 AR, Louis FA Sept 1899 AR, Buena Vista Jan 1898 AR*

More About LEWIS SAMUEL BALLARD:
Burial: Mt. Calvary Cemetery, Dallas, Dallas Co., TX

More About ELIZABETH MARIAH SHERRIL:
Burial: 13 Nov 1941, Mt. Calvary Cemetery, Dallas Co., TX

Children of LEWIS BALLARD and ROSY YOUNG are:
> i. BUENA VISTA[3] BALLARD, *b. 1898.*
> ii. LEWIS BALLARD, *b. Sep 1899.*

8. ELIZABETH NAYWASIE[2] BALLARD (FRANCIS MARION[1]) *was born 31 Jan 1886 in Mountain Home, Baxter Co., AR, and died 13 Nov 1972 in Jasper Co., TX. She married LODA RAYMOND HILL Abt. 1905 in AR.*

He was born 16 Sep 1877 in AL, and died 29 Dec 1962 in Newton Co., TX.

Notes for ELIZABETH NAYWASIE BALLARD:
Source: Jasper County Texas Certificate of Death

More About ELIZABETH NAYWASIE BALLARD:
Burial: Trouth Creek Cemetery, Newton Co., TX

Notes for LODA RAYMOND HILL:
Source: 1910 Independence County Arkansas Federal Census Records, 1920-1930 LeFlore County Oklahoma Federal Census Records, 1940 Matagorda County Texas Federal Census Records
** 1910 - Living in Magness, Independence Co., AR - Hill, Raymon 31 MS MS MS, Bettie 26 - 3 children 2 living AR TN IL, Samuel 4 OK, Carolle 1 7/12 MO*
** 1920 - Living in Milton, LeFlore Co., OK - Hill, Raymond L 41 MS Ireland MS, Betty 33 AR GA IL, Lewis S 13 OK, Myra C 11 MO, William I 8 AR, Olan J 5 OK, Beulah E 3 OK, Lesley R 10/12 OK, Susana Ballard 75 mother in law wd IL TN TN*
** 1930 - Living in Muse, LeFlore Co., OK - Hill, Loda R 51 MS, Elizabeth 44 AR, Samuel L 23 AR, William A 19 AR, James O 16 OK, Berena (hard to read) E 13 OK, Leslie R 11 OK, Lester M 8 AR, Alvin C 6 OK*
** 1940 - Living in Matagorda Co., TX - Hill, L Raymond 63 MS, Betty 54 AR, Olen 26 OK, Alvin 18 OK, Winefford 13 AR*

Children of ELIZABETH BALLARD and LODA HILL are:

> i. LEWIS SAMUEL³ HILL, b. 01 Apr 1906, Spiro, LeFlore Co.,, OK; d. 08 Mar 1975, Houston, Harris Co.,TX.
>
> *Notes for LEWIS SAMUEL HILL:*
> *Source: Harris County Texas Certificate of Death*

> ii. MYRA CAROLLE HILL, b. 16 Sep 1908, MO; d. 18 Apr 1993, Madison Co., TX; m. J. C. CHATHAM; b. 10 Dec 1910; d. 10 Aug 1990.
>
> *Notes for MYRA CAROLLE HILL:*
> *Source: Madison County Texas Certificate of Death*
>
> *More About MYRA CAROLLE HILL:*
> *Burial: Trout Creek, Cemetery, Newton Co., TX*
>
> *More About J. C. CHATHAM:*
> *Burial: Trout Creek, Cemetery, Newton Co., TX*

> iii. WILLIAM ARLIE HILL, b. 10 Jan 1911, Mt. Holly, Union Co., AR; d. 08 Jan 1996.
>
> *Notes for WILLIAM ARLIE HILL:*
> *Source: Union County Arkansas Delayed Birth Certificate*
>
> *More About WILLIAM ARLIE HILL:*
> *Burial: Kilbourne Cemetery, West Carroll Parish, LA*

> iv. JAMES OLEN HILL, b. 29 Jan 1914, Keota, OK; d. 08 Jun 1996; m. ERLINE SUMNER; b. 03 Mar 1913, Collins, MS; d. 28 Nov 1999.
>
> *Notes for JAMES OLEN HILL:*
> *Source: WWII Draft Cards*
>
> *More About JAMES OLEN HILL:*

Burial: Trout Creek Cemetery, Newton Co., TX

Notes for ERLINE SUMNER:
Source: Social Security Records

More About ERLINE SUMNER:
Burial: Trout Creek Cemetery, Newton Co., TX

    v.   BEULAH E. HILL, b. Abt. 1917, OK; d. Aft. 1930.
   vi.   LESLEY RAYMOND HILL, b. 05 Feb 1919, OK; d. 18 Nov 1991, Harris Co., TX; m. OPAL LOUISE PINCKARD; b. 03 Sep 1920, Polk Co., TX; d. 10 Mar 2000.

Notes for LESLEY RAYMOND HILL:
Source: Social Security Records

More About LESLEY RAYMOND HILL:
Burial: Peebles Cemetery, Goodrich, Polk Co., TX

More About OPAL LOUISE PINCKARD:
Burial: Peebles Cemetery, Goodrich, Polk Co., TX

   vii.   LESTER MARTIN HILL, b. 26 Jul 1921, OK; d. 10 Aug 1938, Renner, Matagorda Co., TX.

Notes for LESTER MARTIN HILL:
Source: Matagorda County Texas Standard Certificate of Death

More About LESTER MARTIN HILL:
Burial: Cedarvale Bay City Cemetery, Matagorda Co., TX

   viii.   ALVIN CARL HILL, b. 05 Mar 1924, Albin, Pushmataha Co., OK; d. 12 Jun 2002; m. MARGARET DAVENPORT, 25 Aug 1943, Matagorda Co., TX.

More About ALVIN CARL HILL:
Burial: Rosewood Funeral Home and Cemetery, Humble, Harris Co., TX

   ix.   WIMPFORD HARVE HILL, b. 20 Jul 1926, AR; d. 09 Nov 2007; m. PATRICIA FAY WHITE, 04 Dec 1948, Harris Co., TX.

Generation No. 3

9. EFFIE ELLEN[3] FOLEY (MARY JANE[2] BALLARD, FRANCIS MARION[1]) was born 26 Aug 1905 in Batesville, Independence Co., AR, and died 02 Nov 1983 in Van Buren, Crawford Co., AR. She married PORTER HOUSTON HICKEY 26 Mar 1925 in Crawford Co., AR. He was born 28 Sep 1898 in Crawford Co., AR, and died 13 Jun 1981 in Van Buren, Crawford Co., AR.

Notes for EFFIE ELLEN FOLEY:
Source: Independence County Arkansas Delayed Birth Certificate

More About EFFIE ELLEN FOLEY:
Burial: Gill Cemetery, Van Buren, Crawford Co., AR

Notes for PORTER HOUSTON HICKEY:
Source: 1930-1940 Crawford County Arkansas Federal Census Records

** 1930 - Living in Richland, Crawford Co.,. AR - Hickey, Porter 29, Effie 26, Virginia 4, Lena Jane 1*
** 1940 - Living in Richland, Crawford Co., AR - Hickey, Carter 39 AR, Effie 37 AR, Virginia Love 15 AR, Wanda Jane 12 AR, Eudale 4 AR*

More About PORTER HOUSTON HICKEY:
Burial: Gill Cemetery, Van Buren, Crawford Co., AR

Children of EFFIE FOLEY and PORTER HICKEY are:
  i. VIRGINIA LOVE⁴ HICKEY, b. 02 Feb 1926, Crawford Co., AR; d. 31 Mar 1977; m. COLLINS.

    Notes for VIRGINIA LOVE HICKEY:
    Source: Social Security Records

    More About VIRGINIA LOVE HICKEY:
    Burial: Gill Cemetery, Van Buren, Crawford Co., AR

  ii. WANDA JANE HICKEY, b. 14 Sep 1928, Crawford Co., AR; d. 19 Feb 2008; m. LAWRENCE W. BOLLENGER, 09 Nov 1946, Sebastian Co., AR.
  iii. HUGH DALE HICKEY, b. 20 Jan 1936, Crawford Co., AR; d. 12 Feb 1981, Sequoyah Co., OK; m. MARILYN ANNETTE CLEGG; b. 18 Jul 1937, Van Buren, Crawford Co., AR; d. 13 Jan 1999, AR.

    More About HUGH DALE HICKEY:
    Burial: Gill Cemetery, Van Buren, Crawford Co., AR

    More About MARILYN ANNETTE CLEGG:
    Burial: Bluff Cemetery, Springdale, Washington Co., AR

10. ELVA LO EDITH³ BALLARD (FRANCIS ALBERT MARION², FRANCIS MARION¹) *was born 12 Jul 1916 in OK, and died 12 Jan 2004. She married (1) LUTHER WESSON 25 Jun 1935 in Cecil, Franklin Co., AR. She married (2) JAMES CLEO WHEELER 28 Feb 1938 in Yuma Co., AZ. He was born 27 Jul 1912 in AR, and died Aft. 1940.*

Notes for JAMES CLEO WHEELER:
Source: WWII Draft Cards, 1940 Imperial County California Federal Census Records
** 1940 - Living in Brawley, Imperial Co., CA - Wheeler, James C 27 OK, Elva 23 OK, Gould 4 CA, Patsy 9/12 CA*
** 1942 - Living in Wenatchee, Chelan Co., WA*

Children of ELVA BALLARD and JAMES WHEELER are:
  i. GOULD⁴ WHEELER, b. Abt. 1936, CA; d. Aft. 1940.
  ii. PATSY WHEELER, b. Abt. 1939, CA; d. Aft. 1940.

11. JACOB "JAKE" IRVIN³ BALLARD (JAMES MONROE², FRANCIS MARION¹) *was born 22 Sep 1896 in Baxter Co., AR, and died 23 Dec 1974 in Batesville, Independence Co., AR. He married (1) ETHEL 01 Nov 1906 in AR. He married (2) MABELL WALLACE 01 Mar 1914 in Harrisburg, AR. She was born 09 Apr 1895 in MO, and died 11 Oct 1936 in White Co., AR.*

Notes for JACOB "JAKE" IRVIN BALLARD:

Source: 1920, White Co., AR Federal Census Records, 1930 Barren Co. AR Federal Census Records, 1940 White County Arkansas Federal Census Records

** 1920 - Living in Jackson, White Co., AR - Ballard, Jake 23 AR MO AR, Mary B. 23 MO US OH, Monroe 4 7/12 AR AR MO, Fletcher A 2/12 AR AR MO, Mary F. 11/12 AR AR MO*
** 1930 - Living in Jackson, Barren Co., AR - Ballard, J. F. married 18 yrs 34, MO, E. M. 35 MO, Monroe C. 14 AR,*

Fletcher 12 AR, Mary F. 10 AR, Marion 8 MO, Claire 6, James A. 4 11/12, Hester 1 10/12
** 1940 - Living in Liberty, White Co., AR - Ballard, Jake 43 wd AR, Maison 18 AR, Elsie 15 AR, James 13 AR, Hester 11 AR, Elzie 9 AR, Elvie 9 AR, Earnest 5 AR, Ludene 3 AR*

More About MABELL WALLACE:
Burial: Heard Cemetery, Bradford, White Co., AR

Children of JACOB BALLARD and MABELL WALLACE are:

    i.   *MONROE CLEFTEN[4] BALLARD, b. 24 May 1915, White Co., AR; d. 06 Jun 1990; m. VADA MARIE HUFF, 02 Oct 1941, White Co., AR; b. 21 May 1923, White Co., AR; d. 31 Jan 2012, Cleveland Co., AR.*

        Notes for MONROE CLEFTEN BALLARD:
        Source: WWII Draft Cards

        More About MONROE CLEFTEN BALLARD:
        Burial: Greenwood Cemetery, Rison, Cleveland Co., AR

        More About VADA MARIE HUFF:
        Burial: Greenwood Cemetery, Rison, Cleveland Co., AR

    ii.   *FLETCHER ALBERT BALLARD, b. 27 Oct 1917, White Co., AR; d. Jul 1978; m. ELVA WEATHERS, 28 May 1937, White Co., AR.*

        Notes for FLETCHER ALBERT BALLARD:
        Source: White County Arkansas Birth Certificate, Social Security Records

    iii.   *MARY F. BALLARD, b. 03 Oct 1919, White Co., AR; d. 2009, Longmont, CO; m. (1) ROBERT CANOY, 18 Dec 1944, Forsyth, Rosebud Co., MT; m. (2) WINFRED CHARLES PARKER, 19 Oct 1946, Hardin, Big Horn Co. MT; m. (3) FREEMAN MORRIS, 20 Oct 1937, Poinsett Co., AR.*

        Notes for MARY F. BALLARD:
        Source: White County Arkansas Birth Certificate

    iv.   *MARION BALLARD, b. 04 Nov 1921, White Co., AR; d. 22 Feb 2011, Pulaski Co., AR; m. MARGARET ARMSTRONG, 13 Sep 1941, Cleveland Co., AR; b. 11 Oct 1925, Cleveland Co., AR; d. 05 Oct 2011, Pulaski Co., AR.*

    v.

    v.   *ELSIE MILDRED BALLARD, b. 31 Aug 1924, AR; d. 04 Aug 1998; m. (1) LEROY D. PLUMMER; m. (2) FREEMAN MORRIS, 14 Mar 1941, Poinsett Co., AR; m. (3) ALFRED S. FOSHAY, 10 Jul 1960, San Diego, CA; b. 26 Jun 1927; d. 16 Mar 1989.*

        Notes for ELSIE MILDRED BALLARD:
        Source: Social Security Records

        More About ALFRED S. FOSHAY:
        Burial: Holy Sepulcher Cemetery, Hayward, Alameda Co., CA

    vi.   *JAMES ARTHUR BALLARD, b. 31 May 1926, Sedgwick, Lawrence Co., AR; d. 17 Apr 2009.*

        Notes for JAMES ARTHUR BALLARD:
        Source: WWII Draft Cards

    vii.   *HESTER LAVERNE BALLARD, b. 11 Jul 1928, Boldknob, White Co., AR; d. 15 Apr 1997; m. (1) PENIX; m. (2) F. G. MOSS, 28 Jun 1949, Leachville, Mississippi Co.,, AR.*

viii. ELVIE LUCILLE BALLARD, *b. 20 Apr 1931, Bradford, White Co., AR; d. Aft. 1940.*

ix. ELZA LEE "BUDDY" BALLARD, *b. 20 Apr 1931, Bradford, White Co., AR; d. 26 Jan 1983; m.* MARY ELLEN THARP; *b. 11 Dec 1933, Lawrence Co., AR; d. 24 Oct 2006.*

More About ELZA LEE "BUDDY" BALLARD:
Burial: Pleasant Valley Cemetery, Cushman, Independence Co., AR

More About MARY ELLEN THARP:
Burial: Pleasant Valley Cemetery, Cushman, Independence Co., AR

x. EARNEST DALE BALLARD, *b. 08 Aug 1934, Bradford, White Co., AR; d. 01 Jul 2003, Batesville, Independence Co., AR; m.* GERTIE LEE THARP; *b. 10 Aug 1935; d. 20 Oct 1995.*

Notes for EARNEST DALE BALLARD:
Source: Obit submitted by mstauf@comcast.net

** Batesville Guard-Batesville AR. Spring Mill - Earnest Ballard 68, of Spring Mill died Tuesday, July 1, 2003, in local hospital.*
Info listed: Born Aug 8, 1934, son of Jake and Maebelle Wallace Ballard. Wife: Glenda. Sons: Kenny, Randy and Darrell. Daughters: Doris Foster, Lisa Harris, Christy Harris. Living brothers: James & Marion. Living sisters: Janice Ackerman, Mary Hunsinger, Helen Blevins.
Preceding him in death: parents, three brothers: Monroe, Fletcher and Buddy, three sisters: Elsie Plummer, Lucille Skaggs and Hester Moss.
Funeral: Willis-Hays Funeral Service Chapel in Batesville AR. Burial Pleasant Valley Cem., Cushman AR. Pallbearers: Michael Hall, Jamie Hall, Matthew Henry, J.T. Sandy, John Ballard and James Autry. Honorary pallbearer: Richard Rollins

More About EARNEST DALE BALLARD:
Burial: Pleasant Valley Cemetery, Cushman, Independence Co., AR

More About GERTIE LEE THARP:
Burial: Pleasant Valley Cemetery, Cushman, Independence Co., AR

xi. JANICE BALLARD, *b. Bet. 1935 - 1936, AR; m.* ACKERMAN.

xii. LUCILLE BALLARD, *b. Abt. 1936, AR; d. Bef. 01 Jul 2003; m.* SCAGGS.

xiii. HELEN LUDEAN BALLARD, *b. 27 Sep 1936, AR; d. 27 Apr 2017, Jonesboro, Craighead Co., AR; m. (1)* BILLY BLEVINS; *b. 18 Oct 1940; m. (2)* MARVIN O. MILLER; *b. 27 Sep 1935; d. 27 Apr 1993.*

More About HELEN LUDEAN BALLARD:
Burial: Leachville Cemetery, Mississippi Co., AR

More About BILLY BLEVINS:
Burial: Leachville Cemetery, Mississippi Co., AR

More About MARVIN O. MILLER:
Burial: Leachville Cemetery, Mississippi Co., AR

George Ballard

Generation No. 1

1. GEORGE[1] BALLARD *was born 1823 in TN, and died Aft. 1880. He married* MINERVA CREEK. *She was born 1823 in TN, and died Aft. 1880.*

Notes for GEORGE BALLARD:
Source: 1850, 1860 Coffee County Tennessee Federal Census Records, 1880 Mississippi County Missouri Federal Census Records, Carolyn Paladino (Carolyn.paladino@trz.com)

** 1850 - Living in Coffee Co., TN - Ballard, George 30 TN, Minervy 29 TN, Nancy 2 TN, Amandy 4/12 TN*
** 1860 - Living in Coffee Co., TN - Ballard, George 37 day labor, Minerva 37, Nancy A. 12, Amanda 10, Columbus 8, Sarah 6, William G. 5, Elizabeth 3, John F. 2*
** 1880 - Living in Mississippi Co., MO - Ballard George 57 farmer TN TN TN, Minerva 57 TN TN TN, Betty Cole 23 dau divorced TN TN TN, Richard L Cole 4 MO TN TN, John Ballard 21 TN TN TN*
** 1888 - There is a marriage between a George Ballard and Mary Elizabeth Burton on Sept 15, 1888 in Coffee Co., TN but I don't know that it is the same George.*

Children of GEORGE BALLARD *and* MINERVA CREEK *are:*
2.   i.   NANCY A.[2] BALLARD, *b. 16 Jun 1848, TN; d. 15 Apr 1912, Mississippi Co., MO.*
3.   ii.   AMANDA BALLARD, *b. 1850, TN; d. Aft. 1880.*
4.   iii.   COLUMBUS BALLARD, *b. 1852, TN; d. Aft. 1880.*
          iv.   SARAH BALLARD, *b. 1854, TN; d. Aft. 1860; m.* JOHN STEPHENS, *14 Sep 1870, Coffee Co., TN; b. Abt. 1850, Coffee Co., TN; d. Abt. 1893, DeKalb Co., TN.*
           v.   WILLIAM G. BALLARD, *b. 1855, TN; d. Aft. 1860.*
5.   vi.   ELIZABETH "BETTIE" BALLARD, *b. 1857, TN; d. Bet. 1900 - 1910, Haiti, Pemiscot Co., MO.*
6.   vii.   JOHN FRANKLIN BALLARD, *b. 10 Mar 1858, Coffee Co., TN; d. 01 Jun 1945, Whitwell, Marion Co., TN.*
7.   viii.   JOSEPH S. BALLARD, *b. 10 May 1860, TN; d. 15 Feb 1946, St. Louis Co., MO.*

Generation No. 2

2. NANCY A.[2] BALLARD (GEORGE[1]) *was born 16 Jun 1848 in TN, and died 15 Apr 1912 in Mississippi Co., MO. She married* ROY I. TOLLIVER *25 May 1870 in Coffee Co., TN. He was born Apr 1852 in TN, and died Aft. 1910.*

Notes for ROY I. TOLLIVER:
Source: 1880 Mississippi County Missouri Federal Census Records, 1900 Pemiscot County Missouri Federal Census Records

** 1880 - Living in James Bayou, Mississippi Co., MO - Tolaver, R L 27 TN, Nancy 32 TN, Willie Ann 2 TN, Minrva 4 TN (next door to Columbus Ballard)*
** 1900 - Living in Gayoso, Pemiscot Co., MO - Tolliver, R. L - Apr 1852 TN NC TN farmer, Nancy - June 1848 - 7 children 2 living TN TN TN, Glyde Gibbs 12 servant*

Children of NANCY BALLARD *and* ROY TOLLIVER *are:*
           i.   WILLIE ANN[3] TOLLIVER, *b. Abt. 1878, TN; d. Aft. 1880.*
          ii.   MINAVA TOLLIVER, *b. Abt. 1876, TN; d. Aft. 1880.*

3. AMANDA[2] BALLARD (GEORGE[1]) *was born 1850 in TN, and died Aft. 1880. She married* SAMUEL BURTON. *He was born Abt. 1854, and died Aft. 1880.*

Notes for SAMUEL BURTON:
Source: 1880 Mississippi County Missouri Federal Census Records

** 1880 - Living in James Bayou, Mississippi Co., MO - Burton, Samuel 26 farmer TN TN TN, Melvina 27 TN TN TN, Wm, 2 KY, Joela 1 MO, Sarah 3/12 July MO*

Children of AMANDA BALLARD and SAMUEL BURTON are:
  i. WILLIAM[3] BURTON, b. 1878, KY; d. Aft. 1880.
8. ii. JOELA BURTON, b. 03 Jan 1879, MO; d. 30 Jan 1966, Fulton Co. KY.
  iii. SARAH BURTON, b. 09 Feb 1880, MO; d. 15 Jan 1897, Mississippi Co., MO.
  iv. ALLEN BURTON, b. 1881, MO.
  v. SAMUEL JONES BURTON, b. 26 Nov 1882, MO; d. 14 Jun 1957.

4. COLUMBUS[2] BALLARD (GEORGE[1]) *was born 1852 in TN, and died Aft. 1880. He married* MARTHA. *She was born 1859 in MO, and died Aft. 1880.*

Notes for COLUMBUS BALLARD:
Source: 1880 Mississippi County Missouri Federal Census Records
** 1880 - Living in Mississippi Co., MO - Ballard, Columbus 26 TN TN TN Farmer, Martha 21 MO MO MO, Marietta 2 MO TN MS,*

Child of COLUMBUS BALLARD *and* MARTHA *is:*
  i. MARIETTA[3] BALLARD, b. 1878, MO.

5. ELIZABETH " BETTIE"[2] BALLARD (GEORGE[1]) *was born 1857 in TN, and died Bet. 1900 - 1910 in Haiti, Pemiscot Co., MO. She married (1)* COLE *Bef. 1876. He was born Abt. 1855 in TN, and died Bef. 1880. She married (2)* WILLIAM PALMER HEDGE *03 May 1886 in Charleston, Mississippi Co., MO. He was born 09 Apr 1837 in KY, and died 14 Apr 1922.*

Notes for ELIZABETH " BETTIE" BALLARD:
Source: Carolyn Paladino (carolyn.paladino@trz.com)
** Listed as divorced from Cole on the 1900 census - living with her parents*

Notes for WILLIAM PALMER HEDGE:
Source: 1900 -1910 Pemiscot County Missouri Federal Census Records
** 1900 - Living in Hayti, Pemiscot Co., MO - Hedge, Wm P Jan 1844 KY, Elisabeth 42 Oct 1858 10 children 6 living TN, John - Oct 1883 16 (poss son by his first marriage), Dock - Feb 1889 11 MO, Charles - Mar 1891 9 MO, Elisabeth - Apr 1893 7 MO, Manerva - Dec 1895 MO 5 MO*
** 1910 - Living in Hayti, Pemiscot Co., MO - Hodge, William P 72 wd KY KY KY*

More About WILLIAM PALMER HEDGE:
Burial: White Cemetery, Pemiscot Co., MO

Child of ELIZABETH BALLARD *and* COLE *is:*
  i. RICHARD L.[3] COLE, b. Abt. 1876, MO; d. Aft. 1880.

Children of ELIZABETH BALLARD *and* WILLIAM HEDGE *are:*
  ii. JOHN[3] HEDGE, b. Oct 1883, MO; d. Aft. 1900.
  iii. DOCK ARVEL HEDGE, b. 30 Mar 1889, Charleston, Mississippi Co., MO; d. 13 May 1962, Hayti, Pemiscot Co., MO; m. ROSA E. DAVIS; b. 09 Apr 1890, Hayti, Pemiscot Co., MO; d. 30 Mar 1959, Hayti, Pemiscot Co., MO.

    More About DOCK ARVEL HEDGE:
    Burial: White Cemetery, Pemiscot Co., MO

    More About ROSA E. DAVIS:
    Burial: Woodlawn Cemetery, Hayti, Pemiscot Co., MO

    iv.   *CHARLES REUBEN HEDGE, b. 15 Feb 1891, Charleston, Mississippi Co., MO; d. May 1976, Dunklin Co., MO; m. JEMIMA NODINE; b. 24 Aug 1895, Walnut Ridge, Lawrence Co.,, AR; d. 28 May 1960, Flint, Genesee Co., MI.*

    v.   *MANERVA JANE HEDGE, b. 24 Dec 1894, Wyatt, Mississippi Co., MO; d. 01 Nov 1973, Hayti, Pemiscot Co., MO; m. WILLIAM CURTIS KING; b. 10 Jul 1890, Hopkinsville, Christian Co., KY; d. 07 May 1951, Caruthersville, Pemiscot Co., MO.*

More About MANERVA JANE HEDGE:
Burial: Maple Cemetery, Caruthersville, Pemiscot Co., MO

More About WILLIAM CURTIS KING:
Burial: Maple Cemetery, Pemiscot Co., MO

6. JOHN FRANKLIN[2] BALLARD (GEORGE[1]) *was born 10 Mar 1858 in Coffee Co., TN, and died 01 Jun 1945 in Whitwell, Marion Co., TN. He married* SINTHY CRICK/CREEK *04 Nov 1881 in Coffee Co., TN. She was born 15 Jun 1858 in Coffee Co., TN, and died 14 Aug 1923 in Marion Co., TN.*

Notes for JOHN FRANKLIN BALLARD:
Source: 1900-1940 Marion County Tennessee Federal Census Records, Chuck (candtballard@web-o.net)
** 1900 - Living in Marion Co., TN - Ballard, John - Mar 1858 TN TN TN, Sintha 1858 7 children - 5 living TN TN TN, Pearl - Feb 1884 - 16 TN, Mark - July 1886 -13 TN, Charlie - Nov 1890 - 9 TN, Lillie - Dec 1892 - 7 TN, Barbray - Oct 1894, George - Aug 1888 11 half brother TN, Vance Creek brother in law 52 wd, Joe nephew 19 TN, Willie 13 nephew, Hettie 9, Orbie 7 TN*
** 1910 - Living in Marion Co., TN - Ballard, John 52, Syntha 55 - 8 children 5 living, Lilly 17, Barbra 15, Vance Crick 62 brother in law wd*
** 1920 - Living in Marion Co., TN - Ballard, John H 61, Sinthy 60, Barbreie 24, Vance Creek 65 WD*
** 1930 - Living in Marion Co., TN - Ballard, John, Barbra, Vance Creek*
** 1940 - Living in Whitwell, Marion Co., TN - Ballard, John 83 wd TN, Barbra 42 dau TN, Lillie Contrell dau 46 wd TN, Ocelia Contrell 16 TN grand daughter*
** His death certificate gives parents as Billie Franklin Ballard and Nancy Burton. It's possible that the surviving family members did not know his parents name and it's also possible that two families are incorrectly merged. I don't know at this point.*

More About SINTHY CRICK/CREEK:
Burial: Whitwell Cemetery, Marion Co., TN

Children of JOHN BALLARD *and* SINTHY CRICK/CREEK *are:*
    i.   PEARL[3] BALLARD, *b. Feb 1884, TN; d. 25 Mar 1932, Hamilton Co., TN.*
    ii.   GEORGE MARK BALLARD, *b. 23 Jul 1886, TN; d. 28 Jan 1969, Marion Co., TN.*
    iii.   CHARLES BALLARD, *b. 28 Nov 1890, Marion Co., TN; d. 16 Mar 1924, Marion Co., TN.*
9.   iv.   LILLIE MAE BALLARD, *b. 20 Dec 1893, Marion Co., TN; d. May 1971, Hamilton Co., TN.*
    v.   BARBARA ALLINE BALLARD, *b. 16 Oct 1896, Marion Co., TN; d. 07 Oct 1980, Marion Co., TN.*

       Notes for BARBARA ALLINE BALLARD:
       Source: Delayed Birth Certificate, Coffee County Tennessee

7. JOSEPH S.[2] BALLARD (GEORGE[1]) *was born 10 May 1860 in TN, and died 15 Feb 1946 in St. Louis Co., MO. He married* MATTIE. *She died Bef. 1946.*

Notes for JOSEPH S. BALLARD:
Source: 1910 Fulton County Kentucky Federal Census Records, 1920 St. Clair County Illinois Federal Census Records

** 1910 - Living in Short Creek, Fulton Co., KY - Ballard, Joe 50 TN TN TN carpenter, Mattie 44 - 7 children 3 living TN TN TN, Hattie 19 KY, Ruport 9 KY, Rulove 8 KY*
** 1920 - Living in East St. Louis, St. Clair Co., IL - Ballard, J S 59 TN police, Mattie 53 TN, Hattie Denton dau 26*

KY, Clarence son in law 29 KY, Hazel Marie granddaughter 7/12 IL, Ruport Ballard son 19 KY, Walles, Ruelove dau 17 KY, Cline Wallas son in law 26 TN, Herbert Denton brother to son in law 17 KY

Children of JOSEPH BALLARD and MATTIE are:
10.   i.   *HATTIE³ BALLARD, b. Abt. 1890, KY; d. Aft. 1920.*
       ii.   *RUPORT BALLARD, b. Abt. 1901, KY; d. Aft. 1920.*
     iii. *RULOVE BALLARD, b. Abt. 1902, KY; d. Aft. 1920; m. CLINE WALLACE; b. Abt. 1894, TN; d. Aft. 1920.*

Generation No. 3

8. *JOELA³ BURTON (AMANDA² BALLARD, GEORGE¹) was born 03 Jan 1879 in MO, and died 30 Jan 1966 in Fulton Co. KY. She married JOE PARTLOW WILLIAMS 29 Apr 1896 in Obion Co., TN. He was born 1877 in South Fulton, Obion Co., TN, and died 16 Jan 1963 in Hickman, Fulton Co., KY.*

More About JOELA BURTON:
Burial: Hickman City Cemetery, Hickman, Fulton Co., KY

Notes for JOE PARTLOW WILLIAMS:
Source: 1910-1920 Fulton County Kentucky Federal Census Records
** 1910 - Living in Short Creek, Fulton Co., KY - Williams, Joe 33 TN MO SC, Joella 31 KY TN MO, Ellis 9 KY, Burtha 7 KY, Lavern 5 KY, Guy 2 KY*
** 1920 - Living in Hickman, Fulton Co., KY - Williams, Joe P 43, Joella 41, Laverne 14, Guy 12, Mignone 9, Phebie 5*

More About JOE PARTLOW WILLIAMS:
Burial: Hickman City Cemetery, Hickman, Fulton Co., KY

Children of JOELA BURTON and JOE WILLIAMS are:
     i.   *ELLIS MAE⁴ WILLIAMS, b. 07 Feb 1901, Fulton Co., KY; d. 01 Aug 1995, Union City, Obion Co., TN; m. VIRGIL KEMP; b. 06 Jun 1898; d. 05 Mar 1950.*

           More About ELLIS MAE WILLIAMS:
           Burial: Hickman City Cemetery, Hickman, Fulton Co., KY

           More About VIRGIL KEMP:
           Burial: Mona View Cemetery, Muskegon Heights, Muskegon Co., MI

    ii.   *BERTHA PANSY WILLIAMS, b. 20 Feb 1903, Fulton Co., KY; d. 13 Mar 1921; m. WRIGHT.*

           More About BERTHA PANSY WILLIAMS:
           Burial: Hickman City Cemetery, Hickman, Fulton Co., KY

   iii. *GRACE LAVERNE WILLIAMS, b. 10 May 1905, Fulton Co., KY; d. 13 Aug 1936, Hickman, Fulton Co., KY; m. HATTE JONES.*

           More About GRACE LAVERNE WILLIAMS:
           Burial: Hickman City Cemetery, Hickman, Fulton Co., KY

    iv. *GUY MAXWELL WILLIAMS, b. 24 Nov 1907, Fulton Co., KY; d. Aft. 1940; m. ROBBIE BONDURANT.*

           Notes for GUY MAXWELL WILLIAMS:
           Source: WWII Draft Cards, 1930 Fulton County Kentucky Federal Census Records
           ** 1930 - Living in Hickman, Fulton Co., KY - Williams, Guy M 22, Robbie A 18, Bobbie J*

     v.   *MIGNONE WILLIAMS, b. 17 Jul 1910, Fulton Co., KY; d. 02 Apr 1993, Union City, Obion Co., TN; m. JOSEPH ANTHONY WERNER.*
    vi. *PHOEBE AGNES WILLIAMS, b. 19 Jan 1915, Fulton Co., KY; d. 27 Nov 2002, St. Clair Co., IL;*

m. GEORGE SILAS CISSELL.
More About PHOEBE AGNES WILLIAMS:
Burial: Lake View Memorial Gardens, St. Clair Co., IL

   vii.   *SAMUEL VENTRESS WILLIAMS, b. 21 Jun 1921, Fulton Co., KY; d. 05 Sep 2005, St. Clair Co., IL; m. ANNA.*

        More About SAMUEL VENTRESS WILLIAMS:
        Burial: Mt. Carmel Cemetery, Belleville, St. Clair Co., IL

9. *LILLIE MAE³ BALLARD (JOHN FRANKLIN², GEORGE¹) was born 20 Dec 1893 in Marion Co., TN, and died May 1971 in Hamilton Co., TN. She married JAMES CANTRELL. He was born 23 Dec 1886 in Whitwell, Marion Co., TN, and died 15 Jun 1933 in Chattanooga, Hamilton Co., TN.*

Notes for LILLIE MAE BALLARD:

Source: Marion County Tennessee Delayed Birth Certificate

Notes for JAMES CANTRELL:

Source: 1920-1930 Marion County Tennessee Federal Census Records

** 1920 - Living in Marion Co., TN - Cantrell, James 33, Lillie 25, Paulin 5, Maurine 3, Aline*
** 1930 - Living in Marion Co., TN - Cantrell, Jim, Lilie, Pauline, Maurine, Alleine, Avanelle, Ocellia, Jay H.*

Children of LILLIE BALLARD and JAMES CANTRELL are:

   i.   *PAULINE⁴ CANTRELL, b. Abt. 1915, Marion Co., TN; d. Aft. 1930.*
   ii.   *MAURINE CANTRELL, b. 10 Dec 1916, Marion Co., TN; d. 17 Apr 2008; m. WILLIAM LAWRENCE REEVES; b. 11 Dec 1915, TN; d. Aft. 1940.*

        Notes for MAURINE CANTRELL:
        Source: Social Security Records

        Notes for WILLIAM LAWRENCE REEVES:
        Source: WWII Draft Cards

   iii.   *ALLEINE CANTRELL, b. Abt. 1920, Marion Co., TN; d. Aft. 1930.*
   iv.   *AVENELLE CANTRELL, b. Abt. 1922, Marion Co., TN; d. Aft. 1930.*
   v.   *OCELLIA CANTRELL, b. Abt. 1926, Marion Co., TN; d. Aft. 1940.*
   vi.   *JAY H. CANTRELL, b. Abt. 1928, Marion Co., TN; d. Aft. 1930.*

10. *HATTIE³ BALLARD (JOSEPH S.², GEORGE¹) was born Abt. 1890 in KY, and died Aft. 1920. She married (1) JOHN RIGGS. He was born 1884. She married (2) CLARENCE DENTON Bef. 1920. He was born in KY, and died Aft. 1920.*

Children of HATTIE BALLARD and CLARENCE DENTON are:

   i.   *CLARENCE DENTON⁴ JR., b. Abt. 1916, KY; d. Aft. 1920.*
   ii.   *HAZEL MARIE JR., b. 1920, IL; d. Aft. 1920.*

George P. Ballard

Generation No. 1

1. GEORGE P.[1] BALLARD *was born 1826 in GA, and died Bet. 1860 - 1870. He married* NANCY HOPPER *03 Oct 1847 in Itawamba Co., MS. She was born 1825 in AL, and died Aft. 1870.*

Notes for GEORGE P. BALLARD:
Source: Norma Willoughby, 1850 Marion County Alabama Federal Census Records, 1860 Winston County Alabama Federal Census Records
** Levi Garrison Ballard also lives in Marion Co., AL but I haven't found a connection yet.*
** 1850 - Living in Marion Co., AL - Ballard, George 24 GA, Nancy 17 AL, James 1 AL, Mary 1/12*
** 1860 - Living in Winston Co., AL- Ballard, George W. 36 AL, Nancy 24 AL, James M 12 AL, Mary E 9, Caleb F 7 AL, Jamima 6 AL, George W 5 AL, Elizabeth 3 AL, Thomas 3/12 AL*

Notes for NANCY HOPPER:
Source: 1860 Winston County Alabama Federal Census Records, 1870 Gillis Bluff Butler County Missouri Federal Census Records

** 1870 - Living in Gillis Bluff, Butler Co., MO - Ballard, Nancy 35 AL, James M. 21 MS, Calep 18 AL, Virginia 16, George W 13 AL, Elizabeth 11 AL, Thomas J. 10 AL*

Children of GEORGE BALLARD *and* NANCY HOPPER *are:*
2.   i.   JAMES MAYFIELD[2] BALLARD, *b. 21 Jun 1849, AL; d. 03 Mar 1921, Tuckerman, Jackson Co., AR.*
       ii.   MARY E. BALLARD, *b. 1851, AL; d. Aft. 1860.*
3.   iii.   JEMIMA BALLARD, *b. 1854, AL; d. Aft. 1870.*
       iv.   VIRGINIA BALLARD, *b. 1854, AL; d. Aft. 1850.*
4.   v.   CALEP FRANKLIN BALLARD, *b. 1853, Houston, Winston Co., AL; d. Sep 1895, Lonoke Co., AR.*
5.   vi.   GEORGE W. BALLARD, *b. 24 Jul 1857, AL; d. Aft. 1870.*
       vii.   ELIZABETH BALLARD, *b. 1857, AL; d. Aft. 1870.*
      viii.   THOMAS J. BALLARD, *b. 1860, AL; d. Aft. 1870.*

Generation No. 2

2. JAMES MAYFIELD[2] BALLARD (GEORGE P.[1]) *was born 21 Jun 1849 in AL, and died 03 Mar 1921 in Tuckerman, Jackson Co., AR. He married (1)* SUSAN FRANCES SIMS *Bef. 1881. She died Bet. 1897 - 1900. He married (2)* NANCY LORRINDA LEE YOUNG *23 Dec 1900 in Viola Fulton Co., AR. She was born 11 Oct 1868 in Elizabeth Fulton Co., AR, and died 21 Jul 1928 in Grubbs, Jackson Co., AR.*

Notes for JAMES MAYFIELD BALLARD:
Source: Brenda (bbrown75801@aol.com), Frank Bounds (fbounds@triad.rr.com),1900 Fulton County Arkansas Federal Census Records, 1910 Independence County Arkansas Federal Census Records

** 1900 - Living in Benton, Fulton Co., AR - Ballard, James - Mar 1850 TN, Phillip - Oct 1897 boarding in home. Andrew - Jan 1893 is boarding in a neighbors*
** 1910 - Living in Gainesville twp, Independence Co., AR - Ballard, James M 60 MS, Nancy L 42 AR, Phillip H 12 MO, Nancy E 7 AR, Rosie I 5 AR, Elmer A 2/12 AR, Lillie Ivy 18 step daughter, Walter C Ivy 14 step son AR*

Notes for NANCY LORRINDA LEE YOUNG:
** She had the following Ivie children with her first husband: Marion Jackson Ivie, James Franklin, William, Elizabeth, Louisa, George Washington and Walter.*

More About NANCY LORRINDA LEE YOUNG:

Burial: Elgin Cemetery, Jackson Co., AR

Children of JAMES BALLARD and SUSAN SIMS are:
6.   i.   THOMAS "TOM" HENRY[3] BALLARD, b. 21 Feb 1881, MO; d. 31 Mar 1941, Tuckerman, Jackson Co., AR.
     ii. MILLANDER BALLARD, b. 1882.
7.   iii. JESSE MONROE BALLARD, b. 19 Nov 1889, Pocahontas, AR; d. 22 Feb 1943, Jackson Co., AR.
8.   iv. ANDREW DOLPHUS BALLARD, b. 05 May 1892, MO; d. 12 May 1967, Jonesboro, Craighead Co., AR.
9.   v.   PHILLIP HARK BALLARD, b. 10 Jun 1897, Crouch, Lincoln Co., MO; d. 28 Mar 1930.
     vi. JAMES BALLARD, b. Bef. 1903.
10. vii. NORA BALLARD, b. Bef. 1903.

Children of JAMES BALLARD and NANCY YOUNG are:
     viii. NANCY ELIZABETH[3] BALLARD, b. 25 Jan 1903, Independence Co., AR; d. 03 Oct 1939, Jonesboro, Craighead Co., AR; m. PLEASANT ODA HENSLEY, 1919; b. 03 Feb 1896, AR; d. 12 Nov 1949, Jonesboro, Craighead Co., AR.

          Notes for NANCY ELIZABETH BALLARD:
          Source: Craighead County Arkansas Certificate of Death

11. ix. ROSA IDA MAY BALLARD, b. 13 Jun 1904, Independence Co., AR; d. 10 Jan 1993, Vacaville, Solano Co., CA.
     x.   VIANA GERTRUDE BALLARD, b. 11 Jun 1906, Independence Co., AR; d. Nov 1907, Independence Co., AR.
     xi. ALVIN MAYFIELD BALLARD, b. 30 Dec 1907, Independence Co., AR; d. Dec 1908, Independence Co., AR.
12. xii. ELMER VALENTINE BALLARD, b. 14 Feb 1910, Batesville, Independence Co., AR; d. 16 May 1961, Farmington, St. Francois Co., MO.

3.   JEMIMA[2] BALLARD (GEORGE P.[1]) was born 1854 in AL, and died Aft. 1870. She married WILLIAM HARKINS "HARK" CAUDEL. He was born 03 Feb 1849 in Decatur Co., TN.

Notes for JEMIMA BALLARD:
Source: Jeff Ballard

Child of JEMIMA BALLARD and WILLIAM CAUDEL is:
     i.   WALTER FRANKLIN[3] CAUDEL.

4.   CALEP FRANKLIN[2] BALLARD (GEORGE P.[1]) was born 1853 in Houston, Winston Co., AL, and died Sep 1895 in Lonoke Co., AR. He married (1) HARRIETT SMITH 09 Jun 1872 in Dunklin Co., MO.   He married (2) ISABELLA ATTERBERY 06 Aug 1876 in Stoddard Co., MO. She was born Abt. 1858 in KY, and died Aft. 1880.

Notes for CALEP FRANKLIN BALLARD:
Source: 1880 Dunklin County Missouri Federal Census Records, 1900 Butler County Missouri Federal Census Records, Shirley Garland (sgarland@brick.net), Norma Willoughby (Norma@newwave.comm.net)

** 1880 - Living in Cotton Hill, Dunklin Co., MO - Ballard, CF 27 farmer AL GA MS, 1 - 24 KY KY KY, Geo F P 4/12 MO*
** 1900 - Living in Gillis Bluff, Butler Co., MO - Ballard, Frankie 1852, Hattie E 1853, Millander W 1885, John Wesley 1887, Moni Lee 1888, Oni Jewel 1888, Nancy C 1889, Josephine 1890*

Notes for ISABELLA ATTERBERY:
Source: Shirley Garland (sgarland@brick.net)

Children of CALEP BALLARD and ISABELLA ATTERBERY are:

	i.	GEORGE FRANKLIN P.[3] BALLARD, b. 1880, Dunklin Co., MO; d. Aft. 1880.
13.	ii.	MILLANDER WASHINGTON BALLARD, b. 02 Mar 1885, MO; d. 19 Jan 1970, Jackson Co., MI.
	iii.	JOHN WESLEY BALLARD, b. Abt. 1887.
14.	iv.	NANCY CASSANDER BALLARD, b. 12 Jul 1889, Holcomb, Dunklin Co., MO; d. 13 Oct 1989, Leachville, Mississippi Co., AR.
15.	v.	JOSEPHINE "JOSIE" BALLARD, b. 24 Aug 1893, Lonoke Co., AR; d. 16 Jul 1986, St. Clair Co., IL.
	vi.	ONIE JEWEL BALLARD, b. 1896, Lonoke Co., AR; d. 1932, Mississippi Co., AR; m. JOHN THOMAS TINSLEY; b. 1891; d. 1987.

More About ONIE JEWEL BALLARD:
Burial: Leachville Cemetery Leachville, Mississippi Co., AR

5. GEORGE W.[2] BALLARD (GEORGE P.[1]) was born 24 Jul 1857 in AL, and died Aft. 1870. He married MARY HENSON, daughter of BENONA HENSON and ELVIRA MILLS. She was born 04 Nov 1857 in Pemiscot Co., MO, and died 16 Nov 1918 in Dunklin Co., MO.

Notes for MARY HENSON:
Source: Norma Willoughby

Children of GEORGE BALLARD and MARY HENSON are:

16.	i.	WILLIAM ALFRED[3] BALLARD, b. 11 Jan 1883, Malden, Dunklin Co., MO; d. 22 Feb 1923, Malden, Dunklin Co., MO.
	ii.	ELLA BALLARD, b. Feb 1882, MO; d. Aft. 1900.
	iii.	ETTA MAE BALLARD, b. 07 Oct 1888, MO; d. 19 Mar 1934; m. HENRY HECK.

Notes for ETTA MAE BALLARD:
Source: Norma (norma @newwavecomm.net)

** Death certificate according to Norma:*
Eddie May Heck b. Oct 7, 1888 d. Mar 19 1934 age 45 years 5 mo 12 days Fa: Geo Ballard. Mo: Mary Henson. Info given by Henry Heck (husband)

Generation No. 3

6. THOMAS "TOM" HENRY[3] BALLARD (JAMES MAYFIELD[2], GEORGE P.[1]) was born 21 Feb 1881 in MO, and died 31 Mar 1941 in Tuckerman, Jackson Co., AR. He married (1) SUSAN COPELAND 08 Nov 1905 in Dunklin Co., MO, daughter of GEORGE COPELAND and MARGAERETT HECK. She was born Jun 1885 in Gibson Co., IN, and died 06 Mar 1911 in Dunklin Co., MO. He married (2) MARY FRANCES PURCELL 1916 in Alexander IL. She was born 18 Dec 1894 in IL, and died 03 Dec 1980.

Notes for THOMAS "TOM" HENRY BALLARD:
Source: 1920 Bollinger County Missouri Federal Census Records, 1930-1940 Jackson County Arkansas Federal Census Records, Frank Bounds (fbounds@triad.rr.com), WWI Draft Registration Card, Jackson County Arkansas Certificate of Death

** 1920 - Living in Union, Bollinger Co., MO - Ballard, T. H 39 MO MO MO, Mary 25 IL IL IL, Lena Irene 2 5/12 MO MO MO*
** 1930 - Living in Grubbs, Jackson Co., AR - Ballard, T. H 48 36 MO TN MO, Mary IL IL IL, Irene 12 MO, Joseph 9 MO, Dortha 5 MO, Martha 3 8/12 MO, Albert 5/12 AR*
** 1940 - Living in Bird, Jackson Co., AR - Ballard, Thomas 59 MP, Mary 45 IL, Joseph 19, Dorthy Virginia 16 MO, Martha 12 MO, Albert 10 AR*

More About THOMAS "TOM" HENRY BALLARD:
Burial: Hickory Grove, Diaz, Jackson Co., AR

Notes for SUSAN COPELAND:
Source: Dunklin County Missouri Certificate of Death

More About SUSAN COPELAND:
Burial: Park Cemetery, Malden, Dunklin Co., MO

More About MARY FRANCES PURCELL:
Burial: White Chapel Memorial Gardens, Gladstone, Clay Co., MO

Child of THOMAS BALLARD and SUSAN COPELAND is:
17.   i.   PHILIP HARKES[4] BALLARD, b. 20 May 1908, MO; d. 02 Apr 1974, Poplar Bluff, Butler Co.,MO.

Children of THOMAS BALLARD and MARY PURCELL are:
18.   ii.   LIMA IRENE[4] BALLARD, b. 1917, MO; d. Aft. 1940.
       iii.   JOSEPH BENJAMIN BALLARD, b. 11 Oct 1920, MO; d. 05 Jun 2004; m. HELEN ELIZABETH JACKSON, 07 Aug 1944, Jackson Co., AR; b. 12 Dec 1925, Tuckerman, Jackson Co., AR; d. 14 May 2014, Greenbrier, Faulkner Co., AR.

          More About JOSEPH BENJAMIN BALLARD:
          Burial: Bethlehem Cemetery, Faulkner Co., AR

          More About HELEN ELIZABETH JACKSON:
          Burial: Bethlehem Cemetery, Faulkner Co., AR

       iv.   DOROTHY VIRGINIA BALLARD, b. 07 Jun 1924, Mauldin, Dunklin Co., MO; d. 09 Nov 1997; m. NORMAN EUGENE STARLING, 20 Aug 1948, Jackson Co., AR.
       v.   MARTHA EVA BALLARD, b. 19 Sep 1926, MO; d. 02 Sep 2008; m. (1) GEORGE EDWARD ROE, 02 Jun 1946, Jackson Co., AR; b. 30 Sep 1923, Franklin, MO; d. 27 Sep 1994; m. (2) RAYMOND W. MORGAN, Aft. 1950.

          Notes for MARTHA EVA BALLARD:
          Source: Obituary

          Notes for GEORGE EDWARD ROE:
          Source: WWII Draft Cards

          More About GEORGE EDWARD ROE:
          Burial: Mt. Washington Cemetery, Independence, Jackson Co., MO

       vi.   ALBERT BALLARD, b. 1930, AR; d. Aft. 1940.

7. JESSE MONROE[3] BALLARD (JAMES MAYFIELD[2], GEORGE P.[1]) was born 19 Nov 1889 in Pocahontas, AR, and died 22 Feb 1943 in Jackson Co., AR. He married EVA MAYBELLE RAMSEY 10 Dec 1910 in Pocahontas, Randolph Co., AR. She was born 07 Mar 1892 in Thayer, Oregon Co., MO, and died 12 Oct 1957 in Newport, Jackson Co., AR.

Notes for JESSE MONROE BALLARD:
Source: 1910, 1930-1940 Jackson County Arkansas Federal Census Records

** 1910 - Living in Jefferson, Jackson Co., AR - Ballard, Jess 21 AR MO MO, Eva 18 AR MO MO, Andrew - brother 18 AR MO MO*

** 1930 - Living in Grubbs, Jackson Co., AR - Ballard, Jess 41 AR TN AR, Eva 38 MO IL TN, Clermont 13 AR, Ruby 9 AR, Gaughn W 7 AR, Jaunita 4 1/12 AR, Norman 2 4/12*
** 1940 - Living in Grubbs, Jackson Co., AR - Ballard, Jessie M 51 AR, Eva M 48 MO, Vangel 16 AR, Juanita 14 AR, James N 12 AR, Noramorie 9 AR, Frank Painter 22 AR*

More About JESSE MONROE BALLARD:
Burial: Ballews Chapel Cemetery, Grubbs, Jackson Co., AR

More About EVA MAYBELLE RAMSEY:
Burial: Ballews Chapel Cemetery, Grubbs, Jackson Co., AR

Children of JESSE BALLARD and EVA RAMSEY are:

> i. NORA MARIE[4] BALLARD, b. 19 Aug 1930, Grubbs, Jackson Co., AR; d. 01 Jul 2012, White Co., AR; m. HARLAN REYNOLDS; b. 23 Feb 1927; d. 2010.

> *More About NORA MARIE BALLARD:*
> *Burial: Coffeyville Cemetery, Coffeeville, Jackson Co., AR*

> *More About HARLAN REYNOLDS:*
> *Burial: Coffeyville Cemetery, Coffeeville, Jackson Co., AR*

> ii. VAUGHNCEIL WATSON BALLARD, b. 1923, Grubbs, Jackson Co., AR.
> iii. CLERMONT WESLEY BALLARD, b. 1917, Grubbs, Jackson Co., AR; d. Bef. 1957.
> iv. JUANITA BALLARD, b. 1925, Grubbs, Jackson Co., AR.
> v. JAMES NORMAN BALLARD, b. 19 Aug 1930, Grubbs, Jackson Co., AR; d. 01 Jul 2012, White Co., AR; m. RUBY MAE SMITH; b. 30 Jul 1932; d. 02 Mar 2002.

> *More About JAMES NORMAN BALLARD:*
> *Burial: Ballews Chapel Cemetery, Grubbs, Jackson Co., AR*

> *More About RUBY MAE SMITH:*
> *Burial: Ballews Chapel Cemetery, Grubbs, Jackson Co., AR*

> vi. M. W. BALLARD, b. 23 Aug 1934, Grubbs, Jackson Co., AR; d. 08 Jun 1936.

> *More About M. W. BALLARD:*
> *Burial: Ballews Chapel Cemetery, Grubbs, Jackson Co., AR*

8. ANDREW DOLPHUS[3] BALLARD (*JAMES MAYFIELD[2], GEORGE P.[1]*) *was born 05 May 1892 in MO, and died 12 May 1967 in Jonesboro, Craighead, AR. He married (1) ELVIRA BELL HENSLEY 26 Sep 1911 in Independence Co., AR. She was born 04 Jun 1892 in AR, and died 12 Dec 1918 in Grubbs, Jackson Co., AR. He married (2) MAY HENSLEY 29 Aug 1919 in Grubbs, Jackson Co., AR. She was born 10 May 1901 in AR, and died 31 Oct 1965.*

Notes for ANDREW DOLPHUS BALLARD:
Source: 1930-1940 Jackson County Arkansas Federal Census Records

** 1930 - Living in Grubbs, Jackson Co., AR - Ballard, Andrew 38 MO MO MO, May 28 AR AR MO, Hazel 12, Ray 10, Eveline 7, A D 5, Edith 2 1/12*
** 1940 - Living in Grubbs, Jackson Co., AR - Ballard, Andrew D 47 MO, May 38 AR, Roy 19 AR, Elevine 17 AR, Andrew D Jr. 15 AR, Edith 12 AR*

More About ANDREW DOLPHUS BALLARD:
Burial: Ballews Chapel Cemetery, Grubbs, Jackson Co., AR

More About ELVIRA BELL HENSLEY:
Burial: Ballews Chapel Cemetery, Grubbs, Jackson Co., AR

More About MAY HENSLEY:
Burial: Ballews Chapel Cemetery, Grubbs, Jackson Co., AR

Children of ANDREW BALLARD and ELVIRA HENSLEY are:
  i. EVELYN[4] BALLARD.
  ii. JESSIE BALLARD, b. 1915, AR.

Children of ANDREW BALLARD and MAY HENSLEY are:
  iii. HAZEL PEARL[4] BALLARD, b. 16 Oct 1917, AR; d. 24 May 2004; m. LEONARD LEE WATSON, 11 May 1935, Jackson Co., AR; b. 13 Mar 1915, AR; d. 05 Aug 2001.

    More About HAZEL PEARL BALLARD:
    Burial: Jonesboro Memorial Park Cemetery, Jonesboro, Craighead Co., AR

    Notes for LEONARD LEE WATSON:
    Source: 1940 Jackson County Arkansas Federal Census Records
    * 1940 - Living in Grubbs, Jackson Co., AR - Watson, Leonard B 25 AR farming, Hazel 22 AR

    More About LEONARD LEE WATSON:
    Burial: Jonesboro Memorial Park Cemetery, Jonesboro, Craighead Co., AR

  iv. ROY DANIEL BALLARD, b. 19 Jun 1920, Grubbs, Jackson Co., AR; d. Aft. 1942.
  v. EVELINA BALLARD, b. 16 Sep 1922, Grubbs, Jackson Co., AR; d. 05 Feb 2005; m. (1) LEWIS MAYES, 12 Oct 1955, Jonesboro, Craighead Co., AR; b. 22 Jan 1930, Jonesboro, Craighead Co., AR; d. 21 Sep 2000; m. (2) HARMON WHITEHURST, 05 Sep 1942, Jackson Co., AR.

    More About LEWIS MAYES:
    Burial: Old Enterprise Cemetery, Jonesboro, Craighead Co., AR

  vi. ANDREW DOLPHUS BALLARD JR., b. 10 Sep 1924, AR; d. 03 Jun 1980; m. KATHRYN ROGERS, 05 Mar 1946, Jackson Co., AR; b. Abt. 1928.

    More About ANDREW DOLPHUS BALLARD JR.:
    Burial: Nettleton Cemetery, Jonesboro, Craighead Co., AR

  vii. EDITH BALLARD, b. 1928, AR; d. Aft. 1940; m. FINLEY.

9. PHILLIP HARK[3] BALLARD (*JAMES MAYFIELD[2], GEORGE P.[1]*) was born 10 Jun 1897 in Crouch, Lincoln Co., MO, and died 28 Mar 1930. He married ZELL PERMELIA ZAMONS CRAWFORD. She was born 14 May 1902 in Beedeville, Jackson Co., AR, and died 12 May 1990 in San Antonio, Bexar Co., TX.

More About PHILLIP HARK BALLARD:
Burial: Glen Rest Cemetery, Kerrville, Kerr Co., TX

Notes for ZELL PERMELIA ZAMONS CRAWFORD:
Source: Jackson County Arkansas Certificate of Death, 1930 Kerr County Texas Federal Census Records

* 1930 - Living in Kerrville, Kerr Co., TX - Ballard, Zell P 27 wd AR AR AR, Eulaliah M 9 AR, Doskie E 7 AR, Dempsey E 6 TX

More About ZELL PERMELIA ZAMONS CRAWFORD:
Burial: Austin Memorial Park Cemetery, San Antonio, Bexar Co., TX

Children of PHILLIP BALLARD and ZELL CRAWFORD are:
>   i.   EULALIAH⁴ BALLARD, b. 18 Jun 1920, AR; d. 21 Jul 1991, TX; m. GEORGE W. WEISE; b. 26 Jun 1919; d. 18 Oct 1995.
>
>   *More About EULALIAH BALLARD:*
>   *Burial: Cook-Walden Capital Parks Cemetery and Mausoleum, Pflugerville, Travis Co., TX*
>
>   *More About GEORGE W. WEISE:*
>   *Burial: Cook-Walden Capital Parks Cemetery and Mausoleum, Pflugerville, Travis Co., TX*
>
>   ii.   DOSKIE EDITH BALLARD, b. 05 Sep 1922, Grubbs, Jackson Co., AR; d. 16 Mar 1993, Dallas, TX; m. (1) PENNELL; m. (2) WILLARD C. JOHNSON, 05 May 1971, Bowie, TX.
>
>   *More About DOSKIE EDITH BALLARD:*
>   *Burial: Glen Rest Cemetery, Kerrville, Kerr Co., TX*
>
> iii.   DEMPSEY EARNEST BALLARD, b. 19 Jan 1924, Kerr Co., TX; d. Aft. 1930; m. MARY ALICE PFEIFER, 28 Jan 1950, Burnet Co., TX.
>
>   *Notes for DEMPSEY EARNEST BALLARD:*
>   *Source: Kerr County Texas Birth Certificate, Burnet County Texas Marriage Records*

10. NORA³ BALLARD (*JAMES MAYFIELD²*, *GEORGE P.¹*) was born Bef. 1903. She married DAN ROY.

Child of NORA BALLARD and DAN ROY is:
>   i.   FLOYD⁴ ROY.

11. ROSA IDA MAY³ BALLARD (*JAMES MAYFIELD²*, *GEORGE P.¹*) was born 13 Jun 1904 in Independence Co., AR, and died 10 Jan 1993 in Vacaville, Solano Co., CA. She married WILLIAM PARIS IVIE 06 May 1920 in Jackson Co., AR. He was born 13 Mar 1903 in MO, and died 31 Jan 1970.

More About ROSA IDA MAY BALLARD:
Burial: Vacaville-Elmira Cemetery, Solano Co., CA

Notes for WILLIAM PARIS IVIE:
Source: 1930-1940 Jackson County Arkansas Federal Census Records

** 1930 - Living in Grubbs, Jackson Co., AR - Ivie, W P, Rosie, Louis, Nancy M.*
** 1940 - Living in Grubbs, Jackson Co., AR - Ivie, Parish 37, Rosie 30, William L 17, Nancy M 10, Jessie D 4, Eva E 2*

Children of ROSA BALLARD and WILLIAM IVIE are:

>   i.   WILLIAM LOUIS⁴ IVIE, b. Abt. 1923, Grubbs, Jackson Co., AR; d. Aft. 1940.
>   ii.   NANCY M. IVIE, b. Abt. 1930, Grubbs, Jackson Co., AR; d. Aft. 1940.
> iii.   JESSIE D. IVIE, b. Abt. 1936, Grubbs, Jackson Co., AR; d. Aft. 1940.
>   iv.   EVA E. IVIE, b. Abt. 1938, Grubbs, Jackson Co., AR; d. Aft. 1940.

12. ELMER VALENTINE³ BALLARD (*JAMES MAYFIELD²*, *GEORGE P.¹*) was born 14 Feb 1910 in Batesville,

Independence Co., AR, and died 16 May 1961 in Farmington, St. Francois Co., MO. He married VERNIE DELMER ROBERTS 26 Mar 1927 in Tuckerman, Jackson Co., AR, daughter of AGEE ROBERTS and SARAH WILLIAMS. She was born 26 Nov 1910 in Tuckerman, Jackson Co., AR, and died 08 Feb 1968 in Madison Memorial Hospital, Fredericktown, Madison Co., MO.

Notes for ELMER VALENTINE BALLARD:
Source: 1930 Barry County Missouri Federal Census Records, 1940 St. Genevieve County Missouri Federal Census Records, St. Genevieve County Missouri Death Certificate

** 1930 - Living in Monett, Barry Co., MO - Ballard, Elmer V 23 AR IL AR, Vernie D 22 AR AR AR, Corine B 1/12 MO*
** 1940 - Living in Saline, Ste. Genevieve Co., MO - Ballard, Elmer 30, Vernie 29 AR, Corene 10 AR, Pauline 7 AR, Jerie 2 AR*

More About ELMER VALENTINE BALLARD:
Burial: Genevieve Cemetery, Weingarten, St. Genevieve Co., MO

More About VERNIE DELMER ROBERTS:
Burial: Genevieve Cemetery, St. Genevieve Co., MO

Children of ELMER BALLARD and VERNIE ROBERTS are:

19.　　i.　CORINE BEATRICE[4] BALLARD, b. 07 Mar 1930, St. Genevieve Co., MO; d. 16 Aug 1987, Creek Co., OK.

　　　ii.　PAULINE DELMAR BALLARD, b. 24 Nov 1932, St. Genevieve Co., MO; d. 15 Jul 1970, St. Francois Co., MO; m. CHARLES STEINC; b. 24 Sep 1925, OH; d. 1988, MO.

　　　　　More About PAULINE DELMAR BALLARD:
　　　　　Burial: St. Genevieve Baptist Cemetery, Farmington, St. Francois Co., MO

　　　iii.　GERALD "JERRY" BALLARD, b. 08 Sep 1937, St. Genevieve Co., MO; d. 08 Sep 1937, Jackson Co., AR.
　　　iv.　JOSEPH MICHAEL BALLARD, b. 31 Aug 1944, St. Genevieve Co., MO.
　　　v.　PATRICIA JOYCE BALLARD, b. 31 Aug 1944, St. Genevieve Co., MO; d. 03 Jul 1972, St. Louis Co., MO.
　　　vi.　MARION BALLARD, b. 13 May 1948, St. Genevieve Co., MO; d. 13 May 1948, St. Genevieve Co., MO.

　　　　　Notes for MARION BALLARD:
　　　　　Source: St. Genevieve County Missouri Death Certificate

　　　vii.　NANCY LOIS BALLARD, b. 21 Apr 1951, Bonne Terre, St. Francois Co., MO; d. 05 Oct 2005, Saint Francois Co., MO; m. GROVER CLEVELAND BARTON; b. 23 Apr 1950; d. 01 Jul 2013, MO.

13. MILLANDER WASHINGTON[3] BALLARD (CALEP FRANKLIN[2], GEORGE P.[1]) was born 02 Mar 1885 in MO, and died 19 Jan 1970 in Jackson Co., MI. He married EDITH HOLLAND. She was born 1889 in MO, and died Aft. 1910.

Notes for MILLANDER WASHINGTON BALLARD:
Source: 1910 Shannon County Missouri Federal Census Records, 1930 St. Clair County Illinois Federal Census Records, WWI Draft Registration, Social Security Death Records

** 1910 - Living in Eminence, Shannon Co., MO - Ballard, Millender 26 MO MO MO, Edith 21 MO KY MO, Charley Holland 21 MO KY MO brother in law, Walter 17 MO KY MO brother in law*
** 1917 - WWI Draft Registration - Millinder Washington Ballard - Clay Co., AR Draft Card, Piggott Clay Co., AR Residence b. Mar 3, 1885. Occupation Rail Road, nearest relative: Emma Ballard, Signed Millinder Washington Ballard*

*1930 - Living in E. St. Louis, St. Clair Co., IL - Ballard, Millender W 46 MO, Edith 19 KY, Melbourne C 14 MO
* 1970 - Social Security Death Records: Millinder Ballard b. March 2, 1885 d. Jan 1970. Last Residence, Niles, Berrien Co., MI

More About MILLANDER WASHINGTON BALLARD:
Burial: Woodland Cemetery Jackson, Jackson Co, MI

Child of MILLANDER BALLARD and EDITH HOLLAND is:
      i.   MELBOURNE C.⁴ BALLARD, b. 1925, IL; d. Aft. 1930.

14. NANCY CASSANDER³ BALLARD (CALEP FRANKLIN², GEORGE P.¹) was born 12 Jul 1889 in Holcomb, MO, and died 13 Oct 1989 in Leachville, Mississippi Co., AR. She married WILLIAM ALFRED WOODS 08 Mar 1906 in Gibson, Dunklin Co., MO. He was born 17 Oct 1884 in White Co., IL, and died 05 Sep 1959 in Leachville, Mississippi Co., AR.

Notes for NANCY CASSANDER BALLARD:
* 1906 - Holcomb, Dunklin Co. MO marriage - In the presence of M. W. Ballard and Ellie Shaw, William Alfred Woods and Nancy Cassandra Woods married at Holcomb, Missouri March 8, 1906. J.J. Littlejohn conducted the ceremony.

More About NANCY CASSANDER BALLARD:
Burial: Leachville Cemetery Leachville, Mississippi Co., AR

Notes for WILLIAM ALFRED WOODS:
Source: Find A Grave, 1910-1920 Dunklin County Missouri Federal Census Records, 1930-1940 Mississippi County Arkansas Federal Census Records, Dunklin County Missouri Marriage Records, WWI Draft Registration Card

* 1910 - Living in Dunklin Co., MO - Woods, William A 26 IL IL IL, Nancy C 20 4 children 2 living AR MO MO, Armilla M 1 11/12 MO, Beatris M 1/12, Arey J. Ballard 14 AR MO MO
* 1918 - Living in Dunklin Co., MO - listed as William Alfred Woods living in Holcomb Dunklin co., MO born Oct 17 1883. farmer with Left Eye out. nearest relative Nancy Woods
* 1920 - Living in Dunklin Co., MO - Woods, William 37 IL, Nancy 31 AR, Arville 12 MO, Beatrice 9 MO, Gladis 6 MO, Virgie 3 MO, Jewel 10/12 MO, Tom (father) 61 IL, Nan (mother) 60 IL
* 1930 - Living in Neal, Mississippi Co., AR - Woods, William A 47 IL IL IL, Nancy C 43 AR MO MO, Bettress M 20 MO IL AR, Gladis A 16 MO IL AR, Virgie L 13 MO IL AR, Jewel F 11 MO IL AR, Mary L 8 AR IL AR, Aline C 5 AR IL AR, Vivian V 1 6/12 AR IL AR
* 1940 - Living in Neal, Mississippi Co., AR - Woods, William A 56 IL, Nancy K 50 AR, Jewel T 21 MO, Mary L 18 AR, Aline 15 AR, V Deloris 11 AR

More About WILLIAM ALFRED WOODS:
Burial: Leachville Cemetery Leachville, Mississippi Co., AR

Children of NANCY BALLARD and WILLIAM WOODS are:

      i.   ARMILLA M.⁴ WOODS, b. 1908, Dunklin Co., MO; d. Aft. 1920; m. RUFUS HAMPTON; b. 17 Sep 1908, Poinsett Co., AR; d. 14 Feb 1967, Shelby Co., TN.
     ii.   BEATRICE MELVINA WOODS, b. 16 Mar 1910, Dunklin Co., MO; d. Aft. 1930.
    iii.   GLADIS A. WOODS, b. 1914, Dunklin Co., MO; d. Aft. 1930.
    iv.   VIRGIE L. WOODS, b. 26 Jul 1916, Dunklin Co., MO; d. 23 Dec 2002, Grand Traverse Co., MI; m. PAUL EUGENE POE; b. 11 Nov 1916, Dunklin Co., MO; d. 02 Nov 1993, MI.
    v.   JEWEL THOMAS WOODS, b. 04 Mar 1919, Dallas Co., AL; d. 30 Jun 1988, Mississippi Co., AR; m. ELZNIA TYLER; b. 1922; d. 2013.

More About JEWEL THOMAS WOODS:

Burial: Leachville Cemetery Leachville, Mississippi Co., AR

    vi.   MARY LEE WOODS, *b. 05 May 1922, Mississippi Co., AR; d. 29 Apr 2015, Fayetteville, Washington Co., AR; m.* WARREN DOUGLAS THOMASSON; *b. 23 Jul 1921, Mississippi Co., AR; d. 23 Feb 1990, Mississippi Co., AR.*

        Notes for MARY LEE WOODS:
        Source: Find A Grave

        More About MARY LEE WOODS:
        Burial: Leachville Cemetery Leachville, Mississippi Co., AR

    vii.   ALINE C. WOODS, *b. 1925, Mississippi Co., AR; d. Aft. 1940.*
    viii.   VIVIAN DELORIS WOODS, *b. 1928, Mississippi Co., AR; d. Aft. 1940.*

15. JOSEPHINE "JOSIE"[3] BALLARD (CALEP FRANKLIN[2], GEORGE P.[1]) *was born 24 Aug 1893 in Lonoke Co., AR, and died 16 Jul 1986 in St. Clair Co., IL. She married* EARNEST BUSBY *09 Jan 1910. He was born 10 Aug 1890 in Hickman, Fulton Co., KY, and died 12 Jan 1970 in St. Louis, St. Louis Co., MO.*

More About JOSEPHINE "JOSIE" BALLARD:
Burial: Walnut Hill Cemetery, Belleville, St. Clair Co., IL

Notes for EARNEST BUSBY:
Source: 1920 & 1940 Dunklin County Missouri Federal Census Records, 1930 Mississippi County Arkansas

** 1920 - Living in Holcomb, Dunklin Co., MO - Busby, Earnest 27 KY, Josie 26 AR, Gladis 6 MO*
** 1930 - Living in Neal, Mississippi Co., AR - Busty, Earnest B 37 KY KY KY, Josie 36 AR AR AR, Gladis 17 MO KY AR, Gladis 17 MO KY AR, Ruth 10 MO KY AR, Zilva 8 MO KY AR, Leona 5 MO KY AR, Otis 1 11/12 AR KY AR*
** 1940 - Living in Hornersville, Dunklin Co., MO - Busby, Earnest 49, Josie 47, Odis 11*

More About EARNEST BUSBY:
Burial: Walnut Hill Cemetery, Belleville, St. Clair Co., IL

Children of JOSEPHINE BALLARD *and* EARNEST BUSBY *are:*

    i.   RUTH ELLEN[4] BUSBY, *b. 17 Feb 1920, Dunklin Co., MO; d. 11 Aug 1999; m.* RICHARD WATHERIN; *b. 20 Dec 1919, Belleville, St. Clair Co., IL; d. Jul 1991, Belleville, St. Clair co., IL.*

        More About RUTH ELLEN BUSBY:
        Burial: Valhalla Gardens of Memory and Mausoleum, Belleville, St. Clair Co., IL

        More About RICHARD WATHERIN:
        Burial: Valhalla Gardens of Memory and Mausoleum, Belleville, St. Clair Co., IL

    ii.   GLADIS BUSBY, *b. 1914, Dunklin Co., MO; d. Aft. 1920; m.* WILLIE CROFTON, *08 Oct 1930.*
20.   iii.   SILVIA BUSBY, *b. 29 Dec 1921, Dunklin Co., MO; d. 19 Jan 1995.*
    iv.   LEONA THELMA BUSBY, *b. 02 Apr 1925, Dunklin Co., MO; d. 23 Sep 2016, Brazoria Co., TX; m.* CECIL LUTHER POLK, *24 Nov 1945, Paragould, Greene Co., AR; b. 12 Jan 1922, Delo, Provincia de Luya, Amazonas, Peru; d. 09 Jan 2006.*

        More About LEONA THELMA BUSBY:
        Burial: Cedar Lawn Haven of Rest, West Columbia, Brazoria Co., TX

        More About CECIL LUTHER POLK:

Burial: Cedar Lawn Haven of Rest, West Columbia, Brazoria Co., TX

    v.   ODIS HOWARD BUSBY, *b. 28 May 1928, Dunklin Co., MO; d. 20 Oct 2006.*

Notes for ODIS HOWARD BUSBY:
Source: Social Security Records

16. WILLIAM ALFRED[3] BALLARD (GEORGE W.[2], GEORGE P.[1]) *was born 11 Jan 1883 in Malden, Dunklin Co., MO, and died 22 Feb 1923 in Malden, Dunklin Co., MO. He married* JESSIE MAE CLARK.

Notes for WILLIAM ALFRED BALLARD:
Source: Dunklin County Missouri Certificate of Death, 1900 Dunklin County Missouri Federal Census Records
** 1900 - Living in Cotton Hill, Dunklin Co., MO - Mills, Elvira - May 1837 AL SC AL, Albert Henson - Jan 1868 MO KY AL, William Ballard grandson - Jan 1880 MO TN MO, Ettie granddaughter - Feb 1882 MO TN MO, Ballard Ella grand dau - Sept 1888 MO TN MO*

Child of WILLIAM BALLARD *and* JESSIE CLARK *is:*
    i.   MARIE A.[4] BALLARD, *b. 1907.*

Generation No. 4

17. PHILIP HARKES[4] BALLARD (THOMAS "TOM" HENRY[3], JAMES MAYFIELD[2], GEORGE P.[1]) *was born 20 May 1908 in MO, and died 02 Apr 1974 in Poplar Bluff, Butler Co., MO. He married* DELPHIA GROSS.

Notes for PHILIP HARKES BALLARD:
Source: Frank Bounds (fbounds@triad.rr.com)

Child of PHILIP BALLARD *and* DELPHIA GROSS *is:*

    i.   DIXIE B.[5] BALLARD, *m.* LEONARD BOUNDS.

Notes for DIXIE B. BALLARD:
Source: Frank Bounds (fbounds@triad.rr.com)

18. LIMA IRENE[4] BALLARD (THOMAS "TOM" HENRY[3], JAMES MAYFIELD[2], GEORGE P.[1]) *was born 1917 in MO, and died Aft. 1940. She married* VANNIE TIMMONS *07 Aug 1935 in Jackson Co., AR. He was born 28 Jul 1914, and died 04 Nov 1979 in Watervliet, Berrien Co., MI.*

Notes for VANNIE TIMMONS:
Source: 1940 Jackson County Arkansas Federal Census Records
** 1940 - Living in Bird, Jackson Co., AR - Timmons, Vannie 25 AR, Irene 22 MO, Hazel 10/12 AR, Carroll Sims 16 sister AR, Ester Mae Sims 12 sister AR*

More About VANNIE TIMMONS:
Burial: Watervliet Cemetery, Watervliet, Berrien Co., MI

Child of LIMA BALLARD *and* VANNIE TIMMONS *is:*
    i.   HAZEL[5] TIMMONS, *b. Abt. 1939, AR; d. Aft. 1940.*

19. CORINE BEATRICE[4] BALLARD (ELMER VALENTINE[3], JAMES MAYFIELD[2], GEORGE P.[1]) *was born 07 Mar 1930 in St. Genevieve Co., MO, and died 16 Aug 1987 in Creek Co., OK. She married (1)* ELIJAH HIAWATHA HELM.

She married (2) WILLIAM OTIS POWERS.

Children of CORINE BALLARD and ELIJAH HELM are:
> i.   CORINE MARIE[5] HELM, b. 16 Nov 1946; d. 09 Aug 1991.
> ii. JOYCE HELM, d. 2005.

Child of CORINE BALLARD and WILLIAM POWERS is:
> iii. WILLIAM DELMER[5] POWERS.

20. SILVIA[4] BUSBY (JOSEPHINE "JOSIE"[3] BALLARD, CALEP FRANKLIN[2], GEORGE P.[1]) *was born 29 Dec 1921 in Dunklin Co., MO, and died 19 Jan 1995. She married ALNA GOFF 16 Jan 1938 in Kennett, Dunklin Co., MO. He was born 20 Jul 1918 in Hornersville, Dunklin Co., MO, and died Aft. 1940.*

Notes for SILVIA BUSBY:
Source: Social Security Records

Notes for ALNA GOFF:
Source: WWII Draft Cards, 1940 Dunklin County Missouri Federal Census Records

** 1940 - Living in Clay, Dunklin Co., MO - Goff, Alvin 21 MO, Sylvia 18 MO, Richard 1 MO*

Child of SILVIA BUSBY and ALNA GOFF is:
> i.   RICHARD[5] GOFF, b. 1939, Dunklin Co., MO; d. Aft. 1940.*

Harrison Ballard

Generation No. 1

1. HARRISON[5] BALLARD (GARLAND[4], BLAND[3], THOMAS[2], WILLIAM[1]) *was born 19 Aug 1819 in Todd Co., KY, and died 06 Feb 1886 in Gentry, Jackson Co., MO. He married* FRANCES CULBERTSON *31 Mar 1845 in Todd Co., KY, daughter of* DANIEL CULBERTSON *and* FRANCES GATSON. *She was born 09 Sep 1825 in Todd Co., KY, and died 26 Dec 1897 in Gentry Co., MO.*

Notes for HARRISON BALLARD:
Source: Todd County Kentucky Marriages 1820-1850 pg 1, 1850 Todd County Kentucky Federal Census Records, 1860 - 1880 Gentry County Missouri Federal Census Records, Betty Rhoda, Lesa Pfrommer (lesapfrommer@yahoo.com), 1870 Gentry Jackson County Missouri Federal Census Records

** 1850 - Living in Todd Co., KY - Ballard, Harrison 21 KY, Frances 24 KY, Susan 4 KY, Margarette 12 KY, Sarah 10 KY, Emma 9 KY, Mary 6 KY, Andrew 4 KY, Lucien 2 KY*
** 1860 - Living in Gentry Co., MO - Ballard, Harrison 41 KY, Frances 35 KY, Susan 14 KY,*
** 1870 - Living in Gentry Co., MO - Ballard, Harrison 50 KY, Frances 48 KY, Ellen 18 KY, Mary 16 KY, Andrew L 14 KY, Lucian 12 KY John P. MO, Viola 4 MO, Vinora 4 MO, Lucinda 2 MO*
** 1880 - Living in Jackson, Gentry Co., MO - Ballard, Harrison 61 KY VA VA, Francis E 55 KY NC VA, John B 19 MO, Viola 14 MO, Vinora 14 MO, Lucinda 12 MO*

More About HARRISON BALLARD:

Burial: Cooper Cemetery, Stanberry, Gentry Co., MO

Notes for FRANCES CULBERTSON:
Source: Lesa Pfrommer (lesapfrommer@yahoo.com)

** 1856 - State of Kentucky, Todd Co. Court Clerks office Nov. 7, 1856*
I Ben T. Perkins, Clerk of said Co. court do certify that this Letter of attorney from Hiram Shartzer and Martha J. his wife to F. Culbertson was this day produced to me in my Office together with the certificate of R. R. Junes Notary Public for Santa Clara Co., State of California thereas endorsed and ordered to be recorded. Whereupon I have truly recorded said deed and certificate together with this certificate in my office. Ben T. Perkins
This Indenture made and entered into this 24 day of October in the year of our Lord 1856 between Frances Culbertson widow and relict of Daniel Culbertson, Dec'd and her Children Patterson H. Culbertson, Ellen L. Culbertson, Frances E. Ballard and Harrison Ballard her husband all of Todd county and State of Kentucky, Martha June Shartzer, her husband of the Co. of Santa Clara and State of California by their attorney (Frances Culbertson), John R. G. Culbertson and his wife Rhoda Ann Culbertson of Macoupin Co. of the State of Illinois, Sarah C. Tull, her husband J. R. Tull of Clay Co., State of Missouri this forelast named also by their attorney Frances Culbertson as aforesaid of the first part and Ephraim T. Porter of the second part Witnesseth that this party of the first part for and in consideration of twelve hundred and fifty one Dollars to theirs as have paid by the said Porter the receipt of which is hereby acknowledged the party first named have this day bargained and Sold and by this presents do be____ sell and confirm unto the, said Porter a certain parcel of land in two Separate tracts containing both one hundred and five acres reserving one half acre not sold where the Grave yard of said first party stands the first tract containing one hundred and acres and one half acre lying in Todd county and State of Kentucky on the waters of the Elk fork of Red river and bounded as follows to wit beginning at a Stake near a black oak ranked as a corner thence with said Porters line N66 E80 poles to a black Jack his corner thence S10 E139 poles to a Stake in a flat Sink near the N. W. corner of Isaac Burns old field where there are several Saplings marked as ----- there. S66 W49 poles to a Stake on old corner of Culbertsonis same course continues 80 poles further to a ----- oak and black jack thence at N9 W128 poles to two -----oaks on Frazier line thence with it to a rock in Culbertsonis old line of his Sixty acre survey thence along said line N10 to W to the beginning the other tract of four and one half acres patented to Daniel Culbertson lying in said Co. and State and on the same waters bounded as follows to ----- Beginning at a rock in a field corner to 400 acre Survey patented to Gideon Thompson and William Blackwood -----

a line of a 265 acre Survey patented to Richard Gartin thence with said Gartins S30 W4 poles to a Stake corner to said 265 acre Survey thence with another of its lines S78 W70 poles to a Stake corner to said 265 acres where it ----- for a black Jack there with another of its line N80 W120 poles to a Stake in Chas. Lowryis line thence with it N8 W4 poles to a Stake corner to said 400 acres patented to said Thompson and Blackwood thence with this line S80 E123 poles to a Stake corner to said 400 acre survey thence with its line N78 E70 poles to the Beginning to have and to hold said lands and ----- with Warranty title to the said Porter his him or assigns forever. For Witness whereof said party of the first part hath hereunto Set their hands and Seals the day and date first above Written.

Frances Culbertson (seal) Ellen L. Culbertson (seal)

Patterson H. Culbertson (seal) John R. Culbertson (seal)

Rhoda Ann Culbertson (seal) Hiram Shartzer (seal)

Martha J. Shartzer (seal) J. R. Tull (seal) Sarah C. Tull (seal)

By their atty. Frances Culbertson, Harrison Ballard, Frances E. Ballard

** 1856 - State of Kentucky Todd County Court Clerks Office October 24, 1856*

I D. M. Clagett, Deputy Clerk for Ben T. Perkins Clerk of said Co. Court do certify that this Deed from Frances Culbertson and others to E. T. Porter was this day produced to me in said office and acknowledged by the said Frances Culbertson, Ellen Culbertson and Patterson H. Culbertson to be their act and deed the same was also acknowledged by the said Frances   Culbertson as attorney in fact for John R. Culbertson and Rhoda Ann Culbertson his wife, Hiram Shartzer and Martha J Shartzer his wife, J. R. Tull and Sarah C. Tull his wife to be her act and deed and on the 25 day of October 1856 the same was again produced to me in said office and acknowledged by the said Harrison Ballard and Frances E. Ballard his wife to be their act and deed and ordered to be recorded. Whereupon I have truly recorded the same together with this certificate in said Office   D.   M. Clagett   Ben T. Perkins

More About FRANCES CULBERTSON:
Burial: Cooper Cemetery, Stanberry, Gentry Co., MO

Children of HARRISON BALLARD and FRANCES CULBERTSON are:

2. i. SUSAN FRANCES[6] BALLARD, *b. 24 Mar 1846, Todd Co., KY; d. 09 Sep 1913, Minot, Ward Co., ND.*

3. ii. MARGARET A. BALLARD, *b. 07 Oct 1847, Todd Co., KY; d. 08 Mar 1916, Gentry Co., MO.*

4. iii. SARAH ELLEN BALLARD, *b. 27 Aug 1850, Todd Co., KY; d. 04 Apr 1919, Harley, Blaine Co., ID.*

5. iv. EMMA JANE BALLARD, *b. 06 Nov 1851, Todd Co., KY; d. 22 Mar 1894, Buchanan Co., MO.*

   v. MARY LEE BALLARD, *b. 31 Dec 1853, Todd Co., KY; d. 15 Jun 1938, Lancaster Co., NE; m.* ALLEN O. STOCKTON; *b. 12 May 1848, Platte Co., MO; d. 18 Apr 1933, Perkins Co., NE.*

    More About MARY LEE BALLARD:
    Burial: Fairview Cemetery, Grant, Perkins Co., NE

    More About ALLEN O. STOCKTON:
    Burial: Fairview Cemetery, Grant, Perkins Co., NE

6. vi. ANDREW L. BALLARD, *b. 20 Apr 1856, Todd Co., KY; d. 17 Oct 1908, Gentry Co., MO.*

7. vii. LUCIEN EDWARD BALLARD, *b. 04 May 1858, Todd Co., KY; d. 11 Jan 1939, Los Angeles Co., CA.*

   viii. JOHN PATTERSON BALLARD, *b. 01 Jan 1861, Stanberry, Gentry Co., MO; d. 27 May 1948, Los Angeles Co., CA; m.* DORA E. WHITEAKER, *06 Oct 1889, St. Joseph, Buchanan Co., MO; b. 1868, DeKalb Co., MO; d. 1923, Garfield Co., OK.*

    Notes for JOHN PATTERSON BALLARD:
    Source: Buchanan County Missouri Marriage Records, 1910-1920 Los Angeles County California Federal Census Records
    ** 1910 - Living in Corral, Blaine Co., ID - Ballard, John P 49 MO KY KY*
    ** 1920 - Living in Los Angeles Co., CA - Ballard, John P 59 MO, Lucien E brother 60 KY*

    More About JOHN PATTERSON BALLARD:
    Burial: Forest Lawn Memorial Park, Los Angeles Co., CA

More About DORA E. WHITEAKER:

Burial: Enid Cemetery, Garland Co., OK

8.	ix.	VIOLA S. BALLARD, b. 13 Nov 1865, Stanberry, Gentry Co., MO; d. 14 Feb 1909, Centerville, Appanoose Co., IA.
9.	x.	VINORA BALLARD, b. 13 Nov 1865, Gentry Co., MO; d. 03 Nov 1926, Los Angeles Co., CA.
10.	xi.	LUCINDA CAROLLINE "CARRIE" BALLARD, b. 04 May 1868, Gentry Co., MO; d. 15 May 1952, Johnson Co., KS.

Generation No. 2

2. SUSAN FRANCES[6] BALLARD (HARRISON[5], GARLAND[4], BLAND[3], THOMAS[2], WILLIAM[1]) was born 24 Mar 1846 in Todd Co., KY, and died 09 Sep 1913 in Minot, Ward Co., ND. She married JOHN C. HUSSY 09 Aug 1866 in Stanberry, Gentry Co., MO. He was born 14 May 1841 in NC, and died 19 Nov 1912 in Des Lacs, Ward Co., ND.

More About SUSAN FRANCES BALLARD:
Burial: Des Lacs Cemetery, Ward Co., ND

Notes for JOHN C. HUSSY:
Source: 1870-1880 Gentry County Missouri Federal Census Records

** 1870 - Living in Cooper, Gentry Co., MO - Hussey, John C 27 farmer NC, Susan 23 KY, Frances 2 MO, William 1 MO*
** 1880 - Living in Mt. Pleasant, Gentry Co., MO - Hussey, J. C 37 farmer NC, Susan F 32 KY, Mary 12, William 11, Henry 9, Dora 8, Bertha 4*

More About JOHN C. HUSSY:

Burial: Des Lacs Cemetery, Ward Co., ND

Children of SUSAN BALLARD and JOHN HUSSY are:

11.	i.	MARY FRANCES[7] HUSSY, b. 12 Sep 1867, Gentry Co., MO; d. 11 Sep 1935, Nampa, Canyon Co., ID.
	ii.	JOHN WILLIAM HUSSY, b. 05 Mar 1869, Stanberry, Gentry Co., MO; d. 18 May 1925, Halsey, Linn Co., OR; m. EMMA ALICE WATERMAN; b. 23 Apr 1871, MO; d. 23 Mar 1954, Sutter Co., CA.

More About JOHN WILLIAM HUSSY:
Burial: Pine Grove Cemetery, Peoria, Linn Co., OR

More About EMMA ALICE WATERMAN:
Burial: Pine Grove Cemetery, Peoria, Linn Co., OR

	iii.	HENRY HARRISON HUSSY, b. 07 Dec 1870, Mt. Pleasant, Gentry Co., MO; d. 04 Aug 1943, Nampa, Canyon Co., ID; m. (1) ANNA BELL MASTIN; b. 1873; d. 1903; m. (2) MARY ANN WEATHERWAX; b. 11 Apr 1881, Vinton, Benton Co., IA; d. 08 Apr 1967, Eureka, Humboldt Co., CA.

More About ANNA BELL MASTIN:
Burial: High Ridge Cemetery, Stanberry, Gentry Co., MO

More About MARY ANN WEATHERWAX:
Burial: Kohlerlawn Cemetery, Nampa, Canyon Co., ID

iv.   DORA IRENE HUSSY, b. 03 Mar 1872, Gentry Co., MO; d. 04 Dec 1959, San Francisco Co., CA; m. EDWARD KINCAID; b. 25 Aug 1869, Cook Co., IL; d. 06 Dec 1944, San Mateo Co., CA.

More About DORA IRENE HUSSY:
Burial: Woodlawn Memorial Park, Colma, San Mateo Co., CA

More About EDWARD KINCAID:
Burial: Woodlawn Memorial Park, Colma, San Mateo Co., CA

v.   BERTHA ALVERTA HUSSY, b. 22 Sep 1877, Gentry Co., MO; d. 29 Jun 1920, Ward Co., ND; m. THOMAS E. FOX; b. 1862; d. 1930.

More About BERTHA ALVERTA HUSSY:
Burial: Union Cemetery, Towner, McHenry Co., ND

More About THOMAS E. FOX:
Burial: Union Cemetery, Towner, McHenry Co., ND

3.   MARGARET A.[6] BALLARD (HARRISON[5], GARLAND[4], BLAND[3], THOMAS[2], WILLIAM[1]) was born 07 Oct 1847 in Todd Co., KY, and died 08 Mar 1916 in Gentry Co., MO. She married MOSES GROOM. He was born 13 Feb 1846 in Clinton Co., MO, and died 09 Oct 1915 in Gentry Co., MO.

More About MARGARET A. BALLARD:
Burial: Long Branch Cemetery, Gentry Co., MO

More About MOSES GROOM:
Burial: Long Branch Cemetery, Gentry Co., MO

Children of MARGARET BALLARD and MOSES GROOM are:

i.   JAMES HARRISON[7] GROOM, b. 23 Mar 1868, Gentry Co., MO; d. 15 Apr 1950, Cameron, Clinton Co., MO; m. NELLIE DODGE; b. 19 Mar 1871, Gentry Co., MO; d. 12 Jul 1942, Cameron, Clinton Co., MO.

More About JAMES HARRISON GROOM:
Burial: Graceland Cemetery, Cameron, Clinton Co., MO

ii.   WILLIAM J. GROOM, b. 20 Jan 1870, Gentry Co., MO; d. 01 Dec 1904; m. SARAH ELIZABETH MASTIN; b. 08 Jan 1872, MO; d. 01 Oct 1954, Stanberry, Gentry Co., MO.

More About WILLIAM J. GROOM:
Burial: Long Branch Cemetery, Gentry Co., MO

More About SARAH ELIZABETH MASTIN:
Burial: King City Cemetery, King City, Cemetery, Gentry Co., MO

iii.   CORRINDA E. GROOM, b. 17 Aug 1871, Gentry Co., MO; d. 29 Mar 1931; m. DAVID A. LOCK; b. 1868; d. 1945.

More About CORRINDA E. GROOM:
Burial: Upchurch Cemetery, Norwich, Kingman Co., KS

More About DAVID A. LOCK:
Burial: Upchurch Cemetery, Norwich, Kingman Co., KS

iv. CHARLES L. GROOM, b. 23 Dec 1873, Gentry Co., MO; d. 29 Oct 1949, Albany, Gentry Co., MO; m. (1) FREDRICKA EVA ROBERTS; b. 15 Jan 1876, Darlington, Gentry Co., MO; d. 28 May 1934, Darlington, Gentry Co., MO; m. (2) SARAH SPILLMAN; b. 24 Apr 1875, Louisville, Jefferson Co., KY; d. 14 Apr 1973, Albany, Gentry Co., MO.

More About CHARLES L. GROOM:
Burial: Long Branch Cemetery, Gentry Co., MO

More About FREDRICKA EVA ROBERTS:
Burial: Long Branch Cemetery, Gentry Co., MO

More About SARAH SPILLMAN:
Burial: Grandview Cemetery, Albany, Gentry Co., MO

v. ANN B. GROOM, b. Abt. 1878, Gentry Co., MO.

vi. ORION CURTIS GROOM, b. 03 Dec 1879, Darlington, Gentry Co., MO; d. 18 Apr 1960, Lees Summit, Jackson Co., MO; m. ETHEL CORRINE MCINTURF; b. 17 Feb 1901, MO; d. 01 Jun 1985, MO.

More About ORION CURTIS GROOM:
Burial: High Ridge Cemetery, Stanberry, Gentry Co., MO

More About ETHEL CORRINE MCINTURF:
Burial: Milo Cemetery, Milo, Vernon Co., MO

vii. MYRT ARVEL GROOM, b. 14 Jun 1882, Gentry Co., MO; d. 03 Jan 1955, Darlington, Gentry Co., MO; m. GERTRUDE GILLESPIE; b. 12 Sep 1884, MO; d. 06 Dec 1980, Albany, Gentry Co., MO.

More About MYRT ARVEL GROOM:
Burial: Long Branch Cemetery, Gentry Co., MO

More About GERTRUDE GILLESPIE:
Burial: Long Branch Cemetery, Gentry Co., MO

viii. ELSIE MAY GROOM, b. 19 Feb 1885, Gentry Co., MO; d. 10 Dec 1977, Gentry Co., MO; m. EARL JASPER SHOEMAKER; b. 04 Feb 1884, Gentry Co., MO; d. 20 Aug 1974, Gentry Co., MO.

More About ELSIE MAY GROOM:
Burial: High Ridge Cemetery, Stanberry, Gentry Co., MO

More About EARL JASPER SHOEMAKER:
Burial: High Ridge Cemetery, Stanberry, Gentry Co., MO

4. SARAH ELLEN[6] BALLARD (HARRISON[5], GARLAND[4], BLAND[3], THOMAS[2], WILLIAM[1]) was born 27 Aug 1850 in Todd Co., KY, and died 04 Apr 1919 in Harley, Blaine Co., ID. She married ALVA CURTIS FLOYD. He died Bef. 1919.

Notes for SARAH ELLEN BALLARD:
Source: Blaine County Idaho Certificate of Death

More About SARAH ELLEN BALLARD:
Burial: Hailey Cemetery, Hailey, Blaine Co., ID

Notes for ALVA CURTIS FLOYD:
Source: 1880 Gentry County Missouri Federal Census Records, 1900 Blaine County Idaho Federal Census Records
** 1880 - Living in Gentryville, Gentry, MO - Floyd, A C 33, Sarah 30, Clate 8, Claud 5*
** 1900 - Living in Hailey, Blaine Co., ID - Floyd, Alva C - Oct 1846 KY TN TN, Sarah E - Aug 1850 - 5 children 3 living KY VA VA, Lula G - Sept 1880 MO, Victor C - Jan 1886 ID*

Children of SARAH BALLARD and ALVA FLOYD are:

      i.   CLATO[7] FLOYD, b. 08 Feb 1872, MO; d. 03 Jan 1948, Hailey, Blaine Co., ID; m. SADIE A. GILLIHAN; b. 03 Dec 1875, MO; d. 08 Jun 1940, Boise, Ada Co., ID.

           More About CLATO FLOYD:
           Burial: Hailey Cemetery, Hailey, Blaine Co., ID

           More About SADIE A. GILLIHAN:
           Burial: Hailey Cemetery, Hailey, Blaine Co., ID

     ii.   CLAUD FLOYD, b. Abt. 1875, MO; d. Aft. 1880.
    iii.   LULA G. FLOYD, b. 19 Sep 1880, MO; d. 20 Sep 1965, ID; m. JOSEPH W. FULD; b. 27 Oct 1878, ID; d. 11 Dec 1968, Bannock Co., ID.

           More About LULA G. FLOYD:
           Burial: Hailey Cemetery, Hailey, Blaine Co., ID

           More About JOSEPH W. FULD:
           Burial: Hailey Cemetery, Hailey, Blaine Co., ID

    iv.   VICTOR C. FLOYD, b. 10 Jan 1886, Blaine Co., ID; d. 26 Oct 1936, Hailey, Blaine Co., ID.

           More About VICTOR C. FLOYD:
           Burial: Hailey Cemetery, Hailey, Blaine Co., ID

5.   EMMA JANE[6] BALLARD (HARRISON[5], GARLAND[4], BLAND[3], THOMAS[2], WILLIAM[1]) *was born 06 Nov 1851 in Todd Co., KY, and died 22 Mar 1894 in Buchanan Co., MO. She married* PATRICK WILSON STOCKTON. *He was born 14 Aug 1846 in Perry Co., MO, and died 02 Dec 1936 in Shelby, Toole Co., MT.*

More About EMMA JANE BALLARD:
Burial: Cooper Cemetery, Stanberry, Gentry Co., MO

Notes for PATRICK WILSON STOCKTON:
Source: 1880 Gentry County Missouri Federal Census Records

** 1880 - Living in Cooper, Gentry Co., MO - Stockton, Wilson P 33 farmer MO KY IN, Emma 28 KY KY KY, Ellen 9 MO, George 6 MO, Asberry 1 MO*

More About PATRICK WILSON STOCKTON:
Burial: Mountain View Cemetery, Shelby, Toole Co., MT

Children of EMMA BALLARD and PATRICK STOCKTON are:

      i.   ELLA FRANCES[7] STOCKTON, b. 17 Jul 1870, St. Joseph, Buchanan Co., MO; d. 26 Sep 1950, Shelby, Toole Co., MT; m. ISAAC ALLEN GUNTER; b. 15 May 1877, Warren Co., IL; d. 17 Jul 1929, Andrew Co., MO.

           More About ELLA FRANCES STOCKTON:

Burial: Mountain View Cemetery, Shelby, Toole Co., MT

More About ISAAC ALLEN GUNTER:
Burial: Center Grove Cemetery, Kirkwood, Warren Co., IL

    ii.   *GEORGE WILSON STOCKTON, b. 04 Oct 1872, Stanberry, Gentry Co., MO; d. 17 Jul 1954, CO; m. (1) STELLA M. MCCULLOUGH; b. 13 Dec 1877, Albany, Gentry Co., MO; d. 26 May 1957, Payette Co., ID; m. (2) ETHEL MAY MAROONEY; b. Jun 1881, CO; d. 1924, CO.*

More About GEORGE WILSON STOCKTON:
Burial: Crown Hill Cemetery, Wheat Ridge, Jefferson Co., CO

More About STELLA M. MCCULLOUGH:
Burial: Riverside Cemetery, Payette Co., ID

More About ETHEL MAY MAROONEY:
Burial: Crown Hill Cemetery, Jefferson Co., CO

    iii.   *ASBERRY WILLIAM STOCKTON, b. 23 Apr 1879, Stanberry, Gentry Co., MO; d. 29 Apr 1962, San Diego Co., CA; m. EFFIE IRENE WEATHERWAX; b. 14 Apr 1885, IA; d. 03 Dec 1955, San Diego Co., CA.*

More About ASBERRY WILLIAM STOCKTON:
Burial: Mt. Hope Cemetery, San Diego Co., CA

More About EFFIE IRENE WEATHERWAX:
Burial: Mt. Hope Cemetery, San Diego Co., CA

6. *ANDREW L.[6] BALLARD (HARRISON[5], GARLAND[4], BLAND[3], THOMAS[2], WILLIAM[1]) was born 20 Apr 1856 in Todd Co., KY, and died 17 Oct 1908 in Gentry Co., MO. He married ALICE HALL 09 Feb 1879 in Gentry Co., MO, daughter of P. HALL and MALINDA HUNT. She was born 07 Sep 1858 in IL, and died 28 Aug 1927 in St. Joseph, Buchanan Co., MO.*

Notes for ANDREW L. BALLARD:
Source: 1880-1900 Gentry County Missouri Federal Census Records

** 1880 - Living in Cooper twp., Gentry Co., MO - Ballard, AL 24 IN, Alice 20 IL, Maud 6/12 MO*
** 1900 - Living in Cooper twp., Gentry Co., MO - Ballard, Andrew - May 1856 KY KY KY, Alice - Sept 1854 IL KY KY, Maude - Nov 1879 MO, Grace - Apr 1882 MO, Kate - Dec 1888 MO, Cleo - Aug 1892 MO, Ruth - July 1895 mo*

Notes for ALICE HALL:
Source: 1910 Buchanan County Missouri Federal Census Records, Buchanan County Missouri Death Certificate

** 1910 - Living in St. Joseph, Buchanan Co., MO - Ballard, Alice 52 wd 5 children 5 living, Kate 21 MO, Cleo 17 MO, Ruth 14 MO*

Children of ANDREW BALLARD and ALICE HALL are:
    i.   *MAUDE[7] BALLARD, b. Nov 1879, MO; d. Aft. 1920; m. THOMAS H. COOLEY; b. Abt. 1870, KY; d. Aft. 1920.*

        Notes for THOMAS H. COOLEY:
        Source: 1920 Buchanan County Missouri Federal Census Records
        ** 1920 - Living in St. Joseph, Buchanan Co., MO - Cooley, Thomas H 49 KY, Maude 40 MO, Alice Ballard 60 mother in law 60 wd.*

12.	ii.	GRACE E. BALLARD, b. 10 Apr 1882, MO.
	iii.	KATE BALLARD, b. Dec 1888, MO.
13.	iv.	CLEO L. BALLARD, b. 23 Aug 1893, Stanberry, MO; d. 03 Oct 1939, St. Joseph, Buchanan Co., MO.
	v.	RUTH BALLARD, b. Jul 1895, MO.

7. LUCIEN EDWARD[6] BALLARD (HARRISON[5], GARLAND[4], BLAND[3], THOMAS[2], WILLIAM[1]) *was born 04 May 1858 in Todd Co., KY, and died 11 Jan 1939 in Los Angeles Co., CA. He married* MARY WATSON. *She was born 22 Apr 1875 in MO, and died 22 Apr 1930 in Los Angeles Co., CA.*

Notes for LUCIEN EDWARD BALLARD:
Source: 1900 Buchanan County Missouri Federal Census Records, 1910-1920 Los Angeles County California Federal Census Records

** 1900 - Living in St. Joseph Ward, Buchanan Co., MO - Ballard, Lucian - May 1866 KY VA KY brakeman RR, Marie - Apr 1871 - 2 children - 2 living MO, Germany Germany, Edward - June 1895 MO, Jones - Aug 1897 MO*
** 1910 - Living in Los Angeles Co., CA - Ballard, Lucian E 51 merchant grocery KY KY KY, Mary 39, Edward W 13 MO*
** 1920 - Living in Los Angeles Co., CA with his brother John.*

More About LUCIEN EDWARD BALLARD:
Burial: Forest Lawn Memorial Park, Los Angeles Co., CA

More About MARY WATSON:
Burial: Forest Lawn Memorial Park, Los Angeles Co., CA

Children of LUCIEN BALLARD *and* MARY WATSON *are:*

    i. EDWARD WATSON[7] BALLARD, *b. 27 Jun 1896, St. Joseph, Buchanan Co., MO; d. 28 Dec 1918, Germany.*

        More About EDWARD WATSON BALLARD:
        Burial: Forest Lawn Memorial Park, Glendale, Los Angeles Co., CA

    ii. JONES BALLARD, *b. Aug 1897, Buchanan Co., MO; d. Aft. 1900.*

8. VIOLA S.[6] BALLARD (HARRISON[5], GARLAND[4], BLAND[3], THOMAS[2], WILLIAM[1]) *was born 13 Nov 1865 in Stanberry, Gentry Co., MO, and died 14 Feb 1909 in Centerville, Appanoose Co., IA. She married* CHARLES FRANK SMITH. *He was born Nov 1862 in NY, and died 1929 in Jackson Co., MO.*

Notes for VIOLA S. BALLARD:
Source: Appanoose County Iowa Death Records

More About VIOLA S. BALLARD:
Burial: Oakland Cemetery, Centerville, Appanoose Co., IA

Notes for CHARLES FRANK SMITH:
Source: 1900 Appanoose County Iowa Federal Census Records, 1910 Jackson County Missouri Federal Census Records

** 1900 - Living in Center, Appanoose Co., IA - Smith, C. Frank - Nov 1862 NY NY MO, Ola - Nov 1865 - 4 children 3 living MO KY KY, Ryon - Oct 1892 IA, Beulah - July 1894 IA, Edith - June 1899 IA*
** 1910 - Living in Kansas ward, Jackson Co., MO - Smith, Charles, F 47, Byron 17, Beulah 15, Edith 11,*

More About CHARLES FRANK SMITH:
Burial: Mt. Moriah Cemetery, Kansas City, Jackson Co., MO

Children of VIOLA BALLARD *and* CHARLES SMITH *are:*
      i.   BRYON[7] SMITH, *b. Oct 1892, Des Moines, Polk Co., IA; d. 03 Oct 1944, Kansas City, Wyandotte Co., KY.*

             More About BRYON SMITH:
             Burial: Mt. Moriah Cemetery, Kansas City, Jackson Co., MO

     ii.   BEULAH SMITH, *b. Jul 1894, IA; d. Aft. 1910.*

    iii.   EMMITT MERRILL SMITH, *b. 26 Dec 1896, Appanoose Co., IA; d. 12 Jun 1897, Appanoose Co., IA.*

    iv.   EDITH SMITH, *b. Jun 1899, Appanoose Co., IA; d. 04 Feb 1917, Kansas City, Wyandotte Co., KY.*

     v.   MURRELL A. SMITH, *b. 25 Feb 1902, Appanoose Co., IA; d. 04 May 1973, Kansas City, Wyandotte Co., KY; m.* CLARENCE C. SWENSON; *b. 15 Nov 1900, OK; d. 19 Jan 1988, Madison Co., AL.*

             More About MURRELL A. SMITH:
             Burial: Mt. Moriah Cemetery, Kansas City, Jackson Co., MO

             More About CLARENCE C. SWENSON:
             Burial: Mt. Moriah Cemetery, Kansas City, Jackson Co., MO

9. VINORA[6] BALLARD (HARRISON[5], GARLAND[4], BLAND[3], THOMAS[2], WILLIAM[1]) *was born 13 Nov 1865 in Gentry Co., MO, and died 03 Nov 1926 in Los Angeles Co., CA. She married* JOSEPH STERLLING SCOTT. *He was born 1864 in OH, and died 1933.*

More About VINORA BALLARD:
Burial: Forest Lawn Memorial Park, Los Angeles Co., CA

Notes for JOSEPH STERLLING SCOTT:
Source: 1900-1910 Jackson County Missouri Federal Census Records

** 1900 - Living in Kansas City Ward, Jackson Co., MO - Scott, Joseph S Nov 1864 MO MO MO, Nora - Nov 1865 - 2 children 2 living MO KY KY, Leonard - Apr 1889 MO, Wilbur - Apr 1898 MO*
** 1910 - Living in Kansas City Ward, Jackson Co., MO - Scott, Joseph S 47 MO, Mora C 44 - 6 children 3 living MO, Leonard 21 MO, Wilbur 12 MO, Mildred 5 MO*

Children of VINORA BALLARD *and* JOSEPH SCOTT *are:*

      i.   WILLIAM LEONARD[7] SCOTT, *b. 10 Apr 1889, MO; d. 04 May 1956, Los Angeles Co., CA; m. (1)* MATILDA ANN; *b. 27 Apr 1886, WA; d. 13 May 1949, Los Angeles Co., CA; m. (2)* BESSIE MARGUERITE STETSON; *b. 21 Jul 1892, CA; d. 06 Dec 1994, Ventura Co., CA.*

             More About WILLIAM LEONARD SCOTT:
             Burial: Forest Lawn Memorial Park, Glendale, Los Angeles Co., CA

             More About MATILDA ANN:
             Burial: Forest Lawn Memorial Park, Glendale, Los Angeles Co., CA

             More About BESSIE MARGUERITE STETSON:
             Burial: Mountain View Cemetery and Mausoleum, Altadena, Los Angeles Co., CA

  ii. WALTER SCOTT, b. 1891, MO; d. 25 May 1897, Jackson Co., MO.

    More About WALTER SCOTT:
    Burial: Forest Hill Cemetery, Kansas City, Jackson Co., MO

  iii. ETHEL SCOTT, b. 1893, MO; d. 13 May 1897, Jackson Co., MO.

    More About ETHEL SCOTT:
    Burial: Forest Hill Cemetery, Jackson Co., MO

  iv. HAROLD SCOTT, b. 1895, MO; d. 03 May 1897, Jackson Co., MO.
   v. WILBUR SCOTT, b. 05 Apr 1898, MO; d. 05 Dec 1958, Los Angeles Co., CA; m. GLADYS LEONTINE JACKSON; b. 07 Sep 1895, Andrew Co., MO; d. 26 Sep 1981, Wyandotte Co., KS.

    More About WILBUR SCOTT:
    Burial: Forest Lawn Memorial Park, Glendale, Los Angeles Co., CA

    More About GLADYS LEONTINE JACKSON:
    Burial: Woodlawn Cemetery, Kansas City, Wyandotte Co., KS

  vi. MILDRED SCOTT, b. Abt. 1905, Jackson Co., MO; d. Aft. 1910.

    More About MILDRED SCOTT:
    Burial: Forest Hill Cemetery, Kansas City, Jackson Co., MO

10. LUCINDA CAROLLINE "CARRIE"[6] BALLARD (HARRISON[5], GARLAND[4], BLAND[3], THOMAS[2], WILLIAM[1]) was born 04 May 1868 in Gentry Co., MO, and died 15 May 1952 in Johnson Co., KS. She married (1) CLAUDE WILLIAM PEED. He was born 12 Oct 1887 in IA, and died 04 Aug 1919 in Buchanan Co., MO. She married (2) HARRY CURTIS BRINKLEY 24 Jan 1888 in Albany, Gentry Co., MO. He was born 25 May 1866 in Allegheny Co., PA, and died 23 Oct 1907 in Leavenworth Co., KS. She married (3) MARTIN Abt. 1920. He died Bet. 1920 - 1930.

Notes for LUCINDA CAROLLINE "CARRIE" BALLARD:
Source: 1900 Bourbon County Kansas Federal Census Records, 1910-1920 Jackson County Missouri Federal Census Records, 1930 Los Angeles County California Federal Census Records, 1940 Pulaski County Missouri Federal Census Records

** 1900 - Living in Fort Scott ward, Bourbon Co., KS - Brinkley, Carrie - May 1868 - 2 children 2 living MO KY KY, Garland - Mar 1889 MO, Gladys - Aug 1893 IA*
** 1910 - Living in Kansas Ward, Jackson Co., MO - Brinkley, Carrie 39 wd 2 children 2 living MO KY KY, Gladys 16, May Payne roomer*
** 1920 - Living in Kansas City Ward, Jackson Co., MO - Peed, Caroline L 51 - living with her daughter Garland Nutt and her family.*
** 1930 - Living in Long Beach, Los Angeles Co., CA - Martin, Carrie 67 wd MO KY VA*
** 1940 - Living in Tavern, Pulaski Co., MO - Nutt, Walter H 51 MO, Garland 51 MO, Lucinda C. Martin Mother in law 72 wd MO*

More About LUCINDA CAROLLINE "CARRIE" BALLARD:
Burial: Forest Hill Cemetery, Kansas City, Jackson Co., MO

More About CLAUDE WILLIAM PEED:
Burial: Forest Hill Cemetery, Kansas City, Jackson Co., MO

Notes for HARRY CURTIS BRINKLEY:
Source: 1895 Fort Scott Kansas State Census Records

** 1895 - Living in Fort Scott, MO - Brinkley, H C 29, Carrie C 26, Garland 6, Gladys 1 1/12*

More About HARRY CURTIS BRINKLEY:
Burial: Mt. Muncie Cemetery, Lansing, Leavenworth Co., KS

Children of LUCINDA BALLARD and HARRY BRINKLEY are:
14. i.   GARLAND[7] BRINKLEY, b. 08 Mar 1889, Stanberry, Gentry Co., MO; d. 19 Oct 1978, Kansas City, Wyandotte Co., KY.
     ii. GLADYS BRINKLEY, b. 07 Aug 1893, Des Moines, Polk Co., IA; d. 28 Sep 1912, Kansas City, Wyandotte Co., KY.

          More About GLADYS BRINKLEY:
          Burial: Forest Hill Cemetery, Kansas City, Jackson Co., MO

Generation No. 3

11. MARY FRANCES[7] HUSSY (SUSAN FRANCES[6] BALLARD, HARRISON[5], GARLAND[4], BLAND[3], THOMAS[2], WILLIAM[1]) was born 12 Sep 1867 in Gentry Co., MO, and died 11 Sep 1935 in Nampa, Canyon Co., ID. She married RICHARD POWERS. He was born 30 Mar 1866 in Quincy, Adams Co., IL, and died 30 Sep 1934 in Grants Pass, Josephine Co., OR.

More About MARY FRANCES HUSSY:
Burial: Kohlerlawn Cemetery, Nampa, Canyon Co., ID

More About RICHARD POWERS:
Burial: Grants Pass Masonic Pioneer Cemetery, Grants Pass, Josephine Co., OR

Child of MARY HUSSY and RICHARD POWERS is:
     i.   ROBERT B.[8] POWERS, b. 24 Mar 1896, Stanberry, Gentry Co., MO; d. 02 Jan 1935, Plainfield, Union Co., NJ; m. GERTRUDE E. HANKINS; b. 09 Aug 1897, NJ; d. 18 Oct 1976, Lakewood, Ocean Co., NJ.

          More About ROBERT B. POWERS:
          Burial: Riverside Cemetery, Toms River, Ocean Co., NJ

12. GRACE E.[7] BALLARD (ANDREW L.[6], HARRISON[5], GARLAND[4], BLAND[3], THOMAS[2], WILLIAM[1]) was born 10 Apr 1882 in MO. She married MR. WELLEN.

Child of GRACE BALLARD and MR. WELLEN is:
     i.   GERTRUDE[8] WELLEN, b. Abt. 1910, MO.

13. CLEO L.[7] BALLARD (ANDREW L.[6], HARRISON[5], GARLAND[4], BLAND[3], THOMAS[2], WILLIAM[1]) was born 23 Aug 1893 in Stanberry, MO, and died 03 Oct 1939 in St. Joseph, Buchanan Co., MO. He married THELMA RUTH HARRIS, daughter of CHARLES HARRIS and ELIZABETH HUMPHREY. She was born 04 Oct 1901 in St. Joseph, Buchanan Co., MO, and died 01 Oct 1939 in St. Joseph, Buchanan Co., MO.

Notes for CLEO L. BALLARD:
Source: Buchanan County Missouri Death Certificate, 1920-1930 Buchanan County Missouri Federal Census Records

** 1920 - Living in Buchanan Co., MO - Ballard, Cleo T 27 MO KY IL*
** 1930 - Living with Mother in law in Buchanan Co., MO - Harris, Elizabeth 64 wd Kansas, Wales Wales, Ollie 29*

MO, Etta Crouch 39 wd dau, Laurence grandson 15 MO, Thelma Ballard 28 MO IN KS, CL 37 MO KS IL, Billy L grandson 9/12 MO MO MO

More About CLEO L. BALLARD:
Burial: 05 Oct 1939, Memorial Park.

Notes for THELMA RUTH HARRIS:
Source: Buchanan County Missouri Death Certificate

Child of CLEO BALLARD and THELMA HARRIS is:

> i.   BILLY L.[8] BALLARD, b. 1929, St. Joseph, Buchanan Co., MO; d. Aft. 1930.

14.   GARLAND[7] BRINKLEY (LUCINDA CAROLLINE "CARRIE"[6] BALLARD, HARRISON[5], GARLAND[4], BLAND[3], THOMAS[2], WILLIAM[1]) *was born 08 Mar 1889 in Stanberry, Gentry Co., MO, and died 19 Oct 1978 in Kansas City, Wyandotte Co., KY. She married* WALTER H. NUTT *23 Feb 1909 in Jackson Co., MO. He was born Abt. 1889 in MO, and died Aft. 1940.*

More About GARLAND BRINKLEY:
Burial: Forest Hill Cemetery, Kansas City, Jackson Co., MO

Notes for WALTER H. NUTT:
Source: 1930 Johnson County Kansas Federal Census Records,1940 Pulaski County Missouri Federal Census Records

** 1930 - Living in Shawnee, Johnson Co., KS - Nutt, Walter H 41 MO, Garland 41 MO, Walter G 16 MO, Frances 14 MO, Dorothy M Docker 19, Howard L son in law 20*
** 1940 - Living in Tavern, Pulaski Co., MO - Nutt, Walter H 51 MO, Garland 51 MO, Lucinda C. Martin Mother in law 72 wd MO*

Children of GARLAND BRINKLEY and WALTER NUTT are:

> i.   DOROTHY MILDRED[8] NUTT, b. 26 Jun 1910, Kansas City, Wyandotte Co., KY; d. 05 Nov 1993, Johnson Co., KS; m. HOWARD L. DOCKER; b. 10 Mar 1910; d. 11 Nov 1975, Shawnee Co., KS.
>
> *More About DOROTHY MILDRED NUTT:*
> *Burial: Johnson Co., Chapel and Memorial Gardens, Overland Park, Johnson Co., KS*
>
> *More About HOWARD L. DOCKER:*
> *Burial: Johnson Co., Chapel and Memorial Gardens, Overland Park, Johnson Co., KS*
>
> ii.   WALTER GARLAND NUTT, b. 10 May 1913, MO; d. 10 Dec 1978, Gonzales Co., TX.
>
> *More About WALTER GARLAND NUTT:*
> *Burial: Gonzales Memorial Park Cemetery, Gonzales Co., TX*
>
> iii.   FRANCES C. NUTT, b. Abt. 1916, MO; d. Aft. 1930.

Isaac Newton Ballard

Generation No. 1

1. ISAAC NEWTON[2] BALLARD (JOHN[1]) *was born Mar 1804 in NC, and died Dec 1892 in TN. He married* SARAH ELMER HUTCHINSON *in TN. She was born May 1807 in VA, and died Feb 1894.*

Notes for ISAAC NEWTON BALLARD:
Source: Ballard-Ballord Bits pg 341 X-2538, Gary Farley (gfarley@pickens.net), 1850-1860 Cooper County, 1870-1880 Medicine Putnam County Missouri Federal Census Records

** 1850 - Living in Cooper Co., MO - Ballard, Newton 44 TN, Sarah 40 TN, Huston 20 TN, Granville 16 TN, Mary 12 MO, Jasper 10 MO*
** 1860 - Living in Cooper Co., MO - Ballard, Newton 56 NC, Sally 53 VA, Henry 22 MO, Jasper 19 MO*
** 1870 - Living in Medicine, Putnam Co., MO - Ballard, Newton 66 NC, Sarah 63 VA*
** 1880 - Living in Putnam Co., MO - Ballard, Newton 76 NC, Sarah E 73 VA*

Children of ISAAC BALLARD *and* SARAH HUTCHINSON *are:*
2.   i.   JAMES HUSTON[3] BALLARD, *b. May 1831, TN; d. 1904.*
            ii.   JOHN GRANVILLE BALLARD, *b. Abt. 1833, TN; d. Aft. 1850, TN.*
            iii. MARY BALLARD, *b. 1838, MO; d. Aft. 1850.*
3.   iv.   HENRY COLUMBUS BALLARD, *b. 06 Jun 1838, Cooper Co., MO; d. 03 Dec 1930, Medicine, Putnam Co., MO.*
4.   v.   JASPER NEWTON BALLARD, *b. Bet. 1841 - 1842, Bates Co., MO; d. Aft. 1900, Henry Co., MO (66 yrs).*

Generation No. 2

2. JAMES HUSTON[3] BALLARD (ISAAC NEWTON[2], JOHN[1]) *was born May 1831 in TN, and died 1904. He married* MARY E. COLBERT. *She was born May 1841 in MO, and died Aft. 1900.*

Notes for JAMES HUSTON BALLARD:
Source: 1860 Cooper County Missouri Federal Census Records, 1870-1900 Putnam County Missouri Federal Census Records

** 1860 - Living in Lebanon Cooper Co., MO - Ballard, J. H 29 TN, Mary 19 MO, Duke 3 MO, Newman 3/12 MO*
** 1870 - Living in Medicine, Putnam Co., MO - Ballard, James 39 TN, Mary E MO, Hutchinson 13 MO, Sarah 8 MO, Rhoda C. 5 MO, William N. 2 MO*
** 1880 - Living in Medicine, Putnam Co., MO - Ballard, James H 40 farmer TN, Mary E 39 MO, Duke 22 MO, Isabell 17, Roda 14 MO, William N 12 MO, James H 10 MO, Frank M 8 MO, Mary K 2 MO*
** 1900 - Living in Medicine, Putnam Co., MO - Ballard, James H - May 1831 TN, Mary E - May 1841 MO, Jessie O (f) July 1880 MO*

More About JAMES HUSTON BALLARD:
Burial: Lucerne Cemetery., Lucerne, Putnam Co., MO

Children of JAMES BALLARD *and* MARY COLBERT *are:*
            i.   HUTCHINSON[4] BALLARD, *b. 1857, MO; d. Aft. 1870.*
            ii.   DUKE BALLARD, *b. 1858, MO; d. Aft. 1880.*
            iii. NEWMAN BALLARD, *b. 1860.*
            iv.   SARAH BALLARD, *b. 1862, MO; d. Aft. 1870.*
            v.   ISABELL BALLARD, *b. 1863, MO; d. Aft. 1880.*
            vi.   RHODA C. BALLARD, *b. 1865, MO; d. Aft. 1880.*
            vi.   WILLIAM N. BALLARD, *b. 1868, MO; d. Aft. 1880.*

	viii.	JAMES H. BALLARD, b. 1870, MO; d. Aft. 1880.
5.	*ix.*	JOHN HENRY BALLARD, b. 06 Jun 1870, Lucerne, Putnam Co., MO; d. 23 May 1940, Lucerne, Putnam Co., MO.
	x.	FRANK M. BALLARD, b. 1872, MO; d. Aft. 1880.
	xi.	MARY K. BALLARD, b. 1878, MO; d. Aft. 1880.
	xii.	JESSIE O. BALLARD, b. Jul 1881, MO; d. Aft. 1900.

3. HENRY COLUMBUS[3] BALLARD (*ISAAC NEWTON[2], JOHN[1]*) *was born 06 Jun 1838 in Cooper Co., MO, and died 03 Dec 1930 in Medicine, Putnam Co., MO. He married NANCY PERRY JOHNSON 05 Nov 1868. She was born 06 Apr 1853 in Putnam Co., MO, and died 12 Dec 1925 in Medicine, Putnam Co., MO.*

Notes for HENRY COLUMBUS BALLARD:
Source: Ballard-Ballord Bits pg 341 X-2541, 1870-1910 Putnam County Missouri Federal Census Records, Putnam County Missouri Death Certificate

** 1870 - Living in York, Putnam Co., MO - Ballard, Henry 32 MO, Nancy 17 MO*
** 1880 - Living in York, Putnam Co., MO - Ballard, Henry C 41 farmer MO AL TN, Nancy B 27, Cora E 6*
** 1910 - Living in Medicine, Putnam Co., MO - Ballard, Henry C 71 MO NC VA, Nancy P 51 - 1child/1living MO MO MO*

More About HENRY COLUMBUS BALLARD:
Burial: 05 Dec 1930, Lucerne, MO

Notes for NANCY PERRY JOHNSON:
Source: Medicine, Putnam County Missouri State Board of Health Bureau of Vital Statistics Certificate of Death # 37306

More About NANCY PERRY JOHNSON:
Burial: Lucerne, MO

Child of HENRY BALLARD and NANCY JOHNSON is:

| | *i.* | CORA E.[4] BALLARD, b. 1874, MO; d. lived in Lucerne Co MO in 1912; m. ORVILLE BLACKMAN. |

4. JASPER NEWTON[3] BALLARD (*ISAAC NEWTON[2], JOHN[1]*) *was born Bet. 1841 - 1842 in Bates Co., MO, and died Aft. 1900 in Henry Co., MO (66 yrs). He married JOSEPHINE L. STARKE. She was born 1845 in Cooper Co., MO, and died Aft. 1900.*

Notes for JASPER NEWTON BALLARD:
Source: 1870-1900 Bates County Missouri Federal Census Records

** 1870 - Living in Bates Co., MO - Ballard, Jasper 28 MO, Josephine 25 MO, Eugenia 1 MO*
** 1880 - Living in Bates Co., MO - Ballard, J N 39, Josephine L 35, LB 7, ES 5, Josephine 2, Jassie 4/12*
** 1900 - Living in Bates Co., MO - Ballard, Jasper N - March 1842, Josephine L - Sep 1849, John S - July 1882 MO*

Children of JASPER BALLARD and JOSEPHINE STARKE are:

	i.	EUGENIA[4] BALLARD, b. 1869, MO; d. Aft. 1870.
	ii.	L. B. BALLARD, b. 1873, MO; d. Aft. 1880.
	iii.	EMMETT S. BALLARD, DR., b. 23 Oct 1874, Bates Co., MO; d. 23 Oct 1874, St. Joseph, Buchanan Co., MO; m. GERTRUDE K. STARKE.

Notes for EMMETT S. BALLARD, DR.:
Source: Buchanan County Missouri Death Certificates

More About EMMETT S. BALLARD, DR.:
Burial: Mt. Mora Cemetery, MO

    iv.   JASSIE BALLARD, *b. 1880, MO; d. Aft. 1880.*
    v.   JOHN S. BALLARD, *b. Jul 1882, MO; d. Aft. 1900.*
    vi.   JASPER NEWTON BALLARD, *b. 05 May 1882, Bates Co., MO; d. 18 May 1930, Bates Co., MO.*

Notes for JASPER NEWTON BALLARD:

Source: Bates County Missouri Death Certificate

Generation No. 3

5. JOHN HENRY[4] BALLARD (*JAMES HUSTON*[3], *ISAAC NEWTON*[2], *JOHN*[1]) *was born 06 Jun 1870 in Lucerne, Putnam Co., MO, and died 23 May 1940 in Lucerne, Putnam Co., MO. He married (1) MARY JANET Bef. 1898. She was born Feb 1870 in Monroe Co., VA, and died Aft. 1920. He married (2) NETTIE M. Bef. 1930. She was born 1894 in MO, and died Aft. 1930.*

Notes for JOHN HENRY BALLARD:

Source: Putnam County Missouri Death Certificate, 1900-1920 Putnam County Missouri Federal Census Records

** 1900 - Living in Medicine, Putnam Co., MO - Ballard, John H - June 1870 MO TN MO, Mary J - Feb 1870 MO IL IL, Vivian - Oct 1898 MO, Glenn J - Mar 1900 MO*
** 1910 - Living in Medicine, Putnam Co., MO - Ballard, John 39 MO TN TN, Mary 40 MO IL IL, Vivian 11 MO, Glen J 10 MO*
** 1920 - Living in Medicine, Putnam Co., MO - Ballard, John H 49 wd MO, Vivian 21 MO, Glen J 19 MO*
** 1930 - Living in Union, Putnam Co., MO - Ballard, John H 59 MO, Nettie M 36 MO, Levina Collins 18 step daughter*

More About JOHN HENRY BALLARD:

Burial: Lucerne, Putnam Co., MO

Children of JOHN BALLARD and MARY JANET are:

    i.   VIVIAN[5] BALLARD, *b. Oct 1898, Putnam Co., MO; d. Aft. 1920.*
    ii.   GLENN J. BALLARD, *b. Mar 1900, Putnam Co., MO; d. Aft. 1920.*

James Ballard

Generation No. 1

1. JAMES[5] BALLARD (BLAND WILLIAM[4], BLAND[3], BLAND[2], WILLIAM[1]) *was born 30 Mar 1783 in Linn's Station, Shelby Co., KY, and died 30 Nov 1841 in Oldham Co., KY. He married* ELIZABETH "BETSY" SHACKELFORD *19 Nov 1812 in Shelby Co., KY, daughter of* JOHN SHACKELFORD *and* ANN. *She was born 11 Sep 1785 in GA, and died 01 Mar 1853 in Oldham Co., KY.*

Notes for JAMES BALLARD:
Source: James Harold Smith, LDS Records, Martha Floyd Miller (me2miller@comcast.net)
** Participated in the expedition to White River under John Hardin.*
** Escaped the massacre of the family on 31 March 1788.*

Notes for ELIZABETH "BETSY" SHACKELFORD:
Source: John Shackelford's Will

** 1819 - From the will of John Shackelford, Shelby, KY dated 6-10-1819, To my daughter Milly Shackelford I give three Negroes James and his children Lucy & Richmond (Note Milly did not marry and died in MO), And to the heirs of my daughter Betsy Ballard, two negroes; Sarah & Squire. To Polly Ann Hewlett (Hulett) I give three negroes: Caroline, Phoebe & Laco. My son William Shackelford, my negro boy; Nat. My son Sterling Shackelford, my negro boy; Barber. After the death of my wife Anne Shackelford, all my personal property & my two negroes: Cupid & Dilce to be sold.*

Children of JAMES BALLARD *and* ELIZABETH SHACKELFORD *are:*

2.   i.   ELIZABETH ANN "LIZZIE"[6] BALLARD, *b. Bet. 1820 - 1825, Shelby Co., KY; d. Bet. 1870 - 1880, Hardin Co., KY.*
      ii.   JOHN THOMAS BALLARD, *b. Abt. 1814, Shelby Co., KY.*
      iii.   MARY BALLARD, *b. Abt. 1815, Shelby Co., KY.*
3.   iv.   BENJAMIN H. BALLARD, *b. 23 Jan 1817, Shelby Co., KY; d. 22 Jan 1896, Clark Co., MO.*
      v.   ABSALUM BALLARD, *b. Abt. 1818, KY.*

         Notes for ABSALUM BALLARD:
         Martha Miller states that he is not the son of James and Elizabeth

      vi.   MARTHA BALLARD, *b. Abt. 1820, KY.*

         Notes for MARTHA BALLARD:
         Source: Martha Miller states that this Martha is not the daughter of James and Elizabeth

4.   vii.   BLAND WILLIAM BALLARD, *b. 23 Jul 1824, Oldham Co., KY; d. 18 Mar 1904, Aquilla, Hill Co., TX.*
      viii.   DOROTHY BALLARD, *b. Abt. 1826, Oldham Co., KY; d. Abt. 1838, Oldham Co., KY.*

         Notes for DOROTHY BALLARD:
         Source: Martha Miller (me2miller@comcast.net)

5.   ix.   JAMES THOMAS BALLARD, *b. 30 Sep 1830, Oldham Co., KY; d. 18 Sep 1868, Clark Co., MO.*

Generation No. 2

2. ELIZABETH ANN "LIZZIE"[6] BALLARD (JAMES[5], BLAND WILLIAM[4], BLAND[3], BLAND[2], WILLIAM[1]) *was born Bet. 1820 –*

1825 in Shelby Co., KY, and died Bet. 1870 - 1880 in Hardin Co., KY. She married BLAND HARRISON WILLIAMSON *28 Sep 1837 in Oldham Co., KY, son of* JOHN WILLIAMSON *and* CHARITY WHITAKER. *He was born 1809 in KY, and died Aft. 1870.*

Notes for BLAND HARRISON WILLIAMSON:
Source: 1850 Hardin County Kentucky Federal Census Records, 1860 McLean County Kentucky Federal Census Records, 1870 Mississippi County Arkansas Federal Census Records, Martha Floyd Miller

** His name is found as Blan on some documents and Bland on others.*
** 1845 - Shelby Co., KY - Know all men by these presents that (we/m) Bland. W. Williamson (husband of Elizabeth Williamson the daughter of James Ballard decd) and Benjamin H Ballard; for and in consideration of the sum of two hundred and forty five dollars and Seventy three dollars cents to each of us this day paid by the (execution) of his promissory note for said amount; do hereby give grant Sell and convey unto Bland W. Ballard all our right (unto) and interest in and to the Slaves bequeathed to us by James Ballard decd which were derived from the estate of John Shackleford deceased. (-?-) Fanny and Barber her child and Sam and also all our right (unto) and interest in and to the to the personal property (to wit horses cows (notes) money (-?-) of the Said James Ballard decd; bequeathed to us as a part of his devisees; hereby transferring to the Said Bland W. Ballard all our right (unto) and interest in and to the said property, and forever releasing all claims to the Slaves here in mentioned and to Said personal estate. Witness our hands and Seals this 19th day of August 1845*

  (Test/Wit)   *Benjamin H. Ballard {Seal}*
  M O Rodman   *Blan H Williamson {Seal}*

** 1845 - Transcribed by Martha Floyd Miller on 15 September 2015:*
A document belonging to Bland William Ballard ((1824 KY – 1904 TX), son of James & Elizabeth (Shackelford) Ballard, found in the papers of Bland W.'s daughter, Mary Adeline (Ballard) Hampton, and in the possession of Mary A.'s great grandson, Edgar R. Miller on the above date.
Side 1
Bland H Williamson & Benjamin Ballard

        }
        } Release
        }

Elizabeth Ballard

Side 2
Know all men by these presents that the Bland W Williamson and Benjamin Ballard for and in consideration that Bland W Ballard has this day executed to each of us his promissory note for the sum of two hundred and forty five dollars and Seventy three cents, do hereby release Elizabeth Ballard executrix of James Ballard deceased, from all claims which we hold against her as said executrix hereby acknowledging that we have received our full interest in and to the Slaves bequeathed to us by said James Ballard decd which were devised from the estate of John Shackleford deceased; and other to the personal property so bequeathed to us as his devisees; hereby forever relinquishing all claim or claims against her as such executrix to the will of Said James Ballard only claiming our interest into and to Squire after the death of the Said Elizabeth In witness whereof we have hereunto Set our hands and Seals this 19th day of August 1845

  Test(Wit?)   *Blan H. Williamson {Seal}*
  M O Rodman   *Benjamin H Ballard {Seal}*

** 1850 - Living in Hardin Co., KY - Williamson, Bland H 41 miller KY, Elizabeth A 28 KY, Charity E 11 KY, Mary 8 KY, Malvine 5 KY, Amasetta 0 KY, James Skus 17 farmer KY, Bland Williamson 12 KY*
** 1860 - Living in McLean Co., KY - Williamson, Blan H 51 farmer KY, Elizabeth A 39 KY, Charity E 20 KY, Mary J 17 KY, Malvina 14 KY, Ammasettee 11 KY, Lavinia 7 KY, unnamed (infant) (hard to read - looks like 2 1/12) KY*
** 1870 - Living in Monroe, Mississippi Co., AR - Williamson, B H 62 farmer KY, Eliza 9 KY, Blan 33 farm laborer KY, Loflin, Mary J 27 KY, Alice 7/12, Williamson, Hattie 16 KY, John J 12 KY, Sarah E 5 KY, Mary 40 servant*

Children of ELIZABETH BALLARD *and* BLAND WILLIAMSON *are:*
6.   *i.*   CHARITY E.[7] WILLIAMSON, *b. Abt. 1840, Hardin Co., KY; d. Aft. 1862.*

7.   ii.   *MARY JUNE WILLIAMSON, b. Abt. 1843, Hardin Co., KY; d. Aft. 1880.*
8.   iii.   *MALVENIA WILLIAMSON, b. Abt. 1846, Hardin Co., KY.*
      iv.   *AMASETTA Y. WILLIAMSON, b. Dec 1849, Hardin Co., KY; d. Aft. 1910; m. JAMES A. ASHLIN, 04 Mar 1880, Mississippi Co., AR; b. 13 Mar 1847, TN; d. 20 Feb 1917.*

            Notes for AMASETTA Y. WILLIAMSON:
            Source: Martha Floyd Miller

            Notes for JAMES A. ASHLIN:
            Source: 1900 Mississippi County Arkansas Federal Census Records, Martha Floyd Miller
            ** 1900 - Living in Chickasawba, Mississippi Co., AR - Ashlin, James A - Mar 1847 TN VA VA, Armasetta Y - Dec 1849 KY KY KY, John Williamson bro in law - May 1858 wd KY, Lizzie V - Nov 1895 MO, Blan H - Aug 1897 MO, Ella E Ashlin adopted - Dec 1880 MO, boarders: Daniel M Dunn, James W Smith, Jeff Montgomery, Graham, Thomas Williams*

            More About JAMES A. ASHLIN:
            Burial: Maple Grove Cemetery, Blytheville, Mississippi Co., AR

      v.   *LEVINA WILLIAMSON, b. 27 Apr 1853, Hardin Co., KY.*

            Notes for LEVINA WILLIAMSON:
            Source: Hardin County Kentucky Birth Records

      vi.   *BLAN H. WILLIAMSON, b. 28 Aug 1857, MO; d. Aft. 1870.*
9.   vii. *JOHN JAMES WILLIAMSON, b. 18 May 1858, McLean Co., KY; d. 10 Nov 1952, Cameron Co., TX.*
      viii. *FEMALE WILLIAMSON, b. 09 Aug 1861, McLean Co., KY.*

            Notes for FEMALE WILLIAMSON:
            Source: Kentucky Birth Records

      ix.   *SARAH E. WILLIAMSON, b. 09 Aug 1862, McLean Co., KY; d. Aft. 1880.*

            Notes for SARAH E. WILLIAMSON:
            Source: 1880 Mississippi County Arkansas Federal Census Records, Martha Floyd Miller
            ** 1880 - Living in Monroe, Mississippi Co., AR - Living with brother - Williamson Sarah 16 KY*

3.   *BENJAMIN H.[6] BALLARD (JAMES[5], BLAND WILLIAM[4], BLAND[3], BLAND[2], WILLIAM[1]) was born 23 Jan 1817 in Shelby Co., KY, and died 22 Jan 1896 in Clark Co., MO. He married EMELINE BASKETT 27 Nov 1839 in Shelby Co., KY. She was born 04 Feb 1821 in Shelby Co., KY, and died 24 Mar 1896 in Clark Co., MO.*

Notes for BENJAMIN H. BALLARD:
Source: 1850 Oldham Co., KY Federal Census Records, 1860 - 1880 Clark County Missouri Federal Census Records, Shelby County Kentucky Marriage Records

** 1845 - Know all men by these presents that m Bland W Williamson (husband of Elizabeth Williamson the daughter of James Ballard dec'd) and Benjamin H Ballard for and in consideration of the sum of two hundred and forty five dollars and Seventy three (dollars crossed out) cents to each of us this day paid by the ..... of his promising note for said amount; do hereby give grant sell and convey unto Bland W. Ballard all the rights thereto and in ... in and to the Items bequeathed to us by James Ballard decd which derived from the estate of John Shackelford deceased. .... Fanny and Bets.... her child and Sam. And also all our right ... and interest in and to the personal property (to wit horses ... ... money ... of the said James Ballard decd; bequeathed to us as a part of his devider .... to the said Bland W. Ballard all our right ... and interest in and to said property and forever releasing all claims to the Items here in menchined and to said personal estate witnessed our hand and Seals this 19th day of August 1845 Benjamin H. Ballard, Blan H. Williamson. (Wit. M O Rodman)*

1850 - Living in Oldham Co., KY - Ballard, B H 32 farmer KY, Emeline 28 KY, Sarah 9 KY, Mary 7 KY, Jas W 5 KY, Job 9/12 KY, Elizabeth 60 GA
1860 - Living in Union, Clark Co., MO - Ballard, B. H 43 KY, Emeline 40 KY, Sarah E 19 KY, Mary F. 16 KY, Jas W 14 KY, Job 10 KY, Edmonia R 8 KY, Robt. M 6 MO, Mariat 1 MO
1870 - Living in Lincoln, Clark Co., MO - Ballard, Benj H. 53 KY, Emeline 48 KY, Job 20 KY, Edmonia 18 KY, Robert 15 MO, George 13 MO, Annetta 10 MO
1880 - Living in Clark Co., MO - Ballard, Benjamin H 63 KY KY KY, Emaline 59 KY A VA, Annette L. 19 MO, Walter P. 19 nephew MO KY KY

More About BENJAMIN H. BALLARD:
Burial: Kahoka Cemetery, Clark Co., MO

More About EMELINE BASKETT:
Burial: Kahoka Cemetery, Clark Co., MO

Children of BENJAMIN BALLARD and EMELINE BASKETT are:

10.	i.	SARAH ELIZA[7] BALLARD, b. 02 Dec 1840, KY; d. 31 Jan 1929, Clark Co., MO.
11.	ii.	MARY FRANCES BALLARD, b. 05 Dec 1843, KY; d. 09 Dec 1914, Clark Co., MO.
12.	iii.	WILLIAM JAMES BALLARD, b. 28 Aug 1845, Oldham Co., KY; d. 18 Jun 1918, Fresno Co., CA.
	iv.	JOB BALLARD, b. 1849, Oldham Co., KY; d. 28 Jul 1880, Clark Co., MO.

Notes for JOB BALLARD:
Source: Martha Miller

13.	v.	EDMONIA BALLARD, b. 1852, Oldham Co., KY; d. 03 May 1874, Clark Co., MO.
14.	vi.	ROBERT MITCHELL BALLARD, b. 19 May 1854, MO; d. 21 Apr 1911, Polk Co., OR.
	vii.	GEORGE W. BALLARD, b. 28 Jan 1857, Clark Co., MO; d. 09 Sep 1926, Clark Co., MO; m. SUSAN A. LEWIS, 24 Nov 1881, Clark Co., MO; b. 18 Apr 1856, Clark Co., MO; d. 13 Apr 1929, Clark Co., MO.

Notes for GEORGE W. BALLARD:
Source: Clark County Missouri Death Certificate, Martha Miller, 1900 Clark County Missouri Federal Census Records
1900 - Living in Sweet Home, Clark Co., MO - Ballard, George W - Jan 1857 MO KY KY, Sussan - Apr 1858 - 0 children, 0 living

More About GEORGE W. BALLARD:
Burial: Kahoka, MO

More About SUSAN A. LEWIS:
Burial: Kahoka Cemetery, Kahoka, Clark Co., MO

    viii.   ANNETTA "NETTIE" BALLARD, b. 10 Jul 1861, Clark Co., MO; d. 23 Nov 1927, Clark Co., MO.

Notes for ANNETTA "NETTIE" BALLARD:
Source: Clark County Missouri Death Certificate, Martha Miller, 1900 Clark County Missouri Federal Census Records
1900 - Living in Kahoka, Clark Co., MO - Living with her sister Mary Hickerson family - Ballard, Nettie - July 1861 MO KY KY

More About ANNETTA "NETTIE" BALLARD:
Burial: Kahoka Cemetery, Kahoka, Clark Co., MO

4. BLAND WILLIAM[6] BALLARD (JAMES[5], BLAND WILLIAM[4], BLAND[3], BLAND[2], WILLIAM[1]) *was born 23 Jul 1824 in Oldham Co., KY, and died 18 Mar 1904 in Aquilla, Hill Co., TX. He married* PARTHENA CULL *15 Jul 1845 in Henry Co., KY, daughter of* NATHAN CULL *and* REBECCA RAWLINGS. *She was born 27 Jul 1826 in Henry Co., KY, and died 13 Mar 1888 in Aquilla, Hill Co., TX.*

Notes for BLAND WILLIAM BALLARD:
Sources: Hill County Texas Probate Records Volume 18-19 pages 242-244, Martha Floyd Miller (me2miller@comcast.net), Elijah Nuttle Ballard notes (Rec'd from KY Hist. Soc). KY Marriages Henry County Kentucky 1800-1850 CD#229, 1850 Scotland County Missouri Federal Census Records, 1860-1870 Saline County Missouri Federal Census Records, 1880 - 1900 Hill County Texas Federal Census Records

** 1850 - Living in Scotland Co., MO - Ballard, Bland W 25 KY, Pathina 23 KY, John E. 4 KY, Benjamin W 1 KY, James 19 KY*
** 1860 - Living in Arrow Rock, Saline Co., MO - Ballard, Bland W 36 KY, Mrs. Catherine 34 KY, John E 14 KY, Benjamin 12 KY, Bland A 8 MO, Mary A MO, James T. 2 MO*
** 1870 - Living in Marshall, Saline Co., MO - Ballard, B. W 45 KY, Mrs. Parthena 44 KY, Bland 18 MO, Mary A 15 MO, James J 12 MO, Elijah 9 MO, Annie 2 MO*
** 1880 - Living in Hill Co., TX - (blotched page - hard to read) - Ballard, ?? 56 farmer KY KY GA, P ? 54 has consumption KY KY KY, E N 20 son MO, Annie E 12 MO, Sp ??? 30 male school teacher*
** 1900 - Living in Hill Co., TX - Ballard, B W - July 1824 KY KY GA, Annie E - June 1867 MO KY KY*

** 1904 - Hill Co., TX - page 242 - Proof of Will - The State of Texas County of Hill } - Estate of Bland W. Ballard, Deceased. Proof of Last Will and Testament of Bland W. Ballard Deceased.*
This Day personally appeared in open Court, E. R. Boyd, who being duly sworn as a witness in the above entitled matter, and examined on behalf of the applicant to prove said Will, says: I was well acquainted with Bland W. Ballard deceased, during his lifetime; I knew the above decedent for about thirty years before his death; the signature of said deceased to the instruments now shown to me and offered for probate as his last Will and Testament and codicil thereto, and bearing date Jan Seventh in the year A.D. 1901 and July 2 1904 respectively, was made by the deceased at his home in Aquilla, Texas in the presence of myself, E. R. Boyd and I being over the age of fourteen years. At the time of the making of said Will and Codicil, the Testator was of sound and disposing mind and memory, and he declared the said Will and codicil, so made by him to be his last Will and Testament and Codicil thereto, and I thereupon signed my name as a witness to said will and Codicil and I further state that I am acquainted with the handwriting of said testator and know that said will is written entirely with his own hand at the request of the said Testator, in his presence. The said deceased, at the time of the executing of said instrument was about 76 years of age; the said Bland W. Ballard departed this life on the 18th day of March A. D. 1904, about three years after making said Will. E. R. Boyd.
Sworn to and subscribed before me, this 20th day of May A. D. 1904. M L. Wiginton, Clerk County Court Hill County Texas. By R W Hunt Deputy With Will and Codicils in words and figures as follows, to wit:
page 243 - WILL - A will - In the name of God, I Bland W. Ballard of Aquilla Hill County Texas, being of sound mind, and realizing that all men must die, do make my last will and Testament on earth after defraying my funeral Expenses, and paying all my just debts, I will my sons John E. and Ben W JT and EN Ballard and my daughter Mary A Thompson one Dollard each, having given them money and property previously now give by this my will my daughter Anna E Ballard the remainder of my property, consisting of Lots 8 and 9 and part of 6 & 7 Block 20 with my dwelling and all improvements, also all stock and household goods I may have. Also lots 1,2 and 3 in same block, also lot 1 in Block 21 together with my storehouse and any and all goods therein; to have and to hold the same in consideration of her long painstaking care of me in my old age. I hereby annul all former wills made by me. This seventh day of January one thousand, nine hundred and one. I appoint my son J. T. Ballard my sole executor. Bland W. Ballard. Witness E. R Boyd. Filed Mch 21st day of Mch 1904 M L Wiginton Co Clerk, Hill County TX
** 1904 - Codicil - Aquilla Texas, Feb 2, 1904 - In the name of God, I Bland W. Ballard being of sound mine and knowing death comes to all men I desire to make this my last Will and testament, Having previously made my Will I desire to add this much more to said Will which was duly signed by E. R. Boyd in said Will for the kindness and care that i have received from my Daughter Anna E. Ballard I gave most of my property. Now since said will was written I have accumulated other properties all of which I desire my Daughter Anna E. Ballard shall at my death after paying all my just debts and funeral Expenses have and as in former will I appoint my son James T. Ballard my sole executor. Bland W. Ballard. Witness E. R. Boyd - Filed Mch 21st 1904, ML Wiginton Co Clerk Hill Co., Texas by RW Hunt, Deputy.*

** 1904 - Hill Co., TX - Application for Probate of Will*
In the matter of the Estate of Bland W Ballard Deceased} In County Court Mch Term 1904
To the Honorable L. C. Hill, Judge of the County - County- Court of Hill County, State of Texas:
This the application of J T Ballard respectfully shows: That Bland W. Ballard is dead: that he died on or about the 18th day of March 1904, at his home at Aquilla, Hill County in the State of Texas: that said deceased of the time of his death was a resident of the county of Hill in the State of Texas. That he left estate consisting of Real and personal property: That the nature and probable value of said property: That the nature and probable value of said property (continued on page 244) - are as follows, to wit: Lots 8 and 9 and parts of 6 & 7 in block 20 in Aquilla together with all improvements, also lots 1, 2 & 3 in same block - Lot 1 in Block 21 together with store house and stock of merchandise, and all other property all of the probable value of $2000.00: That said deceased left a written will and codicil having date 7th day of January A. D. 1901, and the codicil having date Feb 2nd 1904 in the possession of Miss Anna E Ballard which your applicant believes and therefore alleges to be the last will and testament and codicil of said deceased, and which is hereunto filed. That J. T. Ballard the person named in said Will as executor thereof, resides at Sauce, Coke County, Texas That said J. T. Ballard is not disqualified by law from accepting Letters - Testamentary up on said estate

Wherefore, applicant pray that citation issue herein, as the law provides, and that up on hearing and the proofs addum said will and codicil be admitted to probate, and that letters issue to applicant and that all other necessary and proper orders be made in the premises. J. T. Ballard applicant. Date: March 21, 1904, Filed March 21, 1904, M. L Wiginton, Clerk County Hill County Texas, by (?), Deputy

More About BLAND WILLIAM BALLARD:
Burial: Hillsboro Cemetery, Hillsboro, Hill Co., TX

Notes for PARTHENA CULL:
Source: me2miller@comcast.net

More About PARTHENA CULL:

Burial: Hillsboro Cemetery, Hillsboro, Hill Co., TX

Children of BLAND BALLARD and PARTHENA CULL are:

       i.   JOHN EDWARD[7] BALLARD, b. 04 May 1846, LaGrange, Oldham Co., KY; d. 21 Jun 1917, Kiowa Co., OK.

15.   ii.   BENJAMIN WILLIAM BALLARD, b. 24 Sep 1848, LaGrange, Oldham Co., KY; d. 08 Oct 1915, Whitney, Hill Co., TX.

      iii.   BLAND AUGUSTUS BALLARD, b. 07 May 1852, Clark Co., MO; d. 29 Nov 1880, Whitney, Hill Co., TX.

          Notes for BLAND AUGUSTUS BALLARD:
          Source: Martha Floyd Miller (me2miller@comcast.net)

          More About BLAND AUGUSTUS BALLARD:
          Burial: Hillsboro Cemetery, Hillsboro, Hill Co., TX

16.   iv.   MARY ADALINE BALLARD, b. 27 Jan 1855, Clark Co., MO; d. 23 Aug 1947, Cleburne, Johnson Co., TX.

      v.   JAMES THOMAS BALLARD, b. 12 Nov 1857, Saline Co., MO; d. 06 Sep 1920, San Angelo, Tom Green Co., TX; m. ETTA E. SWAFFORD, 12 Dec 1889, Limestone Co., TX.

          Notes for JAMES THOMAS BALLARD:
          Source: Martha Floyd Miller (me2miller@comcast.net)

      vi.   ELIJAH NUTTLE BALLARD, b. 24 Dec 1860, Saline Co., MO; d. 22 Jul 1947, La Junta, Otero Co., CO.

Notes for ELIJAH NUTTLE BALLARD:
Source: Elijah Nuttles records, Martha Floyd Miller (me2miller@comcast.net)

More About ELIJAH NUTTLE BALLARD:
Burial: Fairview Cemetery, La Junta, Otero Co., CO

   vii.   HARRIET LEE BALLARD, b. 17 Jun 1863, Saline Co., MO; d. 05 Aug 1868, Saline Co., MO.

           Notes for HARRIET LEE BALLARD:
           Source: Martha Floyd Miller (me2miller@comcast.net)

   viii.   ANNIE ELIZA BALLARD, b. 09 May 1867, Saline Co., MO; d. Aft. 1947, Winslow, Washington Co., AR; m. JAMES J. POE; b. Abt. 1862, AL; d. 24 Sep 1945, Washington Co., AR.

           Notes for ANNIE ELIZA BALLARD:
           Source: Martha Floyd Miller (me2miller@comcast.net)

5.   JAMES THOMAS[6] BALLARD (JAMES[5], BLAND WILLIAM[4], BLAND[3], BLAND[2], WILLIAM[1]) was born 30 Sep 1830 in Oldham Co., KY, and died 18 Sep 1868 in Clark Co., MO. He married LOTSY JANE CROSS 28 Feb 1854. She was born Abt. 1834 in KY, and died 19 Jul 1878 in Clark Co., MO.

Notes for JAMES THOMAS BALLARD:
Source: 1860 Clark County Missouri Federal Census Records, Ann (ROKKYMTNHI@aol.com), LDS data, Martha Floyd Miller
** 1860 - Living in Union, Clark Co., MO - Ballard, J T 30 KY, Lotsey 26 KY, Mary 5 MO, B 3 MO, Martha 2 MO, Sally Howerton 22 teacher*

Notes for LOTSY JANE CROSS:
Source: 1870 Union Clark County Missouri Federal Census Records, Probate records

** 1868 - Clark Co., MO Probate Records - Know all Men by these Presents: That we Lotsey Ballard of Clark County State of Missouri as principal and Henry Black and James Madison Force of Clark Co., Missouri Securities acknowledge ourselves to be held and firmly bound unto the State of Missouri in the Sum of one Thousand Dollars for the payment of Which we bind ourselves our heirs, executors and Administrators firmly by these presents. Sealed with our Seals and dated this Second day of November AD 1868.*
The condition of the above bond if the said Lotsey Ballard, Administratrix of the Estate of James T. Ballard Deceased Shall faithfully administrators Said Estate, account for pay and deliver all money and property of said Estate and performs all other things Touching Said Administration required by Same or the Law or the order on decree of any County having Jurisdiction then the above bound to be void otherwise to remain in full force. Lotsey Ballard (seal), Henry Black (seal), James M Force (seal)
** 1868 - November 2 - State of Missouri County of Clark} - Lotsey Ballard being duly sworn Make oath that James T. Ballard died without will as far as She Knows and believes, leaving the following named heirs Mary E Ballard, Bland W Ballard, Martha J Ballard, Walter P Ballard Sarah Ellen Ballard and that she will make a perfect inventory of and faithfully administer all the Estate of the Deceased and Pay the Debts, as far as the assets will extend and the Law direct and account for and pay all assets which shall come into his possession or knowledge. Subscribed and Sworn to before me this 2nd day of November 1868 James Starr, Justice of the Peace filed Nov 2nd 1868*

** 1870 - Living in Union, Clark Co., MO - Ballard, Lotsy 4 KY, Mary 15 MO, Bland 13 MO, Martha 11 MO, Walter 8 MO, Ella 4 MO*

Children of JAMES BALLARD and LOTSY CROSS are:
      i.   MARY ELIZABETH[7] BALLARD, b. 02 Mar 1855, Clark Co., MO; d. 17 Mar 1923, Clark Co., MO; m.

      GEORGE WASHINGTON BLACK, 06 Sep 1871, Clark Co., MO.

ii. *BLAND W. BALLARD, b. 23 Oct 1856, Clark Co., MO; d. 1923.*

   Notes for BLAND W. BALLARD:
   Source: 1880 Clark County Missouri Federal Census Records, Martha Floyd Miller
   ** 1880 - Living in Union, Clark Co., MO - Ballard, Bland 23 laborer MO East VA KY*

iii. *MARTHA JANE BALLARD, b. 23 Feb 1859, Clark Co., MO; d. Aft. 1868.*
iv. *WALTER P. BALLARD, b. 14 Feb 1861, Clark Co., MO; d. 30 Jan 1944, TX.*
v. *JAMES PRICE BALLARD, b. 23 Feb 1863, Clark Co., MO; d. 1923.*
vi. *GARRIET ELIZA BALLARD, b. 03 Jun 1865, Clark Co., MO; d. 1923.*
vii. *SARA ELLEN BALLARD, b. 06 May 1867, Clark Co., MO; d. 22 Dec 1897; m. ZODAK LOVELACE BROWN, 06 Mar 1888, Wyaconda, Clark Co., MO.*

   Notes for SARA ELLEN BALLARD:
   Source: Martha Floyd Miller

Generation No. 3

6. *CHARITY E.[7] WILLIAMSON (ELIZABETH ANN "LIZZIE"[6] BALLARD, JAMES[5], BLAND WILLIAM[4], BLAND[3], BLAND[2], WILLIAM[1]) was born Abt. 1840 in Hardin Co., KY, and died Aft. 1862. She married JAMES WALKER BAIRD 02 Jan 1862 in McLean Co., KY. He was born 1838, and died 1864.*

Notes for JAMES WALKER BAIRD:
Source: McLean County Kentucky Marriage Records.

Child of CHARITY WILLIAMSON and JAMES BAIRD is:
17.   i. *JAMES B.[8] BAIRD, b. 30 Dec 1862, Daviess Co., KY; d. 18 May 1951, Daviess Co., KY.*

7. *MARY JUNE[7] WILLIAMSON (ELIZABETH ANN "LIZZIE"[6] BALLARD, JAMES[5], BLAND WILLIAM[4], BLAND[3], BLAND[2], WILLIAM[1]) was born Abt. 1843 in Hardin Co., KY, and died Aft. 1880. She married LOFLIN 07 Jun 1868 in AR.*

Notes for MARY JUNE WILLIAMSON:
Source: 1880 Mississippi County Arkansas Federal Census Records

** 1880 - Living in Monroe, Mississippi Co., AR - Living with brother - Loftin, June 36, Bland 10, Frank 7*

Children of MARY WILLIAMSON and LOFLIN are:

i. *ALICE[8] LOFLIN, b. Bet. 1869 - 1870, KY; d. Aft. 1870.*
ii. *BLAND LOFLIN, b. 1870, KY; d. Aft. 1880.*
iii. *BENJAMIN FRANK LOFLIN, b. 14 Jan 1873, KY; d. 03 Apr 1940; m. MARY J. PAUL, 09 Jul 1899, Mississippi Co., AR.*

8. *MALVENIA[7] WILLIAMSON (ELIZABETH ANN "LIZZIE"[6] BALLARD, JAMES[5], BLAND WILLIAM[4], BLAND[3], BLAND[2], WILLIAM[1]) was born Abt. 1846 in Hardin Co., KY. She married JOSEPH B. WHITWORTH 05 Aug 1868 in AR.*

Notes for MALVENIA WILLIAMSON:
Source: Martha Floyd Miller

Notes for JOSEPH B. WHITWORTH:
Source: Martha Floyd Miller

Child of MALVENIA WILLIAMSON and JOSEPH WHITWORTH is:

i.   JAMES E.[8] WHITWORTH, b. 27 May 1869, Union Town, KY; m. LIDA LEE WEEDMAN, 12 Aug 1900, AR.

Notes for JAMES E. WHITWORTH:
Source: Martha Floyd Miller

Notes for LIDA LEE WEEDMAN:
Source: Martha Floyd Miller

9.   JOHN JAMES[7] WILLIAMSON (ELIZABETH ANN "LIZZIE"[6] BALLARD, JAMES[5], BLAND WILLIAM[4], BLAND[3], BLAND[2], WILLIAM[1]) was born 18 May 1858 in McLean Co., KY, and died 10 Nov 1952 in Cameron Co., TX. He married MISS WILSON. She died Bef. 1900.

Notes for JOHN JAMES WILLIAMSON:
Source: 1880-1920 Mississippi County Arkansas Federal Census Records, Kentucky Birth Records, Cameron County Texas Certificate of Death

* 1880 - Living in Monroe, Mississippi Co., AR - Williamson J J 22 KY, June Loftin sister 36 KY, Bland 10 KY, Frank 7 KY, Sarah Williamson 16 sister KY
* 1900 - Living in Chickasawba, Mississippi Co., AR - Living with sister's family - Williamson, John - May 1858 KY KY KY, Lizzie V dau - Nov 1895 MO, Blan H - Aug 1897 MO
* 1910 - Living in Hickman, Mississippi Co., AR - Williamson, J J 51 KY KY KY, Lizzie V 14 MO, Blan H 13 MO, J A Ashlin brother in law, A Y Ashlin, J. W. Williamson
* 1920 - Living in Hickman, Mississippi Co., AR - Williamson, John 61, Blan H 22, Reba 16 dau in law, Alma Ashlan 70 sister

More About JOHN JAMES WILLIAMSON:
Burial: Blytheville Cemetery, Blytheville, AR

Children of JOHN WILLIAMSON and MISS WILSON are:

18.   i.   LIZZIE V.[8] WILLIAMSON, b. 02 Nov 1895, MS or Blythesville, Mississippi Co., AR; d. 02 Mar 1968, LaFeria, Cameron Co., TX.
           ii.   BLAN HARRISON WILLIAMSON, b. 28 Aug 1897, MS; d. 22 Oct 1976; m. REBA CLYDE MILLAY, 07 Dec 1919, Mississippi Co., AR; b. 19 Jan 1903, Owensburg, Owen Co.,, KY; d. 20 Sep 1994.

                  Notes for BLAN HARRISON WILLIAMSON:
                  Source: Martha Floyd Miller

                  More About BLAN HARRISON WILLIAMSON:
                  Burial: Maple Grove Cemetery, Blytheville, Mississippi Co., AR

                  More About REBA CLYDE MILLAY:
                  Burial: Maple Grove Cemetery, Blytheville, Mississippi Co., AR

10.   SARAH ELIZA[7] BALLARD (BENJAMIN H.[6], JAMES[5], BLAND WILLIAM[4], BLAND[3], BLAND[2], WILLIAM[1]) was born 02 Dec 1840 in KY, and died 31 Jan 1929 in Clark Co., MO. She married MILLER AYERS MONCRIEF 20 Feb 1862 in Clark Co., MO. He was born 16 Aug 1840 in IN, and died 13 Jul 1911 in Clark Co., MO.

Notes for SARAH ELIZA BALLARD:
Source: 1920 Clark County Missouri Federal Census Records, Martha Miller

* 1920 - Living in Washington, Clark Co., MO - Moncrief, Sarah E 79 wd KY KY KY, Ora M 46 MO, Fannie E 42 MO, Harry L grandson 25 MO

More About SARAH ELIZA BALLARD:
Burial: New Woodville Cemetery, Wyaconda, Clark Co., MO

Notes for MILLER AYERS MONCRIEF:
Source: 1870-1910 Clark County Missouri Federal Census Records
** 1870 - Living in Wyaconda, Clark Co., MO - Miller, Moncrief 29 IN, Sarah Eliza 29 KY, Wm L 5, Rosaline J 6/12 MO*
** 1880 - Living in Lincoln, Clark Co., MO - Miller, Moncrief 40 IN KY KY farmer, Sarah E 40 KY KY KY, William L 15 MO, Rosalia J 15 MO, Ora May 6 MO, Elizabeth F 3 MO, Elmer 4/12 MO*
** 1910 - Living in Washington, Clark, Co., MO - Moncrief, Miller A 69 IN IN IN, Sarah E 69 - 7 children 5 living K KY KY, William L 45 wd MO, Ora M 36 MO, Elizabeth P 33 MO, Elmer B 30 MO, Harry L grandson 15 MO*

More About MILLER AYERS MONCRIEF:
Burial: New Woodville Cemetery, Wyaconda, Clark Co., MO

Children of SARAH BALLARD and MILLER MONCRIEF are:

      i.   WILLIAM LEE[8] MONCRIEF, *b. 12 Jan 1865, Clark Co., MO; d. 01 Sep 1916, MO; m. ETTA MAY BURKETT; b. 17 May 1872; d. 27 Feb 1895.*

           More About WILLIAM LEE MONCRIEF:
           Burial: Fairmont Cemetery, Clark Co., MO

           More About ETTA MAY BURKETT:
           Burial: Fairmont Cemetery, Clark Co., MO

      ii.   ROSALIA "ROSA" MONCRIEF, *b. 1869, Clark Co., MO; d. 1937; m. GRANVILLE J. HARVEY; b. 1869; d. 1942.*

           More About ROSALIA "ROSA" MONCRIEF:
           Burial: Rest Lawn Memorial Park, Junction City, Lane Co., OR

           More About GRANVILLE J. HARVEY:
           Burial: Rest Lawn Memorial Park, Junction City, Lane Co., OR

      iii.   ORA MAY MONCRIEF, *b. 09 Nov 1873, Clark Co., MO; d. 10 May 1940.*

           More About ORA MAY MONCRIEF:
           Burial: New Woodville Cemetery, Wyaconda, Clark Co., MO

      iv.   ELIZABETH FRANCES MONCRIEF, *b. 29 Jan 1877, Clark Co., MO; d. 26 Mar 1968, Kahoka, Clark Co., MO.*

           More About ELIZABETH FRANCES MONCRIEF:
           Burial: New Woodville Cemetery, Wyaconda, Clark Co., MO

      v.   ELMER BASKETT MONCRIEF, *b. 15 Jan 1880, Clark Co., MO; d. 23 Nov 1953; m. FLODA MAY DORSEY; b. 13 Aug 1883; d. 25 Jun 1971.*

           More About ELMER BASKETT MONCRIEF:
           Burial: New Woodville Cemetery, Wyaconda, Clark Co., MO

           More About FLODA MAY DORSEY:
           Burial: New Woodville Cemetery, Wyaconda, Clark Co., MO

11. MARY FRANCES[7] BALLARD (BENJAMIN H.[6], JAMES[5], BLAND WILLIAM[4], BLAND[3], BLAND[2], WILLIAM[1]) was born 05 Dec 1843 in KY, and died 09 Dec 1914 in Clark Co., MO. She married ELIAS R. HICKERSON 11 Oct 1864 in Clark Co., MO. He was born 01 Mar 1832 in MO, and died 25 Dec 1903.

Notes for MARY FRANCES BALLARD:
Source: Martha Miller

More About MARY FRANCES BALLARD:
Burial: Kahoka Cemetery, Kahoka, Clark Co., MO

Notes for ELIAS R. HICKERSON:
Source: 1870-1900 Clark County Missouri Federal Census Records

* 1870 - Living in Lincoln, Clark Co., MO - Hickerson, Elias farm laborer 38 MO, Mary 25 KY, Walter 4 MO, Alvin 2 MO, Emma 10/12 MO
* 1880 - Living in Lincoln, Clark Co., MO - Hickerson, Elias R 49, Mary 38, Walter 15, Alvin 13, Emma 11
* 1900 - Living in Kahoka, Clark Co., MO - Hickerson, Elias K - Feb 29 1932 TN VA VA, May F - Dec 1843 - 3 children 3 living KY TN KY, Caroline Baskets aunt July 1817
KY, Nettie Ballard, sister in law - July 1861 MO KY KY

More About ELIAS R. HICKERSON:
Burial: Kahoka Cemetery, Kahoka, Clark Co., MO

Children of MARY BALLARD and ELIAS HICKERSON are:

      i.   WALTER[8] HICKERSON, b. 01 Sep 1866, Clark Co., MO; d. 25 Nov 1927, Los Angeles Co., CA; m. JOSEPHINE TRIPLETT.
     ii. ALVIN HICKERSON, b. 31 May 1867, MO; d. 09 Jul 1953, Fresno Co., CA; m. LUELLA WILSON; b. Jun 1868, Clark Co., MO; d. 1933, Fresno Co., CA.

          More About ALVIN HICKERSON:
          Burial: Reedley Cemetery, Reedley, Fresno Co., CA

          More About LUELLA WILSON:
          Burial: Reedley Cemetery, Reedley, Fresno Co., CA

     iii. EMMA HICKERSON, b. 1869, MO; d. 1955; m. LEWIS S. NORCRAFT, 14 Mar 1890, Clark Co., MO; b. 10 Sep 1865, MO; d. 05 Feb 1933, Kirksville, Adair Co., MO.

          More About EMMA HICKERSON:
          Burial: New Woodville Cemetery, Wyaconda, Clark Co., MO

          More About LEWIS S. NORCRAFT:
          Burial: New Woodville Cemetery, Wyaconda, Clark Co., MO

12. WILLIAM JAMES[7] BALLARD (BENJAMIN H.[6], JAMES[5], BLAND WILLIAM[4], BLAND[3], BLAND[2], WILLIAM[1]) was born 28 Aug 1845 in Oldham Co., KY, and died 18 Jun 1918 in Fresno Co., CA. He married JANE "JENNIE" LAURA MCDANIEL 03 Oct 1871 in Clark Co., MO, daughter of JESSE MCDANIEL and WEALTHY ROBERTSON. She was born 28 Jan 1847 in Clark Co., MO, and died 15 Oct 1910 in Kirksville, Adair Co., MO.

Notes for WILLIAM JAMES BALLARD:
Source: Fresno California Probate files No 5166-5215- 1918, 1880 - 1900 Clark County Missouri Federal Census Records, Martha Miller

1880 - Living in Clark Co., MO - Ballard, William 34 farmer KY KY KY, Jane 33 MO KY KY, Benjamin 8 MO, Edwin 5 KY, Mary 3 MO, William 1 M

1900 - Living in Lincoln, Clark Co., MO - Ballard, James - Aug 1845 KY KY KY, Laura J - Jan 1847 MO KY VA, Edwin L - Oct 1875 MO, Jessie G - June 1882 MO, Elsie I - Dec 1883 MO

1918 - Fresno, CA - Probate Files 5166-5215 - Will of William Ballard - Reedley, Calif., May 18th 1915 - I, William Ballard, being of sound and disposing mind; realizing the uncertainty of life and wishing to make proper disposal of my property to my children, hereby make this my last will and testament:

First: I will that my burial expenses and all my just debts be paid

Second: to my son, Benjamin F. Ballard, I will his notes which I hold for money heretofore advanced to him, as his full share of my estate.

Third: I will to my daughter Jessie G. Ballard, my residence property with all furniture and furnishings, and the sum of $2000.00 Two Thousand Dollars in cash as her full share of my estate

Fourth: I will that $5000.00 Five Thousand Dollars be placed in trust for the benefit of my said daughter, Jessie G. Ballard, the interest of which to be paid to her annually while she remains unmarried or until her death.

If She should marry, or die without issue, then the sum of this trust shall revert to my estate and be divided to my legal heirs namely: Benjamin F. Ballard, Edwin L. Ballard, Caroline May Ballard Boley, Jessie G. Ballard, Elsie I Ballard Glasgow, and my granddaughter Marian Ballard and I appoint J. C Glasgow and D. C. Krehbiel to carry out this trust.

Fifth: I will that $3500.00 Three Thousand Five Hundred Dollars be placed in trust for the benefit of my grand daughter Marian Ballard, the only child of my deceased son W. S. Ballard, the interest of which shall be paid annually for her support, until she is 18 years of age, then if necessary for her education, the sum of $400.00 Four Hundred Dollars per year may be paid until she comes of age of 22 years, then all that remains of this trust shall be paid to her. But should she die, without issue, before she comes to the age of twenty-two years, then this trust shall revert to my estate and be divided to my legal heirs, as hereinbefore named.

I appoint my daughters Jessie G. Ballard and Elsie I Glasgow as trustees to carry out this trust.

Sixth: I will that the residue of my estate shall be divided, share and share alike, to my other children not heretofore provided for, and whose names are Edwin L. Ballard, Caroline May Ballard Boley, and Elsie I Ballard Glasgow.

Seventh: I appoint my daughters Jessie G. Ballard and Elsie I Glaslow, as executors of this will and it is my will that they be permitted to serve without bond.

This Will revokes any former will made by me.

Written and signed by my own hand this 18th day of May 1915 signed Wm. Ballard

More About WILLIAM JAMES BALLARD:
Burial: Kahoka Cemetery, Kahoka, Clark Co., MO

Notes for JANE "JENNIE" LAURA MCDANIEL:
Source: Adair County Missouri Death Certificate

More About JANE "JENNIE" LAURA MCDANIEL:
Burial: Kahoka Cemetery, Kahoka, Clark Co., MO

Children of WILLIAM BALLARD and JANE MCDANIEL are:

    i.   BENJAMIN F.[8] BALLARD, b. 1872, MO; d. Aft. 1918.

    ii.   EDWIN L. BALLARD, b. 02 Oct 1875, Kahoka, Clark Co., MO; d. 31 Oct 1963, Odessa, Ector Co., TX; m. PEARL NEVA PANCAKE; b. 06 Jan 1883, Greene Co., MO; d. 03 Feb 1973, Tarrant Co., TX.

        More About EDWIN L. BALLARD:
        Burial: Mt. Hope Cemetery, Belleville, St. Clair Co., IL

        More About PEARL NEVA PANCAKE:
        Burial: Mt. Hope Cemetery, Belleville, St. Clair Co., IL

iii.   CAROLINE MAY BALLARD, b. 24 Jan 1877, Kahoka, Clark Co., MO; d. 13 Apr 1964, Santa Barbara Co., CA; m. JOHN MELVIN BOLEY; b. 25 Sep 1872, Kahoka, Clark Co., MO; d. 18 Jan 1966, Fresno Co., CA.

More About CAROLINE MAY BALLARD:
Burial: Reedley Cemetery, Fresno Co., CA

More About JOHN MELVIN BOLEY:
Burial: Reedley Cemetery, Fresno Co., CA

19.   iv.   WILLIAM S. BALLARD, b. 18 Nov 1878, Clark Co., MO; d. 13 Oct 1909, Santa Rosa, Sonoma Co., CA.

v.   JESSIE GERTRUDE BALLARD, b. 27 Jun 1881, Clark Co., MO; d. 12 Jan 1958, Fresno Co., CA; m. BENJAMIN HARRISON HIESTAND; b. 31 May 1876, IN; d. 11 May 1948, Fresno Co., CA.

More About JESSIE GERTRUDE BALLARD:
Burial: Smith Mountain Cemetery, Dinuba, Tulare Co., CA

More About BENJAMIN HARRISON HIESTAND:
Burial: Smith Mountain Cemetery, Dinuba, Tulare Co., CA

vi.   ELSIE I. BALLARD, b. Dec 1883, Clark Co., MO; d. Aft. 1915; m. J. C. GLASGOW; d. Aft. 1915.

13. EDMONIA[7] BALLARD (BENJAMIN H.[6], JAMES[5], BLAND WILLIAM[4], BLAND[3], BLAND[2], WILLIAM[1]) was born 1852 in Oldham Co., KY, and died 03 May 1874 in Clark Co., MO. She married JAMES MACKEY 16 Jan 1873 in Clark Co., MO.

More About EDMONIA BALLARD:
Burial: Sisson Cemetery, Clark Co., MO

Child of EDMONIA BALLARD and JAMES MACKEY is:

i.   NETTIE G.[8] MACKEY, b. 1874, Clark Co., MO; d. 18 Oct 1874, Clark Co., MO.

14. ROBERT MITCHELL[7] BALLARD (BENJAMIN H.[6], JAMES[5], BLAND WILLIAM[4], BLAND[3], BLAND[2], WILLIAM[1]) was born 19 May 1854 in MO, and died 21 Apr 1911 in Polk Co., OR. He married ALMA DAVIS 27 Nov 1877 in Clark Co., MO. She was born 20 Sep 1852 in Washington Co., OH, and died 12 Jun 1942 in Polk Co., OR.

Notes for ROBERT MITCHELL BALLARD:
Source: 1895 Marion County Oregon State Census Records, 1910 Polk County Oregon Federal Census Records

* 1895 - Living in Marion Co., OR - Ballard, Robert M farmer 40, Alma b. Washington Co., OH 40, Roberta b. Marion Co., OR 3, Annetta b. Marion Co., OR 3, Irving born Washington Co., OH 15, Harry b. Clark Co., MO 9
* 1910 - Living in Polk Co., OR - Ballard, Robert M 55 MO KY KY, Alma 55 - 4 children 4 living, C. Irving 31 MO, Robeta 17 OR, Annetta 17 OR

More About ROBERT MITCHELL BALLARD:
Burial: Dallas Cemetery, Dallas, Polk Co., OR

Notes for ALMA DAVIS:
Source: 1900 Marion County Oregon Federal Census Records, 1920 & 1940 Polk County Oregon Federal Census Records

* 1900 - Living in Silverton, Marion Co., OR - Ballard, Alma - Sept 1854 - 4 children 4 living OH OH OH,

Harry P - July 1885 MO, Roberta - May 1892 MO MO OH, Roberta - May 1892 OR, Annetta - May 1892 OR
** 1920 - Living in Dallas, Polk Co., OR - Ballard, Alma 65 wd OH OH OH, Charles I 41 MO, Roberta 25 OR, Annetta 25 OR*
** 1930 - Living in Oakdale, Polk Co., OR - Ballard, Alma 76 living with son Erven 40 MO and sister Annetta 30*
** 1940 - Living in Oakdale, Polk Co., OR - Ballard, Alma 88 OH, Annetta 39 Oregon*

More About ALMA DAVIS:
Burial: Dallas Cemetery, Dallas, Polk Co., OR

Children of ROBERT BALLARD and ALMA DAVIS are:
> i.   CHARLES IRVING[8] BALLARD, b. 1880, Washington Co., OH; d. Aft. 1930.

> *Notes for CHARLES IRVING BALLARD:*
> *Source: 1930 Polk County Oregon Federal Census Records*
> ** 1930 - Living in Oakdale, Polk Co., OR - Ballard, Ervin 40 MO, Alma mother 76 OH, Annetta sister 30*

> ii.   HARRY BALLARD, b. 02 Jul 1885, Lincoln twp., Clark Co., MO; d. Aft. 1910.
> iii. ANNETTA CAROLINE BALLARD, b. 08 May 1892, Silverton, Marion Co., OR; d. 09 Jun 1961.

> *More About ANNETTA CAROLINE BALLARD:*
> *Burial: Dallas Cemetery, Dallas, Polk Co., OR*

> iv.   ROBERTA E. BALLARD, b. 08 May 1892, Silverton, Marion Co., OR; d. 05 Jun 1965.

> *Notes for ROBERTA E. BALLARD:*
> *Source: Polk County Oregon Registration of Birth*
> ** Delayed certificate created Mar 9 1955*

> *More About ROBERTA E. BALLARD:*
> *Burial: Dallas Cemetery, Dallas, Polk Co., OR*

15. BENJAMIN WILLIAM[7] BALLARD (BLAND WILLIAM[6], JAMES[5], BLAND WILLIAM[4], BLAND[3], BLAND[2], WILLIAM[1]) *was born 24 Sep 1848 in LaGrange, Oldham Co., KY, and died 08 Oct 1915 in Whitney, Hill Co., TX. He married BINA TODD NEAL. She was born 16 Jul 1862 in KY, and died 28 May 1934 in Hill Co., TX.*

Notes for BENJAMIN WILLIAM BALLARD:
Source: Martha Floyd Miller (me2miller@comcast.net), 1880-1900 Hill County Texas Federal Census Records

** 1880 - Living in 1880 Hill County, TX - Ballard, B W 32 BT, J*
** 1900 - Living in 1900 Hill County, TX - Ballard, Benjamin W - Sep 1847 KY KY KY, Vina T F - July 1861 KY KY KY, Nellie - Apr 1886 TX, Desse Stone mother in law - June 1818 KY KY KY*

Notes for BINA TODD NEAL:
Source: 1903-1940 Texas Death Index

Children of BENJAMIN BALLARD and BINA NEAL are:

> i.   NELLIE BLAND[8] BALLARD, b. Apr 1886, TX; d. Aft. 1900.
> 20.   ii.   JOHN NEAL BALLARD, b. 15 Oct 1879, Ft. Graham Co., TX; d. 26 Feb 1960, Whitney, Hill Co., TX.

16. MARY ADALINE[7] BALLARD (BLAND WILLIAM[6], JAMES[5], BLAND WILLIAM[4], BLAND[3], BLAND[2], WILLIAM[1]) *was born*

27 Jan 1855 in Clark Co., MO, and died 23 Aug 1947 in Cleburne, Johnson Co., TX. She married JAMES VALENTINE HAMPTON 20 Feb 1873 in Saline Co., MO, son of JAMES HAMPTON. He was born 22 May 1842 in AR, and died 05 Mar 1916 in Cleburne, Johnson Co., TX.

Notes for MARY ADALINE BALLARD:
Source: Johnson County Texas Certificate of Death, Martha Floyd Miller (me2miller@comcast.net)

More About MARY ADALINE BALLARD:
Burial: Cleburne Memorial Cemetery, Cleburne, Johnson Co., TX

Notes for JAMES VALENTINE HAMPTON:
Source: 1880 Clark County Missouri Federal Census Records, 1900 Hill County Texas Federal Census Records, 1910 Johnson County Texas Federal Census Records
** 1800 - Living in Union, Clark Co., MO - Hampton, J B 36 AR VA TN, Mary 25 MO KY KY, Wade 1 MO*
** 1900 - Living in Hill Co., TX - Hampton, James B - May 1844 AR, Mary A - Jan 1855 MO VA TN, Wade B E June 1879 MO, Thomas B - Oct 1882 MO, John M June 1886 MO, Zuma E July 1891 TX*
** 1910 - Living in Johnson Co., TX - Hampton, James V 65 AR VA TN, Mary A 55 - 5 children 4 living MO KY KY, Blan W 20 MO, John M 23 MO, Zerma E 18 TX*

More About JAMES VALENTINE HAMPTON:
Burial: Cleburne Memorial Cemetery, Cleburne, Johnson Co., TX

Children of MARY BALLARD and JAMES HAMPTON are:

> i.   EDWARD BLAND WADE[8] *HAMPTON, b. 24 Jun 1878, Clark Co., MO; d. 27 Jul 1962, Cleburne, Johnson Co., TX.*
>
> > *Notes for EDWARD BLAND WADE HAMPTON:*
> > *Source: Johnson County Texas Certificate of Death*
> >
> > *More About EDWARD BLAND WADE HAMPTON:*
> > *Burial: Cleburne Memorial Cemetery, Cleburne, Johnson Co., TX*

21.   ii.   *JOHN MORMADUKE HAMPTON, b. 18 Jun 1886, Clark Co., MO; d. 27 Mar 1966, Johnson Co., TX.*
22.   iii.   *THOMAS VALENTINE HAMPTON, b. 12 Oct 1882, Clark Co., MO; d. 22 Jan 1961, Dallas Co., TX.*
       iv.   *VELMA ANNA HAMPTON, b. 27 Jul 1891, Hill Co., TX; d. 04 Aug 1898, Hill Co., TX.*

> > *More About VELMA ANNA HAMPTON:*
> > *Burial: Peoria Cemetery, Hill Co., TX*

23.   v.   *ZUMA ETTA HAMPTON, b. 27 Jul 1891, Hill Co., TX; d. 01 Feb 1977, Godley, Johnson Co., TX.*

Generation No. 4

17.   *JAMES B.*[8] *BAIRD (CHARITY E.*[7] *WILLIAMSON, ELIZABETH ANN "LIZZIE"*[6] *BALLARD, JAMES*[5]*, BLAND WILLIAM*[4]*, BLAND*[3]*, BLAND*[2]*, WILLIAM*[1]*) was born 30 Dec 1862 in Daviess Co., KY, and died 18 May 1951 in Daviess Co., KY. He married ELIZABETH ALLEN DORRIS 10 Nov 1889 in Daviess Co., KY. She was born 15 Mar 1870 in KY, and died 02 Jun 1949.*

Notes for JAMES B. BAIRD:
Source: Davies County Kentucky Certificate of Death, 1910-1920 Daviess County Kentucky Federal Census Records
** 1910 - Living in Daviess Co., KY - Baird, James 47 KY KY KY, Lizzie 40 - 12 children 12 living, KY KY KY, Mona 19 KY, Settee 18 KY, Jessie 15 KY, Walker 13 KY, Willie 11 KY, Mary B 9 KY, Charaty 7 KY, Hettie 5 KY,*

Hatta 5 KY, Eddie 3 KY, Lena 1 2/12 KY, Rena 1 2/12 KY
** 1920 - Living in Vanover, Daviess Co., KY - Baird, James 57 farmer KY KY KY, Elizabeth 48 KY KY KY, William 21 KY, Mary Belle 19 KY, Chariety 17 KY, Hettie 15 KY, Hattie 15 KY, Edward 12 KY, Lena 10 KY, Rena 10 KY, James 8 KY, Catherine 5 KY*

More About JAMES B. BAIRD:
Burial: Utica Baptist Church Cemetery, Daviess Co., KY

More About ELIZABETH ALLEN DORRIS:
Burial: Utica Baptist Church Cemetery, Daviess Co., KY

Children of JAMES BAIRD and ELIZABETH DORRIS are:

      i.   *MONA FRANCES[9] BAIRD, b. 25 Aug 1890, KY; d. 28 May 1991; m. BARNEY T. MACKEY; b. 14 Jun 1892, Beech Grove, McLean Co., KY; d. 08 Jun 1982, Utica, Daviess Co., KY.*

          More About MONA FRANCES BAIRD:
          Burial: Utica Baptist Church Cemetery, Utica, Daviess Co., KY

          More About BARNEY T. MACKEY:
          Burial: Utica Baptist Church Cemetery, Utica, Daviess Co., KY

     ii.   *SETTIE ELIZABETH BAIRD, b. 23 Jul 1892, KY; d. 30 Mar 1981; m. ARCH DAVIS GILL; b. 27 Nov 1891, Daviess Co., KY; d. 15 May 1958, Jefferson Co., TX.*

          More About SETTIE ELIZABETH BAIRD:
          Burial: Utica Baptist Church Cemetery, Utica, Daviess Co., KY

          More About ARCH DAVIS GILL:
          Burial: Utica Baptist Church Cemetery, Utica, Daviess Co., KY

    iii.   *JESSIE BAIRD, b. Abt. 1895, Daviess Co., KY; d. Aft. 1910; m. STATELER S. HOUSTON, 22 Jul 1918, Daviess Co., KY.*
    iv.   *WALKER BAIRD, b. 01 Oct 1896, Daviess Co., KY; d. 04 Apr 1959, Tuscaloosa Co., AL; m. MARY HAMMOND COKE; b. 06 Sep 1902, Daviess Co., KY; d. 10 Feb 1996, El Paso Co., TX.*

          More About WALKER BAIRD:
          Burial: Utica Baptist Church Cemetery, Utica, Daviess Co., KY

          More About MARY HAMMOND COKE:
          Burial: Utica Baptist Church Cemetery, Utica, Daviess Co., KY

     v.   *WILLIAM "WILLIE" ARTHUR BAIRD, b. 30 Sep 1898, Daviess Co., KY; d. 18 May 1966, Owensboro, Daviess Co., KY; m. MAURINE RUBY; b. 17 Nov 1901, McLean Co., KY; d. 24 May 1983, Owensboro, Daviess Co., KY.*

          More About WILLIAM "WILLIE" ARTHUR BAIRD:
          Burial: Utica Baptist Church Cemetery, Daviess Co., KY

          More About MAURINE RUBY:
          Burial: Utica Baptist Church Cemetery, Daviess Co., KY

    vi.   *MARY BELLE BAIRD, b. 13 Sep 1900, Utica, Daviess Co., KY; d. 06 Jan 1988, Munster, Lake Co., IN; m. (1) ROBERT C. MERCER; b. 07 Feb 1900, Daviess Co., KY; d. 07 May 1959, Hammond, Lake Co., IN; m. (2) GEORGE DEWEY COLEMAN; b. 10 Feb 1899, Muhlenberg Co., KY; d. Dec 1974, Hammond, Lake Co., IN.*

More About MARY BELLE BAIRD:
Burial: Chapel Lawn Memorial Gardens, Schereville, Lake Co., IN

More About GEORGE DEWEY COLEMAN:
Burial: Unity Cemetery, Graham, Muhlenberg Co., KY

   vii.   CHARITY BAIRD, *b. Abt. 1903, Daviess Co., KY; d. Aft. 1920; m. WARREN THOMAS VANCE; b. 08 Dec 1902; d. 31 Oct 1999.*

More About WARREN THOMAS VANCE:
Burial: Glenville Baptist Church Cemetery, Daviess Co., KY

  viii.   HATTIE BAIRD, *b. 15 Dec 1904, Daviess Co., KY; d. 07 Jan 1990, McLean Co., KY; m. JOHN HERMAN HUFF; b. 15 Mar 1905, Ohio Co., KY; d. 07 Feb 1984, Owensboro, Daviess Co., KY.*

More About HATTIE BAIRD:
Burial: Utica Baptist Church Cemetery, Utica, Daviess Co., KY

   ix.   HETTIE BAIRD, *b. 15 Dec 1904, Daviess Co., KY; d. 24 Feb 1974, Jasper, Dubois Co., IN; m. GATES LEE MURRAY; b. 06 Nov 1905, KY; d. 06 May 1961, Daviess Co., KY.*

Notes for HETTIE BAIRD:
Source: Dubois County Indiana Certificate of Death

More About GATES LEE MURRAY:
Burial: Utica Baptist Church Cemetery, Utica, Daviess Co., KY

   x.   EDWARD LOUIS BAIRD, *b. 20 Jun 1907, Daviess Co., KY; d. 19 Dec 1971; m. JOSEPHINE SHOCKLEE; b. 20 Oct 1913, McLean Co., KY; d. 04 Dec 2000, McLean Co., KY.*

More About EDWARD LOUIS BAIRD:
Burial: Utica Baptist Church Cemetery, Utica, Daviess Co., KY

More About JOSEPHINE SHOCKLEE:
Burial: Utica Baptist Church Cemetery, Utica, Daviess Co., KY

   xi.   LENA BAIRD, *b. 14 Feb 1909, Daviess Co., KY; d. 24 Nov 1993, Owensboro, Daviess Co., KY; m. CLYDE MAURICE JONES; b. 16 Apr 1914, Daviess Co., KY; d. 16 Apr 1976, Owensboro, Daviess Co., KY.*

More About LENA BAIRD:
Burial: Utica Baptist Church Cemetery, Utica, Daviess Co., KY

  xii.   RENA BAIRD, *b. 14 Feb 1909, Daviess Co., KY; d. 01 Apr 1993, Owensboro, Daviess Co., KY; m. J. EARL JONES; d. 24 Dec 1999.*

More About RENA BAIRD:
Burial: Resurrection Cemetery, Owensboro, Daviess Co., KY

More About J. EARL JONES:
Burial: Resurrection Cemetery, Owensboro, Daviess Co., KY

xiii.   JAMES ALLEN BAIRD, b. 09 Mar 1912, Daviess Co., KY; d. 04 Feb 1989; m. EDNA GRACE DAVIS; b. 14 Mar 1916, Owensboro, Daviess Co., KY; d. 13 Sep 2001, Owensboro, Daviess Co., KY.

More About JAMES ALLEN BAIRD:
Burial: Utica Baptist Church Cemetery, Utica, Daviess Co., KY

More About EDNA GRACE DAVIS:
Burial: Utica Baptist Church Cemetery, Utica, Daviess Co., KY

xiv.   CATHERINE G. BAIRD, b. 23 Apr 1914, Daviess Co., KY; d. 24 Feb 2008, Owensboro, Daviess Co., KY.

More About CATHERINE G. BAIRD:
Burial: Utica Baptist Church Cemetery, Utica, Daviess Co., KY

18.   LIZZIE V.[8] WILLIAMSON (JOHN JAMES[7], ELIZABETH ANN "LIZZIE"[6] BALLARD, JAMES[5], BLAND WILLIAM[4], BLAND[3], BLAND[2], WILLIAM[1]) was born 02 Nov 1895 in MS or Blythesville, Mississippi Co., AR, and died 02 Mar 1968 in LaFeria, Cameron Co., TX. She married LAWRENCE REDMOND MURPHY. He was born 18 Aug 1886 in KY, and died 10 Jun 1952 in LaFeria, Cameron Co., TX.

Notes for LIZZIE V. WILLIAMSON:
Source: Cameron County Texas Certificate of Death

Notes for LAWRENCE REDMOND MURPHY:
Source: 1930-1940 Cameron County Texas Federal Census Records, Cameron County Texas Certificate of Death, Martha Floyd Miller

* 1930 - Living in Cameron Co., TX - Murphy, Laurence R 43 KY, Elizzie V 34 MO, Laurence Jr. 8, AR, Anna Beth 4 3/12 TX, Flay F. 3 TX
* 1940 - Living in Cameron Co., TX - Murphy, Laweronce 53, Lizzie 44, Lawrence Jr. 18, Anna Beth 14, Floy Frances 13

Children of LIZZIE WILLIAMSON and LAWRENCE MURPHY are:
    i.   LAWRENCE REDMOND[9] MURPHY, JR., b. 29 Mar 1922, Cameron Co., TX; d. 15 May 2011.

Notes for LAWRENCE REDMOND MURPHY, JR.:
Source: WWII Draft Cards

24.   ii.   ANNA ELIZABETH MURPHY, b. 20 Jan 1926, Hidalgo Co., TX; d. 27 May 2015.
    iii.   FLAY FRANCIS MURPHY, b. 22 Mar 1927, Cameron Co., TX; d. 20 Jun 1980, Cameron Co., TX; m. L. R. SMITH, 03 Aug 1946, Hidalgo Co., TX.

19.   WILLIAM S.[8] BALLARD (WILLIAM JAMES[7], BENJAMIN H.[6], JAMES[5], BLAND WILLIAM[4], BLAND[3], BLAND[2], WILLIAM[1]) was born 18 Nov 1878 in Clark Co., MO, and died 13 Oct 1909 in Santa Rosa, Sonoma Co., CA. He married GERTRUDE SISSON. She was born 31 Jul 1881 in Kahoka, Clark Co., MO, and died 24 Jun 1968 in Los Angeles Co., CA.

More About WILLIAM S. BALLARD:
Burial: Santa Rosa, Rural Cemetery, Santa Barbara Co., CA

More About GERTRUDE SISSON:
Burial: Forest Lawn Memorial Park, Glendale, Los Angeles Co., CA

Child of WILLIAM BALLARD and GERTRUDE SISSON is:
    i. MARIAN[9] BALLARD.

20. JOHN NEAL[8] BALLARD (BENJAMIN WILLIAM[7], BLAND WILLIAM[6], JAMES[5], BLAND WILLIAM[4], BLAND[3], BLAND[2], WILLIAM[1]) *was born 15 Oct 1879 in Ft. Graham Co., TX, and died 26 Feb 1960 in Whitney, Hill Co., TX. He married WINNIE GREENHILL OR CUNNINGHAM. She was born Abt. 1880.*

Children of JOHN BALLARD and WINNIE CUNNINGHAM are:
    i. REGINALD[9] BALLARD, b. Abt. 1900.
    ii. NELLIE MAE BLAND BALLARD, b. Abt. 1901; m. ROBERT NANCE CASON; b. Abt. 1900.

21. JOHN MORMADUKE[8] HAMPTON (MARY ADALINE[7] BALLARD, BLAND WILLIAM[6], JAMES[5], BLAND WILLIAM[4], BLAND[3], BLAND[2], WILLIAM[1]) *was born 18 Jun 1886 in Clark Co., MO, and died 27 Mar 1966 in Johnson Co., TX. He married RUTH DIXON ANDERSON. She was born 27 Aug 1896 in TX, and died 15 Nov 1981 in Cleburne, Johnson Co., TX.*

More About JOHN MORMADUKE HAMPTON:
Burial: Cleburne Memorial Cemetery, Cleburne, Johnson Co., TX

Child of JOHN HAMPTON and RUTH ANDERSON is:
    i. MARY BLAND[9] HAMPTON, m. JOHN BROWN.

22. THOMAS VALENTINE[8] HAMPTON (MARY ADALINE[7] BALLARD, BLAND WILLIAM[6], JAMES[5], BLAND WILLIAM[4], BLAND[3], BLAND[2], WILLIAM[1]) *was born 12 Oct 1882 in Clark Co., MO, and died 22 Jan 1961 in Dallas Co., TX. He married BIRDIE ROGERS. She was born 06 Sep 1890 in Meridian, Bosque Co., TX, and died 28 Apr 1951 in Dallas Co., TX.*

Notes for THOMAS VALENTINE HAMPTON:
Source: 1920 Johnson County Texas Federal Census Records, 1930 Crook County Wyoming Federal Census Records, 1940 Coleman County Texas Federal Census Records

** 1920 - Living in Cleburne Co., Johnson Co., TX - Hampton, T V 37 MO, Bertie 27 TX, Cecil 8 TX, Vernon 6 TX, James, Delton*
** 1930 - Living in Moorcroft, Crook Co., WY - Hampton, Thomas V 50 MO AR MO, Verdie B 39 TX MS MS, Cecil 19 TX, Vernon 17 TX, James A 14 TX, Delton 12 TX, T. V 7 TX, Annie E 4 TX*
** 1940 - Living in Dawson Co., TX - Hampton, Thomas V Jr. 17 TX mechanic Tractor repair shop, Ruby 15 wife TX, Tommy L 2/12, Thomas V father 59 TX Carpenter building construction, Birdie B 49 TX, Annie E 14 TX, Mary L 8 TX*

More About THOMAS VALENTINE HAMPTON:

Burial: Restland Memorial Park, Dallas Co., TX

Children of THOMAS HAMPTON and BIRDIE ROGERS are:

    i. WILLIAM BLAND[9] HAMPTON, b. 22 Sep 1909, Cleburne, Johnson Co., TX; d. 06 Jul 1910, Cleburne, Johnson Co., TX.
    ii. CECIL HAMPTON, b. 24 Jun 1912, Cleburne, Johnson Co., TX; d. 27 Feb 1936, Kleberg Co., TX.

        Notes for CECIL HAMPTON:
        Source: Nueces County Texas Standard Certificate of Death

    iii. VERNON RANDOLPH HAMPTON, b. 03 May 1913, Cleburne, Johnson Co., TX; d. 06 Sep 1963, Dallas Co., TX; m. MARY LEE DUNCAN.

Notes for VERNON RANDOLPH HAMPTON:
Source: Dallas County Texas Certificate of Death

   iv.   JAMES ALVIN HAMPTON, b. 25 Apr 1916, Cleburne, Johnson Co., TX; d. 15 Jul 1992, Clark Co., NE.
   v.   DELTON MARMADUKE HAMPTON, b. 08 May 1918, Cleburne, Johnson Co., TX; d. 27 Dec 1978, Maricopa Co., AZ; m. TINY GRIFFITH.
   vi.   THOMAS V. HAMPTON, b. 09 Jul 1923, TX; d. 08 Feb 2009, McLennan Co., TX; m. JOY WALKER.
   vii.   ANNIE HAMPTON, b. 06 Mar 1926, Cook Co., TX; d. 03 Jan 1997, Dallas Co., TX.
   viii.   MARY HAMPTON, b. 19 May 1931, Dimmit Co., TX; d. 15 Dec 2003, LeFlore Co., MS.

23. ZUMA ETTA[8] HAMPTON (MARY ADALINE[7] BALLARD, BLAND WILLIAM[6], JAMES[5], BLAND WILLIAM[4], BLAND[3], BLAND[2], WILLIAM[1]) was born 27 Jul 1891 in Hill Co., TX, and died 01 Feb 1977 in Godley, Johnson Co., TX. She married HENRY EARL CULL, son of JAMES WILLIAM CULL. He was born 15 Sep 1890, and died 04 Jan 1955.

More About ZUMA ETTA HAMPTON:
Burial: Rosehill Cemetery, Cleburne, Johnson Co., TX

More About HENRY EARL CULL:
Burial: Rosehill Cemetery, Cleburne, Johnson Co., TX

Children of ZUMA HAMPTON and HENRY CULL are:

   i.   MARY BLAND[9] CULL, b. 1923, Hills Co TX.
   ii.   JOHN VALENTINE CULL, b. 26 Apr 1927, Cleburne, Johnson Co., TX; d. 12 Nov 1983.

      More About JOHN VALENTINE CULL:
      Burial: Restland Memorial Park, Dallas Co., TX

Generation No. 5

24. ANNA ELIZABETH[9] MURPHY (LIZZIE V.[8] WILLIAMSON, JOHN JAMES[7], ELIZABETH ANN "LIZZIE"[6] BALLARD, JAMES[5], BLAND WILLIAM[4], BLAND[3], BLAND[2], WILLIAM[1]) was born 20 Jan 1926 in Hidalgo Co., TX, and died 27 May 2015. She married GERALD RAY 10 Aug 1943 in Cameron Co., TX.

Notes for ANNA ELIZABETH MURPHY:
Source: Texas Standard Certificate of Birth

Child of ANNA MURPHY and GERALD RAY is:
   i.   GERALD[10] RAY.

James Gaines Ballard

Generation No. 1

1. JAMES GAINES[4] BALLARD (CURTIS[3], PHILIP[2], WILLIAM[1]) *was born 14 Feb 1791 in Culpeper Co., VA, and died 23 Jun 1872 in Libertyville, St. Francois Co., MO. He married* RACHEL L. HITT *18 Nov 1830 in Cape, Girardeau Co., MO, daughter of* WILLIAM HITT *and* LEAH PEDDY. *She was born 09 Feb 1809 in Cape Girardeau Co., MO, and died 29 Jul 1897 in Libertyville, St Francois Co., MO.*

Notes for JAMES GAINES BALLARD:
Source: Will of James Ballard, Nancy Johnson, William Curtis Ballard, His Ancestors and Descendents by John Ballard Draper. Cemeteries Madison Co MO Volume 1 by Historical Madison Co. Soc., 1830 Madison County Kentucky Federal Census Records, 1850-1860 Genevieve County Missouri Federal Census Records, Find A Grave

** He was buried Womack, Missouri Ballard Cemetery, 1/2 mile off Highway T in the woods.*
** 1830 - Living in Madison Co., KY*
** 1850 - Living in St. Genevieve Co., MO - Ballard, James 59 VA, Rachel 42 MO, Sarah 18 MO, William C. 15 MO, John 13 MO, Marcissa 11 MO, Fanny D 8 MO, Missouri F. MO*
** 1860 - Living in Saline, St. Genevieve Co., MO - Ballard, James 67 VA, Rachel 51 MO, Sarah M 2 MO, John G 23 MO, Frances D 18 MO, Missouri F 15 MO*
** 1872 - St. Francois Co., MO - 1 James Ballard a citizen of the united States and lately a resident of the County of St. Francois in the State of Missouri, Do make, ordain and declare this instrument which as written by my directions many presence and under my direction my being incapable through sickness and debility to write it myself but which every page thereof is signed with my own signature to be my last will and testament. In Premise, I do leave and bequeath all my real estate which I now own to my beloved wife Rachel Ballard which said estate consists of the North half of the West quarter of section twelve Township thirty-four North of Rouge Seven East also N East half of the south West quarter of section one township thirty-four North of Rouge Seven Containing one hundred and sixty acres more or less. To have and to hold the same during her natural life in full possession in connection also with my daughters Sarah M. Ballard, Narcissa J. Ballard and Missouri F Ballard to have and participate in the same as their lawful homestead during their singleness of life and in case of their death or marriage to come in and participate in the division of the said estate with my other lawful heirs to wit William C. Ballard, Fanny B. Ballard, wife of Samuel J Barren and John G Ballard.*
Secondly, That all the personal property which I shall have on hand and in my possession at the time of my death, I leave in the full possession of my wife to be held by her and disposed of as she shall judge best fit to be most proper for her use and benefit of herself and balance of the family. Thirdly, I wish her to draw the pension which I now draw from my government for her own use and benefit. In witness of and each of the things herein contained I have this day set my hand and seal this tenth day of June A.D. one thousand eight hundred and seventy-two. James Ballard (seal).
Witnesses: Lewis Laborot, John S. Beard, Abraham Barron

** 1872 - October - State of Missouri County of St. Francois - In the Probate Court of said County October Term 1872. Be it remembered that on this 10th day of October A. D. 1872 Then came into the Probate Court of St. Francois County, Missouri, which the same is in the Session, Lewis Laborot and presents the last will and testament of James Ballard, deceased, and also personally appeared in open Court, Lewis Laborot and Abraham Barron subscribing witnesses to the annexed will of said deceased, and being first duly sworn, depose and say that the said James Ballard, the testator, presented them an instrument of writing purporting the last will and testament, and that they submitted the same as witnesses these to in the presence of the testator and at his request; That the said testator acknowledged the signature appended thereto this signature that at the time of this signing as witnesses they heard him publish and dictate the said will the last will and testament; That the said testator was, at the time of publishing his said will of sound mind and more then twenty-one years of age; which said proof so considered by the Court sufficient as to wish the validity of said will and it is ordered that the same be certified accordingly. Abraham Barron, Lewis Laborot.*
In Testimony whereof, I, A. C. McHenry, Judge of Probate within and for the County of St. Francis and State aforesaid, have hereunto subscribed my name and affixed my official seal at office in the town of Farmington the day and year aforesaid. A. C McHenry Judge of probate.

Filed October 10th 172. A. C. McHenry, Judge of Probate

More About JAMES GAINES BALLARD:
Burial: Ballard Cemetery, Womack, St. Francois Co., MO

Notes for RACHEL L. HITT:
Source: 1880 St. Francois County Missouri Federal Census Records
** 1880 - Living in Liberty, St. Francois Co., MO - Ballard, Rachel 71 MO VA GA, Sarah M 48 MO, Jane N 40 MO, Jefferson D 18 grandson Farmer, John G 16 grandson works on farm*

More About RACHEL L. HITT:
Burial: Ballard Cemetery., Womack, St. Francois Co., MO

Children of JAMES BALLARD and RACHEL HITT are:

    i.   VIRGINIA⁵ BALLARD, b. Abt. 1831, Cape Girardeau Co., MO; m. SON HUTCHINSON.

   ii.   SARAH "SALLIE" M. BALLARD, b. 26 Aug 1832, Cape Girardeau Co., MO; d. 12 Apr 1910, Liberty, St. Francois Co., MO.

       Notes for SARAH "SALLIE" M. BALLARD:
       Source: St. Francois County Missouri Death Certificate # 10876

       More About SARAH "SALLIE" M. BALLARD:
       Burial: Ballard Cemetery., Womack , St. Genevieve Co., MO

2.   iii.   WILLIAM CURTIS BALLARD, JUDGE, b. 13 Jan 1836, Cape Girardeau Co., MO; d. 14 Apr 1913, Dickens Co., TX.

3.   iv.   JOHN GAINES BALLARD, b. 03 Apr 1837, Cape Girardeau Co., MO; d. 05 Dec 1911, Farmington, St. Francois Co., MO.

    v.   NARCISSA JANE BALLARD, b. 04 Apr 1839, Cape Girardeau Co., MO; d. 04 Jun 1914, St. Francois Co., MO.

       Notes for NARCISSA JANE BALLARD:
       Source: Obituary, St. Francois County Missouri Death Certificate

       ** Inquest held over Miss Ballard's Body - Dr. English held an inquest last Friday over the body of Narcissus Ballard, near Womack, the account of whose tragic death in the burning of her home was published in last weeks' News. A number of witnesses were examined, but no evidence was brought out indicating that there had been foul play in the connection with the burning of her home and her death, as had been suspected by some. There were no evidence on her body that she had been murdered. The coroner's jury returned a verdict that she came to her death by burning, but did not fix the responsibility upon anyone.*

       More About NARCISSA JANE BALLARD:
       Burial: 05 Jun 1914, Ballard Cemetery.,

4.   vi.   FRANCES "FANNY" DELANEY BALLARD, b. 14 Oct 1841, Cape Girardeau Co., MO; d. 30 Dec 1891, Womack, St. Genevieve Co., MO.

5.   vii.   MISSOURI FRANCIS BALLARD, b. 30 Sep 1844, Cape Girardeau Co., MO; d. 05 Apr 1919, MO.

Generation No. 2

2. WILLIAM CURTIS⁵ BALLARD, JUDGE (*JAMES GAINES⁴, CURTIS³, PHILIP², WILLIAM¹*) was born 13 Jan 1836 in Cape Girardeau Co., MO, and died 14 Apr 1913 in Dickens Co., TX. He married (1) ARTAMISSA M. BOYD 01 May 1856 in St. Genevieve Co., MO. She was born 14 Nov 1840 in MO, and died 13 Sep 1885 in Haskell Co., TX. He married

(2) MARY FRANCES PATTERSON 04 Jan 1887 in poss. Granbury TX. She was born 15 Nov 1852, and died 01 Jan 1929 in Dickens Co., TX.

Notes for WILLIAM CURTIS BALLARD, JUDGE:
Source: William Curtis Ballard, His Ancestors and Descendents by John Ballard Draper, 1860-1880 St. Genevieve County Missouri Federal Census Records, 1900 -1910 Dickens County Texas Federal Census Records

** 1860 - Living in Saline, St. Genevieve Co., MO - Ballard, WC 26 VA, Artemissa 19*
** 1870 - Living in Saline, St. Genevieve Co., MO - Ballard, William 35, A. M 29, Mary 12, Sarah 10, Martha 7, Thomas 3, Cora 2*
** 1880 - Living in St. Genevieve Co., MO - Ballard, WC 45, AM 40, Sarah J 19, Martha 17, Thomas E 13, John J 8, Rachel 6*
** 1900 - Living in Dickens Co., TX - Ballard, William C - Jan 1835 MO VA MO, MF - Nov 1853 MO MO MO, Willie E - Aug 1889 TX MO MO*
** 1910 - Living in Dickens Co., TX - Ballard, William C 75 MO VA VA, Mary F 57 MO MO MO, Willie dau 20 TX*

More About ARTAMISSA M. BOYD:
Burial: Willow Cemetery, Haskell, Haskell Co., TX

Notes for MARY FRANCES PATTERSON:
Source: Dickens County Texas Standard Certificate of Death

More About MARY FRANCES PATTERSON:
Burial: Dickens County Cemetery, Dickens Co., TX

Children of WILLIAM BALLARD and ARTAMISSA BOYD are:

6.	i.	MARY E.[6] BALLARD, b. 22 Jan 1858, Cape Girardeau Co., MO; d. 28 Jun 1938, St. Genevieve Co., MO.
7.	ii.	SARAH JANE BALLARD, b. 11 Jul 1860, Cape Girardeau Co., MO; d. 07 Apr 1948, Silver City, Grant Co., NM.
	iii.	MARTHA L. "MATTIE" BALLARD, b. 03 Apr 1863, St. Genevieve Co., MO; d. 13 Aug 1885, Haskell Co., TX.

More About MARTHA L. "MATTIE" BALLARD:
Burial: Willow Cemetery, Haskell, Haskell Co., TX

8.	iv.	THOMAS EDWIN BALLARD, b. 18 Aug 1866, St. Genevieve Co., MO; d. 15 Feb 1944, Haskell Co., TX.
9.	v.	CORA HELEN BALLARD, b. 16 Mar 1868, Cape Girardeau Co., MO; d. 29 Mar 1941.
10.	vi.	JOHN JAMES BALLARD, b. 15 Jan 1872, St. Genevieve Co., MO; d. 15 Jan 1970, Winnemucca, Humboldt Co., NV.
11.	vii.	RACHEL LOUISE BALLARD, b. 18 Feb 1874, Cape Girardeau Co., MO; d. 31 Aug 1953, Jones Co., TX.
12.	viii.	ESTELLA "ESSIE" CURTIS BALLARD, b. 08 Jul 1881, MO; d. 16 Jun 1962, Dickens Co., TX.
	ix.	WILLIE E. BALLARD, b. Abt. 1882, Dickens Co., TX; d. Aft. 1910.

Children of WILLIAM BALLARD and MARY PATTERSON are:

13.	x.	WILLIE EVELYN[6] BALLARD, b. 25 Aug 1889, Haskell Co., TX; d. 06 Apr 1936, Dickens Co., TX.
	xi.	INFANT SON BALLARD, b. 17 Sep 1894; d. 03 Oct 1894.

3. *JOHN GAINES[5] BALLARD (JAMES GAINES[4], CURTIS[3], PHILIP[2], WILLIAM[1]) was born 03 Apr 1837 in Cape Girardeau Co., MO, and died 05 Dec 1911 in Farmington, St. Francois Co., MO. He married (1) SUSAN ELIZABETH MCDOWELL 28 Oct 1860 in St. Francois Co., MO. She was born Abt. 1838 in MO, and died Bef. 1872 in lived in St. Francois Co., MO with mother in law. He married (2) FANNY IRBY STARBIRD 15 Aug 1872 in MO. She was born 25 Sep 1854 in MA, and died 07 Jul 1931.*

Notes for JOHN GAINES BALLARD:
Source: 1880-1900 Genevieve County Missouri Federal Census Records, mbb13@suddenlink.net, Civil War Draft Registration, Find A Grave
** 1880 - Living in Genevieve Co., MO - Ballard, John G 42 MO VA MA, Fanny I 26, James 6, Irby 4, William C 1*
** 1900 - Living in Liberty, St. Francois Co., MO - wit sisters Sarah and Narcissa, Ballard, John G - Apr 1837 MO VA MO*

More About JOHN GAINES BALLARD:
Burial: Parkview Cemetery, Farmington, St. Francois Co., MO

Notes for FANNY IRBY STARBIRD:
Source: 1900 St. Genevieve County Missouri Federal Census Records
** 1900 - Living in Saline, St. Genevieve Co., MO - Ballard, Frances - Sep 1854 IL 9 children 9 living, Josephine - July 1883 MO, Rachel E - Feb 1884 MO, Sally V - Jan 1886 MO, Phillip H - April 1888 MO, Ada Grace - June 1890 MO, Mary N - June 1898 MO*

More About FANNY IRBY STARBIRD:
Burial: Parkview Cemetery, Farmington, St. Francois Co., MO

Children of JOHN BALLARD and SUSAN MCDOWELL are:

| | i. | JEFFERSON D^6 BALLARD, b. 1862. |
| 14. | ii. | JOHN GAINES BALLARD, b. 31 Jan 1863, Grand Tower IL; d. 31 Oct 1916, Farmington, St. Francois Co., MO. |

Children of JOHN BALLARD and FANNY STARBIRD are:

15.	iii.	JAMES CHARLES^6 BALLARD, b. 01 Sep 1873, IL; d. 25 Jul 1948, St. Francois Co., MO.
	iv.	IRBY FRANCIS BALLARD, b. 28 Jul 1875, IL; d. 04 Jan 1947, MI; Stepchild.
16.	v.	WILLIAM CURTIS BALLARD, b. 21 May 1880, St. Genevieve Co., MO; d. 06 Jun 1941, Cape Girardeau Co., MO; Stepchild.
	vi.	JOSEPHINE BALLARD, b. 15 Sep 1883, MO; d. 1970, St. Louis co., MO; Stepchild.
	vii.	RACHEL EDITH BALLARD, b. Feb 1884, MO; d. Aft. 1900; Stepchild.
	viii.	SARAH VIRGINIA BALLARD, b. 26 Jan 1886, MO; d. 08 Oct 1974, Miami-Dade Co., FL; Stepchild.

More About SARAH VIRGINIA BALLARD:
Burial: Parkview Cemetery, Farmington, St. Francois Co., MO

17.	ix.	PHILLIP HITT BALLARD, b. 01 Apr 1888, Fredericktown, Madison Co., MO; d. 27 Feb 1979, Hot Springs, Garland Co., AR; Stepchild.
	x.	ADA GRACE BALLARD, b. Jun 1890, MO; d. Aft. 1900; Stepchild.
	xi.	MARY N. BALLARD, b. Jun 1898, MO; d. Aft. 1900; Stepchild.

4. FRANCES "FANNY" DELANEY^5 BALLARD (JAMES GAINES^4, CURTIS^3, PHILIP^2, WILLIAM^1) was born 14 Oct 1841 in Cape Girardeau Co., MO, and died 30 Dec 1891 in Womack, St. Genevieve Co., MO. She married SAMUEL JAMES BARRON 30 Aug 1866 in St. Francois MO, son of ABRAHAM BARRON and PHOEBE WELKER. He was born 13 Aug 1841 in Madison, MO, and died 01 Apr 1905 in Womack, St. Genevieve Co., MO.

More About FRANCES "FANNY" DELANEY BALLARD:
Burial: Ballard Cemetery, Womack, St. Francois Co., MO

Notes for SAMUEL JAMES BARRON:
Source: 1870-1880 Saline Missouri Federal Census Records, 1900 St. Genevieve County Missouri Federal Census Records
** 1870 - Living in Perry, Saline Genevieve Co., MO - Barron, Samuel 28 Farmer MO, Delany 28 MO, Sarah 3 MO,*

Lillie 3/12 MO
** 1880 - Living in Saline, St. Genevieve Co., MO - Ballard, Samuel J 37, Fanny D 37, Sarah E 13, Lillie E 10, James E 8, Phoebe E 6, Rachel A 4*
** 1900 - Living in Saline, St. Genevieve Co., MO - Barron, S. J - Aug 1841 58 - wd MO TN MO, Rachel A dau - Aug 1876 23 - MO, Lilly E. Counts - Feb 1870 MO, Gilbert E g son - July 1893 - MO*

Children of FRANCES BALLARD and SAMUEL BARRON are:

	i.	SARAH E.[6] BARRON, b. 1867, MO; d. Aft. 1880.
18.	ii.	LILLIE E. BARRON, b. 16 Feb 1869, MO; d. 29 Jul 1923, St. Francois Co., MO.
	iii.	JAMES EVERETT BARRON, b. 12 Jan 1872, MO; d. 06 May 1918, St. Francois Co., MO; m. MARY BOYD.
	iv.	RACHEL A. BARRON, b. 31 Aug 1876, St. Genevieve Co., MO; d. 01 Jun 1946, St. Francois Co., MO; m. JOHN L. MOORE.
	v.	PHOEBE E. BARRON, b. 1876, MO; d. Aft. 1880.

5.   MISSOURI FRANCIS[5] BALLARD (JAMES GAINES[4], CURTIS[3], PHILIP[2], WILLIAM[1]) was born 30 Sep 1844 in Cape Girardeau Co., MO, and died 05 Apr 1919 in MO. She married WILLIAM HENRY HINES 11 Aug 1872 in St. Francois Co., MO. He was born 10 Mar 1849 in Independence Co., AR, and died 03 Feb 1935.

Notes for MISSOURI FRANCIS BALLARD:
St. Genevieve County Missouri Certificate of Death

More About MISSOURI FRANCIS BALLARD:
Burial: Ballard Cemetery., Womack, St. Francois Co., MO

Notes for WILLIAM HENRY HINES:
Source: 1880-1910 St. Genevieve County Missouri Federal Census Records
** 1880 - Living in Saline, St. Genevieve Co., MO - Hines, Wm H 31, Missouri F 34, Rachel C 6, Carrie A 4, James W 2*
1900 - Living in Saline, St. Genevieve Co., MO - Hines, Wm. H Mar 1849 AR TN TN , Missouri Sep 1844 - 5 children 4 living MO VA MO, William - Jan 1881 MO, Martha Aug 1885 MO
** 1910 - Living in Saline, St. Genevieve Co., MO - Hines, William H 61 AR TN TN, Missouri F 65 MO VA MO, William J 29 MO, Marvin A Wright servant*

More About WILLIAM HENRY HINES:
Burial: McDowell-Lenz Cemetery, St. Francois Co., MO

Children of MISSOURI BALLARD and WILLIAM HINES are:

	i.	RACHEL CORINE[6] HINES, b. 02 Aug 1873, MO; d. 15 Sep 1898, MO; m. JAMES G. TUCKER, 26 Dec 1893, Madison Co., MO.

More About RACHEL CORINE HINES:
Burial: Ballard Cemetery, Womack, St. Francois Co., MO

	ii.	CARRIE ADNEY HINES, b. 23 Nov 1875, Womack, St. Genevieve Co., MO; d. 11 Jan 1931, Womack, St. Genevieve Co., MO; m. GEORGE LENZ; b. 25 Dec 1865; d. 19 Aug 1936.

More About CARRIE ADNEY HINES:
Burial: McDowell-Lenz Cemetery, St. Francois Co., MO

	iii.	JAMES WESLEY HINES, b. 19 Feb 1879, St. Genevieve Co., MO; d. 19 Jun 1944, Memphis, Shelby Co., TN; m. TILDA.
	iv.	WILLIAM JEFFERSON HINES, b. 24 Jan 1881, St. Genevieve Co., MO; d. 14 Nov 1960; m. HATTIE MAE KING, 10 May 1916, Farmington, St. Francois Co., MO; b. 01 Jul 1894; d. 02 May 1992.

More About WILLIAM JEFFERSON HINES:
Burial: Ballard Cemetery, Womack, St. Francois Co., MO

More About HATTIE MAE KING:
Burial: Ballard Cemetery, Womack, St. Francois Co., MO

    v.   MARTHA MISSOURI HINES, b. 05 Aug 1885, St. Francois Co., MO; d. 21 Apr 1922, St. Francois Co., MO.

Generation No. 3

6. MARY E.[6] BALLARD (WILLIAM CURTIS[5], JAMES GAINES[4], CURTIS[3], PHILIP[2], WILLIAM[1]) was born 22 Jan 1858 in Cape Girardeau Co., MO, and died 28 Jun 1938 in St. Genevieve Co., MO. She married JOHN H. PATTERSON 29 May 1879 in St. Genevieve Co., MO. He was born 05 Dec 1854 in MO, and died 29 Jun 1946 in St. Genevieve Co., MO.

Notes for MARY E. BALLARD:
Source: William Curtis Ballard, His Ancestors and Descendents by John Ballard Draper

More About MARY E. BALLARD:
Burial: Stone Cemetery. near Coffman MO

Notes for JOHN H. PATTERSON:
Source: 1900 St. Genevieve County Missouri Federal Census Records

** 1900 - Living in Saline, St. Genevieve Co., MO - Patterson, John - Dec 1854 MO MO MO, Mary - Jan 1858 MO MO MO, Martha - July 1883, Artimissa - Sept 1889, Blanch - June 1892, Zelma - April 1896 MO, Ruth - Feb 1898 MO, William - Feb 1898 MO*

More About JOHN H. PATTERSON:
Burial: Stone Church Cemetery, St. Genevieve Co., MO

Children of MARY BALLARD and JOHN PATTERSON are:

    i.   LORENZO B.[7] PATTERSON, b. 24 Aug 1880, St. Genevieve Co., MO; d. 24 Mar 1896, St. Genevieve Co., MO.

        More About LORENZO B. PATTERSON:
        Burial: Stone Church Cemetery, St. Genevieve Co., MO

    ii.   MATTIE E. PATTERSON, b. 08 Jul 1884, St. Genevieve Co., MO; d. 11 Jun 1956; m. PETE RUDLOFF, 30 Mar 1914.

        More About MATTIE E. PATTERSON:
        Burial: Minnith Cemetery, St. Genevieve Co., MO

    iii.   ARTIE MISSA PATTERSON, b. 17 Sep 1889, St. Genevieve Co., MO; d. 23 Oct 1953, St. Genevieve Co., MO.

        More About ARTIE MISSA PATTERSON:
        Burial: Stone Church Cemetery, St. Genevieve Co., MO

    iv.   BLANCHE PATTERSON, b. 30 Jun 1892, St. Genevieve Co., MO; d. 29 Dec 1963, St. Genevieve Co., MO; m. OTTO SMITH.

More About BLANCHE PATTERSON:
Burial: Crestlawn Cemetery, St. Genevieve Co., MO

    v.   MARY ZELMA PATTERSON, b. 10 Apr 1895, St. Genevieve Co., MO; d. 15 Jul 1940, St. Genevieve Co., MO; m. HENRY RALPH GRIFFITH; b. 19 Apr 1896, St. Genevieve Co., MO; d. 21 Mar 1966, St. Genevieve Co., MO.

More About MARY ZELMA PATTERSON:
Burial: Stone Church Cemetery, St. Genevieve Co., MO

More About HENRY RALPH GRIFFITH:
Burial: Stone Church Cemetery, St. Genevieve Co., MO

    vi.   RUTH PATTERSON, b. 20 Feb 1897, St. Genevieve Co., MO; d. 21 Oct 1978, Farmington, St. Francois Co., MO; m. ROBERT COULTER; b. 26 Dec 1892, MO.

More About RUTH PATTERSON:
Burial: Stone Church Cemetery, St. Genevieve Co., MO

    vii.   WILLIAM J. PATTERSON, b. 20 Feb 1897, St. Genevieve Co., MO; d. 27 May 1976; m. GRETCHEN BLOOM; b. 21 Nov 1905, St. Francois Co., MO; d. 23 Sep 1974, St. Genevieve Co., MO.

More About GRETCHEN BLOOM:
Burial: Stone Church Cemetery, St. Genevieve Co., MO

7. SARAH JANE[6] BALLARD (WILLIAM CURTIS[5], JAMES GAINES[4], CURTIS[3], PHILIP[2], WILLIAM[1]) was born 11 Jul 1860 in Cape Girardeau Co., MO, and died 07 Apr 1948 in Silver City, Grant Co., NM. She married JOHN LEONARD LaBRIERE 24 Jul 1882 in St. Genevieve Co., MO. He was born 02 Jul 1860 in St. Genevieve Co MO, and died 16 Sep 1935.

More About SARAH JANE BALLARD:
Burial: Masonic Cemetery, Silver City, Grant Co., NM

Notes for JOHN LEONARD LaBRIERE:
Source: 1900 Beaver County Oklahoma Federal Census Records, 1910 Prowers County Oklahoma Federal Census Records
** 1900 - Living in Harrison, Beaver Co., OK - Labriere, John - July 1861 MO, Sarah - July 1861 MO, Zeno - Nov 1886, Artie - June 1889 CO, Pearl - Sept 1891 CO, Ashley - Aug 1895 OK*
** 1910 - Living in Lamar, Prowers Co., OK - LaBriere, John 45 MO, Sallie 45 - 7 children 6 living, Artie 20 CO, Pearl 17 CO, Ashley 14 OH, Philamine 11 OK, Ruth 8 OK*

Children of SARAH BALLARD and JOHN LaBRIERE are:
    i.   LUCILLE[7] LaBRIERE, b. 24 Mar 1884, Haskell Co., TX; d. 18 Jan 1886, Haskell Co., TX.
    ii.   ZENO LaBRIERE, b. 24 Nov 1886, Haskell Co., TX; d. 30 Jun 1963, Haskell Co., TX.
    iii.   ARTIE LaBRIERE, b. 19 Jun 1889, CO; d. Aft. 1910; m. WILLIAM J. STEHLE, 10 Jul 1915; d. Jan 1955.
    iv.   PEARL LaBRIERE, b. 30 Sep 1891, CO; d. Aft. 1910; m. ROY HENRY, 27 Nov 1911; d. 1961.
    v.   ASHELY LaBRIERE, b. 23 Aug 1895, OK; d. May 1970; m. LOREE WOOD, 25 Sep 1915, Douglas, AZ.
    vi.   PHILAMINE LaBRIERE, b. 27 Jun 1898, OK; d. 30 Jan 1950; m. CHARLES E. WILLIAMSON.
    vii.   RUTH LaBRIERE, b. 11 Feb 1902, OK; d. Jun 1967; m. I. N. J. PORTER, 1918.

8. THOMAS EDWIN[6] BALLARD (WILLIAM CURTIS[5], JAMES GAINES[4], CURTIS[3], PHILIP[2], WILLIAM[1]) was born 18 Aug 1866 in St. Genevieve Co., MO, and died 15 Feb 1944 in Haskell Co., TX. He married SARAH "EMMA" EMILY POST 12 Dec 1889 in TX. She was born 15 Dec 1871 in Union Parish, LA, and died 03 Mar 1944 in Haskell Co., TX.

Notes for THOMAS EDWIN BALLARD:
Source: 1900 - 1940 Haskell County Texas Federal Census Records
** 1900 - Living in Haskell Co., TX - Ballard, Thomas E - Aug 1867 MO MO MO, Emma - Dec 1871 - 7 children 5 living LA AL AL, John C - Dec 1893 TX, Thomas L - July 1895 TX, Labury E - Apr 1897 TX, Alma E - Dec 1898 TX, Vasti Gilcrease boarder*
** 1910 - Living in Haskell Co., TX - Ballard, TE 42 MO MO MO, Emma 39 - 12 children 7 living LA AL AL, Curtis 16 TX, Thomas 14 TX, Labry 12 TX, Alma 10 TX, Flossie 8 TX, Henry 2 TX, Paul 8/12 TX*
** 1920 - Living in Haskell Co., TX - Ballard, T. E. - (Looks like JE but when compared to other "J"s on the page it's a "T" and not a J. 55 MO, S. E 48 LA, Thomas 24 TX, Flossie 18 TX, Henry 12 TX, Paul 10 TX, Christine 8 7/12 TX*
** 1930 - Living in Haskell Co., TX - Ballard, Thomas E 63 MO MO MO, Emma 58 LA AL AL, Henry 21 TX, Paul 20 TX (next door to Irene Ballard)*
** 1940 - Living in Haskell, Haskell Co., TX - Ballard, T E 73 MO, Emma 68 LA, Henry 32 TX*

More About THOMAS EDWIN BALLARD:
Burial: Willow Cemetery, Haskell, Haskell Co., TX

More About SARAH "EMMA" EMILY POST:
Burial: Willow Cemetery, Haskell, Haskell Co., TX

Children of THOMAS BALLARD and SARAH POST are:

      i.   ROY[7] BALLARD, b. 14 Feb 1891, Haskell Co., TX; d. 13 Aug 1894, Haskell Co., TX.

         More About ROY BALLARD:
         Burial: Willow Cemetery, Haskell, Haskell Co., TX

      ii.   BLAND BALLARD, b. 03 Jun 1892, Haskell Co., TX; d. 29 Aug 1894, Haskell Co., TX.

         More About BLAND BALLARD:
         Burial: Willow Cemetery, Haskell, Haskell Co., TX

19.   iii.   JOHN CURTIS BALLARD, b. 14 Dec 1893, Haskell Co., TX; d. Aug 1968, Pueblo Co., CO.
20.   iv.   THOMAS LYNN BALLARD, b. 14 Jul 1895, Haskell Co., TX; d. Aft. 1930, Haskell Co., TX.
21.   v.   LABRY E. BALLARD, b. 24 Apr 1897, Haskell Co., TX; d. 22 Jul 1921, Haskell Co., TX.
      vi.   ALMA ESTELLA BALLARD, b. 07 Dec 1898, Haskell Co., TX; d. Aft. 1910, Los Angeles Co., CA; m. JAMES CLARENCE PYEATT, 15 Mar 1918, Trinidad, Las Animas Co., CO; b. 08 Oct 1895.
      vii.   ROSS BALLARD, b. 06 Jun 1900, Haskell Co., TX; d. 04 May 1901, Haskell Co., TX.

         More About ROSS BALLARD:
         Burial: Willow Cemetery, Haskell, Haskell Co., TX

      viii.   FLORENCE FLAUCY EMILY BALLARD, b. 31 Jan 1902, Haskell Co., TX; d. 29 Jul 1987, Jackson Co., MO; m. (1) JAMES OTIS GALLOWAY, 1928, Rockwell Co., TX; m. (2) RAYMOND HOLT, Abt. 1945; m. (3) HARRY RALPH STALEY, DR., 1951, Kansas City, MO.
      ix.   LAWRENCE BALLARD, b. 29 Sep 1903, Haskell Co., TX; d. 28 Apr 1906, Haskell Co., TX.

         More About LAWRENCE BALLARD:
         Burial: Willow Cemetery, Haskell, Haskell Co., TX

      x.   GLADYS HESTER BALLARD, b. 19 Sep 1905, Haskell Co., TX; d. 05 May 1907, Haskell Co., TX.

         More About GLADYS HESTER BALLARD:
         Burial: Willow Cemetery, Haskell, Haskell Co., TX

      xi.   HENRY SIDNEY BALLARD, b. 05 Oct 1907, Haskell Co., TX; d. 02 Feb 1991, Jones Co., TX;

m. LOUISE STRICKLAND.

More About HENRY SIDNEY BALLARD:
Burial: Willow Cemetery, Haskell, Haskell Co., TX

   xii.   PAUL BALLARD, *b. 09 Sep 1909, Haskell Co., TX; d. Aft. 1930; m. (1)* VELMA LEMONS, *Abt. 1929; m. (2)* FRONZO CHLOE CRAIGER, *Abt. 1933.*

   xiii.   MELBA CHRISTINE BALLARD, *b. 16 Jun 1911, Haskell Co., TX; d. Aft. 1920; m.* HUGH HUEBSCH; *b. 02 Nov 1908, Chillicothe TX.*

9. CORA HELEN[6] BALLARD (*WILLIAM CURTIS[5], JAMES GAINES[4], CURTIS[3], PHILIP[2], WILLIAM[1]*) *was born 16 Mar 1868 in Cape Girardeau Co., MO, and died 29 Mar 1941. She married* WILLIAM FRANKLIN DRAPER *18 Nov 1885 in Throckmorton Co., TX. He was born Sep 1855 in VA, and died Aft. 1920.*

More About CORA HELEN BALLARD:
Burial: Source: 1900 Haskell County Texas Federal Census Records

Notes for WILLIAM FRANKLIN DRAPER:
Source: 1900 Haskell County Texas Federal Census Records
** 1900 - Living in Haskell Co., TX - Draper, William - Sep 1855 AL, Cora H - March 1868, Mama L - Sep 1888, Ira E - June 1890, John B - Sep 1897, Frank - Nov 1899*
** 1910 - Living in Haskell, Haskell Co., TX - Draper, William F 55 AL AL AL , Cora H 42 MO MO MO, John B 12 TX, Frank C 10 TX*
** 1920 - Living in Haskell Co. TX - Draper, William F 64 AL, Cora H 51 MO, Mamie Barren 31 dau TX, Helen Barron 10 granddaughter TX, Frank C. Draper 20 son TX*

Children of CORA BALLARD and WILLIAM DRAPER are:
      i.   INFANT SON[7] DRAPER, *b. 07 Feb 1887, TX.*
22.   *ii.*   MAMIE LOVELESS DRAPER, *b. 02 Sep 1888, TX; d. Aft. 1900.*
     iii.   IRA ESTELLA DRAPER, *b. 26 Jun 1890, Haskell Co., TX; d. 24 Oct 1975, Seymour, Baylor Co., TX; m.* WILL J. LOWRY, *17 Feb 1908; d. Haskell Co., TX.*

        Notes for IRA ESTELLA DRAPER:
        Source: Baylor county Texas Certificate of Death

     iv.   JOHN BALLARD DRAPER, *b. 14 Sep 1897, Haskell Co., TX; d. Aft. 1910; m.* GILBERTA GREEN, *03 Jun 1920, Spur, TX.*
     v.   FRANK COLEMAN DRAPER, *b. 17 Nov 1899, Haskell Co., TX; d. 18 Nov 1965; m.* RUTH STRICKLAND, *18 Nov 1929, Haskell Co., TX.*

10. JOHN JAMES[6] BALLARD (*WILLIAM CURTIS[5], JAMES GAINES[4], CURTIS[3], PHILIP[2], WILLIAM[1]*) *was born 15 Jan 1872 in St. Genevieve Co., MO, and died 15 Jan 1970 in Winnemucca, Humboldt Co., NV. He married* SARAH LAVINA STEPHENS *10 Jun 1900 in Haskell, Haskell Co .,TX. She was born 08 Mar 1876 in Marengo Co., AL, and died 04 May 1953 in Winnemucca, Humboldt Co., NV.*

Notes for JOHN JAMES BALLARD:
Source: 1910 Prowers County Colorado Federal Census Records, 1920 Las Animas County Colorado Federal Census Records, 1930 Malheur County Oregon Federal Census Records

** 1910 - Living in Lamar, Prowers Co., CO - Ballard, J J 38 MO, Lulu 36AL, Joaquin 8 OK, Eula 7 OK, Clara 5 OK, Brady Pierce 36 roomer, Eula Pierce 25 roomer*
** 1920 - Living in Trinchera, Las Animas Co., CO - Ballard, John J 47 MO MO MO, Sarah L 43 AL AL AL, Eulah 16 OK, Clara 14 OK, Leona 6 OK*
** 1930 - Living in Malheur Co., OR - Ballard, John J 58 MO KY KY Sarah L 54 AL AL AL, Joaquin 29 OK, Leona*

B 17 OK, Grace N dau in law 23 IL, Virgil B grandson 2 11/12 MO, Eulah S Land dau 27 OK, James H son in law 32 NM, Jimmie J grand dau 2 3/12 OR, William Simon lodger

Children of JOHN BALLARD and SARAH STEPHENS are:
23.   i.   JOAQUIN[7] BALLARD, b. 20 Apr 1901, OK; d. 29 Dec 1981, Reno, Washoe Co., NE.
24.   ii.   EULAH BALLARD, b. 24 Mar 1903, OK; d. 29 Dec 1980, Reno, Washoe Co., NE.
        iii. CLARA BALLARD, b. 18 Jan 1905, OK; d. 05 Jan 1958, Elko Co., NE.
        iv. LEONA B. BALLARD, b. 06 Mar 1913, OK; d. 31 Jul 1969, Reno, Washoe Co., NE.

11. RACHEL LOUISE[6] BALLARD (WILLIAM CURTIS[5], JAMES GAINES[4], CURTIS[3], PHILIP[2], WILLIAM[1]) *was born 18 Feb 1874 in Cape Girardeau Co., MO, and died 31 Aug 1953 in Jones Co., TX. She married HENRY SAMUEL POST 07 Sep 1892 in Dickens Co., TX, son of JOHN POST and EMILY BARRON. He was born Nov 1868 in LA, and died Aft. 1920.*

Notes for HENRY SAMUEL POST:
Source: 1900-1920 Haskell County Texas Federal Census Records
** 1900 - Living in Haskell Co., TX - Post, Henry - Nov 1868 LA, Rachel L - Feb 1874 MO, Marvin H - Apr 1894 TX, Bailey - July 1896 TX, Frances L - Apr 1900 TX*
** 1910 - Living in Haskell Co., TX - Post, HS 42 LA AL AL, Rachel 35 MO MO MO, Marvin 15 TX, Bailey 13 TX, Fannie 10 TX, Gaines 8 TX, Artie 1 5/12 TX*
** 1920 - Living in Haskell Co., TX - Post HS 52, Rachel 45, Fannie 19, Gaines 17*

Children of RACHEL BALLARD and HENRY POST are:
        i.   MARVIN HENRY[7] POST, b. 25 Apr 1894, Haskell Co., TX; d. 25 Jun 1988, Kerr Co., TX; m. GLADYS HUCKABEE, 01 Sep 1919, Haskell Co., TX.
        ii.   JOHN BAILY POST, b. 24 Jul 1896, Haskell Co., TX; d. 01 Aug 1979, Corckett Co., TX; m. MYRTLE MARR.
        iii. FRANCES "FANNIE" POST, b. Apr 1900, TX; d. Aft. 1910; m. GEORGE CANNON.

            More About FRANCES "FANNIE" POST:
            Burial: Mission Burial Park South, San Antonio, Bexar Co., TX

        iv. GAINES POST, b. 07 Mar 1902, Haskell Co., TX; d. 19 Dec 1986, Haskell Co., TX; m. KATHERINE RICE; b. 1911.

            More About GAINES POST:
            Burial: Willow Cemetery, Haskell, Haskell Co., TX

        v.   CORA POST, b. 09 Jan 1906, Haskell Co., TX; d. 20 May 1907.

            More About CORA POST:
            Burial: Willow Cemetery, Haskell, Haskell Co., TX

        vi. ARTIE POST, b. 31 Oct 1908, Haskell Co., TX; d. 18 May 1910.

            More About ARTIE POST:
            Burial: Willow Cemetery, Haskell, Haskell Co., TX

        vii. AUSTIN VERNON POST, b. 06 Apr 1911, Haskell Co., TX; d. 04 Jul 1913.

            More About AUSTIN VERNON POST:
            Burial: Willow Cemetery, Haskell Co., TX

12. ESTELLA "ESSIE" CURTIS[6] BALLARD (WILLIAM CURTIS[5], JAMES GAINES[4], CURTIS[3], PHILIP[2], WILLIAM[1]) was born 08 Jul 1881 in MO, and died 16 Jun 1962 in Dickens Co., TX. She married JAMES HUGH MEADORS 06 Jul 1895 in Haskell Co., TX. He was born Abt. 1875 in GA.

Notes for JAMES HUGH MEADORS:
Source: 1910 Haskell County Texas Federal Census Records
* 1910 - Living in Haskell Co., TX - Meador, J H 35, Essie 29 - 5 children 4 living MO, Ollive 13 TX, Cecil 9 TX, Helen 4 AR, Margarite 1 TX

Children of ESTELLA BALLARD and JAMES MEADORS are:
       i.   OLIVE ESTELLE[7] MEADORS, b. 02 Aug 1896, TX; d. Aft. 1910.
      ii.   BERNICE MEADORS, b. 12 Jun 1898; d. Bef. 1910.
     iii.   CECIL H. MEADORS, b. 12 Nov 1900, TX; d. Aft. 1910.
     iv.   CORA HELEN MEADORS, b. 08 Mar 1906, AR; d. Aft. 1910.
      v.   MARGUERITE MEADORS, b. 17 Dec 1907, TX; d. Aft. 1910.

13. WILLIE EVELYN[6] BALLARD (WILLIAM CURTIS[5], JAMES GAINES[4], CURTIS[3], PHILIP[2], WILLIAM[1]) was born 25 Aug 1889 in Haskell Co., TX, and died 06 Apr 1936 in Dickens Co., TX. She married MR. SCOTT.

Child of WILLIE BALLARD and MR. SCOTT is:
       i.   BILLIE[7] SCOTT.

14. JOHN GAINES[6] BALLARD (JOHN GAINES[5], JAMES GAINES[4], CURTIS[3], PHILIP[2], WILLIAM[1]) was born 31 Jan 1863 in Grand Tower IL, and died 31 Oct 1916 in Farmington, St. Francois Co., MO. He married MARY STEELE SHAW. She was born 27 Jan 1871 in Libertyville, St. Francois Co., MO, and died 04 Apr 1913 in Farmington, St. Francois Co., MO.

Notes for JOHN GAINES BALLARD:
Source: St. Francois County Missouri Death Certificate, 1900-1910 St. François County Missouri Federal Census Records

* 1900 - Living in St. Francois Co., MO - Ballard, John G - Jan 1865 IL MO MO, Mary S - Jan 1871 MO MO MO, Willa H - Jan 1871 MO, James A - Jan 1894 MO, Mary R - Oct 1897 MO, Philip A - Nov 1899 MO, Francis J - July 1875 brother IL MO MO
* 1910 - Living in St. Francois Co., MO - Ballard, John 46 MO, Mary 38 MO, Willa 18 MO, James 16 MO, Roberta 12, Jeff 10 MO, Shaw 6 OK

More About JOHN GAINES BALLARD:
Burial: 02 Nov 1916, Parkview Cemetery, Farmington, St. Francois Co., MO

Notes for MARY STEELE SHAW:
Source: St. Francois County Missouri Death Certificate

More About MARY STEELE SHAW:
Burial: Parkview Cemetery, Farmington, St. Francois Co., MO

Children of JOHN BALLARD and MARY SHAW are:
       i.   WILLA H.[7] BALLARD, b. 17 Jan 1892, Farmington, St. Francois Co., MO; d. 02 Jan 1970, Dexter, Stoddard Co., MO; m. FLOYD DAVIS.

          More About WILLA H. BALLARD:
          Burial: Parkview Cemetery, Farmington, St. Francois Co., MO

      ii.   JAMES A. BALLARD, b. Jan 1894, St. Francois Co., MO; d. 01 Jun 1957; m. (1) ELIZABETH LINN;

b. 1896; m. (2) DORAN E. BROWN; b. 1890.

More About JAMES A. BALLARD:
Burial: Parkview Cemetery, Farmington, St. Francois Co., MO

iii.   MARY ROBERTA BALLARD, b. 08 Oct 1897, St. Francois Co., MO; d. 23 Oct 2001, Farmington, St. Francois Co., MO; m. (1) EDWARD ALBERT HAUPT; m. (2) THOMAS W. BYINGTON.

More About MARY ROBERTA BALLARD:
Burial: Sunset Memorial Park, Afton, St. Louis Co., MO

iv.   PHILIP A. BALLARD, b. Nov 1899, St. Francois Co., MO; d. Aft. 1900.
v.   JEFFERSON MADISON BALLARD, b. 21 Nov 1899, Farmington, St. Francois Co., MO; d. 22 Feb 1980, Farmington, St. Francois Co., MO; m. IDA MARY GOVREAU; b. 1900.
vi.   JOHN SHAW BALLARD, b. 12 Feb 1904, St. Francois Co., MO; d. 05 Mar 1977.

Notes for JOHN SHAW BALLARD:
Source: 1920 St. Francois County Missouri Federal Census Records
** 1920 - Living in St. Francois Co., MO - Ballard, Shas 16 MO boarder*

More About JOHN SHAW BALLARD:
Burial: Parkview Cemetery, Farmington, St. Francois Co., MO

15.   JAMES CHARLES[6] BALLARD (JOHN GAINES[5], JAMES GAINES[4], CURTIS[3], PHILIP[2], WILLIAM[1]) was born 01 Sep 1873 in IL, and died 25 Jul 1948 in St. Francois Co., MO. He married (1) EVA L. MARLOW. She was born 23 Nov 1872 in Perry Co., IL, and died 26 Aug 1968. He married (2) ELIZABETH MARY KIEPE. She was born 05 Sep 1873 in St. Francois Co., MO, and died 21 Apr 1934 in St. Francois Co., MO.

Notes for JAMES CHARLES BALLARD:
Source: 1910 - 1930 St. Francois County Missouri Federal Census Records, St. Francois County Missouri Death Certificate
** 1910 - Living in St. Francois Co., MO - Ballard, James C 32 IL, Lizzie M 32 MO, Genevieve A 7 MO, Helen C 4 MO, Marvin L 2 MO*
** 1920 - Living in St. Francois Co., MO - Ballard, James C 46, Lizzie M 46, Genevieve A 17, Ellen C 14, Marion Lynn 11, Frank I 8*
** 1930 - Living in Liberty, St. Francois Co., MO - Ballard, James C 56 IL, Lizzie M 56 MO, Lynn M 22 MO, Frank 18 MO, Earl J Boles 29 son in law MO, Helen C. Boles 24 daughter MO*

More About JAMES CHARLES BALLARD:
Burial: Parkview Cemetery, Farmington, St. Francois Co., MO

More About EVA L. MARLOW:
Burial: Masonic Cemetery, Madison Co., MO

More About ELIZABETH MARY KIEPE:
Burial: Parkview Cemetery, Farmington, St. Francois Co., MO

Children of JAMES BALLARD and ELIZABETH KIEPE are:
i.   GENEVIEVE[7] BALLARD, b. Abt. 1903, St. Genevieve Co., MO; d. Aft. 1920.
ii.   HELEN CORNELIA BALLARD, b. 24 May 1905, St. Genevieve Co., MO; d. 18 Dec 1975, Farmington, St. Francois Co., MO.
iii.   MARVIN LYNN BALLARD, b. Abt. 1908, St. Francois Co., MO; d. Aft. 1930.
iv.   FRANK I. BALLARD, b. 27 Dec 1911, St. Francois Co., MO; d. 30 Nov 2004.

16. WILLIAM CURTIS[6] BALLARD (JOHN GAINES[5], JAMES GAINES[4], CURTIS[3], PHILIP[2], WILLIAM[1]) was born 21 May 1880 in St. Genevieve Co., MO, and died 06 Jun 1941 in Cape Girardeau Co., MO. He married BERTHA WALTHER 20 Nov 1915 in Jackson, Cape Girardeau Co., MO. She was born 07 Nov 1886 in MO, and died 27 Jan 1973.

Notes for WILLIAM CURTIS BALLARD:
Source: 1920-1940 Cape Girardeau County Missouri Federal Census Records
* 1920 - Living in Cape Girardeau Co., MO - Ballard, William B 39 MO, Bertha 33 MO, Rosa - servant - Curtis G Ballard 2 9/12 MO, Robert G 1 7/12 MO
* 1930 - Living in Cape Girardeau Co., MO - Ballard, William C 49 MO MO IL, Bertha M C 43 MO MO LA, Curtis G 13 MO, Robert 11 MO, William W 10 MO, Helen V 8 MO, Mary L 5 MO
* 1940 - Living in Cape Girardeau Co., MO - Bullard, William C 59 MO, Bertha 53 MO, Curtis G 23 MO, Robert G 21 MO, William W 20 MO, Helen V 18 MO, Mary Lee 15 MO

More About WILLIAM CURTIS BALLARD:
Burial: Cape County Memorial Park Cemetery, Cape Girardeau Co., MO

More About BERTHA WALTHER:
Burial: Cape County Memorial Park, Cape Girardeau Co., MO

Children of WILLIAM BALLARD and BERTHA WALTHER are:

     i.   CURTIS G. "CURT"[7] BALLARD, b. 22 Mar 1917, Cape Girardeau Co., MO; d. 31 Jul 1956, Adair Co., MO.

          More About CURTIS G. "CURT" BALLARD:
          Burial: Valhalla Cemetery, Bel-Nor, St. Louis Co., OR

    ii.   ROBERT GAINES BALLARD, b. 07 May 1918, Boone Co., MO; d. 12 Jun 2000, Boone Co., MO.
   iii.   WILLLIAM W. BALLARD, b. Abt. 1920, MO; d. Aft. 1940.
   iv.   HELEN VIRGINIA BALLARD, b. 30 Oct 1921, Cape Girardeau Co., MO; d. 08 Mar 1999; m. MICHAEL GEORGE MINICH; b. 1920.

          More About HELEN VIRGINIA BALLARD:
          Burial: Church of the Red Rocks Columbarium, Coconino Co., AZ

     v.   MARY LEE BALLARD, b. 16 May 1924, Cape Girardeau Co., MO; d. 14 Jul 2013, Yavapai Co., AZ; m. CHARLES OLIVER BOWERS; b. 1918.

17. PHILLIP HITT[6] BALLARD (JOHN GAINES[5], JAMES GAINES[4], CURTIS[3], PHILIP[2], WILLIAM[1]) was born 01 Apr 1888 in Fredericktown, Madison Co., MO, and died 27 Feb 1979 in Hot Springs, Garland Co., AR. He married (1) LAURA FAY PATTON 26 Oct 1913 in New London, Ralls Co., MO, daughter of JOHN PATTON and MARY PHILLIPS. She was born 28 Feb 1891 in Paxton, Ford Co., IL, and died 31 Aug 1927 in Saline twp., Ralls Co., MO. He married (2) CYNTHIA E. COFFEY 29 Jan 1942 in Garland Co., AR. She was born 14 Mar 1900, and died 12 Nov 1971.

Notes for PHILLIP HITT BALLARD:
Source: Missouri marriage records, 1920 Cook County Illinois Federal Census Records, WWI Draft Registration Card, Ralls County Missouri Marriage Records, Garland County Arkansas Marriage Records

* 1920 - Living in Chicago, Cook Co., IL - Ballard, Philip H 32 MO MO MO ship builder government ship yard, Laura P 29 IL NY NY, Richard Halton 3 3/12

More About PHILLIP HITT BALLARD:
Burial: Greenwood Cemetery., Hot Springs, Garland Co., AR

More About CYNTHIA E. COFFEY:

Burial: Greenwood Cemetery, Hot Springs, Garland Co., AR

Child of PHILLIP BALLARD and LAURA PATTON is:
  i. RICHARD P.[7] BALLARD, b. 13 Sep 1916, Chicago, Cook Co., IL; d. 16 Jan 1974, Cincinnati, Hamilton Co., OH; m. SARAH MARGARET BAIN, 06 Jun 1943, Lee Co., NC; b. Abt. 1924.

   Notes for RICHARD P. BALLARD:
   Source: Lee County North Carolina Marriage Record
   ** Marriage records list parents as P. H Ballard and Lora Patton, father living in Hot Springs AR and mother deceased.*

   More About RICHARD P. BALLARD:
   Burial: Goshen Cemetery, Clermont Co., OH

18. LILLIE E.[6] BARRON (FRANCES "FANNY" DELANEY[5] BALLARD, JAMES GAINES[4], CURTIS[3], PHILIP[2], WILLIAM[1]) was born 16 Feb 1869 in MO, and died 29 Jul 1923 in St. Francois Co., MO. She married COUNTS. He died Bef. 1900.

Child of LILLIE BARRON and COUNTS is:
  i. GILBERT E.[7] COUNTS, b. Jul 1896, MO; d. Aft. 1900.

Generation No. 4

19. JOHN CURTIS[7] BALLARD (THOMAS EDWIN[6], WILLIAM CURTIS[5], JAMES GAINES[4], CURTIS[3], PHILIP[2], WILLIAM[1]) was born 14 Dec 1893 in Haskell Co., TX, and died Aug 1968 in Pueblo Co., CO. He married ZELMA FRANCIS FERGUSON 09 Sep 1915. She was born 12 Jul 1894 in TX, and died Aft. 1930.

Notes for JOHN CURTIS BALLARD:
Source: 1920-1940 Las Animas County Colorado Federal Census Records
** 1920 - Living in Las Animas Co., CO - Ballard, John C 26 TX, Zelma F 25 TX, Harlan E 3 5/12 TX, Fairy P 2 5/12 NM, Ella Rhe DeBard companion 26 TX*
** 1930 - Living in Plum Valley, Las Animas Co., CO - Ballard, J Curtis 36 TX MO LA, Zelma F 35 TX TX GA, Harlan E TX, Fairy P 12 NM, Paul 20 brother TX*
** 1940 - Living in Plum Valley, Las Animas Co., CO - Ballard J Curtis 46 TX, Zelma F 45 TX plus lodger*

Children of JOHN BALLARD and ZELMA FERGUSON are:
  i. HARLAN E.[8] BALLARD, b. 1916, TX; d. Aft. 1930.
  ii. FAIRY P. BALLARD, b. 1917, NM; d. Aft. 1930.

20. THOMAS LYNN[7] BALLARD (THOMAS EDWIN[6], WILLIAM CURTIS[5], JAMES GAINES[4], CURTIS[3], PHILIP[2], WILLIAM[1]) was born 14 Jul 1895 in Haskell Co., TX, and died Aft. 1930 in Haskell Co., TX. He married MINNIE ALICE KILLINGSWORTH 01 Jun 1920 in Haskell Co., TX. She was born 1896 in TX, and died Aft. 1930.

Notes for THOMAS LYNN BALLARD:
Source: 1930 Haskell County Texas Federal Census Records

** 1930 - Living in Haskell Co., TX - Ballard, Thomas L 34 TX MO LA, Alise M 34 TX TN TN, David C 7, Maire TX, Velma 5 TX*

Children of THOMAS BALLARD and MINNIE KILLINGSWORTH are:
  i. DAVID C.[8] BALLARD, b. 1923, Haskell Co., TX; d. Aft. 1930.
  ii. EMMA MAIRE BALLARD, b. 30 Mar 1921, Haskell Co., TX; d. 2006, AR.
  iii. ALLOSE VELMA BALLARD, b. 22 Jan 1926, Haskell Co., TX; d. Aft. 1930.

Notes for ALLOSE VELMA BALLARD:
Source: Texas Department of Health Bureau of Vital Statistics

21. LABRY E.[7] BALLARD (*THOMAS EDWIN*[6], *WILLIAM CURTIS*[5], *JAMES GAINES*[4], *CURTIS*[3], *PHILIP*[2], *WILLIAM*[1]) *was born 24 Apr 1897 in Haskell Co., TX, and died 22 Jul 1921 in Haskell Co., TX. He married IRENE PERRIN. She was born 1898 in OK, and died Aft. 1930.*

Notes for LABRY E. BALLARD:
Source: 1920 Haskell County Texas Federal Census Records
** 1920 - Living in Haskell Co., TX - Ballard, LE 26, Irene 22, Helen 4/12, Mrs. CA Bedichecks 68 mother in law wd*

More About LABRY E. BALLARD:
Burial: Willow Cemetery, Haskell, Haskell Co., TX

Notes for IRENE PERRIN:
Source: 1930 Haskell County Texas Federal Census Records

** 1930 - Living in Haskell Co., TX - Ballard, Irene 35 we OK KY MO, Helen 11 TX, Labry 8 TX, David Perrin 33 brother TX KY MO*

Children of LABRY BALLARD and IRENE PERRIN are:
      i.   HELEN[8] *BALLARD, b. 1920, Haskell Co., TX; d. Aft. 1930.*
     ii.   LABRY *BALLARD, b. 1922, Haskell Co., TX; d. Aft. 1930.*

22. MAMIE LOVELESS[7] DRAPER (*CORA HELEN*[6] *BALLARD, WILLIAM CURTIS*[5], *JAMES GAINES*[4], *CURTIS*[3], *PHILIP*[2], WILLIAM[1]) *was born 02 Sep 1888 in TX, and died Aft. 1900. She married BARRON.*

Child of MAMIE DRAPER and BARRON is:
      i.   HELEN[8] *BARRON, b. Abt. 1910, TX; d. Aft. 1920.*

23. JOAQUIN[7] BALLARD (*JOHN JAMES*[6], *WILLIAM CURTIS*[5], *JAMES GAINES*[4], *CURTIS*[3], *PHILIP*[2], *WILLIAM*[1]) *was born 20 Apr 1901 in OK, and died 29 Dec 1981 in Reno, Washoe Co., NE. He married GRACE N.. She was born Abt. 1907 in IL, and died Aft. 1930.*

Child of JOAQUIN BALLARD and GRACE N. is:
      i.   VIRGIL B.[8] *BALLARD, b. Abt. 1927, MO; d. Aft. 1930.*

24. EULAH[7] BALLARD (*JOHN JAMES*[6], *WILLIAM CURTIS*[5], *JAMES GAINES*[4], *CURTIS*[3], *PHILIP*[2], *WILLIAM*[1]) *was born 24 Mar 1903 in OK, and died 29 Dec 1980 in Reno, Washoe Co., NE. She married JAMES H. LANE. He was born Abt. 1898 in NM, and died Aft. 1930.*

Child of EULAH BALLARD and JAMES LANE is:
      i.   JIMMIE J.[8] *LANE, b. Abt. 1927, OR.*

James W. Ballard

Generation No. 1

1. JAMES W.[2] BALLARD (ETHELDRED/ETHERIDGE[1]) *was born Abt. 1808 in NC, and died Aft. 1880 in Newton Co., MO. He married* NANCY JOHNSON *06 Mar 1832 in Greenville, Green Co., TN. She was born 1807 in Raleigh, Wake Co., NC, and died Aft. 1870.*

Notes for JAMES W. BALLARD:
Source: 1850 Hamilton County Tennessee Federal Census Records, 1860 War Eagle Madison County Arkansas Federal Census Records, 1870 - 1880 Franklin Newton County Missouri Federal Census Records, Anderson Boyer (andersonboyer@columbus.rr.com), enh@ticnet.com, Frances Leveille, ginnydbe@windstream.net, Early TN Marriages by Byron & Barbara Sistler

** 1850 - Living in Hamilton Co., TN - Ballard, James 40 VA, Nancy 40 NC, William 18 NC, Sarah 14 NC, John 13 NC, Allen 10 NC, Andrew 8 NC, Joseph 6 NC, Robert 4 NC*
** 1860 - Living in White River Madison Co., AR - Ballard, James 52 VA, Nancy 53 NC, Andrew 18 TN, Joseph 15 TN, Robert 13 TN*
** 1870 - Living in Franklin, Newton Co., MO - Ballard, James 65 NC, Nancy 67 NC*
** 1880 - Living in Franklin, Newton Co., MO - Ballard, James 74 NC*

Children of JAMES BALLARD *and* NANCY JOHNSON *are:*

2.   i.   GEORGE ANDERSON[3] BALLARD, *b. 10 Sep 1834, AL; d. 1863, Washington Co., AR.*
      ii.   SARAH BALLARD, *b. Abt. 1836, TN; d. Aft. 1850.*
3.   iii. WILLIAM H. BALLARD, *b. Apr 1836, AL; d. Aft. 1900.*
4.   iv.   JOHN MARIAN BALLARD, *b. Abt. 1837, Greenville, Green Co., TN; d. Abt. 1880, Dallas Co., MO.*
5.   v.   ALLEN JOHNSON BALLARD, *b. 04 Jul 1840, Greenville, Green Co., TN; d. 08 Sep 1914, Roswell, Chaves Co., NM.*
      vi.   ANDREW BALLARD, *b. 1842, Greenville, Green Co., TN; d. Aft. 1860; m.* ELIZABETH.
6.   vii. JOSEPH BALLARD, *b. Abt. 1844, TN; d. Aft. 1880.*
      viii. ROBERT BALLARD, *b. 1846, TN; d. Aft. 1860.*

Generation No. 2

2. GEORGE ANDERSON[3] BALLARD (JAMES W.[2], ETHELDRED/ETHERIDGE[1]) *was born 10 Sep 1834 in AL, and died 1863 in Washington Co., AR. He married* NANCY LAMB *26 Oct 1854 in Fayetteville, Washington Co., AR. She was born 04 Mar 1837 in AL, and died 1864 in Ozark, MO.*

Notes for GEORGE ANDERSON BALLARD:
Source: Find A Grave, Frances Leveille, Stacy Kendrix (skendrix@swbell.net or langleyb@prodigy.net), Betty Langley (langleyb@prodigy.net), 1860 White River Washington County Arkansas Federal Census Records

** 1860 - Living in White River, Washington Co., AR - Ballard, George 35 AL, Nancy 21 AL, Susan 8 MO, Nancy 4 AR, Mary 2 AR, Martha 9/12 AR*

Notes for NANCY LAMB:
Source: Betty Langley (langleyb@prodigy.net)

Children of GEORGE BALLARD *and* NANCY LAMB *are:*

      i.   SUSAN[4] BALLARD, *b. Abt. 1854, MO; d. Aft. 1860; m.* MR. STAMPS; *b. Abt. 1854.*
      ii.   NANCY ANN BALLARD, *b. 26 May 1856, Washington Co., AR; d. 16 Aug 1938, Adams Co., IL; m. (1)* NEWTON J. KELTNER, *19 Mar 1874, Christian Co., MO; m. (2)* BENJAMIN FRANKLIN BROWN, *19 Sep 1886, Greene Co., MO; b. 27 Apr 1846, Sullivan Co., IN; d. 29 Oct 1943, Adams Co., IL.*

More About NANCY ANN BALLARD:
Burial: Sunset Cemetery, Quincy, Adams Co., IL

More About BENJAMIN FRANKLIN BROWN:
Burial: Sunset Cemetery, Quincy, Adams Co., IL

    iii. MARY ELIZABETH BALLARD, b. 24 Jun 1858, Fayetteville, Washington AR; d. 31 Jan 1916, Elida, NM; m. JAMES W. JOHNSTON, 17 Nov 1874; b. Abt. 1858.

7.   iv. MARTHA "MATTIE" CLEMENTINE BALLARD, b. 12 Sep 1859, Washington Co., AR; d. 05 Dec 1895, Canadian Co., OK.

    v. JAMES WILLIAM BALLARD, b. 05 Jul 1861, Washington Co., AR; d. AR; m. JENNIE M. GIVENS, 29 Mar 1884, Miller Co., AR.

    vi. GEORGE ANDERSON BALLARD, b. 04 Jun 1863, Washington Co., AR; d. 07 Feb 1946, Gregg Co., TX; m. MARY JACKSON PAYNE; b. 27 Feb 1862, Grayson Co., TX; d. 08 Dec 1941, Rusk Co., TX.

3. WILLIAM H.³ BALLARD (JAMES W.², ETHELDRED/ETHERIDGE¹) *was born Apr 1836 in AL, and died Aft. 1900. He married RACHEL. She was born Sep 1838 in AR, and died Aft. 1900.*

Notes for WILLIAM H. BALLARD:
Source: 1860, 1870 White River Washington County Alabama Federal Census Records, 1880 Stephens County Texas Federal Census Records, 1900 Young County Texas Federal Census Records

** 1860 - Living in White River, Washington Co., AL - Ballard, William 23 AL, Rachel 20 AR, Nancy 5 AR, Lucy 2 AR*
** 1870 - Living in White River, Washington Co., AL - Ballard, William 33 AL, Rachael 31 AR, NJ 14 AR, Mary 11 AR, Peter 9 AR, Jackson 8 AR, George AR, John 2 AR*
** 1880 - Living in Stephens Co., TX - Ballard, Wm H 46 farmer AL AL AL, Rachel 42 AR KY IN, Peter B 19 AR, Wm H J 17 AR, Geo H 14 AR, Sarah L 13 AR, John N 10 AR, Ann S 9 AR, Martha M 7 AR, Lydia A 6 AR, Saml I 3 TX, Allice 5/12 TX*
** 1900 - Living in Young Co., TX - Ballard, William Apr 1836 AL, Rachel - Sep 1838 AR, Francis M - May 1882 TX, Samuel J - May 1887 married 3 yrs, Alice L - Sep 1880 (dau in law) MO one child, Alice B Cate (dau) Aug 1899 Indian Territory*

Children of WILLIAM BALLARD and RACHEL are:

    i. NANCY J.⁴ BALLARD, b. 1855, AR; d. Aft. 1870.
    ii. LUCY BALLARD, b. 1858, AR; d. Aft. 1860.
    iii. MARY BALLARD, b. 1860, AR; d. Aft. 1870.
    iv. PETER B. BALLARD, b. 1861, AR; d. Aft. 1880.
    v. WILLIAM H. JACKSON BALLARD, b. 1862, AR; d. Aft. 1880.
    vi. GEORGE H. BALLARD, b. 1864, AR; d. Aft. 1880.
    vii. ELIJAH BALLARD, b. 1866, AR.
    viii. JOHN N. BALLARD, b. 1870, AR; d. Aft. 1880.
    ix. ANN S. BALLARD, b. 1871, AR; d. Aft. 1880.
    x. MARTHA M. BALLARD, b. 1873, AR; d. Aft. 1880.
    xi. LYDIA A. BALLARD, b. 1874, AR; d. Aft. 1880.
8.   xii. SAMUEL BALLARD, b. May 1877, TX; d. Aft. 1900.
    xiii. ALICE BALLARD, b. Dec 1879, TX; d. Aft. 1900; m. MR. CATE.

4. JOHN MARIAN³ BALLARD (JAMES W.², ETHELDRED/ETHERIDGE¹) *was born Abt. 1837 in Greenville, Green Co., TN, and died Abt. 1880 in Dallas Co., MO. He married BARBARA ANN GARRISON 12 Dec 1854 in Dallas Co., MO, daughter of JOSEPH GARRISON and ELIZABETH KING. She was born 1830 in MO, and died 1885 in Benton, Saline Co., AR.*

Notes for JOHN MARIAN BALLARD:
Source: 1860 Madison County Arkansas Federal Census Records, ginnybe@alltel.net
** 1860 - Living in War Eagle, Madison Co., AR - Ballard, Jno 23 TN, Barbary 26 MO, Sarah 5 MO, Wm 2 AR*

Notes for BARBARA ANN GARRISON:
Source: 1880 Saline County Arkansas Federal Census Records

** 1880 - Living in Saline Co., AR - Ballard, Ann 50 MO TN AL, Jennete 13 MO TN MO, Nancy 10 AR TN MO, Josephine 7 AR TN MO, John 4 AR TN MO*

Children of JOHN BALLARD and BARBARA GARRISON are:

9.	i.	SARAH ANN⁴ BALLARD, b. 01 Oct 1856, Camden Co., MO; d. 11 Apr 1936, 5/29/1939 Benton, Saline Co., AR.
10.	ii.	WILLIAM E. BALLARD, b. 02 Jan 1858, AR; d. 03 Feb 1914, 1/17/1932 Benton, Saline Co., AR.
11.	iii.	ADDISON "ALLEN" JACKSON BALLARD, b. 07 Dec 1860, MO; d. Bet. 29 - 30 Jan 1946, Benton, Saline Co., AR.
12.	iv.	MARTHA ELIZABETH BALLARD, b. 26 May 1864, MO; d. 26 Jan 1958, Benton, Saline Co., AR.
13.	v.	JEANETTE "NETTIE" BALLARD, b. 19 Oct 1870, MO; d. 27 Apr 1957, Valliant, McCurtain Co., OK.
14.	vi.	NANCY CLARA BALLARD, b. 1872, AR; d. Bef. 1910.
15.	vii.	JOSEPHINE BALLARD, b. 07 Oct 1874, Benton, Saline Co., AR; d. Oct 1968, Valliant, McCurtain Co., OK.
	viii.	JOHN M. BALLARD, b. 04 Jun 1877, Benton, Saline Co., AR; m. EMILY LOUISA TAYLOR, 10 Feb 1901, Dallas Co., MO.

> *Notes for JOHN M. BALLARD:*
> *Source: 1900 Pulaski County Arkansas Federal Census Records*
> ** 1900 - Living in Roland, Pulaski Co., AR - Living in Roland, Pulaski Co., AR - Ballard, John M - June 1877 AR TN MO, Guy Chenault - partner, Neely Burns boarder, William McLane boarder*

5. ALLEN JOHNSON³ BALLARD (JAMES W.², ETHELDRED/ETHERIDGE¹) *was born 04 Jul 1840 in Greenville, Green Co., TN, and died 08 Sep 1914 in Roswell, Chaves Co., NM. He married* CATHERINE REDING *04 Sep 1865 in Bastrop Co., TX. She was born 10 Dec 1848 in TX, and died 29 Aug 1923 in NM.*

Notes for ALLEN JOHNSON BALLARD:
Source: 1880 Lincoln County New Mexico Federal Census Records 1900 Chaves County New Mexico Federal Census Records

** 1880 - Living in Lincoln Co., NM - Ballard, Allen J 38 farmer TN, Kate 31 NM Charley L 13 TX, Berta 15 TX, Willie 8 TX, Annie 5 TX, Dick 2.TX*
** 1900 - Living in Roswell, Chaves Co., NM - Ballard, A J, Katie, Robt, James*

More About ALLEN JOHNSON BALLARD:
Burial: South Park Cemetery, Roswell, Chaves Co., NM

Children of ALLEN BALLARD and CATHERINE REDING are:

> i. CHARLES LITTLEPAGE⁴ BALLARD, b. 11 Oct 1866, Hays Co., TX; d. 16 Apr 1950, El Paso Co., TX; m. ARAMINTA CORN; b. 31 May 1870; d. 21 Feb 1920.
>
> *More About CHARLES LITTLEPAGE BALLARD:*
> *Burial: South Park Cemetery, Roswell, Chaves Co., NM*
>
> *More About ARAMINTA CORN:*
> *Burial: Evergreen Cemetery, El Paso, Co., T*

ii. BERTA BALLARD, b. 1869, Dripping Springs, Hays Co., TX; d. 1956; m. (1) JAMES A. MANNING; b. 1865; d. 1950; m. (2) JIM JOHNSON.

More About BERTA BALLARD:
Burial: South Park Cemetery, Roswell, Chaves Co., NM

More About JAMES A. MANNING:
Burial: South Park Cemetery, Roswell, Chaves Co., NM

iii. WILLIAM GOOD BALLARD, b. 1873, Dripping Springs, Hays Co., TX; d. 1955, NM; m. CATE CARPER; b. 10 May 1877, Raleigh Co., WV; d. 1956, Eddy Co., NM.

More About WILLIAM GOOD BALLARD:
Burial: Woodbine Cemetery, Eddy Co,, NM

More About CATE CARPER:
Burial: Woodbine Cemetery, Eddy Co,, NM

iv. ANN BALLARD, b. 03 May 1875, Mt. City, Hays Co., TX; d. 09 Oct 1946, Roswell, Chaves Co., NM; m. J. A. MANNING.

More About ANN BALLARD:
Burial: South Park Cemetery, Roswell, Chaves Co., NM

v. RICHARD FRANKLIN BALLARD, b. 14 Oct 1877, Roswell, Chaves Co., NM; d. 18 Jul 1939.

More About RICHARD FRANKLIN BALLARD:
Burial: South Park Cemetery, Roswell, Chaves Co., NM

vi. ROBERT LOVE BALLARD, b. 03 Dec 1880, Roswell, Chaves Co., NM; d. Nov 1964, Roswell, Chaves Co., NM; m. MARIE; b. 1879, KS; d. Jun 1952, Roswell, Chaves Co., NM.

More About ROBERT LOVE BALLARD:
Burial: South Park Cemetery, Roswell, Chaves Co., NM

More About MARIE:
Burial: South Park Cemetery, Roswell, Chaves Co. NM

vii. JAMES BALLARD, b. 1885, Roswell, Chaves Co., NM; d. 1975; m. LAURA ALTA HOBSON; b. 16 Mar 1891, Winnebago Co., IL; d. Nov 1964.

More About JAMES BALLARD:
Burial: South Park Cemetery, Roswell, Chaves Co., NM

More About LAURA ALTA HOBSON:
Burial: South Park Cemetery, Roswell, Chaves Co., NM

viii. KATHERINE "KATE" BALLARD, b. 13 Feb 1888, Roswell, Chaves Co., NM; d. 28 Dec 1895.

More About KATHERINE "KATE" BALLARD:
Burial: South Park Cemetery, Roswell, Chaves Co., NM

6. JOSEPH[3] BALLARD (JAMES W.[2], ETHELDRED/ETHERIDGE[1]) was born Abt. 1844 in TN, and died Aft. 1880.

He married MELVINA MCCOWAN. She was born Abt. 1855.

Notes for JOSEPH BALLARD:
Source: James Tippy (Jimtiping@aol.com), 1870 Makanda, Jackson Co., IL Federal Census Records
** 1870 - Living in Makanda, Jackson Co., IL - Ballard, Joseph 25 AL Farm hand*

Child of JOSEPH BALLARD and MELVINA MCCOWAN is:

    i.   *NORA EDNA[4] BALLARD, b. 27 Oct 1877, Carterville, IL; m. JAMES MONROE TIPPY, 09 Apr 1904, Crainville, Williamson Co. IL.*

        Notes for NORA EDNA BALLARD:
        Source: JSTIPPY@webtv.net

Generation No. 3

7. *MARTHA "MATTIE" CLEMENTINE[4] BALLARD (GEORGE ANDERSON[3], JAMES W.[2], ETHELDRED/ETHERIDGE[1]) was born 12 Sep 1859 in Washington Co., AR, and died 05 Dec 1895 in Canadian Co., OK. She married MARTIN WILLIAM JOHNSTON 10 May 1877 in Kingman, Reno Co., KS, son of GEORGE JOHNSTON and NANCY MCCAFFERTY. He was born 04 Apr 1852 in Greene Co., MO, and died 05 Feb 1926 in Canadian Co., OK.*

Notes for MARTHA "MATTIE" CLEMENTINE BALLARD:
Source: Stacy Kendrix (skendrix@swbell.net)

More About MARTHA "MATTIE" CLEMENTINE BALLARD:
Burial: Yukon Cemetery, Yukon, Canadian Co., OK

Notes for MARTIN WILLIAM JOHNSTON:
Source: 1880 Loda, Reno County Kansas Federal Census Records
** 1880 - Living in Loda, Reno Co., KS - Johnson, Martin Martha, George, Mary*

More About MARTIN WILLIAM JOHNSTON:
Burial: Yukon Cemetery, Yukon, Canadian Co., OK

Children of MARTHA BALLARD and MARTIN JOHNSTON are:

    i.   *GEORGE[5] JOHNSTON, b. 05 Jun 1878, Reno Co., KS; d. 17 Apr 1974, Yukon, Canadian Co., OK; m. LENCIA MARTHA "LUCY" RENFRO; b. 04 Mar 1879; d. 31 Jan 1960.*

        More About GEORGE JOHNSTON:
        Burial: Yukon Cemetery, Yukon, Canadian Co., OK

        More About LENCIA MARTHA "LUCY" RENFRO:
        Burial: Yukon Cemetery, Yukon, Canadian Co., OK

    ii.   *NANCY JANE JOHNSTON, b. 22 Aug 1883, Nixa, MO; m. OLLIE GUNN.*
    iii. *MARTIN CHARLES JOHNSTON, b. 07 Sep 1888, Beaver Co., OK; d. 22 Oct 1934, El Reno KS; m. ATHA BEATRICE BROWN; b. 21 Nov 1909, Yukon, Canadian Co., OK.*

        More About MARTIN CHARLES JOHNSTON:
        Burial: Yukon Cemetery, Yukon, Canadian Co., OK

8. *SAMUEL[4] BALLARD (WILLIAM H.[3], JAMES W.[2], ETHELDRED/ETHERIDGE[1]) was born May 1877 in TX, and died Aft. 1900. He married ALICE L.. She was born Sep 1880 in MO, and died Aft. 1900.*

Child of SAMUEL BALLARD and ALICE L. is:
> i. OSCAR[5] BALLARD, b. Aug 1899, Indian Territory.

9. SARAH ANN[4] BALLARD (JOHN MARIAN[3], JAMES W.[2], ETHELDRED/ETHERIDGE[1]) *was born 01 Oct 1856 in Camden, MO, and died 11 Apr 1936 in 5/29/1939 Benton, Saline Co., AR. She married (1) PAUL M. WRIGHT Abt. 1874. He was born 06 Nov 1839, and died 08 Dec 1920 in AR. She married (2) WILLIAM KING 09 Jan 1879 in Benton, Saline Co., AR. He was born 1857.*

More About SARAH ANN BALLARD:
Burial: McPherson Cemetery.

Children of SARAH BALLARD and WILLIAM KING are:

> i. WALTER[5] KING, b. Aug 1887.
> ii. WILLIAM B. KING, b. Sep 1888.
> iii. LETTA KING, b. Feb 1892, Benton Saline Co., AR; m. HOUSTON MONK.
> iv. MARIETTA KING, b. Jun 1893.
> v. LAFAYETTE KING, b. Apr 1897, Benton Saline Co., AR.

10. WILLIAM E.[4] BALLARD (JOHN MARIAN[3], JAMES W.[2], ETHELDRED/ETHERIDGE[1]) *was born 02 Jan 1858 in AR, and died 03 Feb 1914 in 1/17/1932 Benton, Saline Co., AR. He married HULDA ELIZABETH WILLIS 25 May 1879 in Benton, Saline Co., AR, daughter of WILLIAM WILLIS and ELIZA. She was born 1860 in TN, and died 10 Jun 1944.*

Notes for WILLIAM E. BALLARD:
Source: 1880-1910 Saline County Arkansas Federal Census Records

** 1880 - Living in Saline Co., AR - Ballard, William 23 farmer AR TN MO, Hulda 20 TN TN TN*
** 1900 - Living in Saline Co., AR - Ballard, William Jan 1858, Elizabeth Feb 1860, Thomas 1881, Henry 1883, John 1896*
** 1910 - Living in Saline Co., AR - Ballard, William 52 TN, Elizabeth 49 TN, Samuel 14 AR, Harrison 9 AR*

More About WILLIAM E. BALLARD:
Burial: Sharon

Children of WILLIAM BALLARD and HULDA WILLIS are:

16. i. JOHN THOMAS[5] BALLARD, b. May 1881, Benton, Saline Co., AR; d. 1950, Benton, Saline Co., AR.
17. ii. HENRY W. BALLARD, b. 31 Jan 1883, Benton, Saline Co., AR; d. 01 Jan 1964, Benton, Saline Co., AR.
  iii. SAMUEL HARRISON BALLARD, b. 05 Apr 1896, Benton, Saline Co., AR; d. 10 Feb 1959, Benton, Saline Co., AR; m. MARY L. BUNCH, 05 Aug 1916, Benton, Saline Co., AR; b. 08 Jun 1894; d. 10 Sep 1965, Benton, Saline Co., AR.

> *More About SAMUEL HARRISON BALLARD:*
> *Burial: Sharon Cemetery, Saline Co., AR*
>
> *More About MARY L. BUNCH:*
> *Burial: Sharon Cemetery.*

  iv. GARRISON BALLARD, b. 1901, Benton, Saline Co., AR; d. Aft. 1910.

11. ADDISON "ALLEN" JACKSON[4] BALLARD (JOHN MARIAN[3], JAMES W.[2], ETHELDRED/ETHERIDGE[1]) *was* *born 07 Dec 1860 in MO, and died Bet. 29 - 30 Jan 1946 in Benton, Saline Co., AR. He married SARAH ELIZABETH OWENS 02 Sep 1879 in Benton, Saline Co., AR, daughter of JAMES OWENS and ELIZABETH HOLLINGSWORTH. She was born 18 Mar 1861 in AR, and died 06 Jun 1956 in Benton, Saline Co., AR.*

Notes for ADDISON "ALLEN" JACKSON BALLARD:

Source: LDS-IGI, 1880-1900, 1920-1930 Saline County Arkansas Federal Census Records

** 1880 - Living in Saline Co., AR - Ballard, Addison 19 MO MO TN, Sarah 18 AR SC SC*
** 1900 - Living in Saline Co., AR - Ballard, Allen - Dec 1860 MO TN MO, Sarah - Mar 1861 AR SC SC, Allen - March 1884 AR, Lula - Mar 1888, Anna - Mar 1885, Hattie - Aug 1890, William - Nov 1892, John - Jan 1895, Charlie - Jan 1898 AR*
** 1920 - Living in Saline Co., AR - Ballard, Add 59 MO TN MO, Sarah 58 AR SC SC, Charley 21 AR, Clyde 13 AR, Grace Scott 10 grand dau, Howard Scott 8 grandson, Authur Sanders 14 grandson, Add Peeler 10 grandson*
** 1930 - Living in Saline Co., AR - Ballard, Add 69, Sarah 69, Clyde 23, Howard Scott 19 grandson*

More About ADDISON "ALLEN" JACKSON BALLARD:
Burial: McPherson Cemetery Benton, Saline Co., AR

More About SARAH ELIZABETH OWENS:
Burial: McPherson Cemetery Benton, Saline Co., AR

Children of ADDISON BALLARD and SARAH OWENS are:

    i.   ALLEN PERRY⁵ BALLARD, b. 07 Mar 1883, Benton, Saline Co., AR; d. 25 Jul 1952, Pine Bluff, Jefferson Co.,; m. MARTHA ANN SINGLETON, 19 Jan 1902, Benton, Saline Co., AR; b. 17 Mar 1885; d. 25 Jul 1952, Benton, Saline Co., AR.

        More About ALLEN PERRY BALLARD:
        Burial: McPherson Cemetery, Benton, Saline Co., AR

        More About MARTHA ANN SINGLETON:
        Burial: McPherson Cemetery, Benton, Saline Co., AR

    ii.   ANNA E. BALLARD, b. 1885, Benton, Saline Co., AR; d. 1910, Benton, Saline Co., AR; m. CHARLES PRICE.

        More About ANNA E. BALLARD:
        Burial: McPherson Cemetery, Benton, Saline Co., AR

    iii.   LULA BALLARD, b. 04 Mar 1889, Benton, Saline Co., AR; d. 07 Nov 1969, Benton, Saline Co., AR; m. (1) THOMAS A. SANDERS, 13 Nov 1904, Benton, Saline Co., AR; b. 26 Mar 1879, AR; d. 14 Nov 1917, Saline Co., AR; m. (2) JESSE RICHARD PEELER, 12 Apr 1908, Benton, Saline Co., AR; b. 15 Oct 1879, Benton, Saline Co., AR; d. 28 Aug 1962, Benton, Saline Co., AR; m. (3) JOHN TYSON FLETCHER, 11 Dec 1910, Benton Saline Co., AR; b. 1876, Saline Co., AR; d. 02 Mar 1937, Saline Co., AR.

        Notes for LULA BALLARD:
        Source: ginnybe@alltel.net

        More About LULA BALLARD:
        Burial: McPherson Cemetery, Benton, Saline Co., AR

        More About THOMAS A. SANDERS:
        Burial: Sharon Cemetery, Saline Co., AR

        More About JESSE RICHARD PEELER:

Burial: McPherson Cemetery, Saline Co., AR

More About JOHN TYSON FLETCHER:
Burial: McPherson Cemetery, Saline Co., AR

iv.   HATTIE A. BALLARD, *b. 11 Oct 1890, Benton, Saline Co., AR; d. 21 Oct 1918, Benton, Saline Co., AR; m. WILLIAM E. SCOTT, 27 Sep 1907, Benton, Saline Co., AR; b. 05 Mar 1884; d. 22 Sep 1975.*

Notes for HATTIE A. BALLARD:
Source: ginnybe@alltel.net

More About HATTIE A. BALLARD:
Burial: McPherson Cemetery Benton, Saline Co., AR

More About WILLIAM E. SCOTT:
Burial: Floyd Cemetery, White Co., AR

v.   WILLIAM E. BALLARD, *b. 16 Nov 1893, Benton, Saline Co., AR; d. 07 Sep 1973, Benton, Saline Co., AR; m. MATTIE COLLINS, 24 Dec 1917, Benton, Saline Co., AR; b. 30 Oct 1898; d. 26 May 1992, Benton, Saline Co., AR.*

More About WILLIAM E. BALLARD:
Burial: McPherson Cemetery, Benton, Saline Co., AR

More About MATTIE COLLINS:
Burial: McPherson Cemetery.

vi.   JOHN H. BALLARD, *b. 04 Jan 1895, Benton, Saline Co., AR; d. 06 Nov 1918, Benton, Saline Co., AR.*

More About JOHN H. BALLARD:
Burial: McPherson Cemetery, Benton, Saline Co., AR

vii.   CHARLES EDWARD BALLARD, *b. 30 Jun 1898, Benton, Saline Co., AR; d. 05 Jul 1969, Benton, Saline Co., AR; m. (1) FANNIE COLLINS, 20 Sep 1916, Benton, Saline Co., AR; b. 02 Mar 1898; d. 14 Nov 1917; m. (2) BESSIE O. EMERSON, 13 May 1927; b. 25 Mar 1905, AR; d. 10 Jan 1940; m. (3) FLORA BELLE MAY, 10 May 1941, Benton, Saline Co., AR; b. 30 Oct 1910, Faulkner Co., AR; d. 23 Feb 1998, Little Rock, Pulaski Co., AR.*

Notes for CHARLES EDWARD BALLARD:
Source: ginnybe@alltel.net

More About CHARLES EDWARD BALLARD:
Burial: Sharon Cemetery, Saline Co., AR

More About FANNIE COLLINS:
Burial: Sharon Cemetery, Saline Co., AR

More About BESSIE O. EMERSON:
Burial: Sharon Cemetery, Saline Co., AR

More About FLORA BELLE MAY:
Burial: Bewley Cemetery, Pope Co., AR

viii.   LILLIE A. BALLARD, b. 08 Nov 1900, Benton, Saline Co., AR; d. 27 May 1979, Benton, Saline Co.,
         AR; m. (1) JEFF DOAN; b. 19 Oct 1888; d. 08 Jan 1970; m. (2) AD BRAZIL; m. (3) MR. MIZE; m. (4)
         TOM SINGLETON, 21 Dec 1918, Benton, Saline Co., AR.

         Notes for LILLIE A. BALLARD:
         Source: ginnybe@alltel.net

         More About LILLIE A. BALLARD:
         Burial: McPherson Cemetery Benton, Saline Co., AR

         More About JEFF DOAN:
         Burial: McPherson Cemetery, Benton, Saline Co., AR

ix.   CLYDE DEWELL BALLARD, b. 05 Jul 1906, Benton, Saline Co., AR; d. 17 Jan 1971, Benton, Saline
         Co., AR; m. (1) JOSEPHINE GAUNT, 16 Jun 1930, Benton, Saline Co., AR; b. 17 Sep 1914, AR; d. 18
         Aug 1930, Benton, Saline Co., AR; m. (2) AGGIE BLANCHE MOORE, 05 Feb 1932, Benton, Saline Co.,
         AR; b. 08 Dec 1913, Benton, Saline Co., AR; d. 15 Jul 2010.

         Notes for CLYDE DEWELL BALLARD:
         Source: ginnybe@alltel.net

         More About CLYDE DEWELL BALLARD:
         Burial: McPherson Cemetery Benton, Saline Co., AR

         More About JOSEPHINE GAUNT:
         Burial: Old Rosemont Cemetery, Benton, Saline Co., AR

         More About AGGIE BLANCHE MOORE:
         Burial: McPherson Cemetery Benton, Saline Co., AR

12.   MARTHA ELIZABETH[4] BALLARD (JOHN MARIAN[3], JAMES W.[2], ETHELDRED/ETHERIDGE[1]) was born 26 May 1864 in
MO, and died 26 Jan 1958 in Benton, Saline Co., AR. She married JOHN WILEY WILLIS 26 Jan 1879 in Benton,
Saline Co., AR, son of WILLIAM WILLIS and ELIZA. He was born 19 Oct 1854 in TN, and died 10 Mar 1936 in
Benton, Saline Co., AR.

Notes for MARTHA ELIZABETH BALLARD:
Source: Saline County Arkansas Certificate of Death

More About MARTHA ELIZABETH BALLARD:
Burial: Sharon Cemetery, Saline Co., AR

Notes for JOHN WILEY WILLIS:
Source: 1900-1930 Saline County Arkansas Federal Census Records

* 1900 - Living in Saline Co., AR - Willis, John - Oct 1854 TN TN MS, Martha - Mar MO TN MO, Wylie J - Nov
1883 AR, William H - Nov 1888 AR, Pearl - Apr 1891 AR, Mary M - July 1894 AR, Daisy - Mar 1898 AR
* 1910 - Living in Saline Co., AR - Willis, John 56 US, Mattie E 46 AR, Maggie 15 AR, Daisy 12 AR, George
Howard 7 US
* 1920 - Living in Saline Co., AR - Willis, JW 65 TN TN TN, Martha 55 MO TN MO, Zada 6 grand dau AR AR AR
* 1930 - Living in Saline Co., AR - Willis, John W 75 TN TN MS, Martha E 65 MO US MO, Sadie B 16 g dau AR,
Mittie 12 AR g dau, John W 9 g son, George W 7 g son

More About JOHN WILEY WILLIS:

Burial: Sharon Cemetery, Saline Co., AR

Children of MARTHA BALLARD and JOHN WILLIS are:

    i.   LOUISA KATE[5] WILLIS, b. 28 Oct 1880, Benton, Saline Co., AR; d. 13 Jan 1965, Benton, Saline Co., AR; m. J. LEE NALLEY; b. 09 Nov 1881; d. 14 Feb 1930, Benton, Saline Co., AR.

        Notes for LOUISA KATE WILLIS:
        Source: ginnybe@alltel.net

        More About LOUISA KATE WILLIS:
        Burial: Sharon Cemetery.

    ii.   JOHN W. WILLIS, b. 17 Nov 1882, Benton, Saline Co., AR; d. 22 Jul 1949, Benton, Saline Co., AR; m. (1) JENNIE; m. (2) ELIZABETH BELL ELLIS, 03 May 1916, Littlerock, Pulaski Co., AR.

        Notes for JOHN W. WILLIS:
        Source: ginnybe@alltel.net

        More About JOHN W. WILLIS:
        Burial: Sharon Cemetery.

    iii.   WILLIAM H. WILLIS, b. 10 Nov 1888, Benton, Saline Co., AR; d. 25 Jul 1971, Benton, Saline Co., AR; m. (1) MOLLIE M.; m. (2) THELM STORY, 28 Feb 1915, Benton, Saline Co., AR.

        Notes for WILLIAM H. WILLIS:
        Source: ginnybe@alltel.net

        More About WILLIAM H. WILLIS:
        Burial: Sharon Cemetery.

    iv.   PEARL WILLIS, b. 1891, Benton, Saline Co., AR; d. 1960, Benton, Saline Co., AR; m. (1) C. E. PEELER, 07 Dec 1907; m. (2) ED MANGUM, 16 Mar 1940, Benton, Saline Co., AR.

        More About PEARL WILLIS:
        Burial: Sharon Cemetery.

    v.   MARY MAGLINE WILLIS, b. 31 Jul 1894, Benton, Saline Co., AR; d. 01 Sep 1986, Benton, Saline Co., AR.

        More About MARY MAGLINE WILLIS:
        Burial: McPherson Cemetery Benton, Saline Co., AR

    vi.   DAISY WILLIS, b. 06 Mar 1898, Benton, Saline Co., AR; d. 20 May 1983, Benton, Saline Co., AR; m. CHARLES M. NALLEY, 06 Jul 1914, Benton, Saline Co., AR.

        Notes for DAISY WILLIS:
        Source: ginnybe@alltel.net

        More About DAISY WILLIS:
        Burial: Sharon Cemetery.

13. JEANETTE "NETTIE"[4] BALLARD (JOHN MARIAN[3], JAMES W.[2], ETHELDRED/ETHERIDGE[1]) *was born 19 Oct 1870 in MO, and died 27 Apr 1957 in Valliant, McCurtain Co., OK. She married (1) JACOB COLSTON JAMES 24 Jun 1894 in*

Benton Saline Co., AR, son of WILLIAM JAMES and CHARITY MUSE. He was born 07 Jun 1852 in Saline Co., AR, and died 08 Feb 1916 in Valiant McCurtain Co., OK. She married (2) THOMAS ROW Aft. 1917. He was born 13 Jan 1857 in Floyd Co., KY, and died 31 Jan 1934 in Valliant, McCurtain Co., OK.

Notes for JEANETTE "NETTIE" BALLARD:
Source: ginnybe@alltel.net

More About JEANETTE "NETTIE" BALLARD:
Burial: Felker Free Will Baptist Church Cemetery, McCurtain Co., OK

Notes for JACOB COLSTON JAMES:
Source: 1910 McCurtain County Oklahoma Federal Census Records

** 1910 - Lives in McCurtain Co., OK - James, Jacob 58, Jamette 34 MO, Jacob 13 OK, Rachel 9 OK, Nettie 6 OK, Virgal 3 OK*

More About JACOB COLSTON JAMES:
Burial: Moran Cemetery, Valliant, McCurtain Co., OK

Notes for THOMAS ROW:
Source: 1920-1930 McCurtain County Oklahoma Federal Census Records
** 1920 - Living in Kirk, McCurtain Co., OK - Rowe, Thomas 64, Nettie, Rachel James 18, Nettie James 15, Virgil James 13, Clifton James 7*
** 1930 - Living in Wilson, McCurtain Co., OK - Row, Thomas 76 KY TN KY, Jinett 64 MO TN MO, Clifton 17 OK*

More About THOMAS ROW:
Burial: Felker Free Will Baptist Church Cemetery, McCurtain Co., OK

Children of JEANETTE BALLARD and JACOB JAMES are:
  i.   JACOB COLSTON[5] JAMES, b. 19 Oct 1896, Valliant, McCurtain Co., OK; d. 10 Nov 1980, Valliant, McCurtain Co., OK.
  ii. RACHEL JAMES, b. 11 Jun 1901, Valliant, McCurtain Co., OK; d. 13 Jun 1988, Coalgate, Coal Co., OK; m. EMMETT TATUM, 16 Feb 1920, Valliant, McCurtain Co., OK.
  iii. NETTIE IRENE JAMES, b. 15 Sep 1904, Valliant, McCurtain Co., OK; d. 02 May 1965, Paris, Lamar Co., TX.

       More About NETTIE IRENE JAMES:
       Burial: Felker Free Will Baptist Church Cemetery, McCurtain Co., OK

  iv. VERGIL JAMES, b. 29 Jan 1907, Valliant, McCurtain Co., OK; d. 19 Jan 1972; m. CARMEL L. BARNES, 08 May 1925; b. 11 May 1908; d. 10 Sep 2000, Felker, McCurtain Co., OK.

       More About CARMEL L. BARNES:
       Burial: Felker Free Will Baptist Church Cemetery, McCurtain Co., OK

  v.   CLIFTON JEWEL JAMES, b. 23 Sep 1912, Valliant, McCurtain Co., OK; d. 12 Nov 1956, Valliant, McCurtain Co., OK; m. CLARA MAE BLOUNT; b. 10 Sep 1917; d. 16 Oct 2007.

       More About CLIFTON JEWEL JAMES:
       Burial: Felker Free Will Baptist Church Cemetery, McCurtain Co., OK

       More About CLARA MAE BLOUNT:
       Burial: Felker Free Will Baptist Church Cemetery, McCurtain Co., OK

14. NANCY CLARA[4] BALLARD (JOHN MARIAN[3], JAMES W.[2], ETHELDRED/ETHERIDGE[1]) was born 1872 in AR, and died Bef. 1910. She married WILLIAM JEFFERSON WRIGHT 05 Aug 1891 in Saline Co., AR, son of PAUL WRIGHT and ELIZABETH JAMES. He was born 27 Aug 1865 in AR, and died Aft. 1910.

Notes for NANCY CLARA BALLARD:
Source: ginnybe@alltel.net

Notes for WILLIAM JEFFERSON WRIGHT:
Source: 1900 Garland County Arkansas Federal Census Records, 1910 Saline County Arkansas Federal Census Records

* 1900 - Living in Phillips, Garland Co., AR - Wright, Wm 34, Nancy 27, Henry 3, Lizzie
* 1910 - Living in Kentucky, Saline Co., AR - Wright, William J 48 wd AR TN AR, Henry 13 AR AR AR, Elizabeth 9 AR, Josephine 4 AR

Children of NANCY BALLARD and WILLIAM WRIGHT are:
  i. WILLIAM HENRY STEVENSON[5] WRIGHT, b. 30 Sep 1897, Garland Co., AR; d. 30 Sep 1897; m. (1) ODA; m. (2) BERNICE MASON; b. 02 Sep 1904, AR; d. 12 Sep 1978, AR.

    Notes for WILLIAM HENRY STEVENSON WRIGHT:
    Source: Garland County Arkansas Certificate of Birth

    More About WILLIAM HENRY STEVENSON WRIGHT:
    Burial: Oak Ridge Cemetery, Malvern, Hot Springs Co., AR

    More About BERNICE MASON:
    Burial: Oak Ridge Cemetery, Malvern, Hot Springs Co., AR

  ii. MARY ELIZABETH WRIGHT, b. 15 May 1900, Benton, Saline Co., AR; d. Aft. 1910.

    Notes for MARY ELIZABETH WRIGHT:
    Source: Saline County Arkansas Birth Certificate

  iii. JOSEPHINE WRIGHT, b. 28 Aug 1905, Benton, Saline Co., AR; d. 21 Jul 1991, Benton, Saline Co., AR.

    Notes for JOSEPHINE WRIGHT:
    Source: Vanderburgh County Indiana Certificate of Death

15. JOSEPHINE[4] BALLARD (JOHN MARIAN[3], JAMES W.[2], ETHELDRED/ETHERIDGE[1]) was born 07 Oct 1874 in Benton, Saline Co., AR, and died Oct 1968 in Valliant, McCurtain Co., OK. She married (1) PRESTON TUTTLE 31 Jul 1890 in Benton, Saline Co., AR. He was born 21 Jul 1854 in Laurel Co., KY, and died 28 Jan 1913. She married (2) JASPER NORMAN Bef. 1968.

Notes for JOSEPHINE BALLARD:
Source: ginnybe@alltel.net

More About JOSEPHINE BALLARD:
Burial: Felker Free Will Baptist Church Cemetery, McCurtain Co., OK

Notes for PRESTON TUTTLE:
Source: Laurel County Kentucky Birth Index, 1900 Saline County Arkansas Federal Census Records, 1910 McCurtain County Oklahoma Federal Census Records

** 1900 - Living in Kentucky, Saline Co., AR - Tuttle, Preston - July 1854 KY NC NC, Josephene - Oct 1874 - 5 children - 5 living AR IL IL, Sarah A - July 1891 AR, John W - May 1894 AR, Nancy M - Mar 1896 AR, Lucinda - Jan 1898 AR, Martha E - Apr 1900 AR*
** 1910 - Living in McCurtain Co., OK - Tuttle, Preston 55, Josephine 35 - 7 children 7 living, William 16, Hilda 14, Lucinda 12, Martha 10, Lonie 8, Josephine 4*

More About PRESTON TUTTLE:
Burial: Valliant Cemetery, Valliant, McCurtain Co., OK

Children of JOSEPHINE BALLARD and PRESTON TUTTLE are:

    i.   SARAH ANN[5] TUTTLE, b. 06 Jul 1892, Benton, Saline Co., AR; d. 29 Sep 1959, Texarkana, Miller Co., AR; m. GEORGE ROBERT SHACKELFORD; b. 26 Feb 1878, Searcy, White Co., AR; d. 30 Jul 1962, Texarkana, Miller Co., AR.

       Notes for SARAH ANN TUTTLE:
       Source: Miller County Arkansas Certificate of Death

       More About SARAH ANN TUTTLE:
       Burial: East Memorial Gardens, Texarkana, Miller Co., AR

    ii.   JOHN WILLIAM TUTTLE, b. 19 May 1894, Benton, Saline Co., AR; d. 06 Jul 1954, Kings Co., CA; m. CLAUDIA JAMES; b. 24 Jan 1895, AR; d. 17 Sep 1974, Garvin, McCurtain Co., OK.

       Notes for JOHN WILLIAM TUTTLE:
       Source: Social Security Records, WWI Draft Registration Card

       More About JOHN WILLIAM TUTTLE:
       Burial: Valliant Cemetery, Valliant, McCurtain Co., OK

       More About CLAUDIA JAMES:
       Burial: Forest Hill Cemetery, Garvin, McCurtain Co., OK

    iii. NANCY MATILDA TUTTLE, b. 08 Mar 1896, Benton, Saline Co., AR; d. 28 Jan 1913.

       More About NANCY MATILDA TUTTLE:
       Burial: Valliant Cemetery, Valliant, McCurtain Co., OK

    iv. LUCINDA TUTTLE, b. 26 Jan 1898, Benton, Saline Co., AR; d. 24 May 1970, Hamilton, Ravalli Co., MT; m. LEE BIVENS, 05 Aug 1913, McCurtain, OK.

       Notes for LUCINDA TUTTLE:
       Source: Saline County Arkansas Birth Certificate, Ravalli County Montana Death Certificate

    v.   MARTHA ELIZABETH TUTTLE, b. 10 Apr 1900, Benton, Saline Co., AR; d. 08 Oct 1978, San Louis Obispo Co., CA; m. JOHN H. STARR; b. 17 Feb 1879, TX; d. 23 Jan 1973, Ventura Co., CA.

       Notes for MARTHA ELIZABETH TUTTLE:
       Source: Saline County Arkansas Delayed Birth Certificate

       More About MARTHA ELIZABETH TUTTLE:
       Burial: Pierce Brothers Santa Paula Cemetery, Ventura Co., CA

       More About JOHN H. STARR:
       Burial: Pierce Brothers Santa Paula Cemetery, Ventura Co., CA

vi. LEONA MAE TUTTLE, b. 22 May 1902, Benton, Saline Co., AR; d. 28 Dec 1990, San Louis, Obispo Co., CA; m. (1) WILLIAM THOMAS HARRISON, Bef. 1930; b. 13 Dec 1902, Scottsboro, Jackson Co.,, AL; d. Aft. 1940; m. (2) ELMER HOWELL, Aft. 1940.

Notes for WILLIAM THOMAS HARRISON:
Source: WWII Draft Cards

vii. JOSEPHINE DOVIE TUTTLE, b. 22 Mar 1906, Benton, Saline Co., AR; d. 09 Dec 1985; m. HARRY AUDER SONGER; b. 09 Apr 1904, Little Rock, Pulaski Co., AR; d. 22 Oct 1976, Valliant, McCurtain Co., OK.

More About HARRY AUDER SONGER:
Burial: Valliant Cemetery, Valliant, McCurtain Co., OK

Generation No. 4

16. JOHN THOMAS[5] BALLARD (WILLIAM E.[4], JOHN MARIAN[3], JAMES W.[2], ETHELDRED/ETHERIDGE[1]) was born May 1881 in Benton, Saline Co., AR, and died 1950 in Benton, Saline Co., AR. He married ALICE DUNN 30 Dec 1906 in Benton Saline Co., AR. She was born 1888, and died 1948 in Benton Saline Co., AR.

Notes for JOHN THOMAS BALLARD:
Source: 1910 Saline County Arkansas Federal Census Record

* 1910 - Living in Saline Co., AR - Ballard, Thomas 28, Alice 22 AR, Velmer 2, Miles 1

More About JOHN THOMAS BALLARD:
Burial: McPherson Cemetery, Benton, Saline Co., AR

More About ALICE DUNN:
Burial: Sharon Cemetery.

Children of JOHN BALLARD and ALICE DUNN are:
     i. VELMER[6] BALLARD, b. 1908.
    ii. MILES BALLARD, b. 1909.

17. HENRY W.[5] BALLARD (WILLIAM E.[4], JOHN MARIAN[3], JAMES W.[2], ETHELDRED/ETHERIDGE[1]) was born 31 Jan 1883 in Benton, Saline Co., AR, and died 01 Jan 1964 in Benton, Saline Co., AR. He married ELDA BUNCH 25 Jun 1905 in Benton Saline Co., AR. She was born 03 May 1882, and died 06 Jul 1966 in Benton Saline Co., AR.

Notes for HENRY W. BALLARD:
Source: 1910 Saline County Arkansas Federal Census Records

* 1910 - Living in Saline Co., AR - Ballard, Henry 27 AR, Elda 27 AR, Grace 3 AR, Warren 11/12 AR

More About ELDA BUNCH:
Burial: Sharon Cemetery.

Children of HENRY BALLARD and ELDA BUNCH are:
     i. GRACE[6] BALLARD, b. 1907.
    ii. WARREN BALLARD, b. 1909.

James W. Ballard

Generation No. 1

1. JAMES W.[1] BALLARD was born 21 Mar 1833, and died 29 Mar 1856. He married MARGARET C. KING 03 Jul 1851 in *Laclede, MO. She was born Dec 1834 in MO, and died 05 Dec 1903 in Decaturville, Camden Co., MO.*

More About JAMES W. BALLARD:
Burial: Garrison Cemetery, Decaturville, Camden Co., MO

Notes for MARGARET C. KING:
Source: 1870 Laclede County Missouri Federal Census Records
** 1870 - Living in Hooker, Laclede Co., MO - Kent, John 40 TN, Margaret C 36 MO, Nancy H 11 MO, Frantz 8 MO, Lenceion 7 next door William Ballard 17, James W 16, John K 14*

More About MARGARET C. KING:
Burial: A. B. Union Church Cemetery, Tunas, Dallas Co., MO

Children of JAMES BALLARD and MARGARET KING are:
   i. WILLIAM HAMILTON[2] BALLARD, b. 06 Sep 1852, MO; d. 25 Aug 1874.

     More About WILLIAM HAMILTON BALLARD:
     Burial: A. B. Union Church Cemetery, Tunas, Dallas Co., MO

2. ii. JAMES W. BALLARD, b. Nov 1853, MO.
3. iii. JOHN KING BALLARD, b. 06 Aug 1855, MO; d. 28 Oct 1944, Lebanon, Laclede Co., MO.

Generation No. 2

2. JAMES W.[2] BALLARD (JAMES W.[1]) was born Nov 1853 in MO. He married ALICE AMANDA WRIGHT, daughter of HARVEY WRIGHT and NANCY. She was born Mar 1855.

Children of JAMES BALLARD and ALICE WRIGHT are:
   i. JOHN H.[3] BALLARD, b. Nov 1877, MO.
   ii. NANCY H. BALLARD, b. Abt. 1880, MO.
   iii. ELMA BALLARD, b. Sep 1881, MO; m. JESSE THOMAS HUNT, 07 Feb 1897, Laclede Co., MO; b. TN.
   iv. ELLA BALLARD, b. Nov 1883, MO.
   v. JAMES E. BALLARD, b. Aug 1886, MO.
   vi. ETHEL BALLARD, b. Nov 1888, MO.
   vii. MILLER T. BALLARD, b. Oct 1890, MO.
   viii. NELLIE BALLARD, b. Dec 1892, MO.
   ix. HOMER W. BALLARD, b. Abt. 1895, MO.

3. JOHN KING[2] BALLARD (JAMES W.[1]) was born 06 Aug 1855 in MO, and died 28 Oct 1944 in Lebanon, Laclede Co., MO. He married EMMA LOUISE TAYLOR, daughter of GODFREY TAYLOR. She was born 13 Aug 1855 in MO, and died 30 Dec 1936 in Lebanon, Laclede Co., MO.

Notes for JOHN KING BALLARD:
Source: 1880-1930 Laclede County Missouri Federal Census Records
** 1880 - Living in Hooker, Laclede Co., MO - Ballard, John 25, Ema L 24, Ida M 2, Margaret L 3/12*
** 1900 - Living in Eldridge, Laclede Co., MO - Ballard, John - Aug 1855, Emma - Aug 1855, Emma - Aug 1856, William - Feb 1886, Elizabeth - June 1887, Pearl - Aug 1890, Grover - Nov 1892, Edward - Feb 1895*
** 1910 - Living in Eldridge, Laclede Co., MO - Ballard, John K 54 MO, Emma L 53 MO, Grover C 17 MO, William M 24 MO, Georgia A 16 MO daughter in law*
** 1920 - Living in Eldridge, Laclede Co., MO - Ballard, John K 64 MO MO MO, Emma 63 MO IL IL, Edward K 24 MO, Jewel M 13 grand dau.*
** 1930 - Living in Eldridge, Laclede Co., MO - Ballard, John T 74 MO TN TN, Emma L 73 MO TN TN*

More About JOHN KING BALLARD:

Burial: Holman Ballard Cemetery, Laclede Co., MO

Notes for EMMA LOUISE TAYLOR:
Source: Laclede County Missouri Death Certificate
** Death Certificate lists her date of birth Aug 13 1855 - the 1855 could be 1856. The last number is written over making it difficult to make out clearly. She was born in Illinois. Her father was Godfrey Taylor. Mother is listed as ???? Lee. Died Dec 30, 1936. Burial listed as Holman*

More About EMMA LOUISE TAYLOR:
Burial: Holman Ballard Cemetery, Laclede Co., MO

Children of JOHN BALLARD and EMMA TAYLOR are:
    i.   *IDA MAE[3] BALLARD, b. 01 Mar 1879, Eldridge, Laclede Co., MO; d. 16 May 1931; m. MARTIN CORKERY, 1899.*
    ii.   *MARGARET BALLARD, b. 12 Mar 1880, Eldridge, Laclede Co., MO; d. 06 Sep 1881, Eldridge, Laclede Co., MO.*
    iii. *JAMES FERDINAND BALLARD, b. 29 Nov 1881, Eldridge, Laclede Co., MO; d. 01 Mar 1970, Tulsa Co., OK; m. (1) DORTHA; b. 1881, KY; d. Aft. 1920; m. (2) SUSAN JANE HILDEBRAND; b. 29 Feb 1884, MO; d. Jun 1910, MO.*

        Notes for JAMES FERDINAND BALLARD:
        Source: 1920 Laclede County Missouri Federal Census Records
        ** 1920 - Living in Eldridge, Laclede Co., MO - Ballard, James A 38 MO, Dortha 39 KY*

        More About JAMES FERDINAND BALLARD:
        Burial: Memorial Park Cemetery, Tulsa Co., OK

        More About SUSAN JANE HILDEBRAND:
        Burial: Memorial Park Cemetery, Tulsa Co., OK

    iv. *WILLIAM MCCLANE BALLARD, b. 27 Feb 1886, Eldridge, Laclede Co., MO; d. 04 Sep 1981, Creston, Union Co., IA; m. ALICE GEORGIA HANFORD, 03 Feb 1910; b. 19 Oct 1893, Laclede Co., MO; d. 29 Feb 1988, Ringgold Co., IA.*

        Notes for WILLIAM MCCLANE BALLARD:
        Source: 1920 Laclede County Missouri Federal Census Records
        ** 1920 - Living in Hooker, Laclede Co., MO - Ballard, William M 34, Alice G 25, Ruby L 9, Ralph W 4 11/12, Georgie E 1 6/12*

        More About WILLIAM MCCLANE BALLARD:
        Burial: Blockton Cemetery, Taylor Co., IA

        More About ALICE GEORGIA HANFORD:
        Burial: Blockton Cemetery, Taylor Co., IA

    v.   *TALITHA ELIZABETH BALLARD, b. 25 Jun 1888, Eldridge, Laclede Co., MO; d. 01 Jan 1910, Eldridge, Laclede Co., MO.*
    vi. *PEARL E. BALLARD, b. 06 Aug 1890, Eldridge, Laclede Co., MO; d. 26 Feb 1963; m. BERT DAMPIER, 05 Apr 1908, Laclede Co., MO.*
    vii. *GROVER CLEVELAND BALLARD, b. 29 Nov 1892, Eldridge, Laclede Co., MO; d. 23 Nov 1975; m. LAVINA "VINA" PULLEY, 07 Jan 1914, Laclede Co., MO; d. Aft. 1920.*

        Notes for GROVER CLEVELAND BALLARD:
        Source: 1920 -1930 Laclede County Missouri Federal Census Records
        ** 1920 - Living in Eldridge, Laclede Co., MO - Ballard, Grover C 27 MO, Vina J 26 MO*
        ** 1930 - Living in Eldridge, Laclede Co., MO - Ballard, Grover C 37 MO MO MO, Ina 36 MO MO MO*

    viii. *EDWARD K. BALLARD, b. 01 Feb 1895, Eldridge, Laclede Co., MO; d. 12 Dec 1986, Bastrop, Moorehouse Parish, LA; m. EDITH CUMMINGS.*
    ix. *LILLIE BALLARD, b. 15 Jan 1884, Eldridge, Laclede Co., MO; d. Feb 1893, Eldridge, Laclede Co., MO.*

Jesse W. Ballard

Generation No. 1

1. JESSE W.[1] BALLARD *was born Abt. 1824 in TN, and died 09 Nov 1894 in Stoddard Co., MO. He married (1) ELIZABETH Abt. 1845. She was born 1819 in NC, and died 1869. He married (2) SAMANTHA OGLESBY Abt. 1871. She was born 01 Jul 1850 in Johnson Co., IL, and died 20 Oct 1932 in Dunklin Co., MO.*

Notes for JESSE W. BALLARD:
Source: Application for Letters of Administration Stoddard County Missouri, Bobbie Mills (bjmills@flash.net), 1860 Randolph County Arkansas Federal Census Records, 1870 - 1880 Stoddard County Missouri Federal Census Records
** 1860 - Living in Randolph Co., AR - Bullard, Jesse W 37 farmer AR, Elizabeth C 31 TN, Walter H. 10 TN, Timothy 11 TN, Columbus 9 TN, Nancy J 7 TN, Lucy A. 5 TN, Alexander 2 TN*
** 1870 - Living in Stoddard Co., Castor twp., MO - Ballard, Jesse 48 farmer TN, Walter 22 TN, Timothy 20 TN, Nancy 16 TN, Lucy 14 TN, Allen 12 TN, Tennessee 9 AR, William 2 MO*
** 1880 - Living in Stoddard Co., Castor twp., MO - Ballard, J. W. 56 farmer TN NC NC, Samantha 30 TN, Timothy 30 TN, Allen 21 TN, Lutitia 4 TN, America 1 TN, Stansbery, Van 14 stepson, James James 12 step son, George D James 10 stepson, Martha W. Oglesby 63 Mother in law MO*
** 1894, Nov 28 - Stoddard County Missouri - Application for Letters of Administration - State of Missouri, County of Stoddard } - In the Matter of Jesse W. Ballard Estate, Samantha Ballard says that to the best of her knowledge and belief, the names of the heirs of said Jesse W. Ballard deceased , and their places and residences, are respectively as follows: Samantha Ballard Widow, who resides in the County of Stoddard in the State of Missouri, Timothy M Ballard, who resides in the County of Stoddard In the State of MO, Allen J. Ballard, who resides in the County of Clark in the State of Ark; Lutitia Isaac, who resides in the County of Stoddard in the State of MO; Amy Norman, who resides in the County of Stoddard in the State of MO, Margaret Ballard, who resides in the County of Stoddard in the State of MO; Albert Thomas, who resides in the County of Van Zant in the State of Texas, Sarah E Thomas, who resides in the County of Van Zant in the State of Texas; that the said Jesse W. Ballard died without a will; that she will make a perfect inventory of and faithfully administer all the estate of the deceased, and pay the debts as far as the assets will extend and the law direct, and account for and pay all assets which shall come to her possession or knowledge. Samantha Ballard Subscribed and sworn to before me, this 28 day of Nov AD 1894 Thos Connelly, Recorded this 28th day of November A. D. 1894 Thos Connelly, Probate Judge*
** 1894 - Stoddard County, Missouri - Bond*
Know All Men by These Presents: That we, Samantha Ballard as Principal, and Reuben Horton, W. E. Almond as Securities, acknowledge ourselves indebted to the State of Missouri in the sum of Five Hundred Dollars, for the payment of which we bind ourselves, our heirs, executors and administrators jointly, severally and firmly by these presents, Given under our Hands and Seals this 28th day of Nov 1894.

The Condition of the above Bond is such, that if the said Samantha Ballard, Administrator of the estate of Jesse W. Ballard, deceased, shall faithfully administer said estate, account for and pay and deliver all money and property of said estate, and perform all other touching said administration required by law or the order or Decree of any Court having jurisdiction, then the above bond to be void, otherwise to remain in force. Attest to Mark Thos Connely, Samantha Ballard (seal), Reuben (his x) Horton (seal), W. E. Almond (seal). Recorded this 28th day of Nov A. D. 1894/ Thos Connelly, Probate Judge
** 1894 - County of Stoddard, MO - Letters - The State of Missouri to all Persons whom these Presents shall come -- Greeting: Know ye, that Whereas, Jesse W. Ballard late of the County of Stoddard, died Intestate having, at the time of his death, property in this State which may be lost, destroyed or diminished in value if speedy care be not taken of the same: To the end, thereof that the said property may be collected and disposed of according to law, We do hereby appoint Samantha Ballard Administrator of all and singular, the Goods and Chattels, Rights and Credits, which were of the said Jesse W. Ballard at the time of his death, with full power and authority to secure, preserve and dispose of said property according to the law, and collect all moneys due said deceased, and in general to do the other acts things which are, or hereafter may be, required of him by law.*

In Testimony whereof, I Thos Connelly, Judge of the Probate Court in and for the county of Stoddard aforesaid, have hereunto signed my name an affixed the seal of said Court, at office, this 28th day of Nov A.D. 1894. Recorded this 28th day of November A. D. 1894. Thos. Connelly Probate Judge

More About SAMANTHA OGLESBY:
Burial: Sumach Cemetery, Holcomb, Dunklin Co., MO

Children of JESSE BALLARD and ELIZABETH are:

2.   i.   *TIMOTHY M.^{2} BALLARD, b. 03 Nov 1849, TN; d. 14 Aug 1940, Lipan, Hood Co., TX.*
      ii.   *WALTER W. BALLARD, b. 1850, TN; d. Aft. 1870.*
     iii.   *COLUMBUS BALLARD, b. 1851, TN; d. Aft. 1860.*
3.   iv.   *NANCY J. BALLARD, b. Abt. 1854, TN; d. 19 Mar 1884, Stoddard Co., MO.*
      v.   *LUCY A. BALLARD, b. Abt. 1855, TN; d. Aft. 1870.*
     vi.   *ALEXANDER "ALLEN" J. BALLARD, b. 15 May 1859, TN; d. 12 Feb 1940, Garland Co., AR.*

         More About ALEXANDER "ALLEN" J. BALLARD:
         Burial: Sweet Home Cemetery, Clark Co., AR

    vii.   *TENNESSEE BALLARD, b. 1861, AR; d. Aft. 1870.*
   viii.   *WILLIAM BALLARD, b. 1868, MO; d. Aft. 1870.*

Children of JESSE BALLARD and SAMANTHA OGLESBY are:

     ix.   *LUTICIA LOU^2 BALLARD, b. 13 Jul 1874, Stoddard Co., MO; d. 21 Jun 1945, Van Zandt Co., TX; m. (1) OLIVER PLEASANT ROBERTS; b. 26 Aug 1879, Sebastian Co., AR; d. 27 Dec 1950, Hico, Hamilton Co., TX; m. (2) ABRAHAM "ABE" ISAAC, 18 Mar 1892, Stoddard Co., MO; b. 05 Jan 1862, IL; d. Dec 1920, Van Zandt Co., TX.*

         Notes for LUTICIA LOU BALLARD:
         Source: Van Zandt County Texas Standard Certificate of Death

         More About LUTICIA LOU BALLARD:
         Burial: Starr Cemetery, Canton, Van Zandt Co., TX

         More About OLIVER PLEASANT ROBERTS:
         Burial: Oakwood Cemetery, Hamilton Co., OH

         More About ABRAHAM "ABE" ISAAC:
         Burial: Starr Cemetery., Canton, Van Zandt Co., TX

4.   x.   *AMERICA EMMA "AMY" BALLARD, b. 19 Nov 1876, Stoddard Co., MO; d. 09 Sep 1952, Dallas Co., TX.*
      xi.   *MARGARET BALLARD, b. Bet. 1880 - 1900; d. Aft. 1894.*
5.   xii.   *HATTIE SAMANTHA BALLARD, b. 11 Jan 1884, Stoddard Co., MO; d. 27 Mar 1952, Dunklin Co., MO.*

Generation No. 2

2. *TIMOTHY M.^{2} BALLARD (JESSE W.^{1}) was born 03 Nov 1849 in TN, and died 14 Aug 1940 in Lipan, Hood Co., TX. He married SARAH ELLEN McMILLIAN 14 May 1882 in Clark Co., AR. She was born Abt. 1864 in MO, and died Bet. 1886 - 1900.*

Notes for TIMOTHY M. BALLARD:

Source: 1900 Delta County Texas Federal Census Records, 1940 Hood County Texas Standard Certificate of Death
** 1900 - Living in Delta Co., TX - Ballard, Timothy - Nov 1849 wd farmer TN TN TN, Marvin C - July 1885 MO TN AR, Addie M - Nov 1886 MO TN AR*
** 1940 - Living in Hood Co., TX - Living with Neagle family - Timothy M Ballard (father in law) - 79 wd TN TN TN*

More About TIMOTHY M. BALLARD:
Burial: Evergreen Cemetery Lipan, Hood Co., TX

Children of TIMOTHY BALLARD and SARAH McMILLIAN are:

        i.   MARVIN C.³ BALLARD, b. 06 Jul 1885, Stoddard Co., MO; d. 18 Dec 1964, Sweetwater, Nolan, TX; m. VERA KITCHENS, 02 Mar 1919, Mitchell, TX; b. 29 Aug 1897, TX; d. 07 Jan 1990, Abilene, Taylor Co., TX.

           Notes for MARVIN C. BALLARD:
           Source: Stoddard County Missouri Birth Register, Nolan County Texas Certificate of Death, WWII Draft Registration Card

           More About MARVIN C. BALLARD:
           Burial: Garden of Memories Cemetery, Sweetwater, Nolan Co., TX

           More About VERA KITCHENS:
           Burial: Garden of Memories Cemetery, Sweetwater, Nolan Co., TX

6.   ii.   ADDIE MAE BALLARD, b. 09 Nov 1886, Stoddard Co., MO; d. 30 Jun 1953, Houston, Harris Co., TX.

3. NANCY J.² BALLARD (JESSE W.¹) was born Abt. 1854 in TN, and died 19 Mar 1884 in Stoddard Co., MO. She married JOHN R. THOMAS. He was born 1853 in TN, and died 07 Nov 1914 in OK.

Notes for NANCY J. BALLARD:
Source: Duck Creek Missouri Death Records

Children of NANCY BALLARD and JOHN THOMAS are:

7.   i.   JAMES ALBERT³ THOMAS, b. 14 Jul 1877, Stoddard Co., MO; d. 11 Feb 1918, OK.
         ii.   SARAH E. THOMAS, b. 1880; d. Aft. 1894.

4. AMERICA EMMA "AMY"² BALLARD (JESSE W.¹) was born 19 Nov 1876 in Stoddard Co., MO, and died 09 Sep 1952 in Dallas Co., TX. She married JACOB A. NORMAN 20 Aug 1891 in Stoddard Co., MO. He was born 12 Jul 1867 in MO, and died 09 Nov 1944.

Notes for AMERICA EMMA "AMY" BALLARD:
Source: Dallas County Texas Certificate of Death

More About AMERICA EMMA "AMY" BALLARD:
Burial: Hillcrest Cemetery, Canton, Van Zandt Co., TX

Notes for JACOB A. NORMAN:
Source: 1900 Stoddard County Missouri Federal Census Records, 1910 - 1940 Van Zandt County Texas Federal Census Records

** 1900 - Living in Duck Creek, Stoddard Co., MO - Norman, Jake - Sept 1875 MO NC TN, A. E - Nov 1876 MO TN IL, David - Nov 1892 MO, Walker - Nov 1895 MO, David Fowler boarder*

1910 - Living in Van Zandt Co., TX - Norman, Jacob 42 farmer MO IL IL, Emma A 3 children 3 living MO TN IL, David 17 MO, Walter 13 MO, Hazel 6 TX
1920 - Living in Van Zandt Co., TX - Norman, Jacob A 52 MO NC TN, America C 44 MO TN IL, James W. 23 MO
1930 - Living in Van Zandt Co., TX - Norman, Jacob A 62 MO Germany IL, Merica E 57 MO GA IL, Walker J 33 divorced MO
1940 - Living in Edgewood, Van Zandt Co., TX - Norman, Jacob 72 MO, America E 64 MO

More About JACOB A. NORMAN:
Burial: Hillcrest Cemetery, Canton, Van Zandt Co., TX

Children of AMERICA BALLARD and JACOB NORMAN are:

     i.   *DAVID[3] NORMAN, b. 06 Nov 1892, MO; d. 17 Nov 1979, Van Zandt Co., TX.*
    ii.   *JAMES WALKER NORMAN, b. Nov 1895, MO; d. Aft. 1952.*
   iii.   *HAZEL NORMAN, b. 1904, MO; d. Aft. 1910.*

5. *HATTIE SAMANTHA[2] BALLARD (JESSE W.[1]) was born 11 Jan 1884 in Stoddard Co., MO, and died 27 Mar 1952 in Dunklin Co., MO. She married WILLIAM HENRY SAMPLES 22 Feb 1900 in Stoddard Co., MO. He was born 19 Mar 1880 in Stoddard Co., MO, and died 01 Apr 1963 in Kennett, Dunklin Co., MO.*

More About HATTIE SAMANTHA BALLARD:
Burial: Sumach Cemetery Holcomb, Dunklin Co., MO

Notes for WILLIAM HENRY SAMPLES:
Source: 1940 Dunklin County Missouri Federal Census Records

1940 - Living in Holcomb, Dunklin Co., MO - Samples W. H 60, Hattie 54 MO, Aline 18 MO, Veneda 10 MO

More About WILLIAM HENRY SAMPLES:
Burial: Sumach Cemetery, Holcomb, Dunklin Co., MO

Children of HATTIE BALLARD and WILLIAM SAMPLES are:
     i.   *JAMES EULE[3] SAMPLES, b. 09 Mar 1901; d. 1906.*
    ii.   *MAYMIE MAY SAMPLES, b. 15 Jan 1904; d. 05 Jun 1985.*
   iii.   *RAYMOND SAMPLES, b. 09 Jul 1907, Dunklin Co., MO; d. 11 Aug 1975, MO.*

        More About RAYMOND SAMPLES:
        Burial: Sumach Cemetery Holcomb, Dunklin Co., MO

    iv.   *MARY SAMPLES, b. 02 Oct 1910, Dunklin Co., MO; d. Oct 1913.*
     v.   *MARTIN CLEVELAND SAMPLES, b. 26 Dec 1912, Dunklin Co., MO; d. 24 Mar 1970, Dunklin Co., MO.*

        More About MARTIN CLEVELAND SAMPLES:
        Burial: Sumach Cemetery Holcomb, Dunklin Co., MO

    vi.   *WALTER SAMPLES, b. 20 Oct 1915, Dunklin Co., MO; d. Oct 1915.*
   vii.   *WYONITA SAMPLES, b. 21 Jan 1918, Dunklin Co., MO; d. 30 Oct 1918.*
  viii.   *EVELEE SAMPLES, b. 21 Sep 1920, Dunklin Co., MO; d. 23 Oct 1920.*
    ix.   *EDNA AILENE SAMPLES, b. 28 Jun 1922, Dunklin Co., MO.*
     x.   *VANETA MAXINE SAMPLES, b. 25 May 1929, Dunklin Co., MO; d. 12 Apr 2007.*

        More About VANETA MAXINE SAMPLES:
        Burial: Sumach Cemetery Holcomb, Dunklin Co., MO

Generation No. 3

6. ADDIE MAE[3] BALLARD (*TIMOTHY M.[2], JESSE W.[1]*) was born 09 Nov 1886 in Stoddard Co., MO, and died 30 Jun 1953 in Houston, Harris Co., TX. She married HENRY JOHN ADAM NEAGLE 04 Aug 1901 in Delta Co., TX. He was born 09 Mar 1876 in KY, and died 15 Dec 1943.

Notes for ADDIE MAE BALLARD:
Source: Harris County Texas Certificate of Death

More About ADDIE MAE BALLARD:
Burial: Evergreen Cemetery, Lipan, Hood Co., TX

Notes for HENRY JOHN ADAM NEAGLE:
Source: 1930 Hood County Texas Federal Census Records

** 1930 - Living in Hood Co., TX - Neagle, John A 53 KY KY KY, Eva M 43 MO TN AR, Eva E. 21, Audley A 13 TX, Avoe Spencer dau 24 TX, Robert B Spencer son in law 26 TX TX TX, Timothy M. Ballard - Father in law 79 wd TN TN TN*

More About HENRY JOHN ADAM NEAGLE:

Burial: Evergreen Cemetery, Hood Co., TX

Children of ADDIE BALLARD and HENRY NEAGLE are:

> i.   EVA E.[4] NEAGLE, b. Abt. 1909, TX; d. Aft. 1930.
> ii. AUDLEY A. NEAGLE, b. Abt. 1917, TX; d. Aft. 1930.
> iii. AVOE NEAGLE, b. Abt. 1906, TX; d. Aft. 1930; m. ROBERT SPENCER; b. Abt. 1904, TX; d. Aft. 1930.

7. JAMES ALBERT[3] THOMAS (*NANCY J.[2] BALLARD, JESSE W.[1]*) was born 14 Jul 1877 in Stoddard Co., MO, and died 11 Feb 1918 in OK. He married ALICE MANDY STEWARD. She was born Abt. 1883 in MO, and died 30 Jan 1934 in OK.

Notes for JAMES ALBERT THOMAS:
Source: 1910 Stephens County Oklahoma Federal Census Records

** 1910 - Living in King, Stephens Co., OK - Thomas, James A 32 MO, Manda A 25 MO 5 children, 3 living, Virgil F 5 OK, Clarance E 3 OK, Raymond Alfred 1/12 OK*

Children of JAMES THOMAS and ALICE STEWARD are:

> i.   VIRGIL F.[4] THOMAS, b. Abt. 1905, OK; d. Aft. 1920.
> ii. CLARENCE E. THOMAS, b. Abt. 1907, OK; d. Aft. 1920.
> iii. RAYMOND ALFRED THOMAS, b. Abt. 1910, OK; d. Aft. 1920.
> iv. JEWEL GERALDINE THOMAS, b. Abt. 1914, OK; d. Aft. 1920.
> v.   LESTER THOMAS, b. Abt. 1918, OK; d. Aft. 1920.

Joab Ballard

Generation No. 1

1. JOAB[1] BALLARD *was born 1811 in NC, and died Aft. 1860. He married (1) FIDELLA THOMPSON 14 Dec 1831 in Johnson Co., IN. She was born Abt. 1810 in Halifax, Plymouth Co., MA. He married (2) SARAH RUSSELL 02 Apr 1850 in Jackson Co., IN, daughter of JAMES RUSSELL and ELIZEBETH ZION. She was born 01 Dec 1821, and died Aft. 1860.*

Notes for JOAB BALLARD:
Source: 1850 Jackson County Indiana Federal Census Records, 1860 Carroll County Missouri Federal Census Records
** 1850 - Living in Grassy Fork twp Jackson Co., IN - Job 39 NC, Sarah 29 IN, Rebecca 12 IN, Silas 10 KY, Josephine 7 IN, Leonidas 5 IN, Charles 3 IN*
** 1860 - Living in Grand River, Carroll Co., MO - Ballard, Joel 52 NC wagon maker, Sarah 39 MO, Silas 20 KY, Charles 14 IN, Jas 10 IN, Wm 7 MO*

Child of JOAB BALLARD and FIDELLA THOMPSON is:
2.	i.	SILAS A.[2] BALLARD, *b. 16 Aug 1839, Bedford, Trimble Co., KY; d. 10 Mar 1915, Carrollton, Carroll Co., MO.*

Children of JOAB BALLARD and SARAH RUSSELL are:
	ii.	REBECCA[2] BALLARD, *b. 1838, IN; d. Aft. 1850.*
	iii.	JOSEPHINE BALLARD, *b. 1842, IN; d. Aft. 1850.*
	iv.	LEONIDAS BALLARD, *b. 1840, IN; d. Aft. 1850.*
	v.	CHARLES BALLARD, *b. 1847, IN; d. Aft. 1860.*
	vi.	JAMES BALLARD, *b. Abt. 1850, IN; d. Aft. 1860.*
	vii.	WILLIAM BALLARD, *b. Abt. 1853, MO; d. Aft. 1860.*

Generation No. 2

2.	SILAS A.[2] BALLARD (JOAB[1]) *was born 16 Aug 1839 in Bedford, Trimble Co., KY, and died 10 Mar 1915 in Carrollton, Carroll Co., MO. He married MARY ANN MAY, daughter of ALLEN MAY and ANN PYLES. She was born 31 Aug 1846 in Pocahontas Co., VA, and died 27 Aug 1936 in Carrollton, Carroll Co., MO.*

Notes for SILAS A. BALLARD:
Source: Carroll County Missouri Estate Records, Missouri State Board of Health Death Certificate Carroll County Missouri, 1870-1910 Grand River Carroll County Missouri Federal Census Records
** 1870 - Living in Grand River Carroll Co., MO - Ballard, Silas 38 KY, Mary Ann 23 KY, William 19, David 8 MO, Leonidus 4 MO*
** 1880 - Living in Grand River, Carroll Co., MO - Ballard, S. A 41 farmer KY NC MA, M. A 32 VA VA VA, L. J 14 MO KY VA*
** 1900 - Living in Carrollton, Carroll Co., MO - Ballard, Silas A - Aug 1839 KY NC MA, Mary A - Aug 1849 VA VA VA, Leonides - Feb 1866 MO KY VA*
** 1910 - Living in Carrollton, Carroll Co., MO - Ballard, SA 70 KY NC, Mary A 64 VA VA VA, LJ 44 MO KY VA, Ella M 34 MO IN IN*
** Death by suicide*
** 1915 - Application for Letters of Administration - State of Missouri, County of Carroll} ss. In the Matter of Silas A. Ballard deceased. L. J. Ballard says, that to the best of his knowledge and belief, the names of heirs of the said Silas Ballard deceased, and their places and residences, are respectively as follows: Mary A. Ballard widow who resides in the City of Carrollton in the State of Missouri; L. J. Ballard, son who resides in the city of Carrollton in the State of Missouri; that the said Silas A. Ballard died intestate March 10, 1915 and that he will make a perfect inventory of and faithfully administrator of all the estate of the deceased, and pay the debts as far as the assets will*

extend and the law direct, and account for and pay all assets which shall come to his possession or knowledge. Subscribed and sworn to before me, this 25th day of March A. D. 1915 R. M. Lee, Clerk of Probate Court, Recorded 30th day of March A. D. 1915. L. J Ballard applicant. R. M Lee Clerk of Probate Court

** Bond - State of Missouri, County of Carroll} Sct. We, L. J. Ballard as Principal and Mary A. Ballard and Rush G. Harper as Securities, are held and firmly bound unto the State of Missouri, in the sum of Three Thousand Five Hundred Dollars for the payment of which we do hereby bind ourselves, our heirs, executors and administrators, firmly by these presents. Sealed with our seals, and date at Carrollton in the State aforesaid, this 30th day of March A. D. 1915. The Condition of the above Bond is, that if the said L. J. Ballard Administrator of the estate of Silas A. Ballard deceased, shall faithfully administer said estate account for, pay and deliver all money and property of said estate, and perform all other things touching said administration required by or the order or decree of said Court having jurisdiction, then the above bond to be void; otherwise to remain in full force and effect. Filed, approved and recorded, this 30th day of March A. D. 1915 R. M Lee Clerk of Probate Court}. L. J. Ballard (seal), Mary A. Ballard (seal), Rush G. Harper (seal)*

** Letters of Administration - State of Missouri, County of Carroll } ss. In the Probate Court. To all persons to whom these presents shall come - Greeting:*

Know Ye, That whereas, Silas A. Ballard late of the County of Carroll and State of Missouri, died intestate, as it is said, having at the time of his death, property in this State, which may be lost, destroyed or diminished in value if speedy care be not taken of the same, the end therefore, that the said property may be collected preserved and disposed of according to law, We do Hereby Appoint L. J. Ballard, Administrator of all and singular the Goods and Chattels, Rights and Credits, which were of the said Silas A. Ballard at the time of his death, with full power and authority to secure and dispose of said property according to law, and collect all moneys due said deceased, and in general to do and perform all other acts and things which are or hereafter may be required of him by law. In testimony whereof, I John S. Crawford Judge of the Probate Court, in and for the County of Carroll hereto sign my name and affix the seal of said Court, at office in Carrollton, MO this 30th day of March A. D. 1915. John S. Crawford, Judge of Probate Court

More About SILAS A. BALLARD:
Burial: 11 Mar 1915, Oak Hill Cemetery, Carrollton, Carroll Co., MO

Notes for MARY ANN MAY:
Source: Carroll County Missouri Death Certificate

More About MARY ANN MAY:
Burial: Oak Hill Cemetery, Carrollton, Carroll Co., MO

Children of SILAS BALLARD and MARY MAY are:
> i.   WILLIAM³ BALLARD, b. 1851, Carroll Co., MO; d. Aft. 1870.
> ii.   DAVID BALLARD, b. 1862, Carroll Co., MO; d. Aft. 1870.
> iii.   LEONIDAS J. BALLARD, b. 16 Feb 1866, Carroll Co., MO; d. 18 Sep 1945, Carroll Co., MO; m. ELLA STANLEY; b. 15 Apr 1876, Wakenda, Carroll Co., MO; d. 10 Feb 1922, Carrollton, Carroll Co., MO.

Notes for LEONIDAS J. BALLARD:
Source: Carroll County Missouri Death Certificate, 1910-1920 Carroll County Missouri Federal Census Records
** 1910 - Living in Carrollton, Carroll Co., MO with his parents*
** 1920 - Living in Carrollton, Carroll Co., MO - Ballard, Leonidis 53 MO KY VA, Ella N 44 MO IN IN, Mary A 73 other wd VA*

More About LEONIDAS J. BALLARD:
Burial: Oak Hill Cemetery, Carrollton, Carroll Co., MO

Notes for ELLA STANLEY:
Source: Carroll County Missouri Death Certificate

More About ELLA STANLEY:
Burial: Oak Hill Cemetery, Carrollton, Carroll Co., MO

John Ballard

Generation No. 1

1. JOHN[1] BALLARD *was born 1784 in VA, and died Aft. 1868. He married* NANCY GREEN. *She was born 1798 in TN, and died Aft. 1870.*

Notes for JOHN BALLARD:
Source: Donna Dixon (ddixon@iadfw.net), 1850 - 1870 Smith County Tennessee Federal Census Records, Tennessee Wills and Probate Records

** 1850 - Living in Smith Co., TN - Ballard, John 67 VA, Nancy 50 TN, Eliza 20 TN, Fanny 16 TN, Polly 13 TN, John 8 TN, James H. 28 TN, Allen 4 TN*
** 1860 - Living in Smith Co., TN - Ballard, John 76 VA, Nancy 62 TN, Elizabeth 26 TN, Fanny 22 TN*
** State of Tennessee, Smith County, We, John M. Ballard W Z Ballard & Peter J Ballard & John A Moss are bound to the State of Tennessee in the penalty of Six thousand Dollars. Witness our hands and seals this 2nd day of November A. D. 1868. The Condition of this Obligation is such, That Whereas, the above bound John M Ballard has been appointed executor of the last will and testament of John Ballard deceased. Now if the said John M. Ballard shall well and truly perform all the duties which are or may be required to remain in full force and virtue. John M. Ballard (seal), Wm. Y Ballard (seal), Peter J Ballard (seal), J. A. Moss (seal).*
Securities justified on Bond in open court Acknowledged in and Approved by Court. W. B. Whitley, Judge

Notes for NANCY GREEN:
Source: 1870 Smith County Tennessee Federal Census Records
** 1870 - Living in Smith Co., TN - Ballard, Nancy 70 TN, Eliza 35 TN, Allen 24 farmer TN*

Children of JOHN BALLARD *and* NANCY GREEN *are:*
2.   i.   JAMES H.[2] BALLARD, *b. 24 Feb 1823, Smith Co., TN; d. 01 Jun 1883, Smith Co., TN.*
3.   ii.   ALLEN C. BALLARD, *b. 06 Jun 1825, TN; d. 22 Aug 1883, MO.*
            iii. ELIZABETH "ELIZA" BALLARD, *b. Bet. 1830 - 1834, TN; d. Aft. 1870.*
4.   iv.   FRANCES "FANNY" A. BALLARD, *b. Bet. 1834 - 1838, TN; d. Aft. 1864.*
            v.   MARY "POLLY" BALLARD, *b. Abt. 1837, TN; d. Aft. 1850.*
            vi.   JOHN BALLARD, JR, *b. Bet. 1839 - 1842, TN.*

Generation No. 2

2. JAMES H.[2] BALLARD (JOHN[1]) *was born 24 Feb 1823 in Smith Co., TN, and died 01 Jun 1883 in Smith Co., TN. He married* MARTHA EVANS *15 Dec 1853 in Smith Co., TN. She was born Abt. 1830 in TN, and died Aft. 1870.*

Notes for JAMES H. BALLARD:
Source: Early TN Marriages by Byron & Barbara Sistler, 1850 - 1880 Smith County Tennessee Federal Census Records

** 1850 - Living in Smith Co., TN, with parents - Ballard, James H. 27 Allen 4*
** 1860 - Living in Smith Co., TN, next door to parents - Ballard, James 34 TN, Martha 40 TN, Allen 15 TN*
** 1870 - Living in Smith Co., TN, next door to parents - Ballard, James 47 Farmer TN, Martha 50 laborer TN*
** 1880 - Living in Smith Co., TN - Ballard, James 56 farming TN VA TN, Martha 59 TN VA VA*

Child of JAMES BALLARD *and* MARTHA EVANS *is:*
5.   i.   ALLEN[3] BALLARD, *b. 29 Aug 1845, Smith Co., TN; d. 13 Feb 1913, Smith Co., TN.*

3. ALLEN C.[2] BALLARD (JOHN[1]) *was born 06 Jun 1825 in TN, and died 22 Aug 1883 in MO. He married*

JUDITH KEMP 03 Dec 1846. She was born 20 Aug 1826 in TN, and died 23 Jan 1881 in MO.

Notes for ALLEN C. BALLARD:
Source: Posting on Ballard Family Gen. Forum, 1860 Smith County Tennessee Federal Census Records, 1870, 1880
Carter County Missouri Federal Census Records

* 1850 - Living in Smith Co., TN - Ballard, Allen C. 24 Farmer TN, Judy 23 TN, Alethia 3 TN, Henry 7/12 (next
door to parents)
* 1860 - Living in Cedar Creek, Wayne Co., MO - Ballard, Allen 35 TN, Julia 34 TN, Aletha 12 TN, Henry 10 TN,
Nancy 8 TN, John H 5 TN, James R 3 TN
* 1870 - Living in Carter Co., MO - Ballard, Allen 45 TN, Julia 44 TN, Henry 20 TN, Lucy 18 TN, Henderson J. 16
TN, James 13 TN, William 10 MO, Martha M. 7 MO Letthe 22 TN
* 1880 - Living in Carter Co., MO - Ballard, Allen 54 TN, Julia 53 TN, Henry 28 TN, Henderson 26 TN, James 24
TN, William 18 MO, Emma (granddaughter 18, Hivy 8/12 grandson MO Martha 16 MO, Jobe 5 MO

Children of ALLEN BALLARD and JUDITH KEMP are:
   i. ALETHA³ BALLARD, b. 1848, TN; d. Aft. 1870; m. JOHN A. GRESHAM, 10 Sep 1876, Carter Co., MO.
   ii. HENRY BALLARD, b. Abt. 1852, TN; d. Aft. 1880; m. C. A. GREEN, 11 Apr 1883, Colemanville, Carter
    Co., MO.
   iii. LUCY BALLARD, b. 1852, TN; d. 22 Jul 1922, Carter Co., MO; m. JOHN CARUTHERS; b. 1847, Jackson
    Co., TN; d. 27 Mar 1901, Carter Co., MO.

    More About LUCY BALLARD:
    Burial: Sutherlin Condray Cemetery, Ellsinore, Carter Co., MO

    More About JOHN CARUTHERS:
    Burial: Sutherlin Condray Cemetery, Ellsinore, Carter Co., MO

   iv. NANCY BALLARD, b. 1852, TN; d. Aft. 1860.
6. v. JOHN HENDERSON BALLARD, b. Apr 1856, TN; d. 17 Apr 1911, Dunklin Co., MO.
7. vi. WILLIAM ALLEN BALLARD, b. 23 Oct 1860, MO; d. 28 Dec 1929, Carter Co., MO.
   vii. MARTHA M. BALLARD, b. Bet. 1863 - 1864, MO; d. Aft. 1880.
8. viii. JAMES W. BALLARD, b. 1856, TN; d. Bef. 1900.

4. FRANCES "FANNY" A.² BALLARD (JOHN¹) was born Bet. 1834 - 1838 in TN, and died Aft. 1864. She married
GEORGE SMALLING 10 Oct 1864 in Smith Co., TN. He was born Abt. 1820.

Notes for FRANCES "FANNY" A. BALLARD:
Source: Donna Dixon (donnad@flashnet), Early TN. Marriages by Byron & Barbara Sistler

Child of FRANCES BALLARD and GEORGE SMALLING is:
   i. ELIZABETH³ SMALLING, b. Abt. 1854; m. WILLIAM H. MASSEY, 1882; b. Abt. 1850.

Generation No. 3

5. ALLEN³ BALLARD (JAMES H.², JOHN¹) was born 29 Aug 1845 in Smith Co., TN, and died 13 Feb 1913 in Smith Co.,
TN. He married NANCY ANN HESSION 09 Oct 1870 in Smith Co., TN, daughter of JAMES HASSINE and NANCY KEMP.
She was born 12 Mar 1840 in TN, and died 02 Jan 1929 in Pleasant Shade, Smith Co., TN.

Notes for ALLEN BALLARD:
Source: Early TN Marriages by Byron & Barbara Sistler, 1880 -1910 Smith County Tennessee Federal Census
Records
* 1880 - Living in Smith Co., TN - Ballard, Allen 34 TN TN TN, Nancy 40 TN TN TN, James 4 TN TN TN
* 1900 - Living in Smith Co., TN - Ballard, Allen - Aug 1845 TN TN TN, Nancy - Mar 1840 TN TN TN, Lidy -aunt -
Mar 1830 TN TN TN

** 1910 - Living in Smith Co., TN - Ballard, Allan 64 farmer TN TN TN (next door to son James) , Nancy A 70 TN TN TN, Eliza 80 aunt TN TN TN*

Notes for NANCY ANN HESSION:
Source: Smith County Tennessee Certificate of Death

More About NANCY ANN HESSION:
Burial: Ballard Grave yard

Child of ALLEN BALLARD and NANCY HESSION is:
9.   i.   JAMES ALLEN⁴ BALLARD, b. 23 Jan 1876, Smith Co., TN; d. 30 Jun 1921, Pleasant Shade, Smith Co., TN.

6. JOHN HENDERSON³ BALLARD (ALLEN C.², JOHN¹) was born Apr 1856 in TN, and died 17 Apr 1911 in Dunklin Co., MO. He married EMMA NATTON 21 Aug 1878 in Henry Co., TN. She was born Jul 1858 in IL, and died Aft. 1910.

Notes for JOHN HENDERSON BALLARD:
Source: 1900 Dunklin County Missouri Federal Census Records
** 1900 - Living in Independence, Dunklin Co., MO - Ballard, Henderson - April 1856 TN TN TN farmer, Emma - July 1858 - 14 children 10 living IL IL IL, Ida - Dec 1882 MO, Lula - June 1886 MO, Myrtle - June 1887 MO, Edward - Apr 1888 MO, Tennie - Oct 1889 MO, Clay - May 1892 MO, Virgie - Feb 1894 MO, Mason - Mar 1896 MO*

More About JOHN HENDERSON BALLARD:
Burial: Gregory Cemetery, Kennett, Dunklin Co., MO

Children of JOHN BALLARD and EMMA NATTON are:
10.   i.   IDA⁴ BALLARD, b. Dec 1882, Dunklin Co., MO; d. Aft. 1910.
          ii.   LULA ANN BALLARD, b. 06 Jan 1887, Dunklin Co., MO; d. 11 Jul 1950, St. Louis City, MO.

                More About LULA ANN BALLARD:
                Burial: Gregory Cemetery, Kennett, Dunklin Co., MO

11.   iii. MYRTLE BALLARD, b. Jun 1887, Dunklin Co., MO; d. Aft. 1900.
12.   iv.   EDWARD "ED" BALLARD, b. 11 Apr 1888, Dunklin Co., MO; d. 28 Mar 1961.
          v.   TENNIE BALLARD, b. Oct 1889, Dunklin Co., MO; d. Aft. 1900.
          vi.   CLAY BALLARD, b. May 1892, Dunklin Co., MO; d. Aft. 1910.
          vii. VIRGIE E. BALLARD, b. 20 Feb 1895, Dunklin Co., MO; d. 06 Mar 1972; m. JOHN ELLISON SMITH; b. 06 Nov 1894; d. 06 Apr 1962.

                Notes for VIRGIE E. BALLARD:
                Source: Social Security Records

                More About VIRGIE E. BALLARD:
                Burial: Oak Ridge Cemetery, Kennett, Dunklin Co., MO

                More About JOHN ELLISON SMITH:
                Burial: Oak Ridge Cemetery, Kennett, Dunklin Co., MO

13.   viii. MASON BALLARD, b. 11 Mar 1898, Dunklin Co., MO; d. Nov 1973.

7. WILLIAM ALLEN³ BALLARD (ALLEN C.², JOHN¹) was born 23 Oct 1860 in MO, and died 28 Dec 1929 in Carter Co.,

MO. He married AILSIE ELIZABETH GRESHAM 17 Aug 1890 in Carter Co., MO. She was born 22 Dec 1866 in Carter Co., MO, and died 10 Oct 1943 in Ellsinore, Carter Co., MO.

Notes for WILLIAM ALLEN BALLARD:
Source: 1900-1920 Carter County Missouri Federal Census Records, Carter County Missouri Death Certificate
* 1900 - Living in Jackson, Carter Co., MO - Ballard, William - Oct 1860 MO, Luther L Moss - June 1855 step, Della Ballard - Apr 1893 MO, Charles M - Feb 1895, McKinley - Nov 1896, Edna A 1899 MO
* 1910 - Living in Jackson, Carter Co., MO - Ballard, William 49 MO TN TN, Elsie 44 MO, Della 8 MO, Mathew C 15 MO, Delbert 13 MO, Edna 11 MO, George 8 MO, Earnest 4 MO, Edith 3 MO, Esther L 1/12 MO
* 1920 - Living in Jackson, Carter Co., MO - Ballard, Wm A 60 MO, Alsie E 53 MO, Debert M 23 MO, Edna A 20 MO, George J 18 MO, Ernest 14 MO, Julia E 12 MO, Esther 4 MO, (hard to read W Gresham 45 brother in law

More About WILLIAM ALLEN BALLARD:
Burial: Gresham Cemetery, Carter Co., MO

Notes for AILSIE ELIZABETH GRESHAM:
Source: 1930 Carter County Missouri Federal Census Records
* 1930 - Living in Jackson, Carter Co., MO - Living with son Ernest

More About AILSIE ELIZABETH GRESHAM:
Burial: Gresham Cemetery, Carter Co., MO

Children of WILLIAM BALLARD and AILSIE GRESHAM are:
      i.   DELLA[4] BALLARD, b. 14 Apr 1893, Carter Co., MO; d. 29 Mar 1982; m. JAMES FRANK SMITH; b. 05 Apr 1888, Carter Co., MO; d. 10 Dec 1988, Sapulpa, Creek Co., OK.

          More About DELLA BALLARD:
          Burial: South Heights Cemetery, Sapulpa, Creek Co., OK

          More About JAMES FRANK SMITH:
          Burial: South Heights Cemetery, Sapulpa, Creek Co., OK

      ii.   CHARLES MATHEW BALLARD, b. 19 Feb 1895, Carter Co., MO; d. 29 Jun 1952, St. Louis City, MO; m. CORA JOSEPHINE BOYER; b. 03 May 1894, Mill Spring, Wayne Co., MO; d. 08 Jun 1965, St. Louis City, MO.

          More About CORA JOSEPHINE BOYER:
          Burial: Gresham Cemetery, Carter Co., MO

     iii.   DELBERT MCKINLEY BALLARD, b. 01 Nov 1897, Carter Co., MO; d. 10 Sep 1950.

          Notes for DELBERT MCKINLEY BALLARD:
          Source: Wayne County Missouri, The Division of Health of Missouri Standard Certificate of Death #43976, WWI Draft Registration shows him born Nov 14, 1896 Carter Co. Father William Ballard b. Wayne Co., MO

          More About DELBERT MCKINLEY BALLARD:
          Burial: Gresham Cemetery, Carter Co., MO

     iv.   EDNA A. BALLARD, b. 16 Feb 1899, Carter Co., MO; d. 12 Feb 1920.
          More About EDNA A. BALLARD:
          Burial: Gresham Cemetery, Carter Co., MO

      v.   GEORGE JAMES BALLARD, b. 13 Mar 1901, Carter Co., MO; d. 19 Feb 1992, Wayne Co., MO; m.

EDNA VIOLA CARNAHAN; b. 08 May 1903, Carter Co., MO; d. 24 Jan 1992, Poplar Bluff, Butler Co., MO.

More About GEORGE JAMES BALLARD:
Burial: Carson Hill Cemetery, Mill Spring, Wayne Co., MO

More About EDNA VIOLA CARNAHAN:
Burial: Carson Hill Cemetery, Mill Spring, Wayne Co., MO

    vi.   *VERNIE L. BALLARD, b. 03 Aug 1903, Carter Co., MO; d. 03 Jun 1904, Carter Co., MO.*

More About VERNIE L. BALLARD:
Burial: Gresham Cemetery, Carter Co., MO

    vii.   *ERNEST BALLARD, b. 05 Jun 1905, Carter Co., MO; d. 13 Oct 1973, Poplar Bluff, Butler Co., MO; m. ADA VIOLA LEACH; b. 28 Aug 1911; d. 12 Dec 1968.*

More About ADA VIOLA LEACH:
Burial: Carson Hill Cemetery, Mill Spring, Wayne Co., MO

    viii.   *EDITH JULIA BALLARD, b. 07 Nov 1907, Carter Co., MO; d. 17 Nov 2003, Tulso Co., OK; m. ALBERT SIDNEY LEHR, Bef. 1934; b. 18 May 1892, Ellsinore, Carter Co., MO; d. 29 Sep 1971, Sapulpa, Creek Co., OK.*

More About EDITH JULIA BALLARD:
Burial: Memorial Park Cemetery, Tulsa Co., OK

More About ALBERT SIDNEY LEHR:
Burial: Memorial Park Cemetery, Tulsa Co., OK

    ix.   *ESTHER BALLARD, b. 04 Jan 1910, Carter Co., MO; d. 23 Feb 1990; m. EARL DUNCAN; b. 11 Dec 1900; d. 14 Aug 1972.*

More About ESTHER BALLARD:
Burial: Duncan Cemetery, Williamsville, Wayne Co., MO

More About EARL DUNCAN:
Burial: Duncan Cemetery, Williamsville, Wayne Co., MO

8. *JAMES W.[3] BALLARD (ALLEN C.[2], JOHN[1]) was born 1856 in TN, and died Bef. 1900. He married MARY C. WALLER 04 Feb 1883 in Carter Co., MO. She was born 14 Mar 1864 in Hamilton Co., TN, and died 01 Mar 1944 in Cape Girardeau Co., MO.*

Notes for MARY C. WALLER:
Source: 1900-1910 Carter County Missouri Federal Census Records
** 1900 - Living in Jackson, Carter Co., MO - Kelly, David - May 1850 IL, Mary M - Mar 1863 TN TN TN, John A Ballard stepson - Dec 1883 MO TN TN, Maud G - Mar 1888 MO TN TN, Nancy S - Oct 1889 MO TN TN, Hester W - Sept 1891 MO TN TN, Manly L - Mar 1893 MO TN TN*
** 1920 - Living in Johnson, Carter Co., MO - Ballard, Mary C 56 divorced TN TN TN, Manly, Leroy 36 MO TN TN*

More About MARY C. WALLER:
Burial: Cape County Memorial Park Cemetery, Cape Girardeau Co., MO

Children of JAMES BALLARD and MARY WALLER are:

14.   i.   JOHN ALLEN[4] BALLARD, b. 06 Dec 1883, Carter Co., MO; d. 15 Dec 1967, Poplar Bluff, Butler Co., MO.
          ii. MAUDE GENEVA BALLARD, b. 22 Mar 1888, Carter Co., MO; d. 25 Jun 1915, Carter Co., MO.
          iii. NANCY S. BALLARD, b. 11 Oct 1889, Carter Co., MO; d. 18 Nov 1972, Cape Girardeau Co., MO; m. JOHN WILLIAM O'HOWELL; b. 28 Aug 1885, Carter Co., MO; d. 03 Mar 1964, St. Francois Co., MO.

               More About JOHN WILLIAM O'HOWELL:
               Burial: Cape County Memorial Park Cemetery, Cape Girardeau Co., MO

          iv. HESTER ANNA BALLARD, b. 19 Sep 1891, Carter Co., MO; d. 09 Feb 1960, Joliet, Will Co., IL; m. JOSEPH W. DUNBAR.

               More About HESTER ANNA BALLARD:
               Burial: Woodlawn Memorial Park II, Joliet, Will Co., IL

15.   v.   MANLY LEROY BALLARD, b. Mar 1893, MO; d. Aft. 1930.

Generation No. 4

9. JAMES ALLEN[4] BALLARD (ALLEN[3], JAMES H.[2], JOHN[1]) was born 23 Jan 1876 in Smith Co., TN, and died 30 Jun 1921 in Pleasant Shade, Smith Co., TN. He married SALLY SLOAN 24 May 1896 in Smith Co., TN. She was born 24 May 1876 in Pleasant Shade, Smith Co., TN, and died 03 Apr 1944 in Pleasant Shade, Smith Co., TN.

Notes for JAMES ALLEN BALLARD:
Source: Find A Grave, 1900-1920 Smith County Tennessee Federal Census Records
* 1900 - Living in Smith Co., TN - Ballard, James - Feb 1876 TN, Sally T - May 1876 TN, Fred - May 1898 TN
* 1910 - Living in Smith Co., TN - Ballard, 35 - 4 children 3 living TN TN TN, Sallie T 34 - 4 children 3 living TN TN TN, Fred A 11 TN, Myrtle A 4 TN, Charlie 2 TN
* 1920 - Living in Smith Co., TN - Ballard, J A 44 TN, Sallie 43 TN, Myrtle 14 TN, Charlie 12 TN, Margie 9 TN, Annie 5 TN

More About JAMES ALLEN BALLARD:
Burial: Pleasant Shade Cemetery, Pleasant Shade, Smith Co., TN

Notes for SALLY SLOAN:
Source: 1930 Smith County Tennessee Federal Census Records
* 1930 - Living in Smith Co., TN - Ballard, Sallie T 52 wd TN TN TN, James H 9 TN TN TN, Annie C. Reagan 15 dau, Jasper M Reagan son in law 21 TN TN TN

More About SALLY SLOAN:
Burial: Pleasant Shade Cemetery, Pleasant Shade, Smith Co., TN

Children of JAMES BALLARD and SALLY SLOAN are:
          i.   ALBERT FRED[5] BALLARD, b. 19 May 1898, Pleasant Shade, Smith Co., TN; d. 24 Sep 1975, Nashville, Davidson Co., TN; m. TENNIE PEARL HACKETT; b. 17 Jan 1902, Pleasant Shade, Smith Co., TN; d. 22 Jun 1973, Nashville, Davidson Co., TN.

               More About ALBERT FRED BALLARD:
               Burial: Pleasant Shade Cemetery, Pleasant Shade, Smith Co., TN

               More About TENNIE PEARL HACKETT:
               Burial: Pleasant Shade Cemetery, Pleasant Shade, Smith Co., TN

          ii. GADYS BALLARD, b. 20 May 1904, Smith Co., TN; d. 30 Aug 1905, Smith Co., TN.

iii.	MYRTLE A. BALLARD, b. 03 Dec 1905, Smith Co., TN; d. 09 Jan 1978, Sumner Co., TN; m. WADE COLEMAN SMITH; b. 08 Dec 1901, Smith Co., TN; d. 26 Oct 1972, Sumner Co., TN.

16.	iv.	CHARLIE BROCKKETT BALLARD, b. 11 Jan 1908, Smith Co., TN; d. 10 Jul 1983, Marion Co., IN.

v.	MARJORIE BALLARD, b. 27 Aug 1910, Smith Co., TN; d. 14 Dec 1938, Smith Co., TN; m. WIRT PIPER, 20 Mar 1927, Smith Co., TN.

vi.	ANNIE BALLARD, b. 27 Oct 1914, Smith Co., TN; d. 25 Jan 2001, Sumner Co., TN; m. JASPER REAGAN; b. 03 May 1908, Smith Co., TN; d. 25 Oct 1995, Sumner Co., TN.

vii.	JAMES. H. BALLARD, b. 11 Oct 1920, Smith Co., TN; d. 09 Mar 1976, Smith Co., TN.

Notes for JAMES. H. BALLARD:
Source: 1930 Smith County Tennessee Federal Census Records
* 1930 - Living in Smith Co., TN - Ballard, Sallie T 52 TN, Annie C. Reagan 15 dau TN, Jasper M Reagan son in law 21 TN

10.	IDA[4] BALLARD (JOHN HENDERSON[3], ALLEN C.[2], JOHN[1]) was born Dec 1882 in Dunklin Co., MO, and died Aft. 1910. She married JOHN BILL TRUSH. He was born 1872, and died Aft. 1910.

Notes for JOHN BILL TRUSH:
Source: 1910 Dunklin County Missouri Federal Census Records
* 1910 - Living in Dunklin Co., MO - Trush, John Bill 38, Ida 28, Barned 3, Herman 10/12, Virgie Ballard 17 sister in law, Ed 32 brother in law, Clay 15 brother in law

Children of IDA BALLARD and JOHN TRUSH are:
i.	BARNED[5] TRUSH, b. 1907, Dunklin Co., MO.
ii.	HERMAN TRUSH, b. 1909, Dunklin Co., MO.

11.	MYRTLE[4] BALLARD (JOHN HENDERSON[3], ALLEN C.[2], JOHN[1]) was born Jun 1887 in Dunklin Co., MO, and died Aft. 1900. She married TOM ALEXANDER KINDER.

Children of MYRTLE BALLARD and TOM KINDER are:
17.	i.	URAL[5] KINDER.
ii.	EARL KINDER.

12.	EDWARD "ED"[4] BALLARD (JOHN HENDERSON[3], ALLEN C.[2], JOHN[1]) was born 11 Apr 1888 in Dunklin Co., MO, and died 28 Mar 1961. He married (1) JESSIE HILDERBRAND, daughter of SAMUEL HILDERBRAND. She was born 03 Apr 1891 in MO, and died 29 Sep 1927 in Dunklin Co., MO. He married (2) MARY. She was born 02 May 1892, and died 07 Apr 1960.

Notes for EDWARD "ED" BALLARD:
Source: 1920-1930 Dunklin County Missouri Federal Census Records

* 1920 - Living in Dunklin Co., MO - Ballard, Edward 31 MO KY KY, Jessee 28 MO KY KY, Ansen 8 MO, Harold 5 MO, June 2 8/12 MO
* 1930 - Living in Dunklin Co., MO - (sister) Ida M Potillo 44 TN MO IL, James C Tausty 22 son MO, Edward C Ballard 42 brother wd MO IL MO, Ansin E 17 MO, Harold E 15 MO, June M 12 MO

More About EDWARD "ED" BALLARD:
Burial: Oak Ridge Cemetery, Kennett, Dunklin Co., MO

Notes for JESSIE HILDERBRAND:
Source: Dunklin County Missouri State Board of Health Certificate of Death # 26889

More About JESSIE HILDERBRAND:

Burial: Henson Hill Top Cemetery, Ellsinore, Carter Co., MO

More About MARY:
Burial: Oak Ridge Cemetery, Kennett, Dunklin Co., MO

Children of EDWARD BALLARD and JESSIE HILDERBRAND are:

  i. EDWARD ANSON[5] BALLARD, b. 13 May 1912, Dunklin Co., MO; d. 13 May 1991; m. JERALDINE D.; b. 24 May 1912; d. 06 Jan 1983.

   More About EDWARD ANSON BALLARD:
   Burial: Riverside National Cemetery, Riverside Co., CA

   More About JERALDINE D.:
   Burial: Riverside National Cemetery, Riverside Co., CA

  ii. HAROLD E. BALLARD, b. 24 Jul 1914, Bunker, Reynolds Co., MO; d. 05 Oct 1952, St. Charles Co., MO; m. ZELMA MEYERS; b. 30 Dec 1917, Carter Co., MO; d. 19 Feb 2010, Teller Co., CO.

   Notes for HAROLD E. BALLARD:
   Source: St. Charles Missouri Death Certificate

   More About ZELMA MEYERS:
   Burial: Memorial Park Cemetery, Jennings, St. Louis Co., MO

  iii. AUGUST BALLARD, b. 07 Feb 1917, Dunklin Co., MO; d. 23 Aug 1961, MO.

   More About AUGUST BALLARD:
   Burial: Memorial Park Cemetery, Jennings, St. Louis Co., MO

  iv. JUNE BALLARD, b. 23 Aug 1917, Dunklin Co., MO; d. Apr 1976, MO.

   More About JUNE BALLARD:
   Burial: Calvary Cemetery and Mausoleum, St. Louis City, MO

13. MASON[4] BALLARD (JOHN HENDERSON[3], ALLEN C.[2], JOHN[1]) *was born 11 Mar 1898 in Dunklin Co., MO, and died Nov 1973. He married ORA LEMONDS. She was born 1902 in MO, and died Aft. 1930.*

Notes for MASON BALLARD:
Source: 1920 Dunklin County Missouri Federal Census Records, 1930 St. Louis County Missouri Federal Census Records
** 1920 - Living in Independence, Dunklin Co., MO - Ballard, Mason 20 MO, Ora 18 MO, Vivian 1 2/12 MO*
** 1930 - Living in St. Louis Co.., MO - Balard, Mason A 32 MO, Cora E 28 MO, Viviania 11 MO, Gelberta 7 MO, Mason A Jr. 5 MO, Emma L 2 4/12 MO*

Children of MASON BALLARD and ORA LEMONDS are:

  i. VIVIAN[5] BALLARD, b. 1918, Dunklin Co., MO; d. Aft. 1930.
  ii. UYMAN SYLVESTER BALLARD, b. 30 Jan 1921, Dunklin Co., MO; d. 30 Jun 1921, Dunklin Co., MO.

   Notes for UYMAN SYLVESTER BALLARD:
   Source: 1921 Dunklin County Missouri State Board of Health Certificate of Death # 14515
   ** Death Certificate has cemetery but hard to read. Parents are listed as Mason Ballard and Ora Lemonds*

   More About UYMAN SYLVESTER BALLARD:

Burial: Susuach Cemetery.

 iii. GELBERTA BALLARD, b. 1923, Dunklin Co., MO; d. Aft. 1930.
 iv. MASON A. BALLARD, b. 1925, Dunklin Co., MO; d. Aft. 1930.
 v. EMMA L. BALLARD, b. 1927, Dunklin Co., MO; d. Aft. 1930.

14. JOHN ALLEN[4] BALLARD (JAMES W.[3], ALLEN C.[2], JOHN[1]) *was born 06 Dec 1883 in Carter Co., MO, and died 15 Dec 1967 in Poplar Bluff, Butler Co., MO. He married* MALINDA JANE ODOM. *She was born 12 Oct 1884 in Ripley Co., MO, and died 07 Jan 1926 in Jordan, Ripley Co., MO.*

Notes for JOHN ALLEN BALLARD:
Source: 1910 Carter County Missouri Federal Census Records, 1920 Ripley County Missouri Federal Census Records
** 1910 - Living in Jackson, Carter Co., MO - Ballard, John A 26 MO, Malinda 24 MO, James E 4 MO, Hazel 2 MO, Thelma 2/12*
** 1920 - Living in Johnson, Ripley Co., MO - Ballard, JA 36 MO MO MO, Malinda 35 MO MO MO, Elmer 13 MO, Hazel 11 MO, Thelma 9 MO, Marie 6 MO, William 4 MO, Kathrine 1 3/12*

More About JOHN ALLEN BALLARD:
Burial: Poplar Bluff City Cemetery, Poplar Bluff, Butler Co., MO

More About MALINDA JANE ODOM:
Burial: Bellview Cemetery, Doniphan, Ripley Co., MO

Children of JOHN BALLARD *and* MALINDA ODOM *are:*
 i. ELMER[5] BALLARD, b. 1907, MO; d. Aft. 1920.
 ii. HAZEL BALLARD, b. 28 Mar 1908, MO; d. 25 Nov 1973; m. HANCOCK.

  More About HAZEL BALLARD:
  Burial: Mt. Washington Cemetery, Independence, Jackson Co., MO

 iii. THELMA BALLARD, b. 1911, MO; d. Aft. 1920.
 iv. MARIE BALLARD, b. 1914, MO; d. Aft. 1920.
 v. WILLIAM LEE BALLARD, b. 09 Nov 1915, MO; d. 31 Aug 1936, Ripley Co., MO.

  Notes for WILLIAM LEE BALLARD:
  Source: Ripley County Missouri Death Certificate

  More About WILLIAM LEE BALLARD:
  Burial: Bellview Cemetery, Doniphan, Ripley Co., MO

 vi. KATHRINE BALLARD, b. 1918, MO; d. Aft. 1920.

15. MANLY LEROY[4] BALLARD (JAMES W.[3], ALLEN C.[2], JOHN[1]) *was born Mar 1893 in MO, and died Aft. 1930. He married* LEAH. *She was born 1898 in MO, and died Aft. 1930.*

Notes for MANLY LEROY BALLARD:
Source: 1920 Carter County Missouri Federal Census Records
** 1920 - Living in Johnson, Carter Co., MO - Ballard, Mary C 56 divorced TN TN TN, Manly, Leroy 36 MO TN TN*
** 1930 - Living in Klamath Falls, Klamath Co., OR - Ballard, Manley L 37 MO MO TN, Leah 32 MO MO MO, Jesse 8 MO*

Child of MANLY BALLARD *and* LEAH *is:*

i.   JESSE[5] BALLARD, b. 1922, Klamath Falls, Klamath Co., OR; d. Aft. 1930.

Generation No. 5

16. CHARLIE BROCKKETT[5] BALLARD (JAMES ALLEN[4], ALLEN[3], JAMES H.[2], JOHN[1]) *was born 11 Jan 1908 in Smith Co., TN, and died 10 Jul 1983 in Marion Co., IN. He married GUSTINE FRANCES HIETT 03 Nov 1928 in Smith Co., TN. She was born 1911 in TN, and died 25 Oct 2001 in Indianapolis, Marion Co., IN.*

Notes for CHARLIE BROCKKETT BALLARD:
Source: WWII Draft Cards, 1930-1940 Smith County Tennessee Federal Census Records, Marion County Indiana Certificate of Death

** 1930 - Living in Smith Co., TN - Ballard, Charlie B 22 TN TN TN, Gustine F 19 TN TN TN*
** 1940 - Living in Pleasant Shade, Smith Co., TN - Ballard, 32 farmer TN, Justine 28 TN, Dimple Dean 7 TN, Jerry Ann 4 TN*

More About CHARLIE BROCKKETT BALLARD:
Burial: Washington Park East Cemetery, Indianapolis, Marion Co., IN

More About GUSTINE FRANCES HIETT:
Burial: Washington Park East Cemetery, Indianapolis, Marion Co., IN

Children of CHARLIE BALLARD and GUSTINE HIETT are:

i.   DIMPLE DEAN[6] BALLARD, b. 18 Oct 1932, Pleasant Shade, Smith Co., TN; d. 22 Mar 2005, Macon Co., TN; m. (1) WILLIAM RUSSELL ANGLEA, 24 Nov 1950, Sumner Co., TN; m. (2) JAMES ANTHONY LEATH, Bef. 1958; b. 14 Oct 1929, Sumner Co., TN; d. 06 Feb 1993, Sumner Co., TN.

Notes for DIMPLE DEAN BALLARD:
Source: Social Security Records, 1958 Nashville Tennessee City Directory

More About DIMPLE DEAN BALLARD:
Burial: Sumner Memorial Gardens, Gallatin, Sumner Co., TN

More About JAMES ANTHONY LEATH:
Burial: Sumner Memorial Gardens, Gallatin, Sumner Co., TN

ii.   JERRY ANN BALLARD, b. Abt. 1936, Smith Co., TN; d. Aft. 1978; m. (1) HARRY SWANEY BARNER, 10 Nov 1950, Sumner Co., TN; m. (2) TOMMIE LEE WRIGHT, 08 Jun 1978, Indianapolis, Marion Co., IN; b. Abt. 1935, TN.
iii.   CHARLES BALLARD.
iv.   DEBRA BALLARD, b. Abt. 1950; m. JONES.

Notes for DEBRA BALLARD:
Source: School annual

v.   JACKIE BALLARD, m. BRAWNER.

17. URAL[5] KINDER (MYRTLE[4] BALLARD, JOHN HENDERSON[3], ALLEN C.[2], JOHN[1])

Child of URAL KINDER is:
i.   ROGER[6] KINDER.

John Ballard

Generation No. 1

1. JOHN[1] BALLARD *was born 1835 in Ireland, and died Bet. 1870 - 1880. He married* MARGARET. *She was born 1840 in Ireland, and died Aft. 1920.*

Notes for JOHN BALLARD:
Source: 1870 Carroll County Missouri Federal Census Records
** 1870 - Living in Sugar Tree, Carroll Co., MO - Ballard, John 35 farmer Ireland, Margaret 30 Ireland, James 3 Willard 2 MO*

Notes for MARGARET:
Source: 1880- 1910, 1930 Ray County Missouri Federal Census Records

** 1880 - Living in Crooked River, Ray Co., MO - Cambell, Margaret 39 Ireland Ire Ire, James Ballard 13 MO Ireland Ireland, John Ballard 11 MO, Charles 8 MO, Lillie Cambell 5 MO, Ross Cambell 3 MO*
** 1900 - Living in Crooked River, Ray Co., MO - Campbell, Margaret 59 7 children 4 living Ireland Ireland Ireland, Chas C 29 MO Ire Ire, Lillie Campbell 24 MO, Ross C Campbell 22 MO*
** 1910 - Living in Crooked River, Ray Co., MO - (sometimes he is listed as the head of household and sometimes his mother is. Living with son Charles Ballard, Campbell, Margret 69 Ireland Ire Ire, Charles C Ballard 39 MO Ire Ire, Ross C Campbell 34 MO*
** 1920 - Living in Crooked River, Ray Co., MO - Campbell, Margaret 79 wd Ireland Ire Ire Immigration year 1853, Charley Ballard 48 MO Ire Ire, Ross Cambell 41 MO OH Ire*

Children of JOHN BALLARD *and* MARGARET *are:*

       i.   JAMES[2] BALLARD, *b. 1867, MO; d. Aft. 1870.*
      ii.   WILLARD BALLARD, *b. 1868, MO; d. Aft. 1870.*
2.   iii. JOHN WILLIAM BALLARD, *b. 13 Dec 1868, Carroll Co., MO; d. 14 Nov 1958, Richmond, Ray Co., MO.*
      iv. CHARLES C. BALLARD, *b. 1872, MO; d. Aft. 1930.*

         Notes for CHARLES C. BALLARD:
         Source: Ray County Missouri Federal Census Records
         ** 1910 - Living in Crooked River, Ray Co., MO - Ballard, Charles 39 MO Ireland Ire, Campbell, Margret 69 mother Ireland Ire Ire, Ross C Campbell 34 brother MO*

Generation No. 2

2. JOHN WILLIAM[2] BALLARD (JOHN[1]) *was born 13 Dec 1868 in Carroll Co., MO, and died 14 Nov 1958 in Richmond, Ray Co., MO. He married* RUBY LEE COLLIER *22 Feb 1899 in Ray Co., MO, daughter of* JAMES COLLIER *and* NANCY MILES. *She was born 22 Nov 1880 in Hardin, Ray Co., MO, and died 13 Jun 1946 in Hardin, Ray Co., MO.*

Notes for JOHN WILLIAM BALLARD:
Source: 1900-1940 Ray County Missouri Federal Census Records, Ray County Missouri Standard Certificate of Death
** 1900 - Living in Crooked River, Ray Co., MO - Ballard, John W - Dec 1868 MO Ireland, Ireland farmer, Ruby - Mar 1879 MO KY MO*
** 1910 - Living in Crooked River, Ray Co., MO - Ballard, John W 41 MO Ireland Ireland general farm, Ruby 28 MO KY MO, Leona 9 MO, Harold 8 MO, Mabel 6 MO, Bernard 4 MO, Forest 3 MO, Margurite 1 2/12 MO*
** 1920 - Living in Ray Co., MO - Ballard, William 51 MO Ireland Ireland, Ruby 39 MO KY MO, Harold 17 MO,*

Mabel 16 MO, Bernard 14 MO, Forrest 12 MO, Margaret 11 MO, Russell 9 MO, Opal 7 MO, Miles 5 MO, Elma 3 MO, J W 1 MO (next door to his mother and siblings)

** 1930 - Living in Crooked River, Ray Co., MO - Ballard, John W 61 MO Ire Ire, Ruby 49 MO KY MO, Harold 27 MO, Russell 18 MO, Opal 16 MO, Niles 14 MO, Elma 12 MO, JW 10*
** 1940 - Living in Crooked River, Ray Co., MO - Ballard, J. W 73 MO farmer, Ruby 59 MO, Harold 37 MO, Bernard 34 MO, Russell 29 MO, Niles 25 MO, Elma 24 MO, J. W Jr. 22 MO*

More About JOHN WILLIAM BALLARD:
Burial: Liberty Cemetery, Hardin, Ray Co., MO

Notes for RUBY LEE COLLIER:
Source: Ray County Missouri Death Certificate

More About RUBY LEE COLLIER:
Burial: Liberty Cemetery, Hardin, Ray Co., MO

Children of JOHN BALLARD and RUBY COLLIER are:

> i.   LEONA[3] *BALLARD, b. Abt. 1901, Ray Co., MO; d. Aft. 1910.*
> ii.   *HAROLD BALLARD, b. 08 May 1902, Ray Co., MO; d. 27 Nov 1981; m. DELLA WANNETTA McCORKENDALE; b. 30 Mar 1921; d. 11 Apr 2004.*
>
>   *Notes for HAROLD BALLARD:*
>   *Source: WWII Draft Cards*
>
>   *More About HAROLD BALLARD:*
>   *Burial: Richmond Memory Gardens, Richmond, Ray Co., MO*
>
>   *More About DELLA WANNETTA McCORKENDALE:*
>   *Burial: Richmond Memory Gardens, Richmond, Ray Co., MO*
>
> iii.   *MABEL BALLARD, b. 1904, Ray Co., MO; d. Aft. 1920.*
> iv.   *BERNARD BALLARD, b. 05 Aug 1905, Ray Co., MO; d. 20 Sep 1979, Ray Co., MO; m. LUELLA FAYE; b. 27 Jun 1916; d. 06 Jan 2000.*
>
>   *More About BERNARD BALLARD:*
>   *Burial: Liberty Cemetery, Hardin, Ray Co., MO*
>
>   *More About LUELLA FAYE:*
>   *Burial: Liberty Cemetery, Hardin, Ray Co., MO*

3.   v.   *FORREST BALLARD, b. 14 Apr 1907, Ray Co., MO; d. 01 Dec 1968, Richmond, Ray Co., MO.*
> vi.   *MARGARET K. BALLARD, b. 03 Jan 1909, Ray Co., MO; d. 21 Oct 1985; m. BLAND.*
>
>   *More About MARGARET K. BALLARD:*
>   *Burial: Liberty Cemetery, Hardin, Ray Co., MO*
>
> vii.   *RUSSELL BALLARD, b. 31 Mar 1911, Ray Co., MO; d. 29 Jan 1988.*
>
>   *More About RUSSELL BALLARD:*
>   *Burial: Liberty Cemetery, Hardin, Ray Co., MO*
>
> viii.   *OPAL BALLARD, b. 1913, Ray Co., MO; d. Aft. 1930.*
> ix.   *NILES BALLARD, b. 27 Sep 1914, Ray Co., MO; d. 22 Jan 1985.*

More About NILES BALLARD:
Burial: Liberty Cemetery, Hardin, Ray Co., MO

    x.   *ELMA L. BALLARD, b. 12 Mar 1916, Hardin, Ray Co., MO; d. 03 Nov 1945, Jackson Co., MO.*

        Notes for ELMA L. BALLARD:
        Source: Jackson County Missouri Death Certificates

    xi.   *JOHN WILLIAM BALLARD, b. 18 Feb 1918, Ray Co., MO; d. 14 May 1984; m. BETTY SUE BANDY, 04 Oct 1947, Norborne, Carroll Co., MO; b. 02 Feb 1928, Hardin, Ray Co., MO; d. 17 Jul 1995, Ray Co., MO.*

        Notes for JOHN WILLIAM BALLARD:
        Source: WWII Draft Cards

        More About JOHN WILLIAM BALLARD:
        Burial: Richmond Memory Gardens, Richmond, Ray Co., MO

Generation No. 3

3. *FORREST³ BALLARD (JOHN WILLIAM², JOHN¹) was born 14 Apr 1907 in Ray Co., MO, and died 01 Dec 1968 in Richmond, Ray Co., MO. He married LORENE DeMINT 21 Apr 1929. She was born 05 Feb 1914 in Hardin, Ray Co., MO, and died 01 Apr 2009 in Richmond, Ray Co., MO.*

More About FORREST BALLARD:
Burial: Liberty Cemetery, Hardin, Ray Co., MO

More About LORENE DeMINT:
Burial: Liberty Cemetery, Hardin, Ray Co., MO

Children of FORREST BALLARD and LORENE DeMINT are:

    i.   *PHYLLIS KATHRYN⁴ BALLARD, b. 03 Jan 1932, Hardin, Ray Co., MO; d. 24 Nov 1954, Lexington, Lafayette Co., MO; m. BOWMAN.*

        More About PHYLLIS KATHRYN BALLARD:
        Burial: Liberty Cemetery, Hardin, Ray Co., MO

    ii.   *ROBERT EUGENE BALLARD, b. 1934, Hardin, Ray Co., MO; d. 1951.*

        More About ROBERT EUGENE BALLARD:
        Burial: Liberty Cemetery, Hardin, Ray Co., MO

    iii.   *JAMES WILLIAM BALLARD, b. 07 Jul 1930, Hardin, Ray Co., MO; d. 10 Aug 1975.*

        Notes for JAMES WILLIAM BALLARD:
        Source: Social Security Records

        More About JAMES WILLIAM BALLARD:
        Burial: Liberty Cemetery, Hardin, Ray Co., MO

John B. Ballard, Dr.

Generation No. 1

1. JOHN B.[1] BALLARD, DR. *was born 31 Dec 1812 in VA, and died 19 Nov 1884 in Marshall, Saline Co., MO. He married* ANN N. JOHNSON *08 May 1834 in Albemarle Co., VA. She was born 1814 in VA, and died Bet. 1860 - 1870 in MO.*

Notes for JOHN B. BALLARD, DR.*:*
Source: Buckland (bbuckland@customcpu.com), 1850 Ray County Missouri Federal Census Records, 1860 Carroll County Missouri Federal Census, 1870 Clay County Missouri Federal Census Records

** According to Census Records, he was a physician*
** 1850 - Living in Ray Co., MO - Ballard, John B 36 VA, N N 35 VA, Mary C 15 VA, Ellen E 11 VA, Mildred 10 VA, William L 8 MO, Lucy 6 MO, Thomas R 2 MO*
** 1860 - Living in Carroll Co., MO - Ballard, John B 47 VA, Ann M 47 VA, Wm S 18 MO, Lucinda D 15 MO, Thomas D 13 MO, James W 9 MO, George 5 MO*
** 1870 - Living in Clay Co., MO - Ballard, J. B. 57 physician VA, Mary C 25 MO, Thos. R. 23 medical student, George Ann 16 MO, Sarah A. Walker 8 MO*
** 1880 - Living in Arrow Rock, Saline Co., MO - Ballard, J. B 67 Physician VA VA VA, Sarah Walker 16 grand dau MO KY VA*

More About JOHN B. BALLARD, DR.*:*
Burial: Ridge Park Cemetery, Marshall, Saline Co., MO

Children of JOHN BALLARD *and* ANN JOHNSON *are:*

	i.	MARY C.[2] BALLARD, b. 1835, VA or MO; d. Aft. 1870.
	ii.	ELLEN E. BALLARD, b. 1839, VA; d. Aft. 1850.
	iii.	MILDRED BALLARD, b. 1840, VA; d. Aft. 1850.
2.	iv.	WILLIAM L. BALLARD, b. 1842, MO; d. Aft. 1880.
	v.	LUCY "LUCINDA" BALLARD, b. 1844, MO; d. Aft. 1870.
3.	vi.	THOMAS R. BALLARD, b. 17 Dec 1847, MO; d. 12 Oct 1924, Kansas City, Jackson Co., MO.
	vii.	JAMES W. BALLARD, b. 1851, MO; d. Aft. 1860.
4.	viii.	GEORGE ANNAH BALLARD, b. 31 Mar 1855, Liberty, Clay Co., MO; d. 20 Sep 1885, Cloverland, Asotin Co., WA.

Generation No. 2

2. WILLIAM L.[2] BALLARD (JOHN B.[1]) *was born 1842 in MO, and died Aft. 1880. He married* ZERILDA*. She was born 1848 in MO, and died Aft. 1880.*

Notes for WILLIAM L. BALLARD*:*
Source: 1870-1880 Clay County Missouri Federal Census Records

** 1870 - Living in Clay Co., MO - Ballard, William 28 farmer MO, Zarilda 22 MO, James W 3 MO*
** 1880 - Living in Clay Co., MO - Ballard, William 39 MO KY KY, Zerilda 32 MO Ct VA, James 13 MO, Lucy 7 MO, Arthur 4 MO*

Children of WILLIAM BALLARD *and* ZERILDA *are:*

	i.	JAMES[3] BALLARD, b. 1867, MO; d. Aft. 1880.
	ii.	LUCY BALLARD, b. 1873, MO; d. Aft. 1880.
	iii.	AURTHUR BALLARD, b. 1876, MO; d. Aft. 1880.

3. THOMAS R.² BALLARD (JOHN B.¹) *was born 17 Dec 1847 in MO, and died 12 Oct 1924 in Kansas City, Jackson Co., MO. He married* ALWILDA GEORGE, *daughter of* WILLIAM GEORGE. *She was born 1854 in MO, and died 09 Oct 1936 in Kansas City, Jackson Co., MO.*

Notes for THOMAS R. BALLARD:

Source: Jackson County Missouri Death Certificate, 1880 Clay County Missouri Federal Census Records, 1900-1920 Jackson County Missouri Federal Census Records

** 1880 - Living in Missouri City, Clay Co., MO - Sarens, George 56 (father in law), Ballard, Thos R 32 son in law VA VA VA family grocer, Alwilda 26 MO KY KY, Millie 1*
** 1900 - Living in Kansas City, Jackson Co., MO - Ballard, Thomas R - Dec 1846 VA, Alwilda V - Feb 1859*
** 1910 - Living in Kansas City, Jackson Co., MO - Ballard, Thos R 60 VA, Alwilda V 58*
** 1920 - Living in Kansas City, Jackson Co., MO - Ballard, Thomas R 72 MO, Alwilda V 63, Mattie A 40 MO*

More About THOMAS R. BALLARD:
Burial: Forest Hill Cemetery, Kansas City, Jackson Co., MO

Notes for ALWILDA GEORGE:
Source: Jackson County Missouri Certificate of Death

More About ALWILDA GEORGE:
Burial: Elmwood, Cemetery, Kansas City, Jackson Co., MO

Children of THOMAS BALLARD *and* ALWILDA GEORGE *are:*

> i. MILLIE³ BALLARD, *b. 1879, MO; d. Aft. 1880.*
> ii. MATTIE A. BALLARD, *b. 1880, MO; d. Aft. 1920.*

4. GEORGE ANNAH² BALLARD (JOHN B.¹) *was born 31 Mar 1855 in Liberty, Clay Co., MO, and died 20 Sep 1885 in Cloverland, Asotin Co., WA. She married* LAYTEN YANCY ALDER. *He was born 10 Feb 1828 in Logan Co., OH, and died 16 Mar 1895 in Cloverland, Asotin Co., WA.*

More About GEORGE ANNAH BALLARD:
Burial: Lake Cemetery, Asotin Co., WA

More About LAYTEN YANCY ALDER:
Burial: Lake Cemetery, Asotin Co., WA

Child of GEORGE BALLARD *and* LAYTEN ALDER *is:*

> i. ANN FRANCES³ ALDER, *b. 02 Jul 1876, Idaho Co., ID; d. 15 May 1945, Benton Co., WA; m.* GEORGE FRANK ABEL; *b. 16 Oct 1867, Columbia Co., WA; d. 13 Nov 1950, Benton Co., WA.*
>
> *More About* ANN FRANCES ALDER:
> *Burial: Grandview Cemetery, Yakima Co., WA*
>
> *More About* GEORGE FRANK ABEL:
> *Burial: Grandview Cemetery, Yakima Co., WA*

John Francis Ballard

Generation No. 1

1. JOHN FRANCIS[2] BALLARD (JEFFERSON[1]) *was born Feb 1840 in Bradley Co., TN, and died 19 Apr 1914 in Oxford, Izard Co., AR. He married BARBARA A.. She was born Mar 1842 in TN, and died Aft. 1900 in Oxford, Izard Co., AR.*

Notes for JOHN FRANCIS BALLARD:
Source: 1870 Montgomery County Missouri Federal Census Records, 1880 Fulton County Arkansas Federal Census Records, 1900-1910 Izard County Arkansas Federal Census Records

** 1870 - Living in Montgomery Co., MO - John 30 TN, Barbara 27 TN, James 10 TN, Rebecca 7 GA, George 5 TN, Barnett 2 IL, Sanford 3/12 MO*
** 1880 - Living in Fulton Co., AR - Ballard, J F 40 TN SC MS, Barbara 38 TN TN TN, Rebecca 17 GA, Barnett 12 IL, Sanford 10 MO, Lawrence 8 MO, Jeanette 6 AR, Luther 4 AR*
** 1900 - Living in Izard Co., AR - Ballard, Jno F Feb 1840 TN TN TN, Barbara A Mar 1842 TN TN TN, Rebeca J Nov 1860 GA TN TN, Jenetta Dec 1873 AR, William L. 1882 AR*
** 1910 - Living in Izard Co., AR - Ballard, John 70 TN TN TN married 50 years, Barbara 68 6 children, Rebecka 48 GA*

Children of JOHN BALLARD and BARBARA A. are:

	i.	JAMES[3] BALLARD, b. 1860, TN; d. Aft. 1870.
	ii.	REBECCA J. BALLARD, b. Nov 1860, GA; d. Aft. 1900.
	iii.	GEORGE BALLARD, b. 1865, TN; d. Aft. 1870.
2.	iv.	BARNETT T. "BARNEY" BALLARD, b. 26 Mar 1868, IL; d. 04 Apr 1943, Oxford, Izard Co., AR.
	v.	SANFORD BALLARD, b. 1870, MO; d. Aft. 1870.
3.	vi.	LAWRENCE BALLARD, b. Mar 1871, MO; d. Aft. 1920.
	vii.	JEANETTE BALLARD, b. Dec 1873; d. Aft. 1900.
	viii.	LUTHER BALLARD, b. 1876.
	ix.	WILLIAM L. BALLARD, b. 1882.

Generation No. 2

2. BARNETT T. "BARNEY"[3] BALLARD (JOHN FRANCIS[2], JEFFERSON[1]) *was born 26 Mar 1868 in IL, and died 04 Apr 1943 in Oxford, Izard Co., AR. He married (1) ESTA LOUISA MCBRIDE Bef. 1888, daughter of WILLIAM MCBRIDE and SARAH KIMMER. She was born 29 Jan 1869 in NC, and died 25 Mar 1927. He married (2) BELLE CROUGH 18 Jan 1928 in White Co., AR.*

Notes for BARNETT T. "BARNEY" BALLARD:
Source: 1900 Independence County Arkansas Federal Census Records, 1910-1940 Izard County Arkansas Federal Census Records

** 1900 - Living in Independence Co., AR - Ballard, Barney Mar 1869 IL TN TN, Louisa Jan 1869 NC NC NC, John May 1888 AR, Harrison Dec 1889 AR, Lawrence Jan 1892 AR, George Feb 1894 AR, Emma 1895 AR, Ella 1899 AR*
** 1910 - Living in Izard Co., AR - Ballard, Barney T 42 IL TN TN, Louisa 41 NC NC NC, Harrison R 20 AR, Lawrence 18 AR, George 16 AR, Emma 13 AR, Ella 11 AR, Virgie 9 AR, Thomas R 7 AR, Jefferson 5 AR, Ruby 3 AR*
** 1920 - Living in Izard Co., AR- Ballard, Barney F 51, Louisa 50, Thomas 16, Jefferson 14, Ruby 12, Buck 10*
** 1930 - Living in Izard Co., AR - Ballard, Barney 62 IL TN TN, Laura 56 IL IL IL, Clide Stuart boarder*
** 1940 - Living in New Hope, Izard Co., AR - Ballard, Burney F 72 divorced IL*

More About BARNETT T. "BARNEY" BALLARD:
Burial: Oxford Cemetery, Oxford, Izard Co., AR

More About ESTA LOUISA MCBRIDE:
Burial: Oxford Cemetery., Oxford, Izard Co., AR

Children of BARNETT BALLARD and ESTA MCBRIDE are:

    i.   JOHN BARTON[4] BALLARD, b. 26 May 1888, AR; d. 25 Jul 1969, AR; m. VIRGIE LEE CALDWELL; b. 04 Nov 1892, Izard Co., AR; d. 1979.

Notes for JOHN BARTON BALLARD:
Source: 1910 Izard County Arkansas Federal Census Records

** 1910 - Living in New Hope, Izard Co., AR - Ballard, John 21 AR GA SC farmer, Vergie 17 AR IL AR*
** 1920 - Living in New Hope, Izard Co., AR - Ballard, 31 AR IL NC farming Virgie 27 AR IL AR, Connor 4 9/12 AR, Arlie 1 AR*
** 1930 - Living in New Hope, Izard Co., AR - Ballard, John 42 AR GA AR retail merchant general store, Virgie 37 AR IL AR sales lady general store, Conner 15 AR farmer, Arlin 11 AR farm laborer*
** 1940 - Living in Newburg, Izard Co., AR - Ballard, John B 51 AR farm laborer, Virgie 47 AR*

More About JOHN BARTON BALLARD:
Burial: Oxford Cemetery., Oxford, Izard Co., AR

    ii.   BENJAMIN HARRISON BALLARD, b. 14 Dec 1889, AR; d. 09 Mar 1973, AR; m. MYRTIE; b. 27 Oct 1898, AR; d. 31 Aug 1925.

Notes for BENJAMIN HARRISON BALLARD:
Source: 1920 Izard County Arkansas Federal Census Records, 1930 Fulton County Arkansas Federal Census Records
** 1920 - Living in Izard Co., AR - Ballard, Harrison 30 AR GA US, Myrtie 26 AR IL AR, Marie 8 AR, Cecil 5 2/12 AR, Remmel 3 10/12*
** 1930 - Living in Fulton Co., AR - Ballard, Harrison 40, Marie 18, Cecil 15, Rummel 14, Caroline 8, Pauline 4*

More About BENJAMIN HARRISON BALLARD:
Burial: Union Cemetery., Union, Fulton Co., AR

More About MYRTIE:
Burial: Union Cemetery., Union, Fulton Co., AR

    iii.   WILLIAM LAWRENCE BALLARD, b. Jan 1892, AR; d. 12 Apr 1945, AR; m. TONI; b. 1888; d. 1963, AR.

More About WILLIAM LAWRENCE BALLARD:
Burial: Highland Cemetery., Ozark, Franklin Co., AR

More About TONI:
Burial: Highland Cemetery., Ozark, Franklin Co., AR

    iv.   GEORGE BALLARD, b. Feb 1894, AR; d. Aft. 1920; m. DELILIA; b. 1901, AR; d. Aft. 1920.

Notes for GEORGE BALLARD:
Source: 1920 Izard County Arkansas Federal Census Records, 1930 McClain County Oklahoma Federal Census Records

** 1920 - Living in Newburg, Izard Co., AR - Ballard, George 24, Delilia 19, Jenie, Opal M*
** 1930 - Living in McClain Co., OK - Ballard, George R 33 AR MO AR, Delma C 30 AR AR AR, Joyce T 14 AR, Opal M 13 AR, Boyce R 6 AR*

    v.   EMMA BALLARD, b. 01 Aug 1896, Batesville, Independence Co. AR; d. 17 Nov 1988, Batesville, Independence Co. AR; m. ROBERT B. MARTIN.

    vi.   ELLA BALLARD, b. 09 Jan 1899, AR; d. 21 Feb 1985, Independence Co., AR; m. ALVA JEFF RUPE; b. 1895; d. 1968.

Notes for ALVA JEFF RUPE:

Source: 1930 Jackson County Arkansas Federal Census Records

** 1930 - Living in Grubbs, Jackson Co., AR - Rupe, A J 34, Ella 31, Alice M 8, Harry J 3, Kinchenlin 1*

    vii.   VIRGIE PEARL BALLARD, b. 30 Mar 1901, Oxford, Izard Co., AR; d. 24 Apr 1980, Wenatchee, Chelan Co., WA; m. GEORGE RAY CAMPBELL; b. 09 Oct 1893, Izard Co., AR; d. 15 Jun 1973, Douglas Co., WA.

More About VIRGIE PEARL BALLARD:
Burial: Evergreen Memorial Park, East Wenatchee, Douglas Co., WA

More About GEORGE RAY CAMPBELL:
Burial: Evergreen Memorial. Park, East Wenatchee, Douglas Co., WA

    viii.   THOMAS R. BALLARD, b. 1903, AR; d. Aft. 1920.
    ix.   JEFFERSON BALLARD, b. 1905, AR; d. Aft. 1920.
    x.   RUBY BALLARD, b. 1907, AR; d. Aft. 1920.
    xi.   BUCK BALLARD, b. 1910, AR; d. Aft. 1920.

3. LAWRENCE[3] BALLARD (JOHN FRANCIS[2], JEFFERSON[1]) was born Mar 1871 in MO, and died Aft. 1920. He married AMANDA HARRIIOTT. She was born Sep 1873 in AR, and died Aft. 1920.

Notes for LAWRENCE BALLARD:

Source: 1900-1920 Izard County Arkansas Federal Census Records

** 1900 - Living in Izard Co., AR - Ballard, Lawrence Dec 1871 MO MO MO, Amandy Sep 1873 AR AR AR, George R. June 1896 AR MO AR*
** 1910 - Living in Izard Co., AR - Ballard, Laurence 37 AR, Amanda 35 3 children 2 living, George 15 AR, Barnett 5 AR*
** 1920 - Living in Izard Co., AR - Ballard, Lawrence L 49 MO MO KY, Amanda 46 AR, Teddy R 14 (male) AR*

Children of LAWRENCE BALLARD and AMANDA HARRIIOTT are:

    i.   GEORGE R.[4] BALLARD, b. Jun 1896, AR; d. Aft. 1920.
    ii.   BARNETT BALLARD, b. 1905, AR; d. Aft. 1920.
    iii.   THEADORE ROOSEVELT BALLARD, b. 1905; d. 1968.

Generation No. 1

1.   JOHN P.[1] BALLARD *was born 06 Jul 1836 in KY, and died 20 Sep 1924 in Richmond, Ray Co., MO. He married* WINNIE BALES *Abt. 1860, daughter of* JOHN BALES *and* POLLIE CATES. *She was born 01 Aug 1836 in MO, and died 10 Feb 1919 in Richmond, Ray Co., MO.*

Notes for JOHN P. BALLARD:
Source: 1870 Carroll County Missouri Federal Census Records, 1880 Jasper County Missouri Federal Census Records, 1900-1920 Ray County Missouri Federal Census Records, Ray County Missouri Death Certificate

** 1870 - Living in Wakenda, Carroll Co., MO - Ballard, J P 34 KY, Winney 32 MO, Vina 8 MO, William 6 MO, Andrew 3 MO, Elizabeth 1 MO*
** 1880 - Living in Twin Groves, Jasper Co., MO - Ballard, John P 44 KY KY KY, Winnie 42 MO TN TN, James W 17 MO, Andrew 14 MO, Lizzie 11 MO, John B 8 MO, Carrie 4 MO*
** 1900 - Living in Richmond, Ray Co., MO - Ballard, John - July 1835 KY KY TN, Winnie - Aug 1836 MO TN TN, John Bales father in law - Jan 1817 TN*
** 1910 - Living in Richmond, Ray Co., MO - Ballard, John 74 KY KY KY, Winnie 73 MO TN TN 8 children 6 living*
** 1920 - Living in Richmond, Ray Co., MO - Ballard, John 83 KY MO MO wd - living with son John*

More About JOHN P. BALLARD:

Burial: Dockery Cemetery, Ray Co., MO

More About WINNIE BALES:

Burial: Dockery Cemetery, Ray Co., MO

Children of JOHN BALLARD *and* WINNIE BALES *are:*

> i.   VINA[2] BALLARD, *b. 22 Jul 1861, Ray Co., MO; d. 14 Jul 1948, Clay Co., MO; m.* DAVID C. CATES; *b. 06 Mar 1858; d. 13 Jun 1935.*
>
> More About VINA BALLARD:
> Burial: Richmond Cemetery, Ray Co., MO
>
> More About DAVID C. CATES:
> Burial: Richmond Cemetery, Richmond, Ray Co., MO

2.   ii.   JAMES WILLIAM BALLARD, *b. 22 Mar 1864, Richmond, Ray Co., MO; d. 29 Mar 1937, Cedar Co., MO.*

3.   iii.   ANDREW WALLACE "ANDY" BALLARD, *b. 05 Dec 1867, Ray Co., MO; d. 29 Nov 1953, Richmond, Ray Co., MO.*

> iv.   POLLY ELIZABETH "LIZZIE" BALLARD, *b. 01 Jul 1869, Ray Co., MO; d. 02 Oct 1962, Ray Co., MO; m.* WILLIAM DAVIS, *10 Apr 1889, Ray Co., MO.*
>
> Notes for POLLY ELIZABETH "LIZZIE" BALLARD:
>
> Source: Ray County Missouri Standard Certificate of Death

4.   v.   JOHN BARNEY BALLARD, *b. 27 Sep 1872, Ray Co., MO; d. 19 Aug 1935, Richmond, Ray Co., MO.*
> vi.   CARRIE BALLARD, *b. 1876, Ray Co., MO; d. Aft. 1880.*

Generation No. 2

2. JAMES WILLIAM[2] BALLARD (JOHN P.[1]) *was born 22 Mar 1864 in Richmond, Ray Co., MO, and died 29 Mar 1937 in Cedar Co., MO. He married* EMMA JOHNSON. *She was born 01 May 1873 in Coshocton, OH, and died 15 Aug 1952 in Cedar Co., MO.*

Notes for JAMES WILLIAM BALLARD:
Source: Cedar County Missouri State Board of Health Bureau of Vital Statistics Certificate of Death # 11553, 1900 Woods County Oklahoma Federal Census Records, 1910-1930 Cedar County Missouri Federal Census Records

* 1900 - Living in Deep Creek, Woods Co., OK - Ballard, James - Mar 1864 MO, Emma 1873 5 children 4 living OH, Charles - Jan 1889 MO, John - Dec 1891 MO, Winnie - Oct 1894 MO, Olie - May 1898 OK
* 1910 - Living in Benton, Cedar Co., MO - Ballard, James W 46 MO, Emma J 38, Charley O 21 MO, John B 19 MO, Winnie B 17 MO, Lette A 11, William T 8, Mary O 5
* 1920 - Living in Benton, Cedar Co., MO - Ballard, James W 55 MO KY MO, Emma J 45 MO OH OH, Charles O 28 MO, John B 27 MO, Winnie B 25 MO, Lettie O 21 OK, William T 18 OK, Mary O 16 MO
* 1930 - Living in Benton, Cedar Co., MO - Ballard, James W 66 MO KY TN, Emma J 56 OH OH OH, John B 37 MO, Thomas W 28 OH, Mary O 24 MO

More About JAMES WILLIAM BALLARD:
Burial: Anna-Edna Cemetery, Jerico Springs, Cedar Co., MO

Notes for EMMA JOHNSON:
Source: Cedar County Missouri Standard Certificate of Death

More About EMMA JOHNSON:
Burial: Anna-Edna Cemetery, Jerico Springs, Cedar Co., MO

Children of JAMES BALLARD *and* EMMA JOHNSON *are:*

  5.   i.   CHARLES "CHARLEY" O.[3] BALLARD, b. 25 Jan 1889, MO; d. 17 Nov 1984, Bates Co., MO.
            ii.   JOHN BARNEY BALLARD, b. Dec 1891, MO; d. Aft. 1930.
  6.   iii.   WINNIE B. BALLARD, b. 14 Oct 1893, Cedar Co., MO; d. 1983, Jasper Co., MO.
            iv.   LETTIE OLIE BALLARD, b. May 1898, OK; d. Aft. 1920.
            v.   WILLIAM THOMAS BALLARD, b. 1902, OK; d. Aft. 1930.
            vi.   MARY BALLARD, b. 1905, Benton, Cedar Co., MO; d. Aft. 1930.

3. ANDREW WALLACE "ANDY"[2] BALLARD (JOHN P.[1]) *was born 05 Dec 1867 in Ray Co., MO, and died 29 Nov 1953 in Richmond, Ray Co., MO. He married* ETTA MAY JOINER *23 May 1897 in Ray Co., MO. She was born 1876 in MO, and died Bet. 1920 - 1930.*

Notes for ANDREW WALLACE "ANDY" BALLARD:
Source: Ray County Missouri Standard Certificate of Death, 1910-1930 Ray County Missouri Federal Census Records, Ray County Missouri Death Certificate

* 1910 - Living in Richmond, Ray Co., MO - Ballard, A W 42 MO MO MO, Eddie 34 Virgil 9 MO
* 1920 - Living in Richmond, Ray Co., MO - Ballard, Andy W 54 MO KY MO, Etta 44 MO MO MO
* 1930 - Living in Richmond, Ray Co., MO - Ballard, Andy W 63 MO KY MO Superintendant of County House, Ada M 54 MO MO MO, Virgle D 29 wd MO

More About ANDREW WALLACE "ANDY" BALLARD:
Burial: Dockery Cemetery, Dockery Co., MO

Child of ANDREW BALLARD *and* ETTA JOINER *is:*
            i.   VIRGIL[3] BALLARD, b. 1901, Ray Co., MO; d. Aft. 1930; m. EUNICE; b. 1902, MO; d. Bet. 1920 - 1930.

Notes for VIRGIL BALLARD:
Source: 1920 Ray County Missouri Federal Census Records

** 1920 - Living in Richmond, Ray Co., MO - Ballard, Virgel 9 MO MO MO, Eunice 18 MO MO MO*

4. JOHN BARNEY[2] BALLARD (JOHN P.[1]) was born 27 Sep 1872 in Ray Co., MO, and died 19 Aug 1935 in Richmond, Ray Co., MO. He married DAISY MAUDE NADING. She was born 25 Jul 1881 in Ray Co., MO, and died 15 Feb 1941 in Ray Co., MO.

Notes for JOHN BARNEY BALLARD:
Source: Ray County Missouri Standard Certificate of Death, 1900-1930 Ray County Missouri Federal Census Records, Ray County Missouri Death Certificate

** 1900 - Living in Richmond, Ray Co., MO - Ballard, John - Sept 1872 MO OH MO, Daisy M - July 1881 MO NC MO, Bertha M - Dec 1897 MO*
** 1910 - Living in Richmond, Ray Co., MO - Ballard, J Barney 37 MO MO MO, Daisy 28 3 children 3 living MO AR MO, Bertha M 12 MO, Mildred M 9 MO, Theodore H 5 MO*
** 1920 - Living in Richmond, Ray Co., MO - Ballard, John 46 MO KY MO, Daisy 38 MO NC MO, Harold 15 MO, John 83 father KY MO MO wd*
** 1930 - Living in Richmond, Ray Co., MO - Ballard, John B 57 MO KY MO, Daisy M 48 MO NC MO, John B 7 MO*

Notes for DAISY MAUDE NADING:
Source: Ray County Missouri Standard Certificate of Death

Children of JOHN BALLARD and DAISY NADING are:

    i.   BERTHA M.[3] BALLARD, b. Dec 1897, MO.
    ii.   MILDRED M. BALLARD, b. 1901, MO.
    iii.   THEODORE HAROLD BALLARD, b. 1905, Richmond, Ray Co., MO; d. Aft. 1920.
    iv.   JOHN B. BALLARD, b. 1923, Richmond, Ray Co., MO; d. Aft. 1930.

Generation No. 3

5. CHARLES "CHARLEY" O.[3] BALLARD (JAMES WILLIAM[2], JOHN P.[1]) was born 25 Jan 1889 in MO, and died 17 Nov 1984 in Bates Co., MO. He married MARY SUSAN LILES. She was born 18 Oct 1900 in Richmond, Ray Co., MO, and died 20 Mar 1940 in Cedar Co., MO.

Notes for MARY SUSAN LILES:
Source: Cedar County Missouri Standard Certificate of Death

Children of CHARLES BALLARD and MARY LILES are:

    i.   HELLEN L.[4] BALLARD, b. 1924, Benton, Cedar Co., MO; d. Aft. 1930.
    ii.   MEREDITH E. BALLARD, b. 15 Nov 1926, Benton, Cedar Co., MO; d. 06 Oct 1939, Cedar Co., MO.

        Notes for MEREDITH E. BALLARD:
        Source: Cedar County Missouri Standard Certificate of Death

6. WINNIE B.[3] BALLARD (JAMES WILLIAM[2], JOHN P.[1]) was born 14 Oct 1893 in Cedar Co., MO, and died 1983 in Jasper Co., MO. She married IRA H. POLLEY 24 Sep 1911 in Jerico Springs, Cedar Co., MO. He was born Nov 1892 in MO, and died 28 Apr 1958 in Jasper Co., MO.

More About WINNIE B. BALLARD:

Burial: Park Cemetery, Carthage, Jasper Co., MO

Children of WINNIE BALLARD and IRA POLLEY are:

- i. CHARLES[4] POLLEY.
- ii. JOHN POLLEY.
- iii. WINNIE POLLEY.
- iv. ALICE POLLEY.
- v. ETHEL LETA POLLEY.
- vi. WILLIAM T. POLLEY.
- vii. MARY O. POLLEY.
- viii. WANDA MAXINE POLLEY, b. 20 Feb 1919, Barton Co., MO; d. 26 Aug 2011, Carthage, Jasper Co., MO; m. ROSCOE L. WATTS; b. 03 Jul 1919, Crawford Co., IL; d. 14 Jul 2001, Carthage, Jasper Co., MO.

   More About WANDA MAXINE POLLEY:

   Burial: Park Cemetery, Carthage, Jasper Co., MO

   More About ROSCOE L. WATTS:

   Burial: Park Cemetery, Carthage, Jasper Co., MO

John T. Ballard

Generation No. 1

1. JOHN T.[1] BALLARD *was born 22 Dec 1860 in Waverly, Humphreys Co., TN, and died 06 Jan 1929 in Pemiscot Co., MO. He married* MARY JANE TOTTY. *She was born 12 Feb 1866 in Hickman Co., TN, and died 20 Feb 1916 in Pascola, Pemiscot Co., MO.*

Notes for JOHN T. BALLARD:
Source: Pemiscot County Missouri Death Certificate, 1900 Humphreys County Tennessee Federal Census Records, 1910-1920 Pemiscot County Missouri Federal Census Records

** 1900 - Living in Humphreys Co., TN - Ballard, John - Dec 1859 TN, Mary J - Sept 1868 TN, George W - Aug 1882 TN, Lillie - Aug 1889 MO, Thomas F - Nov 1886 TN, Maude E - Dec 1891 TN, Clara - June 1894 TN*
** 1910 - Living in Hayti, Pemiscot Co., MO - Ballard, John T 52 md 2x TN TN TN, Mary 46 1 child 1 living TN TN TN, William A 9 TN TN TN*
** 1920 - Living in Hayti, Pemiscot Co., MO - Ballard, John T living with daughter Clara and husband Wm. Watts.*

More About JOHN T. BALLARD:
Burial: Ingram Rige Cemetery.

Notes for MARY JANE TOTTY:
Source: Pemiscot County Missouri Death Certificate

More About MARY JANE TOTTY:
Burial: Engram Cemetery.

Children of JOHN BALLARD *and* MARY TOTTY *are:*

2.   i.   GEORGE WASHINGTON[2] BALLARD, *b. 07 Aug 1882, Waverly, Humphreys Co., TN; d. 09 Jan 1947, Hayti, Pemiscot Co., MO.*
        ii.   LILLIE BALLARD, *b. Aug 1889, TN; d. Aft. 1900.*
       iii.   THOMAS F. BALLARD, *b. Nov 1886, TN; d. Aft. 1900.*
       iv.   MAUDE E. BALLARD, *b. Dec 1891, TN; d. Aft. 1900.*
3.   v.   CLARA BALLARD, *b. Jun 1894, TN; d. Aft. 1920.*

Generation No. 2

2. GEORGE WASHINGTON[2] BALLARD (JOHN T.[1]) *was born 07 Aug 1882 in Waverly, TN, and died 09 Jan 1947 in Hayti, Pemiscot Co., MO. He married* EMMA BLACKWELL. *She was born 1888 in Humphries Co., TN, and died Aft. 1930.*

Notes for GEORGE WASHINGTON BALLARD:
Source: 1910-1930 Pemiscot County Missouri Federal Census Records

** 1910 - Living in Pascola, Pemiscot Co., MO - Ballard, George 26 TN TN TN, Emma 22 TN TN TN, Alfred 6 TN, Johnny 4 TN, Ethel M 2 TN*
** 1920 - Living in Pascola, Pemiscot Co., MO - Ballard, Geo 37 TN TN TN, Emma 32 TN TN TN, John 14 MO, Ethel 12 MO, Welborn 9 MO, Clarence 6 MO, Norman 2 MO*
** 1930 - Living in Hayti, Pemiscot Co., MO - Ballard, George W 45 TN, Emma A 42 TN, Norma 13 MO, Murel 10 MO, Woodrow W 3 4/12 MO*

More About GEORGE WASHINGTON BALLARD:

Burial: Woodlawn Cemetery.

Children of GEORGE BALLARD and EMMA BLACKWELL are:

      i.   *ALFRED[3] BALLARD, b. 10 May 1903, Bakersville, Mitchell Co., TN; d. 27 Aug 1910, Pemiscot Co., MO.*

          Notes for ALFRED BALLARD:
          Source: Pemiscot County Missouri Death Certificate

          More About ALFRED BALLARD:
          Burial: Ingram Grave Yard

      ii. *JOHN BALLARD, b. 1906, TN; d. Aft. 1930; m. MARY L. JENNINGS; b. 1906, MO; d. Aft. 1930.*

          Notes for JOHN BALLARD:
          Source: 1930 Pemiscot County Missouri Federal Census Records

          ** 1930 - Living in Little Prairie, Pemiscot Co., MO - Ballard, John W 25 TN TN TN, Mary L 24 MO TN TN, Harris Jennings 50 father in law TN US TN*

     iii. *ETHEL M. BALLARD, b. 1908, TN; d. Aft. 1920.*
     iv. *WELBORN BALLARD, b. 1911, Pascola, Pemiscot Co., MO; d. Aft. 1920.*
      v. *CLARENCE BALLARD, b. 1914, Pascola, Pemiscot Co., MO; d. Aft. 1920.*
     vi. *VURGLE BALLARD FREEMAN, b. 26 Mar 1916, Pascola, Pemiscot Co., MO; d. 15 Apr 1916, Pascola, Pemiscot Co., MO.*

          Notes for VURGLE BALLARD FREEMAN:
          Source: Pemiscot County Missouri Death Certificate

          More About VURGLE BALLARD FREEMAN:
          Burial: Ingram Cemetery.

     vii. *NORMAN BALLARD, b. 1918, Pascola, Pemiscot Co., MO; d. Aft. 1930.*
    viii. *MUREL BALLARD, b. 1920, Pascola, Pemiscot Co., MO; d. Aft. 1930.*
     ix. *WOODROW W. BALLARD, b. 1926, Pemiscot Co., MO; d. Aft. 1930.*

3. *CLARA[2] BALLARD (JOHN T.[1]) was born Jun 1894 in TN, and died Aft. 1920. She married WILLIAM WATTS. He was born 1891 in TN, and died Aft. 1920.*

Notes for WILLIAM WATTS:
Source: 1920 Pemiscot County Missouri Federal Census Records

** 1920 - Living in Hayti, Pemiscot Co., MO - Watts, Wm 29 TN, Clara 24 TN, Virgil 7 MO, Cecil 7 MO, John Ballard 60 wd father in law TN TN TN*

Children of CLARA BALLARD and WILLIAM WATTS are:

      i. *VIRGIL[3] WATTS, b. 1913, Hayti, Pemiscot Co., MO; d. Aft. 1920.*
      ii. *CECIL WATTS, b. 1916, Hayti, Pemiscot Co., MO; d. Aft. 1920.*

John W. Ballard

Generation No. 1

1. JOHN W.[1] BALLARD *was born 1810 in NC, and died Aft. 1876. He married* LUCINDA THOMPSON. *She was born 1817 in KY, and died Aft. 1860.*

Notes for JOHN W. BALLARD:
Source: 1850 Henry County Tennessee Federal Census Records, 1860 Pulaski County Missouri Federal Census Records, Brenda Holman (brenda_99_2000@yahoo.com), Martha Frances Ballard (mduck@citlink.net)

** 1850 - Living in Henry Co., TN - Ballard, John 39 farmer NC, Lucinda 32 KY, Flabel 14 TN, Louisa J. 12 TN, Wm. H. 11 TN, James D. 10 KY, Jesse 8 KY, Margaret 5 KY, Marg 3 KY, John A. 6/12 KY*
** 1860 - Living in Pulaski Co., MO - Ballard, J W 51 NC, Lucinda 50 NC, Louisa 23 MO, Wm H 21 NC, Jesse J 16 TN, Mary M 13 TN, John P 10 TN, Geo W 8 MO, Nancy A 3 MO, Melissa J 3 MO*

Children of JOHN BALLARD *and* LUCINDA THOMPSON *are:*

2.   i.   FLABEL NELSON[2] BALLARD, *b. 1836, TN; d. 1900, Laclede Co., MO.*
      ii.   LOUISA JANE BALLARD, *b. 1838, TN; d. Aft. 1860.*
3.   iii.   WILLIAM HENRY BALLARD, *b. 1839, TN; d. Aft. 1880.*
     iv.   JAMES DAVID BALLARD, *b. 1840, KY.*
      v.   JESSE J. BALLARD, *b. Feb 1843, KY; d. 27 Oct 1925, Cullen, Pulaski Co., MO; m. (1)* LAVINIA MCNAIR; *b. 01 Oct 1854, Gibson Co., TN; d. 05 Nov 1932, Pulaski Co., MO; m. (2)* MAHALA BURTON, *15 Aug 1904, Lebanon, Laclede Co., MO; b. 1838, Crawford Co., MO; d. 27 Nov 1910, Lebanon, Laclede Co., MO; m. (3)* LOUISA AGEE, *28 Mar 1911, Lebanon, Laclede Co., MO.*

         Notes for JESSE J. BALLARD:
         Source: 1880 Pulaski County Missouri Federal Census Records, Pulaski County Missouri Death Certificate

         ** At the time of his death he was an inmate in the County Poor House.*
         ** 1880 - Living in Liberty, Pulaski Co., MO - Ballard, Jesse J 31 - Living with his brother William.*

         More About LAVINIA MCNAIR:
         Burial: Poor Farm Cemetery, Waynesville, Pulaski Co., MO

         More About MAHALA BURTON:
         Burial: Holman Cemetery, Sleeper, Laclede Co., MO

         More About JESSE BALLARD *and* MAHALA BURTON:
         Marriage: 15 Aug 1904, Lebanon, Laclede Co., MO

         More About JESSE BALLARD *and* LOUISA AGEE:
         Marriage: 28 Mar 1911, Lebanon, Laclede Co., MO

     vi.   MARGARET BALLARD, *b. 1845, KY.*
    vii.   MARY BALLARD, *b. 1847, KY; d. Aft. 1860.*
   viii.   JOHN ANDREW BALLARD, *b. 1849, KY; d. Aft. 1860.*
     ix.   GEORGE BALLARD, *b. 1852, MO.*
      x.   MALISSA (TWIN) BALLARD, *b. 1860, MO.*
     xi.   NANCY A. (TWIN) BALLARD, *b. 1860, MO; d. 13 Apr 1946, Pulaski Co., MO; m. (1)* WILLIAM GRAVES; *d. Bet. 1930 - 1940; m. (2)* WILLIS LIGHT, *16 Mar 1904, Laclede Co., MO.*

Notes for NANCY A. (TWIN) BALLARD:
Source: 1940 Pulaski County Missouri Federal Census Records
** 1940 - Living in Cullen, Pulaski Co., MO - Graves, Nancy 86 wd MO*

Notes for WILLIAM GRAVES:
Source: 1930 Pulaski County Missouri Federal Census Records
** 1930 - Living in Cullen, Pulaski Co., MO - Graves, William L 80 KY VA NC, Nancy 70 MO TN TN*

More About WILLIS LIGHT and NANCY BALLARD:
Marriage: 16 Mar 1904, Laclede, MO

Generation No. 2

2. FLABEL NELSON[2] BALLARD (JOHN W.[1]) *was born 1836 in TN, and died 1900 in Laclede Co., MO. He married* SARAH JANE HOPKINS, *daughter of* WILLIAM HOPKINS *and* MARY NICHOLAS. *She was born 30 Jun 1834 in TN, and died Aft. 1880.*

Notes for FLABEL NELSON BALLARD:
Source: 1860 Phelps County Missouri Federal Census Records, 1870 Pulaski County Missouri Federal Census Records, 1880 Laclede County Missouri Federal Census Records, 1900 Ripley County Missouri Federal Census Records, Brenda Holman (brenda_99_2000@yahoo.com), Martha Frances Ballard (mduck@citlink.net)

** 1860 - Living in Liberty, Phelps Co., MO - Ballard, F. N TN, S J. TN EC 4 (f) MO, W. T. (m) 7/12 MO*
** 1870 - Living in Pulaski Co., MO - Ballard, Flavius 36 TN, S Jane 35 TN, Catherine 13 MO, F William 10 MO, F Nelson 7 MO, W John MO, Louiza 3 MO*
** 1880 - Living in Laclede Co., MO - Ballard, Nelson 46 TN NC NC, Sara J 45 TN NC NC, Nelson 18 MO, John W 16 MO, Martha 14 MO*

Children of FLABEL BALLARD *and* SARAH HOPKINS *are:*

	i.	CATHERINE[3] BALLARD, b. 1857, MO; d. Aft. 1870.
4.	ii.	FLABEL NELSON BALLARD, b. 17 Mar 1863, Laclede Co., MO; d. 01 Mar 1933, Ardmore, Carter Co., OK.
5.	iii.	JOHN WILEY BALLARD, b. 18 Feb 1864, Lebanon, Laclede Co., MO; d. 11 Feb 1917, Clay Co., AR.
	iv.	MARTHA BALLARD, b. 1866, Laclede Co., MO; d. Aft. 1880.
	v.	LOUISA BALLARD, b. 1867.

3. WILLIAM HENRY[2] BALLARD (JOHN W.[1]) *was born 1839 in TN, and died Aft. 1880. He married* MARTHA ELIZABETH HOPKINS, *daughter of* WILLIAM HOPKINS *and* MARY NICHOLAS. *She was born 1843 in MO, and died Aft. 1880.*

Notes for WILLIAM HENRY BALLARD:
Source: 1880 Pulaski County Missouri Federal Census Records, Diana Jury Elledge (jurybox@email.msn.com)

** 1880 - Living in Liberty, Pulaski Co., MO - Ballard, William H 41 TN TN TN farmer, Martha E 37 MO TN TN, William B 19 MO, James N 17 MO, Mary L 14 MO, John W 12 MO, Thomas N 9 MO, Davis W 7 MO, Jesse J 31 brother TN TN TN*

Children of WILLIAM BALLARD *and* MARTHA HOPKINS *are:*

6.	i.	WILLIAM BRITEN[3] BALLARD, b. 14 Jun 1861, Phelps Co., MO; d. Aft. 1880.
7.	ii.	JAMES NELSON BALLARD, b. 31 Mar 1863, Ripley Co., MO; d. 02 Mar 1917, Ripley Co., MO.
	iii.	MARY LUCINDA BALLARD, b. 01 Sep 1866, Laclede Co., MO; d. Aft. 1880; m. WILLIAM C. SHIPMAN.

8.   *iv.*   JOHN WILEY BALLARD, b. 19 May 1869, Laclede Co., MO; d. Aft. 1900.

        v.   THOMAS N. BALLARD, b. 26 Feb 1871; d. Aft. 1880; m. MARY EMMA HALL; b. 08 May 1867, Ripley Co., MO; d. 10 May 1955, Fredericktown, Madison Co., MO.

Notes for THOMAS N. BALLARD:
Source: 1900 Ripley County Missouri Federal Census Records
** 1900 - Living in Current River, Ripley Co., MO - Ballard, Thomas N - Feb 1871 MO, Mary E - Oct 1867 MO*

Notes for MARY EMMA HALL:
Source: Madison County Missouri Death Certificate # 15993

More About MARY EMMA HALL:
Burial: Marcus Memorial Park, Madison Co., MO

        vi.   DAVID N. BALLARD, b. 28 Apr 1873; d. Aft. 1880.

Generation No. 3

4. FLABEL NELSON[3] BALLARD (FLABEL NELSON[2], JOHN W.[1]) *was born 17 Mar 1863 in Laclede Co., MO, and died 01 Mar 1933 in Ardmore, Carter Co., OK. He married MARY JANE PRICE 19 Jun 1922 in Ardmore, Carter Co., OK. She was born 13 Aug 1870 in Green Co., MO, and died 17 May 1945 in Ardmore, Carter Co., OK.*

Notes for FLABEL NELSON BALLARD:
Source: 1880 Laclede County Missouri Federal Census Records, 1900 Ripley County Missouri Federal Census Records, 1930 Briscoe County Texas Federal Census Records, Brenda Holman (brenda_99_2000@yahoo.com)
** 1880 - Living in Laclede Co., MO Mayfield township 15-15 - Ballard, Nelson 46 TN-NC-NC, Sarah J 45 ", Nelson 18 MO-TN-TN, John W 16 ", Martha   14   "*
** 1900 - Living in Ripley Co., MO - Ballard, Nelson - May 1863 MO TN TN, Mary J - Aug 1871 TN TN TN, Valley - Mar 1890, Della A - Sep 1892 MO, Sarah M - Nov 1894 MO, Elmer - Mar 1897 MO, Samuel L - Oct 1899 MO*
** 1930 Briscoe Co., TX - Ballard, Flable 67 MO TN TN, Mary J 59 MO MO MO*
** 1933 - Certificate of Death - Oklahoma State Board of Health*
** 1933 - Record of Funeral #128*

More About FLABEL NELSON BALLARD:
Burial: 02 Mar 1933, Provence Cemetery, Ardmore, Carter Co., OK

Notes for MARY JANE PRICE:
Source: Brenda Holman
** 1945 - Record of Funeral # 263*

More About MARY JANE PRICE:
Burial: 18 May 1945, Provence Cemetery, Ardmore, Carter Co., OK

More About FLABEL BALLARD and MARY PRICE:
Marriage: 19 Jun 1922, Ardmore, Carter Co., OK

Children of FLABEL BALLARD and MARY PRICE are:

        i.   CLARENCE VALLEY[4] BALLARD, REV., b. 25 Mar 1890, Doniphan, Ripley Co., MO; d. 09 Jan 1975, Ardmore, Carter Co., OK.

More About CLARENCE VALLEY BALLARD, REV.:

Burial: Provence Cemetery, Ardmore, Carter Co., OK

9.   ii.   DELLA ELIZABETH BALLARD, b. 07 Sep 1892, MO; d. 29 May 1960, Quitaque, Briscoe Co., TX.
      iii.   CHILD BALLARD, b. 07 Sep 1892, Ripley Co., MO.
      iv.   SARAH LINNIE BALLARD, b. 01 Nov 1894, Ripley Co., MO; d. 27 Aug 1982, Ardmore, Carter Co., OK; m. ERNEST EDGAR KENNEDY.

More About SARAH LINNIE BALLARD:
Burial: Rose Hill Cemetery, Ardmore, Carter Co., OK

10.   v.   WILLIAM ELMER BALLARD, b. 22 Mar 1897, Ripley Co., MO; d. 09 Mar 1966, Baytown, Harris Co., TX.
11.   vi.   SAMUEL LEE BALLARD, b. 14 Oct 1899, Joplin, Jasper Co., MO; d. 29 Oct 1988, Ardmore, Carter Co., OK.
      vii.   ORA CECIL BALLARD, b. 10 Nov 1902, Randolph Co., AR; d. 1981, Ardmore, Carter Co., OK; m. WILLIAM A. POLLARD; b. 1900; d. 1981.

More About ORA CECIL BALLARD:
Burial: Provence Cemetery, Ardmore, Carter Co. OK

More About WILLIAM A. POLLARD:
Burial: Provence Cemetery, Ardmore, Carter Co, OK

5. JOHN WILEY[3] BALLARD (FLABEL NELSON[2], JOHN W.[1]) *was born 18 Feb 1864 in Lebanon, Laclede Co., MO, and died 11 Feb 1917 in Clay Co., AR. He married (1) MARY FRANCES POND 18 Sep 1892. She was born 26 Feb 1876 in Ripley Co MO, and died 13 Sep 1907. He married (2) JULIE IRENE RAPERT Bef. 1914, daughter of ALONZO RAPERT and SARA GAMEL.*

Notes for JOHN WILEY BALLARD:
Source: 1900 Ripley County Missouri Federal Census Records, Martha Ballard (mduck@citlink.net), LDS-IGI

** 1900 - Living in Ripley Co., MO - Ballard, John W. - Feb 1864 MO TN TN, Mary F - May 1876 MO TN TN, Elven A - Aug 1893 MO, Louella - Nov 1895 MO, William A - Aug 1898 MO*

More About JOHN BALLARD and MARY POND:
Marriage: 18 Sep 1892

More About JOHN BALLARD and JULIE RAPERT:
Marriage: Bef. 1914

Children of JOHN BALLARD and MARY POND are:
      i.   EDMOND[4] BALLARD, b. 08 Aug 1893, Burr, Ripley Co MO.
      ii.   ELVIN ARLEY BALLARD, b. 16 Aug 1894, Burr, Ripley Co., MO; d. Aft. 1917.

Notes for ELVIN ARLEY BALLARD:
Source: WWI Draft Registration Cards

** 1917 - WWI Draft Registration Card shows him as Elvin Ballard b. Aug 26, 1894 in Missouri. Registered in Clay County Arkansas*

      iii.   LOU ELLA BALLARD, b. 25 Nov 1895, Burr, Ripley Co MO.
      iv.   WILLIAM ALCY BALLARD, b. 19 Aug 1898, Burr, Ripley Co MO.
      v.   THOMAS EARL BALLARD, b. 19 Nov 1901, Burr, Ripley Co., MO; m. LOLA SUE GAMBILL, 02 Sep 1934; b. 28 Sep 1915, Craighead Co., AR; d. 21 Dec 1972, Berrien Co., MI.

More About THOMAS BALLARD and LOLA GAMBILL:
Marriage: 02 Sep 1934

> vi.   ORA BELL "PONZIE" BALLARD, b. 29 Sep 1903, Burr, Ripley Co., MO.
> vii. CARL WASHINGTON BALLARD, b. 18 Jan 1906, Burr, Ripley Co., MO; d. 1907.

Children of JOHN BALLARD and JULIE RAPERT are:
> viii. HAROLD LYNN[4] BALLARD, b. 15 Jan 1914.
> ix.   RUTH ENA BALLARD, b. 30 May 1917.

6. WILLIAM BRITEN[3] BALLARD (WILLIAM HENRY[2], JOHN W.[1]) was born 14 Jun 1861 in Phelps Co., MO, and died Aft. 1880. He married YOURMAN MISSOUIRI ADAMS. She was born in Pulaski Co., MO.

Notes for WILLIAM BRITEN BALLARD:
Source: Laclede County Missouri Birth Certificate

Children of WILLIAM BALLARD and YOURMAN ADAMS are:
> i.   JAMES WILLIAM[4] BALLARD, b. 02 Jan 1884, Laclede Co., MO.
> ii. THOMAS RUSSELL BALLARD, b. 08 Aug 1895, Ripley Co., MO.

7. JAMES NELSON[3] BALLARD (WILLIAM HENRY[2], JOHN W.[1]) was born 31 Mar 1863 in Ripley Co., MO, and died 02 Mar 1917 in Ripley Co., MO. He married SARA "ROCK" MCCAWLEY. She was born Abt. 1870.

Notes for JAMES NELSON BALLARD:
Source: Diane E. (jurybox@msn.com), Ripley County Missouri Death Certificate

Children of JAMES BALLARD and SARA MCCAWLEY are:
> i.   WILLIAM HAMILTON[4] BALLARD, b. 15 Sep 1891, MO; d. 24 Nov 1963, Corning Clay Co., AR.
> ii. MAUDE BALLARD, b. 21 Jun 1894, Weatley Monroe Co., AR; d. 09 Nov 1921; m. RUFUS LLOYD WISNER; d. 23 Jan 1935.
>
>   *Notes for MAUDE BALLARD:*
>   *Source: jurybox@msn.com*

8. JOHN WILEY[3] BALLARD (WILLIAM HENRY[2], JOHN W.[1]) was born 19 May 1869 in Laclede Co., MO, and died Aft. 1900. He married RACHEL ELIZABETH "BETTY" HALL, daughter of JAMES HALL and ELIZABETH DIZMANG. She was born 1871, and died Aft. 1930.

Notes for JOHN WILEY BALLARD:
Source: 1900 Ripley County Missouri Federal Census Records
** 1900 - Living in Current River, Ripley Co., MO - Ballard, John W - May 1868 MO TN TN, Bettie - Nov 1869 MO KY KY, Hettie Kirtley MO IN MO niece - Sept 1845*

Notes for RACHEL ELIZABETH "BETTY" HALL:
Source: 1910-1930 Ripley County Missouri Federal Census Records

** 1910 - Living in Current River, Ripley Co., MO - Ballard, Bettie 40 - 3 children, 3 living MO, Gadays 9 (Gladys) MO, Herbert 7 MO, Denia 6 MO*
** 1920 - Living in Current River, Ripley Co., MO - Ballard, Rachel E 49 wd MO, Gladys V 19 MO, Herbert A 17 AR, Deane I 16 AR*
** 1930 - Living in Current River, Ripley Co., MO - Living with son Herbert*

Children of JOHN BALLARD and RACHEL HALL are:
  - i.   GLADYS V.[4] BALLARD, b. 1901, Ripley Co., MO; d. Aft. 1920.
  - ii.   HERBERT A. BALLARD, b. 1903, AR; d. Aft. 1930; m. RACHEL; b. 1903, MO; d. Aft. 1930.

    Notes for HERBERT A. BALLARD:
    Source: 1930 Ripley County Missouri Federal Census Records

    ** 1930 Living in Current River, Ripley Co., MO - Ballard, 27 AR MO MO, Rachel 27 MO MO MO, Betty 59 Mother in law wd MO TN TN*

  - iii.   DEANE I. BALLARD, b. 1904, Ripley Co., MO; d. Aft. 1930.

Generation No. 4

9.   DELLA ELIZABETH[4] BALLARD (FLABEL NELSON[3], FLABEL NELSON[2], JOHN W.[1]) was born 07 Sep 1892 in MO, and died 29 May 1960 in Quitaque, Briscoe Co., TX. She married HENRY WINFIELD HAMILTON. He was born 06 Nov 1885 in AR, and died 12 Nov 1968 in Lockney, Floyd Co., TX.

More About DELLA ELIZABETH BALLARD:
Burial: Resthaven Cemetery, Quitaque, Briscoe Co., TX

Notes for HENRY WINFIELD HAMILTON:
Source: 1920 Garvin County Oklahoma Federal Census Records, 1930-1940 Briscoe County Texas Federal Census Records

** 1920 - Living in Brady, Garvin Co., OK - Hamilton, Henry 34 AR, Della 27 AR, Iva 10 OK, Leroy 4 2/12 OK, Ivy 2 5/12*
** 1930 - Living in Briscoe Co., TX - Hamilton, Henry W 44 AR, Dela E 37 MO, Lee R 14 OK, Ina M 12 OK, William E 9 OK, Lola M 7 OK, Raymond H 4 1/12 TX, Lynn A 0/12 TX, Glynn E 0/12 TX*
** 1940 - Living in Briscoe Co., TX - Hamilton, Henry W 54 AR, Della E 47 AR, William E 20 OK, Lala M 17 OK, Raymond H 14 TX, Glynn E 10 TX, Lynn A 10 TX, Chester W 6 TX*

More About HENRY WINFIELD HAMILTON:
Burial: Resthaven Cemetery, Quitaque, Briscoe Co., TX

Children of DELLA BALLARD and HENRY HAMILTON are:

  - i.   IRA JANE[5] HAMILTON, b. 13 Oct 1909, Wynnewood, Garvin Co., OK; d. 01 Jun 1965, Groom, Carson Co., TX; m. ROY LERON BRUNSON; b. 16 Aug 1909, Eastland Co., TX; d. 19 Jan 1991, Lubbock Co., TX.

    More About IRA JANE HAMILTON:
    Burial: Resthaven Cemetery, Quitaque, Briscoe Co., TX

    More About ROY LERON BRUNSON:
    Burial: Resthaven Cemetery, Quitaque, Briscoe Co., TX

  - ii.   LEROY WINFIELD HAMILTON, b. 13 Jun 1915, Tuskahoma, OK; d. 16 Sep 1997, TX; m. CLOIE FERN WOODRUFF; b. 06 Oct 1915, Nashville, Howard Co., AR; d. 04 Jun 2010, Lockney, Floyd Co., TX.

    More About CLOIE FERN WOODRUFF:
    Burial: Resthaven Cemetery, Quitaque, Briscoe Co., TX

  - iii.   IVA MAE HAMILTON, b. 09 Jun 1917, Winniewood, Garvin Co., OK; d. 16 Oct 2005, North Richland

Hills, Tarrant Co., TX; m. SIDNEY LESTER MCKENZIE JR.; b. 31 Aug 1920, Anderson Co., TX; d. 09 Jan 2013, Southlake, Tarrant Co., TX.

More About IVA MAE HAMILTON:
Burial: Shannon Rose Hill Memorial Park, Ft. Worth, Tarrant Co., TX

More About SIDNEY LESTER MCKENZIE JR.:
Burial: Shannon Rose Hill Memorial Park, Ft. Worth, Tarrant Co., TX

    iv.   WILLIAM EARL HAMILTON, b. 04 Apr 1920, Wynnewood, Garvin Co., OK; d. 07 Apr 1991, Hall Co., TX; m. CORA ROSE BROWN; b. 29 Dec 1929, Stilwell, Adair Co., OK; d. 26 Nov 2014, Clarendon, Donley Co., TX.

More About WILLIAM EARL HAMILTON:
Burial: Citizens Cemetery, Clarendon, Donley Co., TX

More About CORA ROSE BROWN:
Burial: Citizens Cemetery, Clarendon, Donley Co., TX

    v.   LOLA MAE HAMILTON, b. 1923, OK; d. Aft. 2005; m. (1) EUDY; m. (2) OLIN DOYLE HUFF, 05 Mar 2005, Johnson Co., TX; b. 28 Mar 1919, Lockney, Floyd Co., TX; d. 08 Jun 2015.

More About OLIN HUFF and LOLA HAMILTON:
Marriage: 05 Mar 2005, Johnson Co., TX

    vi.   RAYMOND HAMILTON, b. 21 Feb 1926, Briscoe Co., TX; d. 13 Aug 1986, Quitaque, Briscoe Co., TX; m. MARY JANE JACKS; b. 22 Oct 1925, OK; d. 26 May 2008, Lockney, Floyd Co., TX.

More About RAYMOND HAMILTON:
Burial: Resthaven Cemetery, Quitaque, Briscoe Co., TX

More About MARY JANE JACKS:
Burial: Resthaven Cemetery, Quitaque, Briscoe Co., TX

    vii.   GLYNN ELBERT HAMILTON, b. 11 Mar 1930, Quitaque, Briscoe Co., TX; d. 23 Sep 2010; m. LOIS MAE MOORE.

Notes for GLYNN ELBERT HAMILTON:
Source: Briscoe County Texas Certificate of Birth, Social Security Records

    viii.   LYNN ALBERT HAMILTON, b. 11 Mar 1930, Quitaque, Briscoe Co., TX; d. 08 Jun 1999; m. RUBY LOUETTA JAMES.

Notes for LYNN ALBERT HAMILTON:
Source: Social Security Records

    ix.   CHESTER WAYNE HAMILTON, b. 04 Aug 1933, Quitaque, Briscoe Co., TX; d. 02 Sep 1992.

Notes for CHESTER WAYNE HAMILTON:
Source: Social Security Records

10. WILLIAM ELMER[4] BALLARD (FLABEL NELSON[3], FLABEL NELSON[2], JOHN W.[1]) *was born 22 Mar 1897 in Ripley Co., MO, and died 09 Mar 1966 in Baytown, Harris Co., TX. He married (1) INA MAE SCARBERRY. She was born 24 Dec*

1902 in OK, and died 03 Jun 1961 in Houston, Harris Co., TX. He married (2) VELMA MAE CARTER. She was born 27 Jan 1922, and died 22 Nov 1949.

Notes for WILLIAM ELMER BALLARD:
Source: Harris County Texas Certificate of Death

More About WILLIAM ELMER BALLARD:
Burial: South Park Cemetery, Pearland, Brazoria Co., TX

More About INA MAE SCARBERRY:
Burial: Memorial Oaks Cemetery, Houston, Harris Co., TX

More About VELMA MAE CARTER:
Burial: South Park Cemetery, Pearland, Brazoria Co., TX

Child of WILLIAM BALLARD and INA SCARBERRY is:

> i. WALTER MADISON⁵ BALLARD, b. 13 Sep 1927, Navarro Co., TX; d. 16 Feb 1950, Baytown, Harris Co., TX.
>
> *More About WALTER MADISON BALLARD:*
> *Burial: Cedar Crest Cemetery, Baytown, Harris Co., TX*

11. SAMUEL LEE⁴ BALLARD (FLABEL NELSON³, FLABEL NELSON², JOHN W.¹) *was born 14 Oct 1899 in Joplin, Jasper Co., MO, and died 29 Oct 1988 in Ardmore, Carter Co., OK. He married (1) WILLIE ESTELLE "STELLA" LUTTRELL 19 Jun 1922 in Ardmore, Carter co., OK, daughter of JAKE LUTRELL and CLARA WATTERSON. She was born 21 Apr 1904 in Madill OK, and died 25 Mar 1977 in Ardmore, Carter Co., OK. He married (2) DOVIE RICHARDS Bef. 1988.*

Notes for SAMUEL LEE BALLARD:
Source: Find A Grave, Brenda Holman (brenda_99_2000@yahoo.com)

** 1922 - Marriage records of S. L. Ballard to Stella Luttrell dated 6/19/1922*
** 1937 - US Social Security Application for Account # 446-10-9961*
which shows Samuel Lee Ballard as son of Flabor Nelson Ballard and Mary Jane Price. His birth date as October 14, 1899 in Joplin Missouri.
** 1988 - Death Certificate of Samuel Lee Ballard 10/29/1988*

More About SAMUEL LEE BALLARD:
Burial: Rose Hill Cemetery, Ardmore, Carter Co., OK

Notes for WILLIE ESTELLE "STELLA" LUTTRELL:
Source: Brenda Holman
** 1955 - Application for Social Security Account Number 465-58-6940*
** 1977 - Certificate of Death for Willie Stella (Estell) Ballard*

More About WILLIE ESTELLE "STELLA" LUTTRELL:
Burial: Rose Hill Cemetery, Ardmore, Carter Co., OK

More About SAMUEL BALLARD and WILLIE LUTTRELL:
Marriage: 19 Jun 1922, Ardmore, Carter co., OK

More About SAMUEL BALLARD and DOVIE RICHARDS:
Marriage: Bef. 1988

Children of SAMUEL BALLARD and WILLIE LUTTRELL are:
> i. ORVILE PRUITTE[5] BALLARD, b. 11 Apr 1923, Ardmore, Carter Co., OK; d. 02 Jun 1996, Fannin Co.,
> TX; m. THELMA LOLA BELLE WATTERSON, 18 Mar 1950; b. 27 Feb 1928, Bryan Co., OK; d. 09 Jan
> 2011, Durant, Bryan Co., OK.
>
> *More About ORVILE PRUITTE BALLARD:*
> Burial: Dodd City Cemetery, Dodd City, Fannin Co., TX
>
> *More About THELMA LOLA BELLE WATTERSON:*
> Burial: Dodd City Cemetery, Dodd City, Fannin Co., TX
>
> *More About ORVILE BALLARD and THELMA WATTERSON:*
> Marriage: 18 Mar 1950
>
> ii. WILLIE JUNIOR BALLARD, b. 23 Mar 1925, Ardmore, Carter Co., OK; d. 13 Aug 2011, Plainview,
> Hale Co., TX; m. MINNIE LOU WHITEFIELD; b. 01 May 1930, Quitaque, Briscoe Co., TX; d. 10 Feb
> 2010, TX.
>
> *More About WILLIE JUNIOR BALLARD:*
> Burial: Parklawn Memorial Gardens, Plainview, Hale Co., TX
>
> *More About MINNIE LOU WHITEFIELD:*
> Burial: Parklawn Memorial Gardens Plainview, Hale Co. TX
>
> iii. MELTON RAY BALLARD, b. 27 Mar 1927, Ardmore, Carter Co., OK; d. 25 Dec 2006, Plainview, Hale
> Co., TX; m. ELSIE LUCILLE ADAMS; b. 10 Feb 1929, Hollis, Harmon Co., OK; d. 28 Apr 2011,
> Plainview, Hale Co., TX.
>
> *More About MELTON RAY BALLARD:*
> Burial: Parklawn Memorial Gardens Plainview, Hale Co., TX
>
> *More About ELSIE LUCILLE ADAMS:*
> Burial: Parklawn Memorial Gardens Plainview, Hale Co
>
> iv. THOMAS SAMUEL BALLARD, b. 29 Mar 1929, Mary Nebblack OK; d. 27 Dec 1996, Fannin Co., TX.
>
> *More About THOMAS SAMUEL BALLARD:*
> Burial: Dodd City Cemetery Dodd City, Fannin Co., TX
>
> v. CLAIRE JANE BALLARD, b. 20 Nov 1942, Quitaque, Briscoe Co., TX; d. 08 Jul 2010, Sherman,
> Grayson Co., TX; m. BENNY JOE GEHARDT; b. 26 Sep 1943, Plainview, Hale Co., TX; d. 16 Jan
> 2015, Bonham, Fannin Co., TX.
>
> *More About CLAIRE JANE BALLARD:*
> Burial: Dodd City Cemetery Dodd City, Fannin Co., TX
>
> *More About BENNY JOE GEHARDT:*
> Burial: Dodd City Cemetery Dodd City, Fannin Co., TX

John W. Ballard

Generation No. 1

1. JOHN W.[1] BALLARD *was born 1822 in NY, and died 01 Feb 1899 in MO. He married* MARGARET O'CONNOR *18 Nov 1852 in Will Co., IL, daughter of* JAMES O'CONNOR *and* ELLEN. *She was born 05 Mar 1837 in Jersey City, Hudson Co., NJ, and died 10 Mar 1912 in Washington, Nodaway Co., MO.*

Notes for JOHN W. BALLARD:
Source: 1860 Gentry County Missouri Federal Census Records, 1870-1880 Nodaway County Missouri Federal Census Records
** 1860 - Living in Gentry Co., MO - Ballard, John 32 farmer England, Margarette 24 NJ, Mary 6 IL, Louisa 4 MO, Joseph 2 MO, Amanda 3/12 MO*
** 1870 - Living in Washington, Nodaway Co., MO - Ballard, John W 48 NY, Margaret 41 NY, Mary Ellen 14 IL, Louisa 12 MO, Joseph 10 MO, Amanda 8 MO, Lincoln 6 MO, Charles 4 MO, George 2 MO*
** 1880 - Living in Washington, Nodaway Co., MO - Ballard, John W 58 NY Eng Ireland farmer, Margarett 47 NJ Ireland Ireland, Luiza 21, Joseph 20, Amanda 18, Lincoln 17, Charley 14, George 12*

More About JOHN W. BALLARD:
Burial: St. Columba Cemetery, Conception, Nodaway Co., MO

Notes for MARGARET O'CONNOR:
Source: 1910 Nodaway County Missouri Federal Census Records
** 1910 - Living in Washington, Nodaway Co., MO with her son Charley.*

More About MARGARET O'CONNOR:
Burial: St. Columba Cemetery, Conception, Nodaway Co., MO

More About JOHN BALLARD *and* MARGARET O'CONNOR:
Marriage: 18 Nov 1852, Will Co., IL

Children of JOHN BALLARD *and* MARGARET O'CONNOR *are:*

  i. MARY ELLEN[2] BALLARD, *b. 03 Sep 1854, Joliet, Will Co., IL; d. 25 Jul 1905, Nodaway Co., MO; m.* MATTHEW FRANCIS FARNAN, SR.; *b. 24 Jul 1851, Madison, Jefferson Co., IN; d. 26 Jul 1919, Nodaway Co., MO.*

    More About MARY ELLEN BALLARD:
    Burial: St. Columbia Cemetery, Conception, Nodaway Co., MO

    More About MATTHEW FRANCIS FARNAN, SR.:
    Burial: St. Columbia Cemetery, Conception, Nodaway Co., MO

  ii. LOUISA BALLARD, *b. 02 Oct 1857, Gentry Co., MO; d. 10 Jan 1933, Nodaway Co., MO.*

    More About LOUISA BALLARD:
    Burial: St. Columba Cemetery, Conception, Nodaway Co., MO

  iii. JOSEPH BALLARD, *b. 07 Feb 1859, Gentry Co., MO; d. 03 Feb 1920, Guilford, Nodaway Co., MO.*

    More About JOSEPH BALLARD:
    Burial: St. Columba Cemetery, Conception, Nodaway Co., MO

iv.   *AMANDA BALLARD, b. 21 Feb 1862, Gentry Co., MO; d. 07 Aug 1934, Nodaway Co., MO; m. JOHN ALLEN, 31 Oct 1882, Nodaway Co., MO; b. 01 Mar 1850, Oswego Co., NY; d. 19 Feb 1933, Nodaway Co., MO.*

More About AMANDA BALLARD:
Burial: St. Columba Cemetery, Conception, Nodaway Co., MO

Notes for JOHN ALLEN:
Source: 1900 Nodaway County Missouri Federal Census Records
** 1900 - Living in Jefferson, Nodaway Co., MO - Allen, John - Mar 1850 NY Ireland Ireland, Amanda - Feb 1862 - 5 children 1 living MO, Samuel - Aug 1895 MO, John - Mar 1888 MO, James - Nov 1891 MO, Margaret - Sep 1895 MO, (hired help) Anna Wirth - Nov 1872 Germany, Edward Poe - 1877 IL*

More About JOHN ALLEN:
Burial: St. Columba Cemetery, Conception, Nodaway Co., MO

More About JOHN ALLEN and AMANDA BALLARD:
Marriage: 31 Oct 1882, Nodaway Co., MO

v.   *JAMES LINCOLN BALLARD, b. 26 Jan 1863, Nodaway Co., MO; d. 19 Dec 1934, Washington, Nodaway Co., MO.*

Notes for JAMES LINCOLN BALLARD:
Source: Nodaway County Missouri Death Certificate

More About JAMES LINCOLN BALLARD:
Burial: St. Columba Cemetery, Conception, Nodaway Co., MO

vi.   *CHARLES BALLARD, b. 06 Nov 1864, Gentry Co., MO; d. 22 Sep 1954, Maryville, Nodaway Co., MO.*

Notes for CHARLES BALLARD:
Source: 1910-1920 Nodaway County Missouri Federal Census Records
** 1910 - Living in Washington, Nodaway Co., MO - Ballard, Charley - Nov 1865 MO, George (bro) - July 1868 MO, Louisa - Sept 1857 MO, Margaret 7 children - Y living mother wd NJ Ireland Ireland*
** 1920 - Walter, Nodaway Co., MO - Ballard, Charley 53 MO, George 51 bro MO, Louisa sister 58 next door JE 60 MO*

More About CHARLES BALLARD:
Burial: St. Columba Cemetery, Conception, Nodaway Co., MO

vii.   *GEORGE BALLARD, b. 18 Jul 1867, Guilford, Nodaway Co., MO; d. 24 Jul 1947, Maryville, Nodaway Co., MO.*

Notes for GEORGE BALLARD:
Source: Nodaway County Missouri Death Certificate

More About GEORGE BALLARD:
Burial: 26 Jul 1947, St. Columba Cemetery, Conception, Nodaway Co., MO

Mr. Ballard

Generation No. 1

1. MR.[1] BALLARD *was born Abt. 1780.*

Children of MR. BALLARD are:
2.   i.   JOHN SIDNEY[2] BALLARD, *b. 05 Sep 1817, Baltimore, MD; d. 11 Aug 1912, Elkhorn, Warren Co., MO.*
3.   ii.   JAMES H. BALLARD, *b. 1830, MD; d. Aft. 1870.*

Generation No. 2

2. JOHN SIDNEY[2] BALLARD *(MR.[1]) was born 05 Sep 1817 in Baltimore, MD, and died 11 Aug 1912 in Elkhorn, Warren Co., MO. He married* ARMILDA GILLASPI. *She was born 07 Jan 1818 in KY, and died 15 Mar 1894 in Warren Co., MO.*

Notes for JOHN SIDNEY BALLARD:
Source: Warren County Missouri Death Certificate, 1850 Lincoln County Missouri Federal Census Records, 1860-1880 Warren County Missouri Federal Census Records
** 1850 - Living in Lincoln Co., MO - Ballard, John S 31 MD, Armilda 28 KY, Stephen Masse 10, Thomas 4, Mary 6, James Ballard 22 MD*
** 1860 - Living in Hickory Grove, Warren Co., MO - Ballard, John S 35 MD carpenter, Armilda 32 KY, Thomas Massy 15 MO, Mary Massy 11 MO, George Ballard 8 MO, Henry 4 MO, Ann M 3 MO, Eliza 1 MO, James 37 MO*
** 1880 - Living in Wright City, Warren Co., MO - Ballard, John 58 carpenter MD MD MD, Armilda 58 KY KY KY, Eliza 21 MO*
** 1910 - Living in Elkhorn, Warren Co., MO - Ballard, John 92 wd MO MD KY - Living with daughter Anna Price and family*

More About JOHN SIDNEY BALLARD:
Burial: Wright City Cemetery, Wright City, Warren Co., MO

More About ARMILDA GILLASPI:
Burial: Wright City Cemetery, Wright City, Warren Co., MO

Children of JOHN BALLARD *and* ARMILDA GILLASPI *are:*
      i.   GEORGE[3] BALLARD, *b. 1852, Warren Co., MO; d. Aft. 1860.*
      ii.   HENRY BALLARD, *b. 1856, Warren Co., MO; d. Aft. 1860.*
4.   iii. ANN M. BALLARD, *b. 08 Apr 1857, Warren Co., MO; d. 08 Sep 1928, Pendleton, Warren Co., MO.*
5.   iv. ELIZA VICTORIA BALLARD, *b. 06 Apr 1859, Warren Co., MO; d. 30 Jul 1942, Los Angeles Co., CA.*

3. JAMES H.[2] BALLARD *(MR.[1]) was born 1830 in MD, and died Aft. 1870. He married* LAURA A.. *She was born 1840 in NC, and died Aft. 1870.*

Notes for JAMES H. BALLARD:
Source: 1870 Randolph County Missouri Federal Census Records
** 1870 - Living in Moberly Randolph Co., MO - Ballard, James H. 40 MD, Laura A. 30 NC, George M. 9 MO*
** 1870 - additional listing - they must have moved during the census year - Calumet, Pike Co., MO - Ballard, James H 45 wagon maker MD, Laura A 35 NC, George M 9 MO*

Child of JAMES BALLARD *and* LAURA A. *is:*
      i.   GEORGE M.[3] BALLARD, *b. 1861, MO; d. Aft. 1870.*

Generation No. 3

4. ANN M.[3] BALLARD (JOHN SIDNEY[2], MR.[1]) was born 08 Apr 1857 in Warren Co., MO, and died 08 Sep 1928 in Pendleton, Warren Co., MO. She married SAMUEL PRICE 13 Apr 1876. He was born 05 Apr 1851 in Pendleton, Warren Co., MO, and died 06 Sep 1929 in Butler, Bates Co., MO.

More About ANN M. BALLARD:
Burial: Price Cemetery, Pendleton, Warren Co., MO

Notes for SAMUEL PRICE:
Source: 1880-1920 Warren County Missouri Federal Census Records
* 1880 - Living in Elkhorn, Warren Co., MO - Price, Samuel 29 MO MO VA, Annie 22 MO MD KY, Jobe L 1 MO
* 1900 - Living in Elkhorn, Warren Co., MO - Price, Samuel T - Apr 1851 MO MO VA, Anna M - Apr 1857 9 children 8 living MO MO KY, Samuel T - Mar 1891 MO, Frank M. - Jan 1883 MO, Mary L - July 1885 MO, Annie E - Aug 1887 MO, John M - July 1889 MO, William E - Sept 1891 MO, Armilda K - Nov 1895 MO
* 1910 - Living in Elkhorn, Warren Co., MO - Price, Samuel 59 MO MO VA, Anna 53 9 children 8 living MO MO KY, Luella 24 MO, Edgar 17 MO, Helen 13 MO, John Ballard wd MO MD KY father in law
* 1920 - Living in Elkhorn, Warren Co., MO - Price, Samuel 68 MO, Anna 62, Luella 33 MO
* Mrs. L. D. LaHue of Butler had the remains of her parents Mr. and Mrs. S. T. Price, who passed away at this place in September 1928, 29 removed from the old Price Cemetery near Pendleton Friday to Butler where the remains were interred in the Butler city cemetery at Butler. F. W. Nieburg and son of Warrenton had charge of the work. Walter Taylor of Butler conveyed the remains to Butler.

More About SAMUEL PRICE:
Burial: Price Cemetery, Pendleton, Warren Co., MO

Children of ANN BALLARD and SAMUEL PRICE are:

6. i. JOBE LEE[4] PRICE, b. 28 Mar 1879, Warren Co., MO; d. 14 Jun 1956.
   ii. SAMUEL THOMAS PRICE, b. 18 Mar 1881, Warren Co., MO; d. 14 Jan 1965, Benton, OR; m. FRANCES THOMPSON; b. 1886.
   iii. FRANK M. PRICE, b. 28 Jan 1883, Warren Co., MO; d. 19 Nov 1929, Snohomish Co., WA.
   iv. MARY LUELLA PRICE, b. 28 Jul 1885, Warren Co., MO; d. 13 May 1969, Butler, Bates Co., MO.

    More About MARY LUELLA PRICE:
    Burial: Oak Hill Cemetery, Butler, Bates Co. MO

   v. LYDIA VICTORIA LAHUE, b. 22 Aug 1887, Warren Co., MO; d. 15 Nov 1981, Bates Co., MO; m. LILBURN LAHUE; b. 15 Apr 1887; d. 25 May 1968.
   vi. JOHN MARMADUKE PRICE, b. 14 Jul 1889, Warren Co., MO; d. 26 Aug 1970, Cascade, MT; m. CLARA PATE; b. 21 Dec 1892, Independence Co., AR; d. 14 Apr 1920, Bernalillo Co., NM.
   vii. EDGAR WILLIAM PRICE, b. 28 Aug 1891, Warren Co., MO; d. 08 May 1975; m. LILLIAN MOORE, 22 Oct 1915, Warrenton, Warren Co., MO.

    Notes for EDGAR WILLIAM PRICE:
    Source: WWI Draft Registration, 1920 Buchanan County Missouri Federal Census Records
    * 1920 - Living in St. Joseph, Buchanan Co., MO - Price, Edgar W 28 MO MO MO, Lillian 26 MO MO MO

   viii. AMELDA KATHERINE PRICE, b. 21 Nov 1895, Warren Co., MO; d. 29 Apr 1991, Cook Co., IL; m. OPAL HARRISON LANGFORD; b. 16 Aug 1894, Warren Co., MO; d. 15 Aug 1944, Jackson Co., MO.

5. ELIZA VICTORIA[3] BALLARD (JOHN SIDNEY[2], MR.[1]) was born 06 Apr 1859 in Warren Co., MO, and died 30 Jul 1942 in Los Angeles Co., CA. She married WILLIAM L. GIBSON 22 Sep 1881 in Wright City, Warren Co., MO. He was born May 1854 in KY, and died Aft. 1920.

Notes for ELIZA VICTORIA BALLARD:
Source: California Death Index

More About ELIZA VICTORIA BALLARD:
Burial: Forest Lawn Memorial Park, Glendale, Los Angeles Co., CA

Notes for WILLIAM L. GIBSON:
Source: 1900 Nicholas County Kentucky Federal Census Records, 1910-1920 Craig County Oklahoma Federal Census Records

** 1900 - Living in Huffs Stable, Nicholas Co., KY - Gibson, William L - May 1854 KY KY KY, Eliza V - Apr 1859 - 8 children 7 living KY KY KY, Amelia - Feb 1883 KY, Charles - Sept 1884 KY, George B - Aug 1886 KY, Joseph - Feb 1889 KY, William - June 1892 KY, Mitchell - Sept 1897 KY, Robert - Feb 1899 KY*
** 1910 - Living in Craig Co., OK - Gibson, William L 55 KY VA KY, Eliza V 50 - 9 children 8 living MO MD KY, Finzer 21 KY, Mitchell 12 KY, Dixon E 10 KY, Eliza H 8 KY, Owens, Charley grandson 8 KY, Chas O Gibson 25 KY*
** 1920 - Living in Craig Co., OK - Gibson, William L 65 KY VA KY, Eliza V 60 MO MD KY, Mitchell L 23 KY, Lena dau in law 20 MO, Robert E. D 20 KY, Eliza H 18 KY, Owings, Charles W grandson 17 KY*

Children of ELIZA BALLARD and WILLIAM GIBSON are:

      i.   AMELIA[4] GIBSON, b. Feb 1883, KY; d. Aft. 1900.
     ii.   CHARLES GIBSON, b. Sep 1884, KY; d. Aft. 1910.
    iii.   GEORGE B. GIBSON, b. Aug 1886, KY; d. Aft. 1900.
    iv.   JOSEPH GIBSON, b. Feb 1889, KY; d. Aft. 1900.
     v.   WILLIAM GIBSON, b. Jun 1892, KY; d. Aft. 1900.
    vi.   MITCHELL GIBSON, b. Sep 1897, KY; d. Aft. 1920.
   vii.   ROBERT GIBSON, b. Feb 1899, KY; d. Aft. 1920.
  viii.   EMMETT DICKSON GIBSON, b. 23 Feb 1897, Paris, KY; d. 26 Apr 1990, Big Timber, Sweet Grass Co., MT; m. CHRISTINE BAUER, 09 Oct 1957, Wheatland, MT.

          Notes for EMMETT DICKSON GIBSON:
          Source: Sweet Grass County Montana Certificate of Death, WWII Draft Cards
          ** 1942 - Living in Amarillo, Potter Co., TX*

    ix.   ELIZA H. GIBSON, b. Abt. 1902, KY; d. Aft. 1920.

Generation No. 4

6. JOBE LEE[4] PRICE (ANN M.[3] BALLARD, JOHN SIDNEY[2], MR.[1]) was born 28 Mar 1879 in Warren Co., MO, and died 14 Jun 1956. He married GRACE CATHERINE EVANS 21 Sep 1912. She was born 03 Sep 1884 in Columbus, Cherokee Co., KS, and died 09 Aug 1975.

More About JOBE LEE PRICE:
Burial: Park Cemetery, Columbus, Cherokee Co., KS

More About GRACE CATHERINE EVANS:
Burial: Park Cemetery, Columbus, Cherokee Co., KS

Child of JOBE PRICE and GRACE EVANS is:
      i.   HELEN GERTRUDE[5] PRICE, b. 10 Mar 1915; d. 19 Mar 1915.

          More About HELEN GERTRUDE PRICE:
          Burial: Park Cemetery, Columbus, Cherokee Co., KS

Nathan Ballard

Generation No. 1

1. NATHAN[3] BALLARD (JOHN[2], NATHAN[1] BALLARD/BULLARD) *was born 14 Feb 1847 in Wayne Co., IL, and died 10 Apr 1911 in Richmond twp., Stoddard Co., MO. He married* LOUVINIA TROTTER, *daughter of* JOHN TROTTER *and* CATHERINE SEXTON. *She was born 1850 in Wayne Co., IL, and died Bet. 1880 - 1900.*

Notes for NATHAN BALLARD:
Source: 1870-1880 Wayne County Illinois Federal Census Records, 1900 Stoddard County Missouri Federal Census Records, Missouri State Board of Health Death Certificate

* 1870 - Living in Four Mile, Wayne Co., IL - Ballard, William 24 IL, Louvina A 20 IL, Angeline 2 IL, Martha J 9/12 IL
* 1880 - Living in Four Mile, Wayne Co., IL - Ballard, Nathan 30 IL TN KY, Louvina 30 IL IL IL, Angeline 12 IL, Martha 10 IL, John 8 IL, Mary 6 IL, Daniel 3 IL, Annie 1 IL
* 1900 - Living in Elk, Stoddard Co., MO - Ballard, Nathan - Feb 1846 wd IL IL IL, Anney M dau - Nov 1878 IL IL IL, Orly - Feb 1885 KY KY KY

More About NATHAN BALLARD:
Burial: 12 Apr 1911, Baltimore Cemetery, Wayne City, Wayne Co., IL

Children of NATHAN BALLARD *and* LOUVINIA TROTTER *are:*

2.	i.	ANGELINE[4] BALLARD, b. 20 Dec 1867, Wayne Co., IL; d. 27 Dec 1937, Benton, Franklin Co., IL.
	ii.	MARTHA BALLARD, b. 1870, Wayne Co., IL; d. Aft. 1880.
	iii.	JOHN BALLARD, b. 1872, Wayne Co., IL; d. Aft. 1880.
	iv.	MARY BALLARD, b. 1874, Wayne Co., IL; d. Aft. 1880.
3.	v.	DANIEL "DAN" L. BALLARD, b. 16 Sep 1876, Wayne Co., IL; d. 17 Jul 1948, Flint, Genesee Co., MI.
	vi.	ANNIE BALLARD, b. 1879, Wayne Co., IL; d. Aft. 1880.
	vii.	ORLEY BALLARD, b. 04 Feb 1885, Wayne Co., IL; d. 09 Jul 1961.

> *Notes for* ORLEY BALLARD:
> Source: Social Security Records, WWII Draft Registration Records, Marion County Indiana Coroner's Certificate of Death

Generation No. 2

2. ANGELINE[4] BALLARD (NATHAN[3], JOHN[2], NATHAN[1] BALLARD/BULLARD) *was born 20 Dec 1867 in Wayne Co., IL, and died 27 Dec 1937 in Benton, Franklin Co., IL. She married* WILLIAM WILEY BLACK *05 Jan 1887 in Wayne Co., IL. He was born 17 Mar 1864 in Warrick Co., IN, and died 01 May 1931 in Paragould, Greene Co., AR.*

More About ANGELINE BALLARD:
Burial: Browns Chapel Cemetery, Paragould, Greene Co, AR

Notes for WILLIAM WILEY BLACK:
Source: 1900 Wayne County Illinois Federal Census Records, 1910 - 1920 Stoddard County Missouri Federal Census Records, Child's Lancaster South Carolina Death Certificate, 1930 Greene County Arkansas Federal Census Records

* 1900 - Living in Orel, Wayne Co., IL - Black, William - Mar 1864 IN IN NC farmer, Angline - Dec 1867 7 children 5 living IL IL IL, Verne - Oct 1887 IL, Claud - Mar 1889 IL, Roy - Sept 1890 IL, Ernest P - Sept 1895 IL, Hazel - Nov 1897 IL

** 1910 - Living in Richland, Stoddard Co., MO - Black, William W 46 IN IN NC, Angeline 43 11 children 8 living IL IL IL, Vernie 22 IL, Ray H 19 IL, Purl E 15 MO, Hazel L 13 IL, Charles L 9 MO, Ralph L 9 MO, Pauline A 8/12*
** 1920 - Living in Richland, Stoddard Co., MO - Black, Wm W 55 IN KY NC, Angeline 53 IL IL IL, Charlie 19 MO, Ralph 14 MO, Pauline 10 MO*
** 1930 - Living in Main Shore, Greene Co., AR - Black, William 66 IN, Angeline 60 IL, Charley 27 MO*

More About WILLIAM WILEY BLACK:
Burial: Browns Chapel Cemetery, Paragould, Greene Co., AR

Children of ANGELINE BALLARD and WILLIAM BLACK are:
4.   i.   VERNON[5] BLACK, *b. 20 Oct 1887, Wayne Co., IL; d. 29 Dec 1930, Stoddard Co., MO.*
       ii.   CLAUDE ALVIS BLACK, *b. 05 Mar 1889, Tennyson, Warrick Co., IN; d. 16 Feb 1967, Paragould, Greene Co., AR; m. LORA.*

           Notes for CLAUDE ALVIS BLACK:
           Source: Greene County Arkansas Certificate of Death, 1920 Stoddard County Missouri Federal Census Records
           ** 1920 - Living in Richland, Stoddard Co., MO - Black, Cloud 30 IN, Lora 21 MO*

5.   iii.   HENRY ROY BLACK, *b. 19 Sep 1890, Wayne Co., IL; d. 13 Dec 1969, Paragould, Greene Co., AR.*
6.   iv.   ERNEST PEARL BLACK, *b. 09 Sep 1895, Wayne Co., IL; d. 04 Jan 1970, Essex, Stoddard Co., MO.*
       v.   HAZEL LOUETTA BLACK, *b. 09 Nov 1897, Wayne Co., IL; d. 27 Dec 1976, Franklin Co., IL; m. WILLIAM KENNETH MILLS; b. 11 Sep 1915, Franklin Co., IL; d. 18 Apr 1979, Paducah, McCracken Co., KY.*

           More About HAZEL LOUETTA BLACK:
           Burial: Masonic and Odd Fellows Cemetery, Benton, Franklin Co., IL

           More About WILLIAM KENNETH MILLS:
           Burial: Masonic and Odd Fellows Cemetery, Benton, Franklin Co., IL

       vi.   CHARLES L. BLACK, *b. 06 Jan 1901, Stoddard Co., MO; d. 09 Apr 1947, Lancaster Co., SC; m. MARIE.*

           Notes for CHARLES L. BLACK:
           Source: Death Certificate
           ** The parents names are very clear but the name of the person that passed is faint.*

           More About CHARLES L. BLACK:
           Burial: Browns Chapel

7.   vii.   LELAND RALPH BLACK, *b. 31 Jan 1905, Stoddard Co., MO; d. 03 Sep 1979, Allegan Co., MO.*
8.   viii.   PAULINE BLACK, *b. 16 Aug 1909, Stoddard Co., MO; d. 22 Mar 1990, Johnson Co., IL.*

3. DANIEL "DAN" L.[4] BALLARD (NATHAN[3], JOHN[2], NATHAN[1] BALLARD/BULLARD) *was born 16 Sep 1876 in Wayne Co., IL, and died 17 Jul 1948 in Flint, Genesee Co., MI. He married MARY FRANCES GULLEY 30 Jun 1895 in Stoddard Co., MO. She was born 10 Apr 1878 in MO, and died 15 Apr 1933 in Stoddard Co., MO.*

Notes for DANIEL "DAN" L. BALLARD:
Source: 1900-1930 Stoddard County Missouri Federal Census Records, Stoddard County Missouri Marriage Records

** 1900 - Living in Elk, Stoddard Co., MO - Ballard, Dan - Sept 1876 IL, Mary - Apr 1878 MO, Carrie - Feb 1900*

** 1910 - Living in Elk, Stoddard Co., MO - Ballard, Dan F 34 IL IL IL, Mar F 33 6 children 5 living TN TN TN, Carry F 10 MO, Velma 6 MO, John 4 MO, Erma 3 MO, Earl 9/12 MO*
** 1920 - Living in Elk, Stoddard Co., MO - Ballard, Dan 44 IL IL IL, Mary 48 TN TN TN, Velma 17 MO, John 14 MO, Erma 12 MO, Earl 10, Delmer 8 MO*
** 1930 - Living in Richland, Stoddard Co., MO - Ballard, Dan 54 IL IL IL, Mary 53 MO TN TN, John 24 MO, Erma 22 MO, Delmar 19 MO*

More About DANIEL "DAN" L. BALLARD:
Burial: Essex Cemetery, Stoddard Co., MO

More About MARY FRANCES GULLEY:
Burial: Essex Cemetery, Stoddard Co., MO

Children of DANIEL BALLARD and MARY GULLEY are:

      i.   *CARRIE[5] BALLARD, b. Feb 1900, Stoddard Co., MO; d. Aft. 1948; m. HUX.*
      ii.   *VELMA BALLARD, b. 1904, Stoddard Co., MO.*
      iii. *JOHN BALLARD, b. 15 Jul 1905, Stoddard Co., MO; d. 02 Feb 1940, Liberty, Stoddard Co., MO.*

            Notes for JOHN BALLARD:
            Source: Stoddard County Missouri Death Certificate

            More About JOHN BALLARD:
            Burial: Essex Cemetery, Stoddard Co., MO

      iv. *ERMA BALLARD, b. 1907, Stoddard Co., MO; d. Aft. 1848; m. ALLEN.*
      v.   *EARL BALLARD, b. 1909, Stoddard Co., MO.*
      vi. *DELMER BALLARD, b. 1912, Stoddard Co., MO; d. Aft. 1948.*
      vii. *G. H. BALLARD, d. Aft. 1848.*

Generation No. 3

4. *VERNON[5] BLACK (ANGELINE[4] BALLARD, NATHAN[3], JOHN[2], NATHAN[1] BALLARD/BULLARD) was born 20 Oct 1887 in Wayne Co., IL, and died 29 Dec 1930 in Stoddard Co., MO. He married LULA TUCKER. She was born Abt. 1891 in MO, and died Aft. 1940.*

Notes for VERNON BLACK:
Source: 1930 Greene County Arkansas Federal Census Records

** 1930 - Black, Vernon 42 IN IN IN, Lula 39 MO, Evylin 17 AR, Eunice 6 AR, Elvie 5 AR, Vena J. 1 8/12 AR*

Notes for LULA TUCKER:
Source: 1940 Stoddard County Missouri Federal Census Records

** 1940 - Living in Essex, Stoddard Co., MO - Black, Lulu 49, Eunice J 17*

Children of VERNON BLACK and LULA TUCKER are:
      i.   *EVELYN[6] BLACK, b. Abt. 1913, AR; d. Aft. 1930.*
      ii.   *EUNICE BLACK, b. Abt. 1927, AR; d. Aft. 1940.*
      iii. *ELVIE BLACK, b. Abt. 1925, AR; d. Aft. 1930.*
      iv. *VINA BLACK, b. Abt. 1928, AR; d. Aft. 1930.*
      v.   *BONNIE J. BLACK, b. Abt. 1929, MO; m. ROBERT D. ARNESEN, 12 Mar 1949, Lansing, Ingham Co., MI; b. Abt. 1928, Flint, Genesee Co., MI.*

5. HENRY ROY[5] BLACK (ANGELINE[4] BALLARD, NATHAN[3], JOHN[2], NATHAN[1] BALLARD/BULLARD) *was born 19 Sep 1890 in Wayne Co., IL, and died 13 Dec 1969 in Paragould, Greene Co., AR. He married* LINNIE SKAGGS. *She was born 1897 in IN, and died 1971 in AR.*

Notes for HENRY ROY BLACK:
Source: Greene County Arkansas Certificate of Death

More About LINNIE SKAGGS:
Burial: Greene County Memorial Gardens Cemetery, Paragould, Greene Co., AR

Child of HENRY BLACK *and* LINNIE SKAGGS *is:*

> i. FREEDA WINONA[6] BLACK, *b. 24 Jan 1929; d. 07 Mar 2020, Paragould, Greene Co., AR; m.* GEORGE EDWARD THIEL; *b. 30 Oct 1924; d. 11 Nov 1975.*
>
> > *More About* FREEDA WINONA BLACK:
> > *Burial: Linwood Cemetery, Paragould, Greene Co., AR*
> >
> > *More About* GEORGE EDWARD THIEL:
> > *Burial: Linwood Cemetery, Paragould, Greene Co., AR*

6. ERNEST PEARL[5] BLACK (ANGELINE[4] BALLARD, NATHAN[3], JOHN[2], NATHAN[1] BALLARD/BULLARD) *was born 09 Sep 1895 in Wayne Co., IL, and died 04 Jan 1970 in Essex, Stoddard Co., MO. He married* ADA MAY. *She was born 30 Apr 1898, and died 18 Feb 1933.*

More About ERNEST PEARL BLACK:
Burial: Essex Cemetery, Stoddard Co., MO

More About ADA MAY:
Burial: Essex Cemetery, Stoddard Co., MO

Children of ERNEST BLACK *and* ADA MAY *are:*

> i. LESTER MELVIN[6] BLACK, *b. 01 Jul 1918, Stoddard Co., MO; d. 02 Jun 1987; m.* EDNA LEE ADKISSON; *b. 28 Oct 1917, Roger Mills Co., OK; d. 02 Aug 1986, OK city, Oklahoma Co., OK.*
>
> > *More About* LESTER MELVIN BLACK:
> > *Burial: Sunny Lane Cemetery, Del City, Oklahoma Co., OK*
>
> ii. DORRIS LAVONNE BLACK, *b. 25 Dec 1930, Stoddard Co., MO; d. 09 Feb 1931, Stoddard Co., MO.*

7. LELAND RALPH[5] BLACK (ANGELINE[4] BALLARD, NATHAN[3], JOHN[2], NATHAN[1] BALLARD/BULLARD) *was born 31 Jan 1905 in Stoddard Co., MO, and died 03 Sep 1979 in Allegan Co., MO. He married* GEORGIA BRADHAM *29 Nov 1924 in Essex, Stoddard Co., MO. She was born 16 Aug 1907 in Stoddard Co., MO, and died 17 Feb 1994 in Oakland Co., MI.*

Notes for LELAND RALPH BLACK:
Source: 1930 Greene County Arkansas Federal Census Records

** 1930 - Living in Main Shore, Greene Co., AR - Black, Ralph 25 MO, Georgia 25 MO, Lilan J 4 MO, Charles J 1 MO*

More About LELAND RALPH BLACK:
Burial: Ottawa Park Cemetery, Clarkston, Oakland Co., MI

More About GEORGIA BRADHAM:
Burial: Ottawa Park Cemetery, Clarkston, Oakland Co., MI

Children of LELAND BLACK and GEORGIA BRADHAM are:

> i.   LELAND RALPH[6] BLACK, JR., b. 30 Sep 1925, Stoddard Co., MO; d. 13 Aug 2000, Mesa Co., CO; m. ELAINE GOODWIN; b. 18 Jan 1920, ID; d. 01 Jun 1983, Salt Lake Co., UT.
>
> *More About ELAINE GOODWIN:*
>
> *Burial: Wasatch Lawn Memorial Park, Millcreek, Salt Lake Co., UT*
>
> ii.   CHARLES G. BLACK, b. 01 Dec 1928, Stoddard Co., MO; d. 22 Nov 1999, Lawrence Co., AR; m. JULIA A.; b. 15 Nov 1931; d. 30 Aug 2000.
>
> *More About CHARLES G. BLACK:*
>
> *Burial: Masonic Cemetery, Pocahontas, Randolph Co., AR*

8. PAULINE[5] BLACK (ANGELINE[4] BALLARD, NATHAN[3], JOHN[2], NATHAN[1] BALLARD/BULLARD) *was born 16 Aug 1909 in Stoddard Co., MO, and died 22 Mar 1990 in Johnson Co., IL. She married PAUL CULBERTSON 19 Jul 1929 in Charleston, Mississippi Co., MO.*

Notes for PAULINE BLACK:

Source: 1940 Franklin County Illinois Federal Census Records

** 1940 - Living in Benton, Franklin Co., IL - Culbertson, Pauline 30 divorced MO, Doyle E 9 MO, Betty J 1 MO, Black, Charles brother 39 MO, Marie sister in law 43 OH*

More About PAULINE BLACK:

Burial: Cana Cemetery, Goreville, Johnson Co., IL

Children of PAULINE BLACK and PAUL CULBERTSON are:

> i.   DOYLE E.[6] CULBERTSON, b. Abt. 1931, MO; d. Aft. 1940.
> ii.   BETTY J. CULBERTSON, b. Abt. 1937, MO; d. Aft. 1940.

Reuben Ballard

Generation No. 1

1. REUBEN[1] BALLARD *was born Abt. 1800 in NC, and died 1848. He married (1)* BARBARY SNIDER *25 Sep 1825 in Rowan Co., NC. She was born Abt. 1805. He married (2)* MARY "POLLY" GULLET *19 Jul 1828 in Rowan Co., NC. She was born Abt. 1800 in IN, and died 1886.*

Notes for REUBEN BALLARD:
Sources: 1840 Bartholomew County Indiana Federal Census Records, Kriston Robinson (rootbound@mindspring.com), Georgia Walker (LeeWorld@aol.com), Marriage CD# 4

** 1840 - Reuben Bullard - Rock Creek, Bartholomew, IN -*
Free White Persons - Males - Under 5 - 2, Free White Persons - Males - 5 thru 9 - 1, Free White Persons - Males - 10 thru 14 - 1, Free White Persons - Males - 30 thru 39 - 1, Free White Persons - Females - Under 5 - 2, Free White Persons - Females - 5 thru 9 - 2, Free White Persons - Females - 20 thru 29   - 1, Persons Employed in Agriculture - 1, Free White Persons - Under 20 - 8, Free White Persons - 20 thru 49   - 2, Total Free White Persons 10

Notes for MARY "POLLY" GULLET:
Source: 1850-1860 Jennings County Indiana Federal Census Records

** 1850 - Living in Rock Creek, Bartholomew Co., IN - Ballard, Mary 39 NC, Spencer 20 NC, Luisa 18 NC, Martha F 12 IN, Caroline 16 IN, Van Buran 8 IN, Isabel 7 IN, Huldah A 5 IN, Ephran 3 IN*
** 1860 - Living in Geneva, Jennings Co., IN - Ballard, Mary 45 NC, Isabell 15 IN, Hulda Ann 14 IN, Ephraim D. 11 NC, Isaac W 2 NC, Spencer 30 NC*

Children of REUBEN BALLARD *and* MARY GULLET *are:*

2.	i.	SPENCER[2] BALLARD, b. 1830, NC; d. 1902, Mercer Co., MO.
3.	ii.	LOUISA BALLARD, b. 1832, NC; d. 26 Jun 1889.
4.	iii.	CAROLINE BALLARD, b. 13 Jan 1836, Decatur Co., IN; d. 25 Jan 1921, Putnam Co., MO.
5.	iv.	VAN BURSON BALLARD, b. 05 Aug 1839, Bartholomew Co., IN; d. 16 Sep 1916, Jackson Co., IN.
6.	v.	MARTHA JANE BALLARD, b. 07 Mar 1839, IN; d. 08 Oct 1918, Tulsa OK.
7.	vi.	EPHRAIM BALLARD, b. 10 Apr 1844, IN; d. 11 Jan 1921, Jackson Co., IN.
	vii.	ISABEL BALLARD, b. 1845, IN; d. Aft. 1860.
	viii.	HULDA ANN BALLARD, b. 1846, IN; d. Aft. 1860.

Generation No. 2

2. SPENCER[2] BALLARD (REUBEN[1]) *was born 1830 in NC, and died 1902 in Mercer Co., MO. He married (1)* MARY ANN DYER *11 Jun 1852 in Bartholomew Co., IN. She was born Abt. 1830, and died Aft. 1860. He married (2)* MARGARET MORGAN *12 Dec 1861 in Putnam Co., MO. She was born 1846 in IA, and died 1894 in Princeton, Mercer Co., MO.*

Notes for SPENCER BALLARD:
Source: 1870, 1880 Putnam County Missouri Federal Census records, 1900 Mercer County Missouri Federal Census Records, Vince Leibowitz (vpltz@vzinet.com), Kriston Robinson (rootbound@mindspring.com)
** 1870 - Living in Putnam Co., MO - Ballard, Spencer 40 NC, Margaret 23 MO, Ephraim 18 IA, Isaac W. 11 IN, Deniza W. 7 IA, Jon W 5 IA, Benj. F 3 MO, Leroy V. 1 MO*
** 1880 - Living in Putnam Co., MO - Ballard, Spencer 50, Margaret E 34, David E 23, Daniza A 17, John W 15, Benj F 13, Lefoy VB 11, Burrel C 9, Geo A 7, Mary I M 5*
** 1900 - Living in Princeton, Mercer Co., MO - Ballard, Frank - Nov 1866 MO NC MO, Rebecca - Feb 1873 MO*

MO MO, Emily M - May 1893 MO, Frank - May 1896 MO, Benjamin G - Mar 1898 MO, Rebecca B - Aug 1900 MO, Spencer - Sep 1830 wd grandfather.

More About SPENCER BALLARD:
Burial: Princeton Cemetery, Princeton, Mercer Co., MO

Marriage Notes for SPENCER BALLARD and MARY DYER:
Source: Bartholomew County Indiana Marriage Records Book C5 page 158

More About MARGARET MORGAN:
Burial: Princeton Cemetery, Princeton, Mercer Co., MO

Children of SPENCER BALLARD and MARY DYER are:
    i.   EPHRAIM³ BALLARD, b. 1853, IA; d. Aft. 1870.
    ii.   DAVID E. BALLARD, b. 1857; d. Aft. 1880.
    iii.   ISAAC W. BALLARD, b. 1859, IN; d. Aft. 1870.

Children of SPENCER BALLARD and MARGARET MORGAN are:

8.   iv.   DENISA ANN³ BALLARD, b. 20 Oct 1863, Putnam Co., MO; d. 20 May 1935, Savannah, Andrew Co., MO.
    v.   JOHN WILLIAM BALLARD, b. 06 Nov 1865, IA; d. 16 Apr 1939, Appanoose Co., IA; m. LEORA WALKER, 12 Oct 1898, Princeton, Mercer Co., MO; b. 08 Mar 1882, MO; d. 20 Jan 1910, Seymour, Wayne Co., IA.

    Notes for JOHN WILLIAM BALLARD:
    Source: Appanoose County Iowa Certificate of Death

    More About JOHN WILLIAM BALLARD:
    Burial: Southlawn Cemetery, Seymour, Wayne Co., IA

    More About LEORA WALKER:
    Burial: Southlawn Cemetery, Seymour, Wayne Co., IA

9.   vi.   BENJAMIN FRANKLIN BALLARD, b. 05 Nov 1866, Putnam Co., MO; d. 07 Jun 1943, Unionville, Putnam Co., MO.
    vii.   LEROY W. BALLARD, b. 1869, MO; d. Aft. 1880.
    viii.   BURREL CLINTON BALLARD, b. 12 Jun 1872, 23 June 1871 Putman Co., MO; d. 08 May 1922, Des Moines, Polk Co., IA; m. STELLA DINGWALL, 17 Dec 1912.

    Notes for BURREL CLINTON BALLARD:
    Source: Polk County Iowa Standard Certificate of Death

    More About BURREL CLINTON BALLARD:
    Burial: Southlawn Cemetery, Seymour, Wayne Co., IA

    ix.   GEORGE ALFRED BALLARD, b. 11 Feb 1874, Putnam Co., MO; d. 09 Mar 1943, Des Moines, Polk Co., IA; m. BIRDELLA MEEKER; b. 09 Nov 1877, MO; d. 06 Sep 1965, Des Moines, Polk Co., IA.

    Notes for GEORGE ALFRED BALLARD:
    Source: Iowa State Certificate of Death, Social Security Records

    More About GEORGE ALFRED BALLARD:
    Burial: Southlawn Cemetery, Seymour, Wayne Co., IA

More About BIRDELLA MEEKER:
Burial: Southlawn Cemetery, Seymour, Wayne Co., IA

    x. MARY INGRAM BALLARD, *b. 24 Feb 1876, Princeton, Mercer Co., MO; d. 26 Jan 1924, Bellair, Appanoose Co., IA; m. WADE SMITH.*

      Notes for MARY INGRAM BALLARD:
      Source: Appanoose County Iowa Certificate of Death

10. *xi.* SOLOMON LEVI BALLARD, *b. 17 Sep 1884, Princeton, Mercer Co., MO; d. 22 Apr 1955, Des Moines, Polk Co., IA.*

    xii. SARAH BALLARD, *b. 1881, Princeton, Mercer Co., MO; m. SAMUEL JOHNSON, 10 Nov 1898, Application - Princeton, Mercer Co., MO.*

      Notes for SARAH BALLARD:
      Source: Mercer County Missouri Marriage Application
      ** 1898 - Mercer Co., MO Marriage records - Spencer signed permission, as father - Sarah was 17 years old.*

3. LOUISA[2] BALLARD (REUBEN[1]) *was born 1832 in NC, and died 26 Jun 1889. She married BURREL PADGETT 08 Jun 1851 in Bartholomew Co., IN. He was born Abt. 1830, and died Aft. 1880.*

Notes for BURREL PADGETT:
Source: 1880 Putnam County Missouri Federal Census Records

** 1880 - Living in Sherman, Putnam Co., MO - Padget, Burrel 50, Louisa 49, Benjamin F 16, Joab 13, Isaac 11*

Marriage Notes for LOUISA BALLARD and BURREL PADGETT:
Source: Bartholomew County Indiana Marriage Records Book C5 page 74

Children of LOUISA BALLARD and BURREL PADGETT are:

    i. BENJAMIN F.[3] PADGETT, *b. 1864; d. Aft. 1880.*
    ii. JOAB PADGETT, *b. 1867; d. Aft. 1880.*
    iii. ISAAC PADGETT, *b. 1869; d. Aft. 1880.*

4. CAROLINE[2] BALLARD (REUBEN[1]) *was born 13 Jan 1836 in Decatur Co., IN, and died 25 Jan 1921 in Putnam Co., MO. She married GEORGE WASHINGTON ARNOLD 28 Jun 1860 in Jennings Co., IN. He was born 15 Mar 1833 in KY, and died 13 Aug 1870 in Decatur Co., IN.*

Notes for CAROLINE BALLARD:
Source: 1880 Putnam County Missouri Federal Census Records
** 1880 - Living in Sherman, Putnam Co., MO - Arnold, Caroline 38, Jennie 17, John 14, Charles E 12*

Notes for GEORGE WASHINGTON ARNOLD:
Source: 1870 Jennings County Indiana Federal Census Records
** 1870 - Living in Geneva, Jennings Co., IN - Arnold, George KY, 29 IN, Geni 7 IN, John 4 IN, Charles E 2 IN*

Marriage Notes for CAROLINE BALLARD and GEORGE ARNOLD:
Source: Jennings County Indiana Marriage Records book 6 page 102

Children of CAROLINE BALLARD and GEORGE ARNOLD are:
    i. JENNIE[3] ARNOLD, *b. 07 Sep 1862, IN; d. 25 Nov 1950, Seymour, Wayne Co., IA.*

11. *ii.* JOHN ARNOLD, b. 15 Mar 1866, Jennings Co., IN; d. 12 Jul 1953, Putnam Co., MO.
   iii. CHARLES E. ARNOLD, b. 1868, IN; d. Aft. 1880.

5. VAN BURSON[2] BALLARD (REUBEN[1]) was born 05 Aug 1839 in Bartholomew Co., IN, and died 16 Sep 1916 in Jackson Co., IN. He married MARGARET E. BOWEN. She was born 1839 in IN, and died 1896.

Notes for VAN BURSON BALLARD:
Source: Jackson County Indiana Certificate of Death, 1870 Jennings County Indiana Federal Census Records, 1880 Indiana Census Soundex, Kriston Robinson (rootbound@mindspring.com)

** 1870 - Living in Geneva, Jennings Co., IN - next door to his mother and siblings Vanberson Ballard 20 IN*
** 1880 - Living in Jennings Co., IN*

Children of VAN BALLARD and MARGARET BOWEN are:
   i. WILLIAM[3] BALLARD, b. 1866, IN.
12. *ii.* JAMES E. BALLARD, b. 1867, IN; d. 1940.
   iii. ROSA BALLARD, b. 1873, MO.
   iv. PRESTON BALLARD, b. 1865, MO.
   v. CHESTER BALLARD, b. 1867, MO.
   vi. JOHN BALLARD, b. 1880, IN.

6. MARTHA JANE[2] BALLARD (REUBEN[1]) was born 07 Mar 1839 in IN, and died 08 Oct 1918 in Tulsa OK. She married JOHN W. MORGASON 15 Jun 1856 in Bartholomew Co., IN. He was born Abt. 1835 in of Jefferson Co., IN.

Marriage Notes for MARTHA BALLARD and JOHN MORGASON:
Source: Bartholomew County Indiana Marriage Records Book C6 page 92

Children of MARTHA BALLARD and JOHN MORGASON are:
   i. WILLIAM H.[3] MORGASON, b. 1858, IN.
   ii. LAURA MORGASON, b. 1861, IN.
   iii. MARY MORGASON, b. 1864, MO.
   iv. MARGARET MORGASON, b. 1865, MO.
   v. LOUISA BELL MORGASON, b. 07 Aug 1868, Wayne Co Iowa.

7. EPHRAIM[2] BALLARD (REUBEN[1]) was born 10 Apr 1844 in IN, and died 11 Jan 1921 in Jackson Co., IN. He married (1) SUSAN S. TEMPLE 28 Aug 1879 in Jennings Co., IN. She was born 14 Jan 1859 in KY, and died 03 Mar 1923 in Marion Co., IN. He married (2) MARTHA BOWEN 02 Feb 1871 in Decatur Co., IN. She was born 17 Mar 1847, and died 11 Apr 1878.

Notes for EPHRAIM BALLARD:

Source: 1870-1880 Decatur County Indiana Federal Census Records, 1900-1920 Jackson County Indiana Federal Census Records, Kriston Robinson (rootbound@mindspring.com)

** 1870 - Living in Decatur Co., IN - Ballard, Ephraim 23 b. IN farm laborer (living with the Shera family)*
** 1880 - Living in Jackson, Decatur Co., IN - Ballard, Ephraim 33 IN NC NC, Susan 22 KY KY KY, Omy 7 (m) IN IN IN, William McCleary 12 step son IN IN IN*
** 1900 - Living in Vernon, Jackson Co., IN - Ballard, Ephraim - Apr 1844 MO VA VA, Susan S - Jan 1857 KY KY KY, John W - Mar 1884 IN , Verna - July 1887 IN*
** 1910 - Living in Jackson Co., IN - Ballard, Ephram 65 md 2x IN, Susan 51 md 1x - 4 children 3 living, Wesley 25 IN*
** 1920 - Living in Vernon, Jackson Co., IN - Ballard, Ephram 74 IN, Susan 63 KY*

More About EPHRAIM BALLARD:
Burial: Crothersville Cemetery, Crothersville, Jackson Co., IN

Marriage Notes for EPHRAIM BALLARD and SUSAN TEMPLE:
Source: Jennings County Indiana Marriage Records Book 8 page 463

More About MARTHA BOWEN:
Burial: Jackson twp. Mt. Olivet Cemetery. Decatur Co., IN

Marriage Notes for EPHRAIM BALLARD and MARTHA BOWEN:
Source: Decatur County Indiana Marriage Records Book J Page 498

Children of EPHRAIM BALLARD and SUSAN TEMPLE are:

i. LEOTA[3] BALLARD, b. 13 Jun 1880, IN; d. 20 Apr 1968, Indianapolis, Marion Co., IN; m. ELIJAH BESS; b. 08 Jul 1867, Jennings Co., IN; d. 25 Dec 1953, Indianapolis, Marion Co., IN.

Notes for LEOTA BALLARD:
Source: Marion County Indiana Certificate of Death

More About LEOTA BALLARD:
Burial: Crothersville Cemetery, Crothersville, IN

ii. JOHN WESLEY BALLARD, b. 06 Mar 1886, Jackson Co., IN; d. 26 Jul 1969; m. HATTIE LAURA ULRICH, 02 Sep 1915, Monona, Clayton Co., IA; b. 28 May 1893, Monona, Clayton Co., IA; d. 19 Feb 1984, Monona, Clayton Co., IA.

More About JOHN WESLEY BALLARD:
Burial: Monona, Clayton Co., IA

iii. VERNE F. BALLARD, b. 04 Jul 1888, Jackson Co., IN; d. 14 Sep 1958, Indianapolis, Marion Co., IN; m. WILLIAM FERMAN LLEWELLYN, 05 Oct 1907, IN; b. 27 Jun 1885, Jackson Co., IN; d. 09 Nov 1945, Indianapolis, Marion Co., IN.

Notes for VERNE F. BALLARD:
Source: Marion County Indiana Certificate of Death

Children of EPHRAIM BALLARD and MARTHA BOWEN are:

iv. OMER[3] BALLARD, b. 10 Aug 1872, Jackson Co., IN; d. 23 Nov 1921, Jackson Co., IN; m. ROSA RUDE; b. 13 Jul 1876, Jackson Co., IN; d. 04 Jun 1958, Marion Co., IN.

More About ROSA RUDE:
Burial: Uniontown Cemetery Jackson Co., IN

v. KEANE BALLARD, b. 1873; d. 26 Aug 1874.

More About KEANE BALLARD:
Burial: Jackson twp. Mt. Olivet Cemetery, Decatur Co., IN

vi. DAISY MAY BALLARD, b. 26 Aug 1875, Jennings Co., IN; d. 31 Oct 1877, Jennings Co., IN.

More About DAISY MAY BALLARD:
Burial: Jackson twp. Mt. Olivet Cemetery, Decatur Co., IN

Generation No. 3

8. DENISA ANN[3] BALLARD (SPENCER[2], REUBEN[1]) *was born 20 Oct 1863 in Putnam Co., MO, and died 20 May 1935 in Savannah, Andrew Co., MO. She married* HARLEY ALFRED COOK *20 Mar 1890 in Wayne Co., IA. He was born 18 Dec 1868 in Putnam Co., MO, and died 02 Mar 1932 in Gove Co., KS.*

Notes for DENISA ANN BALLARD:
Source: Andrew County Missouri Certificate of Death

More About DENISA ANN BALLARD:
Burial: Gove Cemetery, Gove Co., KS

More About HARLEY ALFRED COOK:
Burial: Gove Cemetery, Gove Co., KS

Children of DENISA BALLARD *and* HARLEY COOK *are:*

> i. LLOYD ALFRED[4] COOK, *b. 18 Jan 1891, Putnam Co., MO; d. 06 Feb 1955, Sedgwick Co., KS; m.* HAZEL ANN MYERS; *b. 08 Nov 1895, Gove Co., KS; d. 12 Nov 1977, Gove Co., KS.*
>
> > *More About* LLOYD ALFRED COOK:
> > *Burial: Wichita Park Cemetery and Mausoleum, Sedgwick Co., KS*
> >
> > *More About* HAZEL ANN MYERS:
> > *Burial: Wichita Park Cemetery and Mausoleum, Sedgwick Co., KS*
>
> ii. ESSIE M. COOK, *b. 10 Feb 1892, Unionville, Putnam Co., MO; d. 11 Apr 1967, Finney Co., KS; m.* CHARLES ORTEN; *b. 20 Feb 1892, Harrison Co., MO; d. 1944, Gove Co., KS.*
>
> > *More About* ESSIE M. COOK:
> > *Burial: Gove Cemetery, Gove Co., KS*
> >
> > *More About* CHARLES ORTEN:
> > *Burial: Gove Cemetery, Gove Co., KS*

9. BENJAMIN FRANKLIN[3] BALLARD (SPENCER[2], REUBEN[1]) *was born 05 Nov 1866 in Putnam Co., MO, and died 07 Jun 1943 in Unionville, Putnam Co., MO. He married* REBECCA COOK, *daughter of* ISAAC COOK *and* EMMA REDDING. *She was born 08 Feb 1873 in Putnam Co., MO, and died 12 Aug 1929 in Sherman, Putnam Co., MO.*

Notes for BENJAMIN FRANKLIN BALLARD:
Source: 1900 Mercer County Missouri Federal Census Records, 1910 - 1920 Putnam County Missouri Federal Census Records, 1930 Wayne County Iowa Federal Census Records

** 1900 - Living in Princeton, Mercer Co., MO - Ballard, Frank - Nov 1866 MO NC MO, Rebecca - Feb 1873 MO MO MO, Emily M - May 1893 MO, Frank - May 1896 MO, Benjamin G - Mar 1898 MO, Rebecca B - Aug 1900 MO, Spencer - Sep 1830 wd grandfather.*
** 1910 - Living in Sherman, Putnam Co., MO - Ballard, Benjamin F 43 MO, Rebecca 36 MO, Emma M 16 MO, Frank 15 MO, Benjamin 11 MO, R B 9 MO, Lovy 7 MO, Letha 5 MO, Eva M 3 MO, baby 3/12 MO*
** 1920 - Living in Sherman, Putnam Co., MO - Ballard, Frank B 52 MO IN MO, Rebecca 47 MO IN MO, Frank 23 MO, RR 19 MO, Louvie 17 MO, Letha M 15 MO, Eva 12 MO, Clifford 10 MO, Ines 7 MO, Essie 5 MO*
** 1930 - Living in Walnut, Wayne Co., IA - Ballard, Benjamin F 63 MO IN MO, Essie 17 MO, Inez 18 MO*

More About BENJAMIN FRANKLIN BALLARD:
Burial: Union Church Cemetery, Unionville, Putnam Co., MO

More About REBECCA COOK:
Burial: Union Church Cemetery, Unionville, Putnam Co., MO

Children of BENJAMIN BALLARD and REBECCA COOK are:

   i. EMILY MAE⁴ BALLARD, b. May 1893, Mercer Co., MO; d. 1967; m. C. EARNEST BETTIS; b. 1892; d. 1959.

    More About EMILY MAE BALLARD:
    Burial: Corydon Cemetery, Corydon, Wayne Co., IA

    More About C. EARNEST BETTIS:
    Burial: Corydon Cemetery, Corydon, Wayne Co., IA

13. ii. FRANK BALLARD, b. 27 May 1896, Princeton, Mercer Co., MO; d. 03 Feb 1981, Des Moines Co., IA.

14. iii. BENJAMIN GUY BALLARD, b. 02 Apr 1898, Mercer Co., MO; d. 20 Jan 1962.

15. iv. R. B. BALLARD, b. 14 Mar 1900, Mercer Co., MO; d. 18 Apr 1979, Centerville, Appanoose Co., IA.

   v. LOVIE BALLARD, b. 10 Aug 1902, Princeton, Mercer Co., MO; d. 21 May 1980, Los Angeles Co., CA; m. WILBUR THOMPSON; b. 10 Oct 1896, Wayne Co., IA; d. 23 Dec 1978, Los Angeles Co., CA.

    Notes for WILBUR THOMPSON:
    Source: 1930 Wayne County Iowa Federal Census Records, 1940 Los Angeles County California Federal Census Records

    ** 1930 - Living in Corydon, Wayne Co., IA - Thompson, Wilbur 33 IA, Lovey 27 MO, Neal 9 MO, Gilfred grandfather 83 wd IL*
    ** 1940 - Living in Los Angeles Co., CA - Thompson, Wilbur 43, Lovie 37 MO, Neil 19 MO*

   vi. LETHA BALLARD, b. 13 Aug 1904, Princeton, Mercer Co., MO; d. 28 Jul 1963, Davenport, Scott Co., IA; m. FRANK HEILMAN, 07 Jun 1930, Davenport Co., IA; b. 28 Sep 1898, Wayne Co., IA; d. 18 Dec 1988, Davenport, Scott Co., IA.

    More About LETHA BALLARD:
    Burial: Davenport Memorial Park, Davenport, Scott Co., IA

    More About FRANK HEILMAN:
    Burial: Davenport Memorial Park, Davenport, Scott Co., IA

   vii. EVA M. BALLARD, b. 1907, Putnam Co., MO; d. 20 Mar 1971; m. EMMETT EARL MEHLS; b. 21 Sep 1895, Putnam Co., MO; d. 28 May 1973, Unionville, Putnam Co., MO.

    More About EVA M. BALLARD:
    Burial: Unionville Cemetery, Putnam Co., MO

    More About EMMETT EARL MEHLS:
    Burial: Unionville Cemetery, Putnam Co., MO

16. viii. CLIFFORD BALLARD, b. 07 Jul 1909, Putnam Co., MO; d. 06 Sep 1975, Carroll Co., AR.

   ix. INES BALLARD, b. 09 Feb 1912, Putnam Co., MO; d. 25 Aug 1989, Des Moines, Polk Co., IA; m. (1) DELMUS HOMER KING; b. 25 Mar 1906, Clay Co., TN; d. 11 Oct 1989, Des Moines, Polk Co., IA; m. (2) ENNIS.

More About INES BALLARD:
Burial: Avon Cemetery, Des Moines, Polk Co., IA

More About DELMUS HOMER KING:
Burial: Avon Cemetery, Des Moines, Polk Co., IA

     x.   ESSIE BALLARD, *b. 03 Jun 1914, Putnam Co., MO; d. 03 May 2008, Scott Co., IA; m.* HANS HENRY 'KOEHER, *29 Apr 1937, Davenport Co., IA; b. 20 Nov 1911, Davenport, Scott Co., IA; d. 10 Jan 1971, Davenport, Scott Co., IA.*

        More About ESSIE BALLARD:
        Burial: Davenport Memorial Park, Davenport, Scott Co., IA

        More About HANS HENRY 'KOEHER:
        Burial: Davenport Memorial Park, Davenport, Scott Co., IA

10. SOLOMON LEVI[3] BALLARD (SPENCER[2], REUBEN[1]) *was born 17 Sep 1884 in Princeton, Mercer Co., MO, and died 22 Apr 1955 in Des Moines, Polk Co., IA. He married (1)* EMMA L. *Bef. 1906. She was born 1887, and died Aft. 1910. He married (2)* LAURA MYRTLE KNOWLES *Bef. 1910. She was born 30 Dec 1877 in Putnam Co., MO, and died 21 Aug 1971 in Des Moines, Polk Co., IA. He married (3)* DELPHIA LUNIE MOORE *22 Jun 1927 in Des Moines, Polk Co., MO. She was born 15 Dec 1899 in Appanoose Co., IA, and died 21 May 1931 in Oakdale, Johnson Co., IA.*

Notes for SOLOMON LEVI BALLARD:
Source: WWI Draft Registration Cards, WWII Draft Registration Cards, Vince Leibowitz (vpitz@vzinet.com), 1910 Gove County Kansas Federal Census Records, 1920-1930 Appanoose County Iowa Federal Census Records, 1925 Appanoose County Iowa State Census Records

** 1910 - Living in Gove, Gove Co., KS - Ballard, Sollie L 24 MO IN MO, Emma L 23 MO, Carrie C 4 MO, Louise S 3 IA*
** 1917 - WWI Draft Registration - married to Myrtle Laura, living in Appanoose Co., IA*
** 1920 - Living in Bellair, Appanoose Co., IA - Ballard, S L 35 MO, Myrtle 32 MO, Carrie C 14 MO, Seattle L 12 MO, Margaret A 7 MO, Wauneta L 5 IA, Levi 3 2/12 IA, Dorothy D 1 11/12 IA*
** 1925 - Living in Pleasant, Appanoose Co., IA - Ballard, Solomon L 39 Nativity MO Father Spencer Ballard b IN, Mother Margaret Morgan b. MO Carrie 19, Louise 17, Margaret 12, Lorna 10, Levi 8, Deloris 6, Nilu 4*
** 1930 - Living in Pleasant, Appanoose Co., IA - Ballard, Solomon 44 MO IN MO, Delphia 30 IA IA IA, Juanita 15 IA MO IA, Levi 14 IA, Delores 11 IA, Nila 9 IA, Marcella 7 IA, Helen 9/12 IA*
** 1942 - Draft Registration - Residence - Des Moines Polk Co., IA*

More About LAURA MYRTLE KNOWLES:
Burial: Southlawn Cemetery, Seymour, Wayne Co., IA

More About DELPHIA LUNIE MOORE:
Burial: Pleasant Hill Cemetery, Cincinnati, Appanoose Co., ID

Children of SOLOMON BALLARD *and* EMMA L. *are:*

     i.   CARRIE C.[4] BALLARD, *b. 1906, MO; d. Aft. 1920.*
    ii.   LOUISE SEATTLE BALLARD, *b. 17 Feb 1907, 2/7 Seymour Co Wayne Co IA; d. 27 Jul 1997, Centerville, Appanoose Co., IA; m.* CHARLES BURKHISER; *b. 28 Oct 1890, Appanoose Co., IA; d. 31 Jul 1970, IA.*

        More About LOUISE SEATTLE BALLARD:
        Burial: Pleasant Hill Cemetery, Cincinnati, Appanoose Co., IA

More About CHARLES BURKHISER:
Burial: Livingston Cemetery, Cincinnati, Appanoose Co., IA

Children of SOLOMON BALLARD and LAURA KNOWLES are:

 iii. MARGARET A.[4] BALLARD, b. 1913, MO; d. Aft. 1925.
 iv. LAURA JAUNITA BALLARD, b. 26 May 1914, Seymour, Poke Co., IA; d. 18 Jul 1999; m. COBURN.

   Notes for LAURA JAUNITA BALLARD:
   Source: Social Security Records

 v. LEVI BALLARD, b. 1915, IA; d. Aft. 1930.
 vi. DELORES BALLARD, b. 20 Apr 1918, IA; d. 03 Jan 1992; m. ADRON LEE CARTER; b. 12 Jan 1915, Oskaloosa, Mahaska Co., IA; d. 03 Mar 1989, Polk Co., IA.

   More About DELORES BALLARD:
   Burial: Highland Memory Gardens Cemetery, Des Moines, Polk Co., IA

   More About ADRON LEE CARTER:
   Burial: Highland Memory Gardens Cemetery, Des Moines, Polk Co., IA

 vii. NAYLA BALLARD, b. 1921, IA; d. Aft. 1930.
 viii. MARCELLA BALLARD, b. 1923, IA; d. Aft. 1930.
 ix. ORA MARION BALLARD, b. 06 Jun 1924; d. 25 Oct 1996.

   More About ORA MARION BALLARD:
   Burial: Southlawn Cemetery, Seymour, Wayne Co., IA

Children of SOLOMON BALLARD and DELPHIA MOORE are:

 x. FREDA IRENE[4] BALLARD, b. 10 Feb 1928, Appanoose Co., IA; d. 10 Feb 1928, Appanoose Co., IA.

   More About FREDA IRENE BALLARD:
   Burial: Pleasant Hill Cemetery, Cincinnati, Appanoose Co., ID

 xi. HELEN EVELYN BALLARD, b. 11 Jul 1929, Appanoose Co., IA; d. 25 May 2012, AR; m. SMITH.

   Notes for HELEN EVELYN BALLARD:
   Source: Appanoose County Iowa Delayed Birth Certificate

   More About HELEN EVELYN BALLARD:
   Burial: Highland Memory Gardens Cemetery, Des Moines, Polk Co., IA

 xii. PHRONIA ETHEL BALLARD, b. 04 Oct 1930, Des Moines, Polk Co., IA; d. 25 May 1931, MO.

   More About PHRONIA ETHEL BALLARD:
   Burial: Pleasant Hill Cemetery, Cincinnati, Appanoose co., IA

11. JOHN[3] ARNOLD (CAROLINE[2] BALLARD, REUBEN[1]) was born 15 Mar 1866 in Jennings Co., IN, and died 12 Jul 1953 in Putnam Co., MO. He married MARY BELLE COOK. She was born 1868 in MO, and died 21 Feb 1933 in MO.

Notes for JOHN ARNOLD:

Source: 1900 Putnam County Missouri Federal Census Records, 1920 Putnam County Missouri Federal Census Records
** 1900 - Living in Sherman, Putnam Co., MO - Arnold, John - Mar 1866 IN IN IN, Mary B - Apr 1868 - 7 children 7 living MO IL MO, George W - Mar 1887 MO, Lola M - Jan 1889 MO, Phoeba L - Nov 1890 MO, Isaac O - Oct 1892 MO, Lester O - May 1895 IA, Alma E - Apr 1897 MO, Charley C - May 1899*
** 1920 - Living in Sherman, Putnam Co., MO - Arnold, John 58 IN , Merry B 52 MO, George 32 MO, Charlie 20 MO, Verda 12 , Annie 9*

Children of JOHN ARNOLD and MARY COOK are:

    i.   LOLA M.[4] ARNOLD, b. Jan 1889, MO; d. Aft. 1900.
   ii.   PHOEBA L. ARNOLD, b. Nov 1890, MO; d. Aft. 1900.
  iii.   ISAAC O. ARNOLD, b. Oct 1892, MO; d. Aft. 1900.
  iv.   LESTER O. ARNOLD, b. May 1895, IA; d. Aft. 1900.
   v.   ALMA E. ARNOLD, b. Apr 1897, MO; d. Aft. 1900.
  vi.   CHARLEY C. ARNOLD, b. May 1899, MO; d. Aft. 1900.

12. JAMES E.[3] BALLARD (VAN BURSON[2], REUBEN[1]) was born 1867 in IN, and died 1940. He married ALABAMA EVERETT. She was born 1868, and died 1934.

Child of JAMES BALLARD and ALABAMA EVERETT is:
17.   i.   CHARLES W.[4] BALLARD, b. 1890; d. 1962.

Generation No. 4

13. FRANK[4] BALLARD (BENJAMIN FRANKLIN[3], SPENCER[2], REUBEN[1]) was born 27 May 1896 in Princeton, Mercer Co., MO, and died 03 Feb 1981 in Des Moines Co., IA. He married FLOY A. HAMLIN. She was born 28 Sep 1898 in Putnam Co., MO, and died 29 Jul 1973 in Scott Co., IA.

Notes for FRANK BALLARD:
Source: 1930-1940 Putnam County Missouri Federal Census Records, Social Security Records
** 1930 - Living in Sherman, Putnam Co., MO - Ballard, Frank 33 MO, Floy A 31 MO, Ronald B 9 MO*
** 1940 - Living in Davenport, Scott Co., IA - Ballard, Frank 43 MO, Floy 41 MO*

Notes for FLOY A. HAMLIN:
Source: Social Security Records

Child of FRANK BALLARD and FLOY HAMLIN is:

    i.   RONALD B.[5] BALLARD, b. 27 Mar 1921, Sherman, Putnam Co., MO; d. 14 Nov 1971, Davenport, Scott Co., IA; m. VIVIAN ALLENE THOMPSON, 27 Sep 1938, Davenport, Scott Co., IA; b. 27 Sep 1917, Rock Island Co., IL; d. 19 Dec 1964, Davenport, Scott Co., IA.

14. BENJAMIN GUY[4] BALLARD (BENJAMIN FRANKLIN[3], SPENCER[2], REUBEN[1]) was born 02 Apr 1898 in Mercer Co., MO, and died 20 Jan 1962. He married ETHEL M.. She was born 19 Jul 1903, and died 12 Mar 1983.

More About BENJAMIN GUY BALLARD:
Burial: Unionville Cemetery, Putnam Co., MO

More About ETHEL M.:
Burial: Unionville Cemetery, Putnam Co., MO

Child of BENJAMIN BALLARD and ETHEL M. is:

i. ILA JEAN[5] BALLARD, b. 23 Aug 1928, Putnam Co., MO; d. 27 Jul 2019, Boone Co., MO; m. MELVIN CLEO WEBBER; b. 20 Sep 1927; d. 18 Jan 2008.

More About ILA JEAN BALLARD:
Burial: Unionville Cemetery, Putnam Co., MO

More About MELVIN CLEO WEBBER:
Burial: Unionville Cemetery, Putnam Co., MO

15. R. B.[4] BALLARD (BENJAMIN FRANKLIN[3], SPENCER[2], REUBEN[1]) was born 14 Mar 1900 in Mercer Co., MO, and died 18 Apr 1979 in Centerville, Appanoose Co., IA. He married NORA ROBBINS. She was born 07 Nov 1908 in Unionville, Putnam Co., MO, and died 11 Oct 1994 in Unionville, Putnam Co., MO.

Notes for R. B. BALLARD:
Source: 1930 Putnam County Missouri Federal Census Records, WWI & WWII Draft Cards
* 1930 - Living in Union, Putnam Co., MO - Robbins, James E 42, Lula H 41 MO, Nora B Ballard 21 dau MO, R. B Ballard, son in law 29 MO
* 1940-1947 - Registration card - He uses initials only. R B Ballard, living in Unionville, Putnam MO, 41 b. Mercer Co., Date of Birth 14 Mar 1900 MO. Nora Ruth Ballard of Unionville MO self employed.

More About R. B. BALLARD:
Burial: Unionville Cemetery, Putnam Co., MO

More About NORA ROBBINS:
Burial: Unionville Cemetery, Putnam Co., MO

Child of R. BALLARD and NORA ROBBINS is:

i. JAMES FRANKLIN[5] BALLARD, b. 19 Aug 1929, Putnam Co., MO; d. 19 Jan 2014, Des Moines, Polk Co., IA; m. NELLADEAN BALDOCK, 05 Dec 1954; b. 27 Feb 1934, Unionville, Putnam Co., MO; d. 08 Sep 2014, Appanoose Co., IA.

More About JAMES FRANKLIN BALLARD:
Burial: Unionville Cemetery, Putnam Co., MO

More About NELLADEAN BALDOCK:
Burial: Unionville Cemetery, Putnam Co., MO

16. CLIFFORD[4] BALLARD (BENJAMIN FRANKLIN[3], SPENCER[2], REUBEN[1]) was born 07 Jul 1909 in Putnam Co., MO, and died 06 Sep 1975 in Carroll Co., AR. He married (1) LUCILLE DIANA AYOTTE. She was born 13 Mar 1910 in Quebec, Canada, and died 01 Dec 1993 in Des Moines Co., IA. He married (2) FLORENCE MARY CORE 21 Dec 1929 in Kniffin, Wayne Co., IA. She was born 1909 in IA, and died 29 Jun 1962.

Notes for CLIFFORD BALLARD:
Source: 1930 Putnam County Missouri Federal Census Records

* 1930 - Living in Sherman, Putnam Co., MO - Ballard, Florence 21 IA

More About CLIFFORD BALLARD:
Burial: Aspen Grove Cemetery, Burlington, Des Moines Co., IA

More About LUCILLE DIANA AYOTTE:
Burial: Pleasant Point Cemetery, Henry Co., IA

More About FLORENCE MARY CORE:

Burial: Aspen Grove Cemetery, Burlington, Des Moines Co., IA

Children of CLIFFORD BALLARD and FLORENCE CORE are:

> i.   SHIRLEY VIRGINIA[5] BALLARD, b. 01 Mar 1932, Putnam Co., MO; d. 11 Aug 2002, Des Moines Co., IA; m. (1) LOUIS A. PRICE; b. 11 Feb 1931, Maries Co., MO; d. 01 Jan 1996, Des Moines, Polk Co., IA; m. (2) LLOYD WILLIAM BROCKWAY; b. 21 Jun 1927, Des Moines Co., IA; d. 25 Mar 1981, Burlington, Des Moines Co., IA.
>
>   *More About SHIRLEY VIRGINIA BALLARD:*
>   *Burial: Aspen Grove Cemetery, Burlington, Des Moines Co., IA*
>
>   *More About LOUIS A. PRICE:*
>   *Burial: Aspen Grove Cemetery, Burlington, Des Moines Co., IA*
>
>   *More About LLOYD WILLIAM BROCKWAY:*
>   *Burial: Burlington Memorial Park, Burlington, Des Moines Co., IA*
>
> ii.   PATSY RUTH BALLARD, b. 28 Aug 1933, Putnam Co., MO; d. 25 Apr 1995; m. DONALD LEE LEASURE; b. 09 Jul 1932; d. 19 Jul 1976.
>
>   *More About PATSY RUTH BALLARD:*
>   *Burial: Aspen Grove Cemetery, Burlington, Des Moines Co., IA*
>
>   *More About DONALD LEE LEASURE:*
>   *Burial: Aspen Grove Cemetery, Burlington, Des Moines Co., IA*
>
> iii.   ROSEMARY ANN BALLARD, b. 11 Jul 1946, Burlington, Des Moines Co., IA; d. 18 Apr 2018, Burlington, Des Moines Co., IA; m. ANTONIO L. HARMON, 06 Aug 1982, Burlington, Des Moines Co., IA; b. 29 Mar 1941, San Miguel Co., NM; d. 22 Dec 1996, Burlington, Des Moines Co., IA.
>
>   *More About ANTONIO L. HARMON:*
>   *Burial: Aspen Grove Cemetery, Burlington, Des Moines Co., IA*

17.   CHARLES W.[4] BALLARD (*JAMES E.[3], VAN BURSON[2], REUBEN[1]*) was born 1890, and died 1962. He married EDNA MAE COMPTON. She was born 1894, and died 1976.

Child of CHARLES BALLARD and EDNA COMPTON is:

> i.   EDSEL HUBERT[5] BALLARD, b. 09 Mar 1929, Indianapolis, Marion Co., IN.
>
>   *Notes for EDSEL HUBERT BALLARD:*
>
>   *Source: Indianapolis, Marion County Indiana Certificate of Birth*

Thompson R. Ballard

Generation No. 1

1. THOMPSON R.[1] BALLARD *was born 09 Dec 1809 in VA, and died 08 Apr 1886 in Shelby Co., MO. He married* CHARLOTTA WOOD *17 Mar 1831 in 3/14/ Madison Co., KY. She was born 10 May 1811 in NC, and died 16 Jul 1883 in Marion Co., MO.*

Notes for THOMPSON R. BALLARD:
Source: Records of Marriage of Madison County Kentucky for the Period of years 1785-1851 Inclusive pg 13, Marriage CD # 229, Madison County Kentucky Marriages 1823-1851 page 4, Jim Adams (Montanan2@att.net), Tara Perrien (taraperrien@hotmail.com), 1860-1880 Marion County Missouri Federal Census Records.

** 1831 - Records of Marriage, Madison Co., KY - Thompson Ballard married Charlotte Wood bond 3/14/ 1831 bond signed Huston Ballard*
** 1860 - Living in Marion Co, Union Twp, MO - Ballard, Thompson R. 48 Farmer VA, Charlotte 47 VA, Wm. N. 19 KY, John D. 25 KY, Mary E. 16*
** 1870 - Living in Marion Co, Union Twp, MO - Ballard, Thompson R. 52 (62?) KY, Charlotte 50 Keeping House TN next door to son John*
** 1880 - Living in Marion Co, Union Twp, MO - Ballard, Thompson R. 71 farmer VA VA VA Charlotta 68 NC NC NC*
** 1886 - Marion Co., MO Probate Files - Estate of Thompson R. Ballard deceased - Monday 1 Nov 1886 - Now at this day is filed the renunciation of J. W. Ballard and Elizabeth F. Dinwiddie children of said deceased of right to administer and now comes Richard N. Sharp and files application for letters of administration upon the estate of Thompson R. Ballard late of Marion Co. Missouri deceased accompanied with the affidavit required by law and the court being fully advised doth order that he enter into bond to the State of Missouri in the sum of five hundred and fifty dollars with two or more securities to be approved by the court considered for the faithful discharge of the duties of his office according to law. And now comes said Richard N. Sharp and files and submits to the court his official bond in the sum of five hundred and fifty dollars with William H. Raper and Cooper Lufton as securities. Upon examination thereof it is ordered that said bond be and the venue is hereby approved. Wherefore letters of administration of the good and chattles which were of said Thompson R. Ballard deceased are granted to the said Richard N. Sharp and Elwood Wholey and Lycurgus Lafon are appointed witnesses to accompany and aid said administrator in opening and examining the papers money and effects of said deceased and in making an inventory of the same.*

More About THOMPSON R. BALLARD:
Burial: Bethany Baptist Church Cemetery, Philadelphia, Marion Co., MO

More About CHARLOTTA WOOD:
Burial: Bethany Baptist Church Cemetery, Philadelphia, Marion Co., MO

Children of THOMPSON BALLARD *and* CHARLOTTA WOOD *are:*

2.	i.	JOHN DAVID[2] BALLARD, *b. 05 Mar 1835, Shelby Co., MO; d. 01 May 1880.*
3.	ii.	JAMES WILLIAM BALLARD, *b. 23 Nov 1838, Madison Co., KY; d. 18 Jan 1908.*
4.	iii.	ELIZABETH BALLARD, *b. 12 Jun 1833, KY; d. 08 Dec 1895, Marion Co., MO.*
5.	iv.	WILLIAM N. BALLARD, *b. 23 Mar 1843, KY; d. 10 Nov 1911.*

Generation No. 2

2. JOHN DAVID[2] BALLARD (THOMPSON R.[1]) *was born 05 Mar 1835 in Shelby Co., MO, and died 01 May 1880. He married* MARY ELLEN PEPPER, *daughter of* WILLIAM PEPPER *and* MARY. *She was born 09 Aug 1844 in MO, and died 30 Nov 1927 in Jackson twp., Shelby Co., MO.*

Notes for JOHN DAVID BALLARD:
Source: LDS-IGI, 1860-1870 Marion County Missouri Federal Census Records

** 1860 - Living in Union, Marion Co., MO - Ballard, Thompson R 48 farmer VA, Charlotte 47 VA, Wm W 12 KY, John D 25 KY, Mary E 16 MO*
** 1870 - Living in Marion Co., MO - John D. 32 KY, Mary 32 MO, Susan A. 10 MO, Thomas 7 MO, Sarah F. 6 MO, Wade D. 5, James W. 1 MO*

More About JOHN DAVID BALLARD:
Burial: Warren Cemetery, Warren, Marion Co., MO

Notes for MARY ELLEN PEPPER:
Source: 1880 Marion County Missouri Federal Census Records, Shelby County Missouri Death Certificate

** 1880 - Living in Union, Marion Co., MO - Ballard, Mary E MO KY KY, Susan A 19 MO KY MO, Thomas F 17 MO KY MO, Sarah F 15 MO KY MO, Wade D. 13 MO KY MO, James W 11 MO KY MO, Richard T 8 MO KY MO, Lottie B 7 MO KY MO, John D 5 MO KY MO, Charley L 2 MO KY MO, no name (male) 2/12 MO KY MO*

More About MARY ELLEN PEPPER:
Burial: Warren Cemetery, Warren, Marion Co., MO

Children of JOHN BALLARD and MARY PEPPER are:

      i.   SUSAN A.³ BALLARD, b. 10 Dec 1860, Marion Co., MO; d. 22 Oct 1926, Marion Co., MO; m. ENOCH A. PEPPER; b. 26 Aug 1860; d. 12 May 1946, Marion Co., MO.

         More About SUSAN A. BALLARD:
         Burial: Andrew Chapel Cemetery, Warren, Marion Co., MO

         More About ENOCH A. PEPPER:
         Burial: Andrew Chapel Cemetery, Warren, Marion Co., MO

     ii.   THOMAS S. BALLARD, b. 08 Dec 1862, Marion Co., MO; d. 08 Nov 1953, Shelby Co., MO; m. LULU BUFORD; b. 04 Jul 1872, Marion Co., MO; d. 06 Jun 1921, Miller twp., Marion Co., MO.

         Notes for THOMAS S. BALLARD:
         Source: 1900-1910 Marion County Missouri Federal Census Records, Shelby County Missouri Death Certificate
         ** 1900 - Living in Marion Co., MO - Ballard, Thomas - Dec 1863 MO KY MO, Lulu - July 1871 MO MO KY married 9 years no children*
         ** 1910 - Living in Marion Co., MO - Ballard, Thos S 47 MO KY MO, Lou 39 MO MO MO*
         ** 1940 - Living in Jackson, Shelby Co., MO - Living with his brother John D., - Ballard, Thomas S 77 wd MO*

         More About THOMAS S. BALLARD:
         Burial: Emden Memorial Gardens, Shelby Co., MO

         More About LULU BUFORD:
         Burial: Mt. Louis, Shelby Co., MO

    iii.   SARAH F. BALLARD, b. 1864, MO; d. Aft. 1880.
    iv.   WADE DAVIS BALLARD, b. 19 Mar 1867, MO; d. 11 Jul 1942, Fulton, Callaway Co., MO; m. MILTON MONROE WOOD, 27 Aug 1891, Marion Co., MO; b. 04 Jan 1848, TN; d. 30 Jun 1936, Shelby Co., MO.

         More About WADE DAVIS BALLARD:

Burial: Prairie View Baptist Cemetery, Hunnewell, Shelby Co., MO

More About MILTON MONROE WOOD:
Burial: Prairie View Baptist Cemetery, Hunnewell, Shelby Co., MO

      v.   JAMES WILLIAM BALLARD, b. 03 Aug 1869, Marion Co., MO; d. 24 May 1934, Lentner, Shelby Co., MO; m. ANNIE JANE GRAY; b. 06 Jan 1868, Shelby Co., MO; d. 01 Jan 1953, Adair Co., MO.

Notes for JAMES WILLIAM BALLARD:
Source: Shelby County Missouri Death Certificate

More About JAMES WILLIAM BALLARD:
Burial: Morris Cemetery, Shelby Co., MO

More About ANNIE JANE GRAY:
Burial: Morris Cemetery, Shelby Co., MO

6.   vi.   RICHARD T. BALLARD, b. 03 Sep 1871, MO; d. 08 Jun 1927, Union, Marion Co., MO.

    vii.   CHARLOTTA "LOTTIE" B. BALLARD, b. 01 Oct 1873, Shelby Co., MO; d. 19 Jun 1905, Shelby Co., MO; m. SAMUEL B. BOWER; b. Sep 1872, MO; d. Aft. 1900.

Notes for SAMUEL B. BOWER:
Source: 1900 Marion County Missouri Federal Census Records

** 1900 - Living in Marion Co., MO - Bowen, Samuel - Sep 1872 MO PA Germany, Lottie B - Oct 1874 MO KY MO*

    viii.   JOHN DAVID BALLARD, b. 08 Nov 1875, Shelby Co., MO; d. 11 Apr 1969, Marion Co., MO.

Notes for JOHN DAVID BALLARD:
Source: 1920-1940 Shelby County Missouri Federal Census Records

** 1920 - Living in Shelby Co., MO - Ballard, John D 43 MO KY MO farmer Mary E mother 75 MO KY KY, Mina Hines servant 34 MO MO MO*
** 1930 - Living in Shelby Co., MO - Ballard, John D 53 MO MO MO*
** 1940 - Living in Jackson, Shelby Co., MO - Ballard, John D 64 MO, Thomas S 77 wd brother MO*

More About JOHN DAVID BALLARD:
Burial: Emden Memorial Gardens, Shelby Co., MO

    ix.   CHARLES LEE BALLARD, b. 10 Jun 1876, Shelby Co., MO; d. 03 Nov 1918, Shelby Co., MO.

Notes for CHARLES LEE BALLARD:
Source: Missouri State Board of Health Death Certificate

    x.   ESTLE BALLARD, b. 29 May 1880, Marion Co., MO; d. 12 Sep 1883, Shelby Co., MO.

More About ESTLE BALLARD:
Burial: Warren Cemetery, Marion Co., MO

3. JAMES WILLIAM[2] BALLARD (THOMPSON R.[1]) *was born 23 Nov 1838 in Madison Co., KY, and died 18 Jan 1908. He married* LOUISA J. TERRILL *12 Mar 1861, daughter of* JOSEPHUS TERRILL *and* MARY PEPPERS. *She was born 02 May 1841 in Marion Co., MO, and died 09 Feb 1929 in Bethlehem twp., Henry Co., MO.*

Notes for JAMES WILLIAM BALLARD:
Source: 1870-1900 Henry County Missouri Federal Census Records

** 1870 - Living in Henry Co., MO - Ballard, James 57 farmer KY, Louisa 29 MO, Ida May 4 MO, Joseph T 2, Alma 7/12 MO*
** 1880 - Living in Henry Co., MO - J. W. Ballard 40 KY, Louisa 36 MO, Thompson 12 MO, Ernest L. 8 MO, Norman 5 MO, Ida M. 14 MO, Almer 10 MO, Bessie 6 MO, Blanche 4 MO*
** 1900 - Living in Bethlehem, Henry Co., MO - Ballard, James 61 - Nov 1838 KY KY KY, Louisa 59 - May 1841 - 10 children 9 Living MO KY KY, Norman - Feb 1879 MO, Dara 18 - 1881 MO, Lilian 16 - Sept 1883 MO*

More About JAMES WILLIAM BALLARD:
Burial: Bethlehem Cemetery. Henry Co., MO

Notes for LOUISA J. TERRILL:
Source: 1910 Henry County Missouri Federal Census Records, taraperrien@hotmail.com (Tara Perrien), Henry County Missouri Death Certificate, Obituary

Obituary - Death of Mrs. L. J. Ballard - (from Henry Co. Scrapbook, reproductions of old clippings reproduced by the Daily Democrat 1976, Clinton, MO)
Death of Mrs. L. J. Ballard - Louisa J. Terrill was born May 2, 1841, in Marion county, MO, and died at her home 11 miles southeast of Clinton, February 9, 1929, being 87 years, 9 months and 7 days of age. On March 12, 1861, she was married to J. W. Ballard, who passed on before her January 18, 1908. To this union ten children were given, one dying in infancy. Those living are Mrs. Ida Brooks, Holden, MO; J. T. Ballard, Denver, Colo; Mrs. W. N. Evans, Clinton; E. L. Ballard, McMinnville, Ore.; Mrs. Bessie Simmons, Clinton; Mrs. Blanche Evans, Baird, Wash; Misses Dora and Lillian, at home. She leaves 21 grandchildren and 13 great-grandchildren. She was converted when young and in 1866, shortly after its reorganization after the Civil War, she united with the Bethlehem church, and for 63 years she had labored for her Master as a member of this church, rearing her sons and daughters in the light of the Masters' Word, implanting in them a love and reverence for the Great Book and its teaching, which now in these hours without mother shall become their hope and their comfort. Altho, for the last several years, she had become a semi-invalid, seldom leaving her home, she never lost her love for, nor her interest in her church. Thru her beloved daughters, she kept in intimate touch with its needs and interests, never forgetting nor neglecting that it needed her prayers and her material support and always remembering the Orphan's Home on her birthday. She was a quiet, gracious, unassuming woman, whose influence for good can never be measured and her "works do follow" her. Funeral services were conducted by her pastor, Bro. Banks, at Bethlehem, Sunday at 2:30 p. m. from Rev. 14:13--- "Blessed are the dead, which die in the Lord, henceforth." Hers has been a long and useful life, filled with the many things which life and love give, joys and sorrows, duties and pleasures, burdens light and heavy and now death has given her that which is greater than all, the priceless "crown of glory," from everlasting unto everlasting, which is bestowed upon those who die in the Lord. Her children will miss her. Mother's place is vacant, and home has lost its sweetness for she who made it home is there no longer, but they cannot mourn as those having no hope, for with Paul, she has said "I have fought a good fight; I have finished my course; I have kept the faith." She is not dead but sleepeth, and shall waken to a new day. Life, we have been long together, Through sunshine and cloudy weather; It is hard to part when friends are dear Perhaps 'twill cost a sigh and tear; Then steal away, give little warning. Say not goodnight. On some fairer shore ... bid me good morning.
** 1910 - Living in Bethlehem, Henry Co., MO - Ballard, Lousa J 68 wd - 10 children 9 living MO KY KY, Dora 28 MO, Lillian 26 MO*

More About LOUISA J. TERRILL:
Burial: Bethlehem Cemetery. Henry Co., MO

Children of JAMES BALLARD and LOUISA TERRILL are:

7.   i. IDA MAY³ BALLARD, b. Apr 1866, Henry Co., MO; d. 1946.
    ii. JOSEPH THOMPSON BALLARD, b. Abt. 1868, Henry Co., MO; d. Aft. 1880.
    iii. ALMA BALLARD, b. 24 Feb 1870, Henry Co., MO; d. 25 Dec 1960, Clinton, Henry Co., MO; m. WILLIAM NATHAN EVANS; b. 26 Apr 1867, Henry Co., MO; d. 27 Nov 1946, Clinton, Henry Co., MO.

More About ALMA BALLARD:
Burial: Bethlehem Cemetery, Henry Co., MO

More About WILLIAM NATHAN EVANS:
Burial: Bethlehem Cemetery, Henry Co., MO

8.   iv.   ERNEST LLOYD BALLARD, *b. 24 Feb 1872, Henry Co., MO; d. 02 Nov 1959, Yamhill Co., OR.*
      v.   BESSIE BALLARD, *b. 09 Apr 1874, Henry Co., MO; d. 30 Nov 1940; m. JOHN F. SIMMONS; b. 21 Jan 1861, Moniteau Co., MO; d. 15 Oct 1927, Jackson Co., MO.*

More About BESSIE BALLARD:
Burial: Good Hope Cemetery, Coal Henry Co., MO

More About JOHN F. SIMMONS:
Burial: Good Hope Cemetery, Coal Henry Co., MO

      vi.   NORMAN BALLARD, *b. 1875, Henry Co., MO; d. Aft. 1900.*
     vii.   BLANCHE BALLARD, *b. 1876, Henry Co., MO; d. 1961, Douglas Co., WA; m. HAROLD W. EVANS; b. 21 May 1877, Henry Co., MO; d. 28 Oct 1965, Douglas Co., WA.*

More About BLANCHE BALLARD:
Burial: Highland Cemetery, Douglas Co., WA

More About HAROLD W. EVANS:
Burial: Highland Cemetery, Douglas Co., WA

    viii.   DORA BALLARD, *b. 13 Aug 1879, Henry Co., MO; d. 19 Jul 1964, Clinton, Henry Co., MO.*

More About DORA BALLARD:
Burial: Bethlehem Cemetery. Henry Co., MO

     ix.   LILLIAN BALLARD, *b. 02 Sep 1883, Henry Co., MO; d. 26 Nov 1964, Clinton, Henry Co., MO.*

More About LILLIAN BALLARD:
Burial: Bethlehem Cemetery. Henry Co., MO

4. ELIZABETH[2] BALLARD (THOMPSON R.[1]) *was born 12 Jun 1833 in KY, and died 08 Dec 1895 in Marion Co., MO. She married WILLIAM DINWIDDIE. He was born 1824 in KY, and died Aft. 1876.*

Notes for ELIZABETH BALLARD:
Source: 1880 Marion County Missouri Federal Census Records

** 1880 - Living in Union, Marion Co., MO - Dinwiddie, Elizabeth 45 MO, James A 27 MO, John D 22 MO, George L 19 MO, Jackson 17 MO, Fannie 13 MO, Nellie K 9 MO, Marion H 7 MO, Samuel T 4 MO*

Notes for WILLIAM DINWIDDIE:
Source: 1860-1870 Marion County Missouri Federal Census Records

** 1860 - Living Union, Marion Co., MO - Dinwiddle, Wm 36, Elizabeth 22, James A 8, Frank P 6, Wm T 4, John H 2, Mary C 2/12*
** 1870 - Living in Union, Marion Co., MO - Dinwiddle, William 47 KY, Elizabeth 36 KY, James A 18 MO, Franklin 16 MO, William 14 MO, John 12 MO, Mary 10 MO, George 8 MO, Thomas 6 MO, Fannie 4 MO*

Children of ELIZABETH BALLARD and WILLIAM DINWIDDIE are:

    i.   JAMES A.[3] DINWIDDIE, *b. 1852, MO; d. Aft. 1880.*
    ii.   FRANKLIN P. "FRANK" DINWIDDIE, *b. 1854.*
   iii. WILLIAM T. DINWIDDIE, *b. 1856.*
   iv. JOHN DINWIDDIE, *b. 1858, MO; d. Aft. 1880.*
    v.   MARY C. DINWIDDIE, *b. 25 Sep 1859, MO; d. 10 Jun 1880, MO.*

More About MARY C. DINWIDDIE:
Burial: Bethany Baptist Church Cemetery, Philadelphia, Marion Co., MO

   vi. GEORGE DINWIDDIE, *b. 1862, MO; d. Aft. 1880.*
  vii. THOMAS JACKSON DINWIDDIE, *b. 10 Mar 1865, Marion Co., MO; d. 06 Sep 1946, Marion Co., MO;*
       m. ELLA MAE BOHON; b. 28 Mar 1868, Marion Co., MO; d. 25 Mar 1942, Marion Co., MO.

More About THOMAS JACKSON DINWIDDIE:
Burial: Bethany Baptist Church Cemetery, Philadelphia, Marion Co., MO

More About ELLA MAE BOHON:
Burial: Bethany Baptist Church Cemetery, Philadelphia, Marion Co., MO

 viii. FANNIE DINWIDDIE, *b. 24 Jul 1867, Marion Co., MO; d. 21 Dec 1937, Marion Co., MO; m. JORDAN*
       L. PRIOR; b. 28 Jul 1863, Marion Co., MO; d. 05 Jul 1940, Shelby Co., MO.

More About FANNIE DINWIDDIE:
Burial: Bethany Baptist Church Cemetery, Philadelphia, Marion Co., MO

More About JORDAN L. PRIOR:
Burial: Bethany Baptist Church Cemetery, Philadelphia, Marion Co., MO

   ix. MINNIE K. DINWIDDIE, *b. 03 Oct 1870, Marion Co., MO; d. 22 Jun 1882.*

More About MINNIE K. DINWIDDIE:
Burial: Bethany Baptist Church Cemetery, Philadelphia, Marion Co., MO

    x.   MARION DINWIDDIE, *b. 26 Dec 1874, Marion Co., MO; d. 1961; m. AVA MILLER; b. 1890, Shelby*
       Co., MO; d. 06 Apr 1923, Atchison Co., MO.

More About MARION DINWIDDIE:
Burial: Bethany Baptist Church Cemetery, Philadelphia, Marion Co., MO

More About AVA MILLER:
Burial: Bethany Baptist Church Cemetery, Philadelphia, Marion Co., MO

   xi. SAMUEL T. DINWIDDIE, *b. Abt. 1876, Marion Co., MO; d. Aft. 1880.*

5. WILLIAM N.[2] BALLARD (THOMPSON R.[1]) *was born 23 Mar 1843 in KY, and died 10 Nov 1911. He married MARY*
CALISTA SLAVENS. She was born 1854 in Henry Co., MO, and died 1933.

Notes for WILLIAM N. BALLARD:
Source: 1880-1900 Henry County Missouri Federal Census Records, 1910 Kitsap County Washington Federal
Census Records

** 1880 - Living in Bethlehem, Henry Co., MO - Ballard, Wm 35 KY VA VA, Mary C 24 MO OH MO, Albert 6 MO,*
Bertha 4 MO
** 1900 - Living in Bethlehem, Henry Co., MO - Ballard, William - Dec 1844 KY KY KY farmer, Mary - Oct 1854 –*

3 children 3 living MO OH MO, Lottie R - Sept 1844 MO
** 1910 - Living in Port Madison, Kitsap Co., WA - Ballard, William N 64 KY VA TN, Mary C 55 - 3 children 3 living MO OH MO*

More About WILLIAM N. BALLARD:
Burial: Kane Cemetery, Kitsap Co., WA

More About MARY CALISTA SLAVENS:
Burial: Kane Cemetery, Kitsap Co., WA

Children of WILLIAM BALLARD and MARY SLAVENS are:
> i.   ALBERT[3] BALLARD, b. 22 Jan 1874, Henry Co., MO; d. 24 Jun 1925, Snohomish, WA.
> ii. BERTHA BALLARD, b. 05 Mar 1876, Henry Co., MO; d. 17 Sep 1955, Los Angeles Co., CA.
> iii. LOTTIE BALLARD, b. 1884, Henry Co., MO.
> iv. CHARLOTTE JANE BALLARD, b. 11 Sep 1884, Henry Co., MO; d. 29 Dec 1969, Kitsap Co., WA.

Generation No. 3

6. RICHARD T.[3] BALLARD (JOHN DAVID[2], THOMPSON R.[1]) *was born 03 Sep 1871 in MO, and died 08 Jun 1927 in Union, Marion Co., MO. He married DIONA REBECCA SIMMONS, daughter of G. SIMMONS and ELIZABETH LAFOE. She was born 07 Jul 1876 in Philadelphia, MO, and died 10 Mar 1950 in Hannibal, Marion Co., MO.*

Notes for RICHARD T. BALLARD:
Source: 1910 Marion County Missouri Federal Census Records

** 1910 - Living in Marion Co., MO - Ballard, Richard T. 38 MO MO MO, Diona 32 MO KY MO, Beulah 12 MO, Obe 9 MO, David 6 MO*

More About RICHARD T. BALLARD:
Burial: Philadelphia Cemetery, MO

More About DIONA REBECCA SIMMONS:
Burial: Philadelphia Cemetery, MO

Children of RICHARD BALLARD and DIONA SIMMONS are:
> i.   BEULAH[4] BALLARD, b. 09 May 1898, Shelby Co., MO; d. 07 Aug 1913, Union, Marion Co., MO.
>
>   *Notes for BEULAH BALLARD:*
>   *Source: Marion County Missouri Death Certificate*
>
>   *More About BEULAH BALLARD:*
>   *Burial: Philadelphia., MO*
>
> ii. OBIE T. BALLARD, b. 1901, MO; d. Aft. 1910.
> iii. DAVID BALLARD, b. 1904, MO; d. Aft. 1910.

7. IDA MAY[3] BALLARD (JAMES WILLIAM[2], THOMPSON R.[1]) *was born Apr 1866 in Henry Co., MO, and died 1946. She married PHILLIP BROOKS. He was born Jul 1862 in KY, and died 1933.*

More About IDA MAY BALLARD:
Burial: Wall Cemetery, Denton, Johnson Co., MO

Notes for PHILLIP BROOKS:

Source: 1900 - 1910 Henry County Missouri Federal Census Records, 1920 Johnson County Missouri Federal Census Records

** 1900 - Living in Bethlehem, Henry Co., MO - Brooks, Philip M - July 1862 KY KY TN, Ida M - Apr 1866 - 2 children 2 living IL KY MO, Gerald D - May 1892 MO, Ruby - Feb 1896 MO*
** 1910 - Living in Bethlehem, Henry Co., MO - Brooks, Phillip M 46 KY KY TN, Ida M 42 3 children 3 living IL VA MO, Gerald D 18 MO, Ruby P 14 MO, Dora A 6 MO*
** 1920 - Living in Rose Hill, Johnson Co., MO - Brooks, Phillip M 57, Ida M 53, Doris A 16*

More About PHILLIP BROOKS:

Burial: Wall Cemetery, Denton, Johnson Co., MO

Children of IDA BALLARD and PHILLIP BROOKS are:

       i.   GERALD[4] BROOKS, b. 13 May 1892, MO; d. 04 Mar 1979, Sacramento Co., CA.

           More About GERALD BROOKS:
           Burial: Rocklin Cemetery, Placer Co., CA

      ii.   RUBY BROOKS, b. Feb 1896, MO; d. Aft. 1910.
     iii.   DORA A. BROOKS, b. Abt. 1904, Henry Co., MO; d. Aft. 1920.

8. ERNEST LLOYD[3] BALLARD (*JAMES WILLIAM[2], THOMPSON R.[1]*) was born 24 Feb 1872 in Henry Co., MO, and died 02 Nov 1959 in Yamhill Co., OR. He married ETTA ANN WHITLOW. She was born 15 Aug 1875 in MO, and died 04 Feb 1968 in Longview, Cowlitz Co., WA.

Notes for ERNEST LLOYD BALLARD:

Source: 1900 Henry County Missouri Federal Census Records, 1910 Douglas County Washington Federal Census Records, 1920 Yamhill County Oregon Federal Census Records

** 1900 - Living in Henry Co., MO - Ballard, Ernest L Feb 1872 MO KY MO, Etta M Aug 1875 MO KY KY, Evelyn G. Feb 1896 MO, Mary T Apr 1900 MO, Myrtle W Apr 1900 MO*
** 1910 - Living in Douglas Co., WA - Ballard, Ernest L 38 MO VA MO, Etta Ann 35 MO KY KY, Evelyn G 14 MO MO MO, Mary T 10 MO MO MO, Myrtle W 10 MO MO MO*
** 1920 - Living in Yamhill Co., OR - Ballard, Ernest L 48 MO KY KY, Etta M 44 MO KY KY, Evelyn G 23 MO, Mary E 19 MO, Myrtle W 19 MO, Robert E. 7 MO*

More About ETTA ANN WHITLOW:

Burial: Riverview Abbey Mausoleum and Crematory, Portland, Multnomah Co., OR

Children of ERNEST BALLARD and ETTA WHITLOW are:

       i.   EVELYN G.[4] BALLARD, b. Feb 1896, Henry Co., MO; d. Aft. 1920.
      ii.   MARY T. BALLARD, b. Apr 1900, Henry Co., MO; d. Aft. 1920.
     iii.   MYRTLE W. BALLARD, b. Apr 1900, Henry Co., MO; d. Aft. 1920.
     iv.   ROBERT E. BALLARD, b. 1913, MO; d. Aft. 1920.

Welcome Ballard

Generation No. 1

1. WELCOME[1] BALLARD *was born 1793 in NH, and died Aft. 1850. He married* ELIZA. *She was born 1802 in NH, and died Aft. 1850.*

Notes for WELCOME BALLARD:
Source: 1850 Jefferson County New York Federal Census Records

** 1850 - Living in Jefferson Co., NY - Ballard, Welcome 57 NH, Eliza 48 NH, Joseph 19 NH, Olive 17 NY, Mary J 15 NY, Dyer 11 NY, Elsie 7 NY, Emily 4 NY*

Children of WELCOME BALLARD *and* ELIZA *are:*

2.	i.	JOSEPH HENRY[2] BALLARD, b. 11 Apr 1831, NH; d. 16 Apr 1915, Savannah, Andrew Co., MO.
	ii.	OLIVE BALLARD, b. 1833, NY; d. Aft. 1850.
	iii.	MARY J. BALLARD, b. 1835, NY; d. Aft. 1850.
	iv.	DYER BALLARD, b. 1839, NY; d. Aft. 1850.
	v.	EMILY BALLARD, b. 1846, NY; d. Aft. 1850.

Generation No. 2

2. JOSEPH HENRY[2] BALLARD (WELCOME[1]) *was born 11 Apr 1831 in NH, and died 16 Apr 1915 in Savannah, Andrew Co., MO. He married* SOPHIA ARIMINTA LANGWORTH, *daughter of* MARTIN LANGWORTH *and* MISS HASKINS. *She was born 21 Mar 1845 in Syracuse, NY, and died 25 Feb 1924 in Savannah, Andrew Co., MO.*

Notes for JOSEPH HENRY BALLARD:
Source: Andrew County Missouri Death Certificate, 1870-1880 Warren County Pennsylvania Federal Census Records, 1885 Iowa State Census Records, 1900 Holt County Missouri Federal Census Records, 1910 Andrew County Missouri Federal Census Records

** 1870 - Living in Elred, Warren Co., PA - Ballard, JH 39 NY, Sophia A 25 NY, Joseph 2 PA*
** 1880 - Living in Elred, Warren Co., PA - Ballard, Joseph H 49 NY VT NY, Sophia A 36 NY NY NY, Welcome J 13 PA, Myrtle 7 PA, Edith A 5 PA*
** 1885 - Living in Odebolt, Sac Co., IA - Ballard, Joseph 53 engineer Sophiah 47 NY, Welcome J 17 Engineer PA Myrtle F 12 PA, Edith A 10,*
** 1900 - Living in Mound Hill, Holt Co., MO - Ballard, Joseph - Apr 1831 NY NY VT, Sophia - Mar 1845 six children three living NY NY NY, Myrtle - Nov 1872 PA, Well J - Apr 1868 PA*
** 1910 - Living in Suvannah, Andrew Co., MO - Ballard, Joseph H 79 NY CT NY, Sophia A 65 NY, Myrtle 30 PA*

Notes for SOPHIA ARIMINTA LANGWORTH:
Source: 1920 Nodaway County Missouri Federal Census Records
** 1920 - Living in Maryville, Nodaway Co., MO - Ballard, Myrtle 35 PA NY NY, Sophia 75 wd NY NY OH*

More About SOPHIA ARIMINTA LANGWORTH:
Burial: Savannah, Andrew Co., MO

Children of JOSEPH BALLARD *and* SOPHIA LANGWORTH *are:*

3.	i.	WELCOME JOSEPH[3] BALLARD, b. 01 Apr 1868, Bradford Co., PA; d. 15 Oct 1953, St. Joseph, Buchanan Co., MO.
	ii.	MYRTLE BALLARD, b. Nov 1872, PA; d. Aft. 1924.

Notes for MYRTLE BALLARD:

She was the submitter of info on both of her parents death certificates

    iii.   EDITH A. BALLARD, *b. 1875, PA; d. Aft. 1885.*

Generation No. 3

3. WELCOME JOSEPH³ BALLARD (*JOSEPH HENRY²,* WELCOME¹) *was born 01 Apr 1868 in Bradford Co., PA, and died 15 Oct 1953 in St. Joseph, Buchanan Co., MO. He married* CHARLOTTE "LOTTIE" MAE McCASKEY, *daughter of* JAMES McCASKEY *and* SARAH BARNARD. *She was born 03 Jun 1880 in Burlington Junction, MO, and died 05 Jan 1938 in St. Joseph, Buchanan Co., MO.*

Notes for WELCOME JOSEPH BALLARD:

*Source: Buchanan County Missouri Death Certificate, 1910 Lancaster County Nebraska Federal Census Records, 1920 Seward County Nebraska Federal Census Records, 1930 Buchanan County Missouri Federal Census Records
* Death Certificate tells when and where he was born, name of parents, wife and place of burial.*

** 1910 - Living in South Pass, Lancaster Co., KS - Ballard, Welcome J 41 PA NY NY engineer, Lottie 30 MO AL IL (0 children 0 living)
* 1920 - Living in Milford, Seward Co., NE - WJ 51 PA MI PA, Lottie 40 MO AL IL, Glen 1 NE
* 1930 - Living in St. Joseph, Buchanan Co., MO - Ballard, Welcome J 56 PA MI MI, Charlotte 50 MO AL IL, Joseph G 12 NE*

More About WELCOME JOSEPH BALLARD:
Burial: Mt. Hope, Mound City, Holt Co., MO

Notes for CHARLOTTE "LOTTIE" MAE McCASKEY:
Source: Buchanan County Missouri Death Certificate

More About CHARLOTTE "LOTTIE" MAE McCASKEY:
Burial: Mt. Hope Cemetery, Mound City, Holt Co., MO

Child of WELCOME BALLARD *and* CHARLOTTE McCASKEY *is:*
4.   *i.*   JOSEPH GLENN⁴ BALLARD, *b. 1918, NE; d. Aft. 1930.*

Generation No. 4

4. JOSEPH GLENN⁴ BALLARD (WELCOME JOSEPH³, *JOSEPH HENRY²,* WELCOME¹) *was born 1918 in NE, and died Aft. 1930. He married* HAZEL HAYWARD. *She was born Abt. 1920 in St. Joseph, Buchanan Co., MO.*

Child of JOSEPH BALLARD *and* HAZEL HAYWARD *is:*

    i.   GLENN EDWARD⁵ BALLARD, *b. 01 Dec 1938, St. Joseph, Buchanan Co., MO; d. 01 Dec 1938, St. Joseph, Buchanan Co., MO.*

       More About GLENN EDWARD BALLARD:
       Burial: Mt. Hope Cemetery, Mound City, Holt Co., MO

Generation No. 1

1. WILLIAM[1] BALLARD was born 1790 in VA, and died Abt. 1840 in TN. He married AGNESS. She was born Abt. 1800 in VA, and died Aft. 1870.

Notes for WILLIAM BALLARD:
Source: Tabatha Calliou (tshupac@mcsnet.ca)   (mistingsky2000@yahoo.ca)

Notes for AGNESS:
Source: 1850 Montgomery County Missouri Federal Census Records, 1860 Mills County Iowa Federal Census Records, 1870 Cass County Nebraska Federal Census Records

* 1850 - Living in Montgomery Co., MO with daughter Louisa Caldwell
* 1860 - Living in Lyons, Mills Co., IA - Living with son John L. Ballard - Ballard, Agnes 60 VA
* 1870 - Living in Rock Bluffs, Cass Co., NE with Mary J. Murray (daughter in law) - Ballard, Agnes 75 MO

Children of WILLIAM BALLARD and AGNESS are:
2.   i.   LOUISA CALLE[2] BALLARD, b. Abt. 1817, Wilson Co., TN; d. 1856, Schuyler Co., MO.
3.   ii.   JOHN L. NELSON BALLARD, b. 1818, TN; d. Aft. 1885.
4.   iii. ALEXANDER "ALEX" BALLARD, b. Abt. 1825, TN; d. Bet. 1870 - 1880.

Generation No. 2

2. LOUISA CALLE[2] BALLARD (WILLIAM[1]) was born Abt. 1817 in Wilson Co., TN, and died 1856 in Schuyler Co., MO. She married JAMES CALDWELL 22 May 1834 in Wilson Co., TN. He was born 22 Oct 1813 in White Co., TN, and died 20 Nov 1891 in Schuyler Co., MO.

Notes for LOUISA CALLE BALLARD:
Source: Early TN. Marriages by Byron & Barbara Sistler

Notes for JAMES CALDWELL:
Source: 1850 Montgomery County Missouri Federal Census Records, 1860 Schuyler County Missouri Federal Census Records
* 1850 - Living in Montgomery Co., MO - Caldwell, James TN, Louisa 33 TN, Emily 11 TN, William 14 TN, Sarah 9 TN, Nancy 1 MO, James 8/12 MO, Agnes Ballard 50 VA
* 1860 - Living in Independence, Schuyler Co., MO - Kollwell, James 46 farmer TN, Mary 18 (wife), Nancy 14, James 10, Janetta 1, Louisa 1/12

More About JAMES CALDWELL:
Burial: Coffey Cemetery, Downing, Schuyler Co., MO

Children of LOUISA BALLARD and JAMES CALDWELL are:

          i.   WILLIAM[3] CALDWELL, b. 1836, TN; d. Aft. 1850.
5.   ii.   EMILY CALDWELL, b. 09 Feb 1838, Montgomery Co., MO; d. 19 Feb 1923, Schuyler Co., MO.
          iii. SARAH ANN CALDWELL, b. 22 Feb 1840, TN; d. 21 Jun 1925, Schuyler Co., MO; m. MARTIN VANBUREN NEWCUM; b. 08 Jan 1837, MO; d. 18 May 1881.

          More About SARAH ANN CALDWELL:
          Burial: Coffey Cemetery, Downing, Schuyler Co., MO

          More About MARTIN VANBUREN NEWCUM:

Burial: Coffey Cemetery, Downing, Schuyler Co., MO

    iv.   NANCY AGNES CALDWELL, *b. 23 Aug 1845, Montgomery Co., MO; d. 26 Jul 1914, Putnam Co., MO; m. DYE.*

More About NANCY AGNES CALDWELL:
Burial: Unionville Cemetery, Unionville, Putnam Co., MO

    v.   JAMES ALEXANDER CALDWELL, *b. 24 Sep 1849, Montgomery Co., MO; d. 02 Jan 1938, Greentop, Schuyler Co., MO; m. THEODOCIA COFFEY; b. 09 Oct 1858, Schuyler Co., MO; d. 19 Dec 1942, Greentop, Schuyler Co., MO.*

More About THEODOCIA COFFEY:
Burial: Coffey Cemetery, Downing, Schuyler Co., MO

    vi.   JULIA C. CALDWELL, *b. 23 Oct 1851, MO; d. 05 Apr 1930, Downing, Schuyler co., MO; m. JONATHAN PEARCE; b. 10 Mar 1842, Scotland Co., MO; d. 08 Aug 1926, Downing, Schuyler co., MO.*

More About JONATHAN PEARCE:
Burial: Coffey Cemetery, Downing, Schuyler Co., MO

3. JOHN L. NELSON[2] BALLARD (WILLIAM[1]) *was born 1818 in TN, and died Aft. 1885. He married (1) RACHAEL. She was born 1822 in MO, and died Aft. 1860. He married (2) MARY. She was born Abt. 1827 in MO, and died Aft. 1870.*

Notes for JOHN L. NELSON BALLARD:
Source: 1856 Mills County Iowa State Census Records, 1860 Mills County Iowa Federal Census Records, 1880 Monona County Iowa Federal Census Records, 1885 Monona County Iowa State Census Records

** 1856 - Living in Plattville, Mills Co., IA - Ballard, John 33 TN, Eliza 33 TN, Wm 16 MO, Eli F 13 MO, Nancy A 12 MO, Agness 10 MO, Rutha C 8 MO, Rebecca E 4 IA, James R IA*
** 1860 - Living in Lyons, Mills Co., IA - Ballard, J. L 38 farmer TN, Rachael 38 MO, William 18 MO, Eli F 16 MO, Nancy A 14 MO, Agnes 12 MO, Ruth C 10 MO, Rebecca A 6 IA, James R 4 IA, John R 2/12 IA, Agnes Ballard 60 VA, Mary J Snell 15 MO, Martha E. Snell 12 MO*
** 1880 - Living in Lincoln twp., Monona Co., IA - Ballard, John 52 TN VA VA, Mary 53 NC NC NC, John R 20 IA, Henry 17 IA, George 15 IA*
** 1885 - Living in Lincoln, Monona Co., IA - Ballard, John L 62, Mary 60, Henry 21, George 18*

Children of JOHN BALLARD and RACHAEL are:

6.   i.   WILLIAM GOODWIN[3] BALLARD, *b. 23 Aug 1841, MO; d. 08 Jan 1919, Omaha NE.*
7.   ii.   ELI FRANKLIN BALLARD, *b. 29 Feb 1844, MO; d. 02 Apr 1930, Homestead, Baker Co., OR.*
8.   iii.   NANCY A. BALLARD, *b. 1846, MO; d. Aft. 1885.*
9.   iv.   AGNES CATHERINE BALLARD, *b. Apr 1848, MO; d. Aft. 1930.*
       v.   RUTH C. BALLARD, *b. 1850, MO; d. Aft. 1860.*
10.   vi.   REBECCA A. BALLARD, *b. 1854, MO; d. Aft. 1860.*
11.   vii.   JAMES R. BALLARD, *b. 1858, IA; d. Aft. 1880, Living in Monona Co., IA.*
      viii.   JOHN R. BALLARD, *b. May 1860, IA; d. Aft. 1900.*

Notes for JOHN R. BALLARD:
Source: 1900 Cherry County Nebraska Federal Census Records
** 1900 - Living in Schlagle, Cherry Co., NE - Ballard, John - May 1860 IA TN unknown stock ranch*

     ix.   H*ENRY* B*ALLARD*, b. Mar 1864, IA; d. Aft. 1900.

         Notes for H*ENRY* B*ALLARD*:
         Source: 1900 Cherry County Nebraska Federal Census Records
         * 1900 - Living in Schlagle, Cherry Co., NE - Ballard, Henry - Mar 1864 IA TN unknown

     x.   G*EORGE* B*ALLARD*, b. Abt. 1865, IA; d. Aft. 1885.

4. A*LEXANDER* "A*LEX*"[2] B*ALLARD* (W*ILLIAM*[1]) was born Abt. 1825 in TN, and died Bet. 1870 - 1880. He married M*ARTHA* A*NN* M*OORE* 03 Jan 1849 in Pike Co., MO. She was born 1831 in MO, and died Aft. 1900.

Notes for A*LEXANDER* "A*LEX*" B*ALLARD*:
Source: 1850-1860 Montgomery County Missouri Federal Census Records, 1870 Pike County Missouri Federal Census Records

* Possible son of William and Agness Ballard.
* 1850 - Living in Montgomery Co., MO - Ballard, Alexander 32 farming TN, Martha 18 MO, Baby female 1/12 MO
* 1860 - Living in Montgomery Co., MO - Ballard, Alexander 31 farmer TN, Martha A 24 MO, John 9 MO, Zimri 5 MO, Allice 3 MO, James 2 MO, James Forte 20 MO laborer, Jason A. Dempsy 26 laborer OH
* 1870 - Living in Pike Co., MO - Ballard, Alex 42 farmer TN, Martha 39 MO, Jno L. 19 MO, Zach 15 MO, Alice 13 MO, James 11 MO, Jeff D MO, Martha 7 MO

Notes for M*ARTHA* A*NN* M*OORE*:
Source: 1880 Lamar County Texas Federal Census Records
* 1880 - Living in Lamar Co., TX - Shilling, W. A, Martha A, J. D Ballard, Albro

Children of A*LEXANDER* B*ALLARD* and M*ARTHA* M*OORE* are:
     i.   J*OHN* L.[3] B*ALLARD*, b. 1851, Montgomery Co., MO; d. Aft. 1870.
     ii.   Z*ACH* Z*IMRI* B*ALLARD*, b. 1855, Montgomery Co., MO; d. Aft. 1870.
     iii.   A*LICE* B*ALLARD*, b. 1857, Montgomery Co., MO; d. Aft. 1870.
     iv.   J*AMES* B*ALLARD*, b. 1859, Montgomery Co., MO; d. Aft. 1870.
12.   *v.*   J*EFFERSON* D. "J*EFF*" B*ALLARD*, b. 01 Jun 1861, MO; d. 19 Feb 1930, Commerce, Hunt Co., TX.
     vi.   M*ARTHA* B*ALLARD*, b. 1863, MO; d. Aft. 1870.
     vii.   A*LEXANDER* "A*LBRO*" B*ALLARD*, b. 18 Sep 1868, MO; d. 23 Nov 1918, Commerce, Hunt Co., TX.

Generation No. 3

5. E*MILY*[3] C*ALDWELL* (L*OUISA* C*ALLE*[2] B*ALLARD*, W*ILLIAM*[1]) was born 09 Feb 1838 in Montgomery Co., MO, and died 19 Feb 1923 in Schuyler Co., MO. She married J*AMES* P*EARCE*. He was born 19 Jun 1830 in OH, and died 20 Oct 1922 in Schuyler Co., MO.

More About J*AMES* P*EARCE*:
Burial: Greentop Memorial Park, Greentop, Schuyler Co., MO

Children of E*MILY* C*ALDWELL* and J*AMES* P*EARCE* are:
     i.   B*ENJAMIN* S*HANE*[4] P*EARCE*, b. 13 Jun 1859, MO; d. 09 Jan 1947, Greentop, Schuyler Co., MO; m. E*LVIRA* C*OUCH*.
     ii.   E*LVA* D*ORA* P*EARCE*, b. 14 Sep 1865, Scotland Co., MO; d. 19 Dec 1938, Knox Co., MO; m. W*ILLIAM* H*ENRY* P*EARCE*, 03 Dec 1885, Scotland Co., MO.

6. W*ILLIAM* G*OODWIN*[3] B*ALLARD* (J*OHN* L. N*ELSON*[2], W*ILLIAM*[1]) was born 23 Aug 1841 in MO, and died 08 Jan 1919 in Omaha NE. He married F*RANCIS* J*UNE* L*INDSAY* D*E*L*ASHMUTT* in Whiting, Monona Co., IA. She was born 05 Jan 1842 in Eddyville IL, and died 17 May 1928 in Monona Co., IA.

Notes for WILLIAM GOODWIN BALLARD:
Source: 1870-1880 Monona County Iowa Federal Census Records, 1885 Monona County Iowa State Census Records, 1900-1910 Cherry County Nebraska Census Records, Dr. John Ballard (john.ballard@anu.edu.au) submission via the internet of Book on Cherry Co. found on the Cherry Co NE Biographies website, Bev (BGOFORTHCutter@cs.com)

** 1870 - Living in Monona Co., Lincoln twp., IA - Ballard, Wm J 28 MO, Frances J 27 IA, Essce May 2 IA, Jessie L 9/12 IA*
** 1880 - Living in Monona Co., Lincoln twp., IA - Ballard, William 32 farmer MO TN IL, Frances 34 IA VA TN, Jessee M 10 IA, Eddy 8 IA, William 6 IA, Charles 3 IA, Frank 1 IA*
** 1885 - Living in Ashton, Monona Co., NE - Ballard, William 41 farmer, Frances 41, Linsey 14, Edward 13*
** 1900 - Living in Dewey Lake, Cherry Co., NE - Ballard W G 68 - Aug 1831, J. L 29 (m) - Oct 1870 IA MO IA, W N 25 - , C. C 23 - Jan 1877 (m) IA, F. D 22 - Feb 1878 (m) IA, William M 19 - Apr 1880 IA, Ed Brahmstadt 28 employ, Geo R. Horton 50 cook, H. W Husted 23 employee*
** 1910 - Living in Evergreen, Cherry Co., NE - Ballard, William G 68 MO TN TN 7 children 6 living md 1x, Lynn 40 (Jesse Lindsay Ballard) IA MO IA, Hosie Hustead 33 IA NY IN, Ed Ballard 37 wd IA MO IA*

More About WILLIAM GOODWIN BALLARD:

Burial: 11 Jan 1919, Harrison Cemetery, Monona Co., IA

Children of WILLIAM BALLARD and FRANCIS DeLASHMUTT are:

    i.   JESSE LINDSAY[4] BALLARD, b. Oct 1870, Whiting, Monona Co., IA; d. Nov 1966, Dade Co., FL; m. SARAH ELIZABETH KNAPP, 22 Jul 1925, Palm Beach, FL; b. Abt. 1882, MO; d. Feb 1965, Dade Co., FL.

Notes for JESSE LINDSAY BALLARD:
Source: 1930 Dade County Florida Federal Census Records, 1935 Dade County Florida State Census Records, Florida Death Index
** 1930 - Living in Homestead, Dade Co., FL - Ballard, Jesse L 59 IA MO IA, Sarah E 48 MO OH IN*
** 1935 - Living in Dade Co., FL - Ballard, Jesse L 54, Sara E 53*

Notes for SARAH ELIZABETH KNAPP:
Source: Dade County Florida Death Index

    ii.   EDWARD "EDDY" BALLARD, b. 24 Jan 1872, Whiting, Monona Co., IA; d. 28 Oct 1940, Cherry Co., NE.

Notes for EDWARD "EDDY" BALLARD:
Source: 1910 Cherry County Nebraska Federal Census Records
** 1910 - Living in Evergreen, Cherry Co., NE – living with father William G Ballard - Ed 37 wd IA MO IA*

More About EDWARD "EDDY" BALLARD:
Burial: Mt. Hope Cemetery, Valentine, Cherry Co., NE

13.   iii.   WILLIAM NELSON BALLARD, b. 14 Apr 1874, Whiting, Monona Co., IA; d. 19 Mar 1942, Cherry Co., NE.

    iv.   CHARLES C. BALLARD, b. 23 Nov 1876, Whiting, Monona Co., IA; d. May 1966, NE.

14.   v.   FRANK DUDLEY BALLARD, b. 02 Jan 1879, Whiting, Monona Co., IA; d. 1936.

    vi.   ESTHER BALLARD, b. Aft. 1880, Whiting, Monona Co., IA.

    vii.   ETHEL BALLARD, b. Aft. 1880, Whiting, Monona Co., IA.

    viii.   WALTER BALLARD, b. 1882, IA.

ix.   ESSIE MAY BALLARD, b. 26 Jun 1868; d. 07 Mar 1876.

More About ESSIE MAY BALLARD:
Burial: Harrison Cemetery, Whiting, Monona Co., IA

7. ELI FRANKLIN[3] BALLARD (JOHN L. NELSON[2], WILLIAM[1]) was born 29 Feb 1844 in MO, and died 02 Apr 1930 in Homestead, Baker Co., OR. He married (1) MELISSA JANE "LIZZIE" GIBSON 07 Jan 1874 in Seward Co., NE, daughter of AMOS GIBSON and ELIZABETH HAYS. She was born 21 Nov 1846 in Mercer Co., PA, and died 20 Jun 1878 in Hall Co., NE. He married (2) PHOEBE E. DEMPSTER 18 Apr 1880 in NE. She was born 16 Aug 1856 in OH, and died 23 Mar 1891.

Notes for ELI FRANKLIN BALLARD:
Source: 1870 Saline County Missouri Federal Census Records, 1880 Hall County Nebraska Federal Census Record, 1910 Baker County Oregon Federal Census Records

* 1870 - Living in Swan City, Saline Co., MO - Ballard, EF 24 works in saw mill MO
* 1880 - Living in South Platte, Hall Co.,. NE - Ballard, EF 37 farmer MO, Pheobe 23 OH PA OH, Mattie 4 NE, JA 8 NE
* 1900 - Living in Iorn Dyke, Union Co., OR - Ballard, Elie F - Feb 1844 md MO TN PA farmer
* 1910 - Living in Iron Dyke, Baker Co., OR - Ballard, Frank 66 wd MO TN PA, J A 33 NE MO IA, Nora 26 dau in law OR NE MA, Franklin 2 OR, Orman 11/12 OR

More About ELI FRANKLIN BALLARD:
Burial: Pine Haven Cemetery, Baker Co., OR

More About MELISSA JANE "LIZZIE" GIBSON:
Burial: Cedar View Cemetery, Hall Co., NE

More About PHOEBE E. DEMPSTER:
Burial: Anderson Cemetery, Shasta Co., CA

Children of ELI BALLARD and MELISSA GIBSON are:
     i.   DAVID[4] BALLARD.
    ii.   JOHN A. BALLARD.
   iii.   MABLE BALLARD, b. 06 Feb 1871, NE Adopted; d. 14 Feb 1879, IA.

       More About MABLE BALLARD:
       Burial: Fairfax Cemetery, Fairfax, Linn Co., IA

   iv.   MATTIE BALLARD, b. 08 Aug 1874, Hall Co., NE; d. 18 Sep 1930, Baker Co., OR.

       More About MATTIE BALLARD:
       Burial: Pine Haven Cemetery, Baker Co., OR

15.   *v.*   JAY A. BALLARD, b. 1876, NE; d. 30 Jun 1960, Baker Co., OR.

8. NANCY A.[3] BALLARD (JOHN L. NELSON[2], WILLIAM[1]) was born 1846 in MO, and died Aft. 1885. She married (1) HALL Abt. 1863. She married (2) JAMES C. STOKES 19 Sep 1869 in Omaha, NE. He was born 04 Aug 1840 in PA, and died 24 Jan 1898.

Notes for JAMES C. STOKES:
Source: Omaha Nebraska Marriage Records, 1870-1880 Washington County Nebraska Federal Census Records, 1885 Washington County Nebraska State Census Records

** 1870 - Living in Grant, Washington Co., NE - Stokes, James C 30, Nancy 24*
** 1880 - Living in Herman, Washington Co., NE - Stokes, James 41 PA PA VA Nancy 34 MO TN TN, Josphene 8 NE*
** 1885 - Living in Washington Co., NE - Stokes, 45 farming PA PA PA, Nancy Ann 38, Josephine 18 NE. William 11 NE (this child is not found on the 1880 census)*

More About JAMES C. STOKES:
Burial: Blair Cemetery, Washington Co., NE

Children of NANCY BALLARD and JAMES STOKES are:

> i.   JOSEPHINE[4] STOKES, b. Abt. 1872, Washington Co., NE; d. Aft. 1885.
> ii.   WILLIAM STOKES, b. Abt. 1874, Washington Co., NE; d. Aft. 1885.

9.   AGNES CATHERINE[3] BALLARD (JOHN L. NELSON[2], WILLIAM[1]) *was born Apr 1848 in MO, and died Aft. 1930. She married JACOB JAY LONG 31 Dec 1865 in Shenandoah Page Co., IA. He was born 24 Nov 1839 in PA, and died 07 May 1927 in Blair, Washington Co., NE.*

Notes for AGNES CATHERINE BALLARD:
Source: 1930 Hall County Nebraska Federal Census Records

** 1930 - Living in Grand Island, Hall Co., NE Soldiers and Sailor's Home - Long, Agnes C 82 wd MO TN MO*

Notes for JACOB JAY LONG:
Source: 1870 Fremont County Iowa Federal Census Records, 1880-1900 Pottawattamie County Iowa Federal Census Records, 1885 Pottawattamie County State Census Records, 1910 – 1920 Washington County Nebraska Federal Census Records

** 1870 - Living in Fisher, Fremont Co., I A - Long, Jacob 28 farmer PA, Agnes 22 MO, Frances 1 IA*
** 1880 - Living in Pottawattamie Co., IA - Long, Jacob 38 PA Germany PA, Agnes 30 MO TN ?, John 8 IA, Effie L 3 IA, Winnie 5/12 IA*
** 1885 - Living in Knox, Pottawattamie Co., IA - Long, Jacob J 45, Lucinda 40, Agness 37 John 13, Effie 7, Bell 5, Fred B 2*
** 1895 - Living in Cayton, Pottawattamie Co., IA Long, Jacob J*
** 1900 - Living in Pottawattamie Co., IA - Long, Jacob J - Nov 1939 PA, Agnes C - Apr 1848 - 6 children 3 living MO, Effie L - Sept 1877, Fred B - Nov 1882 IA IA*
** 1910 - Living in Washington Co., NE - Long, Jacob J 70 PA, Agnes C 62 MO*
** 1920 - Living in Blair, Washington Co., NE - Long, Jacob J 80 PA Germany PA, Agnes C 72 MO TN TN, Effie L 45 IA wd*

More About JACOB JAY LONG:
Burial: Graceland Cemetery, Pottawattamie Co., IA

Children of AGNES BALLARD and JACOB LONG are:
> i.   FRANCES[4] LONG, b. Abt. 1869, IA; d. Bef. 1870.
> ii.   JOHN LONG, b. 1872, IA; d. 01 Jul 1898, El Caney, Cuba.
>
> > *More About JOHN LONG:*
> > *Burial: Pottawattamie Co., IA*
>
> iii.   EFFIE LULU LONG, b. 30 Sep 1878, Shenandoah Co., IA; d. Aft. 1940; m. (1) WILBER IRA HOKLAS, 11 Jul 1900, Pottawattamie Co., IA; b. 11 Jul 1877, Adams Co., IA; d. 11 Jan 1957, Denver, CO; m. (2) AUGUST SYLVESTER WALTERS, 31 May 1922, Pottawattamie Co., IA; b. 17 Jun 1879, IA; d. 25 Apr 1931; m. (3) BLY, Aft. 1941.
>
> > *Notes for AUGUST SYLVESTER WALTERS:*

Source: 1920-1930 Pottawattamie County Iowa Federal Census Records
* 1920 - Living in Pottawattamie Co., IA - Walters, August S 41, Annie 38, Earl 17, Elmer 14, Edna 6
* 1930 - Living in Walnut, Pottawattamie Co., IA - Walters, August S 50, Effie L 50, Edna C. 16

More About AUGUST SYLVESTER WALTERS:
Burial: Layton twp Cemetery, Pottawattamie Co., IA

16.   iv.   BELL MINNIE LONG, b. 09 Feb 1880, Pottawattamie Co., IA; d. 17 Oct 1961, Hall Co., NE.
17.   v.   FRED B. LONG, b. 02 Nov 1882, IA; d. 08 Oct 1972.

10. REBECCA A.³ BALLARD (JOHN L. NELSON², WILLIAM¹) was born 1854 in MO, and died Aft. 1860. She married JOHN POLIN. He was born Abt. 1855.

Children of REBECCA BALLARD and JOHN POLIN are:
          i.   EDGAR L.⁴ POLIN, b. 14 Oct 1873, Plattsmouth, Douglas Co., NE; d. 14 Oct 1975; m. CLARA BILLSTEIN, 26 Dec 1895, NE; b. 22 Nov 1874, Cass Co., NE; d. 11 Sep 1947, Lancaster Co., NE.

                 More About EDGAR L. POLIN:
                 Burial: Lincoln, Lancaster Co., NE

                 More About CLARA BILLSTEIN:
                 Burial: Lincoln, Lancaster Co., NE

          ii.   JAY POLIN, b. 18 Sep 1883, Pottawattamie Co., IA.
          iii.   ESTELLA POLIN.
          iv.   EDITH POLIN.

11. JAMES R.³ BALLARD (JOHN L. NELSON², WILLIAM¹) was born 1858 in IA, and died Aft. 1880 in Living in Monona Co., IA. He married HARRIET. She was born 1859 in NY, and died Aft. 1880.

Notes for JAMES R. BALLARD:
Source: 1880 Monona County Iowa Federal Census Records
* 1880 - Living in Lincoln, Monona Co., IA - Ballard, James 22 IA TN NC, Harriet 21 NY Ireland NY, Mary 2 IA, Baby - Apr 2/12 IA

Children of JAMES BALLARD and HARRIET are:
          i.   MARY⁴ BALLARD, b. 1878, IA; d. Aft. 1880.
          ii.   BABY BALLARD, b. 1880, IA; d. Aft. 1880.

12. JEFFERSON D. "JEFF"³ BALLARD (ALEXANDER "ALEX"², WILLIAM¹) was born 01 Jun 1861 in MO, and died 19 Feb 1930 in Commerce, Hunt Co., TX. He married NANCY ANN HORN. She was born 03 Sep 1866 in TN, and died 03 Jan 1948 in Commerce, Hunt Co., TX.

Notes for JEFFERSON D. "JEFF" BALLARD:
Source: Hunt County Texas Death Certificate, 1900 Kaufman County Texas Federal Census Records, 1910-1920 Hunt County Texas Federal Census Records

* 1900 - Living in Kaufman Co., TX - Ballard, Jeff - May 1861 MO TN MO, Nancy A - Sep 1866 TN NC NC, Martha E - July 1888 TX, Martha J Shilling mother - Nov 1831 wd 11 children 6 living MO VA KY
* 1910 - Living in Commerce, Hunt Co., TX - Ballard, Jeff D 48, Nancy 42, Mattie 21, Jeff D 5
* 1920 - Living in Commerce, Hunt Co., TX - Ballard, Jeff D 58, Nancy Ann 42, J D 1

** 1930 - Commerce, Hunt Co., TX death certificate. J D Ballard Sr born June 1, 1861 died Feb 19, 1930 - parents A Ballard of MO, Martha A Moore of MO*

More About JEFFERSON D. "JEFF" BALLARD:
Burial: Commerce, Hunt Co., TX

Notes for NANCY ANN HORN:
Source: 1940 Hunt County Texas Federal Census Records
** 1940 - Living in Commerce, Hunt Co., TX - Ballard, Nancy 73 wd tN, Mattie Kennedy daughter 51 wd TX*

More About NANCY ANN HORN:
Burial: Rosemound Cemetery, Commerce, Hunt Co., TX

Children of JEFFERSON BALLARD and NANCY HORN are:

      i.   *MATTIE E.[4] BALLARD, b. 18 Jul 1888, Commerce, Hunt Co., TX; d. 15 Feb 1970, Commerce, Hunt Co., TX; m. JOHN M. KENNEDY, 1913, Hunt Co., TX; b. 18 Apr 1884, Hunt Co., TX; d. 12 Aug 1936, Commerce, Hunt Co., TX.*

           More About MATTIE E. BALLARD:
           Burial: Rosemound Cemetery, Commerce, Hunt Co., TX

           Notes for JOHN M. KENNEDY:
           Source: Hunt County Texas Death Certificate

           More About JOHN M. KENNEDY:
           Rosemound Cemetery, Commerce, Hunt Co., TX

     ii.   *JOHN A. BALLARD, b. 08 Aug 1898; d. 28 Apr 1899.*

           More About JOHN A. BALLARD:
           Burial: Cottonwood Cemetery, Cottonwood, Kaufman Co., TX

    iii.   *JEFFERSON "JEFF" D. BALLARD, b. 1905, TX; d. Aft. 1920.*

Generation No. 4

13.   *WILLIAM NELSON[4] BALLARD (WILLIAM GOODWIN[3], JOHN L. NELSON[2], WILLIAM[1]) was born 14 Apr 1874 in Whiting, Monona Co., IA, and died 19 Mar 1942 in Cherry Co., NE. He married CATHERINE "CASSIE" EDITH RICHARDSON 15 Oct 1902, daughter of WILLOUGHBY RICHARDSON. She was born 18 Mar 1882 in Kearney, Buffalo Co., NE, and died 10 Mar 1966 in Cherry Co., NE.*

Notes for WILLIAM NELSON BALLARD:
Source: Family Bible records (Helen Ballard Eatinger of Valentine, NE, 1910 - 1940 Cherry County Nebraska Federal Census Records

** 1910 - Living in Dewey Lake, Cherry Co., NE - Ballard, William W 36 stock rover cattle ranch, Catherine E 28, Edward W 6, Walter G 5, Lindsey W 3, Mary E 2, Esther 0, Haney A Newman*
** 1920 - Living in Evergreen, Cherry Co., NE - Ballard, William 45 rancher, Catherine 38, Edward 16, Walter 14, William 12, Mary 11, Esther 10, Dudley 9, Ruth 7, Thomas 6, James 5, Billie 2, Vera 0*
** 1930 - Living in Evergreen, Cherry Co., NE - Ballard, William M 56 rancher, Katherine E 48, Walter 25, Esther M 20, Dudley F 19, Ruth C 18, Thomas C 16, James 15, Billy 12, Vera 11, John A 9, Helen 4, Theodore Chaffin 18, Cecil Hamilton 33*
** 1940 - Living in Evergreen, Cherry Co., NE - Ballard, William N 65 rancher, Mary E 32, James E 25, William 22, John A 19*

More About WILLIAM NELSON BALLARD:
Burial: Mt. Hope Cemetery, Wood Lake, Cherry Co., NE

Notes for CATHERINE "CASSIE" EDITH RICHARDSON:
** She taught school at Wood Lake, Cherry Co., NE*

More About CATHERINE "CASSIE" EDITH RICHARDSON:
Burial: Mt. Hope Cemetery, Cherry Co., NE

Children of WILLIAM BALLARD and CATHERINE RICHARDSON are:

      i.   EDWARD WILLOUGHBY[5] BALLARD, b. 02 Jan 1904, Cherry Co., NE; d. 03 Jul 2000, Cherry Co., NE.

          More About EDWARD WILLOUGHBY BALLARD:
          Burial: Mt. Hope Cemetery, Wood Lake, Cherry Co., NE

      ii.   WALTER GOODWIN BALLARD, b. 03 Mar 1905, Cherry Co., NE; d. 04 Dec 1998, Cherry Co., NE; m. MARGARET TYLOER; b. 19 Apr 1915, NE; d. 25 Jul 2002, Cherry Co., NE.

          More About WALTER GOODWIN BALLARD:
          Burial: Mt. Hope Cemetery, Wood Lake, Cherry Co., NE

          More About MARGARET TYLOER:
          Burial: Mt. Hope Cemetery, Wood Lake, Cherry Co., NE

     iii.   WILLIAM "BILL" LINDSEY BALLARD, b. 12 Feb 1907, Cherry Co., NE; d. 05 Feb 2002, Pulaski Co., AR; m. ELAINE MITCHELL; b. 05 Jan 1916; d. 26 Apr 2008, Little Rock, Pulaski Co., AR.

          More About WILLIAM "BILL" LINDSEY BALLARD:
          Burial: Arkansas State Veterans Cemetery, Little Rock, Pulaski Co., AR

          More About ELAINE MITCHELL:
          Burial: Arkansas State Veterans Cemetery, Little Rock, Pulaski Co., AR

     iv.   MARY ELIZABETH BALLARD, b. 31 Mar 1908, Cherry Co., NE; d. 14 Mar 2001, Dawson Co., NE; m. (1) ROBERT ELLWORTH MORGAN; m. (2) PARKHURST, Bef. 2001.

          More About MARY ELIZABETH BALLARD:
          Burial: Mt. Hope Cemetery, Cherry Co., NE

      v.   ESTHER MARGARET BALLARD, b. 21 Jun 1909, Cherry Co., NE; d. 30 Mar 2000, Lincoln Co., NE; m. GEORGE W. JOHNSON, 28 Jun 1930.

          More About ESTHER MARGARET BALLARD:
          Burial: North Platte Cemetery, Lincoln Co., NE

     vi.   FRANK DUDLEY BALLARD, b. 04 Dec 1910, Cherry Co., NE; d. 18 May 1995, King Co., WA; m. IVIAN ELLIOT.

          More About FRANK DUDLEY BALLARD:
          Burial: Mt. Olivet Cemetery, King Co., WA

    vii.   RUTH KATHERINE BALLARD, b. 12 Mar 1912, Cherry Co., NE; d. 25 Oct 2002, Cherry Co., NE; m. FRED FRITZ.

More About RUTH KATHERINE BALLARD:
Burial: Mt. Hope Cemetery, Cherry Co., NE

    viii.   THOMAS CONNER BALLARD, *b. 13 Jun 1913, Cherry Co., NE; d. 1939.*

More About THOMAS CONNER BALLARD:
Burial: Mt. Hope Cemetery, Wood Lake, Cherry Co., NE

    ix.   JAMES ELLIS BALLARD, *b. 03 Jun 1914, Cherry Co., NE; d. 15 May 2004, Las Vegas, Clark Co., NV.*

Notes for JAMES ELLIS BALLARD:
Source: Social Security Application

    x.   CHARLES DONALD BALLARD, *b. 17 Jun 1915, Cherry Co., NE; d. 07 Sep 1917.*

More About CHARLES DONALD BALLARD:
Burial: Mt. Hope Cemetery, Wood Lake, Cherry Co., NE

    xi.   BILLIE BALLARD, *b. 07 Sep 1917, Cherry Co., NE; d. 19 Apr 1995, Cherry Co., NE; m. MARY ETHEL WHIPP; b. 04 Aug 1921, Philadelphia Co., PA; d. 12 Mar 2007, Clark Co., NE.*

More About BILLIE BALLARD:
Burial: Mt. Hope Cemetery, Wood Lake, Cherry Co., NE

More About MARY ETHEL WHIPP:
Burial: Southern Nevada Veterans Memorial Cemetery, Clark Co., NE

    xii.   VERA MATILLA BALLARD, *b. 09 Mar 1919, Cherry Co., NE; d. 29 Oct 1992, Cherry Co., NE; m. CARLYLE GRAY, 04 Nov 1934.*

More About VERA MATILLA BALLARD:
Burial: Mt. Hope Cemetery, Wood Lake, Cherry Co., NE

    xiii.   JOHN ALBERT BALLARD, *b. 24 Dec 1920, Cherry Co., NE; d. Aft. 1940, Of Hemet, CA.*

    xiv.   HOMER CORNELIAS "NEAL" BALLARD, *b. 03 Jan 1924, Cherry Co., NE; d. 07 Sep 1969, OR; m. GLORIA.*

More About HOMER CORNELIAS "NEAL" BALLARD:
Burial: Mt. Hope Cemetery, Wood Lake, Cherry Co., NE

    xv.   HELEN SYLVIA BALLARD, *b. 29 Jan 1926, Cherry Co., NE; d. 14 Jan 2010, Lincoln Co., NE; m. CLARIS EALINGER; b. 24 Apr 1921; d. 05 Feb 1981.*

More About HELEN SYLVIA BALLARD:
Burial: Mt. Hope Cemetery, Wood Lake, Cherry Co., NE

More About CLARIS EALINGER:
Burial: Mt. Hope Cemetery, Wood Lake, Cherry Co., NE

14. FRANK DUDLEY[4] BALLARD (WILLIAM GOODWIN[3], JOHN L. NELSON[2], WILLIAM[1]) *was born 02 Jan 1879 in Whiting, Monona Co., IA, and died 1936. He married* MATILDA "MATTIE" C. THOMPSON *15 Oct 1903 in Valentine, NE,* *daughter of* A RCHIBALD T HOMPSON *and* S ARAH C ONNOR. *She was born 03 Feb 1884 in Stanley Buff, NE, and died 1957.*

Notes for F RANK D UDLEY B ALLARD:
Source: 1910-1930 Cherry County Nebraska Federal Census Records
** 1910 - Living in Dewey Lake, Cherry Co., NE - Ballard, Frank D 30 IA MO MO stock rover Cattle Ranch, Mattie C 26 - 3 children 3 living NE Ireland Ireland, Edna V 4 NE, Della May 1 8/12 NE, Leta Francis 4/12 NE*
** 1920 - Living in Dewey Lake, Cherry Co., NE - Ballard, Frank B 41 IA, Matilda C 37 IA, Della 12 NE, Edith 6 NE, Vernice 3 4/12 NE, Lydia Cook, Clifford Oakes 24 boarder, Simon Reinhart 47 boarders*
** 1930 - Living in Valentine, Cherry Co., NE - Ballard, Frank D 51 IA US US, Mathilda C 46 NE IA IA, Della M 21 NE IA NE, Eva R 16 NE, Vernice A 13 NE*

More About F RANK D UDLEY B ALLARD:
Burial: Mt. Hope Cemetery, Valentine, Cherry Co., NE

Notes for M ATILDA "M ATTIE" C. T HOMPSON:
Source: Social Security Records, 1940 Cherry County Nebraska Federal Census Records

** 1940 - Living in Valentine, Cherry Co., NE - Ballard, Matilda 56 wd NE, Della 31 NE, Helen Heller 20 lodger, Alice Schmaltz 24 lodger, Ileene Boucher 21 lodger*

More About M ATILDA "M ATTIE" C. T HOMPSON:
Burial: Mt. Hope Cemetery, Valentine, Cherry Co., NE

Children of F RANK B ALLARD *and* M ATILDA T HOMPSON *are:*
      i.   E DNA V IOLET[5] B ALLARD, *b. 18 Aug 1905, Cherry Co., NE; d. 25 Aug 1918.*

          More About E DNA V IOLET B ALLARD:
          Burial: Mt. Hope Cemetery, Valentine, Cherry Co., NE

      ii.   D ELLA M AY B ALLARD, *b. 06 Aug 1908, Cherry Co., NE; d. 25 Oct 1971; m.* T ROY C OX, *Divorced.*

          More About D ELLA M AY B ALLARD:
          Burial: Mt. Hope Cemetery, Valentine, Cherry Co., NE

      iii.   L ETA F RANCIS B ALLARD, *b. 09 Dec 1909, Cherry Co., NE; d. 20 Jan 1918.*

          More About L ETA F RANCIS B ALLARD:
          Burial: Mt. Hope Cemetery, Valentine, Cherry Co., NE

      iv.   F RANK D UDLEY B ALLARD, J R., *b. 08 Feb 1912, Cherry Co., NE; d. 12 Aug 1913.*

          More About F RANK D UDLEY B ALLARD, J R.:
          Burial: Mt. Hope Cemetery, Valentine, Cherry Co., NE

18.   v.   E DITH R OSE B ALLARD, *b. 21 Nov 1913, Cherry Co., NE; d. 07 Jul 1971, Canyon Co., ID.*

      vi.   V ERNICE A. B ALLARD, *b. 22 Oct 1916, Cherry Co., NE; d. 28 Sep 1996; m.* R OBET H UNTER K OONTZ; *b. 25 Nov 1906; d. 05 Jan 1977.*

          Notes for V ERNICE A. B ALLARD:
          Source: Social Security Death Records

          More About V ERNICE A. B ALLARD:
          Burial: Mt. Hope Cemetery, Valentine, Cherry Co., NE

More About ROBET HUNTER KOONTZ:
Burial: Mt. Hope Cemetery, Valentine, Cherry Co., NE

15. JAY A.[4] BALLARD (ELI FRANKLIN[3], JOHN L. NELSON[2], WILLIAM[1]) *was born 1876 in NE, and died 30 Jun 1960 in Baker Co., OR. He married NORA J. TITUS 24 Jun 1907 in Baker City, Union Co., OR. She was born 1884 in OR, and died 18 Apr 1970.*

Notes for JAY A. BALLARD:
Source: 1920-1930 Baker County Oregon Federal Census Records, Union County Oregon Marriage Records

** 1920 - Living in Pine, Baker Co., OR - Ballard, Jay A 43 NE MO TN, Nora J 36 OR IL MA, Franklin A 11 OR, Ormin A 9 OR, Harold J 7 OR, Elif F 74 MO unk unk*
** 1930 - Living in Pine, Baker Co., OR - Ballard, JA 53, Nora J 45, Ormin A 20, Harold J 18*

More About JAY A. BALLARD:
Burial: Pine Haven Cemetery, Baker Co., OR

Children of JAY BALLARD and NORA TITUS are:
> i.   FRANKLIN A.[5] BALLARD, *b. 16 Apr 1908, Baker Co., OR; d. 25 Oct 1970, Lane Co., OR; m. DORIS BELL MCCARVER; b. 09 Apr 1911, MO; d. 06 Aug 1987, Lane Co., OR.*
>
>> *More About DORIS BELL MCCARVER:*
>> *Burial: Brumbaugh Cemetery, Lane Co., OR*
>
> ii. ORMIN ALTON BALLARD, *b. 17 Mar 1910, Baker Co., OR; d. 26 Aug 1982, Baker Co., OR; m. ANNA NAVE; b. 25 May 1908, Yellowstone Co., MT; d. 26 Jan 1979, Baker Co., OR.*
>
>> *More About ORMIN ALTON BALLARD:*
>> *Burial: Eagle Valley Cemetery, Baker Co., OR*
>>
>> *More About ANNA NAVE:*
>> *Burial: Eagle Valley Cemetery, Baker Co., OR*
>
> iii. HAROLD J. BALLARD, *b. Abt. 1913, Baker Co., OR; d. Aft. 1920.*

16. BELL MINNIE[4] LONG (AGNES CATHERINE[3] BALLARD, JOHN L. NELSON[2], WILLIAM[1]) *was born 09 Feb 1880 in Pottawattamie Co., IA, and died 17 Oct 1961 in Hall Co., NE. She married ASHLEY THOMAS CONGER. He was born 21 Dec 1874 in Essex Co., NY, and died 28 Aug 1958 in Sherman Co., NE.*

More About BELL MINNIE LONG:
Burial: Evergreen Cemetery, Sherman Co., NE

More About ASHLEY THOMAS CONGER:
Burial: Evergreen Cemetery, Sherman Co., NE

Child of BELL LONG and ASHLEY CONGER is:
> i.   ASHLEY T.[5] CONGER, *m. CLARA GERKLING, 28 Jun 1924, Pottawattamie Co., IA.*

17. FRED B.[4] LONG (AGNES CATHERINE[3] BALLARD, JOHN L. NELSON[2], WILLIAM[1]) *was born 02 Nov 1882 in IA, and died 08 Oct 1972. He married BERTHA M. GREEN 25 Dec 1901 in Pottawattamie Co., IA. She was born 28 Jun 1879, and died 02 Jul 1954.*

Notes for FRED B. LONG:
Source: 1910-1920 Washington County Nebraska Federal Census Records

** 1910 - Living in Herman, Washington Co., NE - Long, Fred B 27 IA, Bertha M 30 IA, Lua T 7 IA, Weston R 5 IA, Arthur J 1 1/12 IA*
** 1920 - Living in Blair, Washington Co., NE - Long, Fred B 37, Bertha M 40, L. Thelma 17, Weston I 15, Arthur F 10, Howard J. 5*

More About FRED B. LONG:
Burial: Blair Cemetery, Washington Co., NE

More About BERTHA M. GREEN:
Burial: Blair Cemetery, Washington Co., NE

Children of FRED LONG and BERTHA GREEN are:

> i.   LUA THELMA⁵ LONG, b. 22 Oct 1902, Pottawattamie Co., IA; d. 27 Jul 2002, Douglas Co., NE; m. EARL CLAYTON CALDWELL; b. 18 Apr 1897, Washington Co., NE; d. 27 Sep 1978, Warren Co., IA.
>
> > *More About LUA THELMA LONG:*
> > *Burial: Blair Cemetery, Washington Co., NE*
> >
> > *More About EARL CLAYTON CALDWELL:*
> > *Burial: Blair Cemetery, Washington Co., NE*
>
> ii.   WESTON R. LONG, b. Abt. 1905, Pottawattamie Co., IA; d. Aft. 1920.
> iii.   ARTHUR F. LONG, b. Abt. 1909, Washington Co., NE; d. Aft. 1920.
> iv.   HOWARD J. LONG, b. Abt. 1915, Washington Co., NE; d. Aft. 1920.

Generation No. 5

18.   EDITH ROSE⁵ BALLARD (*FRANK DUDLEY⁴, WILLIAM GOODWIN³, JOHN L. NELSON², WILLIAM¹*) was born 21 Nov 1913 in Cherry Co., NE, and died 07 Jul 1971 in Canyon Co., ID. She married PATRICK R. CAYLER 07 Oct 1933 in Jackson Co., SD. He was born 12 Jul 1914 in Nobles Co., MN, and died 24 Jun 1999 in Canyon Co., ID.

More About EDITH ROSE BALLARD:

Burial: Hillcrest Memorial Gardens, Canyon Co., ID

Notes for PATRICK R. CAYLER:
Source: 1940 Okanogan County Washington Federal Census Records

** 1940 - Living in Washington Co., SD - Cayler, Pat R 25   MN, Edith R 26 NE, Ratsy Gean 5 NE, Frank Michel 4 NE*

More About PATRICK R. CAYLER:
Burial: Hillcrest Memorial Gardens, Canyon Co., ID

Children of EDITH BALLARD and PATRICK CAYLER are:

> i.   PATSY GEAN⁶ CAYLER, b. Abt. 1935, NE; d. Aft. 1940.
> ii.   MICHEL FRANK CAYLER, b. Abt. 1936, NE; d. Aft. 1940.

William Ballard

Generation No. 1

1. WILLIAM[1] BALLARD *was born 1793 in KY, and died 1863. He married* SUSAN CRAWFORD *1837 in Greenup Co., KY. She was born 1814 in Montgomery Co., TN, and died Aft. 1850.*

Notes for WILLIAM BALLARD:
Source: 1850 Greenup County Kentucky Federal Census Records
** 1850 - Living in Greenup Co., KY - Ballard, Wm 57 farmer KY, Susan 36 TN, Sanders 13 KY, Eliza 12 KY, Jas 6 KY, Carlisle 5 KY*

Children of WILLIAM BALLARD *and* SUSAN CRAWFORD *are:*
2.   i.   SAUNDERS[2] BALLARD, *b. 1837, Greenup Co., KY; d. 30 Sep 1899, St. Joseph, Buchanan Co., MO.*
3.   ii.   WILLIAM ELGRY BALLARD, *b. 03 Dec 1837, Mt. Sterling, Owen Co., KY; d. 07 Jun 1912, Kearney, Clay Co., MO.*
       iii.   ELIZA BALLARD, *b. 1838, KY.*
       iv.   JAMES BALLARD, *b. 1843, KY; d. 18 Aug 1918, Buchanan Co., MO.*

          Notes for JAMES BALLARD:
          Source: Buchanan County Missouri Death Certificate

          More About JAMES BALLARD:
          Burial: 19 Aug 1918, New King Hill Cemetery, St. Joseph, Buchanan Co., MO

4.   v.   CHARLES CARLISLE BALLARD, *b. 01 Jan 1847, Greenup Co., KY; d. 13 Sep 1908, Starke Co., IN.*
5.   vi.   JOHN WESLEY BALLARD, *b. 27 Apr 1849, KY; d. 09 May 1925, St. Joseph, Buchanan Co., MO.*

Generation No. 2

2. SAUNDERS[2] BALLARD (WILLIAM[1]) *was born 1837 in Greenup Co., KY, and died 30 Sep 1899 in St. Joseph, Buchanan Co., MO. He married* CAROLINE BALDWIN SUITER *Abt. 1860 in Adams Co., OH, daughter of* JOHN SUTERS *and* NANCY COCHRAN. *She was born 04 Mar 1833 in Adams Co., OH, and died 11 Sep 1883.*

Notes for SAUNDERS BALLARD:
Source: 1870 Buchanan County Missouri Federal Census Records

** Find a Grave shows a different burial: New King Hill Cemetery, St. Joseph Buchanan Co., MO*
** Find a Grave shows a son Henry Amison Ballard born 19 Apr 1873 Plattsmouth, Cass Co., NE - I haven't proven this one yet. He is buried in Dadeville City Cemetery., Dadeville, Tallapoosa Co., Al*
** 1870 - Living in Buchanan Co.,, St. Joseph MO - Ballard, Saunders 34 KY game dealer, Caroline 37 OH, Miranda 8 OH, William 7 OH, Virginia 5 OH, not named 6/12 MO, John W. 21 KY Game Dealer KY*

More About SAUNDERS BALLARD:
Burial: New King Hill Cemetery, St. Joseph, Buchanan Co., MO

Notes for CAROLINE BALDWIN SUITER:
Source: 1880 Adams County Ohio Federal Census Records
** 1880 - Living in Bratton, Adams Co., OH - Ballard, Carolina 47 OH OH OH, Maranda E 18 OH KY OH, William C 17 OH KY OH, Virginia F. 15 OH KY OH, Mary E 8 OH KY OH*

More About CAROLINE BALDWIN SUITER:
Burial: Louisville Cemetery, Louisville, Adams Co., OH

Children of SAUNDERS BALLARD and CAROLINE SUITER are:

     i.   MIRANDA EMMALINE[3] BALLARD, b. 07 Nov 1861, Adams Co., OH; d. 02 Nov 1938, Clinton Co., OH; m. LEVI TURNER MOORE; b. 11 Sep 1865, OH; d. 05 May 1953.

         More About MIRANDA EMMALINE BALLARD:
         Burial: Martinsville 100F Cemetery, Martinsville, Clinton Co., OH

         More About LEVI TURNER MOORE:
         Burial: Martinsville 100F Cemetery, Martinsville, Clinton Co., OH

    ii.   WILLIAM CRAWFORD BALLARD, b. 10 Jan 1863, Adams Co., OH; d. 21 Feb 1922, Little Rock, Pulaski Co., AR.

         Notes for WILLIAM CRAWFORD BALLARD:
         Lived in Winthrop AR

         More About WILLIAM CRAWFORD BALLARD:
         Burial: Greenwood Cemetery, Hot Springs, Garland Co., AR

   iii. FLORENCE VIRGINIA "JENNIE" BALLARD, b. 1864, Adams Co., OH; d. 1895, Adams Co., OH; m. JOHN WYLIE; b. 1861, Adams Co., OH; d. 1893, Adams Co., OH.

         More About FLORENCE VIRGINIA "JENNIE" BALLARD:
         Burial: Lawshe Cemetery., Lawshe, Adams Co., OH

         More About JOHN WYLIE:
         Burial: Lawshe Cemetery., Lawshe, Adams Co., OH

    iv. MARY ELIZABETH BALLARD, b. 13 Nov 1871, Adams Co., OH; d. 01 Apr 1947; m. JACOB LAYTON WISECUP; b. 19 Apr 1868, Highland Co., OH; d. 19 Aug 1959, Montgomery Co., OH.

         More About MARY ELIZABETH BALLARD:
         Burial: Marble Furnace Cemetery., Adams Co., OH

         More About JACOB LAYTON WISECUP:
         Burial: Marble Furnace Cemetery., Adams Co., OH

3. WILLIAM ELGRY[2] BALLARD (WILLIAM[1]) was born 03 Dec 1837 in Mt. Sterling, Owen Co., KY, and died 07 Jun 1912 in Kearney, Clay Co., MO. He married NANCY A.. She was born Jun 1842 in OH, and died 26 Dec 1923.

Notes for WILLIAM ELGRY BALLARD:
Source: Clay County Missouri Will Records, Clay County Missouri Probate Records, Clay County Missouri Death Certificate, 1880 - 1910 Clay County Kentucky Federal Census Records,
** 1880 - Living in Washington twp., Clay Co., MO - Ballard, Wm E 43 KY, Nancy A 38 OH, WJC 16 OH, Mary L 14 OH, E A 5 MO, JW 3 MO, Ida M 1 MO*
** 1900 - Living in Liberty twp., Clay Co., MO - Ballard, William - Dec 1837 KY KY TN, Nancie A - June 1842 OH Ireland OH, Eva A - June 1875 MO*
** 1910 - Living in Clay Co., MO - Ballard, William E 73 KY, US KY, Nancy A 68 OH US US 9 children 2 living*
** 1910 - Clay Co., MO - Will of William E. Ballard – (with an attempt to use original spelling)*
I, W. E. Ballard, make this, my first, last and only Will! in good health, mind and Spirit at this day: June 1, 1910 twenty minites to one oclock. P.M. to my wife Nancy my Real Estate consisting of House and 2 Lots at Kearney MO, all household Goods and Chattel, also My wife shall have Procession and full Control of said Property during her lifetime.

In case of her dead this Property shall be equally devited between the Children: vis: Mrs. Lou Smith, Mrs. Conrad (Eva) Fisher, and W. E. Ballard (Sumerset Kansas) the Part of the Estate willed here to W. E. Ballard Junior shall be kept in trust by Conrad Fisher of Clay Co., MO) until said heir is of the age of 21 years.
I appoint Conrad Fisher Administrator of this will without Bond!
I have signed this will now in the present of witnesses. William E. Ballard - W. B. Cheek, T J Cuthbertson

** 1912 - State of Missouri, County of Clay } ss. In the Probate Court In Vacation - Be It Remembered, That on the 15th day of June 1912, personally appeared before the undersigned, Clerk of the Probate Court, of the county and State aforesaid, W. B. Cheek and T J Cuthbertson, the subscribing witnesses to the annexed will of William E. Ballard, deceased, and being by me first duly sworn depose and say that the said William E. Ballard, the testate subscribed the same in their presence, and published the said will or instrument of writing, as his last will; that he, the said testator, was at the time of publishing his said will, of sound mind and more than twenty - one years of age, and that they, the said deponents, attested the said will as witnesses thereto, at the request of said testator by subscribing their names to the same, in the presence of the said testator and in the presence of each other. And said deponents further state that said decedent died, while a resident of Clay County, Missouri, on the seventh day of June. A. D. 1912. W. B. Cheek, T. J Cuthbertson*
Sworn to and subscribed before me, they day and year first above written.
In Witness whereof, I have here unto set my hand and affixed the seal of said Court, at office, in the City of Liberty, in said County, this 15th day of June, A.D. 1912. (seal) Frances B. Hopkins, Clerk

** 1912 - Clay co., MO Will records - State of Missouri, County of Clay } ss. I, Frances B. Hopkins, Clerk of the Probate Court of the county and State aforesaid, having examined the foregoing instrument of writing, signed by William E. Ballard, and purporting to be the last will and testament of said William E. Ballard, deceased, and having heard the testimony of W. B. Cheek and T. J Cuthbertson, subscribing witnesses thereto in relation to the execution of the same, do declare and adjudge said instrument of writing to be the last will and testament of William E. Ballard, deceased, late of Clay County, and record the same as such.*
In Witness Whereof, I have hereunto set my hand and affixed the seal of said Court, at office, in the city of Liberty, in said County, this 15th day of June, 1912. (seal) Frances B. Hopkins, Clerk.

** 1912 - Clay Co., MO Application For Letter of Administrators, Vol B-C, 1907-1923 - Letters of Testamentary - State of Missouri County of Clay } ss. In the Probate Court of Clay County, Missouri. In the Matter of the estate of William E. Ballard, deceased, Conrad Fisher, Executor named in and by the last will and testament of said deceased, to execute the same, says that to the best of his knowledge and belief, the names of the widow and heirs of the said William E. Ballard, deceased, and their places of residence, are respectively as follows: Nancy Ballard, widow, who resides in the County of Clay, in the State of Missouri; Lou Smith, (wife of David Smith,) daughter, who resides in the County of Clay, in the State of Missouri; Eva Fischer, (wife of Conrad Fisher,) daughter, who resides in the County of Clay i the State of Missouri, William E. Ballard, (only child and heir) of William E. Ballard deceased son of said decedent,) grandson, who resides in the County of Somerset in the State of Kansas, that the said William E. Ballard on the seventh day of June, 1912 died with a will; that he will make a perfect inventory of and faithfully administer all the estate of the deceased; and pay the debts as far as the assets will extend and the law direct, and account for and pay all assets which shall come to his possession or knowledge. Conrad Fisher*
Subscribed and sworn to before me, this 15th day of June A.D. 1912 (seal) Frances B. Hopkins, Clerk, Filed June 15th, 1912 and recorded the 12th day of August, 1912,. Frances B. Hopkins, Clerk

More About WILLIAM ELGRY BALLARD:
Burial: Muddy Fork Cemetery, Kearney, Clay Co., MO

More About NANCY A.:
Burial: Muddy Fork Cemetery, Kearney, Clay Co., MO

Children of WILLIAM BALLARD and NANCY A. are:

       i.   *W. J. C.[3] BALLARD, b. 1865, Clay Co., MO; d. Bef. 1912.*
6.   ii.   *MARY LOU BALLARD, b. 1866, Clay Co., MO; d. 1915.*

7.	iii.	*EVA ALICE BALLARD, b. Jun 1875, Clay Co., MO; d. Aft. 1940.*
	iv.	*J. W. BALLARD, b. 1877, Clay Co., MO; d. Aft. 1880.*
	v.	*IDA M. BALLARD, b. 1879, Clay Co., MO; d. Aft. 1880.*
8.	vi.	*WILLIAM E. BALLARD, d. Bef. 1912.*

4. *CHARLES CARLISLE[2] BALLARD (WILLIAM[1]) was born 01 Jan 1847 in Greenup Co., KY, and died 13 Sep 1908 in Starke Co., IN. He married SARAH ELIZABETH ACKLES 15 Nov 1865 in Highland Co., OH. She was born 05 Dec 1854 in Highland Co., OH, and died 09 Sep 1928 in Grant Co., IN.*

Notes for CHARLES CARLISLE BALLARD:
Source: Stark County Indiana Certificate of Death, Highland Co. Ohio birth records, Judy Waggoner Green (rgreen@comteck.com), 1870 Highland County Ohio Federal Census Records, 1880 Brown County Ohio Federal Census Records, 1900 Grant County Indiana Federal Census

** 1870 - Living in Danville, Highland Co., OH - Ballard, Carlisle 25 Feathering KY, Sarah 18 OH, William 1 OH*
** 1880 - Living in Sterling, Brown Co., OH - Ballard, Charles 33 horse trader KY, Sarah E 27 OH, Thomas 7 OH Elizabeth 3*
** 1900 - Living in Grant Co., IN - Ballard, Charles - Jan 1850 50 KY KY KY vet, Sarah - Jan 1852 OH OH OH 9 children - 8 living, Leray - Jan 1888 OH KY OH, Leroy - Jan 1888 OH KY OH*

More About CHARLES CARLISLE BALLARD:
Burial: Grandview Cemetery, Terre Haute, Vigo Co., IN

Notes for SARAH ELIZABETH ACKLES:
Source: Grant County Indiana Certificate of Death

More About SARAH ELIZABETH ACKLES:
Burial: Estates of Serenity, Marion, Grant Co., IN

Children of CHARLES BALLARD and SARAH ACKLES are:

9.	i.	*THOMAS JEFFERSON[3] BALLARD, b. 02 Jan 1872, Highland Co., OH; d. 14 Nov 1919, Grant Co., IN.*
	ii.	*ELIZABETH BALLARD, b. 1877, Highland Co., OH; d. Aft. 1880.*
	iii.	*CLINTON FRANCES "CALLIE" BALLARD, b. 09 Jun 1884, Highland Co., OH; d. 26 Jan 1918, Grant Co., IN; m. JESSE ALBERT PULLEY, 27 Dec 1899, Grant Co., IN.*

More About CLINTON FRANCES "CALLIE" BALLARD:
Burial: Van Buren Cemetery, Grant Co., IN

iv. *LERAY BALLARD, b. 27 Jan 1888, Highland Co., OH; d. 19 Nov 1937, Marion, Grant Co., IN; m. MABEL BUSH; b. 09 Apr 1891; d. 17 Nov 1968.*

More About LERAY BALLARD:
Burial: Estates of Serenity, Marion, Grant Co., IN

More About MABEL BUSH:
Burial: Beech Grove Cemetery, Muncie, Delaware Co., IN

v. *LEROY BALLARD, b. 26 Jan 1888, White Oak Twp, Highland Co., OH; d. 12 Feb 1912; m. MABEL COX, 10 Dec 1909, Winamac, Pulaski Co., IN; b. 19 Sep 1892, Pulaski Co., IN.*

Notes for LEROY BALLARD:
Source: Winamac, Pulaski County Indiana Marriage Registration

More About LEROY BALLARD:
Burial: Estates of Serenity, Marion, Grant Co., IN

5. JOHN WESLEY[2] BALLARD (WILLIAM[1]) *was born 27 Apr 1849 in KY, and died 09 May 1925 in St. Joseph, Buchanan Co., MO. He married* SUSAN ELLA MCQUEEN *17 Feb 1879 in Buchanan Co., MO. She was born 25 Dec 1864 in Buchanan Co., MO, and died 15 Aug 1972 in St. Joseph, Buchanan Co., MO.*

Notes for JOHN WESLEY BALLARD:
Source: 1900-1910 Buchanan County Missouri Federal Census Records, Buchanan County Missouri Death Certificate

** 1900 - Living in Washington, Buchanan Co., MO - Ballard, John W - Apr 1847 KY KY KY, Susan - Dec 1863 MO MO VA, James W - June 1881 MO, Grace E - May 1886 MO, John E - Mar 1889 MO, Katie E - June 1899 MO, Nellie Reed - Nov 1886 niece KS VA KY*
** 1910 - Living in Washington, Buchanan Co., MO - Ballard, John W 39 KY KY KY, John E 20 MO, Kattie 13 MO*
** 1920 - Living in Washington, Buchanan Co., MO - Ballard, John 69 OH, Elisha Pinter 18 KS*

More About SUSAN ELLA MCQUEEN:
Burial: Ashland Cemetery, St. Joseph, Buchanan Co., MO

Children of JOHN BALLARD *and* SUSAN MCQUEEN *are:*

10.   i.   JAMES W.[3] BALLARD, *b. 01 Jun 1881, Buchanan Co., MO; d. 08 Jul 1949, St. Joseph, Buchanan Co., MO.*

       ii.   GRACE ELIZABETH BALLARD, *b. 25 May 1886, Buchanan Co., MO; d. 22 Jan 1926, St. Joseph, Buchanan Co., MO; m.* CHARLES E. FITZJOHN; *b. 28 Jun 1889, Pike Co., IL; d. 08 Dec 1942, St. Joseph, Buchanan Co., MO.*

             More About GRACE ELIZABETH BALLARD:
             Burial: Ashland Cemetery, St. Joseph, Buchanan Co., MO

             More About CHARLES E. FITZJOHN:
             Burial: Ashland Cemetery, St. Joseph, Buchanan Co., MO

       iii.   JOHN EDWARD BALLARD, *b. 18 Mar 1889, Buchanan Co., MO; d. 13 Dec 1940, Buchanan Co., MO; m.* MARY; *b. 1890, MO; d. Aft. 1940.*

             Notes for JOHN EDWARD BALLARD:
             Source: 1930 Buchanan County Missouri Federal Census Records, Buchanan County Missouri Death Certificate
             ** 1930 - Living in Washington, Buchanan Co., MO - Ballard, John E 40 MO MO MO, Mar 31 MO MO MO*

             More About JOHN EDWARD BALLARD:
             Burial: Ashland Cemetery, St. Joseph, Buchanan Co., MO

       iv.   KATHERINE "KATIE" EDNA BALLARD, *b. 26 Dec 1896, Buchanan Co., MO; d. 21 Aug 1942, St. Joseph, Buchanan Co., MO; m.* WILLIAM E. BANDEL; *b. 01 Nov 1881; d. 17 Aug 1957.*

             More About KATHERINE "KATIE" EDNA BALLARD:
             Burial: Ashland Cemetery, St. Joseph, Buchanan Co., MO

             More About WILLIAM E. BANDEL:

Burial: Pacific Crest Cemetery, Los Angeles Co., CA

Generation No. 3

6. MARY LOU[3] BALLARD (WILLIAM ELGRY[2], WILLIAM[1]) *was born 1866 in Clay Co., MO, and died 1915. She married* DAVID SMITH *19 Jan 1884 in Clay Co., MO. He was born Mar 1858 in MO, and died 1945.*

More About MARY LOU BALLARD:
Burial: Muddy Fork Cemetery, Kearney, Clay Co., MO

Notes for DAVID SMITH:
Source: 1900 Clay County Missouri Federal Census Records
** 1900 - Living in Kearney, Clay Co., MO - Smith, David - Mar 1858 MO KY KY, Mary L - Apr 1866 - 3 children 3 living OH KY OH, Bernard - Nov 1885 MO, Homer - Dec 1887 MO, Virgil - Feb 1893 MO*

More About DAVID SMITH:
Burial: Muddy Fork Cemetery, Kearney, Clay Co., MO

Children of MARY BALLARD *and* DAVID SMITH *are:*
       i.   BERNARD[4] SMITH, *b. Nov 1885, MO; d. Aft. 1900.*
      ii.   HOMER SMITH, *b. Dec 1887, MO; d. Aft. 1900.*
     iii. VIRGIL SMITH, *b. Feb 1893, MO; d. Aft. 1900.*

7. EVA ALICE[3] BALLARD (WILLIAM ELGRY[2], WILLIAM[1]) *was born Jun 1875 in Clay Co., MO, and died Aft. 1940. She married* CONRAD FISHER. *He was born Abt. 1874 in MO, and died Aft. 1940.*

Notes for CONRAD FISHER:
Source: 1920-1940 Clay County Missouri Federal Census Records

** 1920 - Living in Platte, Clay Co., MO - Fisher, Conrad 46 MO, Eva Alice 45, Gracie May 17 MO, Albert L 12 MO, Helen Irene 7 MO, Mrs. Nancy Ballard mother in law 77 wd OH*
** 1930 - Living in Liberty, Clay Co., MO - Fishcher, Conrad 54 MO Germany Germany, Eva A 54 MO KY OH, Albert L 23 MO, Helen I 18 MO*
** 1940 - Living in Liberty, Clay Co., MO - Fisher, Conrad 64 MO, Eva 65 MO*

Children of EVA BALLARD *and* CONRAD FISHER *are:*
       i.   GRACIE MAY[4] FISHER, *b. Abt. 1903, MO; d. Aft. 1920.*
      ii.   ALBERT L. FISHER, *b. Abt. 1908, MO; d. Aft. 1930.*
     iii. HELEN IRENE FISHER, *b. Abt. 1913, MO; d. Aft. 1930.*

8. WILLIAM E.[3] BALLARD (WILLIAM ELGRY[2], WILLIAM[1]) *died Bef. 1912.*

Child of WILLIAM E. BALLARD *is:*
       i.   WILLIAM E.[4] BALLARD, *b. of Somerset, Miami Co., KS.*

9. THOMAS JEFFERSON[3] BALLARD (CHARLES CARLISLE[2], WILLIAM[1]) *was born 02 Jan 1872 in Highland Co., OH, and died 14 Nov 1919 in Grant Co., IN. He married* ALICE LUCINDA WALLACE *10 Oct 1905 in Grant Co., IN. She was born 18 Apr 1880, and died 08 Feb 1946 in Grant Co., IN.*

Notes for THOMAS JEFFERSON BALLARD:
Source: Grant County Indiana Certificate of Death

More About THOMAS JEFFERSON BALLARD:
Burial: Estates of Serenity, Marion, Grant Co., IN

More About ALICE LUCINDA WALLACE:
Burial: Estates of Serenity, Marion, Grant Co., IN

Child of THOMAS BALLARD and ALICE WALLACE is:

     i.   THOMAS ALBERT[4] BALLARD, b. 16 Mar 1904, Grant Co., IN; d. Dec 1967, Miami-Dade Co., FL; m. GRACE P. SEXTON; b. 16 Oct 1909, Montgomery Co., KY; d. 12 Sep 1947, Grant Co., IN.

        More About THOMAS ALBERT BALLARD:
        Burial: Estates of Serenity, Marion, Grant Co., IN

        More About GRACE P. SEXTON:
        Burial: Estates of Serenity, Marion, Grant Co., IN

10. JAMES W.[3] BALLARD (JOHN WESLEY[2], WILLIAM[1]) was born 01 Jun 1881 in Buchanan Co., MO, and died 08 Jul 1949 in St. Joseph, Buchanan Co., MO. He married ANNA. She was born 1892 in MO, and died Aft. 1920.

Notes for JAMES W. BALLARD:
Source: 1910-1920 Buchanan County Missouri Federal Census Records, Buchanan County Missouri Death Certificate

* 1910 - Living in Washington, Buchanan Co., MO - Ballard, James 27 MO MO MO, Ana 18 MO MO MO, Charles 3 MO, Flossie infant
* 1920 - Living in Washington, Buchanan Co., MO - Ballard, James 38 MO, Anna 26 MO, Charles 12 MO, Flossie 10 MO, James 8 MO, Junita 1 2/12 MO

Children of JAMES BALLARD and ANNA are:

     i.   CHARLES[4] BALLARD, b. 1907, Buchanan Co., MO; d. Nov 1978, St. Joseph, Buchanan Co., MO.
    ii.   FLOSSIE BALLARD, b. 09 Jun 1909, Buchanan Co., MO; d. 18 Jun 1975, Multnomah Co., OR; m. PHILLIP GOERKE, 09 Feb 1934, St. Joseph, MO; b. 03 Mar 1902; d. Sep 1982, Gresham, Multnomah, Co., OR.
   iii.   JAMES BALLARD, b. 1912, Buchanan Co., MO; d. Aug 1979, St. Joseph, Buchanan Co., MO.
   iv.   JUANITA BALLARD, b. 1918, Buchanan Co., MO; d. Aft. 1920.

William Riley Ballard

Generation No. 1

1. WILLIAM RILEY[1] BALLARD *was born 1811 in KY, and died 24 Apr 1865 in Boone Co., MO. He married* CAROLINE G. PULLIAM *04 Oct 1833 in Garrard Co., KY, daughter of* WOODSON PULLIAM *and* NANCY SPELLMAN. *She was born 15 Jul 1817 in KY, and died 22 May 1890 in Saline Co., MO.*

Notes for WILLIAM RILEY BALLARD:

Source: Garrard County Kentucky Marriage Records, 1840 Lincoln County Kentucky Federal Census Records, 1850 Anderson County Kentucky Federal Census Records, 1860 Boone County Missouri Federal Census Records, Winifred Schwab, CD# 229 Garrard Co., KY, Bill Fairly, Rocky Mt. NC, Michael D. Ballard (mike0047@juno.com), Mike Ballard (mike5117@worldnet.att.net)

** More than likely the brother of James Ballard of Lincoln Co., KY*
** William Riley Ballard - name source - Death certificate of Eliza Ballard Masters*
** 1833 - Living in Garrard Co., KY - marriage Oct 4, 1833. Bondsman: James P. Letcher, daughter of Woodson G. Pulliam*
** 1840 - Living in Lincoln Co., KY - Ballard, William R - Males - Under 5 - 3 Males - 5 thru 9 - 1, Males - 30 thru 39 -1, Females - 20 thru 29 - 1*
** 1850 - Living in Anderson Co., KY - Ballard, William R 39 farmer KY, Caroline 33 KY, Woodson 15 laborer KY, James 13 KY, Abner 10 KY, Mary J 8 Ky, Nancy 5 KY, Franklin 3 KY*
** 1860 - Living in Bourbon, Boone Co., MO - Ballard, Wm R 49 KY, Caroline 43 KY, Abner 20 KY, Nancy 15 KY, Franklin 12 KY, Edward 8 KY, Sarah A 6 KY, Eliza 5 MO, not named 10/12 MO*

Notes for CAROLINE G. PULLIAM:
Source: 1870-1880 Saline County Missouri Federal Census Records
** 1870 - Living in Elmwood, Saline Co., MO - Ballard, Caroline 53 KY, Franklin 22 farmer KY, Edward 18 farmer KY, Eveline 12 MO, Albert 8 MO*
** 1880 - Living in Liberty, Saline Co., MO - Ballard, Caroline 68, Albert 16*

Children of WILLIAM BALLARD *and* CAROLINE PULLIAM *are:*

2.	i.	SQUIRE WOODSON "WOOD" A.[2] BALLARD, b. 27 Aug 1834, KY; d. 17 Apr 1912, Miami, Saline Co., MO.
3.	ii.	JAMES LIVINGSTON BALLARD, b. 29 Feb 1836, Garrard Co., KY; d. 05 Aug 1923, Union, Wright Co., MO.
4.	iii.	ABNER "AB" GREEN BALLARD, b. 07 Apr 1840, KY; d. 10 Oct 1917, Saline Co., MO.
5.	iv.	MARY J. BALLARD, b. 1842, KY; d. Aft. 1870.
	v.	NANCY "NAN" BALLARD, b. 1845, KY; d. 21 May 1915; m. MR. GIBSON.
6.	vi.	BENJAMIN FRANKLIN "FRANK" BALLARD, b. 17 Mar 1848, KY; d. Bef. 1900.
	vii.	WILLIAM R. BALLARD, b. 1850, KY.
7.	viii.	EDWARD "BOB" SPELLMAN BALLARD, b. 25 Jan 1851, KY; d. 13 Nov 1928.
	ix.	SARAH BALLARD, b. 25 Mar 1854, Garrard Co., KY; d. Aft. 1860.

Notes for SARAH BALLARD:
Source: Garrard County Kentucky Birth Records

8.	x.	ELIZA DILLARD BALLARD, b. 08 Feb 1856, Boone Co., MO or Greene Co., KY; d. 13 Oct 1955, Marshall, Saline Co., MO.
9.	xi.	EVALINE "EVA" BALLARD, b. 1859, KY; d. Aft. 1900.
	xii.	ALBERT "ALLIE" BALLARD, b. 1862, MO; d. Aft. 1880.

Generation No. 2

2. SQUIRE WOODSON "WOOD" A.[2] BALLARD (WILLIAM RILEY[1]) *was born 27 Aug 1834 in KY, and died 17 Apr 1912 in Miami, Saline Co., MO. He married* MARY ELLEN DICKERSON *20 Apr 1856 in Garrard Co., KY, daughter of* HIRAM DICKERSON. *She was born 17 Mar 1834 in KY, and died 26 Feb 1913 in Miami, Saline Co., MO.*

Notes for SQUIRE WOODSON "WOOD" A. BALLARD:
Source: 1860-1880 Garrard County Kentucky Federal Census Records,1900 Saline County Missouri Federal Census Records, Saline County Missouri Certificate of Death

** 1860 - Living in Garrard Co., MO - Ballard, Woodson 35 KY, Ellen 2 KY, SB 3, John W 2 KY, Hiram 1 KY*
** 1870 - Living in Bryantsville, Garrard Co., MO - Ballard, Woodson 45 farmer, Ellen 40 KY, Sarah B 12, John W 10, Hiram 8, Valentine 7, Susan M 6, Mundosa 5, Robert 4, Edward 2 (or Edmond - hard to read), Carra 4/12*
** 1880 - Living in Bryantsville, Garrard Co., KY - Ballard, Woodson 45 farming KY KY KY, Mary E 46 KY, Charles 21 KY, Valentine 18 KY, Susan 17 KY, Nancy 16 KY, Robert 15 KY, Edward 14 KY, Carrie 10 KY*
** 1900 - Living in Miami, Saline Co., MO - Ballard, S W 70 KY VA KY, Mary E - Aug 1833 KY VA KY, E. F - Apr 1864 KY, Robt E - May 1873 KY, Nannie - Mar 1866 KY, Nannie - Mar 1890 MO*
** 1910 - Living in Miami, Saline Co., MO - Ballard, Squire M 75 KY VA VA, 78 - 10 children 7 living KY VA VA, Charlie 49 KY, Robert 40 KY, George Figgins grandson 10 MO*

Notes for MARY ELLEN DICKERSON:
Source: Saline County Missouri Death Certificate

Children of SQUIRE BALLARD *and* MARY DICKERSON *are:*

10.	i.	SARAH BELL[3] BALLARD, *b. 27 Jan 1857, Garrard Co., MO; d. 17 Apr 1938, KS.*
11.	ii.	JOHN WILLIAM BALLARD, *b. 12 Jan 1858, Garrard Co., MO; d. 30 Jan 1943, Marshall, Saline Co., MO.*
	iii.	CHARLES HIRAM BALLARD, *b. 20 May 1859, Garrard Co., MO; d. 24 Jan 1936, Marshall, Saline Co., MO.*

Notes for CHARLES HIRAM BALLARD:
Source: Garrard County Kentucky Birth Records, Saline County Missouri Certificate of Death

	iv.	SUSAN M. BALLARD, *b. 10 May 1864, Garrard Co., MO; d. Nov 1881.*

More About SUSAN M. BALLARD:
Burial: Neff Family Cemetery, Saline Co., MO

12.	v.	VALENTINE BALLARD, *b. 01 Apr 1862, Garrard Co., MO; d. 14 Dec 1925, Saline Co., MO.*
	vi.	MUNDOSA BALLARD, *b. 1865, Garrard Co., MO; d. Aft. 1870.*
13.	vii.	ANN "NAN" "ANNIE" DORA BALLARD, *b. 22 Mar 1866, Garrard Co., MO; d. 31 Jan 1956, Marshall, Saline Co., MO.*
	viii.	EDWARD T. BALLARD, *b. 1867, Garrard Co., MO; d. Aft. 1900.*
	ix.	ROBERT E. BALLARD, *b. 20 May 1868, Garrard Co., MO; d. 30 Jan 1951, Saline Co., MO.*

More About ROBERT E. BALLARD:
Burial: Malta Bend Cemetery, Malta Bend, Saline Co., MO

	x.	CARRIE LEE BALLARD, *b. 19 Mar 1870, Garrard Co., MO; d. 26 Aug 1946, Marshall, Saline Co., MO; m.* CHARLES ROBERT FIGGINS, *12 Sep 1902; b. 18 Mar 1870, Saline Co., MO; d. 05 Nov 1929, Norway, Republic Co., KS.*

More About CARRIE LEE BALLARD:
Burial: Pleasant Hill Cemetery, Cloud Co., KS

More About CHARLES ROBERT FIGGINS:
Burial: Pleasant Hill Cemetery, Cloud Co., KS

     xi.   MIRANDA BALLARD, b. 1872, Garrard Co., MO; d. Aft. 1870.
    xii.   WILLIAM J. BALLARD, b. 1878, Garrard Co., MO; d. Bef. 1880.

3. JAMES LIVINGSTON[2] BALLARD (WILLIAM RILEY[1]) was born 29 Feb 1836 in Garrard Co., KY, and died 05 Aug 1923 in Union, Wright Co., MO. He married MARY CALIFORNIA HENDERSON, daughter of SAMUEL HENDERSON. She was born 19 Sep 1855 in MO, and died 21 Jan 1932 in Union, Wright Co., MO.

Notes for JAMES LIVINGSTON BALLARD:
Source: 1900-1910 Wright County Missouri Federal Census Records, Wright County Missouri Death Certificate
** 1900 - Living in Union, Wright Co., MO - Ballard, James - Feb 1836 KY KY KY, Mary - Sept 1853 9 children 7 living TN TN TN, Harrison - Apr 1889 MO, Walter - Oct 1891 MO, Ilu - Mar 1892 MO, James - Sept 1893 MO, Estie - Jan 1895 MO, Claudie - July 1896 MO Step child Emma Stephens - Sept 1881 MO*
** 1910 - Living in Union, Wright Co., MO - Ballard, James L Sr. 78 TN TN TN, Mary C 50 19 children 11 living, Harrison 21 MO, Walter 20 MO, May 18 MO, James Jr 17 MO, Esty 15 MO, Claud 13 MO*

More About JAMES LIVINGSTON BALLARD:
Burial: Shaddy Cemetery, Grovespring, Wright Co., MO

Notes for MARY CALIFORNIA HENDERSON:
Source: Wright County Missouri Death Certificate

More About MARY CALIFORNIA HENDERSON:
Burial: Shaddy Cemetery, Grovespring, Wright Co., MO

Children of JAMES BALLARD and MARY HENDERSON are:
14.   *i.*   HARRISON "HARRY" STREETER[3] BALLARD, b. 23 Apr 1889, Grovespring, Wright Co., MO; d. 28 Jun 1976, Springfield, Greene Co., MO.
15.   *ii.*   WALTER DAYTON BALLARD, b. 15 Oct 1890, MO; d. 03 Jan 1976.
       iii. ILA BALLARD, b. Mar 1892, MO; d. Aft. 1910.
       iv. JAMES SAMUEL BALLARD, b. 13 Sep 1893, MO; d. Aft. 1910.

           More About JAMES SAMUEL BALLARD:
           Burial: Shaddy Cemetery, Grovespring, Wright Co., MO

       v.   ESTIE BALLARD, b. 29 Dec 1894, MO; d. Aft. 1910.

           More About ESTIE BALLARD:
           Burial: Shaddy Cemetery, Grovespring, Wright Co., MO

16.   *vi.* CLAUDE CHARLES BALLARD, b. 02 Jul 1896, Grovespring, Wright Co., MO; d. 13 Jul 1982, Webster Co., MO.

4. ABNER "AB" GREEN[2] BALLARD (WILLIAM RILEY[1]) was born 07 Apr 1840 in KY, and died 10 Oct 1917 in Saline Co., MO. He married SARAH ELIZABETH SCHOOLING 05 Jul 1869 in Boone Co., MO, daughter of WILLIAM SCHOOLING and NANCY POLLARD. She was born 12 Apr 1844 in Boone Co., MO, and died 31 Mar 1926 in Aarow Rock, Saline Co., MO.

Notes for ABNER "AB" GREEN BALLARD:
Source: 1880-1910 Saline County Missouri Federal Census Records, Saline County Missouri State Board of Health Death Certificate

1880 - Living in Arrow Rock, Saline Co., MO - Ballard, Abner 40 farmer KY KY KY, Sarah 36 MO MO MO MO, Abner 11 IL farm laborer, Ada 7 MO, Carrie 5 MO, James 3 MO, Mary 2 MO, Spellman 4/12 MO
1900 - Living in Arrow Rock, Saline Co., MO - Ballard, A G - Apr 1840 KY KY KY, Sarah - Apr 1840 MO MO MO, Ada Boyd dau - Nov 1872 wd MO, Cathl D Ballard - Apr 1887, John W Boyd - Sept 1895 grandson MO
1910 - Living in Arrow Rock, Saline Co., MO - Ballard, Abner B 69 KY KY KY, Sarah E 66 md 2x MO MO KY, John W Boyd 14 grandson MO KY MO

More About ABNER "AB" GREEN BALLARD:
Burial: 13 Oct 1917, Arrow Rock Cemetery, Arrow Rock, Saline Co., MO

Notes for SARAH ELIZABETH SCHOOLING:
Source: 1920 Saline County Missouri Federal Census Records
1920 - Living in Arrow Rock, Saline Co., MO - Living with daughter Kathleen and her husband Thomas G. McRudy. - Ballard, Sarah 75 wd MO MO KY

More About SARAH ELIZABETH SCHOOLING:
Burial: Arrow Rock Cemetery, Arrow Rock, Saline Co., MO

Children of ABNER BALLARD and SARAH SCHOOLING are:

     i.   ELIZA R.³ BALLARD, b. 1870, MO; d. 05 Mar 1872, Boone Co., MO.

        More About ELIZA R. BALLARD:
        Burial: Winn Cemetery, Sturgeon, Boone Co., MO

     ii.   SARAH BALLARD, b. 1870, MO; d. 06 Mar 1872, Boone Co., MO.

        More About SARAH BALLARD:
        Burial: Winn Cemetery, Sturgeon, Boone Co., MO

     iii.   ABNER D. BALLARD, b. 21 Jun 1872, MO; d. 30 Jun 1938, Higbee, Randolph Co., MO; m. (1) LULA E. TOALSON, 01 Apr 1895, Boone Co., MO; b. Feb 1875, MO; d. 1925; m. (2) BELLE BURTON, 04 Mar 1929, Randolph Co., MO; b. 1874, MO; d. Aft. 1938.

        Notes for ABNER D. BALLARD:
        Source: Randolph County Missouri Certificate of Death, Boone County Missouri Marriage Records, Randolph County Missouri Marriage Record, 1900 Boone County Missouri Federal Census Records, 1905 Moberly Missouri City Directory, 1910 Randolph County Missouri Federal Census Records, 1920 Craig County Oklahoma Federal Census Records, 1930 - Living in Randolph County Missouri Federal Census Records

        1900 - Living in Perche, Boone Co., MO - Ballard, AD - June 1872 MO MO KY, Lula E - Feb 1875 MO MO KY, Girtie M Holt sister in law - July 1884 MO MO KY
        1905 - Living in Moberly, Raldolph Co., MO - Ballard, Abner D (wf Lula E) lab Wab r 1006 W. Franklin
        1910 - Living in Union, Randolph Co., MO - Ballard, Abner D 55 MO KY KY, Lula E 35 MO ? VA
        1920 - Living in Craig Co., OK - Ballard, Abner D 51 MO IL IL, Lulie E 43 MO MO VA
        1929 - Living in Fulton, Boone Co., MO at the time of his marriage to Belle Burton in Randoph Co., MO. Her residence was Moberly, Randolph Co., MO
        1930 - Living in South Sugar Creek, Randolph Co., MO - Ballard, AD 56 MO KY MO, Belle 56 md 5 yrs MO WV NC, Waldo Burton 30 step son MO MO MO, Roseo 18 step son MO MO MO

        More About ABNER D. BALLARD:
        Burial: Rocky Fork Baptist Church Cemetery, Hinton, Boone Co., MO

More About LULA E. TOALSON:
Burial: Rocky Fork Baptist Church Cemetery, Hinton, Boone Co., MO

17.   iv.   ADA BALLARD, b. Nov 1872, Saline Co., MO; d. Aft. 1900.
      v.   CLAIR MABLE BALLARD, b. 13 Mar 1874, Saline Co., MO; d. 17 Apr 1954, Marshall, Saline Co., MO; m. JOHN DOW SANDIDGE; b. 1854; d. 1935.

            More About CLAIR MABLE BALLARD:
            Burial: Mt. Olive Cemetery, Marshall, Saline Co., MO

      vi.   JAMES RILEY BALLARD, b. 19 Apr 1876, Saline Co., MO; d. 14 Feb 1944, Saline Co., MO; m. HOMIE VESTA WEBB, 30 Oct 1913, Claiborne Par., LA.

            More About JAMES RILEY BALLARD:
            Burial: Arrow Rock Cemetery, Arrow Rock, Saline Co., MO

      vii. MARY BALLARD, b. 1878, Saline Co., MO.
18.   viii. SPILLMAN EDWARD BALLARD, b. 25 Jan 1880, Saline Co., MO; d. 25 May 1948, Boone Co., MO.
      ix.   CHILD BALLARD, b. 23 Nov 1883, Arrow Rock twp, Saline Co., MO.
      x.   GROVER CLEVELAND BALLARD, b. 29 Nov 1883, Saline Co., MO; d. 28 Sep 1895, Saline Co., MO.

            More About GROVER CLEVELAND BALLARD:
            Burial: Arrow Rock Cemetery, Arrow Rock, Saline Co., MO

19.   xi.   KATHLEEN PEARL BALLARD, b. 23 Apr 1887, Saline Co., MO; d. 25 Jan 1963, MO.

5. MARY J.[2] BALLARD (WILLIAM RILEY[1]) was born 1842 in KY, and died Aft. 1870. She married WILLIAM MARTIN SMITH. He was born Abt. 1827 in NC, and died Aft. 1870.

Notes for WILLIAM MARTIN SMITH:
Source: 1870 Johnson County Missouri Federal Census Records

* 1870 - Living in Kingsville, Johnson Co., MO - Smith, W M 43 farmer NC, Mary J 26 KY, William H 14 IL, Louisa V 8 IL, Sterline P 5 IL, Martha L MO, William Lee 21 works on farm MO, Sarah Ballard 17 house keeper KY, M H Smith 20 IL works on farm

Children of MARY BALLARD and WILLIAM SMITH are:

      i.   WILLIAM H.[3] SMITH, b. Abt. 1856, IL; d. Aft. 1870.
      ii.   LOUISA V. SMITH, b. Abt. 1862, IL; d. Aft. 1870.
      iii. STERLING P. SMITH, b. Abt. 1865, IL; d. Aft. 1870.
      iv.   MARTHA L. SMITH, b. Abt. 1869, MO; d. Aft. 1870; m. WALLACE W. GAFNEY, 01 Mar 1893, Jerseyville, Jersey Co., IL.

6. BENJAMIN FRANKLIN "FRANK"[2] BALLARD (WILLIAM RILEY[1]) was born 17 Mar 1848 in KY, and died Bef. 1900. He married MARY "MOLLIE" GERTRUDE BAILEY 30 Mar 1875. She was born Feb 1858 in MO, and died Aft. 1910.

Notes for BENJAMIN FRANKLIN "FRANK" BALLARD:
Source: 1880 Saline County Missouri Federal Census Records

*1880 - Living in Liberty, Saline Co., MO - Ballard, Frank 32 KY VA KY, Mary G 22 MO, Rosetta 4 MO, Richard 2 MO, Lillie J 11/12 MO

Notes for MARY "MOLLIE" GERTRUDE BAILEY:

Source: 1900-1910 Saline County Missouri Federal Census Records
** 1900 - Living in Liberty, Saline Co., MO - Ballard, Mary G - Feb 1858 wd - 8 children 5 living MO VA IN, Rosa -*
Jan 1876 MO, Elmer - Mar 1881 MO, Lois - Jan 1885 MO, Lewis - Nov 1886 MO, Homer - May 1895 MO
** 1910 - Living in Salt Pond, Saline Co., MO - Lee, John 56, Mary Lee 54, Ethel Ballard 24, Homer Ballard 15*

Children of BENJAMIN BALLARD and MARY BAILEY are:

	i.	ROSETTA "ROSA"[3] BALLARD, b. Jan 1876, Saline Co., MO; d. Aft. 1900.
	ii.	RICHARD BALLARD, b. 1878, Saline Co., MO; d. Aft. 1880.
	iii.	LILLIE J. BALLARD, b. 1879, Saline Co., MO; d. Aft. 1880.
20.	iv.	ELMER C. BALLARD, b. 21 Mar 1881, Saline Co., MO; d. 04 Aug 1944, Canyon Co., ID.
	v.	LOIS BALLARD, b. Jan 1885, Saline Co., MO; d. Aft. 1900.
21.	vi.	LEWIS NATHANIEL BALLARD, b. 06 Nov 1886, Saline Co., MO; d. 24 Dec 1947, Marshall, Saline Co., MO.
22.	vii.	HOMER OLIVER BALLARD, b. 23 May 1895, Saline Co., MO; d. Aft. 1930.

7. EDWARD "BOB" SPELLMAN[2] BALLARD (WILLIAM RILEY[1]) *was born 25 Jan 1851 in KY, and died 13 Nov 1928. He married LUCY P. WINN. She was born 1861 in MO, and died Aft. 1880.*

Notes for EDWARD "BOB" SPELLMAN BALLARD:
Source: 1880 Missouri Federal Census Records Soundex
** 1880 - Living in Boone Co. Missouri*

Children of EDWARD BALLARD and LUCY WINN are:
    i. ALMAREATTE[3] BALLARD, b. 1879, MO.
    ii. U. O. BALLARD, b. 1880, MO.

8. ELIZA DILLARD[2] BALLARD (WILLIAM RILEY[1]) *was born 08 Feb 1856 in Boone Co., MO or Greene Co., KY, and died 13 Oct 1955 in Marshall, Saline Co., MO. She married GEORGE WASHINGTON MASTERS 17 Jun 1873 in Saline Co., MO. He was born 28 Aug 1845 in Green Co., KY, and died 18 Jul 1934 in Marshall, Saline Co., MO.*

Notes for ELIZA DILLARD BALLARD:
Source: Saline County Missouri Standard Certificate of Death
** Father listed as William Rylie Ballard on Death Certificate*

More About ELIZA DILLARD BALLARD:

Burial: Source: 1920-1930 Sheridan County Wyoming Federal Census Records, WWI Draft Registration Card, WWII Draft Registration Cards

More About GEORGE WASHINGTON MASTERS:
Burial: Hazel Grove Cemetery, Herndon, Saline Co., MO

Children of ELIZA BALLARD and GEORGE MASTERS are:
    i. LUTHER BENJAMIN[3] MASTERS, b. 28 May 1874; d. 15 Jan 1950.

        More About LUTHER BENJAMIN MASTERS:
        Burial: Ridge Park Cemetery, Marshall, Saline Co., MO

    ii. MAUDE E. MASTERS, b. 25 Feb 1876; d. 04 Dec 1963; m. ANDY COOK.

        More About MAUDE E. MASTERS:
        Burial: Fairview Cemetery, Sweet Springs, Saline Co., MO

iii. OLLIE VIRGINIA MASTERS, *b. 04 Oct 1879; d. 14 Jul 1963; m. EDWIN M. BEATY.*

More About OLLIE VIRGINIA MASTERS:
Burial: Oak Hill Cemetery, Siloam Springs, Benton Co., AR

9. EVALINE "EVA"[2] BALLARD *(WILLIAM RILEY[1]) was born 1859 in KY, and died Aft. 1900. She married* WILLIAM PRICE WYNN *10 Feb 1884 in Boone Co., MO, son of* JACKSON WINN *and* MARTHA SIMS. *He was born Nov 1861 in MO, and died Aft. 1900.*

Notes for WILLIAM PRICE WYNN:
Source: 1900 Randolph County Missouri Federal Census Records, Social Security Records
** 1900 - Living in Moberly, Randolph Co., MO - Winn, William P - Nov 1861 VA MO MO, Eva - Aug 1859 - 2 children 2 living MO KY KY, Ethel - July 1885 MO, Herbert - June 1888 MO*

Children of EVALINE BALLARD and WILLIAM WYNN are:
    i. ETHEL[3] WYNN, *b. Jul 1885, MO; d. Aft. 1900.*
    ii. HERBERT WYNN, *b. Jun 1888, MO; d. Aft. 1900.*

Generation No. 3

10. SARAH BELL[3] BALLARD *(SQUIRE WOODSON "WOOD" A.[2], WILLIAM RILEY[1]) was born 27 Jan 1857 in Garrard Co., MO, and died 17 Apr 1938 in KS. She married* JAMES ROBERT FIGGINS *14 Jun 1883 in Saline Co., MO. He was born 1841 in VA, and died 01 Jul 1911 in MO.*

Notes for JAMES ROBERT FIGGINS:
Source: 1900 Saline County Missouri Federal Census Records

** 1900 - Living in Arrow Rock, Saline Co., MO - Ballard, J R 58 VA VA VA (hard to read), Sarah B - Jan 1837 KY KY KY, Sam D - Dec 1873 MO, Katie - May 1874 MO, Roy - Feb 1886 MO, Jno - Sept 1888 MO, Arthur - June 1891 MO, Henry - Aug 1893 MO, Lula - Sep 1894 MO*

More About JAMES ROBERT FIGGINS:
Burial: Arrow Rock Cemetery, Saline Co., MO

Children of SARAH BALLARD and JAMES FIGGINS are:
    i. SAM D.[4] FIGGINS, *b. Dec 1873, Arrow Rock, Saline Co., MO; d. Aft. 1900.*
    ii. ANNA KATHRYN "KATIE" FIGGINS, *b. 14 May 1884, Arrow Rock, Saline Co., MO; d. 26 Jan 1959; m.* WILLIAM H. WENDLETON; *b. 22 Jan 1883, Cooper Co., MO; d. 18 Nov 1918, Cooper Co., MO.*

        More About ANNA KATHRYN "KATIE" FIGGINS:
        Burial: Walnut Grove Cemetery, Boonville, Cooper Co., MO

        More About WILLIAM H. WENDLETON:
        Burial: Walnut Grove Cemetery, Boonville, Cooper Co., MO

    iii. ROY WOODSON FIGGINS, *b. Feb 1886, Arrow Rock, Saline Co., MO; d. 1932; m.* CHRISTINA PERSINGER; *b. 01 Dec 1904, KS; d. 06 Jan 2004, Sarpy Co., NE.*

        More About ROY WOODSON FIGGINS:
        Burial: Valley Cemetery, Norway, Republic Co., KS

        More About CHRISTINA PERSINGER:
        Burial: Westlawn - Hillcrest Memorial Park, Omaha, Douglas Co., NE

iv. ARTHUR FIGGINS, b. Jun 1891, Arrow Rock, Saline Co., MO; d. Aft. 1900.
v. HENRY FIGGINS, b. 06 Aug 1892, Arrow Rock, Saline Co., MO; d. 03 Dec 1969, Republic Co., KS.

More About HENRY FIGGINS:

Burial: Valley Cemetery, Norway, Republic Co., KS

vi. LULA BELLE FIGGINS, b. 06 Sep 1894, Arrow Rock, Saline Co., MO; d. 09 Jul 1955, Norway, Republic Co., KS; m. CLARENCE GREER; b. 18 Aug 1890, Putnam Co., MO; d. 23 Oct 1960, Wichita, Sedgwick Co., KS.

More About LULA BELLE FIGGINS:
Burial: Norway Cemetery, Norway, Republic Co., KS

More About CLARENCE GREER:
Burial: Norway Cemetery, Norway, Republic Co., KS

vii. JOHN W. FIGGINS, b. 02 Sep 1888, Arrow Rock, Saline Co., MO; d. 16 Apr 1940; m. MAUDE HAZEL WILSON, 04 Nov 1908; b. 17 Sep 1887, Sioux Co., NE; d. 22 May 1977, Walla Walla Co., WA.

More About JOHN W. FIGGINS:
Burial: Valley Cemetery, Norway, Republic Co., KS

More About MAUDE HAZEL WILSON:
Burial: Blue Mountain Memorial Garden, College Place, Walla Walla Co., WA

11. JOHN WILLIAM[3] BALLARD (SQUIRE WOODSON "WOOD" A.[2], WILLIAM RILEY[1]) was born 12 Jan 1858 in Garrard Co., MO, and died 30 Jan 1943 in Marshall, Saline Co., MO. He married MARGARET KATHRYN HILL. She was born 30 Jan 1874 in Saline Co., MO, and died 30 Jan 1950 in Jackson Co., MO.

Notes for JOHN WILLIAM BALLARD:
Source: 1900-1910 Saline County Missouri Federal Census Records

* 1900 - Living in Grand Pass, Saline Co., MO - Ballar (d), William - Jan 1858 KY KY KY, Maggie C - Jan 1874 - 5 children 5 living MO KY MO, (Anderson step children) Nolica Anderson step dau - Nov 1891 MO, James Anderson - July 1893 MO, Bessie L Anderson - July 1895 MO, Louis A Anderson - Dec 1897 MO, Edith M. Ballard - Feb 1900 MO
* 1910 - Living in Marshall, Saline Co., MO - Ballard, Wm 53 KY KY KY, Maggie 36 MO MO KY, (Anderson step children) James, Bessie, Lewis Anderson, Ballard, Edith 10 MO, Marie 8 MO, Mildred 5 MO, Earle 12/12 MO

Notes for MARGARET KATHRYN HILL:
Source: 1920 St. Louis County Missouri Federal Census Records

* 1920 - Living in St. Louis Co., MO - Anderson, James 26 MO, Louis 22 MO, Mrs. Marie Winchell 17 dau, James D Roberts 32 bro. in law Bessie Roberts 23, Mildred Ballard 15 sister, Earl 11, Edward 6, Janey Hill 50, Patrick Collins boarder 19

More About MARGARET KATHRYN HILL:
Burial: Memorial Park Cemetery, Kansas City, Jackson Co., MO

Children of JOHN BALLARD and MARGARET HILL are:

i. EDITH MARTHA[4] BALLARD, b. Feb 1900, Saline Co., MO; d. Aft. 1910.
ii. MARIE BALLARD, b. Abt. 1902, Saline Co., MO; d. Aft. 1920; m. HARRY WINCHELL.
iii. MILDRED BALLARD, b. Abt. 1905, Saline Co., MO; d. Aft. 1920.

     iv. ROBERT EARLE BALLARD, b. Abt. 1909, Saline Co., MO; d. Aft. 1920.
     v. EDWARD SAMUEL BALLARD, b. 1913, Saline Co., MO; d. Aft. 1920.

12. VALENTINE[3] BALLARD (SQUIRE WOODSON "WOOD" A.[2], WILLIAM RILEY[1]) was born 01 Apr 1862 in Garrard Co., MO, and died 14 Dec 1925 in Saline Co., MO. He married NANCY KNOX 28 Apr 1906 in Marshall, Saline Co., MO. She was born 1886.

Notes for VALENTINE BALLARD:
Source: 1910 Saline County Missouri Federal Census Records
* 1910 - Living in Saline Co., MO - Ballard, Valentine 48 KY KY KY, Nancy L or L 24 IN IN IN, Mary W 1 8/12 MO

More About VALENTINE BALLARD:
Burial: Malta Bend Cemetery, Saline Co., MO

Child of VALENTINE BALLARD and NANCY KNOX is:
     i. MARY W.[4] BALLARD, b. 1908.

13. ANN "NAN" "ANNIE" DORA[3] BALLARD (SQUIRE WOODSON "WOOD" A.[2], WILLIAM RILEY[1]) was born 22 Mar 1866 in Garrard Co., MO, and died 31 Jan 1956 in Marshall, Saline Co., MO. She married JOSEPH BENEDICT MESCHEDE. He was born 02 Feb 1868 in MO, and died 26 Jun 1931.

More About ANN "NAN" "ANNIE" DORA BALLARD:
Burial: Mt. Saint Marys Cemetery, Shackleford, Saline Co., MO

Notes for JOSEPH BENEDICT MESCHEDE:
Source: 1920-1930 Saline County Missouri Federal Census Records
* 1920 - Living in Saline Co., MO - Meschede, Joe 51 MO, Nanny 53 KY, Richard 16 MO, Frederick 15 MO, Clara 12, Robert Ballard boarder (brother) 52 KY
* 1930 - Living in Saline Co., MO - Meschede, Joseph B 62 MO Germany Germany, Nannie 64 KY KY KY, Clara B 22 MO, Clarence Stockman nephew 31 MO, Robert E. Ballard brother in law 61 KY KY KY

More About JOSEPH BENEDICT MESCHEDE:
Burial: Mt. Saint Marys Cemetery, Shackleford, Saline Co., MO

Children of ANN BALLARD and JOSEPH MESCHEDE are:
     i. RICHARD[4] MESCHEDE, b. Abt. 1904, MO; d. Aft. 1920.
     ii. FREDERICK MESCHEDE, b. Abt. 1905, MO; d. Aft. 1920.
     iii. CLARA B. MESCHEDE, b. Abt. 1908, MO; d. Aft. 1930.

14. HARRISON "HARRY " STREETER[3] BALLARD (JAMES LIVINGSTON[2], WILLIAM RILEY[1]) was born 23 Apr 1889 in Grovespring, Wright Co., MO, and died 28 Jun 1976 in Springfield, Greene Co., MO. He married SARAH JANE KINKADE. She was born 26 Jun 1902 in MO, and died 30 Oct 1996 in Springfield, Greene Co., MO.

Notes for HARRISON "HARRY " STREETER BALLARD:
Source: 1920-1940 Wright County Missouri Federal Census Records

* 1920 - Living in Union, Wright Co., MO - Ballard, Harry S. 30 MO KY TN, Sarah J 17 MO MO MO, Lore May 1 1/12 MO
* 1930 - Living in Boone, Wright Co., MO - Ballard, Harry 41 MO KY TN, Sarah J 27 MO MO IN, Lovie 11 MO, Lois 9 OK, Lawrence 8 OK, Mary 4 OK, Harry Jr 1 3/12 MO
* 1940 - Living in Union, Wright Co., MO - Ballard, HS 50 MO farmer, Sarah 38, Lawrence 18 MO, Mary 14 OK,

Junior 11 MO, Dorothy 8 MO, Fora Lee 5 MO

More About HARRISON "HARRY" STREETER BALLARD:
Burial: Little Vine Cemetery, Grovespring, Wright Co., MO

More About SARAH JANE KINKADE:
Burial: Little Vine Cemetery, Grovespring, Wright Co., MO

Children of HARRISON BALLARD and SARAH KINKADE are:

    i.   LOVIE[4] BALLARD, b. 1919, Wright Co., MO; d. Aft. 1930.

    ii.   LOIS MARIE BALLARD, b. 21 May 1920, OK; d. 27 Sep 2007; m. GEORGE RAYMOND KING; b. 30 Aug 1913, MO; d. 04 Sep 1996, MO.

        More About LOIS MARIE BALLARD:
        Burial: Little Vine Cemetery, Grovespring, Wright Co., MO

    iii.   LAWRENCE A. BALLARD, b. 18 Aug 1921, OK; d. 25 Dec 1989, TX; m. (1) OLIVE GERTRUDE TOBALT; b. 18 Dec 1926; d. 06 Jan 2019; m. (2) GARNET JEWEL HENDRICKSEN; b. 12 Jan 1928, Denver Co., CO; d. 05 Feb 2010, SC.

        More About LAWRENCE A. BALLARD:
        Burial: Copperas Cove Cemetery, Copperas Cove, Coryell Co., TX

        More About OLIVE GERTRUDE TOBALT:
        Burial: Copperas Cove Cemetery, Copperas Cove, Coryell Co., TX

        More About GARNET JEWEL HENDRICKSEN:
        Burial: St. Joseph Parish Cemetery, Natrona Heights, Allegheny Co., PA

    iv.   MARY LOUISE BALLARD, b. 25 Apr 1926, Sapulpa, Creek Co., OK; d. 15 Jul 2015, Springfield, Greene Co., MO.

        More About MARY LOUISE BALLARD:
        Burial: Little Vine Cemetery, Grovespring, Wright Co., MO

    v.   HARRY BALLARD, JR., b. 26 Dec 1928, MO; d. 11 Feb 2020, Mt. Vernon, Lawrence Co., MO; m. THEDA JEANETTE DOUGLAS; b. 17 Apr 1929, Orangeburg Co., SC; d. 12 Nov 1994, Springfield, Greene Co., MO.

        More About HARRY BALLARD, JR.:
        Burial: Springfield National Cemetery, Springfield, Greene Co., MO

        More About THEDA JEANETTE DOUGLAS:
        Burial: Springfield National Cemetery, Springfield, Greene Co., MO

    vi.   DOROTHY BALLARD, b. 1932, MO; d. Aft. 1940.

    vii.   FLORA LEE BALLARD, b. 27 Jul 1934, Grovespring, Wright Co., MO; d. 22 May 2018, Springfield, Greene Co., MO; m. BILL BUTTRAM; b. 08 Aug 1927, Grovespring, Wright Co., MO; d. 24 Mar 2017, Springfield, Greene Co., MO.

        More About FLORA LEE BALLARD:
        Burial: Little Vine Cemetery, Grovespring, Wright Co., MO

15. WALTER DAYTON[3] BALLARD (JAMES LIVINGSTON[2], WILLIAM RILEY[1]) was born 15 Oct 1890 in MO, and died 03 Jan 1976. He married BERTHA MAY HENDERSON. She was born 01 Feb 1888, and died 01 Nov 1982 in Grovespring, Wright Co., MO.

Notes for WALTER DAYTON BALLARD:
Source: 1920-1930 Wright County Missouri Federal Census Records
** 1920 - Living in Boone, Wright Co., MO - Ballard, Walter B 29 MO KY US, Bertha M 31 MO MO MO, Mitchell Ollie 7 step son MO, Mary 4 5/12 step son MO, Richard Ollie 2 step child MO*
** 1930 - Living in Boone, Wright Co., MO - Ballard, Walter 38 MO MO MO, Bertha 42 MO US MI, Ottie Ollie 18 MO Palestine MO, step children, Mary 14 step son, Richard 13 step child, Wallace Ballard 9 MO*

More About WALTER DAYTON BALLARD:
Burial: Shaddy Cemetery, Grovespring, Wright Co., MO

More About BERTHA MAY HENDERSON:
Burial: Shaddy Cemetery, Grovespring, Wright Co., MO

Child of WALTER BALLARD and BERTHA HENDERSON is:

      i.   WALLACE L.[4] BALLARD, b. 05 May 1920, Union, Wright Co., MO; d. 31 Jan 1932, Wright Co., MO.

          Notes for WALLACE L. BALLARD:
          Source: Wright County Missouri State Board of Health Bureau of Vital Statistics Certificate of Death - Death Certificate #3600

          More About WALLACE L. BALLARD:
          Burial: 31 Jan 1932, Shaddy Cemetery, Grovespring, Wright Co., MO

16. CLAUDE CHARLES[3] BALLARD (JAMES LIVINGSTON[2], WILLIAM RILEY[1]) was born 02 Jul 1896 in Grovespring, Wright Co., MO, and died 13 Jul 1982 in Webster Co., MO. He married BESSIE MAY GUINN. She was born 03 Nov 1901 in Grovespring, Wright Co., MO, and died 29 Jun 1986 in Webster Co., MO.

Notes for CLAUDE CHARLES BALLARD:
Source: 1920-1940 Wright County Missouri Federal Census Records

** 1920 - Living in Union, Wright Co., MO - Ballard, Claude 20 MO KY MO, James L 81 KY Ireland Ireland father, Mary C 65 mother MO MO MO*
** 1930 - Living in Union, Wright Co., MO - Ballard, Claude 33 MO MO MO, Bessie 28 MO TN MO, Lowell 6 MO MO MO, Athel 3 4/12 MO MO MO, Baby (son) 1/12 MO MO MO, Robert Pearson lodger.*
** 1940 - Living in Union, Wright Co., MO - Ballard, C C 43, Bessie May 38 MO, Hugh Lowell 16 MO, Athol Waldo 15 MO, Donald Kirth 10 MO, Claudine 4 MO*

More About CLAUDE CHARLES BALLARD:
Burial: Prospect Baptist Cemetery, Niangua, Webster Co., MO

Children of CLAUDE BALLARD and BESSIE GUINN are:

      i.   HUGH LOWELL[4] BALLARD, b. 15 Jun 1923, Union, Wright Co., MO; d. 28 Mar 2014, MO; m. JOY M..

          More About HUGH LOWELL BALLARD:
          Burial: Missouri Veterans Cemetery Springfield, Greene Co., MO

     ii.   ATHOL WALDO BALLARD, b. 02 Sep 1924, Union, Wright Co., MO; d. 28 May 2007; m. FAY LEONE COATS; b. 23 Sep 1926, MO; d. 23 Jan 2020, Webster Co., MO.

More About ATHOL WALDO BALLARD:
Burial: Spokane Cemetery, Spokane, Christian Co., MO

   iii.   DONALD KIRTH BALLARD, b. 04 Apr 1930, Union, Wright Co., MO; d. 29 Nov 2007; m. VIVIAN MARIE FILLMER; b. 14 Apr 1926, Niangua, Webster Co., MO; d. 07 Aug 2013, Springfield, Greene Co., MO.

     More About DONALD KIRTH BALLARD:
     Burial: Prospect Baptist Cemetery, Niangua, Webster Co., MO

   iv.   CLAUDINE BALLARD, b. 1936, Union, Wright Co., MO; d. Aft. 1940.

17. ADA[3] BALLARD (ABNER "AB" GREEN[2], WILLIAM RILEY[1]) was born Nov 1872 in Saline Co., MO, and died Aft. 1900. She married MR. BOYD.

Child of ADA BALLARD and MR. BOYD is:
   i.   JOHN W.[4] BOYD, b. Sep 1895, Saline Co., MO; d. Aft. 1910.

18. SPILLMAN EDWARD[3] BALLARD (ABNER "AB" GREEN[2], WILLIAM RILEY[1]) was born 25 Jan 1880 in Saline Co., MO, and died 25 May 1948 in Boone Co., MO. He married LUCILLE MAE ALLEN. She was born 30 Jul 1887 in Boone Co., MO, and died 11 Jan 1942 in Boone Co., MO.

Notes for SPILLMAN EDWARD BALLARD:
Source: Boone County Missouri Death Certificate
* States he was widowed

More About SPILLMAN EDWARD BALLARD:
Burial: 27 May 1948, Locust Grove Baptist Church Cemetery, Sturgeon, Boone Co., MO

Children of SPILLMAN BALLARD and LUCILLE ALLEN are:
   i.   BENJAMIN ROY[4] BALLARD, b. 09 Jul 1909, Sturgeon, Boone Co., MO; d. 18 Jul 1963, Gravois Mills, Morgan Co., MO; m. MARY MARTIN; b. 19 Sep 1917, Columbia, Boone Co., MO; d. 14 Nov 2010, Versailles, Morgan Co., MO.

     More About BENJAMIN ROY BALLARD:
     Burial: Versailles Cemetery, Morgan Co., MO

     More About MARY MARTIN:
     Burial: Versailles Cemetery, Morgan Co., MO

   ii.   LEON G. BALLARD, b. 23 Nov 1914, Sturgeon, Boone Co., MO; d. 14 Jul 1997, Columbia, Boone Co., MO; m. THELMA HINSHAW; b. 31 Jul 1911, Boone Co., MO; d. 17 Oct 1994, Hallsville, Boone Co., MO.

     More About LEON G. BALLARD:
     Burial: Memorial Park Cemetery, Columbia, Boone Co., MO

   iii.   GLEN BALLARD, b. 06 May 1918, Sturgeon, Boone Co., MO; d. 27 Apr 1968, Little Elm, Denton Co., TX.

     More About GLEN BALLARD:
     Burial: Walnut Grove Cemetery, Boonville, Cooper Co., MO

iv. WILLIAM ALLEN BALLARD, b. 26 Apr 1925, Boone Co., MO; d. 21 Aug 1993, Sturgeon, Boone Co.,
MO; m. MONA RUTH ROBERTS; b. 24 Jun 1927, MO; d. 10 May 1991, Boone Co., MO.

More About WILLIAM ALLEN BALLARD:
Burial: Mt. Horeb Cemetery, Sturgeon, Boone Co., MO

19. KATHLEEN PEARL[3] BALLARD (ABNER "AB" GREEN[2], WILLIAM RILEY[1]) was born 23 Apr 1887 in Saline Co., MO,
and died 25 Jan 1963 in MO. She married THOMAS GILMER MCRADY. He was born 17 Feb 1883 in Caddo Par., LA,
and died 20 Jan 1952 in St. Joseph, Buchanan Co., MO.

More About KATHLEEN PEARL BALLARD:
Burial: Arrow Rock Cemetery, Arrow Rock, Saline Co., MO

Notes for THOMAS GILMER MCRADY:
Source: 1920 Saline County Missouri Federal Census Records
* 1920 - Living in Arrow Rock, Saline Co., MO - McRudy, Thomas G. 36 LA LA LA, Kathleen P 32 MO KY MO,
Kathleen M 11 MO, Alda M 7 MO, Sarah Ballard 75 wd mother in law MO MO KY

More About THOMAS GILMER MCRADY:
Burial: Arrow Rock Cemetery, Arrow Rock, Saline Co., MO

Children of KATHLEEN BALLARD and THOMAS MCRADY are:
i. KATHLEEN M.[4] MCRUDY, b. 17 Oct 1908, Saline Co., MO; d. 03 Jan 1988; m. JULIUS HOMER DEAL;
b. 21 Feb 1904, Mt. Leonard, Saline Co., MO; d. 09 Sep 1986, Caddo Par., LA.

More About KATHLEEN M. MCRUDY:
Burial: Arrow Rock Cemetery, Arrow Rock, Saline Co., MO

ii. ALDA M. MCRUDY, b. 1913, Saline Co., MO; d. Aft. 1920.

20. ELMER C.[3] BALLARD (BENJAMIN FRANKLIN "FRANK"[2], WILLIAM RILEY[1]) was born 21 Mar 1881 in Saline Co., MO,
and died 04 Aug 1944 in Canyon Co., ID. He married EUNICE CAROLINE KELLEY. She was born 09 Aug 1889 in
Warrensburg, Johnson Co., MO, and died 10 Nov 1965 in Nampa, Canyon Co., ID.

Notes for ELMER C. BALLARD:
Source: Nampa Canyon Idaho Certificate of Death, 1940 Canyon County Idaho Federal Census Records
* 1940 - Living in Melba, Canyon Co., ID - Ballard, Elmer C 59 MO, Eunice C 50 MO, Jackie L 10 ID

Child of ELMER BALLARD and EUNICE KELLEY is:
i. JACKIE[4] BALLARD, b. Abt. 1930, ID; d. Aft. 1940.

21. LEWIS NATHANIEL[3] BALLARD (BENJAMIN FRANKLIN "FRANK"[2], WILLIAM RILEY[1]) was born 06 Nov 1886 in Saline
Co., MO, and died 24 Dec 1947 in Marshall, Saline Co., MO. He married MARY MAUDE THOMAS 25 Dec 1907 in
Nelson, Saline Co., MO. She was born 07 Jul 1891 in MO, and died 18 Jul 1979.

Notes for LEWIS NATHANIEL BALLARD:
Source: 1910 & 1930-1940 Saline County Missouri Federal Census Records, 1920 Sheridan County Wyoming
Federal Census Records, Saline county Missouri Standard Certificate of Death

* 1910 - Living in Liberty, Saline Co., MO - Ballard, Lewis N 23 MO, Mary M 18 MO, Edna M 12/12 MO
* 1920 - Living in Clearmont, Sheridan Co., WY - Ballard, Lewis 34 farmer MO, Maud 27, Edna 10, Gertrude 7,
Georgia 4

** 1930 - Living in Marshall, Saline Co., MO - Ballard, Louis N 43 tinner MO, Mary Maude 37 MO, Gertrude 17 MO, Georgia 13 MO*
** 1940 - Living in Marshall, Saline Co., MO - Ballard, Lewis N 53 plumber MO, Mary Maude 47 MO*

More About LEWIS NATHANIEL BALLARD:
Burial: Nelson Cemetery, Nelson, Saline Co.,, MO

More About MARY MAUDE THOMAS:
Burial: Nelson Cemetery, Nelson, Saline Co.,, MO

Children of LEWIS BALLARD and MARY THOMAS are:

      i.   *EDNA MAE[4] BALLARD, b. 03 Apr 1909, Liberty, Saline Co., MO; d. 24 Jun 1989, Marshall, Saline Co., MO; m. SAMUEL HOBSON WILSON; b. 1899.*

          More About EDNA MAE BALLARD:
          Burial: Sunset Gardens Cemetery, Marshall, Saline Co., MO

     ii.   *MARY JOYCE BALLARD, b. 10 Aug 1938, Marshall, Saline Co., MO; d. 08 Nov 1938, Marshall, Saline Co., MO.*
    iii.   *EVA LEWIS BALLARD, b. 11 Oct 1923, Marshall, Saline Co., MO; d. 25 Nov 1923, Marshall, Saline Co., MO.*
    iv.   *GERTRUDE BALLARD, b. Abt. 1913, Marshall, Saline Co., MO; d. Aft. 1930.*
     v.   *GEORGIA BALLARD, b. 30 Sep 1916, Marshall, Saline Co., MO; d. 14 May 2008; m. CHARLES DONREATH PAGE, 14 Feb 1937, Warsaw, Benton Co., MO; b. 25 Sep 1913, Sweet Springs, MO.*

          More About GEORGIA BALLARD:
          Burial: Ridge Park Cemetery, Marshall, Saline Co., MO

          Notes for CHARLES DONREATH PAGE:
          Source: WWII Draft Cards

22. *HOMER OLIVER[3] BALLARD (BENJAMIN FRANKLIN "FRANK"[2], WILLIAM RILEY[1]) was born 23 May 1895 in Saline Co., MO, and died Aft. 1930. He married ELLEN BELLE GRANGER 01 Apr 1920 in Sheridan Co., WY, daughter of WALTER A. GRANGER. She was born Abt. 1892 in IA, and died Aft. 1930.*

Notes for HOMER OLIVER BALLARD:
Source: 1920-1930 Sheridan County Wyoming Federal Census Records, WWI Draft Registration Card, WWII Draft Registration Cards

** 1920 - Living in Clearmont, Sheridan Co., WY - next door to his brother - Ballard, Homer, 24 MO KY IN farmer*
** 1930 - Living in Clearmont, Sheridan Co., WY - Ballard, Homer O 35 MO, Ellen B 38 IA, Marianna B 9 WY, Marion B 5 WY, Janet E 4 WY, Phyllis B 1 WY, Walter A Granger father in law 64 IA, Clyde McCarty lodger 23*

Children of HOMER BALLARD and ELLEN GRANGER are:

      i.   *MARIANNA[4] BALLARD, b. Abt. 1921, WY; d. Aft. 1930.*
     ii.   *MARION B. BALLARD, b. Abt. 1925, WY; d. Aft. 1930.*
    iii.   *JANET E. BALLARD, b. Abt. 1926, WY; d. Aft. 1930.*
    iv.   *PHYLLIS B. BALLARD, b. Abt. 1929, WY; d. Aft. 1930.*

William H. Ballard

Generation No. 1

1. WILLIAM H.[2] BALLARD (JOHN P.[1]) *was born 25 Jan 1835 in Madison Co., KY, and died Aft. 1870 in lived in Platte Co., MO. He married (1)* MARGARET. *She was born 1842 in IN, and died Aft. 1870. He married (2)* MARY "MOLLIE" A. GABBERT *24 Mar 1863, daughter of* JAMES GABBERT *and* POLLY SULLIVAN. *She was born 31 Aug 1840 in Clay Co., MO, and died 15 Jun 1927 in Clay Co., MO.*

Notes for WILLIAM H. BALLARD:
Source: Ballard-Ballord Bits pg 350 X-2735, 1870 Platte County Missouri Federal Census Records
** 1870 - Living in Weston Platte Co., MO - William A. 35 KY, Margaret 28 IN, Perry A. 6 KY*

Notes for MARY "MOLLIE" A. GABBERT:
Source: Clay County Missouri Death Certificate

Children of WILLIAM BALLARD *and* MARY GABBERT *are:*

2.	i.	PERRY A.[3] BALLARD, b. 04 Dec 1863, KY; d. Bet. 1900 - 1910.
3.	ii.	OAKLEY GABBERT BALLARD, b. 09 Jul 1873, MO; d. 08 Apr 1952, Clay Co., MO.

Generation No. 2

2. PERRY A.[3] BALLARD (WILLIAM H.[2], JOHN P.[1]) *was born 04 Dec 1863 in KY, and died Bet. 1900 - 1910. He married* ELIZABETH A. "LIZZIE" GEORGE *07 Mar 1886, daughter of* WILLIAM GEORGE *and* FANNIE DUNCAN. *She was born 01 Oct 1866 in MO, and died 21 Jan 1914 in Camden, Green twp., Platte Co., MO.*

Notes for PERRY A. BALLARD:
Source: 1900 Platte County Missouri Federal Census Records, Ballard-Ballord Bits pg 350 X2735

** 1900 - Living in Greene, Platte Co., MO - Ballard, Perry A. - -Dec 1863 KY KY KY, Lizzie A - Oct 1866 MO VA MO, Austin K - Dec 1889, William H - Jan 1892, Bryan W - Oct 1894, Marcy - July 1896*

Notes for ELIZABETH A. "LIZZIE" GEORGE:
Source: Platt County Missouri Death Certificate, 1920 Platte County Missouri Federal Census Records
** 1910 - Living in Platte Co., MO - Ballard, Lizzie A 42 wd MO VA MO, Bryan W 15 MO KY MO, Marcellus 13 MO KY MO*

Children of PERRY BALLARD *and* ELIZABETH GEORGE *are:*

	i.	OSCAR K.[4] BALLARD.
4.	ii.	AUSTIN KARR BALLARD, b. 13 Dec 1889; d. Aft. 1900.
5.	iii.	WILLIAM A. BALLARD, b. 1891, MO; d. Aft. 1916.
	iv.	WILLIAM GABBERT BALLARD, b. Jan 1892.
	v.	BRYAN WYATT BALLARD, b. Oct 1894; d. Aft. 1910.
	vi.	MARCELLUS BALLARD, b. Jul 1896; d. Aft. 1910.

3. OAKLEY GABBERT[3] BALLARD (WILLIAM H.[2], JOHN P.[1]) *was born 09 Jul 1873 in MO, and died 08 Apr 1952 in Clay Co., MO. He married (1)* GENEVIEVE MAXWELL. *He married (2)* LULA FIELD *14 Feb 1897. She was born 11 Nov 1876.*

Notes for OAKLEY GABBERT BALLARD:
Source: Clay County Missouri Death Certificate

Child of OAKLEY BALLARD and LULA FIELD is:
      i.   MARY HELEN[4] BALLARD, b. 19 Jul 1901.

Generation No. 3

4. AUSTIN KARR[4] BALLARD (PERRY A.[3], WILLIAM H.[2], JOHN P.[1]) *was born 13 Dec 1889, and died Aft. 1900. He married* EMILY HERICK.

Notes for AUSTIN KARR BALLARD:
Source: Ballard-Ballord Bits pg 350 X----2739

Children of AUSTIN BALLARD *and* EMILY HERICK *are:*

      i.   RAYMOND S.[5] BALLARD, b. 1926; d. 30 Apr 1950, Berlin Brandenburg Germany.
     ii.   MARY ELIZABETH BALLARD, m. LEROY SHAFER.

5. WILLIAM A.[4] BALLARD (PERRY A.[3], WILLIAM H.[2], JOHN P.[1]) *was born 1891 in MO, and died Aft. 1916. He married* CALLIE SLANCH. *She was born 1894 in MO, and died Aft. 1920.*

Notes for WILLIAM A. BALLARD:

Source: 1920 Platte County Missouri Federal Census Records

** 1920 - Living in Green, Platte Co., MO - Ballard, William 29 MO MO MO, Callie C 26 MO MO MO, William 8 MO, Mary 7 MO, Everett 5 MO, Harry 3 MO*

Children of WILLIAM BALLARD *and* CALLIE SLANCH *are:*

      i.   EVERETT[5] BALLARD, b. 1915, MO; d. Aft. 1920.
     ii.   WILLIAM BALLARD, b. 1912, MO; d. Aft. 1920.
    iii.   MARY BALLARD, b. 1913, MO; d. Aft. 1920.
    iv.   DAVID FRANKLIN "HARRY" BALLARD, b. 17 Mar 1916, MO; d. 29 Apr 1916, Platt Co., MO.

        Notes for DAVID FRANKLIN "HARRY" BALLARD:

        Source: Death Certificate names his parents

        More About DAVID FRANKLIN "HARRY" BALLARD:

        Burial: Camden Point Masonic Cemetery., MO

William Ballard

Generation No. 1

1. WILLIAM[1] BALLARD *was born Jun 1846 in England, and died Bet. 1900 - 1910. He married* RACHEL ANN PERRELL, *daughter of* BRAXEN PERILL *and* EVELINE BAKER. *She was born 17 Jun 1839 in Capenbridge, Hampshire Co., WV, and died 16 Mar 1914 in Kingsville, Johnson Co., MO.*

Notes for WILLIAM BALLARD:
Source: 1870-1880 Montgomery County Missouri Federal Census Records, 1900 Johnson County Missouri Federal Census Records
** 1870 - Living in Danville, Montgomery Co., MO - Ballard, William 31 England, Rachel 30 VA, Mary 13 MO, Henry 4 IL, Franklin 2 IL*
** 1880 Living in Montgomery City, Montgomery Co., MO - Ballard, William 40 Butcher - England England England, Rachel A 41 VA VA VA, Thomas F 12 IL, Saml 9 MO, George R 6 IL, Claud 4 MO, Corine 7/12 MO*
** 1900 - Living in Kingsville, Johnson Co., MO - Ballard, William - June 1846 Eng, Eng. Eng, Rachel - June 1839 VA VA VA, Richard - Sept 1873 IL, Thomas - Mar 1876 MO, John - Mar 1881 MO, Cora B - Sept 1879 MO*

Notes for RACHEL ANN PERRELL:
Source: Johnson County Missouri Death Certificate

Children of WILLIAM BALLARD *and* RACHEL PERRELL *are:*

	i.	HENRY[2] BALLARD, *b. 1866, IL.*
2.	ii.	THOMAS FRANKLIN BALLARD, *b. 06 Mar 1868, Arcole, Douglas Co., IL; d. 10 Jan 1945, Cass Co., MO.*
3.	iii.	SAMUEL ERNEST BALLARD, *b. 04 May 1872, Jonesburg, MO; d. 15 Jun 1947, Kingsville, Johnson Co., MO.*
4.	iv.	GEORGE RICHARD BALLARD, *b. Sep 1873, IL; d. Aft. 1930.*
	v.	CLAUDE EDWARD BALLARD, *b. 06 Mar 1877, New Florence, MO; d. 12 Mar 1950, Johnson Co., MO.*

Notes for CLAUDE EDWARD BALLARD:
Source: Johnson County Missouri Death Certificate, 1930 Johnson County Missouri Federal Census Records
** Never married*
** 1930 - Living in Kingsville, Johnson Co., MO - Clause 53 MO Birmingham England, MO*

More About CLAUDE EDWARD BALLARD:
Burial: Elms Springs, Elm, MO

	vi.	CORINE B. BALLARD, *b. Sep 1879, MO.*
5.	vii.	JOHN ELMER BALLARD, *b. 28 Feb 1882, Montgomery City, Cass Co., MO; d. 03 Feb 1947, Kingsville, Johnson Co., MO.*

Generation No. 2

2. THOMAS FRANKLIN[2] BALLARD (WILLIAM[1]) *was born 06 Mar 1868 in Arcole, IL, and died 10 Jan 1945 in Cass Co., MO. He married (1)* NANNIE. *She was born Mar 1868 in MO. He married (2)* MARY JANE OUTON, *daughter of A. OUTON and MARY PENROD. She was born 14 Sep 1871 in Cass Co., MO, and died 08 Apr 1937 in Polk, Cass Co., MO.*

Notes for THOMAS FRANKLIN BALLARD:
Source: Cass County Missouri Death Certificate, 1880 - 1900 Johnson County Missouri Federal Census Records, 1910-1930 Cass County Missouri Federal Census Records

** 1880 - Living in Kingsville, Johnson Co., MO - Ballard, Frank - Mar 1868 IL, Nannie J - Feb 1874 MO, Jessie L - Jan 1894 MO, Luther - Feb 1896 MO, Charlie - Mar 1897 MO*
** 1900 - Living in Kingsville, Johnson Co., MO - Ballard, Frank - Mar 1868 IL, Nannie J - Feb 1874 MO, Jessie L - Jan 1894 MO, Luther - Feb 1896 MO, Charlie - Mar 1897*
** 1910 - Living in Polk, Cass Co., MO - Ballard, Thomas F 43 (md 2x) MO, Mary J 39 (md 2x) MO, Jesse W 16 MO, Charles W 13 MO, Robert F 5 MO, Mary R 2 MO*
** 1920 - Living in Polk, Cass Co., MO - Ballard, Franklin 51 IL, Mary J 45 MO, Charles 22 MO, Robert 15 MO, Mary Rose 12 MO*
** 1930 - Living in Polk, Cass Co., MO - Ballard, Thomas 62 IL Eng MO, Mary J 58 MO IL IL, Mary 22*

Children of THOMAS BALLARD *and* NANNIE *are:*
      i.   JESSE[3] BALLARD, *b. Jan 1894, MO; d. Aft. 1910.*
     ii.   LUTHER BALLARD, *b. Feb 1896, MO; d. Aft. 1900.*
   iii.   CHARLES W. BALLARD, *b. Mar 1897, MO; d. Aft. 1920.*

Children of THOMAS BALLARD *and* MARY OUTON *are:*
   iv.   ROBERT F.[3] BALLARD, *b. 1905, MO; d. Aft. 1920.*
    v.   MARY ROSE BALLARD, *b. 1908, MO; d. Aft. 1930.*

3. SAMUEL ERNEST[2] BALLARD (WILLIAM[1]) *was born 04 May 1872 in Jonesburg, MO, and died 15 Jun 1947 in Kingsville, Johnson Co., MO. He married* MARTHA "MATTIE" ISABELL LAWSON, *daughter of* PATRICK LAWSON *and* MARY HALL. *She was born 14 Nov 1877 in KY, and died 07 Jul 1954 in Kingsville, Johnson Co., MO.*

Notes for SAMUEL ERNEST BALLARD:
Source: 1900-1930 Johnson County Missouri Federal Census Records, Johnson County Missouri Death Certificate
** 1900 - Living in Jackson, Johnson Co., MO - Ballard, Samuel E - June 1872 MO Eng IL, Mattie J - Nov 1877 MO KY KY, Henrietta R - May 1898 MO MO MO, Mary B - Agu 1899 MO*
** 1910 - Living in Jackson, Johnson Co., MO - Ballard, Samuel E 36 MO Eng VA, Martha E 32 - 7 children 7 living, MO KY KY, Ruth H 11 MO, Mary B 10 MO, Nina J 8 MO, Fred 7 MO, Gladys L 5 MO, Imogene 3 MO, Bessie P. 11/12 MO*
** 1920 - Living in Jackson, Johnson Co., MO - Ballard, SE 47 MO Eng IL, Martha E MO KY KY, Ruth 21 MO, Mary 20 MO, Nina 18 MO, Amos 16 MO, Gladys 15 MO, Bessie 10 MO, Rufy 8 MO, Mabel 3 4/12 MO*
** 1930 - Living in Jackson, Johnson Co., MO - Ballard, Sam E 7 MO Eng WV, Martha F 52 MO KY KY, Bessie P 20 MO MO MO, Ruby E 18 MO MO MO, Matalia (hard to read) 13 MO MO MO*

More About SAMUEL ERNEST BALLARD:
Burial: Elm, MO

Children of SAMUEL BALLARD *and* MARTHA LAWSON *are:*
      i.   HENRIETTA RUTH[3] BALLARD, *b. May 1898, MO; d. Aft. 1920.*
     ii.   MARY B. BALLARD, *b. Aug 1899, MO; d. Aft. 1920.*
   iii.   NINA J. BALLARD, *b. 1902, MO; d. Aft. 1920.*
6.   iv.   AMOS FRED BALLARD, *b. 1903, MO; d. Aft. 1930.*
    v.   GLADYS BALLARD, *b. 1905, MO; d. Aft. 1920.*
   vi.   IMOGENE BALLARD, *b. 21 Sep 1906, Johnson Co., MO; d. 27 Feb 1925.*
  vii.   BESSIE P. BALLARD, *b. 1909, MO; d. Aft. 1930.*
 viii.   RUBY E. BALLARD, *b. 1912, MO; d. Aft. 1930.*
   ix.   MABEL BALLARD, *b. 1916; d. Aft. 1920.*

4. GEORGE RICHARD[2] BALLARD (WILLIAM[1]) *was born Sep 1873 in IL, and died Aft. 1930. He married* LYDIA ALICE BURKS, *daughter of* JOHN BURKS *and* NANCY PROCTER. *She was born 14 Oct 1879 in MO, and died 25 Feb 1934 in Kingsville, Johnson Co., MO.*

Notes for GEORGE RICHARD BALLARD:
Source: 1910-1930 Johnson County Missouri Federal Census Records
** 1910 - Living in Knoxville, Johnson Co., MO - Ballard, GR 35 IL KY VA, LA 30 MO MO MO, Elsie M 7 MO, Roy 4 MO, CE 33 brother MO Eng VA, R. A mother 70 10 children, 5 living*
** 1920 - Living in Knoxville, Johnson Co., MO - Ballard, George R 43 IL Eng VA, Allace 40 MO, Ellsie M 17 MO, Roy E 14 MO, Jake H Caryle 72 uncle VA, Claude Ballard 43 MO Eng VA*
** 1930 - Living in Knoxville, Johnson Co., MO - Ballard, Dick 54 MO Birmingham England, VA, Alice 50 MO MO MO, Ray 25 MO MO MO*

Notes for LYDIA ALICE BURKS:
Source: Johnson County Missouri Death Certificate

More About LYDIA ALICE BURKS:
Burial: Elm Cemetery, Johnson Co., MO

Children of GEORGE BALLARD and LYDIA BURKS are:

> i.   ELSIE M.[3] BALLARD, b. 1903, MO; d. Aft. 1920.
> ii. ROY E. BALLARD, b. 1906, MO; d. Aft. 1930.

5. JOHN ELMER[2] BALLARD (WILLIAM[1]) *was born 28 Feb 1882 in Montgomery City, Cass Co., MO, and died 03 Feb 1947 in Kingsville, Johnson Co., MO. He married* MINNIE E.. *She was born 1885 in MO, and died Aft. 1930.*

Notes for JOHN ELMER BALLARD:
Source: 1920-1930 Cass County Missouri Federal Census Records, Cass County Missouri Death Certificate

** 1920 - Living in Polk, Cass Co., MO - Ballard, John 37 MO Eng VA, Minnie E 35 MO MO MO, John R 7 MO, Sylvia 5 MO*
** 1930 - Living in Polk, Cass Co., MO - Ballard, John E 48 MO Eng VA, Minnie E 45 MO MO MO, Raymond 18, MO MO MO, Jeanette 15 MO MO MO*

Children of JOHN BALLARD and MINNIE E. are:

> i.   JOHN RAYMOND[3] BALLARD, b. 1912, MO; d. Aft. 1930.
> ii. SYLVIA JEANETTE BALLARD, b. 1915, MO; d. Aft. 1930.

Generation No. 3

6. AMOS FRED[3] BALLARD (SAMUEL ERNEST[2], WILLIAM[1]) *was born 1903 in MO, and died Aft. 1930. He married* DOROTHY. *She was born 1903 in MO, and died Aft. 1930.*

Notes for AMOS FRED BALLARD:
Source: 1930 Johnson County Missouri Federal Census Records

** 1930 - Living in Centerview, Johnson Co., MO - Ballard, Amos F 27 MO MO MO, Dorothy 20 MO MO MO, Opal 2 MO, Everett 1 8/12 MO*

Children of AMOS BALLARD and DOROTHY are:

> i.   OPAL[4] BALLARD, b. 1928, Johnson Co., MO; d. Aft. 1930.
> ii. EVERETT BALLARD, b. 1928, Johnson Co., MO; d. Aft. 1930.

William Ballard

Generation No. 1

1. WILLIAM[1] BALLARD *was born Feb 1862 in KY, and died Aft. 1900 in lived Buchanan Co., MO 1900. He married JULIA ANN WALLER. She was born Oct 1864 in MO.*

Notes for WILLIAM BALLARD:

Source: 1900 Buchanan County Missouri Federal Census Records

** 1900 - Living in Buchanan Co., MO - Ballard, William - July 1864 MO KY MO, Clarence - July 1882, Effie - July 1884 MO, Thomas - Apr 1886*

Children of WILLIAM BALLARD and JULIA WALLER are:

2.   i.   CLARENCE[2] BALLARD, b. Jul 1882, MO; d. Aft. 1920.
            ii.   EFFIE MAY BALLARD, b. 30 Jul 1884, Agency MO; m. MR. MCLEAN.
           iii.   THOMAS BALLARD, b. Apr 1886, MO.

Generation No. 2

2. CLARENCE[2] BALLARD (WILLIAM[1]) *was born Jul 1882 in MO, and died Aft. 1920. He married FLORA. She was born 1887 in KS, and died Aft. 1930.*

Notes for CLARENCE BALLARD:

Source: 1910 -1920 Buchanan County Missouri Federal Census Records

** 1910 - Living in St. Joseph, Buchanan Co., MO - Ballard, Clarence B 27 MO KY US, Flora 23, Ferrel C 4, Ina L 1*
** 1920 - Living in St. Joseph, Buchanan Co., MO - Ballard, Clarence 36 MO, Flora 3, Ferol 14, Ina 11*

Notes for FLORA:

Source: 1930 Buchanan Federal Census Records

** 1930 - Living in St. Joseph, Buchanan Co., MO - Ballard, Flora 42 divorced KS IA KS, Farroll 24 MO KS IS, Ina Danbury 21 MO, Ellia son in law 24 England England England*

Children of CLARENCE BALLARD and FLORA are:

           i.   FARROL[3] BALLARD, b. 1906, St. Joseph, Buchanan Co., MO.
          ii.   INA BALLARD, b. 1909, St. Joseph, Buchanan Co., MO; d. Aft. 1930; m. ELLIA DANBURY; b. 1906, England; d. Aft. 1930.

Hamilton, Glynn Elbert: 192
Hamilton, Grace D.: 42
Hamilton, Henry Winfield: 191
Hamilton, Ira Jane: 191
Hamilton, Iva Mae: 191, 192
Hamilton, Leroy Winfield: 191
Hamilton, Lola Mae: 192
Hamilton, Lynn Albert: 192
Hamilton, Minnie F.: 42
Hamilton, Raymond: 192
Hamilton, Robert F.: 42
Hamilton, Thomas Phelix: 42
Hamilton, William Earl: 192
Hamilton, Zelma L.: 42
Hamlin, Floy A.: 214
Hammock, Nathalee: 45
Hammons, Juanita: 28
Hampton, Annie: 123
Hampton, Cecil: 122
Hampton, Delton Marmaduke: 123
Hampton, Edward Bland Wade: 118
Hampton, James: 118
Hampton, James Alvin: 123
Hampton, James Valentine: 118
Hampton, John Mormaduke: 118, 122
Hampton, Mary: 123
Hampton, Mary Bland: 122
Hampton, Rufus: 85
Hampton, Thomas V.: 123
Hampton, Thomas Valentine: 118, 122
Hampton, Velma Anna: 118
Hampton, Vernon Randolph: 122, 123
Hampton, William Bland: 122
Hampton, Zuma Etta: 118, 123
Hancock, Unnamed: 170
Hancock, Ida: 52
Hancock, s. Ken C.: 52
Hanford, Alice Georgia: 154
Hankins, Gertrude E.: 99
Harmon, Antonio L.: 216
Harriet, Unnamed: 233
Harriiott, Amanda: 179
Harris, Charles: 99
Harris, Thelma Ruth: 99, 100
Harrison, Charles Bland: 37
Harrison, Daniel Harden: 37
Harrison, Elmer Roscoe: 37
Harrison, George Robert: 37
Harrison, James Robert: 14
Harrison, James Samuel: 37
Harrison, Ora M.: 37
Harrison, William Robert: 36, 37
Harrison, William Thomas: 152
Harvey, Granville J.: 113
Haskins, Miss: 225
Hassine, James: 163
Hathcoat, Joseph Arthur: 21
Haun, Jessie Maud: 56
Haupt, Edward Albert: 135
Hays, Elizabeth: 231
Hayward, Hazel: 226
Heck, Henry: 79

Heck, Margaerett Isabelle: 79
Hedge, Charles Reuben: 74
Hedge, Dock Arvel: 73
Hedge, John: 73
Hedge, Manerva Jane: 74
Hedge, William Palmer: 73
Heilman, Frank: 211
Helm, Corine Marie: 88
Helm, Elijah Hiawatha: 87, 88
Helm, Joyce: 88
Henderson, Bertha May: 257
Henderson, Mary California: 249
Henderson, Samuel: 249
Hendricksen, Garnet Jewel: 256
Henry, Roy: 130
Hensley, Elvira Bell: 81, 82
Hensley, May: 81, 82
Hensley, Pleasant Oda: 78
Henson, Benona: 79
Henson, Mary: 79
Herick, Emily: 262
Hession, Nancy Ann: 163, 164
Hickerson, Alvin: 114
Hickerson, Elias R.: 114
Hickerson, Emma: 114
Hickerson, Walter: 114
Hickey, Hugh Dale: 69
Hickey, Porter Houston: 68, 69
Hickey, Virginia Love: 69
Hickey, Wanda Jane: 69
Hiestand, Benjamin Harrison: 116
Hiett, Gustine Frances: 171
Higgins, Catherine: 30
Hildebrand, Susan Jane: 154
Hilderbrand, Jessie: 168, 169
Hilderbrand, Samuel: 168
Hill, Alvin Carl: 68
Hill, Beulah E.: 68
Hill, James Olen: 67
Hill, Lesley Raymond: 68
Hill, Lester Martin: 68
Hill, Lewis Samuel: 67
Hill, Loda Raymond: 66, 67
Hill, Margaret Kathryn: 254
Hill, Myra Carolle: 67
Hill, William Arlie: 67
Hill, Wimpford Harve: 68
Hilton, Naomi "Oma": 16
Hines, Carrie Adney: 128
Hines, James Wesley: 128
Hines, Martha Missouri: 129
Hines, Rachel Corine: 128
Hines, William Henry: 128
Hines, William Jefferson: 128, 129
Hinshaw, Thelma: 258
Hitchman, Charles M.: 54
Hitt, Rachel L.: 124, 125
Hitt, William: 124
Hobbs, Joe L.: 42
Hobbs, Leroy Jasper: 41
Hobson, Laura Alta: 142
Hodge, William F.: 62

Norman, Jacob A.: 157, 158
Norman, James Walker: 158
Norman, Jasper: 150
Norris, Charles Ross: 47
Nutt, Dorothy Mildred: 100
Nutt, Frances C.: 100
Nutt, Walter Garland: 100
Nutt, Walter H.: 100
Oakley, Barbara: 18
Oakley, Edward: 18
Oakley, Ellison W.: 18
Oakley, Rhesa: 18
Oakley, Willis E.: 18
Oakley, Woodard Franklin: 18
Oakley, Yancey: 17, 18
Oakley, Yancey J.: 18
O'Connor, James: 195
O'Connor, Margaret: 195
Oda, Unnamed: 150
Odle, Benjamin Wesley: 29
Odle, Isaac C.: 28, 29
Odom, Malinda Jane: 170
Oglesby, Samantha: 155, 156
O'Howell, John William: 167
Oliver, Mary Elizabeth: 45
Ollie, Unnamed: 23
Orten, Charles: 210
Oursbourn, Athol C.: 44
Oursbourn, Aubrey Joseph: 45
Oursbourn, Cecil F.: 45
Oursbourn, Ernest C.: 44
Oursbourn, Joseph Edward: 44
Oursbourn, Lillian L.: 44
Oursbourn, Mildred L.: 45
Oursbourn, Robert Monroe: 44
Oursbourn, William R.: 44
Outon, A. C.: 263
Outon, Mary Jane: 263, 264
Owens, James: 145
Owens, Sarah Elizabeth: 145
Padgett, Benjamin F.: 207
Padgett, Burrel: 207
Padgett, Isaac: 207
Padgett, Joab: 207
Page, Charles Donreath: 260
Pancake, Pearl Neva: 115
Parker, Barbara Marie: 44
Parker, Winfred Charles: 70
Parkhurst, Unnamed: 235
Pate, Clara: 198
Pate, John W.: 18
Patterson, Artie Missa: 129
Patterson, Blanche: 129, 130
Patterson, John H.: 129
Patterson, Lorenzo B.: 129
Patterson, Mary Frances: 126
Patterson, Mary Zelma: 130
Patterson, Mattie E.: 129
Patterson, Ruth: 130
Patterson, William J.: 130
Patton, John: 136
Patton, Laura Fay: 136, 137

Paul, Mary J.: 111
Payne, Mary Jackson: 140
Pearce, Benjamin Shane: 229
Pearce, Elva Dora: 229
Pearce, James: 229
Pearce, Jonathan: 228
Pearce, William Henry: 229
Peddy, Leah: 124
Peed, Claude William: 98
Peeler, C. E.: 148
Peeler, Jesse Richard: 145
Penix, Unnamed: 70
Pennell, Unnamed: 83
Penrod, Mary M.: 263
Pepper, Enoch A.: 218
Pepper, Mary Ellen: 217, 218
Pepper, William: 217
Peppers, Mary Beakley: 219
Perill, Braxen: 263
Perrell, Rachel Ann: 263
Perrin, Irene: 138
Perry, Unnamed: 32
Persinger, Christina: 253
Pfeifer, Mary Alice: 83
Phillips, Marion C.: 56
Phillips, Mary: 136
Pilant, Thomas S.: 21
Pinckard, Opal Louise: 68
Piper, Andy Denis: 36
Piper, Wirt: 168
Plummer, Leroy D.: 70
Poe, James J.: 110
Poe, Paul Eugene: 85
Polin, Edgar L.: 233
Polin, Edith: 233
Polin, Estella: 233
Polin, Jay: 233
Polin, John: 233
Polk, Cecil Luther: 86
Pollard, Nancy: 249
Pollard, William A.: 189
Polley, Alice: 183
Polley, Charles: 183
Polley, Ethel Leta: 183
Polley, Ira H.: 182, 183
Polley, John: 183
Polley, Mary O.: 183
Polley, Wanda Maxine: 183
Polley, William T.: 183
Polley, Winnie: 183
Pond, Mary Frances: 189
Porter, I. N. J.: 130
Post, Artie: 133
Post, Austin Vernon: 133
Post, Cora: 133
Post, Frances "Fannie": 133
Post, Gaines: 133
Post, Henry Samuel: 133
Post, John Baily: 133
Post, John Sidney: 133
Post, Marvin Henry: 133
Post, Sarah "Emma" Emily: 130, 131